Analyzing Financial Statements: A Decision Tree Approach
Part 1

Analyzing Financial Statements: A Decision Tree Approach, Part 1
Eighth Edition

This publication is designed to provide accurate and authoritative information in regard to the subject matter covered. It is sold with the understanding that the publisher is not engaged in rendering legal, accounting, or other professional services. If legal advice or other expert assistance is required, the services of a competent professional person should be sought.

From a Declaration of Principles jointly adopted by a Committee of the American Bar Association and a Committee of Publishers and Associations.

The American Bankers Association is committed to providing innovative, high-quality products and services that are responsive to its members' critical needs. To comment about this product, or to learn more about the American Bankers Association and the many products and services it offers, please call **1-800-BANKERS** or visit us at our website: **www.aba.com.**

> This textbook has been approved by the American Institute of Banking for use in courses for which AIB certificates or diplomas are granted. The American Institute of Banking is the professional development and training affiliate of the American Bankers Association. Instructional materials endorsed by AIB have been developed by bankers for bankers.

© 2013 by the American Bankers Association
Eighth Edition

All rights reserved. No part of this publication may be reproduced, stored in a retrieval system, or transmitted in any form or by any means—electronic, mechanical, photocopying, recording, or otherwise—without prior written permission from the American Bankers Association.

Printed in the United States of America

10 9 8 7 6 5 4 3 2 1

Catalog Number: 3009774
ISBN-10: 0-899-82681-4
ISBN-13: 978-0-089-82681-3

CONTENTS

LIST OF FIGURES Xiii
ACKNOWLEDGMENT Xviii
INTRODUCTION Xix
    The Commercial Lending Decision Tree Xx

SECTION 1 UNDERSTANDING BUSINESS BORROWERS
CHAPTER 1: BUSINESS SECTORS AND OPERATING CYCLES 1
    Introduction 2
        Relationship to the Commercial Lending Decision Tree 2
    Operating Cycles 3
    Operating Cycle Purpose 3
    Agricultural Businesses 4
    Manufacturers 5
        General Characteristics 7
    Wholesalers 7
        Assessing the Risk of a Wholesale Borrower 8
    Retailers 9
        Evaluating a Retailer's Financial Statements 10
    Service Businesses 11
        Financial Statements of a Service Business 11
        Other Service Related Businesses 12
    Construction Businesses 12
        Construction Industry Financial Risks. 14
        Evaluating the Construction Business Financial Statements. 15
    Operating Cycle Application 16
    Analyzing the Financial Data 16
    Evaluating the Risks 17
    Summary 18
    Questions for Discussion. 19
    Exercise 1 19
        Application to Dry Supply Background 19
        Instructions 19
    Exercise 2 20
CHAPTER 2: WHY BUSINESSES BORROW 21
    Introduction 22
        Relationship to the Commercial Lending Decision Tree. 22
    Cash Flow Cycles 22
    Understanding Cash Flow Cycles 23
    Uses of Cash 23
    Sources of Cash. 26
        Capital 26
        Trade Credit 28
        Accruals 29
        Reduction of Credit Sale Terms 29
    Long-Term Uses of Cash. 30
    Long-Term Sources of Cash 32
    Reasons Why Businesses Borrow. 32
    Borrowing Needs By Business Type or Industry. 32
    General Borrowing Needs by All Businesses 35

Borrowing Cause Vs. Purpose (Use of Funds)	35
Typical Borrowing Causes	35
Types of Borrowing Arrangements	36
Borrowing Arrangements Offered by Banks	36
Special Commitment Loan	36
Operating Line of Credit	36
Standby Letter of Credit	37
Term Loan	38
Lease Financing	38
Matching of Purpose to Repayment Sources	39
Competing and Complementing Financing	39
Full-Range Competitors to Banks	40
Brokerage Firms	40
Credit Unions	40
Competitors with Limited Products	40
Commercial Finance Companies	40
Factoring	40
Captive Finance Companies	41
Credit Card Issuers	41
Leasing Companies	41
Life Insurance Companies	41
Complementary Financing or Partners to Banks	42
Trade Credit	42
Investors	42
Government Loan Programs, Guarantees, and Grants	42
Industrial Revenue Bonds	43
Participations and Syndications	43
Summary	44
Questions for Discussion	45
Exercise 1	45
Exercise 2	46
Chapter 3: Business Legal Structures and Life Cycles	**47**
Introduction	48
Relationship to the Commercial Lending Decision Tree	48
Legal Structures	48
Types of Legal Structures	49
Sole Proprietorship	51
Business Responsibility and Taxation	51
Business Liability	51
Assumed Name	51
General Partnership	52
Partnership Agreement	52
Business Responsibility and Taxation	53
Business Liability and Activities	53
Limited Partnership	53
Certificate of Limited Partnership	54
Business Taxation and Liability	54
C Corporation	54
Income Taxes for the Owners	54
Business Liability	55
How C Corporations Differ from Other Entities	55
Articles of Incorporation	55
S Corporation	56
Taxation	56
S Corporation Ownership	56
Distribution of Income and Cash	56
Limited Liability Company (LLC)	57
LLC Ownership	57
Limited Liability Partnership	57

Lending to an LLC	57
Business Life Cycles	58
What is a Business Life Cycle?	58
General Characteristics of the Life Cycle Stages	58
Matching Products	58
The Start-Up Stage	60
The Growth Stage	61
The Mature Stage	62
The Decline Stage	63
What Are the Key Risk Factors in a Business Life Cycle?	64
Summary	66
Questions for Discussion	67
Exercise 1	67
Exercise 2	67
Background	67
Instructions	67
CHAPTER 4: INTRODUCTION TO BUSINESS FINANCIAL STATEMENTS	**69**
Introduction	70
Relationship to the Commercial Lending Decision Tree	70
Financial Statement Analysis Process	71
Role and Purpose of Financial Statement Analysis	71
Financial Statement Analysis Defined	71
Technical and Interpretive Analysis	72
Financial Analysis Overview	72
Step 1: Obtaining Statements	73
Step 2: Processing Statements	74
Step 3: Spreading Statements	74
Step 4: Technical Analysis	75
Step 5: Interpretive Analysis	76
Financial Statement Basics	78
Statement Spreading Guidelines	79
Other Considerations	80
More on Technical And Interpretive Analysis Revisited	81
Limitations of Financial Analysis	82
Quality of Information	82
Accounting Methods	82
External Environment	82
Unlisted Information	83
Distortion in Numbers	83
Aggregate Accounts	83
Basic Analytical Techniques	84
Strengths — Weaknesses > Uncertainties	85
Evaluating Statement Quality And Reliability	86
Accounting Standards	86
Internally Prepared Statements	88
Externally Prepared Statements	89
Compiled Statements	89
Compilation Qualifications	92
Reviewed Statements	92
Audited Statements	93
Unqualified Audit Opinion	94
Qualified Audit Opinion	95
Adverse Audit Opinion	96
Going Concern Disclosure	97
Disclaimer of Opinion	99
Management Letter	101
Other Component Analysis	102
Management Plans and Reports	102
Analyzing the Financial Statements	103

    Income Statement Analysis.. 103
    Balance Sheet Analysis 103
    Ratio Analysis... 104
    Cash Flow Analysis.. 104
Preparing Forecasts 104
    Cash Budget.. 104
    Pro Formas.. 105
Limitations of Analysis 105
Questions for Discussion... 106
Exercise 1 106
    Instructions 106

Chapter 5: How Business Financial Statements are Constructed 109
Introduction 110
    Relationship to the Commercial Lending Decision Tree.................................. 110
Overview of Accounting Methods.. 110
Cash Method 111
Accrual Method 112
What is Income Tax Basis?... 112
Cash Vs. Accrual Basis 113
    Practical Example of Cash Vs. Accrual Basis.. 113
Accounting Refresher 115
Gadgets Etc. First Year on Accrual-Basis Accounting... 116
    Accounts After Transaction A.. 116
    Accounts After Transaction B.. 117
    Accounts After Transaction C.. 118
    Accounts After Transaction D.. 119
    Accounts After Transaction E.. 120
    Accounts After Transaction F.. 121
    Accounts After Transaction G.. 122
    Accounts After Transaction H 123
    Accounts After Transaction I 124
    Accounts After Transaction J 125
    Accounts After Transaction K.. 126
    Gadgets Etc. Summary Balance Sheet and Income Statement on Accrual-Basis Accounting 127
Gadgets Etc. First Year on Cash-Basis Accounting 128
    Accounts After Transaction A 128
    Accounts After Transaction B 129
    Accounts After Transaction C 130
    Accounts After Transaction D 131
    Accounts After Transaction E 132
    Accounts After Transaction F.. 133
    Accounts After Transaction G 134
    Accounts After Transaction H 135
    Gadgets Etc. Summary Balance Sheet and Income Statement on Cash-Basis Accounting 136
Comparing Gadgets Etc. Balance Sheets and Income Statements 136
Build Financial Statements 137
Summary... 137
Exercise 1 138
    Instructions.. 138
        Widgets, Inc. Accounting Transactions Worksheet 139

Section 2: Analyzing Business Financial Statements and Tax Returns

Chapter 6: Income Statement Analysis 143
Introduction 144
    Relationship to the Commercial Lending Decision Tree 144
Income Statement Analysis—Part 1: Sales and Cost of Goods Sold Analysis 145
    The Income Statement Structure and Preliminary Considerations........................ 146
    How the Type of Business Affects the Structure.. 147
    Preliminary Considerations.. 147

	Types of Businesses	148
	Management Objectives	149
Revenue Analysis		149
	Net Sales	149
	Example	150
	Method of Accounting for Revenues and Expenses	150
	Sales Volume and Price Trends	150
	Sales Mix	151
	Order Backlogs	152
	Large, Nonrecurring Sales	152
	Sales on Extended Terms or to Marginal Customers	152
Cost of Goods Sold		153
Inventory Valuation		154
	Changing the Inventory Method Used	155
	Reconciling LIFO to FIFO	155
	Inventory as a Deferred or Capitalized Cost	155
	Inventory Valuation—Weighted-Average Cost Method	156
	Inventory Valuation—Retail Method	157
Gross Profit		157
Gross Margin Trends		158
Income Statement Analysis—Part 2: Operating Expense and Net Profit Analysis		158
	Operating Expense Analysis	159
	Operating Income	161
	Operating Leverage	161
	Other Income and Expense Analysis	163
	Other Income	163
	Other Expenses	164
	Analysis of Net Profit Before Tax and After Tax	165
	Net Profit Before Tax	165
	Income Taxes	165
	Net Profit After Tax	165
	Reconciliation of Net Worth	166
	Reconciling Net Worth	166
	Retained Earnings	167
Summary		168
Questions for Discussion		168
Exercise 1		169
	Background	169
	Dry Supply Case Study	169
Chapter 7: Balance Sheet Analysis		171
Introduction		172
	Relationship to the Commercial Lending Decision Tree	172
Business Balance Sheet Considerations		172
	Key Considerations	172
	Balance Sheet Equation	174
Asset Analysis		174
	Current Assets	175
	Cash	176
	Marketable Securities	176
	Accounts Receivable	177
	Accounts Receivable: Aged Listings and Concentrations	178
	Allowance for Doubtful Accounts	180
	Inventory	180
	Raw Materials Inventory	181
	Work-In-Process	182
	Finished Goods Inventory	182
	Other Current Assets	183
	Noncurrent Assets	183
	Fixed Assets	183

| Fixed-Asset Valuation 184
         Depreciation 184
         Fixed-Asset Capacity, Efficiency, and Specialization 186
         Leasehold Improvements 187
         Valuing Fixed Assets 187
         Dry Supply's Fixed Assets 187
         Other Securities. 188
         Notes Receivable 188
         Due From Officers and Employees, or Loans to Shareholders 188
         Due From Affiliates 189
         Prepaid Expenses 189
         Cash-Value Life Insurance 189
         Intangibles 189
   Liabilities And Equity Analysis 190
      Current Liabilities 190
         Overdrafts 191
         Notes Payable to Banks 192
         Accounts Payable 193
         Notes Payable to Others 194
         Due To Affiliates or Officers, or Loans From Shareholders 194
         Current Maturities of Long-Term Debt 194
         Accrued Expenses 195
         Other Current Liabilities 195
      Noncurrent Liabilities 196
         Long-Term Debt 196
         Bonds And Debentures 196
         Subordinated Debt 197
         Reserves 197
      Equity (Net Worth) 198
         Equity (Net Worth) for Different Business Entities 199
         C Corporations 199
         Equity Accounts for Other Entities 200
         Concept of Tangible Net Worth 201
   Summary 203
   Exercise 1 203
      Background 203
      Instructions 203

Chapter 8: Ratio Analysis 207
   Introduction 208
      Relationship to the Commercial Lending Decision Tree 208
   Ratio Analysis Considerations 208
      Ratios and Accounting Methods 209
         Income Statement 209
      Ratio Characteristics 211
   Types of Ratios 211
      Liquidity Ratios 212
         Current Ratio 212
         Quick Ratio 213
         Dollar Amount of Working Capital 213
      Financial Leverage Ratios 214
         Debt-To-Worth or Leverage Ratio 214
         Tangible Leverage Ratio 215
         Tangible Effective Leverage Ratio 215
      Profitability Ratios 216
         Return-on-Assets Ratio 218
         Return-on-Equity Ratio 218
      Efficiency Ratios 219
         Accounts Receivable Turnover 220
         Inventory Turnover Ratio 221

Accounts Payable Turnover Ratio	221
Sales to Total Assets	222
Coverage Ratios	223
Traditional Cash Flow Coverage	223
Interest Coverage	223
Fixed Charge Coverage	224
Dividend Payout Ratio	226
Industry Data	229
Primary Sources of Industry Data	230
Rma's Annual Statement Studies	230
Industry and Trade Associations	230
Trend and Comparative Analysis	231
Trend Analysis	232
Comparative Analysis	232
Summary	233
Questions for Discussion	234
Exercise 1	234
Exercise 2	234
Background	234
Dry Supply Case Study	234
Part 1	235
Part 2	236
CHAPTER 9: CASH FLOW ANALYSIS	**237**
Introduction	238
Relationship to the Commercial Lending Decision Tree	238
Overview Of Cash Flow Statements And Reports	238
Why Bankers Focus on Cash Flow	239
Profit	239
Working Capital	239
Cash Flows	240
Sources and Uses of Cash—Liabilities and Equity Accounts	240
Asset Accounts	241
Statement of Cash Flows—Indirect Method	241
Cash Flow Formats: Indirect Vs. Direct Method	242
Statement of Cash Flows (SCF)—Indirect Method	242
UCA Cash Flow Model—Direct Method	243
Cash Flows from Operating Activities—Indirect Method	244
Cash Flows from Investing Activities—Indirect Method	246
Cash Flows from Financing Activities—Indirect Method	247
Completed Statement of Cash Flows—Indirect Method	249
Statement of Cash Flows (Operating Activities)—Direct Method	250
Calculations Using the Direct Method	251
Cash Flow Reports and Other Tools	254
Abbreviated Cash Flow Report	254
Impact of Sales Growth and Other Significant Changes on Cash Flow	256
Summary	258
Question for Discussion	258
Exercise 1	259
Background	259
Exercise 2	259
Background	259
Exercise 3	260
Background	260
Exercise 4	260
Instructions	260
Part 1	260
Part 2	260

CHAPTER 10: THE UCA MODEL 263
    Introduction 264
        Relationship to the Commercial Lending Decision Tree 264
    UCA Cash Flow Model—Direct Method 264
        UCA Format Compared to SCF 265
        UCA Calculations Using the Direct Method—Net Cash From Operations (NCAO) 268
        UCA Calculations Using the Direct Method—Cash After Debt Amortization 271
        UCA Calculations Using the Direct Method—Financing Surplus (Requirement) 273
        UCA Calculations Using the Direct Method—Cash After External Financing 273
        Advantages of UCA. 274
    Summary 276
    Question for Discussion 276
    Exercise 1 277
        Background. 278
    Exercise 2 278
        Background. 279
    Exercise 3 279
        Background. 279
    Exercise 4 279
        Background. 280
    Exercise 5 280
        Instructions. 280
            Part 1 280
                Dry Supply UCA Cash Flow Model for 20xy 280
            Part 2 280

CHAPTER 11: CASH BUDGETS AND PRO FORMA STATEMENTS 283
    Introduction 284
        Relationship to the Commercial Lending Decision Tree 284
    Analyzing Cash Budgets 284
        Cash Budget Overview 285
        Inflows and Outflows of Cash, Plus Other Building Blocks of a Cash Budget 285
        Use of Cash Budgets 286
        Cash Budget Format 287
            Example: Cash Budget for a Growing Company (Designs by Dezine, Inc.). 288
            Cash Budget Analysis 294
        The Role Of A Cash Budget 294
            Interrelationship Between the Operating Cycle and Cash Needs 294
            Interrelationship Between Working Capital and Capital Expenditures. 295
    Calculating and Interpreting Pro Forma Financial Statements. 295
        Considerations for Constructing and Reviewing Projections 296
            Projection Assumptions. 296
            Pro Forma Framework. 297
            Realistic Assumptions 297
            Financial Statement Background. 297
            Dependability of Performance. 297
            Time Intervals. 298
            External Factors. 298
            Internal Factors. 299
            Example: Designs by Dezine, Inc.. 299
            Summary of External Factors. 300
            Summary of Internal Factors. 301
            Analyzing Pro Forma Statements. 301
            Past Performance. 301
        Forecasting an Income Statement 302
            Sales 302
            Cost of Goods Sold. 303
            Operating Expenses. 304
            Operating Profit 304
            Other Income and Expense. 304

Income Taxes	305
Forecasting the Balance Sheet	305
Assets	306
Liabilities and Net Worth	309
The Plug Accounts	311
Analyzing Each Scenario	311
Uncertainties in Forecasts	313
Summary	313
Exercise 1	314
Instructions	314
Part 1	314
Part 2	314
Exercise 2	315
Instructions	315
Exercise 3	316
Instructions	316

SECTION 3: ANALYZING PERSONAL FINANCIAL STATEMENTS AND TAX RETURNS

CHAPTER 12: TYPES OF PERSONAL FINANCIAL STATEMENTS 321

Introduction	322
Relationship to the Commercial Lending Decision Tree	322
Personal Financial Statement Overview	322
Basic Formats	322
Sample Format and Preliminary Analysis	323
Personal Financial Statement Components	327
Personal Information	327
Income & Expenditure Statement	327
Income Analysis	327
Expenditures Analysis	329
Balance Sheet	330
Asset Analysis	330
Liability Analysis	335
Net Worth	336
Contingent Liabilities	337
Other Information Requested	337
Representations and Warranties	337
Summary	338
Questions for Discussion	339
Exercise 1	339
Instructions	339

CHAPTER 13: KEY RATIOS AND ADJUSTED NET WORTH 341

Introduction	342
Relationship to the Commercial Lending Decision Tree	342
Key Ratios From Personal Financial Statements	342
Sample PFS Format	343
Liquidity Ratio	343
Unsecured Debt Ratio	346
Debt-To-Income Ratio	347
Adjusted Net Worth	348
Components of Adjusted Net Worth	348
Outside Net Worth	349
Calculating Adjusted Net Worth	349
Summary	351
Questions for Discussion	352
Exercise 1	352
Background	352
Instructions	352
Exercise 2	355
Instructions	355
Exercise 3	355

   Instructions. 355
CHAPTER 14: PERSONAL TAX RETURNS AND CASH FLOW 357
  Introduction 358
   Relationship to the Commercial Lending Decision Tree 358
  Introduction to Personal Tax Returns 358
   Key Uses of Personal Tax Returns and Common Forms. 358
   Income Vs. Cash 359
   Personal Tax Return Components 360
    Initial Review 360
    Analysis of Income and Form 1040. 360
   Related Analysis of Income and Form 1120S (S Corporation). 366
  Personal Cash Flow Analysis 367
   Calculating Personal Cash Flow. 367
    Key Sections and Calculations. 368
  Summary. 373
  Question for Discussion 373
  Appendix A: Dezine Personal Tax Return 374
CHAPTER 15: COMBINING BUSINESS AND PERSONAL CASH FLOW INTO GLOBAL CASH FLOW 397
  Introduction 398
   Relationship to the Commercial Lending Decision Tree 398
  Global Cash Flow Overview 398
   Why is Global Cash Flow Needed? 399
   Two Analytical Issues. 400
    No Single "Correct" Method for GCF. 401
   Global Cash Flow Example 402
   Calculating Global Cash Flow. 403
  Summary. 406
  Question for Discussion 407
  Exercise 1 407
   Instructions. 407
  Appendix A: Personal Cash Flow 408
GLOSSARY TERMS 411
INDEX 415

List of Figures

Chapter 1

Figure 1.1 Agricultural Operating Cycle 5

Figure 1.2 Agricultural Lending Summary 5

Figure 1.3 Manufacturing Business Cycle 6

Figure 1.4 Manufacturer Lending Summary 7

Figure 1.5 Wholesale Business Cycle. 8

Figure 1.6 Wholesaler Lending Summary 9

Figure 1.7 Retail Business Cycle 9

Figure 1.8 Retailer Lending Summary. 10

Figure 1.9 Service Business Cycle 11

Figure 1.10 Service Business Lending Summary 12

Figure 1.11 Other Service-Related Businesses 13

Figure 1.12 Construction Business Cycle 14

Figure 1.13 Construction Lending Summary 15

Figure 1.14 Typical Financial Profiles for Various Businesses (Dining Tables Example) 17

Figure 1.15 Industry Risks Summary 18

Chapter 2

Figure 2.1 Cash Flow Cycle Comparison 24

Figure 2.2 Cash Flow Cycle of Harris Table Company 25

Figure 2.3 Cash Flow Cycle of Harris Table Company with Accounts Receivable 26

Figure 2.4 Cash Flow Cycle of Harris Table Company with Lower Initial Capital. 27

Figure 2.5 Cash Flow Cycle of Harris Table with Trade Credit to Fund Shortfall 28

Figure 2.6 Cash Flow Cycle of Harris Table Company with Labor Accrual to Fund Shortfall 29

Figure 2.7 Cash Flow Cycle of Harris Table Company with Reduced Sales Terms to Fund Shortfall 30

Figure 2.8 Fixed Asset Cycle 31

Figure 2.9 Borrowing Needs by Business Type or Industry 33

Figure 2.10 Summary of Borrowing Arrangements Offered by Banks 39

Chapter 3

Figure 3.1 Business Legal Structures 50

Figure 3.2 Business Life Cycle. 59

Figure 3.3 General Issues for Start-up Businesses 60

Figure 3.4 General Issues for Growth Businesses. 61

Figure 3.5 General Issues for Mature Businesses 62

Figure 3.6 General Issues for Decline Businesses. 63

Figure 3.7 Commercial Lending Business Life Cycle Characteristics. 65

Chapter 4

Figure 4.1 Financial Statement Analysis Process 73

Figure 4.2 Income Statement Spread: Dry Supply. 77

Figure 4.3 Balance Sheet Spread: Dry Supply 78

Figure 4.4 Footnotes to Financial Statements of Dry Supply. 90

Figure 4.5 Accountant's Cover Letter Excerpt—Dry Supply Compiled Financial Statements 91

Figure 4.6 Accountant's Cover Letter Excerpt—Dry Supply Reviewed Financial Statements 93

Figure 4.7 Accountant Cover Letter Excerpt—Dry Supply Audited Financial Statement—Unqualified Opinion. 94

Figure 4.8 Accountant Cover Letter Excerpt—Dry Supply Audited Financial Statement—Qualified Opinion 96

Figure 4.9 Accountant Cover Letter Excerpt—Dry Supply Audited Financial Statement—Adverse Opinion. 98

Figure 4.10 Accountant Cover Letter Excerpt—Dry Supply Audited Financial Statement—Going Concern Disclosure 99

Figure 4.11 Accountant Cover Letter Excerpt—Dry Supply Audited Financial Statement—Disclaimer of Opinion 100

Figure 4.12 Management Letter—Dry Supply Audited Financial Statement. 101

Chapter 5

Figure 5.1 Accounts of Gadgets Etc. After Transaction A 116

Figure 5.2 Accounts of Gadgets Etc. After Transaction B 117

Figure 5.3 Accounts of Gadgets Etc. After Transaction C 118

Figure 5.4 Accounts of Gadgets Etc. After Transaction D 119

Figure 5.5 Accounts of Gadgets Etc. After Transaction E 120

Figure 5.6 Accounts of Gadgets Etc. After Transaction F. 121

Figure 5.7 Accounts of Gadgets Etc. After Transaction G 122

Figure 5.8 Accounts of Gadgets Etc. After Transaction H 123

Figure 5.9 Accounts of Gadgets Etc. After Transaction I 124

Figure 5.10 Accounts of Gadgets Etc. After Transaction J 125

Figure 5.11 Accounts of Gadgets Etc. After Transaction K and All Transactions 126

Figure 5.12 Gadgets Etc. Accrual-Basis Balance Sheet and Income Statement for 20xy. 127

Figure 5.13 Gadgets Etc. Accounts after Transaction A. 128

Figure 5.14 Gadgets Etc. Accounts after Transaction B 129

Figure 5.15 Gadgets Etc. Accounts after Transaction C. 130

Figure 5.16 Gadgets Etc. Accounts after Transaction D. 131

Figure 5.17 Gadgets Etc. Accounts after Transaction E 132

Figure 5.18 Gadgets Etc. Accounts after Transaction F 133

Figure 5.19 Gadgets Etc. Accounts after Transaction G. 134

Figure 5.20 Gadgets Etc. Accounts after Transaction H and All Transactions 135

Figure 5.21 Gadgets Etc. Cash-Basis Balance Sheet and Income Statement for 20xy. 136

Figure 5.22 Gadgets Etc. Comparative Balance Sheets and Income Statements for Year Ended October 31, 20xy 136

Chapter 6

Figure 6.1 Income Statement Structure. 144

Figure 6.2 Income Statement Structure. 145

Figure 6.3 Income Statement Structure. 146

Figure 6.4 Income Statement Spread: Dry Supply. 148

Figure 6.5 Net Sales Calculation: Dry Supply ($ in 000s). 150

Figure 6.6 Dry Supply Sales Mix ($ in 000s). 152

Figure 6.7 Calculations of Cost of Goods for Businesses. 153

Figure 6.8 Inventory Purchases Illustration 155

Figure 6.9 LIFO and FIFO Inventory Valuation Comparison. 156

Figure 6.10 Weighted-average Cost Inventory Valuation Example
(Cost of Goods for Sale ÷ Units Available for Sale) 156

Figure 6.11 Inventory Valuation Comparison: Weighted-ave. Cost, LIFO, FIFO 157

Figure 6.12 Dry Supply Gross Profit ($ in 000s). 157

Figure 6.13 Income Statement Structure. 159

Figure 6.14 Dry Supply Operating Expense Trends ($ in 000s). 160

Figure 6.15 Operating Leverage Examples ($ in 000s) 162

Figure 6.16 Operating Leverage and Fixed Assets Example* 162

Chapter 7

Figure 7.1 Key Balance Sheet Accounts by Industry Type 173

Figure 7.2 Balance Sheet Spread: Dry Supply 175

Figure 7.3 Income Statement Spread: Dry Supply. 178

Figure 7.4 Abbreviated Accounts Receivable Aged Listing
for Dry Supply as of December 31, 20xz (from Invoice Date). 179

Figure 7.5 Depreciation Calculation Examples 185

Figure 7.6 Summary of Balance Sheet Categories 202

Chapter 8

Figure 8.1 Income Statement Spread: Dry Supply. 209

Figure 8.2 Balance Sheet Spread: Dry Supply 210

Figure 8.3 Definitions of Ratios 227

Figure 8.4 Trend and Comparative Analysis: Dry Supply 232

Chapter 9

Figure 9.1 Income Statement Spread: Dry Supply. 244

Figure 9.2 Balance Sheet Spread: Dry Supply 245

Figure 9.3 Dry Supply Statement of Cash Flows for the Year Ending 12/31/20xz ($ in 000s) 246

Figure 9.4 Dry Supply Statement of Cash Flows for the Year Ending 12/31/20xz ($ in 000s). 246

Figure 9.5 Dry Supply Capital Expenditures for the Year Ending 12/31/20xz ($ in 000s). 247

Figure 9.6 Dry Supply Statement of Cash Flows for the Year Ending 12/31/20xz ($ in 000s). 248

Figure 9.7 Dry Supply Debt Change Calculations for the Year Ending 12/31/20xz ($ in 000s) 249

Figure 9.8 Dry Supply Dividends Paid Calculation for the Year Ending 12/31/20xz ($ in 000s). 249

Figure 9.9 Dry Supply Statement of Cash Flows for the Year Ending 12/31/20xz ($ in 000s). 250

Figure 9.10 Dry Supply Cash Received from Customers Calculation
for the Year Ending 12/31/20xz ($ in 000s) 252

Figure 9.11 Dry Supply Cash Paid to Suppliers Calculation
for the Year Ending 12/31/20xz ($ in 000s) 252

Figure 9.12 Dry Supply Cash Paid for Operating Expenses
Calculation for the Year Ending 12/31/20xz ($ in 000s) 253

Figure 9.13 Dry Supply Cash Paid for Interest, Income Taxes, and Extraordinary Items
Calculation for the Year Ending 12/31/20xz ($ in 000s) 253

Figure 9.14 Dry Supply Statement of Cash Flows Operating
Activities (Direct Method) for the Year Ending 12/31/20xz ($ in 000s) 254

Figure 9.15 Dry Supply for the Year Ending 12/31/20xz ($ in 000s) Statement of Cash Flows 255

Figure 9.16 Abbreviated Cash Flow Report Format: Dry Supply
for the Year Ending 12/31/20xz ($ in 000s) 256

Figure 9.17 Dry Supply Statement of Cash Flows for the Year Ending 12/31/20xz ($ in 000s) 257

CHAPTER 10

Figure 10.1 Income Statement Spread: Dry Supply 265

Figure 10.2 Balance Sheet Spread: Dry Supply 266

Figure 10.3 Comparison of UCA and SCF Formats 268

Figure 10.4 Dry Supply Cash From Sales UCA Calculation for 20xz ($ in 000s) 269

Figure 10.5 Dry Supply Cash Production Costs UCA Calculation for 20xz ($ in 000s) 269

Figure 10.6 Dry Supply Cash Operating Expenses UCA Calculation for 20xz ($ in 000s) 270

Figure 10.7 Dry Supply Total Miscellaneous UCA Calculation for 20xz ($ in 000s) 270

Figure 10.8 Dry Supply Cash Paid for Taxes UCA Calculation for 20xz ($ in 000s) 271

Figure 10.9 Dry Supply UCA Cash Flow Model Net Cash After Operations for 20xz ($ in 000s) ... 271

Figure 10.10 Dry Supply Cash After Debt Amortization UCA Calculation for 20xz ($ in 000s) 272

Figure 10.11 Dry Supply Financing Surplus (Requirement) UCA Calculation for 20xz ($ in 000s) .. 273

Figure 10.12 Dry Supply Cash After External Financing UCA Calculation for 20xz ($ in 000s) ... 274

Figure 10.13 Dry Supply for the Year Ending 12/31/20xz ($ in 000s) 275

CHAPTER 11

Figure 11.1 Designs by Dezine—Monthly Sales ($ in 000s) 289

Figure 11.2 Designs by Dezine Summary Financial Information 289

Figure 11.3 Designs by Dezine 20yx Cash Budget ($ in 000s) 290

Figure 11.4 Company-Prepared Pro Forma Statement ($ in 000s) 300

Figure 11.5 Designs by Dezine Summary Financial Information 301

Figure 11.6 Designs by Dezine, Inc. for 20yx 303

Figure 11.7 Designs by Dezine, Inc. for 12/31/20yx 306

Figure 11.8 Designs by Dezine Fixed Asset Projection for 20yx ($ in 000s) 308

Figure 11.9 Designs by Dezine UCA Cash Flow Worksheet for
Year Ended 12/31/20yx Company-Prepared Projection ($ in 000s) 312

CHAPTER 12

Figure 12.1 Personal Financial Statement Format for Kaitlyn Nieson 324

CHAPTER 13

Figure 13.1 PFS for Ed and Linda Dezine 344

Chapter 14

Figure 14.1 Summary of Personal Balance Sheets of Linda C. and Edward G. Dezine 367

Figure 14.2 Dezines' Personal Cash Flow Statement 368

Chapter 15

Figure 15.1 Differences Between DSC and DTI 401

Figure 15.2 Summary of Personal Balance Sheets
of Linda C. and Edward G. Dezine 402

ACKNOWLEDGMENT

This new edition was updated by Richard Hamm, who has spent his entire career in banking, primarily in commercial lending and credit. His training work includes both creating and teaching courses for the American Bankers Association (ABA) and the Risk Management Association (RMA), plus regional banking schools, numerous state banking and community banking associations, and individual banks. He is based in Huntsville, AL and has owned/operated Advantage Consulting & Training since 2005, after a 22-year banking career including senior positions in lending and credit, plus actively training bankers since 1991. He earned BS and MBA degrees from the University of Alabama, and holds the CTP (Certified Treasury Professional) designation.

The American Bankers Association also wants to acknowledge George E. Ruth, who has made many contributions towards the education of bankers. Ruth began his banking career in 1965 and is a graduate of the American Bankers Association's Stonier Graduate School of Banking. Currently, he serves as Senior Vice President and Chief Credit Officer for Klein Bank. For the ABA, he authored the previous edition of Analyzing Financial Statements and the Commercial Lending textbooks. Ruth has also taught at ABA's National Commercial Lending School.

A special thanks to American Bankers Association's Bob Seiwert, who made valuable contributions to this new edition as an editor and reviewer.

Introduction

THE COMMERCIAL LENDING DECISION TREE

Commercial lending remains the primary income source for most community banks. The Commercial Lending Decision Tree approach is derived from two American Bankers Association (ABA) textbooks, *Analyzing Financial Statements* and *Commercial Lending* that have been combined and divided into **two textbooks**: *Analyzing Financial Statements: A Decision Tree Approach, Part 1* and *Commercial Lending: A Decision Tree Approach, Part 2*. The books focus on commercial and industrial lending (C&I), and exclude commercial real estate or investment properties. Although the textbooks together make up the content for the Commercial Lending Decision Tree curriculum, each can stand alone as well. However, used together they provide community bankers with an effective and efficient way to learn the commercial lending process.

The business lending process involves many steps. The process is grouped into a number of steps within different stages, and the steps do not necessarily occur in a particular order though for ease we will approach them in order for the two books. The first stage is emphasized where early screening and qualifying steps should prevent the lender from spending time on opportunities that have a low probability of being approved within the bank. Other steps in this stage involve determining the type of business, including its characteristics and structure, in order to better anticipate possible borrowing needs.

The second stage involves development of the credit proposal and possible approval of the request. After the preliminary screening, this stage is usually the most time consuming. The focal point of this part of the textbook is on analyzing business and personal financial statements and tax returns, which are key parts of these stages. The first and second stages together make up this textbook: *Analyzing Financial Statements: A Decision Tree Approach*.

The subsequent stages are covered in the *Commercial Lending: A Decision Tree Approach* textbook. These stages include dealing with non-financial issues and risks, negotiating and finalizing the terms and conditions of the request, plus dealing with problems that can occur during the monitoring of the loan over its repayment.

As mentioned, the commercial lending process involves many steps, and while these steps do not necessarily occur in a particular order, the chart below places them in a likely sequence that is grouped into six major stages. These are the stages that comprise the two textbooks. This process emphasizes early screening and qualifying steps that will prevent the lender from spending too much time on opportunities that have a low probability of being approved within the bank, and better recognizing key weaknesses that will require mitigating factors in order to move forward.

COMMERCIAL LENDING DECISION TREE

STAGES AND STEPS

STAGE ONE:
Preliminary Opportunity Assessment

- Initial Meetings with Business Owners/Managers or Development of Targeted Bank Call List
- Preliminary Screen for Business and Portfolio Fit
- Preliminary Screen for Business Financial and Nonfinancial Qualifications

Analyzing Financial Statements: A Decision Tree Approach, Part 1

SECTION 1
Understanding Business Borrowers

STAGE TWO:
Credit Proposal Development and Approval

- Develop Credit Proposal Structure; Assign a Risk Rating to the Transaction and/or Borrower
- Bank Approves, Modifies, or Denies Credit Proposal

SECTION 2
Analyzing Business Financial Statements and Tax Returns

SECTION 3
Analyzing Personal Financial Statements and Tax Returns

Commercial Lending: A Decision Tree Approach, Part 2

SECTION 1
Qualitative Analysis and Determining a Credit Risk Rating

STAGE THREE:
Presentation of Loan Proposal

- Customer Accepts, Declines, or Seeks Modified Credit Proposal

STAGE FOUR:
Loan Documentation and Closing

- Loan Agreement Is Structured Based Upon Agreed Terms and Conditions; Loan Is Closed

STAGE FIVE:
Loan Monitoring

- Monitor Loan Performance and Credit Risk Rating

SECTION 2
Loan Structuring, Documentation, Pricing, and Problem Loans

STAGE SIX:
Problem Loan Assessment and Action Steps

- Take Appropriate Problem Loan Actions if Business Does Not Perform as Planned

Negotiating and cross-selling of other bank products and services should occur throughout the credit decision

Section 1 of the *Analyzing Financial Statements: A Decision Tree Approach* focuses on understanding business industries and types, plus why they borrow money. It also introduces basic concepts of business financial accounting and entity structures. Section 2 covers the analysis of business financial statements and tax returns, including cash flow statements. Section 3 moves into personal financial statements and tax returns, including combining business and personal cash flows into a global analysis.

Successful business lending has always involved an understanding of the borrower that goes beyond the quantitative analysis covered in Sections 1 through 3. These qualitative factors include some of the following considerations:

- How the business is managed and key employees
- Primary products and services and how they are made or provided
- Competition with other businesses
- Local, regional, national, and international economic conditions and how they may affect the business
- Banking products and services that the business currently utilizes

Accordingly, Section 1 of the *Commercial Lending: A Decision Tree Approach* covers qualitative analysis and how to assess industry risk, market risk, and management risk. It also provides an understanding of the role of loan policy and the need to summarize the borrower's various risks into an appropriate credit risk rating.

Finally, Section 2 of the *Commercial Lending: A Decision Tree Approach* completes the lending process by providing guidance on loan structuring and documentation issues in response to the analysis of the quantitative and qualitative risks. This will include an overview of key documents, loan agreements, and covenants, as well as negotiating and pricing. This Section concludes with an introduction to problem loans.

Section 1
Understanding Business Borrowers

1

Business Sectors and Operating Cycles

OBJECTIVES

After studying *Business Sectors and Operating Cycles*, you will be able to—

- Describe the purpose of the operating cycle
- Analyze the financial data from an operating cycle
- Evaluate the risks within the major industry types

INTRODUCTION

Unlike most other companies that deal with a select group of suppliers and customers, banks establish financial relationships with businesses of all types, from the smallest dry-cleaning shop to the largest construction company. The variety of business industries is not only challenging but also professionally and intellectually rewarding to a business banker. A business banker is continuously learning, widening experiences, meeting interesting people, participating in the economic life of the community and region, and expanding awareness about global effects on the industries to which the bank lends. Most business bankers find this experience very enriching, and for many it becomes a reason to choose banking as a career.

The wide variety of businesses also places particular demands on business bankers, who must not only understand the business of banking, but also have a working knowledge of the businesses they call on. The type and size of businesses a business banker deals with, of course, depend on the size of the bank, the lender's expertise and lending authority, and the bank's defined market area. In addition, most businesses can be classified in one of the following categories:

- Agricultural
- Manufacturing
- Wholesaling
- Retailing
- Service
- Construction

Each category performs a different economic function and has unique operational characteristics.

Familiarity with these categories and their functions can help the business banker recognize the particular assets and financing needs of different businesses. An appreciation of the similarities and differences among businesses regarding their operating cycles, assets, liabilities, income data, lending needs, and other basic characteristics is important to the assessment of the business's creditworthiness.

Relationship to the Commercial Lending Decision Tree

In the textbook Introduction, we discussed the Commercial Lending Decision Tree as a way to think about the stages and steps involved in the commercial lending process. Although these steps do not necessarily occur in a particular order, the Decision Tree places them in a likely sequence. As shown in the Introduction illustration, this process emphasizes early screening and qualifying steps, which is where this textbook will help you. A business banker can greatly enhance the preliminary screening process by understanding the typical operational cycles of businesses.

Specifically, the lender needs to screen for general fit within the portfolio and goals of the bank. This involves the following types of questions:

- Is the firm in an acceptable or targeted industry?
- Is the firm within the bank's defined market area?
- Does adding this relationship cause the bank to exceed bank limits for the industry or the type of loan to be made?

- Does the loan meet regulatory requirements (such as allowable advance rates for margined collateral)?
- Does this loan opportunity allow the bank to earn an acceptable return, given the probable transaction risk?

Because most credits have weaknesses or may not clearly fit one of the above parameters, the lender should identify ways to mitigate the weaknesses before moving forward.

Similarly, the lender begins assessing financial and nonfinancial qualifications of the business to borrow from the bank. Understanding the industry, type of business, and operating cycles helps in developing this assessment, since it is typically done prior to an in-depth analysis of detailed financial information. As such, in this chapter we will focus on how a lender can begin this assessment process before receiving detailed financial statements and other data.

OPERATING CYCLES

The **operating cycle** of a business is an important factor to understand before making a financial analysis and lending decision.

As shown in the commercial lending decision tree, once initial meetings and preliminary screening of the business have taken place, one of the next steps in the lending process is to understand the type of business and its operating cycle. Businesses may be categorized as agricultural, manufacturing, wholesaling, retailing, service, or construction. The ways in which each business category produces or distributes a product or service illustrate how each has a distinct operating cycle.

> **Operating cycle**
> The time required to purchase or manufacture inventory or provide service, sell the product or provide the service, and collect the cash.

OPERATING CYCLE PURPOSE

A business operating cycle illustrates how a company uses cash to produce a product or provide a service. The cycle begins and ends with cash. It reveals information about the nature and amount of financing needed, appropriate sources of repayment, timing of repayment, and risks associated with repayment. An infusion of cash is used to buy raw materials (in manufacturing and agriculture) or finished goods (in wholesaling or retailing) or hire labor (for service and construction companies). This cash comes from a variety of sources, including equity supplied by the owners of the business, trade creditors, or bank loans. As sales increase, the amount of cash needed increases. If fixed assets support sales, at some point the assets will reach capacity, and more will need to be purchased.

> **Working capital**
> A firm's investment in current assets, namely cash, marketable securities, accounts receivable, and inventory. Working capital is liquid and therefore is available to meet current business needs. The difference between a firm's current assets and current liabilities is called working capital.

The length of the operating cycle varies among industries and businesses. It affects the amount of **working capital** needed. Working capital, the owners' investment and long-term debt holders' loans used in the operating cycle, is calculated as current assets less current liabilities. The longer it takes to complete the operating cycle, the greater the need for working capital. A printing press manufacturer, for example, has a longer operating cycle than an ice cream shop. Working capital is a firm's investment in current assets, namely cash, marketable securities, accounts receivable, and inventory. Working capital is liquid and therefore is available to meet current business needs. The difference between a firm's current assets and current liabilities is called working capital. *See also* net working capital.

It is also important to understand whether a change in the operating cycle is temporary or permanent. A temporary need to fund increases in current assets should be financed by short-term debt or a revolving line of credit. An ongoing need to fund increases in current assets should be financed with long-term debt or even a permanent working capital loan if the company is growing rapidly.

The nature of sales also affects the need for cash. A large warehouse grocery store has greater cash needs than a local convenience store, because the warehouse grocery store needs to stock more inventory to support its sales.

Cash from a profitable operating cycle is used to repay short-term debt and reduce long-term debt. It also is distributed as dividends and used to begin another operating cycle. Bank loans are structured in many ways to inject cash at crucial points in the operating cycle to ensure its completion. Seasonal and term loans as well as lines of credit are examples of loan types that provide cash when it is needed most.

The operating cycle—a valuable tool in understanding the characteristics of a business—is a way for the business banker to visualize the business structure. It provides a framework that a business banker can use to prepare for customer interviews and to know what to investigate and what to analyze in financial statements. By isolating each step and understanding internal and external factors that influence or disrupt each step, the business banker will discover opportunities for the bank to provide products and services to help the business and its management achieve its goals.

AGRICULTURAL BUSINESSES

The agricultural industry is important to the economy of many communities. The umbrella term "agricultural industry" encompasses many businesses that can also be considered manufacturers, wholesalers, retailers, or service companies.

In many ways, an agricultural operating cycle is similar to that of a manufacturer (Figure 1.1). Cash is used to purchase seeds, fertilizer, livestock, equipment, and other materials for growing inventory. However, unlike manufacturing, agricultural inventory is not necessarily a finished good but a crop, milk, livestock, or other farm product such as logs. The product is sold on the market, creating accounts receivable that, when paid, generate cash used in the next operating cycle. Figure 1.2 provides a summary of Agricultural Lending.

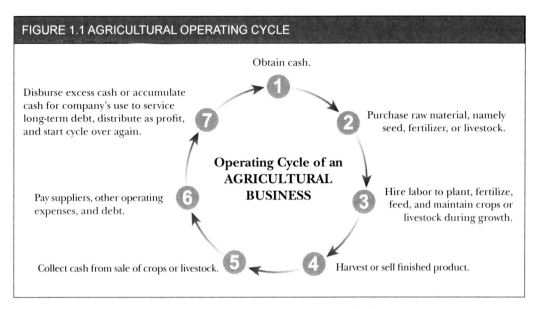

Note: The more acres planted or more livestock grown, the more cash needed in the operating cycle.

FIGURE 1.2 AGRICULTURAL LENDING SUMMARY

AGRICULTURAL BUSINESS LOAN PURPOSES	AGRICULTURAL BUSINESS RISKS	AGRICULTURAL BUSINESS FINANCIAL CHARACTERISTICS
• Purchase seed, plants, fertilizer, or livestock • Purchase equipment • Finance land • Fund living and operating expenses • Pay labor	• Adverse weather • Falling crop prices • Increasing seed, fertilizer, and operating costs • Maintenance and repair costs • Quality of labor • Declining land values	• Fixed assets are largest asset at about 50 percent of total assets • Inventory is next largest asset, but only 18 percent of total assets • Liabilities evenly split between current and long-term • Leverage as high as 4.0x • Gross profits about 35 percent of sales

MANUFACTURERS

A manufacturer is engaged in transforming raw material or assembling parts into a finished product, which is then sold to wholesalers or retailers. Some manufacturers, called fabricators, buy raw materials and change their form. A wood furniture company (fabricator) does this when it buys lumber from a forester (processor) and transforms it into dining room tables. Other manufacturers, called assemblers, purchase finished parts, such as screws and steel, and make finished products, such as metal boxes.

The operating cycle for manufacturers starts with cash to finance the purchase of raw materials. Some raw materials purchases are financed by suppliers. This form of credit is called trade credit, trade payables, or accounts payable (Figure 1.3). Using the raw materials, finished goods inventory is manufactured and then sold on credit to create accounts receivable. When the accounts receivable are collected, the cash generated is used to purchase more raw materials, pay dividends, pay debt, and begin the cycle again. As sales grow, the operating cycle expands, creating a greater need for cash. This cash can come from trade credit, owners' equity, or bank debt.

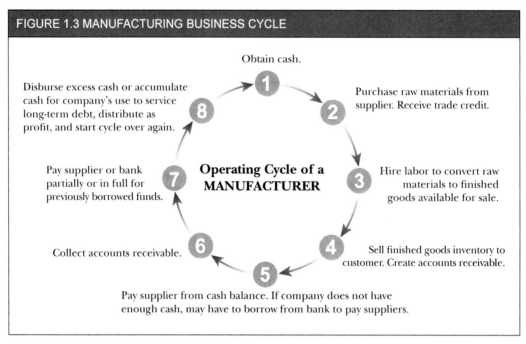

Note: The longer it takes a company to complete each step in the cycle, the more money the company will need in order to complete its operating cycle.

It is important that the business banker differentiate between seasonal and nonseasonal businesses, because the nature of the financing need and the bank's loan structure will be very different. A seasonal business may have large, short-term financing needs that are repaid when the season is completed. The business banker distinguishes between completing the operating cycle and having cash to repay short-term debt (seasonal need) and completing the operating cycle and reinvesting cash to maintain the viable core business (permanent need).

For example, before a dining room table reaches the home of a consumer, one or more agricultural, manufacturing, wholesaling, retailing, service, or construction businesses may have been involved in the process that began with growing or harvesting wood. A manufacturer of wood furniture first buys raw lumber from an agricultural company (forestry) to produce dining room tables for thousands of homes. Rather than form an account relationship with each furniture store, the manufacturer can utilize a wholesaler, which buys large quantities of tables for eventual distribution to its retail business customers.

In this example, cash is used to purchase lumber (raw material) and hire labor to cut, sand, and glue the lumber, thereby producing the finished table (finished goods inventory). When the tables are sold to wholesalers or retailers, for example, on 30-day credit terms, accounts receivable are created.

To make a profit, a manufacturer's cash sales must exceed the expense of producing and selling inventory. The business banker's job is to determine how much cash is generated and available through the operating cycle to service the company's debt.

Another consideration is any factor that may disrupt the operating cycle and, therefore, the flow of cash. For the wood furniture manufacturer, obvious factors include rising lumber prices and outdated or deteriorating equipment that needs to be replaced. These factors increase the cost of manufacturing inventory. Each risk can interrupt the operating cycle that produces the cash to repay debts and keep the company a going concern.

General characteristics

In general, manufacturing businesses are more capital-intensive than labor-intensive. Manufacturers require a large amount of debt and equity to carry assets that support their operations. Before a wood furniture manufacturer can make its first dining room table, it must obtain substantial capital to build or lease a plant and purchase equipment. Manufacturing companies usually hold most of their assets in inventory, accounts receivable, and fixed assets.

A manufacturer's income statement has gross margins approximately the same as agricultural businesses. This is partially explained by the value added by labor and equipment in the manufacturing process. The total of all costs is the "cost price" prior to any markup. Markup is the amount added to the cost price to calculate the selling price after taking into consideration overhead and profit. Figure 1.4 provides a summary of Manufacturer Lending.

FIGURE 1.4 MANUFACTURER LENDING SUMMARY

MANUFACTURER LOAN PURPOSES	MANUFACTURER RISKS	MANUFACTURER FINANCIAL CHARACTERISTICS
• Fund raw materials purchases • Fund work-in-process and labor • Carry accounts receivable • Purchase plant or make improvements • Purchase equipment	• Inability to sell product • Quality of raw material used • Labor costs and availability • Collection of accounts receivable • Efficiency of plant operations • Knowledge of operating costs • Accurately assigning costs to products	• Inventory is largest asset at about 40 percent of total assets • Fixed assets are next largest at about 25 percent of total assets • Current liabilities more than double amount of long-term liabilities • Leverage as high as 2.5x • Gross profits about 33 percent of sales • Very thin (1 percent) net profit margin

WHOLESALERS

Wholesalers are inventory managers that typically operate as intermediaries for manufacturers. They do not produce goods, but purchase finished goods from manufacturers and then sell the items to retailers or end users for a profit. Retailers are the typical final distributors of products.

The operating cycle of a wholesaler begins with cash to purchase finished goods inventory from manufacturers. Unlike the manufacturer, the wholesaler adds no value to these finished goods, other than possibly packaging (Figure 1.5). When the inventory is sold, accounts receivable are created, which on payment are converted to cash, thus completing the cycle. The large amount of inventory purchased and sold is a notable characteristic of the operating cycle of wholesalers. With the high rate of inventory turnover, the gross profit, as a percentage of sales, is usually low and of limited added value.

For example, a wholesaler paid cash for dining room tables and distributes the dining room tables to retail furniture stores, which generates accounts receivable for the wholesaler. As the accounts receivable were paid, cash was produced, which will be used to purchase more inventory, repay debts, and start the cycle again. Occasionally, the wholesaler overestimates the retailer's demand for tables and ends up with more inventory than needed. Instead of selling the tables at less than cost and absorbing a loss, the wholesaler may decide to keep the tables at a storage company until they are needed. The storage company, which has had no direct hand in the manufacturing, distribution, or sale of the furniture, is a service company.

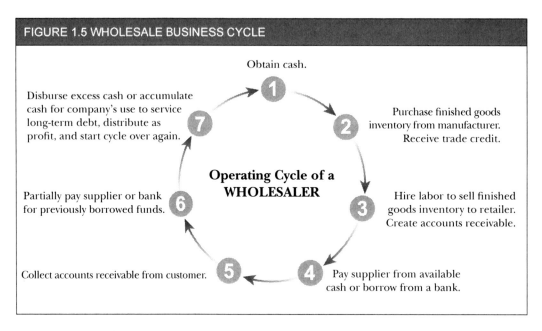

FIGURE 1.5 WHOLESALE BUSINESS CYCLE

Note: The longer it takes a company to complete each step in the cycle, the more money the company will need in order to complete its operating cycle.

Assessing the risk of a wholesale borrower

With wholesalers, the business banker assesses the risks that might disrupt the operating cycle. In evaluating a loan to a furniture wholesaler, a concentration of receivables and the special use of inventory may warrant consideration.

A significant portion of a wholesaler's assets are in accounts receivable and inventory with relatively low fixed asset needs. Because wholesalers are not location-specific businesses and basically need storage or warehouse space, most wholesalers have fewer fixed assets than manufacturers. Of a wholesaler's liabilities, a significant portion is in accounts payable. For wholesalers in general, fixed assets average about 15 percent of total assets, which are minimal but expected when the principal fixed assets are items such as storage racks. The 15 percent for fixed assets is about half that of manufacturers.

For furniture wholesalers, accounts receivable and inventory totaled about 67 percent of all assets. Their 29 percent gross margin is high for wholesalers. Most wholesalers' gross margins range from 8 percent to 15 percent net sales. The low gross margin for wholesalers reflects limited value added for the finished product being sold. Figure 1.6 provides a summary of Wholesaler Lending.

FIGURE 1.6 WHOLESALER LENDING SUMMARY

WHOLESALER LOAN PURPOSES	WHOLESALER RISKS	WHOLESALER FINANCIAL CHARACTERISTICS
• Fund finished goods purchases • Fund new product purchases • Carry accounts receivable • Purchase plant or expansions • Purchase equipment	• Quality of product • Inability to market product • Credit approval policies • Collection of accounts receivable • Relationship with vendors	• Inventory and accounts receivable are largest assets at about 30 percent each of total assets • Fixed assets are next largest at about 15 percent of total assets • Current liabilities comprise about 80 percent of total liabilities, with accounts payable as largest liability (about 25 percent of total) • Leverage as high as 2.5x • Gross profits about 8–15 percent of sales • Stronger (2.2 percent) net profit margin

RETAILERS

Retailers buy finished products through wholesalers or directly from manufacturers, and then sell those products to consumers, usually for cash. Retailing businesses are diverse, ranging from sellers of diamond rings to gasoline service stations. Cash required to finance a retail operation is a function of sales volume and type of business. A company with high sales volume usually holds a significant amount of inventory, which requires more cash. However, because retailing is a cash or credit card business, there are generally few, if any, accounts receivable.

The operating cycle of a retailer begins with purchasing a finished product either directly from a manufacturer or through a wholesaler (Figure 1.7). Inventory usually is sold directly to the public. For this reason, most sales are cash rather than accounts receivable. Cash is used to purchase additional inventory and thus begin

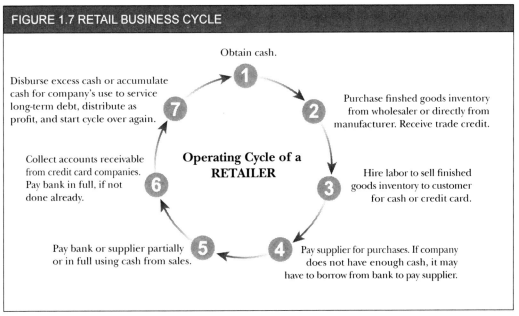

Note: The longer it takes a company to complete each step in the cycle, the more money the company will need in order to complete its operating cycle.

another cycle. However, there are exceptions to cash sales only. A retail drugstore with a pharmacy, for example, will have accounts receivable from insurance companies for prescriptions filled. In the dining room table example, a furniture wholesaler sold tables to a furniture store, where the tables were placed in the store's display area and bought with cash by consumers. The cash then was used to pay suppliers and purchase additional inventory.

Evaluating a retailer's financial statements

Because many retailers lease space, fixed-asset needs are usually limited. They may require leasehold improvements, such as carpet or lighting financed by the lender or the property owner. Retailing is a location-specific business, which may inflate certain expenses, such as lease (rental) expense.

A key in evaluating a retailer is to evaluate inventory turnover. Retailers, particularly those such as grocery stores that sell large amounts of low-ticket and perishable items, must move large amounts of inventory quickly. Low consumer demand and other factors can disrupt the operating cycle.

Balance sheet items, such as inventory and fixed assets, vary considerably among retailers. Gasoline service stations have a high proportion of fixed assets. This is not surprising in an industry where the principal expense items are buildings and improvements. On the other hand, the gasoline service station's accounts receivable are minimal. With a jewelry or clothing store, the asset situation is somewhat reversed, with inventory the primary asset and fixed assets relatively insignificant.

Furniture retailers have several differences in financial characteristics compared with furniture manufacturers and wholesalers. Some differences can be attributed to a lack of receivables, since manufacturers and wholesalers sell products on credit. Also, to produce a product, manufacturers need more fixed assets.

For the furniture store in the dining room table example, we can expect a small proportion of receivables (about 15 percent) because some furniture is bought on credit. We can expect the percentage of assets held as inventory to be high, as well a relatively high gross margin of about 40 percent. Manufacturers have a lower gross margin because of the costs involved in making the product. Wholesalers, in general, have a lower gross margin because of fewer price markups. A retailer's operating ex-

FIGURE 1.8 RETAILER LENDING SUMMARY

RETAILER LOAN PURPOSES	RETAILER RISKS	RETAILER FINANCIAL CHARACTERISTICS
• Fund permanent inventory purchases • Fund seasonal inventory purchases • Fund leasehold improvements • Purchase equipment	• Inability to sell product • Product quality and mix • Service provided by employees • Employee theft (shrinkage) • Relationship with vendors	• Inventory is largest asset at about 50 percent of total assets • Fixed assets are next largest at about 20 percent of total assets • Current liabilities (mostly accounts payable) about 2.5x the amount of long-term liabilities • Leverage as high as 2.5x • Gross profits about 40 percent of sales • Net profit margin of about 2 percent

penses (or overhead) are higher because of sales costs and the cost of carrying a larger inventory to provide adequate selection for purchasers, plus space rental expense. Figure 1.8 provides a summary of Retailer Lending.

SERVICE BUSINESSES

Unlike manufacturers, wholesalers, or retailers, businesses in the service industry do not sell a tangible product. Their product—service—can include financial consultation, legal advice, medical treatment, or, as in the wood furniture example, warehousing. Banking is a service industry and, just as with other service industries, success depends on the quality of service delivered and the ideas offered to customers that will help them achieve their goals or improve their financial condition.

Because there is no inventory, a service business operating cycle is different from those of a manufacturer, wholesaler, or retailer (Figure 1.9). Cash pays for the labor to provide a service that generates cash or accounts receivable. When accounts receivable are paid, the cash created is used to pay debt and begin the cycle again. The warehouse service firm in the furniture example used space in a leased or owned facility to perform a service for which the furniture wholesaler was billed. When the wholesaler paid bills (accounts receivable), cash was created for the warehouse business. This cash was used to pay electric bills, rent, salaries, debt, and other expenses incurred.

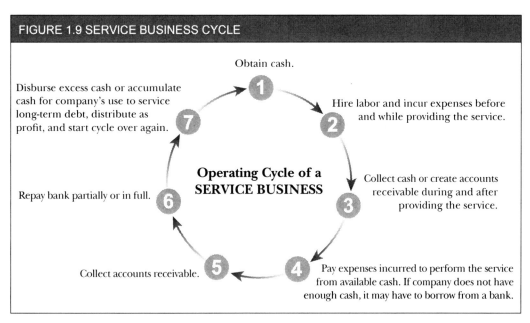

FIGURE 1.9 SERVICE BUSINESS CYCLE

Note: The longer it takes a company to complete each step in the cycle, the more money the company will need in order to complete its operating cycle.

Financial statements of a service business

A service business may have inventory on the balance sheet, which represents parts and supplies used in providing the service. However, the business typically will not have cost of goods sold.

For the transportation-general warehousing industry pertinent to our furniture example, the balance sheet should be similar to that of most service industries. Warehousing businesses have significant cash and accounts receivable amounts, but low inventory. Unlike other service industries, however, a warehousing firm's fixed assets are high, which is attributable to holdings in real estate—primarily warehouse space.

Service businesses have few or no product costs and, therefore, the gross profit is often near 100 percent of revenues. For service firms, net sales are known as revenues. However, for comparison purposes, analysts commonly use the term "net sales." All expenses to provide the service are included in operating expenses.

The risks that may disrupt the operating cycle vary by the type of service industry. For example, the collection of accounts receivable may disrupt the operating cycle of a doctor, but the capacity constraints of the fixed assets would disrupt the operating cycle of a bus company. Figure 1.10 provides a summary of Service Business Lending.

FIGURE 1.10 SERVICE BUSINESS LENDING SUMMARY		
SERVICE BUSINESS LOAN PURPOSES	**SERVICE BUSINESS RISKS**	**SERVICE BUSINESS FINANCIAL CHARACTERISTICS**
• Carry accounts receivable • Fund fixed asset purchases • Fund leasehold improvements	• Quality of service provided • Credit approval process • Collection of accounts receivable • Quality and capacity of fixed assets • Demand for service	• Accounts receivable is largest asset at about 35 percent of total assets • Fixed assets are next largest at about 30 percent of total assets • Liabilities evenly split between current and long-term • Leverage as high as 2.5x • Gross profits about 100 percent of sales • Net profit margin of about 7.5 percent

Other service related businesses

Because nothing tangible is produced, most service businesses have few physical assets and thus, comparatively low long-term debt needs. There are exceptions, however, because the service industry encompasses everything from airports to operators of apartment buildings to school bus operators. These capital-intensive industries require long-term debt to support large fixed assets. Other types of service businesses, such as law firms, require financing for assets such as accounts receivable. A concentration of accounts receivable or a large number of uncollected receivables may indicate a potential disruption of the operating cycle and, therefore, a risk to the lender. Inventory, however, is usually an insignificant asset, which is not surprising in an industry that primarily sells knowledge and expertise. Figure 1.11 provides a table of Other Service-Related Businesses.

CONSTRUCTION BUSINESSES

Some lenders would consider a construction business to be part of the service industry. However, the construction industry is usually categorized separately. Construction businesses range from local homebuilders to bridge builders. Included in this industry are **subcontractors**, which are businesses or individuals (sole pro-

> **Subcontractor**
>
> One who takes a portion of a contract from the principal contractor or from another subcontractor.

FIGURE 1.11 OTHER SERVICE-RELATED BUSINESSES

The United States Census Bureau breaks the service industry into major categories for its North American Industry Classification System (NAICS) codes. The structure of the six-digit NAICS codes is similar to ten-digit phone numbers. Whereas the first three digits of a phone number is an area code, the first two digits of the NAICS code is a broad industry category, such as wholesale trade (42) and retail trade (44 and 45).

FIRST TWO NAICS CODE DIGITS	CATEGORY	INDUSTRIES INCLUDED
48 and 49	Transportation and warehousing	Railroads, local passenger transportation, bus charter, school buses, local trucking, courier, farm product warehousing, marine cargo airports, and packing
51	Information	Newspapers, periodicals, book publishing, radio and television, direct mail, computer processing, motion picture, and prepackaged software
52	Finance and insurance	Banking, business credit institutions, loan brokers, title insurance, insurance carriers, and real estate investment trusts
53	Real estate and rental and leasing	Operators of apartment buildings, real estate agents, heavy construction equipment rental, computer rental, and passenger car leasing
54	Professional, scientific and technical services	Veterinary services, title abstract offices, photographic studios, outdoor advertising, engineering, legal, commercial research, and public relations
55	Management of companies and enterprises	Offices of bank holding companies and offices of holding companies not classified elsewhere
56	Administration and support and waste management and remediation services	Travel agencies, tour operators, refuse systems, pest control services, employment agencies, security systems services and facilities support management services
61	Educational services	Dance studios and halls, elementary and secondary schools, junior colleges and vocational schools
62	Health care and social assistance	Offices of clinics and doctors, dentists, chiropractors, nursing and personal care facilities, general medical and surgical hospitals, home health care, job training and residential care
71	Arts, entertainment and recreation	Marinas, theatrical producers, bowling centers, public golf courses and amusement parks
72	Accommodation and food services	Restaurants, drinking places, hotels, motels and recreational vehicle parks
81	Other services (except public administration)	Power laundries, linen supply, dry-cleaning plants, beauty shops, funeral homes and car washes
92	Public administration	Fire protection, general government and administration of public housing programs

prietors) a general contractor may hire to complete portions of the work. Subcontractors take a portion of a contract from the principal contractor or from another subcontractor. Architects, carpenters, masons, plumbing, heating, and electrical companies typically are subcontracted to perform construction work.

A construction company may be involved in any of the previously mentioned businesses. It may have built the factory used by the manufacturer to produce the furniture, the wholesaler's transport facility to deliver the furniture to the retailer, the store used by the retailer to sell the furniture to the consumer, and the warehouse used to store surplus furniture for future sales to retailers.

The operating cycle of a construction business begins with cash used to hire labor and purchase materials (Figure 1.12). One unique feature of the construction industry is how most suppliers of materials and subcontractors are paid. For small, shorter-term projects, the supplier or subcontractor is paid on completion of the project. For large projects that may take up to several years to complete, a progress payment is collected and paid to the supplier or subcontractor. A portion of the payment is retained until the project is completed. This amount is called **retainage** and listed as an account receivable on the balance sheet. Retainage is usually paid at the end of the project. If a subcontractor performs work early in the project, such as the foundation, the subcontractor may not be paid retainage until the building is complete.

> **Retainage**
> The amount of a contractor's bill that is withheld until the job has been completed.

Construction industry financial risks

Because of the complex nature of building homes and commercial buildings, many things may disrupt the operating cycle of a construction business. A notable risk for contractors is performance issues. Collecting receivables for work completed to the

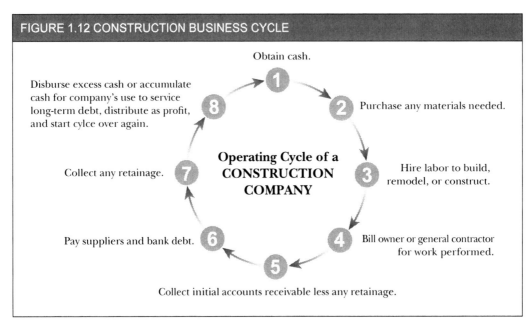

FIGURE 1.12 CONSTRUCTION BUSINESS CYCLE

Operating Cycle of a CONSTRUCTION COMPANY

1. Obtain cash.
2. Purchase any materials needed.
3. Hire labor to build, remodel, or construct.
4. Bill owner or general contractor for work performed.
5. Collect initial accounts receivable less any retainage.
6. Pay suppliers and bank debt.
7. Collect any retainage.
8. Disburse excess cash or accumulate cash for company's use to service long-term debt, distribute as profit, and start cylce over again.

Note: The more jobs performed, the greater the need for cash to keep the operating cycle going.

building owner's satisfaction may be delayed because of a dispute or problem on work currently being performed. Business bankers also should be wary of accounts receivable from contracts requiring strict adherence to payment specifications. If the specifications are not met, accounts receivable may not be paid. Figure 1.13 provides a summary of Construction Lending.

FIGURE 1.13 CONSTRUCTION LENDING SUMMARY		
CONSTRUCTION BUSINESS LOAN PURPOSES	CONSTRUCTION BUSINESS RISKS	CONSTRUCTION BUSINESS FINANCIAL CHARACTERISTICS
• Fund construction materials purchases • Pay subcontractors • Fund equipment purchases • Pay operating expenses • Standby letters of credit	• Underbidding projects • Labor costs and availability • Collection of accounts receivable and retainages • Subcontractor work quality • Completing projects on time (weather and other disruptions) • Unexpected conditions such as poor soil • Change orders	• Accounts receivable is largest asset at about 40 percent of total assets and consisting primarily of progress billings • Cash and equivalents are next largest at about 20 percent of total assets, with a relatively small 15 percent in fixed assets • Liabilities primarily short-term, with about one-half in trade payables • Leverage as high as 2.5x • Gross profits low at about 17 percent of sales • Net profit margin of about 2.5 percent

Evaluating the construction business financial statements

Contractors using the percentage of completion accounting are allowed to recognize revenues, expenses, and profits periodically as work on a contract proceeds. This results in two unusual balance sheet accounts as follows:

- **Underbillings**, or the asset account called "costs and estimated earnings in excess of billings," is the difference between the sum of total costs and recognized estimated earnings-to-date versus the total billings-to-date. Basically, this is work performed by the contractor that has not been billed to the customer nor collected. Increases in underbillings may indicate internal accounting or processing problems, or even a dispute with the customer over the percentage of work completed.
- **Overbillings**, or the liability "billings in excess of costs and estimated earnings," is the difference between the total billings-to-date and sum of the total of cost and unrecognized estimated earnings-to-date. In effect, the contractor is speeding up its cash flow by billing more than the costs-to-date.

An alternative to percentage of completion accounting is completed contract. With this method, income is recognized only when the project is completed. During construction, costs and expenses accumulate as construction-in-progress, very similar to work-in-progress inventory for a manufacturer.

In this section, you learned about the operating cycle of each business type, their typical activities, and general financing needs that match the operating cycle steps. You also learned some possible risks associated with each business industry. You should now feel more confident in assisting your business customers with their day-to-day financial needs.

OPERATING CYCLE APPLICATION

The operating cycle and typical financial data for agriculture, manufacturers, wholesalers, retailers, service, and construction companies vary greatly.

The operating cycle indicates a business's true liquidity. By comparing the historical record of a company with its peer groups in the same industry, you can apply the information and evaluate the financial picture of a business.

Accounts receivable are highest for the contractor, which is a normal situation considering that little or no inventory is sold. Because it is their primary asset, inventory is highest for retailers. Fixed assets are highest for the service company in warehousing, which is unusual, because in many service companies accounts receivable is the primary asset.

Because of the high fixed assets in the service company example, the long-term debt also is high. Most manufactures fund equipment purchases with high levels of long-term debt. Frequently, because no costs are involved in selling or producing their service, gross profit is highest for service companies, often near 100 percent.

ANALYZING THE FINANCIAL DATA

The nature of a company's business determines whether a loan should be made and under what terms. For the furniture manufacturer, suppose that 60 percent of the assets are accounts receivable and 10 percent are inventory. Based on this information, would it be advisable to grant a loan? In a different business, such as the wholesale furniture industry, this situation might not be unusual. However, accounts receivable average about 22 percent and inventory averages 33 percent in the furniture manufacturing industry.

The Dining Tables Example, shown in Figure 1.14, along with the different business types or industries that you have learned in this chapter, allows you to look at the various industry financial profiles side by side. Understanding, or at least anticipating, these profiles is key in the lending decision process as part of the initial screening of the credit. Understanding the financial profile helps the lender in the following ways:

- It expedites the gathering of data by knowing important areas to investigate
- It provides key areas for questioning of the managers and owners
- It anticipates typical financing needs prior to in-depth financial analysis
- It highlights key areas for attention in the subsequent written analysis and discussion

In a sense, the relative proportions shown in Figure 1.14 can serve as a guideline for allocating space and time in the analytical process and written output. For example, the dominant asset for a service business involved in warehousing is fixed assets. One of the smaller assets is inventory. Accordingly, the financial analysis should not focus heavily on trends and issues with inventory—they simply are not likely to be important to the credit decision. However, small changes and trends in fixed assets, because of the sheer size of this account relative to the others, should receive intense analysis and scrutiny during the financial analysis.

Deviations from these expected profiles can help uncover important management strategies or issues that the borrower may face. These deviations from the profile are also important for the business banker to explore and understand, because they set a framework of expectations before receiving detailed financial information and allow the lender to make progress within the Commercial Lending Decision Tree you read about in the Introduction.

FIGURE 1.14 TYPICAL FINANCIAL PROFILES FOR VARIOUS BUSINESSES (DINING TABLES EXAMPLE)

	AGRICULTURE (LOGGING)	MANUFACTURER (WOOD FURNITURE)	WHOLESALER (FURNITURE)	RETAILER (FURNITURE)	SERVICE (WAREHOUSING)	CONTRACTOR (INDUSTRIAL BUILDINGS)
Accounts Receivable	10%*	22%	37%	14%	18%	40%
Inventory	13%*	33%	29%	50%	2%	2%
Net Fixed Assets	53%*	28%	13%	18%	55%	16%
Accounts Payable	5%*	15%	22%	18%	8%	30%
Long-Term Debt	30%*	21%	9%	11%	7%	7%
Gross Profit	31%**	31%	29%	41%	100%	15%
Operating Expenses	28%**	28%	27%	39%	83%	13%
Profit Before Taxes	<1%**	1%	1%	2%	8%	2%

* Percentage of total assets or total liabilities and equity. **Percentage of sales.

EVALUATING THE RISKS

A business banker who is aware of the difference between manufacturers and wholesalers would seriously question granting credit to the manufacturer discussed above, with 60 percent of assets composed of accounts receivable and 10 percent in inventory. This business may be having trouble collecting accounts receivable and maintaining sufficient inventory.

By reviewing the risks within the major industry types, a business banker can visualize why one entity, such as a service company, should have a greater gross margin than another.

In Figure 1.15, you will see the industry risks summary for the various business types.

In this section, you learned how to analyze data derived from the operating cycle of each business industry. You also learned how to evaluate the risks associated within the major industry types. You are now better prepared to ask your business customers financial questions that relate to their operating cycle and industry type.

FIGURE 1.15 INDUSTRY RISKS SUMMARY					
AGRICULTURE	MANUFACTURER	WHOLESALER	RETAILER	SERVICE	CONSTRUCTION
Adverse weather	Inability to sell product	Quality of product	Inability to sell product	Quality of service provided	Underbidding projects
Falling crop prices	Quality of raw material used	Inability to market product	Product quality and mix	Credit approval process	Labor costs and availability
Increasing seed, fertilizer, and operating costs	Labor costs and availability	Credit approval process	Service provided by employees	Collection of accounts receivable	Completing a project on time (weather and other disruptions)
Maintenance and repair costs	Collection of accounts receivable	Collection of accounts receivable	Employee theft (shrinkage)	Quality and capacity of fixed assets	Unexpected conditions such as poor soil
Quality of labor	Efficiency of plant operation	Relationship with vendors	Relationship with vendors	Demand for service	Subcontractor work quality
Declining land values	Knowledge of operating costs				Change orders
	Accurately assigning costs to products				Collection of accounts receivable and retainages

SUMMARY

Most business industries are considered to be agricultural, manufacturing, wholesaling, retailing, service, or construction companies. Companies that fall within each category have similar operating cycles, balance sheets, income data, and risks. A business banker who understands these distinctions can anticipate a business's financial strengths and weaknesses.

By completing this chapter, you have learned the preliminary steps in Stage One of the commercial lending process. You have gained a better understanding of the characteristics, operating cycles, typical borrowing purposes, and risks within the major industry types.

QUESTIONS FOR DISCUSSION

1. What might be the risks in lending to a manufacturer of shoes?
2. A retail drugstore decides to offer credit terms to customers, rather than require cast payments at the time products are purchased. What effect does this change in payment policy have on the store's operating cycle?

EXERCISE 1

Application to Dry Supply Background

Dry Supply is a wholesaler of dry-cleaning equipment, cleaning supplies, and laundry soap. The company, which is located in central Kansas, has been in business more than 50 years. Anne Schippel, business banker, has made a couple of introductory calls and knows that Dry Supply currently is owned by two sisters and is organized as an S corporation. Based on this understanding, she can begin making a preliminary assessment of the loan request.

While performing her preliminary screening of the business, Schippel found the typical financial profile for the industry (see table below).

WHOLESALE LAUNDRY AND DRY-CLEANING EQUIPMENT AND SUPPLIES (TYPICAL FINANCIAL DATA)

Assets	Percent
Accounts receivable	30%
Inventory	35%
Total current assets	76%
Net fixed assets	16%

Liabilities	Percent
Notes payable (short-term debt)	15%
Current maturities of long-term debt	3%
Accounts payable	20%
Total current liabilities	47%
Long-term debt	13%
Total liabilities	65%
Net worth	35%

Income Statement	Percent
Net sales	100%
Gross profit	35%
Operating expenses	32%
Operating profit	3%
Profit before taxes	2%

Instructions

Answer the following questions using the operating cycle information in this chapter- and the industry data shown above.

A. As a wholesaler, what is the company's operating cycle likely to involve?
B. What is the largest asset and the largest liability?
C. What risks may disrupt the operating cycle?
D. What additional questions should Anne Schippel ask, consistent with Stage One of the Commercial Lending Decision Tree, as illustrated in the textbook Introduction?

EXERCISE 2

In the table below, each asset, liability, and net worth account is a percentage of total assets and each income account is a percentage of net sales.

Identify which of the businesses in the table below is a manufacturer of mattresses, wholesaler of fish, retailer of recreational vehicles, cleaning and maintenance business, or retail drugstore. Give reasons for your answer.

Business	A	B	C	D	E
	Percentage of Balance Sheet or Income Statement				
Assets					
Accounts receivable	39	42	3	29	19
Inventory	28	4	76	27	47
Net fixed assets	16	24	11	27	15
Liabilities					
Notes payable (short-term debt)	20	12	46	7	7
Current maturities of long-term debt	3	4	3	4	4
Accounts payable	27	12	8	23	25
Total current liabilities	59	44	66	42	45
Long-term debt	6	14	9	14	15
Total liabilities	70	62	77	61	63
Net worth	30	38	23	39	37
Income Statement					
Net sales	100	100	100	100	100
Gross profit	14	100	20	31	29
Operating expenses	12	97	17	27	26
Operating profit	2	4	3	4	3
Profit before taxes	1	3	2	4	2

2

WHY BUSINESSES BORROW

OBJECTIVES

After studying *Why Businesses Borrow*, you will be able to—

- Explain how a firm's cash flow cycle can affect debt requirements and repayment sources
- Identify the reasons why businesses need to borrow
- Identify the various borrowing arrangements used to structure a business loan
- Describe how alternative lending sources compete with or complement community banks

INTRODUCTION

Loan purpose is the immediate need that brings the business customer into your financial institution. Your customer might say, "I need a loan to buy more inventory," or "I need to buy a new delivery truck." This chapter will extend the concept of a business operating cycle to the related cash flow. You will learn about the connection between the cash flow needs and the types of borrowing needs these businesses have, plus the borrowing arrangements that provide the best fit.

Relationship to the Commercial Lending Decision Tree

In the textbook Introduction, we explored the Commercial Lending Decision Tree as a way to think about the stages and steps involved in the commercial lending process. As you have learned, the process emphasizes early screening and qualifying steps to match the bank's portfolio and goals. Similarly, the lender begins assessing financial and non-financial qualifications of the business. In this chapter you will learn the typical cash flow cycles of various business types and the related borrowing needs, which will help you in developing this assessment.

Specifically, this chapter is related to Stage One as shown in the illustration in the Introduction. A business banker can greatly enhance the preliminary screening process, prior to receiving detailed financial statements and other data, by understanding the typical cash flow cycles of businesses and the related borrowing needs that are likely to emerge. The borrowing needs could lead directly to possible borrowing arrangements, which may involve other financing sources beyond your bank.

When addressing borrowing needs, you should ask the following three questions:

- What are the likely needs?
- What borrowing arrangements meet those needs?
- Is a bank or a nonbank lender a likely source?

Even if a bank is the final conclusion for the likely source, your own bank may not offer the specific borrowing arrangement. This is important to know as early as possible, in order to be efficient within the Commercial Lending Decision Tree and avoid spending too much time in Stage Two, where detailed financial analysis occurs.

CASH FLOW CYCLES

The various characteristics of a business **operating cycle** are important to business lending and financial statement analysis because they affect cash flow, which in turn affects a firm's need for bank financing and its ability to repay debt. Most businesses rely on accounts payable, bank loans, owner equity contributions, earnings retained in the business, or cash as their primary sources of financing. These funds may be used to purchase inventory, which in turn is used to produce goods or deliver ser-

> **Operating cycle**
> The time required to purchase or manufacture inventory or provide a service, sell the product or provide the service, and collect the cash.

vices, and then returns to cash (or accounts receivable, and then to cash). This cash enables the business to purchase more inventory to begin the cash flow cycle again.

UNDERSTANDING CASH FLOW CYCLES

Understanding cash flow, including how cash is generated and used, is a critical and difficult part of the financial statement analysis process.

Cash flow in financial statement analysis includes all of the economic resources available to a business—not just the balance in the cash account. Although most business transactions involve cash or cash equivalents, business bankers also consider such seemingly noncash economic resources as **accrued expenses** (accruals) and accounts payable (**trade credit**) as part of the cash flow. Trade credit results from the common practice of purchasing goods from vendors on account, meaning that the goods are paid for some time after they are received. During the time between the purchase of and payment for a supplier's goods, trade credit serves as a source of cash. Salary, vacation, and bonus accruals are noncash resources involving a promise to pay later for a service performed now. A bank, for example, may pay employees weekly for work performed the previous week. Such owed but unpaid labor costs constitute another source of cash.

> **Accrued expenses**
> Expenses incurred but not yet paid during an accounting period.

> **Trade credit**
> Credit extended to a company by its suppliers, usually to cover inventory purchases or other normal operating expenses.

The analysis of cash flows, therefore, involves not only cash and cash-equivalent accounts, but also other tangible resources or assets (such as inventory or machinery) and intangible economic power (such as the ability to incur debt in the form of trade credit and accruals). Because loans are repaid in cash, a firm's cash flow cycle is of particular importance to the business banker. By measuring the amount of cash allocated in each step of the operating cycle, the business banker can evaluate the firm's ability to manage the operating cycle and the risks associated with any loans made to the firm. The key question the financial analyst or business banker should ask is, "What might disrupt the firm's normal operating cycle?"

USES OF CASH

Uses of cash are those transactions that reduce the amount of money on hand, such as payment of installment loans, payment of salaries, cash purchase of an asset, and payment of taxes. Other uses of cash include increases in assets other than cash where a business foregoes collecting cash, such as extending credit to customers via accounts receivable. Decreases in liabilities are also uses of cash because the business has decreased the amount of funds it has essentially borrowed from or owes to another business. This can include decreases in the amount of trade accounts payable used when purchasing inventory.

To illustrate a simple cash flow cycle, consider the Harris Table Company, a manufacturing business that assembles all types of tables and resells them at a profit.

Figure 2.1 shows a comparison of the cash flow cycles of the different types of business operations, each selling a product or providing a service for $1.00. It also shows the effect on the timing of cash needs.

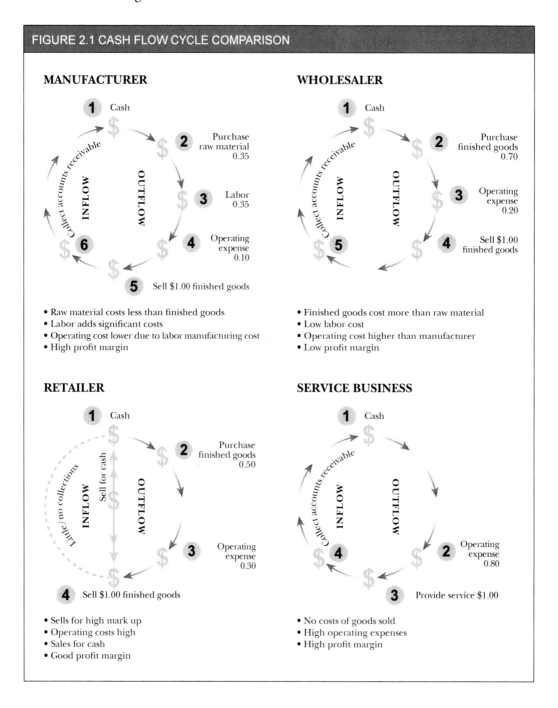

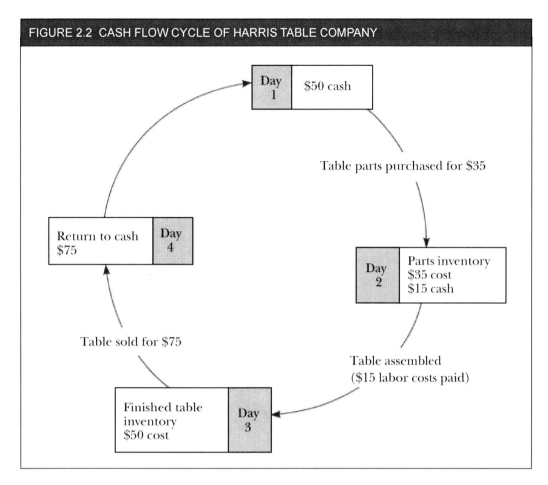

Harris Table Company buys unassembled table parts, employs a person to assemble the tables in its shop, and then sells the completed tables.

Figure 2.2 shows that on Day 1, the Harris Table Company has $50 in its bank account. On Day 2, the company pays $35 for table parts. On Day 3, the employee assembles the table and places it on the showroom floor. The employee is paid $15. On Day 4, the table is sold for $75 cash. Harris Table makes a $25 profit on its original $50 investment.

As Figure 2.3 illustrates, the length of the company's cash flow cycle increases further if the table is sold on credit. In the example, a table is sold on Day 4 on 30-day terms. This creates accounts receivable and lengthens the cash flow cycle, assuming that the customer waits until Day 34 or longer to pay for the table. Meanwhile, the company has no cash to purchase parts for more tables or to pay its employee.

These examples illustrate that the cash flow cycle is directly affected by the operating cycle of the business. They also illustrate how management decisions can affect the cash flow cycle (in this case, management's decision to sell the tables on credit).

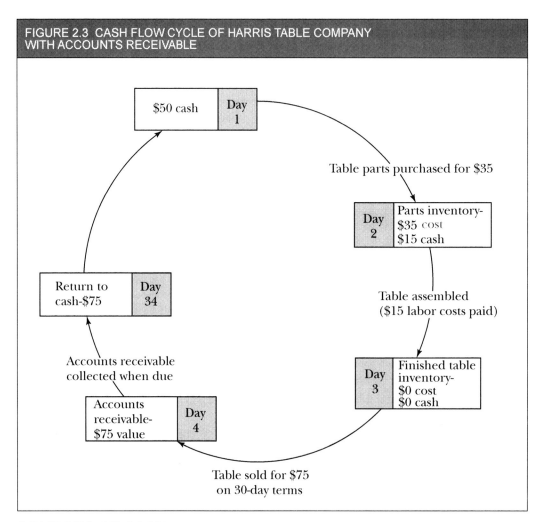

FIGURE 2.3 CASH FLOW CYCLE OF HARRIS TABLE COMPANY WITH ACCOUNTS RECEIVABLE

SOURCES OF CASH

The initial source of cash for most businesses is the owner's original equity investment and any loans. Ongoing sources of cash include the following:

- Collecting accounts receivable
- Selling inventory for cash
- Receiving trade credit (from suppliers)
- Receiving additional loans
- Retaining profits in the business

Up to this point, the Harris Table Company's use of cash in its operations (to buy inventory and pay for labor) has been considered, but the question of where the cash came from (the sources of cash) has not been addressed. It was assumed that the company had sufficient cash to purchase parts, pay for labor, and wait 30 days to collect the proceeds of a sale.

Capital

Capital, one of the major sources of cash available to a business, may be the only source of cash available to

> **Capital**
>
> The funds invested in a firm by the owners for use in conducting business.

a new business. The amount of money the owner invested in the Harris Table Company's operation(the original $50) is considered capital. But what happens if a business does not have sufficient capital to sustain its entire cash flow cycle? What would happen if, for example, the Harris Table Company started out with only $40 worth of capital? Figure 2.4 illustrates this situation.

After spending $35 on table parts, the company has only $5 left, whereas labor to assemble the table costs $15. The Harris Table Company faces a classic business dilemma—a shortage of cash. The shortfall is only $10, but the company needs that money to hire the labor to assemble the table. Once assembled, if the table is sold for cash, the worker can be paid. But if the company cannot complete its operating cycle, it will fail. Failure to complete the operating cycle is a common cause of problem loans.

How can a company with insufficient capital raise money to enable it to complete its operating cycle? It could go to its bank and request a short-term loan. However, because loans cost money in the form of interest payments and thus reduce the company's profits, it might want to consider other sources of cash first, such as trade credit, labor accruals, a reduction of selling credit terms, or starting the business with more capital.

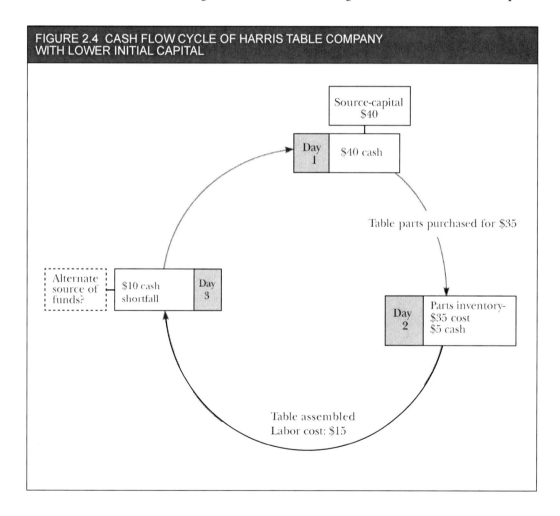

FIGURE 2.4 CASH FLOW CYCLE OF HARRIS TABLE COMPANY WITH LOWER INITIAL CAPITAL

Trade credit

The Harris Table Company can try to negotiate credit terms with its supplier of table parts. Supplier credit is also referred to as trade credit, trade payables, or accounts payable. Strictly speaking, accounts payable is a broader term including various types of payables the business may have, in addition to suppliers or trade credit. Figure 2.5 illustrates this type of credit.

In the above scenario, the Harris Table Company has $40 in its account on Day 1. The next day, the company purchases $35 worth of table parts and agrees to pay for them in 30 days. Thus, the company still has $40 cash at its disposal. On the Day 3, the company uses $15 of its cash reserve to hire a laborer to assemble the table parts. On Day 4, the table is sold on 30-day terms. On Day 32, the bill for table parts is due, and the Harris Table Company faces a $10 shortfall again.

Unless the company can raise the additional $10, its supplier must wait for payment until Day 34, when the customer's payment of $75 becomes due. If this fails to satisfy the supplier, the company may still need to request a short-term loan or inject more cash into the operating cycle. However, if the customer pays on time, the company now needs to borrow the $10 for only two days, rather than for 30 days (as required in the previous scenario).

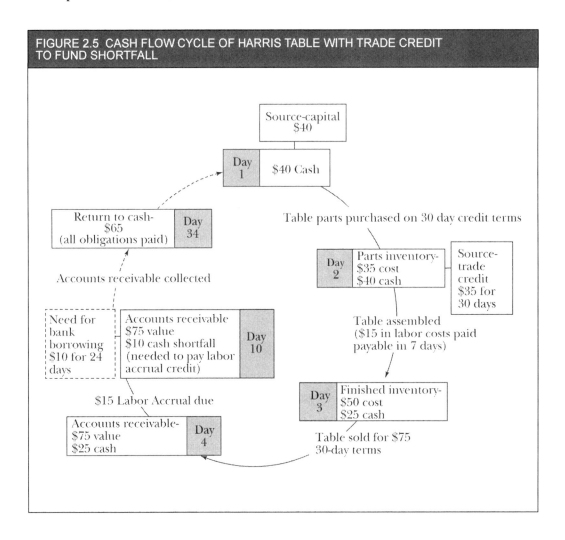

FIGURE 2.5 CASH FLOW CYCLE OF HARRIS TABLE WITH TRADE CREDIT TO FUND SHORTFALL

Accruals

Another strategy the Harris Table Company might use to complete its cash flow cycle would be to defer the payment of its labor for a week. This is, in effect, a source of cash called accrued expenses—wages payable. The company's cash flow cycle would then look like the one in Figure 2.6.

Again, the Harris Table begins with $40 in capital and spends $35 for table parts. Since it pays cash for the supplies, it now has a $5 balance. On Day 3, the employee assembles the table but agrees to be paid one week later. On Day 4, a customer purchases the table on 30-day terms. On Day 10, the $15 salary expense comes due, but the company has only a $5 cash balance. Once more, the company finds itself $10 short and must borrow from the bank for 24 days, extend trade credit, or inject more capital into the company until the customer's $75 payment is made. Although this strategy is preferred over borrowing for 30 days, it is not as effective as negotiating extended trade credit terms.

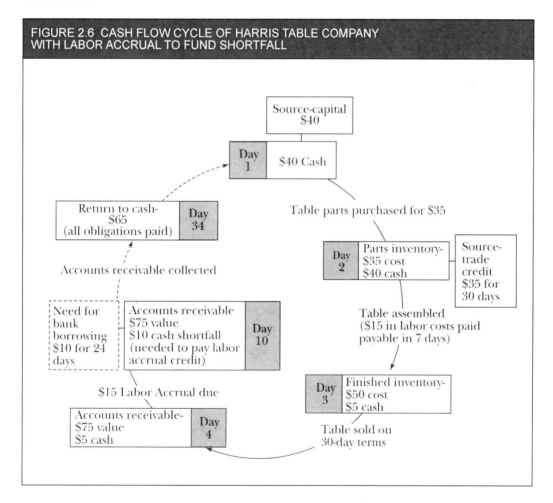

FIGURE 2.6 CASH FLOW CYCLE OF HARRIS TABLE COMPANY WITH LABOR ACCRUAL TO FUND SHORTFALL

Reduction of credit sale terms

Another strategy the Harris Table Company could adopt to alleviate its cash shortfall would be to reduce the credit terms it offers its customers. Suppose the company reduced the credit terms extended to its customers from 30 days to 18 days and was also able to negotiate a 20-day trade credit with its supplier. The company's cash flow cycle would now look like the one in Figure 2.7.

On Day 1, the company has $40 in its account. On Day 2, the company purchases $35 in table parts on credit, promising to pay for them in 20 days. The employee assembles the table on Day 3 and receives $15 in payment. On Day 4, a customer purchases the table for $75 on 18-day terms.

On Day 22, both the company's $35 bill for table parts and the customer's $75 payment for the table come due, enabling Harris Table to meet its debt obligation (assuming the customer pays by the due date). Moreover, the company makes a $25 profit on its original investment, which may be used to start the operating cycle once again.

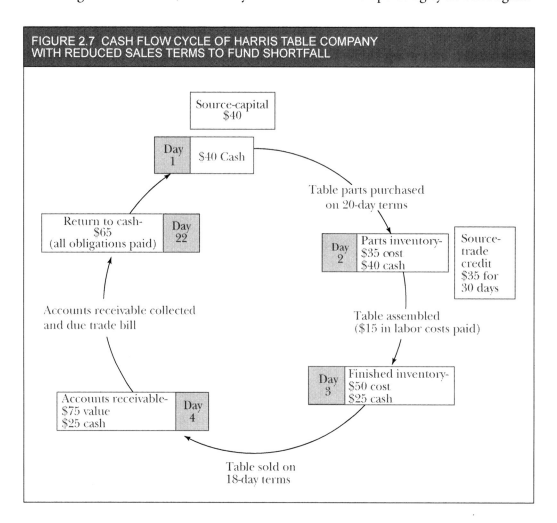

LONG-TERM USES OF CASH

So far, the discussion of cash flow has been concerned with the short-term or current operating cycle, which involves converting cash into working assets and then back into cash within a short period. But that cash conversion process does not take place in a vacuum. Businesses need facilities to house their operations and equipment to perform their tasks.

The Harris Table Company, for example, might need offices for its sales and administrative staff, space for the assembly process, and a warehouse for its inventory.

It also might need production equipment (such as a drill press) and other equipment (such as a delivery van). Assets needed to support, rather than be consumed by, a company's operation are referred to as fixed assets. The acquisition, funding, use, and replacement of fixed assets is called the fixed asset cycle because the company reuses the assets throughout a number of operating cycles rather than expending them or converting them to cash within a single operating cycle.

The fixed asset cycle (Figure 2.8), like the operating cycle, begins with the expenditure of cash to acquire an asset, such as a drill press. The business does not, however, directly convert the fixed asset back into cash by selling its drill press to create an accounts receivable later collected to produce cash. Nevertheless, fixed assets do play a critical part in the operating cycle. The business's products cannot be created and its services cannot be delivered without the support of its fixed assets. Further, it does recover the original cash expenditure for the fixed asset, but only over time and only through the profitable sale of the products that the fixed asset helps to create.

Most fixed assets, however, are eventually expended through their repeated use in the production process and must be replaced. Because replacement usually occurs several years after the initial purchase, replacement costs become higher and need to be considered in cash flow analysis.

During this time, the fixed assets generally have declined in value. Fixed assets generally are financed over their useful life, which usually exceeds one year. The loan is repaid from successfully completing multiple operating cycles.

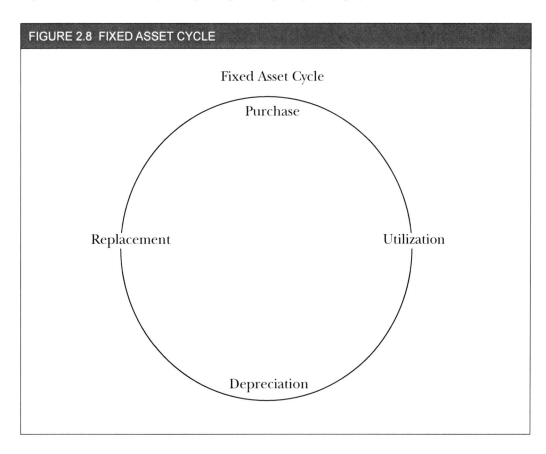

FIGURE 2.8 FIXED ASSET CYCLE

LONG-TERM SOURCES OF CASH

A business must have adequate accounts receivable, inventory, and fixed assets to support its current operating cycle. Additionally, it must structure its payments for accounts receivable, inventory, and fixed assets to avoid disrupting its current operations. Initial payment for the permanent accounts receivable, permanent inventory, and fixed assets can come from three sources: excess cash, capital contribution, or debt. Of these, debt and excess cash are the most common. Permanent accounts receivable are those amounts the company will carry on average each month. Permanent inventory is the amount of inventory that the company needs to maintain to generate a constant level of sales. Multiple operating cycles generate the cash to repay the intermediate or long-term debt used to finance a company's permanent level of accounts receivable, inventory, or fixed assets.

However, cash generated through the current operating cycle must first be used to replenish the company's inventory and accounts receivable. Accounts receivable include all cash due to a company for goods or services sold to customers on credit.

To the extent that it is not used for some other purpose, the cash generated from operations is normally available to purchase fixed assets or to service debt. Therefore, the business banker should structure payment terms on loans for the funding of permanent accounts receivable, permanent inventory, and fixed assets in such a way that a business can repay these debts with cash generated from multiple completions of the operating cycle.

You learned about the various cash flow cycles of different types of businesses. You now know how uses of cash and sources of cash can affect the business's cash flow cycle. You also learned about the relationship between long-term uses of cash and the fixed asset cycle, along with how, as a business banker, you need to structure loan repayment based on the long-term sources of cash.

REASONS WHY BUSINESSES BORROW

As we have seen with the Harris Table example, the operating cycle of a business directly influences its cash flow cycle. In this chapter, you will define the typical debt requirements of a business in two ways—borrowing needs by type of industry and general needs that are fairly common across most industries.

BORROWING NEEDS BY BUSINESS TYPE OR INDUSTRY

Figure 2.9 summarizes the business functions, working assets, operating cycles, and capital requirements for all the various business types.

FIGURE 2.9 BORROWING NEEDS BY BUSINESS TYPE OR INDUSTRY

AGRICULTURAL BUSINESSES

WORKING ASSETS	STAGES IN OPERATING CYCLE	CAPITAL REQUIRED	INVESTMENT IN FIXED ASSETS	TYPICAL FINANCING NEEDS
Inventory and equipment	• Purchase seed, plants, fertilizer, or livestock • Hire/pay • Purchase land and equipment • Fund operating and living expenses	Large	Modest or large	Long-term to finance fixed assets or permanent levels of inventory; short-term to finance seasonal inventory needs

Agricultural businesses have fixed asset needs, primarily for equipment, as well as annual purchases of feed, seed, and labor that start the cash cycle. This results in long-term financing needs for equipment, as well as short-term financing needed for the start-up costs.

MANUFACTURERS BUSINESSES

WORKING ASSETS	STAGES IN OPERATING CYCLE	CAPITAL REQUIRED	INVESTMENT IN FIXED ASSETS	TYPICAL FINANCING NEEDS
Plant and equipment	• Purchase raw materials • Hire labor to manufacture finished goods inventory • Sell on credit, creating receivable to cash	Large	Large	Long-term to finance fixed assets or permanent investment in inventory and accounts receivable. May require short-term financing for temporary buildups in receivables and inventory

Manufacturers tend to have a large investment in fixed assets, including machinery and equipment necessary to make a product. This generates long-term financing needs for the fixed assets. A secondary financing need can arise with long-term financing for any permanent investment in accounts receivable and inventory. If the business is seasonal, short-term financing for temporary increases in accounts receivable and inventory may be necessary.

WHOLESALERS

WORKING ASSETS	STAGES IN OPERATING CYCLE	CAPITAL REQUIRED	INVESTMENT IN FIXED ASSETS	TYPICAL FINANCING NEEDS
Inventory and accounts receivable	• Purchase inventory (finished goods) • Sell, creating receivable • Convert receivable to cash	Function of volume and length of operating cycle	Limited to such items as warehouse space and material-handling equipment	Long-term to finance permanent investment in inventory and accounts receivable. May require short-term financing for temporary buildups in receivables and inventory

Wholesalers do not have as strong a need for fixed assets and related financing. Their primary assets tend to be accounts receivable and inventory. Accordingly, there is a limited need for long-term financing of fixed assets, but a greater need for long-term financing for permanent levels of inventory, accounts receivable, warehouse space, and material-handling equipment. A wholesaler also is likely to need short-term financing for seasonal or other temporary buildups in accounts receivable and inventory.

FIGURE 2.9 BORROWING NEEDS BY BUSINESS TYPE OR INDUSTRY (CONTINUED)

RETAILERS

WORKING ASSETS	STAGES IN OPERATING CYCLE	CAPITAL REQUIRED	INVESTMENT IN FIXED ASSETS	TYPICAL FINANCING NEEDS
Inventory and real estate	• Purchase inventory (finished goods) • Sell inventory for cash	Function of volume and length of inventory cycle plus investment in real estate	Modest to large	Long-term to finance permanent investment in inventory and real estate. May require seasonal financing to support temporary buildups in inventory

Retailers tend to have a large investment in inventory, followed by fixed assets if a store location is owned. As a result, long-term financing usually is needed for permanent levels of inventory, along with short-term financing for seasonal or other temporary buildups in inventory.

SERVICE BUSINESSES

WORKING ASSETS	STAGES IN OPERATING CYCLE	CAPITAL REQUIRED	INVESTMENT IN FIXED ASSETS	TYPICAL FINANCING NEEDS
Accounts receivable	• Hire/pay labor • Perform service creating accounts receivable	Limited to large	Nominal (large if not renting location)	Long-term to finance permanent levels of accounts receivable; short-term to finance temporary levels of accounts receivable

Service businesses generally do not carry inventory, so financing needs are primarily centered on accounts receivable. Long-term financing usually is needed for permanent levels of accounts receivable, along with short-term financing for seasonal or other temporary buildups of accounts receivable. Depending on the type of service provided, fixed asset investment may not be very prominent.

CONSTRUCTION BUSINESSES

WORKING ASSETS	STAGES IN OPERATING CYCLE	CAPITAL REQUIRED	INVESTMENT IN FIXED ASSETS	TYPICAL FINANCING NEEDS
Accounts receivable and fixed assets	• Hire/pay labor • Purchase materials • Perform construction, creating accounts receivable	Limited to large	Nominal to large	Long-term to finance fixed assets and permanent levels of accounts receivable; short-term to finance temporary levels of accounts receivable based on contract payment terms

Construction businesses have cash needs for materials and labor. However, many subcontractors are not paid until a job is completed, resulting in long-term financing needs and short-term financing needs for the buildup of accounts receivable, depending on the nature of the contracts involved. Some long-term financing may be needed for equipment, but this need is usually secondary to the financing for accounts receivable.

GENERAL BORROWING NEEDS BY ALL BUSINESSES

A business banker can anticipate the types of borrowing needs that many companies will have simply by understanding cash flow cycles of different industries and business types. Nevertheless, businesses of all types have some common borrowing needs.

Borrowing cause vs. purpose (use of funds)

Borrowing cause relates to why the business has a cash shortfall compared with how the funds are being used—usually the loan purpose. Depending on the situation, the cause and purpose may not be the same. One example is the owner taking money out of the business to purchase an airplane for personal use, leaving the business unable to finance seasonal buildup of accounts receivable and inventory. Another example is a business using excess cash on hand to purchase machinery, leaving it unable to fund payroll on the following Friday. Both examples illustrate a "disconnect" between the borrowing cause and the use of funds.

Because loan repayment most likely will come from events related to the borrowing cause (even an outright reversal of the borrowing cause), understanding the true borrowing cause is a key task for the business banker. Also important is recognizing other potential sources of repayment (such as additional capital contributions by the owners or sale of collateral). In most cases, a business banker will identify a primary source of repayment that is closely related to the reversal of the borrowing cause. A secondary source of repayment will include items such as sale of collateral or guarantor support.

Understanding why the business needs to borrow is a key part of the lending decision process and is a critical component for appropriately structuring a loan that the bank may approve.

Typical borrowing causes

Borrowing causes fall into two categories.

Primary borrowing causes
- Growth in business sales
  - Permanent accounts receivable and permanent inventory
  - Temporary or seasonal buildup
- Declining efficiency of working capital accounts (current assets and current liabilities)
  - Slower collection of accounts receivable due to increased dating terms granted to customers, or customers taking too long to pay invoices
  - Slower utilization of inventory due to length of manufacturing process or reduced demand for a product
  - Faster payment of suppliers due to reduced dating terms or taking discounts for more prompt payment
- Fixed asset purchases
  - Expansion of fixed asset base
  - Replacement of existing fixed assets

Other borrowing causes
- Restructuring of business liabilities
    - Pay off existing accounts payable or accruals
    - Refinance or pay off existing short-term or long-term debt
    - Convert short-term debt to long-term debt
- Owner buyouts
- Distributions or dividends to owners
- Unprofitable business operations
- Miscellaneous onetime expenses such as litigation settlements and bulk or large-volume materials purchases

With an understanding of the business type, cash flow cycle, and the general types of borrowing needs of most businesses, the lender can now begin to identify possible lending arrangements.

You learned about the typical borrowing needs of each business type and industry. You also learned how to identify general borrowing needs of most companies by understanding the cash flow cycles of different industries and business types. This information makes you more knowledgeable about primary borrowing causes and other borrowing causes.

TYPES OF BORROWING ARRANGEMENTS

When a business customer comes to you with a lending request, choosing the correct borrowing arrangement requires matching the purpose of the loan, the source of repayment, the required loan amount, and the term of the loan. Borrowing arrangements may be a special commitment loan, seasonal line of credit, revolving line of credit, permanent working capital loan, standby letter of credit, term loan, or lease financing.

BORROWING ARRANGEMENTS OFFERED BY BANKS

The small business customer has a greater need for borrowing than most individuals. Because of the variety and size of these needs, more lending instruments are available to businesses based on their borrowing needs.

Special commitment loan

A special commitment loan supports an isolated increase in current assets needed for an unusual circumstance. The loan is disbursed all at once and repaid from the sale of the assets financed. Repayment is required within a designated period, usually 30, 60, or 90 days. These loans are repaid with the cash generated by the conversion of noncash current assets to cash.

For example, a retailer of sporting goods has an opportunity to sell basketballs and jerseys to the local school district. This is a onetime opportunity. The loan will be structured as a special commitment loan disbursed to pay for the basketballs and jerseys and repaid when the funds due from the school district are collected.

Operating line of credit

An operating line of credit is typically used to fund daily operations, and is repaid by converting current assets to cash. The outstanding amount will vary by the daily collection of cash. The facility will generally be reviewed for renewal on an annual basis. In general, an operating line of credit is fairly small in relation to the current assets of the business, and the principal balance frequently reaches $0, or "cleans up."

The following are two specialized versions of operating lines of credit:

- A permanent working capital line of credit tends to always have a principal balance outstanding, supporting a business that is rapidly growing or with limited capital and long-term debt to support working capital needs. Because the principal balance is often limited to a formula or percentage of current assets serving as collateral, this type of loan is often referred to as a type of asset-based lending.

    The principal portion of the loan will never be repaid as long as the company's sales volume requires a level of accounts receivable and inventory in excess of the company's internally generated capital. The primary users of permanent working capital lines of credit are rapidly growing businesses that have inadequate cash flow and trade credit to finance the accounts receivable and inventory necessary to support their growing sales volume. A loan agreement with specific terms, such as periodic aged listings of accounts receivable and listings of inventory, usually supports the loans.

    For example, a manufacturer of plastic pipe needs to finance inventory and fund accounts receivable to support sales growth from increasing the product line and territory. The sales growth is expected to continue for some time and has created an operating cycle where the business does not generate sufficient cash to fund the increases in accounts receivable and inventory. It needs a permanent working capital line of credit. As long as sales increase at a rapid rate, the principal portion of the loan will not be repaid in full. Interest usually is collected monthly by the lender.

- A seasonal line of credit is used to support a seasonal increase in current assets. Funds are used to purchase seasonal inventory, which is sold for cash or credit. If inventory is sold on credit, a seasonal line of credit is needed until the accounts receivable are collected. The loan is repaid when the inventory is sold for cash or accounts receivable are collected. The loan is usually structured with a short-term maturity to match the completion of the operating cycle.

    For example, a retailer of lawn mowers and garden equipment needs to purchase seasonal inventory in late winter. The loan will be repaid over the spring and summer months from the sale of inventory for cash.

Standby letter of credit

A standby letter of credit (SLOC) is an unfunded extension of credit through which a bank guarantees payment by the underlying business upon presentation of specific documents by the beneficiary. For underwriting and monitoring purposes, a SLOC is treated as a loan. If the beneficiary draws on the SLOC, most banks trigger a secured promissory note or loan whereby the underlying business that requested the SLOC will repay the draw amount. SLOCs are often used to support domestic inventory purchases or provide a short-term warranty to cover installation of equipment.

In some cases, a documentary letter of credit (DLOC) can be issued to support international purchases of inventory.

For example, a retailer of computers purchases large orders of inventory from Asia. The seller wants to be guaranteed payment when the computers are shipped. The bank customer requests a DLOC that will be funded and actually serve as the payment mechanism upon receipt of the shipment. Community banks issue DLOCs via larger correspondent banks that have international banking relationships and capabilities.

Term loan

A term loan is used to finance fixed assets—namely equipment, land, and buildings. Repayment comes from operating cash flow generated by multiple completions of the operating cycle. The term or length of the loan matches the useful life of the asset purchased and the cash flow generated by the borrower. Typically, the longer the useful life of the fixed asset, the longer the term of the loan. Since real estate has a longer life than a telephone system, a term loan to finance real estate may have an amortization of 15 to 20 years. A telephone system loan will likely be for five years or less. In either situation, principal and interest payments are made monthly.

In addition to financing fixed assets, a term loan may be used to fund permanent accounts receivable and permanent inventory that could not be supported by profits or excess cash as a firm grows or expands. The repayment source for this type of term loan is the same, via multiple, successful operating cycles.

For example, a pediatrician wants to expand her practice to include a new examination room. She requests a loan to remodel the existing building and purchase new equipment. She repays the loan using the excess cash flow generated from the new patient load and increased procedures.

Lease financing

Lease financing is also used to finance fixed assets, but with several features that can be an advantage over term loans. Since a lease provides 100 percent financing of an asset, it helps new or growing companies with little capital available for a down payment. In other situations, rent (lease) expense may provide a tax advantage compared with owning the asset, with related depreciation expense combined with a term loan and interest expense. In still other situations, leases can be short term and give the business a way to periodically upgrade equipment that is subject to frequent technological advances. A nonbank leasing company may also provide servicing and repairs to the underlying equipment during the course of the lease.

For example, the owners of a movie theater desire to extend their area of operation and build additional screens. They wish to lease new audio equipment as well. The lease will be repaid from the growth of sales and existing cash flow of the business.

MATCHING OF PURPOSE TO REPAYMENT SOURCES

The business banker also needs to keep in mind that the purpose of a loan and the repayment source for the loan may not always match a specific borrowing arrangement. For example, a company may need to purchase a new piece of equipment that normally is financed as a term loan. However, if the source of repayment is not excess cash flow over time but rather the sale of another piece of equipment, then the borrower needs a short-term note until the equipment sells. Matching the purpose and repayment sources is key to good loan structuring.

Sometimes the most difficult task for a business owner is finding the money to fund operations. You learned about the different types of borrowing arrangements banks offer (Figure 2.10). By knowing the loan types and purposes, you can now better assist your business customers with their borrowing needs.

COMPETING AND COMPLEMENTING FINANCING

Banks are not the sole source of the various borrowing arrangements you have learned about so far. A business customer can turn to a variety of other types of financing, depending on factors such as what the loan will be used for and the type of financing desired. In this section, you will learn about the sources and types of financing that either compete with or complement financing offered by community banks.

FIGURE 2.10 SUMMARY OF BORROWING ARRANGEMENTS OFFERED BY BANKS

TYPE	PURPOSE	REPAYMENT	TERMS
Special commitment	Support isolated increases in current assets	Sale of current assets	Short (30–90 days)
Operating line of credit	Support daily operations of business	Conversion of current assets to cash	Annual renewal with interest monthly, principal reduced to $0 periodically
Permanent working capital line of credit	Permanent increases in accounts receivable and inventory	Excess cash generated from increased sales	Annual renewal with interest monthly, principal limited to collateral formula
Seasonal line of credit	Inventory purchases, support accounts receivable	Sale of inventory or collection of accounts receivable	Short, matched to operating cycle
Standby letter of credit	Facilitate domestic inventory purchases	Cash flow or sale of collateral	Unfounded extension of credit, annual fee charged
Term loan	Fixed assets	Cash flow from operations	Principal and interest monthly over useful life of fixed assets purchased or cash flow, whichever is shorter
Lease financing	Fixed assets	Cash flow from operations	Monthly rent over the useful life of fixed assets or lease term, whichever is shorter

FULL-RANGE COMPETITORS TO BANKS

In the business loan market, brokerage firms and credit unions are full-range competitors to banks that offer similar financial services and products.

Brokerage firms

In today's financial services marketplace, brokerage firms have become strong competitors of banks for personal and small business loans. Brokerage firms typically offer quick turnaround of loan requests and are staffed with professionally trained sales representatives. Many offer a full range of borrowing arrangements, similar to a commercial bank.

Credit unions

Credit unions are nonprofit financial institutions organized to provide checking and savings accounts, loans, and other financial services to their members. They are both owned and controlled by their members, with each member having a vote and the opportunity to serve on the board of directors. Credit unions are either state or federally chartered. State-chartered credit unions are supervised by a state regulatory agency. Those with federal charters are supervised by the National Credit Union Administration. Credit unions can often offer higher rates on deposits and lower interest rates on loans thanks to their tax-exempt status. The size and number of commercial loans they make varies by market, and size of a credit union's commercial loan portfolio (in relation to its total assets) is limited by regulations.

COMPETITORS WITH LIMITED PRODUCTS

Several financial firms compete with or complement banks, but have a narrower range of products.

Commercial finance companies

Operating within the larger group called "asset-based lenders," commercial finance companies specialize in making working capital or investment capital loans to small businesses secured by accounts receivable, inventory, or, on occasion, equipment. These firms can compete with banks to provide working capital financing, but can also complement bank financing where increased risk is present.

Asset-based lenders make loans based primarily on the value of the assets or collateral the borrower agrees to pledge, instead of the company's financial condition. Asset-based lending can include dealer floor plans (secured by inventory) and some leasing arrangements.

Factoring

Another way to support working capital needs for growing or young firms is via factoring—where accounts receivable are sold at a discount to a factor, which then assumes the credit risk of the account debtors and receives cash as the debtors pay. The factor makes a profit by collecting the full amount due or more than the discounted purchase price paid for the accounts. Factoring is prevalent in some industries such as garment and textile manufacturing. The financial condition of the business selling the accounts is not a key issue, and the focus of the factor (purchaser) is the credit quality of the account debtors. The factor can determine to whom and for how much total exposure a business can make sales, and essentially become the credit department of the business.

Captive finance companies

Captive finance companies tied to a large manufacturer's industrial or agricultural equipment can compete with banks for term loans and sometimes provide lease financing. These firms can make direct equipment loans and leases, or can support a dealer by purchasing loans or leases made by the dealer. These firms attempt to support the sales of the manufacturer and often have sources of funding that are different from bank funding. Consequently, they can offer competitive terms such as 100 percent financing, a lower interest rate, or a longer amortization period than typically offered by a community bank. In consumer banking, similar firms dominate the financing of automobiles.

Credit card issuers

Many credit card issuers offer business lines of credit that can be used for any type of purchase. Although the interest rates may be high compared with a bank loan, the convenience of a onetime application for credit has value to the small business owner.

In recent years, business credit card marketing has intensified, with programs offering new levels of information, such as categorized spending summaries and improved spending control. Cards can be restricted to selected employees, with customized limits put on the types of transactions, dollar amounts, and participating merchants. Banks—even community banks—can issue these cards, although larger banks tend to dominate this area.

Leasing companies

Leasing companies are a major source of credit for financing equipment for businesses. Leasing is an attractive alternative because the initial capital outlay is often smaller, and there may be tax benefits to deducting the full lease payments versus deducting depreciation and only the interest expense portion of the loan payments. Also, equipment with quickly changing technology is often leased. Fast-growing companies can choose to lease equipment in order to use their capital to fund the growth rather than down payments on equipment. Many large banks have leasing company subsidiaries.

Life insurance companies

Nonrecourse (no personal guarantee), long-term, fixed-rate financing for large commercial real estate (CRE) projects has been provided for many years by life insurance companies. Life insurance companies are more of a competitor for larger banks than for community banks. The general terms provided by life insurers, such as term of the loan and ability and willingness to offer fixed rate financing, are usually more favorable than those offered by banks. Commercial mortgage-backed securities are also a large provider of financing for large CRE projects. In consumer finance, property and casualty insurers have become more active in automobile finance.

COMPLEMENTARY FINANCING OR PARTNERS TO BANKS

The remaining firms and types of financing appear to be competitors, but in most cases provide complementary funding or support, or routinely partner directly with banks.

Trade credit

Manufacturers and wholesalers often extend credit to purchasers of their inventory. The terms are usually 30 days or fewer, depending on the type of industry and the nature of the items being sold. Vendors or trade creditors generally do not charge customers interest on the amount owed. However, they may charge interest or a late fee if payment is not received on time. In general, it makes sense for most businesses to utilize vendor or trade credit as much as possible because of its lower cost and the fact that it is usually unsecured. Indirectly, this reduces credit risk to the bank. Because trade credit usually comprises most of the accounts payable on the balance sheet, the terms trade credit, trade payables, and accounts payable are used interchangeably.

Investors

Various types of investors can provide funding for start-ups, as well as significant business expansions.

Start-up investing usually comes from founders, individuals, and angels. Angel investing has long been an important source of financial support and mentoring for new and growing businesses, bridging the gap between individuals (friends and family) and institutional venture capital rounds of financing. Angels generally are wealthy individuals who provide personal funds for capital for a business start-up, usually in exchange for convertible debt or ownership equity. Many angels are successful business owners themselves.

Venture capitalists generally invest funds from a pool or investment group, seeking more mature firms. These groups cannot provide a broad range of financing services, but can be a critical piece of the entire financing picture for businesses that utilize banking products and services. They can even create a "senior" lending role for the bank that has priority liens on collateral and cash flow, with the investors taking secondary positions at greater risk and higher compensation.

Government loan programs, guarantees, and grants

The Small Business Administration (SBA), the U.S. Department of Agriculture Business and Industry Program, and the Export-Import Bank are examples of the federal government's direct and indirect support for business loans.

For example, the SBA's 504 Program provides direct loans to businesses by partnering with banks. A typical 504 loan involves real estate and equipment acquisition where the businesses contributes a 10 percent down payment, the SBA loans another 40 percent, and a community bank provides another loan for the remaining 50 percent. Often, the 40 percent SBA loan is for a slightly longer amortization and has a lower interest rate than a bank can offer. The SBA also provides indirect support via the 7(a) Program, where operating lines of credit and other loans made by a community bank are enhanced by a guarantee from the SBA, usually for 50 percent or more of the total credit.

Many states have other programs and grants to support job growth and economic development. Even utility companies can assist. For instance, in its seven-state service area, the Tennessee Valley Authority can provide direct loans to new and expanding businesses.

Industrial revenue bonds

Another variation of state government assistance to businesses occurs in the form of tax-exempt financing to support industrial development, particularly for manufacturers. Although the state does not provide direct financing, it allows a loan structure whereby the business can borrow at a lower, tax-exempt interest rate. Banks can provide a SLOC that is a key to this loan structure.

Industrial revenue bond (IRB) structures work generally as follows. A local board (usually an industrial development board) purchases land and equipment, and constructs a building to the specifications of a new or expanding qualifying business. The board issues tax-exempt bonds to finance the project. However, a lease is created whose terms mirror the bond principal and interest, and essentially pass the credit obligation to the underlying business, not to the municipality or county that formed the board.

This is where a bank SLOC comes in. The bank SLOC can provide credit enhancement and a reduced interest rate on the bonds (in addition to tax-exempt status) that more than covers the SLOC's annual fee. The bank is essentially taking on the full credit risk of the bonds.

An alternative to the public bond issue being supported by a bank SLOC is a single bond being issued by the board and then purchased by the bank. In this variation, a profitable bank can utilize the tax-exempt bond interest income and offer a corresponding tax-exempt borrowing rate to the underlying business. Either way, the business will have lower borrowing costs. Further, most IRB structures provide additional savings to the business in the form of property tax abatements or reductions, plus exemption from paying sales tax on all materials and equipment purchased for the project. Even in situations where a state has already granted its limit of tax-exempt IRB financing, it can still grant taxable IRB status and give the business the property tax and sales tax benefits.

Participations and syndications

Some lending situations involve more than one bank. A **participation** occurs when one bank actually sells a portion of a loan to one or more other banks. The borrower may or may not know that the participation has occurred. A **syndication** occurs when two or more banks jointly lend to the business and the business deals directly with the members of the group.

Other differences exist between participations and syndications, but the main issue for this chapter is that

> **Participation**
>
> An interest in a loan acquired by a third party, such as another lender or a group of lenders, from the lender that originates and services the loan.

> **Syndication**
>
> A loan made by a group of banks to one borrower. In most cases, the dollar amount requested exceeds the amount the individual banks are either willing or able to lend. Each bank receives a pro-rated share of the income based on its level of participation of credit.

these structures allow a bank to make a larger loan than it can on its own. This can allow the bank to serve a larger, growing customer or balance the risk parameters of the bank's overall loan portfolio, as shown in the Commercial Lending Decision Tree.

You learned about the full range competitors to banks—brokerage firms and credit unions. You also learned about bank competitors with a narrower range of products, such as commercial finance companies, credit card issuers, and leasing companies. In addition, you gained a better understanding of complementary financing and affiliates to banks that appear to be competitors, but in most cases support or partner directly with banks to provide financial services to small business customers.

SUMMARY

In addition to the various funding needs that are characteristic of each industry, you also learned some of the more general reasons why businesses borrow. These include primary borrowing causes, such as growth in sales, as well as other causes such as restructuring of liabilities. It is important to be able to distinguish between the true cause of borrowing and the use of funds (purpose), since they will not always be the same.

By completing this chapter, you have learned that it is important for the business banker to understand thoroughly the applicant company's industry or business type. Knowing each of the basic industry types—manufacturers, wholesalers, retailers, construction companies, service firms, and agricultural businesses—and how each has a characteristic operating cycle that creates differing funding needs is key to understanding the purpose, repayment source, and risk of a loan. Understanding the company's business operations will also help a business banker understand its cash cycle. You are now able to explain how a company's cash flow cycle can affect debt requirements and repayment sources. You gained a better understanding of how the operating cycle and the fixed asset cycle must generate sufficient cash to replenish current working assets, provide for growth, and repay debt.

With an understanding of a business's operating, cash flow, and fixed asset cycles, plus an understanding of why a business needs to borrow funds, the business banker can consider possible lending arrangements. You learned about the various borrowing arrangements used to structure a business loan, such as special commitment loans, operating lines of credit, seasonal lines of credit, permanent working capital loans, letters of credit, term loans, and lease financing. You also learned about possible alternative lending sources that may compete with or complement community banks. These include brokerage firms, credit unions, commercial finance companies, captive finance companies, credit card issuers, leasing companies, life insurance companies, trade credit, government loan programs, industrial revenue bonds, and participations and syndications.

QUESTIONS FOR DISCUSSION

1. In addition to the balance in the cash account of a business, what does cash flow include?

2. What is the term or wording used for assets needed to support, rather than be consumed by, a company's operations?

3. Why is it important to determine the borrowing cause (beyond the use of funds or purpose)?

4. What is a key competitive advantage of brokerage firms?

5. In terms of Stage One of the Commercial Lending Decision Tree, why is it important to understand the borrowing cause, use of funds, and likely borrowing arrangement?

EXERCISE 1

What borrowing arrangement would you recommend for the following loan purposes?

A. Purchase winter coats and gloves

B. Purchase a printing press

C. Open a new location in an adjacent city

D. Import German auto parts

E. Gradually expand existing customer base

EXERCISE 2

Match each competitor on the left to its description on the right.

_____ 1. Commercial finance companies

_____ 2. Factoring

_____ 3. Commercial sales

_____ 4. Credit card issuers

_____ 5. Leasing companies

_____ 6. Life insurance companies

A. A major source of credit for financing equipment for businesses

B. Offer business lines of credit that can be used for any type of purchase

C. Another way to support working capital needs for growing or young firms

D. Nonrecourse, long-term, fixed-rate financing for large commercial real estate projects

E. Tied to large manufacturer's industrial or agricultural equipment

F. Specialize in making working capital or investment capital loans

3

BUSINESS LEGAL STRUCTURES AND LIFE CYCLES

OBJECTIVES

After studying *Business Legal Structures and Life Cycles*, you will be able to—

- Define the basic types of legal structures available to a business
- Describe the general characteristics of the four stages in the business life cycles

INTRODUCTION

Business bankers should have a thorough understanding of the basic legal structures of businesses and the general pattern of growth, or life cycle stages, that they experience. It is important for you to know this information because the legal structure and life cycle stage will affect the analysis of the related financial statements.

Legally, most businesses are structured as a sole proprietorship, general partnership, limited partnership, C corporation, S corporation, or limited liability company. Each type is treated differently under the law in such areas as ownership, liability, taxation, transfer of ownership, duration (life), management, and continuity. A business banker needs to determine the legal status of the business, its structure, legal stipulations for operations, who has the authority to sign for the business, and who is liable for its debt obligations.

Just as important as the legal structures is an awareness of the stages involved in the typical life cycle of a business. By understanding the characteristics of each stage, a banker is more perceptive of a business customer's needs and is therefore better able to match lending arrangements to those needs. In addition, being knowledgeable about the life cycle stages allows the business banker to be more alert regarding possible credit risks at each stage.

Relationship to the Commercial Lending Decision Tree

In the textbook Introduction, we explored the Commercial Lending Decision Tree as a way to think about the stages and steps involved in the commercial lending process. As you have already learned, the process emphasizes early screening and qualifying steps to match the opportunity to the portfolio and goals of the bank. Similarly, the lender begins assessing financial and nonfinancial qualifications of the business. In this chapter, you will gain a better understanding of business legal structures, along with the stages in the typical life cycle, which will help you in making the preliminary assessment in the screening steps.

In terms of the Commercial Lending Decision Tree illustration in the Introduction, this chapter relates to Stage One, where the lending opportunity is screened before beginning the time-consuming process of analyzing detailed financial statements and other data. By understanding the legal structure of the business and its stage in the life cycle, a business banker is better positioned to anticipate certain issues that are likely to arise in the financial statements. For instance, the legal structure will determine at which level(s) income taxes are paid by the business, passed through to the owners, or paid by both. In the same way, the life cycle stage provides clues about the cash flow needs of the business and likely financing needs. Additionally, the life cycle stages have different sets of risks, which are important to understand when developing a full assessment of the lending opportunity. At times, the legal structure and life cycle stage risks will require strong mitigating factors or conditions in order to remain in the commercial lending process—uncovering these issues and risks as early as possible is the goal.

LEGAL STRUCTURES

How do you know the person at your desk has the authority to apply for a business loan or sign the loan documents for the business? Knowing the various business legal structures provides critical information such as the principals who have the authority to make decisions, who has ownership in the business or management responsibilities, tax liability, and much more.

As a business banker, it is important for you to know the legal structures available to businesses. Whether a customer is opening a deposit account or making a business loan, banks require documented evidence to verify that the business is operating as a legal entity.

Types of legal structures

Business legal structures affect such critical business issues as the owner's liability and the ease with which capital can be raised. Knowing the legal structure of your small business customer will provide the following valuable information:

- Names of individuals with the authority to make decisions
- Names of individuals with ownership and management responsibilities
- Appropriate products for this type of business
- Documentation required to open an account or make a loan
- Names of individuals with signing authority

The first step in evaluating a business borrower is understanding the business's type of legal structure and how this affects its financial statements. Most commercial borrowers are structured as one of the following legal structures:

- Sole proprietorships
- General partnerships
- Limited partnerships
- Regular ("C") corporations
- S corporations
- Limited liability companies (LLCs)

Each entity receives different considerations under the tax code and law. Similarly, each entity creates different levels of personal liability to the owners. Since the two primary reasons for choosing a legal entity are taxes and personal liability, it is important for the lender to fully understand the business legal status. Figure 3.1 summarizes the key aspects of the legal structures.

> **NOTE**
> Because state requirements and bank policies vary, this textbook is limited to the documentation typically used to establish the primary business legal structures. Check your bank's requirements for a complete listing of required documentation for your business clients.

FIGURE 3.1 BUSINESS LEGAL STRUCTURES

LEGAL STRUCTURE	COST AND EASE TO ESTABLISH	LIABILITY OF OWNERS	BUSINESS CONTINUITY	MANAGEMENT CONTROL	EASE OF RAISING CAPITAL	TAX IMPLICATIONS
SOLE PROPRIETORSHIP	Least expensive Simplest form to establish	Unlimited personal liability	No provision for continuity in case of death of proprietor	Owner has control over all management decisions	Borrowing by owner or from owner's personal assets	Owner pays taxes at the individual rate on net income of business
GENERAL PARTNERSHIP	Minimal expense Written or verbal agreement	Unlimited personal liability or each partner for any and all partnership debts	May be dissolved by death or withdrawal of general partner	Management by majority rule among partners	Borrowing or bringing in other partners	Each partner pays taxes at the individual rate on his or her share of net income
LIMITED PARTNERSHIP	Statutory requirements usually include written agreement and statement of limited and general partners	Limited partner's liability limited to investment General partner's liability unlimited	Limited partner's death or withdrawal does not affect partnership General partner's death or withdrawal can dissolve partnership	Limited partners not allowed to participate Management by majority rule among general partners	Borrowing or bringing in other partners	Each partner pays taxes at the individual rate on his or her share of net income
LIMITED LIABILITY COMPANY	Statutory requirements include Operating Agreement and Articles of Organization	Limited to the amount invested	Creates degree of continuity; continues despite death or withdrawal of member	Management by majority rule of members	Borrowing, other debt instruments, addition of members	Each member pays taxes at the individual rate on his or her share of net income
CORPORATION (C CORPORATION)	Statutory requirements include Articles of Incorporation	Limited to the amount invested	Creates degree of continuity; continues despite death or withdrawal of stockholder	Board of directors elected by shareholders	Borrowing, other debt instruments, sale of stock	Pays taxes at the corporate rate
S CORPORATION	Same as a C corporation, plus must meet certain criteria (including no more than 100 shareholders)	Limited to the amount invested	Creates degree of continuity; continues despite death or withdrawal of stockholder	Board of directors elected by shareholders	Borrowing, other debt instruments, sale of stock	Each shareholder pays taxes at the individual rate on his or her share of net income

> **NOTE**
>
> Taxation issues can change, and legal structures are generally regulated at the state level and can vary slightly from state to state. Therefore, this is intended as a general introduction to common tax and legal issues. Please refer to tax experts, legal counsel, and/or your bank's policies for the specific issues for a customer and a given location.

Sole Proprietorship

The most common business entity in the United States is the sole proprietorship. Many small businesses, such as accountants, dentists, computer programmers, carpenters, or other service professionals, operate as sole proprietorships. One reason sole proprietorships are so prevalent is because they are the easiest business structure to set up, since there are few or no documents to file. There is minimal additional involvement with government, other than perhaps obtaining federal, state, or municipal licenses that verify the professional training of the proprietor, or registering a trade name.

Business responsibility and taxation

In a sole proprietorship, the owner controls the business, makes all the important decisions, and is responsible for its operations. All business profits and losses are those of the proprietor, regardless of how the business income is used. For example, if the net income of a sole proprietorship is $100,000, of which $20,000 is reinvested in the business, the owner's personal tax liability is calculated on the entire $100,000 at the individual, not corporate, income tax rate. Further, the assets, debt, income, and expenses of the owner and business are one and the same.

Business liability

Because of this inseparable relationship, the sole proprietor's legal exposure or liability is greater than that of owners of a regular or C corporation. Any legal claims against the assets of the business are treated as a claim against the owner's personal assets. Although the personal liability of a sole proprietorship poses a risk for the owner, it is a benefit to a lender that wants to secure the loan. A business banker can consider personal and business assets and cash flow in evaluating the creditworthiness of a sole proprietor.

Many banks integrate business and personal cash flow when underwriting loans to small business owners to calculate a global cash flow. Global cash flow analysis determines the business and personal income available to service all business and personal debt. You will learn more about global cash flow in an upcoming chapter.

Assumed name

Although many sole proprietors do business under the name of the individual owner, it is also common for them to operate under an assumed name or "**doing business as**" (dba). Many states require individuals using an assumed name to file an assumed name certificate with a local or state office, and the certificate becomes part of the public record.

> **dba**
>
> An abbreviation for "doing business as." Some entities may have one name but conduct business under another name.

For banking purposes, an account for a sole proprietorship is opened in the owner's legal name. If the business uses an assumed name, that name is recorded on the account—for example, "Samuel Brown dba Acme Cleaners." If the account is opened in the assumed name and not the owner's name, the bank should obtain a copy of the assumed name certificate.

A bank may transact business with a sole proprietorship as it does with an individual. The owner is generally responsible for the sole proprietorship. Loan documents may be signed by the sole proprietor as an individual or along with the assumed name, as in the example, "Samuel Brown **dba** Acme Cleaners." Be sure to check with your bank's legal counsel and documentation policies for the correct procedures to use in your location.

> **DID YOU KNOW?**
> More than 14 million sole proprietorships in the United States are considered nonemployers because they have no other employees.

General Partnership

Like a sole proprietorship, a general partnership is relatively easy to set up. A business jointly owned by two or more persons, companies, or organizations can be a general partnership. It is a legal entity separate from the partners.

Suppose, for example, a lamp salesman working evenings out of his basement develops a revolutionary new light bulb for consumer use. Rather than devote time and energy to manufacturing the light bulb, an area in which he lacks expertise, the salesman may choose to form a general partnership with someone who can supply additional capital and who has expertise in manufacturing. The salesman can concentrate on refining the invention or selling the product. An oral or written agreement is all that is necessary. In many states, if there is a written document, it is not filed, nor is the partnership registered.

Partnership agreement

For a business banker, a written **partnership agreement** is preferable because it documents any stipulations, such as buyout provisions, that may be important in assessing credit risk. In theory, each partner in a general partnership has an equal right to participate in the management of the business. In practice, however, control and authority are usually divided according to areas of expertise. The division of responsibility frequently falls between the technical and management aspects of the operation.

> **Partnership agreement**
> The partnership agreement usually contains provisions for the following:
> - Partnership's name and place of business
> - Nature of the partnership business
> - Dates when the relationship is to begin and end
> - Amount of capital contributed by each partner
> - When and in what form capital will be contributed
> - Each partner's share in the partnership

The partnership agreement may discuss other terms as well, such as partnership management and partner authorities. Any terms that are not covered in the agreement are governed by a state's Uniform Partnership Act, which details partners' rights and responsibilities to each other and regulates the obligations of individual partners to partnership creditors.

As mentioned earlier, some states do not require official filing of the partnership agreement. Therefore, all partnerships should supply the bank a partnership resolution that contains language certifying the name of the partnership and who is authorized to write checks and sign for loans.

Business responsibility and taxation

Profits or losses in a general partnership are divided among the partners according to the terms of the partnership agreement. As with sole proprietorships, all business income is regarded as owners' income. If, for example, a partnership has net income of $150,000, of which $100,000 is reinvested in the business, the partners must, between or among them, declare all $150,000 as taxable income. The income is considered personal and is taxed at individual, not corporate, rates.

In many general partnerships, the responsibilities and income are not divided equally among partners. One partner may have more authority or receive a greater percentage of the profits than others. However, it is fairly common for profit distribution to be based on each partner's equity contribution. If one partner initially contributed $300,000 to the partnership, and the other partner contributed $100,000, they will likely split the profits on a 75 percent to 25 percent basis, respectively. This would be specified in a written partnership agreement.

Business liability and activities

All partners are liable, separately and without limitation, for the indebtedness of the general partnership. When one partner obtains debt in the name of the partnership, all partners are liable for that debt. Further, the liability for indebtedness is not limited by any division of profit or any other factor. In the previous example, if the 75 percent owner disappears, leaving an $80,000 partnership debt, the 25 percent owner is liable for the entire $80,000—not just 25 percent of the amount.

In most other ways, general partnerships are similar to sole proprietorships. General partnerships can engage in business activities in any state, provided the state's licensing requirements and other standards are met. A business banker, when evaluating creditworthiness, can consider both the personal assets of each partner and the general partnership's assets.

Limited Partnership

In a limited partnership there must be at least one general partner and other limited partners. Different from a general partnership, some of the partners' liability can be limited to the amount invested or to a specified amount. However, if the restrictions placed on a limited partnership are violated, the limited liability of each partner is jeopardized.

Certificate of limited partnership

Unlike a general partnership, a limited partnership cannot be created informally and the limited partners do not actively participate in the management of the business. To qualify as a limited partnership, a **certificate of limited partnership** must be filed, typically in the office of the state's secretary of state.

The certificate of limited partnership is a public record and is considered legal notice that the partnership is a limited partnership and that the designated persons are general partners. This allows third parties to know which partners have authority to bind the partnership.

Certificate of limited partnership

This certificate must furnish the following information:

- Name of the partnership, including the words "limited partnership"
- Office address, and name and address of an agent on whom a summons can be served if the partnership is sued
- Name and business address of each general partner
- Latest date on which the partnership is to dissolve

Most states also require that the certificate of limited partnership include the following:

- Description of the partnership's business
- Names and addresses of limited partners
- Description of the value of partnership contributions
- Method for changing partners

Business taxation and liability

In limited partnerships, like general partnerships, the income is passed through to the partners, and the resulting personal income is taxed at the individual tax rate.

Limited partners are not liable for the partnership obligations unless they materially participate in the management of the business or otherwise obligate themselves personally in a partnership's activities. If limited partners materially participate in management of the business, usually they are liable only to those with whom they transact business.

C Corporation

A regular or "C" corporation is a legal entity with a distinct existence apart from its owners. C corporations pay taxes, buy and sell assets, incur liabilities, and can sue or be sued. Unlike a sole proprietorship, general partnership, or limited partnership, a corporation is highly regulated by both the federal government and any state in which it is organized or conducts business. C corporations can be held privately by a single owner or held publicly by thousands of shareholders.

Income taxes for the owners

Because a C corporation is recognized as an entity separate from its owners, it pays income taxes on all net income at corporate rates. If all net income is retained within the business, then the owners have no personal income and resulting tax obligation. However, some of business net income can be paid in dividends to its owners (shareholders), and this personal income is then taxed at the individual tax rate. This double taxation of income (at both the corporate and individual levels) is perhaps the greatest disadvantage in forming a C corporation.

Most C corporations that a business banker encounters are private, closely held businesses with a small number of owners. Profits generated are either retained as equity in the company or distributed as salaries and benefits to its owners. Unlike dividends, salaries are a pretax corporate expense.

Business liability

An advantage of a corporate structure is that it protects owners from personal liability for corporate indebtedness. If a corporation is sued or fails to meet a loan obligation, the personal and business assets of its owners are not at risk, unless they have personally guaranteed the loan. However, the owners can lose the amount of their investment in the business should the business fail or go bankrupt. There is no danger of losing their personal assets as well.

Limited liability exposure is essential for growth of large, publicly held C corporations. Shareholders of publicly held corporations would be extremely reluctant to invest in the company if stock ownership constituted unlimited liability for corporate debt.

Sometimes, the absence of an owner's personal liability for debt may hinder a larger corporation's ability to obtain credit. When analyzing the creditworthiness of a large corporation, the business banker may review the corporation's financial standing only. These loans are made without recourse to the corporation's owners. In contrast, most loans to small, closely held corporations are contingent on the owners personally guaranteeing the debt.

How C corporations differ from other entities

C corporations differ from sole proprietorships and general partnerships in two respects:

- C corporations retain legal existence irrespective of changes in ownership. If a group of stockholders sell their shares or if the principal officers resign, a corporation still retains its existence. Upon the death of its owners or partners, a sole proprietorship or a general partnership ceases to exist.
- C corporations are legal entities registered by the state and do not have the right to operate where they please. They must be recognized by the state in which they are formed (registered or organized) and perhaps even by states in which they desire to do business, and they must comply with the state laws and regulations regarding corporations.

Articles of incorporation

If a loan is being made to a C corporation, the business banker is responsible for ensuring that all documents are signed by an officer who has legal authority to obligate the company and create the liability. The corporate officer signing the loan documents is not personally liable for the loan.

The usual documents required to authenticate a C corporation are the **articles of incorporation** and the state's charter or certificate of incorporation. Articles of incorporation define the corporation and are filed with the appropriate state agency. Upon approval, the state usually charters the corporation and issues a certificate of incorporation. To document the authority of the corporate officers, banks rely on the corporate resolution signed by the secretary of the board of directors.

> **Articles of incorporation**
>
> Articles of incorporation usually define the following:
> - Name of the corporation
> - Name and address of each incorporator
> - Broad purposes or objectives of the corporation
> - Street address of the corporation's principal office, and the name of its agent upon whom a summons can be served if the corporation is sued
> - Length of time the corporation is to last (often called the maximum duration)
> - Number of shares of stock the corporation is authorized to issue
> - Par value of the stock (amount of money in corporate assets represented by each share of stock)

S Corporation

Taxation

How income is treated for tax purposes is one of the most significant differences between S corporations and C corporations. With an S corporation, similar to sole proprietorships and partnerships, all net income from the business is passed through to the owners as personal income and is taxed at the individual income tax rate. As noted in the previous section, the net income of a C corporation is taxed at the business level at the corporate tax rate. Then, any distribution to the owners in the form of dividends is taxed a second time as personal income at the individual tax rate.

S corporation ownership

This difference in the treatment of income makes an S corporation preferable for many small, closely held businesses, as opposed to a C corporation. However, the business banker needs to be careful not to give double credit for the income earned by S corporations—once at the corporate level and again at the personal level. Although the income is passed through to the individual, it may not actually be distributed as cash and contribute to personal cash flow available for debt service. In an upcoming chapter, we will examine how S corporations report income and cash distributions to their owners on what is called a Schedule K-1.

S corporations also differ from C corporations in that an S corporation usually has a limited number of shareholders, most recently 100 natural persons. A C corporation can have an unlimited number of shareholders, and they can be non-natural persons (e.g., other corporations, trusts). In many other ways, S corporations are identical to C corporations.

Distribution of income and cash

Compared with partnerships, perhaps the greatest difference is in distribution of income and cash from the business. As we have seen, in a general or limited partnership, the partners can agree to income pass-through percentages that are different than the ownership percentages. For instance, a partnership with two owners, each with a 50 percent ownership, can have a 25 percent income pass-through and cash distribution to one of the partners, with the remaining 75 percent to the other partner. In an S corporation, the income pass-through and cash distribution percentages must be the same as the ownership percentages.

Limited Liability Company (LLC)

Limited liability companies (LLCs) are the fastest growing form of legal structure. A common usage is to hold a single-purpose asset such as a commercial building. LLCs offer several advantages to business owners. First, business income is passed through for tax purposes to the owners, resulting in personal income that is taxed at the individual tax rate. Second, like the owners of a corporation, the owners of an LLC have limited personal liability.

LLC ownership

Flexibility in ownership structure is a third attractive feature of LLCs. There is no limit on the number and type of owners. Owners may include a single individual, two or more individuals, corporations, trusts, and partnerships. Most states refer to the owners as "members." Unlike corporations, though, LLCs have a limited life, and ownership interests are not freely transferable. LLCs terminate on a specified termination date or the death, withdrawal, expulsion, bankruptcy, or dissolution of a member.

Limited Liability Partnership

LLCs are now widely used for all types of businesses, and the legal form has been adopted in all states. In most states, professionals cannot use the LLC corporate form but can use a limited liability partnership (LLP). The LLP offers unique protections to professionals but has not been adopted in all states, nor are the protections the same in all states.

Lending to an LLC

When making a loan to an LLC, a business banker should carefully review all documentation, such as articles of organization and the **operating agreement**—a document similar to a corporation's bylaws—which denotes member powers and duties, such the ability to enter into contracts (like a promissory note). Because LLC members are not personally liable for the debts of the LLC, personal guaranties are necessary. Further, the limited duration and possible dissolution of an LLC can affect the decision to extend long-term financing.

> **Operating agreement**
>
> The document that sets forth how the business of a limited liability company will be conducted. It is similar to a corporation's bylaws.

In this section, you learned about the most common types of legal structures and the characteristics of each business structure. Being acquainted with these characteristics provides you with an important foundation that will enable you to lend and service your business customers more effectively. By having this information, you now know if your business customer has the authority to perform a banking transaction and what documentation is needed to transact the business.

BUSINESS LIFE CYCLES

Understanding the concept of a business life cycle gives you an overall or "big picture" perspective of a business borrower. Knowing its life cycle stage will help when analyzing a credit request, assessing possible risks, and matching the correct lending arrangement to the borrowing need.

WHAT IS A BUSINESS LIFE CYCLE?

A **business life cycle** is a macro look at how businesses generally develop over time. From the beginning, the needs of a business change and evolve as the business grows and matures. It is important to understand this process in general, and the stages in the cycle in particular, to anticipate the borrowing needs of a business and possible risks associated with its life cycle stages. Experts have identified as many as seven or eight stages within a business life cycle, but the most common models involve at least four basic stages. In this section, you will learn the general characteristics to the following business life cycle stages (Figure 3.2):

- Start-up
- Growth
- Mature
- Decline

> **Business life cycle**
>
> The business life cycle is a macro look at how most businesses typically change and develop over time. Every business starts as a concept or idea. After that stage, businesses "age" through four main life cycle stages (start-up, growth, mature, and decline), which affect the need for particular bank products and services.

General characteristics of the life cycle stages

When determining the life cycle stage of a business, certain characteristics can be your guide. These characteristics change as a business "ages." However, the exact stage can be difficult to identify, and sometimes it is clear only in hindsight. Also, businesses do not always progress from cycle to cycle. For example, by developing a new product or acquiring another company, a mature business can shift back into the growth stage.

Matching products

As you recognize the life cycle stages of a business, you will be better able to identify likely borrowing needs and offer appropriate borrowing arrangements. For example, a business in the mature stage likely would not require a loan to expand the business; rather, refinancing of existing debt might be necessary. A business in the growth stage, by contrast, might require funding for working capital or expansion of fixed assets.

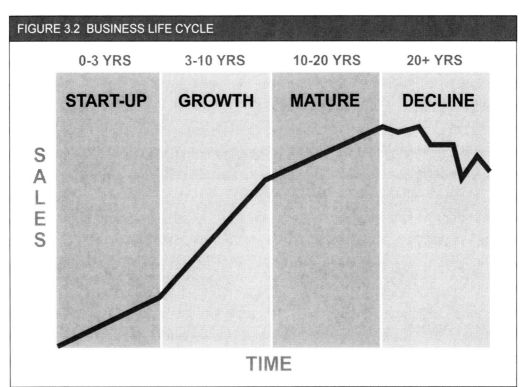

FIGURE 3.2 BUSINESS LIFE CYCLE

STAGE	START-UP	GROWTH	MATURE	DECLINE
Typical industries	Bio-engineering, alternative fuels, mobile application design, tea and healthy beverages	Social media, environmental consulting, exam prep and tutoring, language translation services	Automobile manufacturers, wireless carriers, television cable companies	Commodity chemicals, automobile dealers, department stores
Focus	Research and development, establishing a customer base	Marketing and production, developing formal management and financial systems	Operational efficiency, automation and outsourcing, search for new opportunities	Value of business, succession planning and ownership transition strategy
Funding issues	Operating cash, raising capital, venture capital	Working capital to fund growth, fixed-asset expansion	Strong operating cash flow, refinance fixed assets	Return of capital to investors, reduction of debts

THE START-UP STAGE

Typically, the *start-up stage* of a new business occurs within the first three years of operation. Depending on the business, the start-up stage may be several months to several years, or longer. Some companies have spent 10 years or more researching and developing a product before the product is offered on the market. See Figure 3.3 for general characteristics for start-up businesses.

FIGURE 3.3 GENERAL ISSUES FOR START-UP BUSINESSES

Management abilities	Business owners in the start-up stage generally have the following characteristics: • Limited experience • Strengths in one area, but weaknesses in others Also, start-up businesses might be able to develop a product but may lack the skill to market it.
Business assets	Businesses in the start-up stage generally are funded by the owners' savings and personal loans. In this stage, the balance sheet typically shows the following: • Low levels of cash • Minimal fixed assets
Cash flow	Commonly, all initial cash is used to get the business off the ground. Typical expenses include research and development, inventory, equipment, advertising, and other promotions. There are minimal sales at this stage. The cash flow during the start-up stage is one of the following: • Nonexistent • Undercapitalized • Heavily dependent on suppliers
Priorities	Finding customers and developing sales are the highest priorities at this stage. A start-up will emphasize the following: • Marketing • Product delivery Time is very important to the new business owner; usually, only one or two people are managing all aspects of the business.

THE GROWTH STAGE

The *growth stage* is the second phase of the business life cycle and is characterized by increasing sales over many operating cycles. This stage typically occurs between the third and tenth years of business. A business is not limited to just one growth stage in its life cycle; it reenters this stage periodically throughout its development. For example, a business might successfully market a product line and then reach a plateau because of market saturation or changing consumer tastes. At this point, the business may change to a new product line and find itself back in the growth stage. See Figure 3.4 for general issues for growth businesses.

FIGURE 3.4 GENERAL ISSUES FOR GROWTH BUSINESSES	
Management abilities	The owner of a growing business generally has little available time. He or she is faced with the challenge of juggling the demands of managing the business operations and managing the additional staff needed to support the business. Management abilities in the growth stage are in the following situation: • Competent, but stretched for time
Business assets	During the growth stage, business assets are generally tied up in the following areas: • Little or no cash assets • Accounts receivable • Inventory • Equipment
Cash flow	Although profits are earned in the operating cycle, cash flow during the growth stage is usually tight. Increased sales cause a need for more money to support the operations. This is due to increases in the following areas: • Operating expenses • Inventory • Accounts receivable For example, collection of receivables takes 60 to 90 days. New orders are received while those receivables are still outstanding.
Priorities	Finding resources to support sales growth (highest priority) • Ownership of the business may change during the growth stage For example, a sole proprietor might take on partners as an additional source of capital and management expertise.

THE MATURE STAGE

When rapid sales growth diminishes, the business enters the *mature stage* of the life cycle. Generally, this stage occurs after the business has achieved at least 10 years of profitable operations. Sales are still increasing, but at a much slower rate. See Figure 3.5 for general issues for mature businesses.

FIGURE 3.5 GENERAL ISSUES FOR MATURE BUSINESSES	
Management abilities	The business no longer depends only on the owner's vision and energy. Instead, there is a capable management team. Management ability for a business in the mature stage is the following: • Seasoned professionals
Business assets	Equipment and other fixed assets have been in use throughout many operating cycles. The business's mature stage assets include the following characteristics: • Fixed, may need to be replaced or updated • Strong cash assets
Cash flow	Cash flow increases at the mature stage. Sales have reached a plateau, so cash flow is not needed to fuel sales growth. Receivables support purchase of new inventory and pay new staff. • Cash flow is increasing or excessive
Priorities	Business owners might be content to stay with level, steady sales. This would cause cash flow to remain strong and would allow business and personal wealth to grow. Owners also might focus on new markets or products that would allow them to enter another growth stage. The owners have the following priorities at the mature stage: • Identify new markets and new products • Build wealth (personal and business), such as purchasing a building for the business rather than leasing it

THE DECLINE STAGE

A business in the *decline stage* of its life cycle is characterized by level or slightly declining sales. Typically, a company reaches the decline stage after 20 or more years of operation. See Figure 3.6 for general issues for decline businesses.

FIGURE 3.6 GENERAL ISSUES FOR DECLINE BUSINESSES	
Management abilities	Management at the decline stage generally has the following attributes: • Planning for retirement • Looking for new owners
Business assets	The business is attempting to maintain its assets, but it is unlikely to invest heavily in new equipment. The business is cash heavy, meaning that profits remain in the form of cash rather than being invested in new equipment or increased inventory. The following are examples of assets in the decline stage: • Cash heavy • Dated equipment, with no significant updating planned
Cash flow	Cash flow from profitable operations might be down because sales are declining. Because of decreases in supporting accounts receivable and inventory levels, the following may occur: • Overall cash flow may still be stable, or slightly declining
Priorities	Business owners typically are unlikely to take risks at this stage. They do not want to endanger the assets and net worth that have accumulated during years of hard work. The owners may have nonbusiness priorities such as family or community responsibilities that are taking more of their time. They might be looking to phase out of the business. The following are examples of priorities in a decline stage: • Retaining or transferring assets • Selling the business

If you recall, a business does not necessarily have only one growth stage. When you look at companies in a decline stage, be aware that changing management or owners—injecting "new blood"—could lead to a new growth stage.

WHAT ARE THE KEY RISK FACTORS IN A BUSINESS LIFE CYCLE?

Identifying what business life cycle stage a company is in can help the business banker anticipate various issues, such as depth of management experience to strength of cash flow and cash levels. By knowing the life cycle stage, a business banker is better equipped to explore the company's borrowing needs and then select the appropriate lending arrangement. As part of the screening process, it also beneficial to understand some of the key risk factors present in the four stages.

- **Start-up businesses**—In this stage, the risk is highest, while cash flow and collateral are very weak. Because the owner has likely utilized most of his or her resources in getting the business started, the owner is not an attractive borrower. The business does not have a proven market or track record, so it also is not an attractive borrower. Further, the business lacks experienced management and has depleted most of the initial investment by the owners. Business bankers generally are not in a position to provide loans to start-up companies, but can provide transactional products and services where credit risk can be controlled. The marketing challenge for the business banker is to maintain a dialogue with the business until it grows into a more profitable and bankable customer.

- **Growth businesses**—The growth stage is perhaps the earliest stage at which bank lending is appropriate. This is also where the owner must decide how to finance the business. Other investors or even venture capitalists may emerge as viable alternatives to bank loans. The key risk factor in this stage is the degree to which sales growth, although profitable, cannot be financed by internal cash flow. Few business owners understand this issue, and they pursue even more sales as a cash flow cure. A business banker can help the owner understand how sales growth causes corresponding increases in accounts receivable, inventory, and fixed assets. Related risks may include lack of depth in the supply chain or even a labor shortage. In short, the sales growth may be beyond the company's ability to manage or deliver. This leads to another risk—how quickly the business can develop a more professional and experienced management team. This includes a chief financial officer, treasurer, controller, or some other professional-level manager who directly affects the quality and timeliness of financial reporting, which is critical to a bank's ability to fully analyze and monitor the credit.

- **Mature businesses**—In this stage, businesses will likely provide the most attractive financial profile to a bank, while having fewer lending needs because of strong cash flow. The key risk of lending to a mature firm is expecting its stable pattern of sales and cash flow to continue into the future. A business banker must be alert to impending strategies to develop new products or market, or even to acquire other businesses, where the profile may shift back to a growth stage business. Other key risk factors include fixed assets becoming outdated, compression of profit margins, and competition for raw materials and labor.

- **Decline businesses**—Businesses in the decline stage also have an attractive financial profile of relatively low balance sheet leverage and strong cash positions, which may mask some of the lending risks. The business in decline may have complacent management or obsolete products. The industry may be consolidating as total sales for all firms decline. Sales decreases may leave the business with excess product or service delivery capacity and employees. Long-term financing becomes particularly risky in the face of further sales declines. The business may lose substantial market value in this phase, which can jeopardize the wealth and support provided by the owners via a personal guarantee.

In this section, you learned about the general characteristics and business needs of the four stages in a business life cycle—the start-up, growth, mature, and decline stages. You also learned about possible credit risk factors associated with these four stages. You should now feel more confident when analyzing a business's credit request and determining the most appropriate credit product to match its needs. Figure 3.7 summaries the characteristics of the four life cycle stages of businesses.

FIGURE 3.7 COMMERCIAL LENDING BUSINESS LIFE CYCLE CHARACTERISTICS

STAGE	DESCRIPTION	CHARACTERISTICS	
Start-Up	In this stage, there usually will be cash outflow for recurring expenses with little or no sales income. This stage occurs within the first three years of operation.	Management ability:	Limited experience, one-person operation, undermanaged
		Business assets:	Cash poor, minimal fixed assets
		Cash flow:	None, business undercapitalized
		Priorities:	Marketing, increased sales
Growth	This stage is characterized by increasingly higher sales over many operating cycles. This stage typically begins after Year 3 and continues until Year 10.	Management ability:	Competent, but stretched for time
		Business assets:	Additional assets needed to support sales growth
		Cash flow:	All cash put back into business
		Priorities:	Find resources to support growth
Mature	Generally, this stage is defined by having achieved at least 10 years of profitable operations. Sales are still increasing, but at a much slower rate.	Management ability:	Seasoned professionals
		Business assets:	Builtup fixed assets support sales growth
		Cash flow:	Increasing or excess cash flow
		Priorities:	Identify new markets, new products, build wealth (personal and business)
Decline	This stage is characterized by level sales that may begin to decline slightly. Typically, a company reaches the decline stage after 20 or more years in operation.	Management ability:	Looking to retire, looking for "new blood"
		Business assets:	Cash heavy, no new purchases of equipment
		Cash flow:	Steady or declining
		Priorities:	Retain or transfer assets, sell business

SUMMARY

By completing this chapter, you learned about the basic types of legal structures available to businesses. Whether the business is a sole proprietorship, partnership, C corporation, S corporation, or limited liability company, this information is important when determining how the profits of the business are taxed, whether the owners have liability for business debts, and other factors that will affect the financial statements to be analyzed and any subsequent borrowing arrangements you propose.

You also learned the general characteristics associated with the four basic stages in a business life cycle. Most businesses have a start-up phase characterized by a lack of management experience, with untested products seeking markets that have not been fully developed. The initial investment by the owners is the key funding source, but can be easily depleted. In the growth stage, the firm generally struggles to meet demand, and any cash flow from profits is stretched by the corresponding growth in accounts receivable and inventory. As a business matures, profitable sales may reach a plateau, and cash flow strengthens as accounts receivable and inventory are not expanding. If the firm is not successful in developing new products or markets, then it may move into the decline stage, where sales can decrease, and the owners may seek to sell or otherwise exit the business. These stages help a business banker anticipate funding needs, but more important, to anticipate key risk factors that will accompany these needs. By having this knowledge, you will be better positioned for subsequent analysis of detailed financial information and, if a loan is approved, better mitigate the risk factors with your loan structure and documentation.

QUESTIONS FOR DISCUSSION

1. What are the two primary reasons for choosing a legal entity?
2. What is the difference between a business life cycle and the operating cycle of a business?
3. What is the key risk of lending to a mature business?

EXERCISE 1

Match each business life cycle on the left to its description on the right.

____ 1. Start-up stage   A. Positive cash flow, has fixed assets

____ 2. Growth stage   B. Undermanaged, minimum fixed assets

____ 3. Mature stage   C. Needs to conserve or transfer wealth

____ 4. Decline stage   D. Additional assets needed to support sales

EXERCISE 2

Background

Dry Supply is a wholesaler of dry-cleaning equipment, cleaning supplies, and laundry soap. The company, which is located in central Kansas, has been in business more than 50 years. Anne Schippel, business banker, in conjunction with her manager, has determined that this business is consistent with the industries targeted by her bank, as well as being within the bank's designated market area. She has made introductory calls, and knows that Dry Supply currently is owned by two sisters and is organized as an S corporation. Based on this information, she can begin making a preliminary assessment of the loan request.

Instructions

Answer the following questions using the legal structure and life cycle information in this chapter.

A. What initial assessment can Anne Schippel make based on the legal structure of Dry Supply?

B. Based on the age of the business, what life cycle stage is Dry Supply? What characteristics or additional information would help you make this assessment?

C. What key risk factors should be considered?

D. Based on the Commercial Lending Decision Tree (see illustration in the textbook Introduction), what are some additional issues Anne Schippel should consider?

4

INTRODUCTION TO BUSINESS FINANCIAL STATEMENTS

OBJECTIVES

After studying *Introduction to Business Financial Statements*, you will be able to—

- Describe the financial statement analysis process
- Describe basic guidelines for preparing a spreadsheet and analyzing the data
- Identify and evaluate a borrower's financial strengths, weaknesses, and uncertainties
- Explain the different types of financial statement preparation
- Describe the other components associated with financial analysis

INTRODUCTION

"Numbers talk and bankers need to listen." For business bankers, this statement is very true, and often it is learned the hard way.

A fictitious business banker, Thomas Scott, presents a case in point. It is 8 a.m. on a bright, sunny day when Scott enters his office. He is feeling optimistic, full of energy. In one hand he holds a cup of coffee and in the other he holds a thick file. He places the file on his desk, takes a sip of coffee, turns on his computer, and sits down. Looking at the file, Scott smiles and says, "Okay, from what I've learned so far, it appears that—

- You operate the type of business we want to have as a customer
- You are located in my bank's defined market area
- The loan purpose is compatible with our loan policy
- The loan request has a defined source of repayment

Now let's go over your statements and see whether your past financial performance is also satisfactory and whether all signs indicate that it will remain so throughout the life of the loan." The steps that Scott has just performed show that he is progressing through the Commercial Lending Decision Tree. With positive results so far, Scott now accesses his spreading program, takes a pencil in hand, opens the file, and starts the analysis of the customer's financial statements.

By performing **financial statement analysis**, Scott is "listening to the numbers," assessing the customer's financial performance to date, and drawing conclusions about the future prospects for loan repayment. Although entire textbooks have been devoted to financial analysis as used in commercial lending, this textbook will focus on the role and purpose of financial analysis, the basic steps in financial statement analysis (from obtaining and processing statements to analyzing and interpreting the information in those statements), some basic analytical techniques, and the types of statements prepared and analyzed.

> **Financial statement analysis**
>
> The examination and interpretation of financial data to evaluate a business's past performance, present condition, and future prospects.

Relationship to the Commercial Lending Decision Tree

In the textbook Introduction, we explored the Commercial Lending Decision Tree as a way to think about the stages and steps involved in the commercial lending process, just as Scott did in the previous example. As you have already learned, this process emphasizes early screening and qualifying steps to match the portfolio and goals of your bank. The business banker also begins assessing the financial and nonfinancial qualifications of the business. By understanding how the financial statements of the business have been constructed, you will gain greater insight into making the preliminary assessment in the screening steps.

In terms of the Commercial Lending Decision Tree illustration in the Introduction, this chapter relates to Stage One, where the lending opportunity is screened in a variety of ways before beginning the time-consuming process of analyzing detailed financial statements and other data. By understanding the role and purpose of the business financial statement, plus the type of statement being provided, you take yet another preliminary step that will better position the business banker to anticipate certain issues that are likely to arise in the financial statements. In addition, you will learn the steps in the upcoming financial analysis process and key issues for spreading financial statements. This knowledge will better position you to collect all the data needed and maximize the efficiency of the analysis that will occur in Stage Two of the Commercial Lending Decision Tree.

FINANCIAL STATEMENT ANALYSIS PROCESS

The focus of financial statement analysis depends on the specific purpose of the examination. For example, a loan request to fund a temporary increase in inventory or to acquire new equipment will be analyzed in a different way than interim data to monitor an existing loan. The purpose of the analysis will affect the nature and depth of the investigation.

The size of the requested loan (relative to the size of the bank) and its terms also affect the range of financial statement analysis. A large loan requires more effort by the bank than a small loan because a loss on the larger loan would have a greater impact on bank earnings. This is not to say that small loans do not involve a considerable amount of uncertainty concerning repayment, but the smaller interest income does not always profitably allow for extensive analysis. A $50,000 loan for 90 days, adequately secured with a defined source of repayment, for example, should involve less analysis than a $350,000 loan for five years to finance an equipment purchase.

Nevertheless, when conducting a financial analysis, most banks follow a systematic approach to obtain statements, organize and present the information from those statements, and evaluate and interpret the data by using several analytical techniques.

ROLE AND PURPOSE OF FINANCIAL STATEMENT ANALYSIS

The purpose of financial statement analysis is to examine past and current financial data so that a company's performance and financial position can be evaluated and future risks and potential can be estimated. Financial statement analysis can yield valuable information about trends and relationships, the quality of a company's earnings, and the strengths and weaknesses of its financial position.

FINANCIAL STATEMENT ANALYSIS DEFINED

Financial statement analysis is a systematic examination and interpretation of the past performance of a business in order to predict future profitability and capacity of the business to repay debt. Financial statement analysis helps the business banker decide whether a loan should be made, determine possible terms and conditions, and identify the monitoring needed until the loan is repaid. It is a critical component of the business lending process, which begins with an initial meeting with the business customer, then moves on to the stages of financial statement analysis, loan structuring and pricing, loan negotiation, loan documentation and closing, and monitoring.

Financial statement analysis focuses on the company's past, current, and projected financial performance as reflected in its financial statements, rather than on its management style or credit history. Nevertheless, such nonfinancial considerations do help establish the frequency and the depth of the financial statement analysis.

Technical and interpretive analysis

Technical manipulation of the data is only a small part of a comprehensive and effective financial statement analysis. Once the technical analysis of a business and its industry has been completed, the business banker must interpret the results to determine whether to make a loan.

- **Technical**—whenever they examine available financial information, business bankers apply research techniques based on sound business logic and generally accepted accounting principles. Technical applications include spreading information for clarity, comparing ratios with those of other businesses, preparing cash flow calculations for analysis, and projecting future operating results.
- **Interpretive**—the goal of interpretive analysis is to learn not only what is happening, but also why it is happening. In this process, how past events and current trends might affect a company's future repayment ability are important considerations.

The importance of interpreting the financial statements is echoed in the communication theme that opened this chapter. Good communication and analytical skills are required when conducting a proper financial statement analysis. However, in a financial analysis, the financial statements of the business do the "talking." By knowing what questions to ask and how to "listen" and interpret the answers, a business banker can pinpoint a business's strengths, weaknesses, and critical issues. From these determinations, the lender can begin to predict a customer's future capacity to repay debt. Financial statement analysis is fundamentally important to the lending decision and to the monitoring process that begins once the loan is closed, including early identification of problem loans.

Another issue in interpreting the "talk" of financial statements is that the results are a direct result of management actions, or sometimes lack of action. Beyond some issues influenced by the type of business and its industry, the business owners and managers decide the products and markets to develop. They decide how to respond to a competitor, set the terms for selling a product or service on credit and who to sell to, and the levels of inventory to hold. Overall, they are responsible for and directly affect all the numbers the business banker will be analyzing. The cover letters for the different types of accountant-prepared financial statements all include the phrase "these statements are the responsibility of management."

FINANCIAL ANALYSIS OVERVIEW

In a large bank with separate lending and credit departments, different individuals may be responsible for receiving and logging in statements, spreading statements and calculating ratios, and interpreting data. In a small bank, the business banker may be responsible for every aspect of financial analysis. Another practice followed by some banks is for the business banker to spread and analyze financial statements received on active loans as part of an ongoing periodic monitoring process, whereas the credit department performs these functions for statements received from business prospects.

Financial analysis, regardless of the division of labor or responsibility, involves the same basic process at all banks. The first step is for the banker to obtain all necessary financial information. Figure 4.1 shows the financial Statement Analysis Process.

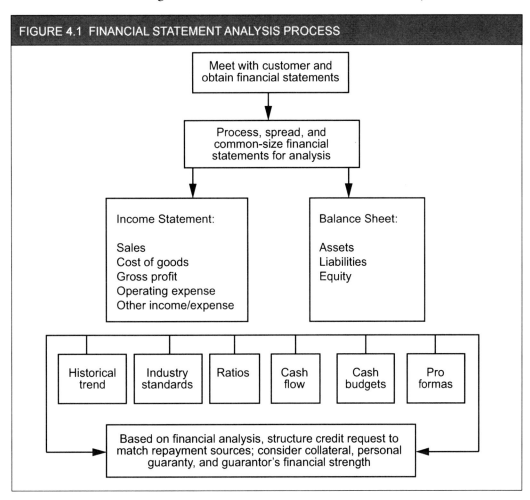

Step 1: Obtaining Statements

Most banks have guidelines for the type and number of statements to obtain for a comprehensive financial analysis. When considering a loan request from a new customer who operates an established business, a bank might require income statements and balance sheets for the most recent three years, and two or three interim statements for consecutive periods (such as quarterly or monthly) of the current year. The business banker may ask for this information during the initial meetings with the customer.

As the business banker learns more about the business, more information may become necessary. For example, the customer may have prepared statements internally, rather than by an external accountant. One way to verify that the internal financial information is reasonably accurate is to obtain the business tax returns for the same period and compare the general levels of revenues and profits, and assets and liabilities. In other cases, pro forma statements (projections) or cash budgets may be necessary to discern the firm's future direction if substantial strategic changes are occurring or being planned. In still other cases, such as privately held businesses, personal financial statements of the owners may need to be reviewed as part of assessing the financial strength of the potential guarantors.

Step 2: Processing Statements

Whether mailed or e-mailed to the bank, or even delivered personally by the customer, all statements should indicate the following:

- The date of the statement
- The signature and date by the customer or the customer's accountant

Where possible, the statements should include a disclosure that affirms that they are meant for use by the bank to which they are submitted. The statements are then placed in the customer's credit file, with the subsequent spread and summary comments to be included later. Most banks use a computerized database to track when each statement is received and when the next statement should be received. As the due date of the next financial statement approaches, the program assists the business banker in making a timely, advance request for updates. If the due date passes, the same program generates an exception list of items not received from the customer.

Credit files contain—
- Copies of loan documents such as the promissory note and the security agreement
- Financial information such as tax returns and financial statements
- Credit inquiries and reports
- Collateral information
- Correspondence, e-mails, and memos
- Other company-related information such as annual reports and brochures

Step 3: Spreading Statements

Spreading financial statements is the process of extracting information from multiple years of (and likely separate) financial statements of a business and inputting the data into a spreadsheet in a consistent format from which various ratios can be computed. The result has been referred to by bankers as a "spread" or "spreadsheet" for many years, even before the introduction of general data spreadsheet computer programs such as Lotus® and Microsoft Excel®. Bankers prepared spreads prior to the advent of computerized tools.

Having all the data in a condensed and easily readable format allows a banker to spot trends more quickly and facilitates better comparisons. Various types of financial spreading programs are available for banks, ranging from off-the-shelf software to internally developed spreadsheets. The choice of a spreading program depends on the number of statements to be spread, the nature of the typical analysis, and preferences for formats and data-tracking features.

If a business banker works extensively with businesses in a particular industry, many spreading programs have specialized formats specific to certain industries. Common examples include the construction industry, auto dealerships, and insurance companies.

Step 4: Technical Analysis

To give additional perspective to financial analysis, the numbers in the statements are subjected to various examinations of a technical nature. These include common-sizing, trend analysis, and comparative analysis.

- **Common-sizing**—expresses each account on the income statement as a percentage of net sales and each account on the balance sheet as a percentage of total assets. If net sales are $100 and operating expenses are $34, for example, common-sized operating expenses are expressed as 34 percent. When financial statements are common-sized, the business banker may compare related information quickly and note changes over time. For example, if a shoe retailer remodels the business-owned building, the value of those improvements as a percentage of total assets will increase. When a business remodels space, sales often are expected to increase. Depending on the type of inventory carried in the new space, the mix of sales may change. If the sales mix changes, the cost of inventory as a percentage of sales will probably change. Common-sized statements show these percentages and results of these strategic moves in a readable format.

- **Trend analysis**—involves comparing financial data and ratios during similar periods or at comparable times for the same business. It is used to detect favorable or unfavorable changes in the financial position of a business, as reflected in revenues, expenses, assets, liabilities, or net worth accounts.

- **Comparative analysis**—parallels the financial information of at least two businesses, preferably of the same size and industry. Making industry comparisons enables the business banker to see where competitors stand in relation to the business of the loan applicant. Industry comparisons, too, are used to detect favorable or unfavorable conditions, but more on an industry-wide basis.

By using the Annual Statement Studies compiled by the Risk Management Association (RMA), a business banker can match many companies to the subject company by North American Industry Classification System (NAICS) code and draw statistical conclusions. RMA's data are collected from member banks' spreads of roughly 200,000 customers.

ROUNDING

Many numbers are used in this textbook, and typically they have been rounded up, either as dollars to the nearest thousand, or as fractions only to one-tenth. The focus should not be on whether the numbers add up, but on what they mean. Most commercial loans made today are greater than $100,000, with financial data being rounded to thousands. A $1,000 or $2,000 difference caused by rounding or typographical error should not be a material issue. However, a large error caused by poor preparation of financial statements should concern the lender and be investigated.

Step 5: Interpretive Analysis

In addition to the financial and technical assessments showing what is happening, the business banker needs to determine why it is happening. This includes a continuity analysis and the ultimate, written analysis of all findings.

- **Continuity analysis**—involves determining whether a firm likely will remain in business, in its present form, for long enough to use its assets for their intended purpose, which is to generate cash flow to repay liabilities in the ordinary course of business. This concept also is known as a "going concern." If a business is not a going concern, then the immediate practical problem for the business banker is to determine whether the company's assets are properly valued for financial presentation. If the assets are not properly valued, the business banker will need to determine whether the net worth is overstated.

    Again, the underlying assumption of continuity is that assets will be used for their original purpose—to generate future revenues and long-term net cash flow. If a business fails, the assets could be liquidated for the sole purpose of immediately repaying debt. Under such distressed conditions, this would produce a result substantially less than any value appearing on the financial statements. If there is reason to question the ability of the business to maintain its status as a going concern, the accountant must bring this question to the attention of the reader of the financial statements; however, such statements are rare unless the company already is in default on its various obligations or liabilities.

- **Written analysis**—occurs after the statements are spread and common-sized and other mathematical calculations (such as ratios, cash flow figures, or projections) are completed. The business banker writes an objective, not speculative, analysis, or interpretation. The interpretation should include an explanation of what actually caused any changes and avoid the so-called "elevator language" of just stating that something went up or down. For example, the analysis should not be worded, "sales increased 4 percent." Rather, the analysis should read, "sales increased 4 percent due to a 3 percent price increase and a small increase in product volume sold."

> **Common-sizing**
>
> A form of financial ratio analysis that allows the comparison of companies with different levels of sales or total assets by introducing a common denominator. A common-sized balance sheet expresses each item on the balance sheet as a percentage of total assets and each item on the income statement as a percentage of net sales.

Dry Supply is a fictitious example company that will be used throughout the textbook to illustrate various financial statements. Dry Supply is a wholesaler of dry-cleaning and laundry products. It is an established company owned by two sisters. As a primary tool, you will use the income statement and balance sheet spreads that summarize multiple years of financial information about this business. Statement spreading is the heart of financial statement analysis and places financial data, ratios, and **common-sizing** information in a concise format to facilitate the analysis process. Your purpose, for now, is to focus on the format and content of this example—the income statement and balance sheet spread. In upcoming chapters you will learn about each of the data components, how to calculate the various ratios, and how to interpret the results.

Figures 4.2 and 4.3 show the income statement and balance sheet spreads for Dry Supply. You will refer to these financial statement spreads through out the chapter.

As you have read, the financial statement analysis process demands attention to detail and an ability to perform or review certain mathematical tasks, including calculating ratios, preparing cash flow statements, and determining the amount and percentage of change in accounts from one statement to the next. The process can be time-consuming and costly. Many banks, for these and other reasons, have computerized as much of the statement-spreading function as possible. Even with this level of automation, the banker must understand how the numbers originated, how the mathematical calculations were made, and how to interpret the results.

In this section, you learned about the financial analysis process and the types and number of statements you need to obtain from the customer to perform a comprehensive financial analysis. You also learned about the statement components that need to be reviewed when processing statements. You can now explain the process of spreading financial statements, the three types of technical analysis, and the two types of interpretive analysis.

FIGURE 4.2 INCOME STATEMENT SPREAD: DRY SUPPLY

Income Statement ($ in 000s)	Review 20xx		Review 20xy		Review 20xz	
	Amount	%	Amount	%	Amount	%
Net sales	$895	100.0	$937	100.0	$918	100.0
Cost of goods sold	<u>645</u>	<u>72.1</u>	<u>667</u>	<u>71.2</u>	<u>631</u>	<u>68.7</u>
Gross profit	250	27.9	270	28.8	287	31.3
Selling, gen. and admin. expense	157	17.5	173	18.5	180	19.6
Officer's compensation	36	4.0	31	3.3	28	3.1
Rent expenses	15	1.7	18	1.9	20	2.2
Bad debt expense	2	0.2	1	0.1	0	0.0
Profit-sharing expense	7	0.8	7	0.7	0	0.0
Depreciation expense	<u>12</u>	<u>1.3</u>	<u>12</u>	<u>1.3</u>	<u>13</u>	<u>1.4</u>
Total operating expenses	229	25.6	242	25.8	241	26.3
Operating income	21	2.3	28	3.0	46	5.0
Other income	0	0.0	0	0.0	0	0.0
Interest income	2	0.2	2	0.2	2	0.2
Rental income	3	0.3	3	0.3	3	0.3
Interest expense	<u>6</u>	<u>0.7</u>	<u>7</u>	<u>0.7</u>	<u>11</u>	<u>1.2</u>
Net profit before tax	20	2.2	26	2.8	40	4.4
Taxes	<u>11</u>	<u>1.2</u>	<u>12</u>	<u>1.3</u>	<u>17</u>	<u>1.9</u>
Net profit after tax	$ 9	1.0	$ 14	1.5	$ 23	2.5

FIGURE 4.3 BALANCE SHEET SPREAD: DRY SUPPLY

Common-sized report ($ in $000s)	Review 12/31/20xx		Review 12/31/20xy		Review 12/31/20xz	
Assets	Amount	%	Amount	%	Amount	%
Cash	$ 3	1.2	$ 12	4.6	$ 22	8.1
Accounts receivable	114	46.9	118	45.4	117	43.3
Less: allowance for doubtful accounts	5	2.1	5	1.9	5	1.9
Net accounts receivable	109	44.9	113	43.5	112	41.5
Inventory	73	30.0	72	27.7	67	24.8
Total current assets	185	76.1	197	75.8	201	74.4
Furniture and fixtures	76	31.3	75	28.8	78	28.9
Leasehold improvements	1	0.4	1	0.4	0	0.0
Transportation equipment	53	21.8	70	26.9	85	31.5
Gross fixed assets	130	53.5	146	56.2	163	60.4
Less: Accum. depreciation	85	35.0	97	37.3	110	40.7
Net fixed assets	45	18.5	49	18.8	53	19.6
Cash-value life insurance	13	5.3	14	5.4	16	5.9
Total assets	$243	100.0	$260	100.0	$270	100.0

	Review 12/31/20xx		Review 12/31/20xy		Review 12/31/20xz	
Liabilities	Amount	%	Amount	%	Amount	%
Notes payable bank short-term	$81	33.3	$68	26.2	$59	21.8
Accounts payable—trade	42	17.3	46	17.7	31	11.5
Accrued taxes	5	2.1	6	2.3	7	2.6
Accrued bonuses	10	4.1	11	4.2	12	4.4
Total current liabilities	138	56.8	131	50.4	109	40.4
Subordinated debt officers	48	19.8	58	22.3	67	24.8
Total liabilities	186	76.5	189	72.7	176	65.2
Net Worth						
Common stock	2	0.8	2	0.8	2	0.7
Retained earnings	55	22.6	69	26.5	92	34.1
Total net worth	57	23.5	71	27.3	94	34.8
Total liabilities and net worth	$243	100.0	$260	100.0	$270	100.0

FINANCIAL STATEMENT BASICS

Financial statements provide a standardized way to record and communicate important financial information about the operations and financial conditions of businesses, other types of organizations, and individuals. To obtain detailed information about businesses and individuals, banks generally rely on the following three components of financial statements:

- **Balance Sheet**—a detailed list of assets, liabilities, and owner's equity, showing a company's or individual's financial position at a given date

- **Income Statement**—a summary of a company's or individual's income and expenses over a given period (also referred to as a profit and loss statement, operating statement, and earnings statement)
- **Statement of Cash Flows**—a summary of a company's operating, financing, and investing activities (cash receipts and payments) over a specific period (also referred to as a sources and uses of funds statement)

It is considered a complete set of financial statements when the accountant's cover letter, a reconciliation of owner's equity, disclosures (**footnotes**), the balance sheet, income statement, and statement of cash flows are packaged together. In many cases, where an internally prepared balance sheet and income statement are all a business provides, together they may be referred to as a "financial statement," but they are not considered complete. We will look more closely at the differences between internally and externally prepared financial statements later in this chapter.

> **Footnotes**
>
> A detailed explanation attached to and considered an integral part of audited or reviewed financial statements prepared by a certified public accountant that allow the auditor to comment on the statements relative to GAAP.

STATEMENT SPREADING GUIDELINES

Before analyzing a company's financial statements, bankers should use the following basic guidelines for preparing a spreadsheet:

- Reverse the order of data columns as presented by the accountant. Accountant-prepared financial statements usually present data for the current year in the left-most column, followed by prior years to the right—the reverse of chronological order. The spreadsheet format, however, typically begins with the oldest year on the left and succeeding years on the right, in chronological order. Lenders should be careful to avoid transposing data from the accountant's statements to the bank spreadsheet, to ensure that the dates are in proper order.
- Spread and analyze annual and interim statements separately. Compare interim statements only with interim statements of the same date from previous years. If quarterly or monthly statements are available, the lender makes multiple spreadsheets that contain fiscal years, first quarters, second quarters, third quarters, and fourth quarters. Spreadsheets allow the lender to review several years of financial performance simultaneously.
- Read the accountant's cover letter and disclosures (including footnotes) before spreading the statement and beginning the analysis. Footnotes and other disclosures generally detail basic methods used to construct financial statements. It is essential, therefore, that they be read and understood before spreading the statement. Information in some footnotes does not appear on the balance sheet, income statement, statement of cash flows, or reconciliation of equity. This information may pertain to potential lawsuits, warranties, and events that will take place after the statement date. The footnotes for Dry Supply can be found later in this chapter.

- Round numbers to thousands, with ratio decimal places limited to one or two. This practice makes the spreadsheet easier to read. Additionally, smaller, non-material items that do not evenly round up to at least $1,000 are eliminated. If financial statement entries are very small, it may make sense not to round.

Before spreading the statements, a lender also thinks about the following situations:

- Methods the company uses to recognize revenue and expenses (i.e., cash or accruals)
- Sales trends, product or service mix, order backlogs, discounts, allowances, returns, large nonrecurring sales, seasons, and cyclical factors
- Cost of goods sold calculations
- Larger changes in expenses in relation to sales
- How bad debt is recognized
- The inventory valuation method used
- The depreciation method used for fixed assets
- Taxation issues

When analyzing spreadsheets, a business banker uses many techniques. One way to assess a company's performance is to look at the trend figured by a specific account over several consecutive periods. Examining the net profit after tax posted at the end of four or five consecutive years, for example, reveals whether it declined, increased, remained stable, or fluctuated. After considering the company's operating environment, a business banker may use the trend in net profits to support a prediction of the company's future profits.

OTHER CONSIDERATIONS

Financial analysis is more than just adding and subtracting figures, calculating ratios and percentages, and extrapolating numbers based on past trends. For analytical purposes, these numbers have little meaning unless the business banker understands the internal and external factors affecting the company's performance. Later in Level 3, you will learn more about these nonfinancial factors. As a brief overview, the following are some factors to consider:

- **Economic and regulatory issues**—In addition to examining a business and its financial performance, a business banker also pays close attention to general business conditions, including inflation, interest rate forecasts, pending regulations, and taxation policies. All of these factors may influence a company's ability to repay loans.
- **The industry**—A business banker determines whether the industry and its products are growing, declining, or stagnant. For example, is the industry highly competitive or controlled by a few companies? What is the customer's position within the company and the industry? Business cycles affect some industries. Cyclical industries include housing, auto, and clothing. Some industries are noncyclical (not affected by business cycles), such as food, medical

care, and education. Still others are countercyclical, actually improving when other industries are in declining business cycles. Auto servicing, home repair, and employment agencies tend to be counterclyclical.

- **The market**—Business bankers consider whether the company's market is diversified or restricted, growing, or stagnant. Demographic and consumer preference trends influence sales, expenses, and key balance sheet accounts.
- **The business**—The legal structure of the business, management goals and objectives, and operating characteristics affect spreadsheet analysis. A corporation's balance sheet, for example, will indicate an entry for common stock. Because a sole proprietor's net worth is composed of business and personal assets, the balance sheet will not have a common stock entry.
- **Other events**—Other events may affect numbers on a spreadsheet. The poor health or death of an owner or a key manager, for example, influences events. The availability of well-trained, capable employees is important, especially to the growing number of service companies.

MORE ON TECHNICAL AND INTERPRETIVE ANALYSIS REVISITED

To analyze financial statements effectively, a business banker must possess both the technical skills of an accountant and the interpretive skills of an investigator.

First, financial analysis involves understanding the structure, organization, and contents of financial statements. An experienced business banker, for example, knows what "cost of goods sold" means, where it can be found on a financial statement, which accounts make up its structure, how it is calculated, and how the choice of inventory valuation methods affects it. In short, a business banker must have an accountant's familiarity with the terminology of financial statements.

Second, mathematical proficiency is essential. Data are calculated in specific, sometimes complex, ways. During technical analysis, the applications used include statement spreading, comparing ratios, preparing cash flow calculations, and projecting future operating results. The business banker must be knowledgeable about the following approaches to calculations:

- Calculating the numerical and percentage changes in an account over time
- Understanding how the calculations were made
- Making comparisons with data from other statements
- Calculating ratios and a cash flow statement
- Working with numbers
- Interpreting the results

In financial analysis, an inability to look beyond the numbers is a serious failing. One of the first duties of a business banker is to get behind the numbers and not take them at face value. This is equally important whether the numbers are good or bad. A major objective of interpretive analysis, therefore, is to help a business banker understand a firm's financial strengths and weaknesses better through technical calculation and data interpretation.

LIMITATIONS OF FINANCIAL ANALYSIS

The financial condition of a business is not always accurately portrayed by calculating and interpreting financial data, because the raw data may be misleading, inconsistent, or erroneous. Before analyzing statements, therefore, a business banker must be familiar with limitations, especially accuracy, involving the quality of information, accounting methods used, external environment, unlisted information, distortion in numbers, and aggregate accounts.

The bankruptcy filings of Enron, WorldCom, and Adelphia within the past decade are good examples of limitations to financial analysis. The financial failures of these firms illustrate the importance of being able to draw independent conclusions and to not rely solely on the accounting experts. Although these firms were very large and seemingly irrelevant to community banks, many smaller, related businesses were caught up in their financial difficulties and ultimately failed or had operating losses that affected loans at community banks.

Quality of information

Financial analysis is only as good as the information upon which it is based. Lenders often borrow a phrase from the computer industry ("garbage in, garbage out") when referring to the quality of financial information and its effect on the quality of the related financial analysis.

For example, if accounts receivable are erroneously reported on a balance sheet, the resulting calculation of the current ratio or accounts receivable turnover will be faulty. Statements prepared and attested to by a reputable accounting firm are more likely to be complete and accurate than those prepared by an inexperienced internal controller. Business bankers must be wary of any statement that appears to have been drawn up at the last minute or in an unprofessional manner.

Accounting methods

In preparing financial statements, many different accounting alternatives are available and acceptable. Three inventory valuation methods commonly used are first-in, first-out (FIFO); last-in, first-out (LIFO); and weighted average cost. When production costs are rising, the FIFO method of valuing inventory can result in higher gross profits relative to current costs. Comparing a company that uses the FIFO method to a company that uses LIFO can result in erroneous conclusions. The accounting methods used are usually described in the footnotes to the financial statement.

External environment

Economic, competitive, and regulatory conditions influence the environment in which a business operates. What may appear as a weakness on an income statement, such as a small decline in profits from one year to the next, may actually be a strength, if the economy took a sharp downturn during that period. The constantly changing external environment can limit conclusions drawn from comparing statements from different periods.

Unlisted information

Honesty, willingness to repay debts, and other measures of character cannot be quantified and listed on a financial statement. This information is obtained primarily through loan interviews and credit investigation. Financial statements also do not include other information that may be relevant, such as a list of order backlogs, unfunded pension liabilities, proposed capital expenditures, pending lawsuits, or assets used by the business that may belong to the owner. For example, Dry Supply's financial statements do not reflect that the company has a $150,000 backlog in orders, is approaching shipping capacity, and is projecting an increase in capital expenditures for the next year.

Distortion in numbers

A firm's management may decide to distort the picture portrayed in its financial statements. For example, an owner may write off the accumulated bad debts (unpaid accounts receivable) of the business over a single accounting period, or obsolete inventory may not be written off quickly. Such actions make it difficult for the business banker to accurately assess historical profitability, accounts receivable turnover rates, and inventory value.

Aggregate accounts

Many of the data in financial statements are aggregated. Sales generated for each product are combined and listed as one account (net sales) on the income statement. Aggregation may limit a business banker's observations when assessing the financial condition and prospects of a company. Dry Supply's statements, for example, do not break out sales by dry-cleaning and laundry products. Most businesses can provide breakdowns of accounts and items shown in the financial statement, including product mix of sales, if needed.

To review the information you read regarding the distinction between technical and interpretive skills and their application to financial analysis, look at the trend in sales as shown in the income statement of Dry Supply.

SALES TREND	
Year	Sales
20xx	$895
20xy	$937
20xz	$918

The **technical analysis** of these numbers begins by looking at the annual increase in sales on both a numerical and percentage basis.

ANNUAL INCREASE IN SALES		
Period	Numerical growth	Percentage growth
20xx - 20xy	$42	4.7%
20xy - 20xz	($19)	(2.0%)

To make the percentage calculation for 20xx-20xy, the dollar difference between the two years is divided by the base year of 20xx and then multiplied by 100.

$$\frac{(\$937 - \$895)}{\$895} \times 100 = 4.69\% \text{ or } 4.7\% \text{ rounded}$$

If financial analysis consisted only of technical manipulation of numbers, then it would be safe to say that Dry Supply figured minor sales growth and, based on this trend, predict that sales should continue to increase annually at 1 percent or less. Interpretive analysis, however, requires a more penetrating look. A business banker will want to know what caused this growth in sales. If inflation was 5 percent per year over that period, then the growth in sales was mostly a result of inflation. If sales of all other similar wholesalers increased by an average of 8 percent between 20xx and 20xz, then the performance of this particular business was below inflation as well as the industry rate. The numbers must always be put in the proper context.

Interpretive analysis requires business bankers to know the reasons for the technical results obtained from financial analysis. All the background information from the interviews and investigations—ownership, industry, markets, economy, onsite visits, and more—are used. The key to financial analysis lies, therefore, in the ability to determine not only what happened in a business but also why it happened and how it may influence future financial results.

As you have discovered, working with numbers, zeroing in on a final result while excluding other necessary considerations, may lead to invalid conclusions. Financial analysis is one way of identifying the strengths and weaknesses of a business and making educated assumptions about the firm's future capacity to repay debt.

In this section, you learned about the basic guidelines for preparing a spreadsheet. You are now able to identify the other considerations, both internal and external, that may affect a company's performance. You also learned that to analyze financial statements effectively, you must possess technical and interpretive skills. In addition, you are now familiar with the limitations of financial analysis—especially accuracy—involving the quality of information, accounting methods used, external environment, unlisted information, distortion in numbers, and aggregate accounts.

BASIC ANALYTICAL TECHNIQUES

Just as with the other steps in the first two stages of the Commercial Lending Decision Tree, the underlying objective of financial statement analysis is to gauge a customer's ability to repay the loan. The focus is on past, current, and projected financial performance and not on, for example, personal character and credit history.

Nonfinancial considerations revealed in the interview help establish the direction and depth of financial analysis. A long-term loan to a business with a short operating record and an uncertain future carries a high-risk value, for example. To make the loan decision, the business banker must conduct an in-depth evaluation using all available income statements, balance sheets, customer-prepared pro forma statements, and cash budgets.

STRENGTHS — WEAKNESSES > UNCERTAINTIES

Financial analysis is not a crystal ball that allows a business banker to peer into the future and predict, with absolute certainty, how a business will fare in the coming years. Uncertainty is ever present. Examples are the chance the economy will take a turn for the worse, that a well-financed competitor will set up shop down the street, or that a business's customers may stop paying their bills.

Financial analysis requires a constant process of inquiry to identify and evaluate a borrower's financial strengths and weaknesses. When done properly, financial analysis allows the business banker to understand all of the risks involved in extending credit and how to minimize those risks through proper credit underwriting and loan structuring. If all the strengths outweigh the accumulated weaknesses by a margin sufficient to cover for uncertainties, the loan represents an acceptable credit risk. This conclusion is written as follows:

Strengths — Weaknesses > Uncertainties

For example, consider a loan request for a line of credit by Dry Supply. The most recent balance sheet submitted by the customer shows current assets of $201,000 and current liabilities of $109,000. The $92,000 differential is generally favorable. If demand for the product surges unexpectedly or, conversely, if demand falls off, the company has a margin of funds available to purchase inventory or to sustain short-term operating losses.

However, of the $201,000 in current assets, $67,000 is inventory—primarily liquid dry-cleaning products purchased by the company. Inventory is not as easily converted to cash as other forms of current assets, and cash is needed to repay loans. The concentration of current assets in inventory should raise the following questions:

- What is the demand for the product?
- Will dry cleaning prices be rising?
- When will the inventory be sold and the accounts receivable collected?

Next, uncertainties are considered. A prime uncertainty is the future demand for various types of dry-cleaning products. If, for example, for environmental reasons, many dry-cleaners switch from using liquid to using powder in dry-cleaning, then the inventory will not be sold and the cash the business needs to repay and meet operating costs will not be generated.

Of course, financial analysis involves more than looking at the amount of current assets, current liabilities, inventory, and the characteristics of a particular industry. For efficiency, a bank may even credit score certain business loans. Every financial statement should draw out numerous questions about every aspect of a business's financial performance. Applying specific analytical techniques to this task begins with a look at the types of financial statements and the quality of information they contain.

Financial statement analysis is a systematic examination and interpretation of information to assess a business's past performance for the purpose of predicting future profitability and its capacity to repay debt.

In this section, you learned about the process of identifying and evaluating a business borrower's financial strengths, weaknesses, and uncertainties. Using these standard analytical techniques, you will now understand the risks involved in extending credit and how to minimize those risks when you examine financial statements.

> **CREDIT SCORING VERSUS FINANCIAL ANALYSIS**
>
> For efficiency, a bank may credit score certain commercial loans. Credit scoring is the process of giving points for a variety of factors, such as length of time in business, number of years of consecutive profits, amount of debt verses equity, type of collateral, and loan term. The total of the points helps a business banker estimate repayment probability based the financial statements. An applicant who scores high enough is granted the loan. A full financial analysis is completed on the larger loan requests only.
>
> When credit scoring is used, one or more senior lenders may have authority to override the credit score and approve loans on an exception basis. Approval may be warranted based on other factors not considered in the credit score, such as a financially strong guarantor.
>
> Community banks normally perform a complete credit analysis on all commercial loans, including nonfinancial considerations such as character, number of jobs in the community, and length of time in business. Full financial analysis involves investigating the business to understand the "story" behind the numbers.

EVALUATING STATEMENT QUALITY AND RELIABILITY

Financial statements are the report card of a business. They help the lender understand the borrower's ability to repay debt, assist in loan monitoring, and document management's ability to make decisions and manage changes. Financial statements may be prepared internally or externally. Internal statements are prepared by an employee of the business. External statements are generally prepared on a fee basis by someone from outside the business. In general, bankers require borrowers to move from internal to external statements, and then to different levels of external statements (compiled to reviewed to audited) as credit exposure to the bank grows.

When analyzing financial statements, a critical consideration is the quality and reliability of information. Statement quality and reliability can vary significantly depending on who prepared the statement and how it was prepared. The least reliable statements are prepared internally by the owner or company controller and have not been compiled, reviewed, or audited by an accountant. This is particularly true when the person preparing the statements has no background in accounting. Although it is desirable to obtain accountant-prepared statements whenever possible, the expense of bringing in an independent accountant may be unwarranted, especially when the loan request is small or presents little risk. If accepted, borrower-prepared statements should be verified by checking the information in the statements against other company records and income tax returns.

ACCOUNTING STANDARDS

When analyzing financial statements, a business banker can be reasonably certain that consistent accounting practices were applied to calculating the numbers in those statements, particularly if the statements were internally prepared by a certified public accountant (CPA), or were externally compiled, reviewed, or audited by a CPA. It is critically important that consistent standards be applied in preparing statements so that valid comparisons can be made, both between statements from two different time periods and between statements of similar companies.

A set of rules called **generally accepted accounting principles (GAAP)** is the framework that ensures information accountants report in financial statements follows consistent accounting techniques. These rules are for accountants and companies that analyze and summarize records to make financial statements. GAAP is continuously being refined to accommodate the following:

- Innovations in the ways credit is extended and debt financed
- Innovations by accountants as to calculating and presenting financial information
- Legal considerations such as changes in tax laws
- Continued efforts to move closer to **international financial reporting standards (IFRS)**

The principal group responsible for setting accounting policy is the **Financial Accounting Standards Board (FASB)**, a private organization made up of accounting professionals. FASB usually has the final say in **adopting accounting standards**. However, the **Securities and Exchange Commission (SEC)** is the final arbiter when it comes to publicly traded companies. The SEC is the federal agency that regulates the public sale of securities and related disclosures.

Because FASB and SEC cooperate in developing standards, it is rare that the SEC would override a FASB decision. FASB also works closely with the accountant's trade group, the American Institute of Certified Public Accountants (AICPA); and public companies, financial institutions, regulatory agencies, and trade associations are given an opportunity to comment before any standard is approved.

Accounting standards are constantly being changed and updated. When a standard is adopted, it has the potential to significantly change the financial statements of certain businesses. FASB publishes up-to-date changes on its Web site, and business bankers need to understand how proposed and approved changes can affect their customers.

> **Generally accepted accounting principles (GAAP)**
>
> The rules, conventions, practices, and procedures that form the foundation for financial accounting.

> **International Financial Reporting Standards (IFRS)**
>
> International Financial Reporting Standards (IFRS) are principles-based standards, interpretations, and the framework (1989)[1] adopted by the International Accounting Standards Board (IASB).

> **Financial Accounting Standards Board (FASB)**
>
> The public accounting profession's private self-regulatory organization that is authorized to establish financial accounting and reporting standards, commonly referred to as generally accepted accounting principles (GAAP). FASB publishes the widely used Statements of Financial Accounting Standards (SFAS).

> **Securities and Exchange Commission (SEC)**
>
> The federal agency that regulates the public sale of securities and related disclosures. The SEC monitors issuers, underwriters, exchanges, and over-the-counter dealers and publishes regulations pertaining to financial information submitted by businesses reporting the results of their financial condition and their operations.

MIGRATION TO IFRS

Perhaps the most sweeping change looming for accounting standards is a Securities and Exchange Commission (SEC) proposal to require U.S. firms to move to IFRS by 2015. U.S. and international regulators have been working for years to eliminate many of the biggest differences between GAAP and IFRS. Even if a formal decision to require U.S. firms to adopt IFRS is not made, the Financial Accounting Standards Board (FASB) is continuing to absorb new IFRS rules into GAAP, as well as modify some features of GAAP to match more closely IFRS.

In general, GAAP is a detailed set of rules, whereas IFRS is less detailed and more principles oriented. The financial statement formats generated by each system are very different. Beyond learning an entirely new format and presentation of information, businesses and bankers will see certain accounting techniques change. For instance, the LIFO inventory discussed earlier in this section is allowed by GAAP but is not allowed under IFRS.

Another key issue in the GAAP-to-IFRS conversion will be the stance of the Internal Revenue Service for standards allowed for business tax returns. For now, most bankers remain focused on understanding GAAP, while keeping abreast of the IFRS conversion issue.

INTERNALLY PREPARED STATEMENTS

Internally prepared financial statements by the company owner, controller, or other employees are typically created either monthly or quarterly. For smaller companies, these statements are considered the least reliable because the preparer typically does not have all the required accounting expertise. Larger companies may employ a CPA to prepare these statements. Although generally reliable, they are usually less accurate than externally prepared financial statements. Most internal statements need adjustments at fiscal year-end, such as adjustments for depreciation expense—an account often omitted in internally

EXAMPLE OF A FASB RULING

Summary of Statement No. 142 *Goodwill and Other Intangible Assets* (Issued 6/2001)

Summary
This Statement addresses financial accounting and reporting for acquired goodwill and other intangible assets and supersedes Accounting Principles Board (APB) Opinion No. 17, *Intangible Assets*. It addresses how intangible assets that are acquired individually or with a group of other assets (but not those acquired in a business combination) should be accounted for in financial statements upon their acquisition. This Statement also addresses how goodwill and other intangible assets should be accounted for after they have been initially recognized in the financial statements.

Reasons for issuing this statement
Analysts and other users of financial statements, as well as company managements, noted that intangible assets are an increasingly important economic resource for many entities and are an increasing proportion of the assets acquired in many transactions. As a result, better information about intangible assets was needed. Financial statement users also indicated that they did not regard goodwill amortization expense as being useful information in analyzing investments.

Differences between this statement and opinion 17
This Statement changes the unit of account for goodwill and takes a very different approach to how goodwill and other intangible assets are accounted for subsequent to their initial recognition. Because goodwill and some intangible assets will no longer be amortized, the reported amounts of goodwill and intangible assets (as well as total assets) will not decrease at the same time and in the same manner as under previous standards. There may be more volatility in reported income than under previous standards because impairment losses are likely to occur irregularly and in varying amounts.

prepared interim statements. Most banks use internally prepared financial statements primarily to compare year-to-year trends at interim dates such as month-ends or quarter-ends. To verify the accuracy of the financial statements, all internally prepared fiscal year-end financial statements should be supported by an externally prepared tax return.

The following is a list of internally prepared financial statements:

- Income statement
- Balance sheet
- Cash flow statement
- Interim financial statement
- Tax returns
- Personal financial statements

EXTERNALLY PREPARED STATEMENTS

External financial statements, usually prepared by independent CPAs, are classified as compilations, reviews, or audits. Externally prepared financial statements include the following components:

- Accountant's cover letter
- Balance sheet and income statement
- Statement of retained earnings
- Statement of cash flows
- Footnotes and disclosures

After reading the footnotes, the business banker writes out any questions or comments that come to mind. In the case of Dry Supply, Anne Schippel will want to address some of the following questions with the owner or controller of the business:

- How many customers are in Kansas?
- When are estimates used in financial reports?
- What has been the amount of bad debts expensed to the allowance?
- What is the inventory?
- How long has the company had a credit line?
- Does the credit line have any covenants?
- What are terms of officer debt?
- Which employees are eligible for the profit-sharing plan?

COMPILED STATEMENTS

Compiled statements, available to privately owned entities only and providing no assurance of the quality or value of the statement data, are the least informative of the externally prepared financial statements. One reason is that the numbers are simply restated or reformatted from company records with little or no verification. Also, most compiled statements omit GAAP disclosures, including a statement of cash flows and footnotes. Persons preparing a

> **Compiled statement**
>
> The least informative externally CPA-prepared financial statement, in which the numbers are restated from company records with little or no verification. These statements are available to nonpublic entities only.

compilation statement do not have to be independent of the customer's business, and this must disclosed when applicable. Although a compilation focuses on the format of the financial statements, an accountant is still required to document any communications to the appropriate level of management regarding fraud or illegal acts.

Although footnotes appear at the end of the financial statement, they should be read first. Footnotes tell business bankers what they are about to analyze. Footnotes allow the auditor to comment on the statements and their compliance with GAAP. Usually, they are found only in audited or reviewed financial statements prepared by a CPA. Figure 4.4 is an example of footnotes for Dry Supply.

FIGURE 4.4 FOOTNOTES TO FINANCIAL STATEMENTS OF DRY SUPPLY

December 31, 20xx and 20xy

Note 1	**Description of business** Dry Supply is a wholesaler of dry-cleaning and other laundry supplies. The primary area served is central Kansas.	
Note 2	**Summary of significant accounting polices** **Estimates.** Management uses estimates and assumptions in preparing financial statements in accordance with generally accepted accounting principles. Those estimates and assumptions affect the reported amounts of assets and liabilities, the disclosure of contingent assets and liabilities, and the reported revenues and expenses. Actual results could vary from the estimates used. **Cash.** Cash includes demand deposits held at a financial institution. At times, the amount held on deposit may exceed federally insured limits. **Accounts receivable.** Accounts receivable uses the allowance method and is shown net of an allowance for doubtful accounts of $5,000 on December 31, 20xx and 20xy. The company actively monitors its receivable balances and generally requires no collateral. In certain instances, the company requires a partial or full-advance deposit from customers prior to delivery. **Inventory.** Inventories are valued using the last-in first-out (LIFO) method. **Depreciation.** Depreciation of property and equipment is computed using accelerated methods during the estimated useful lives of the assets as follows:	
	Furniture and fixtures	5 to 10 years
	Machinery and equipment	5 years
	Leasehold improvements	10 years
	Automobiles and trucks	5 years
	Income taxes. By unanimous consent of the shareholders, the company has elected to be treated as a corporation under the Internal Revenue Code.	
Note 3	**Inventory** Inventories consist of finished products only.	
Note 4	**Notes payable—bank** **Notes payable—bank** consists of a revolving credit note payable to State bank. The note is secured by substantially all assets of the company and the personal guarantees of the shareholders. Interest is due monthly at prime plus 0.75 percent (6.25 percent on December 31, 20xy). The maximum borrowing under the agreement is the lesser of $150,000 or availability under a borrowing base, as defined. The note agreement expires April 30, 20xz. The outstanding balances on December 31, 20xy and 20xx, were $59,000 and $68,000, respectively.	
Note 5	**Long-term debt** Note Payable to Officers—Unsecured were $58,000 and $67,000 in 20xx and 20xy, respectively.	
Note 6	**Profit-sharing plan** Effective January 1, 20xx, the company adopted a profit-sharing plan covering substantially all employees. Contributions to the plan are at the discretion of management.	

Figure 4.5 shows the Accountant's Cover Letter Excerpt—Dry Supply Compiled Financial Statements. Note: This example includes wording where the CPA has omitted a statement of cash flows and footnotes.

In late 2009, AICPA issued new provisions in the *Statement on Standards for Accounting and Review Services, Compilation and Review Engagements* (SSARS 19) for statements for periods ending after December 15, 2010. SSARS 19 adds materiality and evidence features to compilations and reviews, as well as requiring engagement letters. For compilations, an accountant is now allowed to disclose the following reason(s) for lack of independence, such as a member of the engagement team:

- Having a direct financial interest in the business
- Having an immediate family member employed by the business
- Serving along with the business owner or executive as an officer or major shareholder in another, separate business

FIGURE 4.5 ACCOUNTANT'S COVER LETTER EXCERPT—DRY SUPPLY COMPILED FINANCIAL STATEMENTS

To the Management of Dry Supply:

We have compiled the accompanying balance sheet of Dry Supply as of December 31, 20xx, and the related statements of income and retained earnings for the year then ended. We have not audited or reviewed the accompanying financial statements and, accordingly, do not express an opinion or provide any assurance about whether the financial statements are in accordance with accounting principles generally accepted in the United States of America.

Management is responsible for the preparation and fair presentation of the financial statements in accordance with accounting principles generally accepted in the United States of America and for designing, implementing and maintaining internal control relevant to the preparation and fair presentation of financial statements.

Our responsibility is the conduct the compilation in accordance with statements on Standards for Accounting and Review Services issued by the American Institute of Certified Public Accountants. The objective of a compilation is to assist management in presenting financial information in the form of financial statements without undertaking to obtain or provide any assurance that there are no material modifications that should be made to the financial statements. During our compilation, we did become aware of departures from accounting principles generally accepted in the United States of America and are described in the following paragraphs.

A statement of cash flows for the year ended December 31, 20xx, has not been presented. Accounting principles generally accepted in the United States of America require that such a statement be presented when financial statements purport to present financial position and results of operations.

Management has elected to omit substantially all of the disclosures required by accounting principles generally accepted in the United States of America. If the omitted disclosures were included in the financial statements, they might influence the user's conclusions about the company's financial position, results of operations, and cash flows. Accordingly, these financial statements are not designed for those who are not informed about such matters.

Compilation qualifications

In preparing a compilation statement, the preparer must—

- Possess general understanding of the customer's industry, business transactions, and the form of accounting records
- Be familiar with stated qualifications of the customer's accounting personnel to consider the need for adjustments to the account records
- Read the financial statements and consider whether they are appropriate in form and content and free from obvious material errors

Most externally prepared financial statements provided by bank customers are compiled. Because of the limited process used by the accountant, the lender must thoroughly understand all the entries on the statement and the related accounting principles.

REVIEWED STATEMENTS

Bankers generally consider **reviewed statements** to be an improvement over compiled statements because of the inclusion of additional information, such as a statement of cash flows and footnotes explaining the statement. Reviewed statements are so named because an outside CPA reviews but does not verify the balance sheet and income statement. Similar to a compilation, this level of accounting engagement is available to privately owned entities only.

Also similar to compilations, SSARS 19 has added new general procedures that CPAs must follow for reviews, including materiality and evidence concepts, plus an engagement letter requirement. The materiality and evidence concepts require the CPA to accumulate review evidence that will provide a reasonable basis for obtaining limited assurance that there are no material modifications that should be made to the financial statements. Overall, this process prevents CPAs from using a canned list of analytical and inquiry provisions. Rather, a tailored approach is needed, based on areas where the CPA believes increased risk for misstatements exists. Nevertheless, a review remains significantly less comprehensive than an audit and does not provide a **management letter** that expresses concerns or deficiencies not referred to in the audit.

> **Reviewed statement**
>
> The degree of work performed by a public accounting firm in conjunction with the issuance of financial statements of a nonpublic entity that is greater in scope than a compilation but less in scope than an audit and does not provide a basis for the expression of an opinion on the financial statements. The accountant's report would generally state, however, that, based on his or her review, the accountant is not aware of any material modifications that should be made to the financial statements for them to conform to generally accepted accounting principles.

> **Management letter**
>
> Letter sent to the board of directors or management of the company expressing concerns or deficiencies not referred to in the audit. The auditing CPA includes information describing the reportable condition, as well as information about any material weaknesses that do not reduce risk of error or irregularities.

Review qualifications

In constructing a review statement (Figure 4.6), the preparer must—

- Know the accounting principles and practices of the customer's industry
- Understand the customer's business, including its organization and operations
- Inquire about accounting policies, record keeping procedures, and actions of owners and management that may affect financial statements and changes in business, activitiesor transactions
- Identify and explain unusual items or trends in the financial statements
- Determine that financial statements conform to GAAP
- Be independent of the company

FIGURE 4.6 ACCOUNTANT'S COVER LETTER EXCERPT—DRY SUPPLY REVIEWED FINANCIAL STATEMENTS

To the Management of Dry Supply:

We have reviewed the accompanying balance sheet of Dry Supply as of December 31, 20xx, and the related statements of income, retained earnings, and cash flows for the year then ended. A review includes primarily applying analytical procedures to management's financial data and making inquiries of company management. A review is substantially less is scope than an audit, the objective of which is the expression of an opinion regarding the financial statements as a whole. Accordingly, we do not express such an opinion.

Management is responsible for the preparation and fair presentation of the financial statements in accordance with accounting principles generally accepted in the United States of America and for designing and implementing internal control relevant to the preparation and fair presentation of the financial statements.

Our responsibility is to conduct the review in accordance with Statements on Standards for Accounting and Review Services issued by the American Institute of Certified Public Accountants. Those standards require us to perform procedures to obtain limited assurance that there are no material modifications that should be made to the financial statement. We believe that the results of our procedures provide a reasonable basis for out report.

Based on our review, we are not aware of any material modifications that should be made to the accompanying financial statements in order for them to be in conformity with accounting principles generally accepted in the United States of America.

AUDITED STATEMENTS

Audits are more thorough and expensive than compilations or reviews, and therefore are least often available to the community bankers. Most small, privately held companies cannot justify the cost and time involved. Audits are required for public companies, which are usually very large businesses. Bankers, however, may require their borrowers to provide them with an audited financial statement when the bank's loan policy dictates it. Loan policy may require **audited statements** when the following situations occur:

> **Audited statement**
>
> A financial statement that has been audited in conformity with generally accepted auditing standards by a certified public accountant and is accompanied by the auditor's opinion.

- Loan is of a large size
- Risk is high relative to the financial strength of the borrower
- Term of the loan is long

In an audit, the accountant performs a comprehensive evaluation of the borrower's accounting systems to determine the accuracy of the financial information and to verify that the statements conform to GAAP. Depending on the CPA's findings, several types of opinions can be rendered—unqualified, qualified, adverse, and disclaimer.

Unqualified audit opinion

An **unqualified audit opinion** is often called a "clean" opinion, where the CPA feels that management has accurately reported its financial position, along with any changes and the operating results for the reported periods.

The term "clean" can be misleading, and is not equivalent to "clean bill of health." An audit does not provide assurance about any positive or satisfactory rating of financial condition. In fact, the financial condition may be weak. The audit simply certifies the relative accuracy of the data reported. It is up to the user to determine the "health" of

> **Unqualified audit opinion**
>
> An unqualified audit opinion is issued when the auditor concludes that the financial statements give a true and fair view in accordance with the financial reporting framework used for the preparation and presentation of the financial statements. The auditor does not have any significant reservation in respect of matters contained in the financial statements.

FIGURE 4.7 ACCOUNTANT COVER LETTER EXCERPT—DRY SUPPLY AUDITED FINANCIAL STATEMENT—UNQUALIFIED OPINION

To the Management of Dry Supply:

We have audited the accompanying balance sheets of Dry Supply as of December 31, 20xy, and December 31, 20xx, and the related statements of income, retained earnings and cash flows for the years then ended. These financial statements are the responsibility of the Company's management. Our responsibility is to express an opinion of these financial statements based on our audits.

We conducted our audit in accordance with auditing standards generally accepted in the United States of America. Those standards require that we plan and perform the audit to obtain reasonable assurance about whether the financial statements are free of material misstatement. An audit includes examining, on a test basis, evidence supporting the amounts and disclosures in the financial statements. An audit also assesses the accounting principles used and significant estimates made by management, as well as evaluating the overall financial statement presentation. We believe that our audits provide a reasonable basis for our opinion.

In our opinion, the financial statements referred to above present fairly, in all material respects, the financial position of Dry Supply at December 31, 20xy, and December 31, 20xx, and the results of its operations and its cash flows for the years then ended, in conformity with accounting principles generally accepted in the United States of America.

the underlying business.

The three paragraphs of an opinion (Figure 4.7) are described best as what the auditors found (introductory), how they found it (scope), and what the auditors think about the findings (opinion).

Qualified audit opinion

A **qualified audit opinion** occurs when the CPA has encountered one of two types of situations that do not comply with GAAP. Despite these departures, the rest of the financial statements are fairly presented. This type of opinion is very similar to an unqualified or "clean" opinion, but the report states that the financial statements are fairly presented with a certain exception, which is misstated. Lenders need to fully understand the exception that was noted, but can otherwise treat the financial statements similar to an unqualified audit.

> **Qualified audit opinion**
>
> A qualified audit opinion is issued when the auditor encountered one of two types of situations that do not comply with generally accepted accounting principles; however, the rest of the financial statements are fairly presented.

The following are two types of situations that can cause a CPA to issue a qualified opinion:

- *Single deviation from GAAP*—when one or more areas of the financial statements do not conform with GAAP, or misstate an item, but do not affect the rest of the financial statements from being "fairly" presented when taken as a whole. Examples include a company that did not correctly calculate the depreciation expense of its building. Even if this expense is considered material, since the rest of the financial statements do conform with GAAP, the auditor qualifies the opinion by describing the depreciation misstatement in the report and issues an unqualified opinion on the rest of the financial statements.
- *Limitation of scope*—when the auditor could not audit one or more areas of the financial statements, and although they could not be verified, the rest of the financial statements were audited and they conform with GAAP. Examples include an auditor not being able to observe and test a company's inventory in a prior period. This can happen if the business has changed accounting firms, or the current CPA may not have access to the older inventory records, which can happen after a natural disaster. If the CPA audited the rest of the financial statements and is reasonably sure that they conform with GAAP, then the auditor simply states that the financial statements are fairly presented, with the exception of the inventory which could not be audited.

The wording of the qualified opinion is very similar to the unqualified opinion, but an *explanatory* paragraph is added. The scope and the opinion paragraphs receive a slight modification in line with the qualification in the explanatory paragraph. The key phrasing to look for is "*Except as discussed in the following paragraph*, we conducted our audit . . . ." Some bankers refer to a qualified audit as an "except for" opinion. Some opinions include the wording "subject to."

Figure 4.8 shows a qualified opinion for Dry Supply. In this example, the company has not capitalized or has excluded from reported liabilities some of its lease obligations, which violates GAAP in certain situations.

> **FIGURE 4.8 ACCOUNTANT COVER LETTER EXCERPT—DRY SUPPLY AUDITED FINANCIAL STATEMENT—QUALIFIED OPINION**
>
> To the Management of Dry Supply:
>
> We have audited the accompanying balance sheets of Dry Supply as of December 31, 20xy, and December 31, 20xx, and the related statements of income, retained earnings and cash flows for the years then ended. These financial statements are the responsibility of the Company's management. Our responsibility is to express an opinion of these financial statements based on our audits.
>
> We conducted our audit in accordance with auditing standards generally accepted in the United States of America. Those standards require that we plan and perform the audit to obtain reasonable assurance about whether the financial statements are free of material misstatement. An audit includes examining, on a test basis, evidence supporting the amounts and disclosures in the financial statements. An audit also assesses the accounting principles used and significant estimates made by management, as well as evaluating the overall financial statement presentation. We believe that our audits provide a reasonable basis for our opinion.
>
> The Company has excluded from property and debt in the accompanying balance sheets certain lease obligations that, in our opinion, should be capitalized in order to conform to accounting principles generally accepted in the United States of America. If these lease obligations were capitalized, property would be increased by $X thousand and $X thousand, long-term debt would be increased by $X thousand and $X thousand, the current portion of long-term debt would be increased by $X thousand and $X thousand, and retained earnings would increase by $X thousand and $X thousand as of December 31, 20xy and 20xx, respectively. Additionally, net income would be increased by $X thousand and $X thousand and earnings per share would be increased by $X.XX and $X.XX, respectively, for the years ended December 31, 20xy and 20xx, respectively.
>
> In our opinion, except for the effects of not capitalizing certain lease obligations as disclosed in the above paragraph, the financial statements referred to above present fairly, in all respects the financial position of Dry Supply at December 31, 20xy, and December 31, 20xx, and the results of its operations and cash flows for the years then ended, in conformity with accounting principles generally accepted in the United States of America.

Adverse audit opinion

An **adverse audit opinion** occurs when the CPA determines that the financial statements are materially misstated and, considered as a whole, do not conform with GAAP. It is considered the opposite of an unqualified opinion, essentially saying that the information is materially incorrect, unreliable, and inaccurate in order to assess financial position and results of operations of the business. Most investors and bankers

> **Adverse audit opinion**
>
> An adverse audit opinion is issued when the auditor determines that the financial statements of a business are materially misstated and, considered as a whole, do not conform with GAAP.

very rarely accept an audit with an adverse opinion, and usually ask the business to correct the financial statements and obtain another audit report.

Generally, an adverse opinion is given only if the financial statements pervasively differ from GAAP. An example of such a situation would be failure of a company to consolidate a material subsidiary. Further, the wording of the adverse report is similar to a qualified report. The scope paragraph is modified accordingly and an explanatory paragraph is added to cover the reason for the adverse opinion. However, the most significant change in the adverse report from the qualified report is in the opinion paragraph, where the auditor clearly states that the financial statements are not in accordance with GAAP, which means that they, as a whole, are unreliable, inaccurate, and do not present a fair view of the company's position and operations. Look for wording similar to "In our opinion, *because of the situations mentioned above* (in the explanatory paragraph), the financial statements referred to in the first paragraph do not present fairly, in all material respects, the financial position of . . . ."

Figure 4.9 shows an adverse opinion for Dry Supply. In this example the company has been valuing fixed assets at appraised values, compared with GAAP's cost basis, with subsequent effects on depreciation expense, deferred taxes, cost of goods sold, and other accounts.

Going concern disclosure

A **going concern disclosure** opinion is perhaps the only audit result where an indication of the "health" of the underlying business is made. *Going concern* means that the business will continue to operate in the near future, or generally more than next 12 months, so long as it generates or obtains enough resources to operate. If the business is not a going concern, this means that it is dissolved, bankrupt, or closed. If the CPA considers that the business is not a going concern, or will not be a going concern in the near future, then the audit cover letter includes an explanatory paragraph explaining the situation, which is commonly referred to as the going concern disclosure—such as an opinion is also called an "unqualified modified opinion."

For obvious reasons, a disclosure for a lack of going concern is viewed negatively by investors and bankers, and therefore reduces the chance that the business may obtain the capital or borrowing it needs to survive once the disclosure is made.

> **Going concern disclosure**
>
> A going concern disclosure opinion is issued when the auditor considers that the business is not a going concern, or will not be a going concern in the near future. The auditor is then required to include an explanatory paragraph before the opinion paragraph or following the opinion paragraph in the audit report explaining the situation. Such an opinion is called an "unqualified modified opinion."

Figure 4.10 shows a going concern disclosure opinion for Dry Supply. For illustration purposes, and not consistent with the financial data for Dry Supply presented earlier in this chapter, in this example the company has generated net losses over several years and has a negative net worth.

> **FIGURE 4.9 ACCOUNTANT COVER LETTER EXCERPT—DRY SUPPLY AUDITED FINANCIAL STATEMENT—ADVERSE OPINION**

To the Management of Dry Supply:

We have audited the accompanying balance sheets of Dry Supply as of December 31, 20xy, and December 31, 20xx, and the related statements of income, retained earnings and cash flows for the years then ended. These financial statements are the responsibility of the Company's management. Our responsibility is to express an opinion of these financial statements based on our audits.

We conducted our audit in accordance with auditing standards generally accepted in the United States of America. Those standards require that we plan and perform the audit to obtain reasonable assurance about whether the financial statements are free of material misstatement. An audit includes examining, on a test basis, evidence supporting the amounts and disclosures in the financial statements. An audit also assesses the accounting principles used and significant estimates made by management, as well as evaluating the overall financial statement presentation. We believe that our audits provide a reasonable basis for our opinion.

As discussed in Note X to the financial statements, the Company carries its property, plant, and equipment accounts at appraisal values, and provides depreciation on the basis of such values. Further, the Company does not recognize deferred income taxes with respect to differences between financial income and taxable income arising because of the use, for income tax purposes, of the installment method of reporting gross profit from certain types of sales. Accounting principles generally accepted in the United States of America require that property, plant and equipment be stated at an amount not in excess of cost, reduced by depreciation based on such amount, and that deferred income taxes be recognized.

Because of the departures from accounting principles generally accepted in the United States of American ands discussed in the preceding paragraph, as of December 31, 20xx, inventories have been increased by $X thousand and $X thousand by inclusion in manufacturing overhead of depreciation in excess of that based on cost; property, plant and equipment, less accumulated depreciation, is carried at $X thousand and $X thousand in excess of an amount based on the cost to the company; and deferred income taxes of $X thousand and $X thousand have not been recognized, resulting in an increase of $X thousand in retained earnings and in appraisal surplus of $X thousand and $X thousand, respectively. For the years ended December 31, 20xy, and December 31, 20xx, cost of goods sold has been increased $X thousand and $X thousand, respectively, because of the effects of the depreciation accounting referred to above, and deferred income taxes of $X thousand and $X thousand have not been recognized, resulting in an increase in net income of $X thousand and $X thousand, respectively.

In our opinion, because of the effects of the matters discussed in the preceding paragraphs, the financial statements referred to above do not present fairly, in conformity with accounting principles generally accepted in the United States of America, the financial position of Dry Supply at December 31, 20xy, and December 31, 20xx, or the results of its operations or its cash flows for the years then ended.

> **FIGURE 4.10 ACCOUNTANT COVER LETTER EXCERPT—DRY SUPPLY AUDITED FINANCIAL STATEMENT—GOING CONCERN DISCLOSURE**
>
> To the Management of Dry Supply:
>
> We have audited the accompanying balance sheets of Dry Supply as of December 31, 20xy, and December 31, 20xx, and the related statements of income, retained earnings and cash flows for the years then ended. These financial statements are the responsibility of the Company's management. Our responsibility is to express an opinion of these financial statements based on our audits.
>
> We conducted our audit in accordance with auditing standards generally accepted in the United States of America. Those standards require that we plan and perform the audit to obtain reasonable assurance about whether the financial statements are free of material misstatement. An audit includes examining, on a test basis, evidence supporting the amounts and disclosures in the financial statements. An audit also assesses the accounting principles used and significant estimates made by management, as well as evaluating the overall financial statement presentation. We believe that our audits provide a reasonable basis for our opinion.
>
> In our opinion, the financial statements referred to above present fairly, in all material respects, the financial position of Dry Supply at December 31, 20xy, and December 31, 20xx, and the results of its operations and its cash flows for the years then ended, in conformity with accounting principles generally accepted in the United States of America.
>
> The accompanying financial statements have been prepared assuming that the Company will continue as a going concern. As discussed in Note X to the financial statements, the Company has suffered recurring losses and has a net capital deficiency. These conditions raise substantial doubt about its ability to continue as a going concern.
>
> Management's plans in regard to these matters are also described in Note X. The financial statements do not include any adjustments relating to the recoverability and classification of asset carrying amounts or the amount and classification of liabilities that might result should the Company be unable to continue as a going concern.

Disclaimer of opinion

A disclaimer of opinion is not really an opinion at all. This type of report is issued when the CPA tried to audit an entity but for various reasons could not complete the work and does not issue an opinion. *Statements on Auditing Standards* (SAS) list the following situations where a disclaimer of opinion may be appropriate:

- A lack of independence or material conflict(s) of interest between the CPA and the business
- Significant scope limitations, whether intentional or not, that hinder the CPA's work in obtaining evidence and performing procedures
- Substantial doubt about the company's ability to continue as a going concern
- Significant uncertainties within the business

Although this type of opinion is rarely used, a common example includes an audit where the company willfully hides or refuses to provide evidence and information in significant areas of the financial statements, where the company is facing significant legal and litigation issues in which the outcome is uncertain (usually government investigations), and where going concern issues exist. Investors and bankers typically reject such financial statements and will ask the company to correct the situations the auditor mentioned and obtain another report.

A disclaimer of opinion differs substantially from the rest of the auditor's reports because it provides little information regarding the audit itself, although it includes an explanatory paragraph stating the reasons for the disclaimer. Almost every paragraph is modified extensively, and the scope paragraph is entirely omitted since the auditor is basically stating that an audit opinion could not be formed. Other differences include the following:

- In the introductory paragraph, the first phrase changes from "We have audited" to "We were engaged to audit" and does not mention that the auditor necessarily completed the audit.
- The auditor refuses to accept any responsibility by omitting the last sentence of the first paragraph.
- The opinion paragraph changes completely, stating that an opinion could not be formed and is not expressed because of the situations mentioned in the previous paragraphs.

Figure 4.11 shows a disclaimer of opinion report for Dry Supply. For illustration purposes, Dry Supply did not count its inventory or provide documents to support the cost of property and equipment. GAAP requires inventory to be counted at least annually. Furthermore, GAAP requires companies to retain records to support the cost of fixed assets.

To summarize the types of audit cover letters and opinions, a qualified opinion is generally comparable to an unqualified opinion and, depending on the reason for the qualification, is usually acceptable to lenders. A financial statement with the disclaimer opinion would be considered unaudited, but could be prepared in accordance with

---

FIGURE 4.11 ACCOUNTANT COVER LETTER EXCERPT—DRY SUPPLY AUDITED FINANCIAL STATEMENT—DISCLAIMER OF OPINION

To the Management of Dry Supply:

We were engaged to the accompanying balance sheets of Dry Supply as of December 31, 20xy, and December 31, 20xx, and the related statements of income, retained earnings and cash flows for the years then ended. These financial statements are the responsibility of the Company's management.

The company did not make a count of its physical inventory in 20xy or 20xx, stated in the accompanying financial statements at $X thousand as of December 31, 20xy, and at $X thousand as of December 31, 20xx. Furthermore, evidence supporting the cost of property and equipment acquired prior to December 31, 20xy, is no longer available. The company's records do not permit the application of other auditing procedures to inventories or property and equipment.

Because the company did not take physical inventories and we were not able to apply other auditing procedures to satisfy ourselves as to inventory quantities and the cost of property and equipment, the scope of our work was not sufficient to enable us to express, and we do not express, an opinion on these financial statements.

GAAP. The adverse opinion is of questionable value in a financial analysis, as is a going concern disclosure.

MANAGEMENT LETTER

A CPA usually issues a management letter along with audited financial statements. This letter, sent to the board of directors or management of the company, expresses concerns or deficiencies not referred to in the audit. The auditing CPA includes information describing the reportable conditions as well as information about any material weaknesses that do not reduce risk of error or irregularities. Reportable conditions include accuracy of computer-generated information due to obsolete software or lack of dual control over certain procedures. Material weaknesses include inventory not properly monitored or employee theft.

Figure 4.12 shows a management letter for the Dry Supply example. Because it is

---

FIGURE 4.12 MANAGEMENT LETTER—DRY SUPPLY AUDITED FINANCIAL STATEMENT

To the Management of Dry Supply:

In planning and performing our audit of the financial statements of Dry Supply for the year ended December 31, 20xy, we considered its internal control structure in order to determine our auditing procedures for the purpose of expressing our opinion on the financial statements and not to provide assurance on the internal control structure. However, we noted certain matters involving the internal control structure and its operation that we consider to be reportable conditions under standards established by the American Institute of Certified Public Accountants. Reportable conditions involve matters coming to our attention relating to significant deficiencies in the design or operation of the internal control structure that, in our judgment, could adversely affect the organization's ability to record, process, summarize, and report financial data consistent with the assertions of management in the financial statements.

Note: The auditor would include paragraph(s) to describe any reportable conditions noted. If material conditions were present, the auditor would include the following discussion and then describe the material weakness found.

A material weakness is a reportable condition in which the design or operation of one or more of the internal control structure elements do not reduce to a relatively low level the risk that errors or irregularities in amounts that would be material in relation to the financial statements being audited may occur and not be detected within a timely period by employees in the normal course of performing their assigned functions.

Our consideration of the internal control structure would not necessarily disclose all matters in the internal control structure that might be reportable conditions and, accordingly, would not necessarily disclose all reportable conditions that are considered to be material weaknesses as defined above.

Note: The auditor would include paragraph(s) here to disclose any material weaknesses noted.

This report is intended solely for the information and use of the audit committee (board of directors, board of trustees, or owners in owner-managed enterprises), management, and others within the organization.

not part of the audit, the commercial lender may need to request a copy.

Statement quality and reliability can vary significantly depending on who prepared the statement and how it was prepared.

In this section you learned why it is important that GAAP are applied when financial statements are prepared. In addition, you learned about the various preparation options available for financial statements such as, internally versus externally prepared statements, compiled statements, reviewed statements, and audited statements. You also learned about the CPA's management letter and how it expresses concerns or deficiencies not referred to in the audit.

OTHER COMPONENT ANALYSIS

After examining the opinion and footnotes, the business banker should analyze management reports, the income statement, balance sheet, statement of retained earnings, and statement of cash flows as part of completing calculations based on the financial statements.

MANAGEMENT PLANS AND REPORTS

Information from business and personal financial statements is, by itself, insufficient to measure performance because the information may not be adequately detailed. Management plans and reports can provide additional insight, but the usefulness of these reports varies among businesses.

- **Business and strategic plan**—many businesses prepare an annual business and strategic plan that summarizes the company's goals in the market, types of products, management structure, and projected sales growth and financial results for the coming year. The level of detail of a business and strategic plan vary by the size of the business and the organizational ability of the owner.
- **Operations and capital budgets**—most well-run businesses develop operational and capital budgets that specify how funds are to be spent in the coming year. Operations budgets show a company's plans for allocating personnel and other sales support resources. Capital budgets provide insight into future financing needs for fixed-asset purchases.
- **Accounts receivable aged listing**—this report lists individual customer accounts and the related amounts due by billing dates in aged categories. A single account may have invoices or portions of invoices that are current or 30, 60, or 90 days past due. This report also identifies amounts that may be uncollectible.
- **Inventory analysis**—businesses often analyze inventory from a number of different perspectives, such as age (time on hand), type, location, and quantity. A schedule with an aged listing of inventory often identifies slow-moving products. Depending on the type of industry, inventory may be raw material, work-in-process, and/or finished goods. Many businesses have multiple locations, and the quantity of inventory needed will vary by location.

ANALYZING THE FINANCIAL STATEMENTS

Income statement analysis

The income statement (also called a profit and loss statement, P&L statement, or earnings statement) is one of the most important sources of information about a business. One reason is that the income statement influences most balance sheet accounts. The following chart shows the components of a balance sheet that are taken from the income statement:

Income Statement	Balance Sheet
Cash sales	Cash
Credit sales	Accounts receivable
Cost of goods sold	Inventory, accounts payable
Depreciation	Fixed assets
Net profit (loss)	Retained earnings

Over a period of time, the income statement reflects how total sales (or revenues) and expenses lead to the net profit (or loss) for that period. The terms "sales" and "revenues" often are used interchangeably, although sales generally are derived from a tangible product being sold, while revenues generally are derived from services being provided.

The analysis of an income statement starts with the quality and consistency of sales/revenues and accuracy of the expenses. The income statement identifies a company's growth as evidenced by the increases in sales/revenues and also reveals the its viability through profitable operations. A consistently unprofitable company would not be considered viable. Income statement analysis also includes analyzing the break-even point of the business, which is the level of sales where fixed costs are covered such that the business has a net profit of $0. You will learn more about specific techniques and examples of income statement analysis in later chapters.

Balance sheet analysis

The balance sheet is a point-in-time financial picture of the business, usually as of the last day of a month, quarter, or fiscal year. The basic structure of the balance sheet can be stated in the following the simple equation:

$$\text{Assets} - \text{Liabilities} = \text{Net Worth}$$

Balance sheet analysis entails a line-by-line evaluation of the firm's assets and liabilities (or debt) and the difference between the two—its net worth (or equity). Net worth and equity are often used interchangeably.

The purpose of balance sheet analysis is to determine the liquidity and solvency of the business. Liquidity is the ability of the company to convert its assets to cash in time to pay its liabilities as they become due. Solvency is the ability of the company to sell its assets for sufficient cash to pay all of its liabilities. You will learn more about specific techniques and examples of balance sheet analysis in Section 2.

Ratio analysis

Ratios are not only the best known and most widely used of all financial statement analysis tools, but they are also the most overrated and most widely misused. Ratios allow the business banker to study the relationship and trends over time between various components of financial statements, such as assets and liabilities or expenses and revenues. Although ratios are easily calculated, their correct interpretation is problematic. The primary classes of ratios are liquidity, financial leverage, profitability, efficiency, and coverage, which will be covered in Section 2.

Cash flow analysis

The remaining primary component of a financial statement to be analyzed is the statement of cash flows. As its name implies, this statement of a firm's operations shows how it obtains and uses its cash resources. The data to construct a statement of cash flows come from the income statement and the balance sheet.

Because debt is repaid with cash, the statement of cash flows helps the business banker assess both the funding needs of the business and its potential sources of repayment. It shows inflows and outflows of cash categorized as operating, investing, and financing activities. If the financial statement is audited or reviewed, the accountant includes a statement of cash flows. In compiled statements, the cash flow statement may or may not be included.

If possible, borrowers should be required to submit a statement of cash flows that conforms to SFAS number 95. Some borrowers, especially those submitting statements that have not been prepared by outside auditors, may not be able to prepare a statement of cash flows. In such cases, the business banker can create similar information in the spreading process, particularly if a computerized statement spreading model is used. Cash flow analysis, the statement of cash flows, and related models will be covered in later in the book.

PREPARING FORECASTS

Forecasts, basic to loan analysis, are presented in numerical form and help determine what conditions are needed for the borrower to be able to repay the principal and interest. Two tools used in this analysis are cash budgets and pro formas.

Cash budget

A cash budget projects the cash position of a company during a short period of time (usually less than one year). Presented in a monthly format, a cash budget forecasts a company's cash receipts and payments for each period. This enables the business banker to gauge a firm's peak credit needs and its ability to generate sufficient cash to repay short-term loans during the term of its operating cycle.

The cash budget also helps a business banker determine whether a company's borrowing needs are long or short term. Cash budgets are particularly useful in determining the financial needs of borrowers with seasonal operating cycles (such as a toy store that rings up half of its total sales in the last two months of each year). Because management controls the outflows of cash, a company's management should prepare cash budgets.

Pro formas

Using revenues/sales as its primary basis, a pro forma statement forecasts what the income statement and balance sheet of a business will look like after any new debt is added. Creating one- to three-year forecasts (referred to as pro forma statements) forces the lender to apply information gathered from historical financial statements to estimate future levels of sales. Examining a company-provided forecast involves evaluating the company's underlying assumptions as well as the expected economic, competitive, and regulatory environments in which it will operate. For example, if the business is forecasting sales growth of 10 percent per year and the expected economic and industry growth is 4 percent, the business banker clearly will want to understand why the company expects to grow faster.

Normally, the type of projections needed by the banker depend on the size and term of the requested loan. Because management-submitted pro formas tend to be optimistic, business borrowers often create their own prognosis for a company, based on what they consider to be more likely assumptions (such as lower profit margins).

LIMITATIONS OF ANALYSIS

Although financial statement analysis is a critical tool in business lending activities, it has some important limitations. First, its success depends on the reliability and completeness of the information being analyzed. Second, the financial statements may have amounts that were estimated, many accounts are aggregated, and different accounting methods may be used by different businesses. Even with unqualified audit opinions, financial statement analysis is not an exact science providing absolute conclusions. Because analysis deals with future uncertainties, it is better at formulating questions and projecting possibilities than it is at providing definitive answers. You will learn more about these limitations later in the book.

Beyond the limitations, technical analysis alone cannot provide a complete understanding of the borrower. Banks do not base loan decisions solely on financial statement analysis; a borrower's nonfinancial strengths and weaknesses must be considered. Nonfinancial issues include the management, company's plant capacity, pending lawsuits, technology changes, and industry trends. These concerns are not always apparent in the financial statements. Pricing, negotiation of specific terms, the bank's willingness to assume risk, and the availability of funds are other important aspects of the decision to extend or deny credit.

In this section, you learned about the other components associated with financial analysis. You are now able to identify the management plans and reports you need when analyzing financial statements. You also gained a better understanding of the purpose for the income statement, balance sheet, statement of cash flow, and ratio analyses as components for the analysis. You also learned how to prepare forecasts to help determine what conditions are needed for the borrower to repay the debt, and the limitations sometimes involved in financial analysis.

Financial statement analysis is used to help determine the amount of risk involved in a lending situation. It involves the technical calculation and interpretation of financial information to assess a company's past performance, present condition, and future viability.

In this chapter, you learned the role and purpose of the financial analysis in the business lending process. You now know the financial statement process, the basic guidelines for preparing a spreadsheet and analyzing the data. You also learned how to identify and evaluate a borrower's financial strengths, weaknesses, and uncertainties. You are able to explain the different types of financial statement preparation—internally and externally prepared, compiled statements, reviewed statements, and audited statements. You also gained a better understanding of the other components that may be involved in financial analysis.

QUESTIONS FOR DISCUSSION

1. What is the role of financial statement analysis?
2. What are the basic steps in the financial analysis process?
3. What type of external financial statement is the least reliable? Why?
4. What is common-sizing and why is it important in financial statement analysis?
5. Explain the difference between technical and interpretive analysis.
6. What might a business banker ask for during the initial meetings with a new customer who operates an established business and is requesting a loan?
7. What two things should all statements indicate?
8. What are some internal and external factors affecting the company's performance that a business banker should consider when analyzing a financial statement?
9. Most banks use internally prepared financial statements for what purpose?
10. What is a management letter?
11. What are the four common management plans and reports used in financial analysis?
12. What are two limitations of financial analysis?

EXERCISE 1

Instructions

Read the footnotes included in the financial statements for H & B Bakery (on following page), then answer the following questions:

    A. What questions do you have based on the footnotes?
    B. What questions do you have relative to the Commercial Lending Decision Tree?
    C. What general questions should you ask about the accountant or accounting firm?

Note 1 Description of business

H & B Bakery is a retailer of fresh bakery products. The primary area served is Colorado Springs.

Note 2 Summary of significant accounting polices

Estimates. Management uses estimates and assumptions in preparing financial statements in accordance with accounting principles generally accepted in the United States of America. Those estimates and assumptions affect the reported amounts of assets and liabilities, the disclosure of contingent assets and liabilities, and the reported revenues and expenses. Actual results could vary from the estimates that were used.

Cash. Cash includes demand deposits held at a financial institution. At times, the amount held on deposit may exceed federally insured limits.

Accounts receivable. Accounts receivable uses the allowance method and is shown net of an allowance for doubtful accounts of $15,000 on December 31, 20xy and 20xx. The company actively monitors its receivable balances and generally requires no collateral. In certain instances, the company requires a partial or full-advance deposit from customers prior to delivery.

Inventory. Inventories are valued using the first-in first-out (FIFO) method.

Depreciation. Depreciation of property and equipment are computed using accelerated methods during the estimated useful lives of the assets as follows:

Furniture and fixtures	5 to 10 years
Machinery and equipment	5 years
Leasehold improvements	10 years
Automobiles and trucks	5 years

Income taxes. By unanimous consent of the shareholders, the company has elected to be treated as a partnership and therefore no company taxes are paid.

Note 3 Inventory

Inventory consists of raw materials and finished products only.

Note 4 Notes payable-bank

Note payable—bank consists of a revolving credit note payable to Colorado Springs Bank. The note is secured by substantially all assets of the company and the personal guarantees of the partners. Interest is due monthly at prime plus 1.75 percent (7.25 percent on December 31, 20xy). The maximum borrowing under the agreement is the lesser of $50,000 or availability under a borrowing base, as defined. The note agreement expires April 30, 20xz. The outstanding balances on December 31, 20xy and 20xx, were $20,000 and $5,000, respectively.

Note 5 Long-term debt

Long-term debt consists of a note payable to Colorado Springs Bank secured by equipment. The outstanding balances on December 31, 20xy and 20xx, were $25,000 and $50,000, respectively.

Note 6 Profit-sharing plan

Effective January 1, 19xx, the company adopted a profit-sharing plan covering substantially all employees. Contributions to the plan are at the discretion of management. In 20xy, the company contributed $23,000 to the plan.

Notes to Financial Statements, H&B Bakery, LLC for December 31, 20xy and 20xx

5

How Business Financial Statements Are Constructed

OBJECTIVES

After studying *How Business Financial Statements Are Constructed*, you will be able to—

- Compare and contrast the cash method and accrual method of accounting
- Construct a balance sheet and income statement on the accrual basis for an example business

INTRODUCTION

Financial statements are the "report card" of a business. Understanding the structure of financial statements and the underlying accounting processes used to construct them is an important skill for a business banker. It is difficult to interpret the information presented in a financial statement if you do not have some basic knowledge of how business activities translate into the numbers you see on the statement. Not all business bankers have extensive training or experience in financial accounting. For this reason, this chapter will serve as an accounting refresher with a detailed look at a sample business, its transactions, how they are processed, and the financial statement that emerges. This basic knowledge of financial accounting provides the foundation for analyzing the financial statements submitted by a borrower.

In this chapter, you will learn the accounting methods used by businesses and how these methods can affect the financial statements. It also explores how basic financial statements are compiled from these different methods, and discusses how businesses typically use these different methods.

Relationship to the Commercial Lending Decision Tree

So far in the Section 1 chapters, the emphasis has been on "front-end" issues that influence how a business banker analyzes a commercial borrower, as shown in the Commercial Lending Decision Tree illustration in the Introduction. As you have already learned, this series of stages and steps emphasizes early screening and qualifying steps, such as general fit with the portfolio and goals of your bank. The business banker also begins assessing financial and nonfinancial qualifications of the business. Understanding accounting methods and how the financial statements of the business have been constructed provides the framework for the subsequent analysis that we will cover in Section 2 of this textbook (also shown as Stage Two in the Commercial Lending Decision Tree).

In terms of the Commercial Lending Decision Tree, this chapter relates to Stage One, where the lending opportunity is screened before beginning the time-consuming process of analyzing detailed financial statements and other data. By knowing the accounting methods used by a business, as well as how business activities and transactions affect income statement and balance sheet accounts, another preliminary step is achieved that better positions the business banker to anticipate certain issues that are likely to arise in the financial statements. Some issues may involve situations like those you have studied so far about why businesses borrow money—how the company's legal structure and stage in the life cycle affect borrowing needs and financial results. The end result of these Stage One activities is to maximize the efficiency and accuracy of the analysis that will occur in Stage Two of the Commercial Lending Decision Tree.

OVERVIEW OF ACCOUNTING METHODS

Accounting methods refer to the basic rules and guidelines that a business can utilize to record transactions, keep other records, and prepare financial reports. Businesses can use one of two comprehensive methods of accounting—**the cash basis** and the **accrual basis**. Business owners and

> **Cash basis**
>
> Income and expenses recorded when cash is received or paid out, regardless of when income was earned or expenses were incurred.

managers must decide which method to use depending on the legal form of the business, its sales volume, whether it extends credit to customers, and also tax return requirements. The method used will affect the financial statement presentation and other issues that the business banker must understand.

In addition to the importance of a business banker understanding the underlying accounting method used by a business, it is important for the business to make the best choice up front. Although it is possible to change methods later on, the process can be complicated.

> **Accrual basis**
>
> A method of accounting in which revenue is recognized when earned, expenses are recognized when incurred, and other changes in financial condition are recognized as they occur, without regard to the timing of the actual cash receipts and expenditures.

CASH METHOD

Businesses that use the cash method of accounting recognize income and expenses as cash is received and expended. Income is recognized when funds are received, not when a product or service has been delivered or provided. Expenses are recognized when they are paid, rather than when they were incurred.

The cash method offers businesses the following advantages:

- It is simpler to implement and use than the accrual method
- It provides a clearer picture of business cash flow
- Income is not subject to taxes until funds are received

> **DID YOU KNOW?**
>
> Tax returns filed by businesses can be based on either the cash or accrual accounting method, with the disclosure of the method shown as follows (based on 2010 tax forms):
>
> - Sole proprietorships, Form 1040, Schedule C, row F
> - Partnerships and most LLCs, Form 1065, page 1, row H
> - S corporations, Form 1120S, Schedule B, row 1
> - C corporations, Form 1120, Schedule K, row 1

Deferring revenue combined with accelerating expenses usually can defer the recognition of taxable income, either at the business level, or (as you learned in Chapter 1) as taxable income passed through to the owners. One way to defer revenue is to delay billing so that payment is received in the next accounting period. Similarly, expenses can be accelerated by paying bills as soon as they are received—in advance of the due date.

As a practical matter, most business borrowers at the community bank level will employ the cash accounting method. It is a good fit when the owners of the business are heavily involved in most day-to-day operations, and also when the business sells for cash or credit card payments.

ACCRUAL METHOD

Businesses that use the accrual method of accounting recognize revenue when earned—when sales are transacted—regardless of when the company receives cash from the sale. All expenses—the costs to produce a product or provide a service—are likewise recognized when costs are incurred rather than when cash payment is made.

Under the accrual method, if a company with a calendar-year fiscal period sold $2,000 worth of products on December 20, 20xx, with payments collected on January 20, 20xy, the $2,000 would be recognized as 20xx revenues; under the cash method, it would be recognized as 20xy revenues.

As a practical matter, larger businesses tend to use the accrual method because it better matches revenues to expenses, resulting in a more accurate measure of profitability. At certain revenue sizes, many businesses are required to use accrual accounting for tax purposes, and all publicly traded firms are required to use it.

Accrual accounting can be more complicated to implement because it requires compliance with **generally accepted accounting principles (GAAP)**. As you learned in Chapter 3, GAAP is a set of standardized rules for business accounting principles. GAAP provides a level of consistency and comparability among business financial statements, which allows business lenders to take a more consistent approach to analyzing the statements. Although GAAP does not eliminate personal interactions vital to the bank and borrower relationship, it makes it possible to thoroughly examine a business's past financial performance, primarily through its financial statements. GAAP also enables different companies to use the same concepts in their accounting activities. Even though many smaller companies today do not issue financial statements prepared by an independent accountant using GAAP, most banks require larger companies to prepare statements in accordance with GAAP.

> **Generally accepted accounting principles (GAAP)**
>
> The standards that govern the practice of external auditing. They comprise general standards, fieldwork standards, and reporting standards.

WHAT IS INCOME TAX BASIS?

Before we examine the differences between cash and accrual accounting more closely, business bankers must also realize that financial statements of a business can be compiled using the income tax basis. Although this is not a full "method of accounting," the numbers are based on either the cash or accrual method and then are adjusted to conform to the following tax return guidelines:

- Limits on deductibility of meals and entertainment expenses
- Certain types of nontaxable interest income
- Limits and exclusions of deductibility of key person life insurance premiums
- Accelerated depreciation methods allowed on tax returns only, including the Section 179 deduction that allows fully writing off certain purchases when acquired in the tax year
- Presentation of land as a separate, nondepreciable asset on the balance sheet

There are schedules on a business tax return that reconcile the differences in net income between the internal books and the related tax return. These differences can occur even if both the internal books and the tax return are constructed using the same accounting method. Even more differences can result if a business elects to keep its internal books on a different basis (accrual, for instance) than the tax return (cash basis, for instance). For this reason, most business bankers try to get a set of multiple years of financial statements on the same basis of accounting from period to period, as well as the same source—either internal books or tax returns—from year to year.

CASH VS. ACCRUAL BASIS

As previously mentioned, there are two comprehensive methods of accounting—the cash basis and the accrual basis. The method a company uses depends on various factors, such as the legal form of the business, its sales volume, whether it extends credit to customers, and tax return requirements.

The following example illustrates how the type of method used affects the financial statement presentation of Gadgets Etc. when using the cash and accrual basis of accounting.

Practical example of cash vs. accrual basis

Assume that Gadgets Etc. opened for business on November 1, 20xx. The company buys various electronic items (gadgets) for $125 each, paying at the time of purchase. It rents office and warehouse facilities for $500 per month and pays an average of $200 per month for utilities. The company pays the rent and utility bills in cash on the fifteenth of each month.

On November 1, Gadgets Etc. purchases 40 gadgets for $125 each (for a total of $5,000). The next day, the company sells 30 gadgets at $200 each to a commercial business. The gadgets will be delivered to the customer in November. They are sold on 30-day terms, so the invoice will be due December 1.

From December 8 to 20, Gadgets Etc. sells 10 gadgets to consumers at $100 each—a 50 percent year-end discount intended to move the remaining **inventory**. These gadgets are delivered at the time of purchase in December, with payment due upon receipt.

Inventory

The materials owned and held by a business, such as raw materials, intermediate products and parts, work-in-progress, and finished goods. These materials may be intended for sale or internal consumption.

On a cash basis, the business lost money in November, whereas profits in December were excellent. The company's interim

GADGETS ETC. INCOME STATEMENT (CASH BASIS)		
Item	Month Ended 11/30/xx	Month Ended 12/31/xx
Sales (revenues)*	—	$7,000*
Purchases**	$5,000**	—
Gross Profit	($5,000)	$7,000
Utilities and rent expense	700	700
Profit (loss)	($5,700)	$6,300
*30 gadgets at $200 and 10 gadgets at $100 **40 gadgets at $125 each		

American Bankers Association

income statements for November and December, prepared on the cash basis, are shown on the previous page.

Accrual accounting matches revenues with expenses and tells a different story. It shows that November was a profitable month for Gadgets Etc., whereas December was unprofitable. During November, Gadgets Etc. sold 30 gadgets for $200 each, for a $75 profit on each gadget. In December, the company sold 10 gadgets for $100 each, for a $25 loss per gadget.

Although the business showed strong profits in December, as shown in the cash-basis statement, the extra profit was not the result of an effective sales strategy. The company's interim income statement calculated on an accrual basis is shown below.

GADGETS ETC. INCOME STATEMENT (ACCRUAL BASIS)		
Item	Month Ended 11/30/xx	Month Ended 12/31/xx
Sales (revenues)	$6,000*	$1,000**
Purchases	3,750***	1,250****
Gross Profit	$2,250	($250)
Utilities and rent expense	700	700
Profit (loss)	$1,550	($950)

*30 gadgets at $200 ***30 gadgets at $125
**10 gadgets at $100 ****10 gadgets at $125

In the two income statements for Gadgets Etc., the total profits for the two-month period equal the amount of cash generated ($600 in each case). In an actual situation, the amount of profit or loss shown on an accrual-basis income statement usually would be quite different from the company's cash flow, because of transactions from preceding months. Analyzing cash flow allows the business banker to better understand the timing and amount of a company's cash requirements from period to period and its ability to repay debt—information that may not be evident from examining a company's accrual-basis financial statements. Nevertheless, the income statement, constructed using the accrual method, is a better reflection of true company profits.

The components of the income statement involve a company's recognition of income and related expenses as well as the resulting profit or loss. It is important to understand that recognition of profit in accrual accounting does not always coincide with a company's cash flow. In fact, while all companies seek to maximize their cash flow in order to pay loans, salaries, dividends, and so on, not all companies try to maximize profits.

Many smaller businesses use cash-basis accounting to minimize taxable income in a current period. However, taxes are being deferred, not eliminated, so this is only a temporary situation. Eventually, revenues will be recognized with fewer or no offsetting expenses. The business banker needs to be aware of this future tax liability and determine whether the company is reserving sufficient money for future taxes.

Although the business banker can determine which method is being used by the disclosure on the tax return, the actual financial statement may be trickier, if it is not prepared by an accountant with a footnote that discloses the accounting method. Cash-basis financial statements generally will not have **accounts receivable** or **accounts payable** listed, because a sale is not recognized until collected nor a related expense until paid. It is important to understand that these companies often have accounts receivable and accounts payable, even though they do not appear on the balance sheet. These companies typically keep a separate listing or ledger of accounts receivable and accounts payable.

In this section, you learned the advantages of using the cash method of accounting: It is simpler to implement and use than the accrual method; it provides a clearer picture of business cash flow; and, the income is not subject to taxes until funds are received. You also learned about the accrual method of accounting and now have a better understanding of why many larger businesses at certain revenue levels, along with all publicly traded firms, are required to use accrual accounting for tax purposes. In addition, this chapter presented another accounting method for business financial statements using the income tax basis—the numbers are based on either the cash or accrual method, and then adjusted to conform to tax return guidelines. You should now feel more confident about the different types of accounting methods that a business can utilize to record transactions, keep other records, and prepare financial reports.

> **Accounts receivable**
> Assets on a balance sheet that arise from the extension of trade credit to a company's customers where the customers have not paid by the reporting date. These are generally short-term assets. *Also called* receivables.

> **Accounts payable**
> Amounts owed to vendors and suppliers for delivered products or services used in normal operations and bills that must be paid in one year or less. *Also called* payables.

ACCOUNTING REFRESHER

To demonstrate how a business keeps its financial records, we will expand on the Gadgets Etc. example used earlier in this chapter. Each transaction or summary of a group of transactions will be identified by a letter code so that we can track the corresponding entries in t-accounts. Debits will be posted to the left side of each t-account, and credits posted to the right. Balance sheet accounts will have a beginning balance at the top and an ending balance at the bottom.

- For asset accounts, debits will increase the account balance and credits will decrease it
- For liability accounts, credits will increase the account balance and debits will decrease it

GADGETS ETC. FIRST YEAR ON ACCRUAL-BASIS ACCOUNTING

The following transactions will summarize the first year of operations for Gadgets Etc. and will be recorded using the accrual basis of accounting.

Accounts after Transaction A

Mr. Smith starts Gadgets Etc. by investing $25,000 on November 1, 20xx. The business elects to use the accrual basis of accounting.

The cash account has a debit (increase) of $25,000 applied. The beginning balance of all of the accounts used in this sample is $0 since the business has just started. In fact, all of the accounts we will be using in this example will start with a $0 balance. The offsetting credit is applied as an increase to the **capital stock** account within owner's equity. Figure 5.1 summarizes the accounts of Gadgets Etc. after Transaction A.

> **Capital stock**
>
> (1) All the outstanding shares of a company's stock representing ownership, including preferred and common stock. (2) The total amount of stock, common and preferred, that a corporation is authorized to issue under its certificate of incorporation or charter. It is typical to have more shares authorized than are issued.

FIGURE 5.1 ACCOUNTS OF GADGETS ETC. AFTER TRANSACTION A

GADGETS ETC. T-ACCOUNTS — **TRANSACTION OR EVENT A** — **ACCRUAL BASIS**

BALANCE SHEET

ASSETS

CASH
- Beginning Bal. $ -
- A $ 25,000
- Ending Balance $ 25,000

Beginning Bal. $ -
Transactions:
Ending Balance $ -

Beginning Bal. $ -
Transactions:
Ending Balance $ -

Beginning Bal. $ -
Transactions:
Ending Balance $ -

Beginning Bal. $ -
Transactions:
Ending Balance $ -

Total Assets $ 25,000

LIABILITIES

Beginning Bal. $ -
Transactions:
Ending Balance $ -

Beginning Bal. $ -
Transactions:
Ending Balance $ -

Total Liabilities $ -

OWNER'S EQUITY

CAPITAL STOCK
- Beginning Bal. $ -
- Transactions: $ 25,000 A
- Ending Balance $ 25,000

RETAINED EARNINGS
- Beginning Bal. $ -
- Net Income $ - **
- Ending Balance $ -

Owner's Equity $ 25,000

Total Liabs. & Owner's Eq. $ 25,000

INCOME STATEMENT

Transactions:
Cumulative Total $ -

Transactions:
Cumulative Total $ -

Transactions:
Cumulative Total $ -

Transactions:
Cumulative Total $ -

Transactions:
Cumulative Total $ -

Transactions:
Cumulative Total $ -

Net Income ** $ -

Accounts after Transaction B

Gadgets Etc. purchases store fixtures for cash of $12,000.

The net **fixed assets** account is debited (increased) by $12,000 (from a starting balance of $0) and the cash account is credited (decreased) by $12,000. Total assets do not change, since one of the asset accounts increased and another decreased by the same amount. Figure 5.2 summarizes the accounts of Gadgets Etc. after this transaction.

> **Fixed assets**
>
> Those items of a long-term nature required for the normal conduct of a business and not converted into cash during a normal operating period. Fixed assets include furniture, buildings, and machinery, and are subject to depreciation.

FIGURE 5.2 ACCOUNTS OF GADGETS ETC. AFTER TRANSACTION B

GADGETS ETC. T-ACCOUNTS — TRANSACTION OR EVENT B — ACCRUAL BASIS

BALANCE SHEET

ASSETS

CASH
- Beginning Bal. $ -
- A $ 25,000 $ 12,000 B
- Ending Balance $ 13,000

Beginning Bal. $ -
Transactions:
Ending Balance $ -

Beginning Bal. $ -
Transactions:
Ending Balance $ -

NET FIXED ASSETS
- Beginning Bal. $ -
- Transactions: B $ 12,000
- Ending Balance $ 12,000

Total Assets $ 25,000

LIABILITIES

Beginning Bal. $ -
Transactions:
Ending Balance $ -

Beginning Bal. $ -
Transactions:
Ending Balance $ -

Total Liabilities $ -

OWNER'S EQUITY

CAPITAL STOCK
- Beginning Bal. $ -
- Transactions: $ 25,000 A
- Ending Balance $ 25,000

RETAINED EARNINGS
- Beginning Bal. $ -
- Net Income $ -   **
- Ending Balance $ -

Owner's Equity $ 25,000

Total Liabs. & Owner's Eq. $ 25,000

INCOME STATEMENT

Transactions:
Cumulative Total $ -

Transactions:
Cumulative Total $ -

Transactions:
Cumulative Total $ -

Transactions:
Cumulative Total $ -

Transactions:
Cumulative Total $ -

Transactions:
Cumulative Total $ -

Net Income   ** $ -

Accounts after Transaction C

Gadgets Etc. purchases merchandise for resale, all on account, for $42,000 during the fiscal year.

The inventory account is debited (increased) by $42,000 from a starting balance of $0. The purchases have occurred all during the fiscal year ended October 31, 20xy. The accounts payable account is credited (increased) by $42,000 from a starting balance of $0. Figure 5.3 summarizes the accounts of Gadgets Etc. after this transaction.

FIGURE 5.3 ACCOUNTS OF GADGETS ETC. AFTER TRANSACTION C

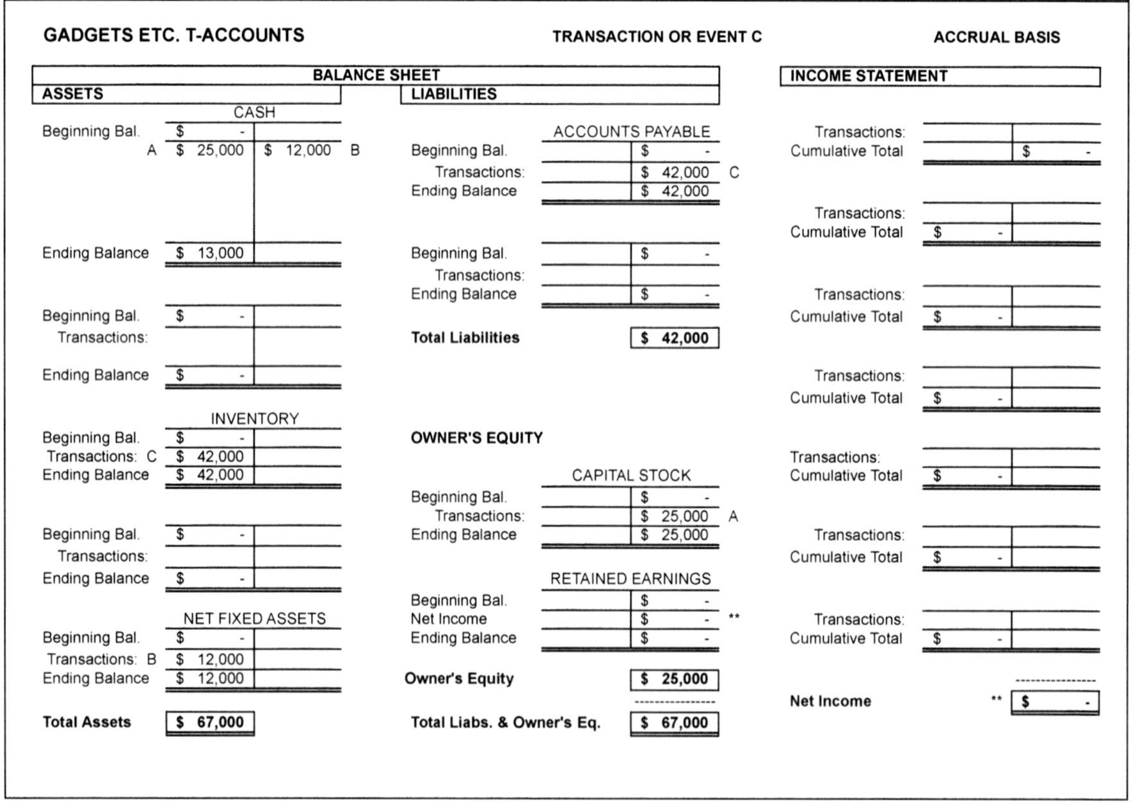

GADGETS ETC. T-ACCOUNTS — **TRANSACTION OR EVENT C** — **ACCRUAL BASIS**

BALANCE SHEET

ASSETS

CASH
- Beginning Bal. $ -
- A $ 25,000 | $ 12,000 B
- Ending Balance $ 13,000

Beginning Bal. $ -
Transactions:
Ending Balance $ -

INVENTORY
- Beginning Bal. $ -
- Transactions: C $ 42,000
- Ending Balance $ 42,000

Beginning Bal. $ -
Transactions:
Ending Balance $ -

NET FIXED ASSETS
- Beginning Bal. $ -
- Transactions: B $ 12,000
- Ending Balance $ 12,000

Total Assets $ 67,000

LIABILITIES

ACCOUNTS PAYABLE
- Beginning Bal. $ -
- Transactions: $ 42,000 C
- Ending Balance $ 42,000

Beginning Bal. $ -
Transactions:
Ending Balance $ -

Total Liabilities $ 42,000

OWNER'S EQUITY

CAPITAL STOCK
- Beginning Bal. $ -
- Transactions: $ 25,000 A
- Ending Balance $ 25,000

RETAINED EARNINGS
- Beginning Bal. $ -
- Net Income $ - **
- Ending Balance $ -

Owner's Equity $ 25,000

Total Liabs. & Owner's Eq. $ 67,000

INCOME STATEMENT

Transactions:
Cumulative Total $ -

Transactions:
Cumulative Total $ -

Transactions:
Cumulative Total $ -

Transactions:
Cumulative Total $ -

Transactions:
Cumulative Total $ -

Transactions:
Cumulative Total $ -

Transactions:
Cumulative Total $ -

Net Income ** $ -

Accounts after Transaction D

Gadgets Etc. sells merchandise, all on account, for $53,000 during the fiscal year. At October 31, 20xy, an adjusting entry is made to show that inventory on hand amounted to $12,000.

The accounts receivable asset account is debited (increased) by $53,000 from a starting balance of $0, while the sales account is credited (increased) by $53,000. The income statement accounts accumulate transactions during the year, resetting to $0 at the start of each year. The sales have occurred all during the fiscal year ended October 31, 20xy.

To complete the accounting, we also need to use the ending balance of $12,000 in the inventory account to solve for the cost of sales recognized during the fiscal year. Since inventory started at $0 and ended at $12,000, a debit (increase) of $30,000 is made to cost of sales account in the income statement, along with a credit (decrease) to the inventory account. Figure 5.4 summarizes the accounts of Gadgets Etc. after this transaction.

Notice that the resulting net income from the income statement is "closed" into the retained earnings account on the balance sheet. Since this is the first year of the business, the beginning balance of retained earnings is $0. For now, the gross profit of $23,000 is the net income. In subsequent transactions, will we account for the operating expenses in the income statement?

FIGURE 5.4 ACCOUNTS OF GADGETS ETC. AFTER TRANSACTION D

GADGETS ETC. T-ACCOUNTS — TRANSACTION OR EVENT D — **ACCRUAL BASIS**

BALANCE SHEET

ASSETS

CASH
- Beginning Bal. $ -
- A $ 25,000 | $ 12,000 B
- Ending Balance $ 13,000

ACCOUNTS REC.
- Beginning Bal. $ -
- Transactions: D $ 53,000
- Ending Balance $ 53,000

INVENTORY
- Beginning Bal. $ -
- Transactions: C $ 42,000 | $ 30,000 D
- Ending Balance $ 12,000 D

- Beginning Bal. $ -
- Transactions:
- Ending Balance $ -

NET FIXED ASSETS
- Beginning Bal. $ -
- Transactions: B $ 12,000
- Ending Balance $ 12,000

Total Assets $ 90,000

LIABILITIES

ACCOUNTS PAYABLE
- Beginning Bal. $ -
- Transactions: $ 42,000 C
- Ending Balance $ 42,000

- Beginning Bal. $ -
- Transactions:
- Ending Balance $ -

Total Liabilities $ 42,000

OWNER'S EQUITY

CAPITAL STOCK
- Beginning Bal. $ -
- Transactions: $ 25,000 A
- Ending Balance $ 25,000

RETAINED EARNINGS
- Beginning Bal. $ -
- Net Income $ 23,000 **
- Ending Balance $ 23,000

Owner's Equity $ 48,000

Total Liabs. & Owner's Eq. $ 90,000

INCOME STATEMENT

SALES
- Transactions: $ 53,000
- Cumulative Total $ 53,000

COST OF SALES
- Transactions: D $ 30,000
- Cumulative Total $ 30,000

- Transactions:
- Cumulative Total $ -

- Transactions:
- Cumulative Total $ -

- Transactions:
- Cumulative Total $ -

- Transactions:
- Cumulative Total $ -

Net Income ** $ 23,000

Accounts after Transaction E

Gadgets Etc. collects $37,000 of cash on accounts (from customers) during the fiscal year.

Cash is debited (increased) by $37,000 and accounts receivable is credited (decreased) for $37,000. The collections have occurred all during the fiscal year ended October 31, 20xy. Total assets do not change, since one asset account is decreased while another asset account is increased by the same amount. Figure 5.5 summarizes the accounts of Gadgets Etc. after this transaction.

FIGURE 5.5 ACCOUNTS OF GADGETS ETC. AFTER TRANSACTION E

GADGETS ETC. T-ACCOUNTS — **TRANSACTION OR EVENT E** — **ACCRUAL BASIS**

BALANCE SHEET

ASSETS

CASH
- Beginning Bal. $ -
- A $ 25,000 | $ 12,000 B
- E $ 37,000
- Ending Balance $ 50,000

ACCOUNTS REC.
- Beginning Bal. $ -
- Transactions: D $ 53,000 | $ 37,000 E
- Ending Balance $ 16,000

INVENTORY
- Beginning Bal. $ -
- Transactions: C $ 42,000 | $ 30,000 D
- Ending Balance $ 12,000 D

- Beginning Bal. $ -
- Transactions:
- Ending Balance $ -

NET FIXED ASSETS
- Beginning Bal. $ -
- Transactions: B $ 12,000
- Ending Balance $ 12,000

Total Assets $ 90,000

LIABILITIES

ACCOUNTS PAYABLE
- Beginning Bal. $ -
- Transactions: $ 42,000 C
- Ending Balance $ 42,000

- Beginning Bal. $ -
- Transactions:
- Ending Balance $ -

Total Liabilities $ 42,000

OWNER'S EQUITY

CAPITAL STOCK
- Beginning Bal. $ -
- Transactions: $ 25,000 A
- Ending Balance $ 25,000

RETAINED EARNINGS
- Beginning Bal. $ -
- Net Income $ 23,000 **
- Ending Balance $ 23,000

Owner's Equity $ 48,000

Total Liabs. & Owner's Eq. $ 90,000

INCOME STATEMENT

SALES
- Transactions: $ 53,000
- Cumulative Total $ 53,000

COST OF SALES
- Transactions: D $ 30,000
- Cumulative Total $ 30,000

- Transactions:
- Cumulative Total $ -

- Transactions:
- Cumulative Total $ -

- Transactions:
- Cumulative Total $ -

- Transactions:
- Cumulative Total $ -

Net Income ** $ 23,000

120 Analyzing Financial Statements — American Bankers Association

Accounts after Transaction F

Gadgets Etc. disburses cash of $32,000 to creditors (on account) during the fiscal year.

Cash is credited (decreased) by $32,000 and accounts payable is debited (decreased) by $32,000. The disbursements (payments) have occurred all during the fiscal year ended October 31, 20xy. Figure 5.6 summarizes the accounts of Gadgets Etc. after this transaction.

FIGURE 5.6 ACCOUNTS OF GADGETS ETC. AFTER TRANSACTION F

GADGETS ETC. T-ACCOUNTS — **TRANSACTION OR EVENT F** — **ACCRUAL BASIS**

BALANCE SHEET | **INCOME STATEMENT**

ASSETS

CASH
Beginning Bal.		$ -		
A	$ 25,000	$ 12,000	B	
E	$ 37,000	$ 32,000	F	
Ending Balance	$ 18,000			

ACCOUNTS REC.
Beginning Bal.	$ -			
Transactions: D	$ 53,000	$ 37,000	E	
Ending Balance	$ 16,000			

INVENTORY
Beginning Bal.	$ -			
Transactions: C	$ 42,000	$ 30,000	D	
Ending Balance	$ 12,000			

Beginning Bal.	$ -	
Transactions:		
Ending Balance	$ -	

NET FIXED ASSETS
Beginning Bal.	$ -	
Transactions: B	$ 12,000	
Ending Balance	$ 12,000	

Total Assets $ 58,000

LIABILITIES

ACCOUNTS PAYABLE
Beginning Bal.		$ -		
Transactions: F	$ 32,000	$ 42,000	C	
Ending Balance		$ 10,000		

Beginning Bal.		$ -
Transactions:		
Ending Balance		$ -

Total Liabilities $ 10,000

OWNER'S EQUITY

CAPITAL STOCK
Beginning Bal.	$ -	
Transactions:	$ 25,000	A
Ending Balance	$ 25,000	

RETAINED EARNINGS
Beginning Bal.	$ -	
Net Income	$ 23,000	**
Ending Balance	$ 23,000	

Owner's Equity $ 48,000

Total Liabs. & Owner's Eq. $ 58,000

SALES
| Transactions: | $ 53,000 |
| Cumulative Total | $ 53,000 |

COST OF SALES
| Transactions: D | $ 30,000 |
| Cumulative Total | $ 30,000 |

| Transactions: | |
| Cumulative Total | $ - |

| Transactions: | |
| Cumulative Total | $ - |

| Transactions: | |
| Cumulative Total | $ - |

| Transactions: | |
| Cumulative Total | $ - |

| Transactions: | |
| Cumulative Total | $ - |

Net Income   ** $ 23,000

Accounts after Transaction G

Gadgets Etc. disburses cash of $9,700 to employees (for wages) during the fiscal year. On October 31, 20xy, an adjusting entry is made to show that earned but unpaid wages amounted to $600.

Cash is credited (decreased) by $9,700 and wages payable is debited (decreased) by $9,700 from a starting balance of $0. The disbursements (payments) have occurred all during the course of the fiscal year ended October 31, 20xy.

To complete the accounting, we also need to use the ending balance of $600 in the wages payable account to solve for the wage expense recognized during the fiscal year. Since wages payable started at $0 and ended at $600, a wage expense credit (increase) of $10,300 is made to wages payable, along with a debit (increase) to the wage expense account within the income statement. Figure 5.7 summarizes the accounts of Gadgets Etc. after this transaction.

FIGURE 5.7 ACCOUNTS OF GADGETS ETC. AFTER TRANSACTION G

GADGETS ETC. T-ACCOUNTS — **TRANSACTION OR EVENT G** — **ACCRUAL BASIS**

BALANCE SHEET

ASSETS

CASH
Beginning Bal.	$ -			
A	$ 25,000	$ 12,000	B	
E	$ 37,000	$ 32,000	F	
		$ 9,700	G	
Ending Balance	$ 8,300			

ACCOUNTS REC.
Beginning Bal.	$ -			
Transactions: D	$ 53,000	$ 37,000	E	
Ending Balance	$ 16,000			

INVENTORY
Beginning Bal.	$ -			
Transactions: C	$ 42,000	$ 30,000	D	
Ending Balance	$ 12,000		D	

Beginning Bal.	$ -		
Transactions:			
Ending Balance	$ -		

NET FIXED ASSETS
Beginning Bal.	$ -	
Transactions: B	$ 12,000	
Ending Balance	$ 12,000	

Total Assets $ 48,300

LIABILITIES

ACCOUNTS PAYABLE
Beginning Bal.		$ -		
Transactions: F	$ 32,000	$ 42,000	C	
Ending Balance		$ 10,000		

WAGES PAYABLE
Beginning Bal.		$ -		
Transactions: G	$ 9,700	$ 10,300	G	
Ending Balance		$ 600	G	

Total Liabilities $ 10,600

OWNER'S EQUITY

CAPITAL STOCK
Beginning Bal.	$ -	
Transactions:	$ 25,000	A
Ending Balance	$ 25,000	

RETAINED EARNINGS
Beginning Bal.	$ -	
Net Income	$ 12,700	**
Ending Balance	$ 12,700	

Owner's Equity $ 37,700

Total Liabs. & Owner's Eq. $ 48,300

INCOME STATEMENT

SALES
Transactions:	$ 53,000	
Cumulative Total	$ 53,000	

COST OF SALES
Transactions: D	$ 30,000	
Cumulative Total	$ 30,000	

Transactions:		
Cumulative Total	$ -	

WAGE EXPENSE
Transactions: G	$ 10,300	
Cumulative Total	$ 10,300	

Transactions:		
Cumulative Total	$ -	

Transactions:		
Cumulative Total	$ -	

Net Income ** $ 12,700

Accounts after Transaction H

Gadgets Etc. disburses cash of $3,900 for rental of the store facility (building). At October 31, 20xy, an adjusting entry is made to show that prepaid rent amounted to $300. That is, one month of rent was prepaid, and the payment of $3,900 was for 13 months of rent, starting on November 1, 20xx.

Cash is credited (decreased) by $3,900, and prepaid rent (sometimes more broadly labeled "**prepaid assets**" since insurance also is often paid in advance) is debited (increased) by $3,900.

To complete the accounting, we need to use the ending balance of $300 in the prepaid rent account to solve for the rent expense recognized during the fiscal year. Since prepaid rent started at $0 and ended at $300, a rent expense credit (increase) of $3,600 is made to prepaid rent, along with a debit (increase) to the rent expense account within the income statement. Figure 5.8 summarizes the accounts of Gadgets Etc. after this transaction.

> **Prepaid assets**
>
> Assets that you have paid for in advance, but whose benefits you do not realize the benefits until later. The easiest examples to understand are insurance or rent.

FIGURE 5.8 ACCOUNTS OF GADGETS ETC. AFTER TRANSACTION H

GADGETS ETC. T-ACCOUNTS — **TRANSACTION OR EVENT H** — **ACCRUAL BASIS**

BALANCE SHEET

ASSETS

CASH
- Beginning Bal. $ -
- A $ 25,000 | $ 12,000 B
- E $ 37,000 | $ 32,000 F
-           | $ 9,700 G
-           | $ 3,900 H
- Ending Balance $ 4,400

ACCOUNTS REC.
- Beginning Bal. $ -
- Transactions: D $ 53,000 | $ 37,000 E
- Ending Balance $ 16,000

INVENTORY
- Beginning Bal. $ -
- Transactions: C $ 42,000 | $ 30,000 D
- Ending Balance $ 12,000 | D

PREPAID RENT
- Beginning Bal. $ -
- Transactions: H $ 3,900 | $ 3,600 H
- Ending Balance $ 300 | H

NET FIXED ASSETS
- Beginning Bal. $ -
- Transactions: B $ 12,000
- Ending Balance $ 12,000

Total Assets $ 44,700

LIABILITIES

ACCOUNTS PAYABLE
- Beginning Bal. $ -
- Transactions: F $ 32,000 | $ 42,000 C
- Ending Balance $ 10,000

WAGES PAYABLE
- Beginning Bal. $ -
- Transactions: G $ 9,700 | $ 10,300 G
- Ending Balance $ 600 G

Total Liabilities $ 10,600

OWNER'S EQUITY

CAPITAL STOCK
- Beginning Bal. $ -
- Transactions: $ 25,000 A
- Ending Balance $ 25,000

RETAINED EARNINGS
- Beginning Bal. $ -
- Net Income $ 9,100 **
- Ending Balance $ 9,100

Owner's Equity $ 34,100

Total Liabs. & Owner's Eq. $ 44,700

INCOME STATEMENT

SALES
- Transactions: $ 53,000
- Cumulative Total $ 53,000

COST OF SALES
- Transactions: D $ 30,000
- Cumulative Total $ 30,000

RENT EXPENSE
- Transactions: H $ 3,600
- Cumulative Total $ 3,600

WAGE EXPENSE
- Transactions: G $ 10,300
- Cumulative Total $ 10,300

- Transactions:
- Cumulative Total $ -

- Transactions:
- Cumulative Total $ -

- Transactions:
- Cumulative Total $ -

Net Income ** $ 9,100

Accounts after Transaction I

Gadgets Etc. disburses cash of $2,900 for miscellaneous expenses during the fiscal year.

Cash is credited (decreased) by $2,900 and the miscellaneous expenses account within the income statement is debited (increased) by $2,900. The disbursements (payments) have occurred all during the fiscal year ended October 31, 20xy. Figure 5.9 summarizes the accounts of Gadgets Etc. after this transaction.

FIGURE 5.9 ACCOUNTS OF GADGETS ETC. AFTER TRANSACTION I

GADGETS ETC. T-ACCOUNTS — **TRANSACTION OR EVENT I** — **ACCRUAL BASIS**

BALANCE SHEET

ASSETS

CASH
Beginning Bal.	$ -			
A	$ 25,000	$ 12,000	B	
E	$ 37,000	$ 32,000	F	
		$ 9,700	G	
		$ 3,900	H	
		$ 2,900	I	
Ending Balance	$ 1,500			

ACCOUNTS REC.
Beginning Bal.	$ -			
Transactions: D	$ 53,000	$ 37,000	E	
Ending Balance	$ 16,000			

INVENTORY
Beginning Bal.	$ -			
Transactions: C	$ 42,000	$ 30,000	D	
Ending Balance	$ 12,000	D		

PREPAID RENT
Beginning Bal.	$ -			
Transactions: H	$ 3,900	$ 3,600	H	
Ending Balance	$ 300	H		

NET FIXED ASSETS
Beginning Bal.	$ -	
Transactions: B	$ 12,000	
Ending Balance	$ 12,000	

Total Assets $ 41,800

LIABILITIES

ACCOUNTS PAYABLE
Beginning Bal.		$ -		
Transactions: F	$ 32,000	$ 42,000	C	
Ending Balance		$ 10,000		

WAGES PAYABLE
Beginning Bal.		$ -		
Transactions: G	$ 9,700	$ 10,300	G	
Ending Balance		$ 600	G	

Total Liabilities $ 10,600

OWNER'S EQUITY

CAPITAL STOCK
Beginning Bal.	$ -
Transactions:	$ 25,000 A
Ending Balance	$ 25,000

RETAINED EARNINGS
Beginning Bal.	$ -
Net Income	$ 6,200 **
Ending Balance	$ 6,200

Owner's Equity $ 31,200

Total Liabs. & Owner's Eq. $ 41,800

INCOME STATEMENT

SALES
Transactions:	$ 53,000
Cumulative Total	$ 53,000

COST OF SALES
Transactions: D	$ 30,000
Cumulative Total	$ 30,000

RENT EXPENSE
Transactions: H	$ 3,600
Cumulative Total	$ 3,600

WAGE EXPENSE
Transactions: G	$ 10,300
Cumulative Total	$ 10,300

Transactions:	
Cumulative Total	$ -

Transactions:	
Cumulative Total	$ -

MISC. EXPENSE
Transactions: I	$ 2,900
Cumulative Total	$ 2,900

Net Income ** $ 6,200

Accounts after Transaction J

*Gadgets Etc. made an adjusting entry on October 31, 20xy, to record **depreciation** of store fixtures for the fiscal year of $1,500.*

Net fixed assets are credited (decreased) by $1,500, and depreciation expense is debited (increased) by $1,500. Figure 5.10 summarizes the accounts of Gadgets Etc. after this transaction.

FIGURE 5.10 ACCOUNTS OF GADGETS ETC. AFTER TRANSACTION J

GADGETS ETC. T-ACCOUNTS — **TRANSACTION OR EVENT J** — **ACCRUAL BASIS**

BALANCE SHEET

ASSETS

CASH
- Beginning Bal. $ -
- A $ 25,000 | $ 12,000 B
- E $ 37,000 | $ 32,000 F
- | $ 9,700 G
- | $ 3,900 H
- | $ 2,900 I
- Ending Balance $ 1,500

ACCOUNTS REC.
- Beginning Bal. $ -
- Transactions: D $ 53,000 | $ 37,000 E
- Ending Balance $ 16,000

INVENTORY
- Beginning Bal. $ -
- Transactions: C $ 42,000 | $ 30,000 D
- Ending Balance $ 12,000 | D

PREPAID RENT
- Beginning Bal. $ -
- Transactions: H $ 3,900 | $ 3,600 H
- Ending Balance $ 300 | H

NET FIXED ASSETS
- Beginning Bal. $ -
- Transactions: B $ 12,000 | $ 1,500 J
- Ending Balance $ 10,500

Total Assets $ 40,300

LIABILITIES

ACCOUNTS PAYABLE
- Beginning Bal. $ -
- Transactions: F $ 32,000 | $ 42,000 C
- Ending Balance | $ 10,000

WAGES PAYABLE
- Beginning Bal. $ -
- Transactions: G $ 9,700 | $ 10,300 G
- Ending Balance | $ 600 G

Total Liabilities $ 10,600

OWNER'S EQUITY

CAPITAL STOCK
- Beginning Bal. $ -
- Transactions: | $ 25,000 A
- Ending Balance | $ 25,000

RETAINED EARNINGS
- Beginning Bal. $ -
- Net Income | $ 4,700 **
- Ending Balance | $ 4,700

Owner's Equity $ 29,700

Total Liabs. & Owner's Eq. $ 40,300

INCOME STATEMENT

SALES
- Transactions: | $ 53,000
- Cumulative Total | $ 53,000

COST OF SALES
- Transactions: D | $ 30,000
- Cumulative Total | $ 30,000

RENT EXPENSE
- Transactions: H | $ 3,600
- Cumulative Total | $ 3,600

WAGE EXPENSE
- Transactions: G | $ 10,300
- Cumulative Total | $ 10,300

- Transactions: |
- Cumulative Total | $ -

DEPRECIATION EXP.
- Transactions: J | $ 1,500
- Cumulative Total | $ 1,500

MISC. EXPENSE
- Transactions: I | $ 2,900
- Cumulative Total | $ 2,900

Net Income ** $ 4,700

Depreciation

In accounting, a process of allocating the cost of a fixed asset less salvage value, if any, over its estimated useful life. A depreciation charge is treated as a noncash expense. For income tax purposes, depreciation is determined by a formula, not by any actual loss of value. This aspect of depreciation applies to many types of assets, not just real property.

Accounts after Transaction K

Gadgets Etc. estimated that uncollectible accounts at October 31, 20xy, were $400, and no accounts had been written off during the fiscal year. Instead of charging the estimate against revenues, it was recorded as a bad debt expense on the income statement.

Accounts receivable is credited (decreased) by $400, and bad debt expense is debited (increased) by $400. This is a fiscal year-end adjusting entry. Figure 5.11 summarizes the accounts of Gadgets Etc. after this transaction, as well as all of the transactions in this example.

FIGURE 5.11 ACCOUNTS OF GADGETS ETC. AFTER TRANSACTION K AND ALL TRANSACTIONS

GADGETS ETC. T-ACCOUNTS — TRANSACTION OR EVENT K — **ACCRUAL BASIS**

BALANCE SHEET

ASSETS

CASH
Beginning Bal.	$ -			
A	$ 25,000	$ 12,000	B	
E	$ 37,000	$ 32,000	F	
		$ 9,700	G	
		$ 3,900	H	
		$ 2,900	I	
Ending Balance	$ 1,500			

ACCOUNTS REC.
Beginning Bal.	$ -			
Transactions: D	$ 53,000	$ 37,000	E	
		$ 400	K	
Ending Balance	$ 15,600			

INVENTORY
Beginning Bal.	$ -			
Transactions: C	$ 42,000	$ 30,000	D	
Ending Balance	$ 12,000		D	

PREPAID RENT
Beginning Bal.	$ -			
Transactions: H	$ 3,900	$ 3,600	H	
Ending Balance	$ 300	H		

NET FIXED ASSETS
Beginning Bal.	$ -			
Transactions: B	$ 12,000	$ 1,500	J	
Ending Balance	$ 10,500			

Total Assets $ 39,900

LIABILITIES

ACCOUNTS PAYABLE
Beginning Bal.		$ -		
Transactions: F	$ 32,000	$ 42,000	C	
Ending Balance		$ 10,000		

WAGES PAYABLE
Beginning Bal.		$ -		
Transactions: G	$ 9,700	$ 10,300	G	
Ending Balance		$ 600	G	

Total Liabilities $ 10,600

OWNER'S EQUITY

CAPITAL STOCK
Beginning Bal.	$ -	
Transactions:	$ 25,000	A
Ending Balance	$ 25,000	

RETAINED EARNINGS
Beginning Bal.	$ -	
Net Income	$ 4,300	**
Ending Balance	$ 4,300	

Owner's Equity $ 29,300

Total Liabs. & Owner's Eq. $ 39,900

INCOME STATEMENT

SALES
Transactions:	$ 53,000	
Cumulative Total	$ 53,000	

COST OF SALES
Transactions: D	$ 30,000	
Cumulative Total	$ 30,000	

RENT EXPENSE
Transactions: H	$ 3,600	
Cumulative Total	$ 3,600	

WAGE EXPENSE
Transactions: G	$ 10,300	
Cumulative Total	$ 10,300	

BAD DEBT EXPENSE
Transactions: K	$ 400	
Cumulative Total	$ 400	

DEPRECIATION EXP.
Transactions: J	$ 1,500	
Cumulative Total	$ 1,500	

MISC. EXPENSE
Transactions: I	$ 2,900	
Cumulative Total	$ 2,900	

Net Income ** $ 4,300

Gadgets etc. summary balance sheet and income statement on accrual-basis accounting

As a final step in the Gadgets Etc. accrual basis example, we show the ending balances of the various accounts in the formats of a balance sheet and income statement in Figure 5.12. Total assets have an ending balance of $39,900. The business had a profit of $4,300 on sales of $53,000.

FIGURE 5.12 GADGETS ETC. ACCRUAL-BASIS BALANCE SHEET AND INCOME STATEMENT FOR 20xy

Balance Sheet as of October 31, 20xy				FY 20xy Income Statement	
Assets		Liabilities		Sales	$53,000
Cash	$1,500	Accounts Payable	$10,000	Cost of Sales	30,000
Accounts Rec.	15,600	Accrued Expenses	600	Gross Profit	$23,000
Inventory	12,000	Current Liabilities	$10,600	Rent Expense	3,600
Prepaid Assets	300	Total Liabilities	$10,600	Wage Expense	10,300
Current Assets	29,400	Capital Stock	$25,000	Bad Debt Expense	400
Net Fixed Assets	10,500	Retained Earnings	4,300	Depreciation Exp.	1,500
Total Assets	$39,900	Owner's Equity	$29,300	Misc. Expenses	2,900
		Tot. Liabs.& Owner's Eq.	$39,900	Total Op. Exp.	$18,700
				Net Profit	$ 4,300

GADGETS ETC. FIRST YEAR ON CASH-BASIS ACCOUNTING

The following transactions will summarize the first year of operations for Gadgets Etc. and will be recorded using the cash basis of accounting.

Accounts after Transaction A

Mr. Smith starts Gadgets Etc. by investing $25,000 on November 1, 20xx. The business elects to use the cash basis of accounting.

The cash account has a debit (increase) of $25,000 applied. The beginning balance of all of the accounts used in this sample is $0 since the business has just started. The offsetting credit is applied as an increase to the capital stock account within owner's equity.

Figure 5.13 summarizes the accounts of Gadgets Etc. after this transaction.

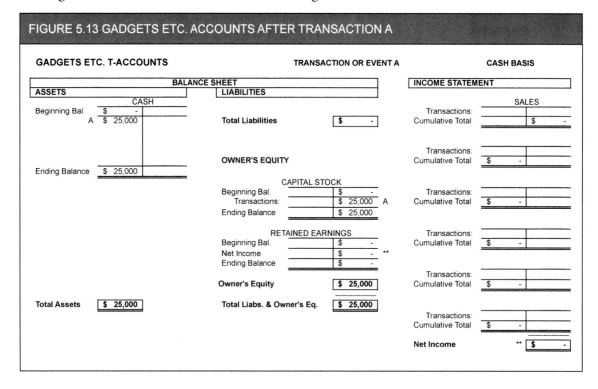

Accounts after Transaction B

Gadgets Etc. purchases store fixtures for cash of $12,000.

The net fixed assets account is debited (increased) by $12,000 (from a starting balance of $0) and the cash account is credited (decreased) by $12,000. Total assets does not change, since one of the asset accounts increased and another decreased by the same amount. Figure 5.14 summarizes the accounts of Gadgets Etc. after this transaction.

FIGURE 5.14 GADGETS ETC. ACCOUNTS AFTER TRANSACTION B

GADGETS ETC. T-ACCOUNTS — TRANSACTION OR EVENT B — CASH BASIS

BALANCE SHEET | **INCOME STATEMENT**

ASSETS | LIABILITIES

CASH
- Beginning Bal. $ -
- A $ 25,000 | $ 12,000 B
- Ending Balance $ 13,000

Total Liabilities $ -

OWNER'S EQUITY

CAPITAL STOCK
- Beginning Bal. $ -
- Transactions: $ 25,000 A
- Ending Balance $ 25,000

RETAINED EARNINGS
- Beginning Bal. $ -
- Net Income $ - **
- Ending Balance $ -

NET FIXED ASSETS
- Beginning Bal. $ -
- Transactions: B $ 12,000
- Ending Balance $ 12,000

Owner's Equity $ 25,000

Total Assets $ 25,000 | **Total Liabs. & Owner's Eq.** $ 25,000

SALES
- Transactions:
- Cumulative Total $ -

- Transactions:
- Cumulative Total $ -

- Transactions:
- Cumulative Total $ -

- Transactions:
- Cumulative Total $ -

- Transactions:
- Cumulative Total $ -

Net Income ** $ -

Accounts after Transaction C

Gadgets Etc. purchases merchandise for resale, all on account, for $42,000 during the fiscal year. The company sells merchandise, all on account, for $53,000 during the fiscal year. Gadgets Etc. collects $37,000 of cash on accounts (from customers) during the fiscal year.

The purchases of inventory do not create any accounting entries (such as an increase to inventory), since no cash was disbursed. Therefore, no corresponding accounts payable are created. Similarly, the sales do not create any accounting entries (such as an increase to accounts receivable), since no cash was collected.

As collections are made (and since cash is involved), the sales account is credited (increased) by $37,000. The income statement accounts accumulate transactions during the year, resetting to $0 at the start of each year. The sales have occurred all during the fiscal year ended October 31, 20xy.

Figure 5.15 summarizes the accounts of Gadgets Etc. after this transaction.

FIGURE 5.15 GADGETS ETC. ACCOUNTS AFTER TRANSACTION C

GADGETS ETC. T-ACCOUNTS — **TRANSACTION OR EVENT C** — **CASH BASIS**

BALANCE SHEET

ASSETS

CASH
- Beginning Bal. $ -
- A $ 25,000 | $ 12,000 B
- C $ 37,000
- Ending Balance $ 50,000

NET FIXED ASSETS
- Beginning Bal. $ -
- Transactions: B $ 12,000
- Ending Balance $ 12,000

Total Assets $ 62,000

LIABILITIES

Total Liabilities $ -

OWNER'S EQUITY

CAPITAL STOCK
- Beginning Bal. $ -
- Transactions: $ 25,000 A
- Ending Balance $ 25,000

RETAINED EARNINGS
- Beginning Bal. $ -
- Net Income $ 37,000 **
- Ending Balance $ 37,000

Owner's Equity $ 62,000

Total Liabs. & Owner's Eq. $ 62,000

INCOME STATEMENT

SALES
- Transactions: $ 37,000
- Cumulative Total $ 37,000

- Transactions:
- Cumulative Total $ -

- Transactions:
- Cumulative Total $ -

- Transactions:
- Cumulative Total $ -

- Transactions:
- Cumulative Total $ -

- Transactions:
- Cumulative Total $ -

Net Income ** $ 37,000

Accounts after Transaction D

Gadgets Etc. disburses cash of $32,000 to creditors (on account) during the fiscal year. At October 31, 20xy, an adjusting entry is made to show that inventory on hand amounted to $12,000.

Cash is credited (decreased) by $32,000 and inventory is debited (increased) by $32,000. The disbursements (payments to creditors) have all occurred during the fiscal year ended October 31, 20xy.

To complete the accounting, we need to use the ending balance of $12,000 in the inventory account to solve for the cost of sales recognized during the fiscal year. Since inventory started at $0 and ended at $12,000, a credit (increase) of $20,000 is made to cost of sales account in the income statement, along with a credit (decrease) to the inventory account. Figure 5.16 summarizes the accounts of Gadgets Etc. after this transaction.

Notice that the resulting net income from the income statement is "closed" into the retained earnings account on the balance sheet. Since this is the first year of the business, the beginning balance of retained earnings is $0. For now, the gross profit of $17,000 is the net income. In subsequent transactions, will we account for the operating expenses in the income statement.

FIGURE 5.16 GADGETS ETC. ACCOUNTS AFTER TRANSACTION D

GADGETS ETC. T-ACCOUNTS — TRANSACTION OR EVENT D — CASH BASIS

BALANCE SHEET

ASSETS

CASH
- Beginning Bal. $ —
- A $ 25,000 | $ 12,000 B
- C $ 37,000 | $ 32,000 D
- Ending Balance $ 18,000

INVENTORY
- Beginning Bal. $ —
- Transactions: D $ 32,000 | $ 20,000 D
- Ending Balance $ 12,000

NET FIXED ASSETS
- Beginning Bal. $ —
- Transactions: B $ 12,000
- Ending Balance $ 12,000

Total Assets $ 42,000

LIABILITIES
- Total Liabilities $ —

OWNER'S EQUITY

CAPITAL STOCK
- Beginning Bal. $ —
- Transactions: $ 25,000 A
- Ending Balance $ 25,000

RETAINED EARNINGS
- Beginning Bal. $ —
- Net Income $ 17,000 **
- Ending Balance $ 17,000

Owner's Equity $ 42,000

Total Liabs. & Owner's Eq. $ 42,000

INCOME STATEMENT

SALES
- Transactions: $ 37,000
- Cumulative Total $ 37,000

COST OF SALES
- Transactions: D $ 20,000
- Cumulative Total $ 20,000

- Transactions:
- Cumulative Total $ —

- Transactions:
- Cumulative Total $ —

- Transactions:
- Cumulative Total $ —

- Transactions:
- Cumulative Total $ —

Net Income ** $ 17,000

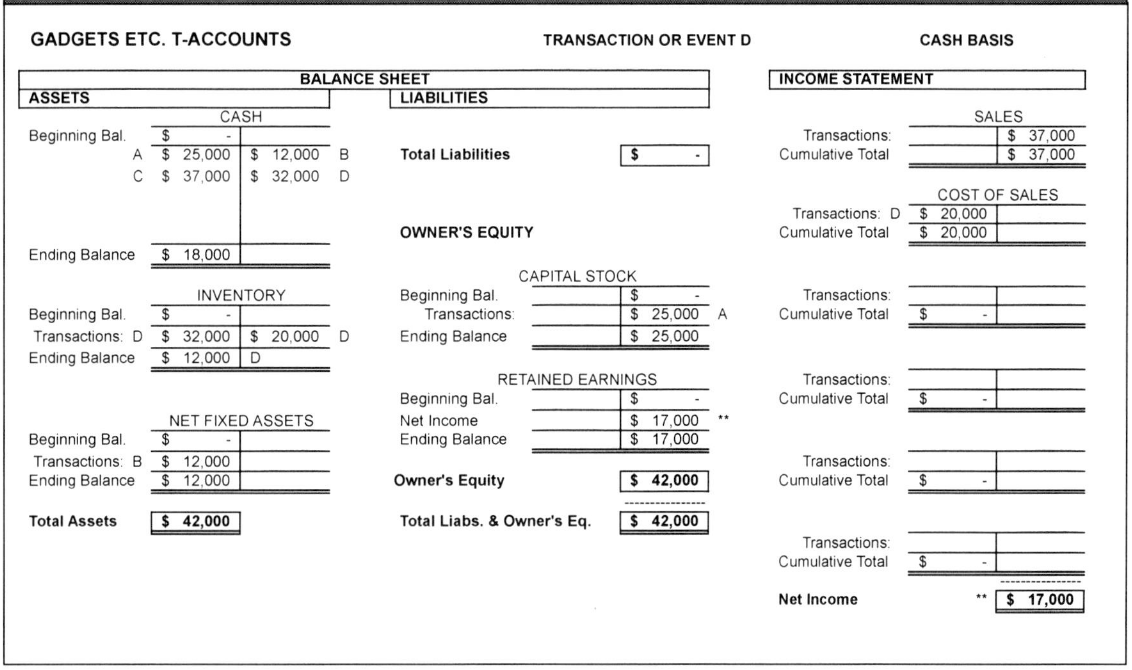

Accounts after Transaction E

Gadgets Etc. disburses cash of $9,700 to employees (for wages) during the fiscal year.

Cash is credited (decreased) by $9,700 and wage expense is debited (increased) by $9,700 from a starting balance of $0. The disbursements (payments) have occurred all during the fiscal year ended October 31, 20xy. Unlike the accrual method example, an adjusting entry is not made to recognize the ending balance of $600 in the wages payable account. Figure 5.17 summarizes the accounts of Gadgets Etc. after this transaction.

FIGURE 5.17 GADGETS ETC. ACCOUNTS AFTER TRANSACTION E

GADGETS ETC. T-ACCOUNTS — TRANSACTION OR EVENT E — **CASH BASIS**

BALANCE SHEET

ASSETS					LIABILITIES		
		CASH					
Beginning Bal.		$ -			Total Liabilities	$ -	
A	$ 25,000	$ 12,000	B				
C	$ 37,000	$ 32,000	D				
		$ 9,700	E				
Ending Balance	$ 8,300				**OWNER'S EQUITY**		
		INVENTORY				CAPITAL STOCK	
Beginning Bal.	$ -				Beginning Bal.	$ -	
Transactions: D	$ 32,000	$ 20,000	D		Transactions:	$ 25,000	A
Ending Balance	$ 12,000	D			Ending Balance	$ 25,000	
						RETAINED EARNINGS	
		NET FIXED ASSETS			Beginning Bal.	$ -	
Beginning Bal.	$ -				Net Income	$ 7,300	**
Transactions: B	$ 12,000				Ending Balance	$ 7,300	
Ending Balance	$ 12,000						
					Owner's Equity	$ 32,300	
Total Assets	$ 32,300				**Total Liabs. & Owner's Eq.**	$ 32,300	

INCOME STATEMENT

		SALES	
Transactions:		$ 37,000	
Cumulative Total		$ 37,000	
		COST OF SALES	
Transactions: D		$ 20,000	
Cumulative Total		$ 20,000	
Transactions:			
Cumulative Total	$ -		
		WAGE EXPENSE	
Transactions: E		$ 9,700	
Cumulative Total		$ 9,700	
Transactions:			
Cumulative Total	$ -		
Transactions:			
Cumulative Total	$ -		
Net Income	**	$ 7,300	

Accounts after Transaction F

Gadgets Etc. disburses cash of $3,900 for rental of the store facility (building). The payment of $3,900 was for 13 months of rent, starting on November 1, 20xx.

Cash is credited (decreased) by $3,900 and rent expense (sometimes called "prepaid assets" since insurance also is often paid in advance) is debited (increased) by $3,900. Unlike the accrual method example, an adjusting entry is not made to recognize the ending balance of $300 in the prepaid assets account. Under the cash method, the business is able to fully expense the entire payment for rent, even the prepaid portion. Figure 5.18 summarizes the accounts of Gadgets Etc. after this transaction.

FIGURE 5.18 GADGETS ETC. ACCOUNTS AFTER TRANSACTION F

GADGETS ETC. T-ACCOUNTS — **TRANSACTION OR EVENT F** — **CASH BASIS**

BALANCE SHEET

ASSETS					LIABILITIES	
CASH						
Beginning Bal.	$ -				Total Liabilities	$ -
A	$ 25,000	$ 12,000	B			
C	$ 37,000	$ 32,000	D			
		$ 9,700	E		OWNER'S EQUITY	
		$ 3,900	F			
Ending Balance	$ 4,400				CAPITAL STOCK	
					Beginning Bal.	$ -
INVENTORY					Transactions:	$ 25,000 A
Beginning Bal.	$ -				Ending Balance	$ 25,000
Transactions: D	$ 32,000	$ 20,000	D			
Ending Balance	$ 12,000	D			RETAINED EARNINGS	
					Beginning Bal.	$ -
NET FIXED ASSETS					Net Income	$ 3,400 **
Beginning Bal.	$ -				Ending Balance	$ 3,400
Transactions: B	$ 12,000					
Ending Balance	$ 12,000				Owner's Equity	$ 28,400
Total Assets	$ 28,400				Total Liabs. & Owner's Eq.	$ 28,400

INCOME STATEMENT

	SALES	
Transactions:		$ 37,000
Cumulative Total		$ 37,000
	COST OF SALES	
Transactions: D	$ 20,000	
Cumulative Total	$ 20,000	
	RENT EXPENSE	
Transactions: F	$ 3,900	
Cumulative Total	$ 3,900	
	WAGE EXPENSE	
Transactions: E	$ 9,700	
Cumulative Total	$ 9,700	
Transactions:		$ -
Cumulative Total		$ -
Net Income	**	$ 3,400

Accounts after Transaction G

Gadgets Etc. disburses cash of $2,900 for miscellaneous expenses during the fiscal year.

Cash is credited (decreased) by $2,900 and the miscellaneous expenses account within the income statement is debited (increased) by $2,900. The disbursements (payments) have all occurred during the fiscal year ended October 31, 20xy. Figure 5.19 summarizes the accounts of Gadgets Etc. after this transaction.

FIGURE 5.19 GADGETS ETC. ACCOUNTS AFTER TRANSACTION G

GADGETS ETC. T-ACCOUNTS — TRANSACTION OR EVENT G — CASH BASIS

BALANCE SHEET

ASSETS

CASH
- Beginning Bal. $ -
- A $ 25,000 | $ 12,000 B
- C $ 37,000 | $ 32,000 D
- | $ 9,700 E
- | $ 3,900 F
- | $ 2,900 G
- Ending Balance $ 1,500

INVENTORY
- Beginning Bal. $ -
- Transactions: D $ 32,000 | $ 20,000 D
- Ending Balance $ 12,000

NET FIXED ASSETS
- Beginning Bal. $ -
- Transactions: B $ 12,000
- Ending Balance $ 12,000

Total Assets $ 25,500

LIABILITIES

Total Liabilities $ -

OWNER'S EQUITY

CAPITAL STOCK
- Beginning Bal. $ -
- Transactions: $ 25,000 A
- Ending Balance $ 25,000

RETAINED EARNINGS
- Beginning Bal. $ -
- Net Income $ 500 **
- Ending Balance $ 500

Owner's Equity $ 25,500

Total Liabs. & Owner's Eq. $ 25,500

INCOME STATEMENT

SALES
- Transactions: $ 37,000
- Cumulative Total $ 37,000

COST OF SALES
- Transactions: D $ 20,000
- Cumulative Total $ 20,000

RENT EXPENSE
- Transactions: F $ 3,900
- Cumulative Total $ 3,900

WAGE EXPENSE
- Transactions: E $ 9,700
- Cumulative Total $ 9,700

- Transactions:
- Cumulative Total $ -

MISC. EXPENSE
- Transactions: G $ 2,900
- Cumulative Total $ 2,900

Net Income ** $ 500

Accounts after Transaction H

Gadgets Etc. made an adjusting entry on October 31, 20xy, to record depreciation of store fixtures for the fiscal year of $1,500. The company also determines that $400 of invoices is uncollectible.

Net fixed assets is credited (decreased) by $1,500, and depreciation expense is debited (increased) by $1,500. Because depreciation is a noncash expense, technically it would not be reflected on a cash-basis income statement. However, because the IRS requires capital assets to be depreciated, even for cash-basis taxpayers, the common practice is to record depreciation expense, similar to accrual-basis accounting.

Under cash-basis accounting, since sales are not recognized until the invoice (account receivable) is collected, there is no entry to reflect the uncollectible invoices. Figure 5.20 summarizes the accounts of Gadgets Etc. after this transaction, as well as all of the transactions in this example.

FIGURE 5.20 GADGETS ETC. ACCOUNTS AFTER TRANSACTION H AND ALL TRANSACTIONS

GADGETS ETC. T-ACCOUNTS — TRANSACTION OR EVENT H — **CASH BASIS**

BALANCE SHEET

ASSETS

CASH
Beginning Bal.	$ -			
A	$ 25,000	$ 12,000	B	
C	$ 37,000	$ 32,000	D	
		$ 9,700	E	
		$ 3,900	F	
		$ 2,900	G	
Ending Balance	$ 1,500			

INVENTORY
Beginning Bal.	$ -			
Transactions: D	$ 32,000	$ 20,000	D	
Ending Balance	$ 12,000	D		

NET FIXED ASSETS
Beginning Bal.	$ -			
Transactions: B	$ 12,000	$ 1,500	H	
Ending Balance	$ 10,500			

Total Assets $ 24,000

LIABILITIES

Total Liabilities $ -

OWNER'S EQUITY

CAPITAL STOCK
Beginning Bal.	$ -
Transactions:	$ 25,000 A
Ending Balance	$ 25,000

RETAINED EARNINGS
Beginning Bal.	$ -
Net Income	$ (1,000) **
Ending Balance	$ (1,000)

Owner's Equity $ 24,000

Total Liabs. & Owner's Eq. $ 24,000

INCOME STATEMENT

SALES
Transactions:	$ 37,000
Cumulative Total	$ 37,000

COST OF SALES
Transactions: D	$ 20,000
Cumulative Total	$ 20,000

RENT EXPENSE
Transactions: F	$ 3,900
Cumulative Total	$ 3,900

WAGE EXPENSE
Transactions: E	$ 9,700
Cumulative Total	$ 9,700

DEPRECIATION EXP.
Transactions: H	$ 1,500
Cumulative Total	$ 1,500

MISC. EXPENSE
Transactions: G	$ 2,900
Cumulative Total	$ 2,900

Net Income ** $ (1,000)

Gadgets etc. summary balance sheet and income statement on cash-basis accounting

As a final step in the Gadgets Etc. cash-basis example, we show the ending balances of the various accounts in formats of a balance sheet and income statement in Figure 5.21. Total assets have an ending balance of $24,000. The business had a profit (loss) of ($1,000) on sales of $37,000.

FIGURE 5.21 GADGETS ETC. CASH-BASIS BALANCE SHEET AND INCOME STATEMENT FOR 20xy

Balance Sheet as of October 31, 20xy				FY 20xy Income Statement	
Assets		Liabilities		Sales	$37,000
Cash	$1,500	Total Liabilities	$0	Cost of Sales	20,000
Inventory	12,000	Capital Stock	$25,000	Gross Profit	$17,000
Current Assets	$13,500	Retained Earnings	(1,000)	Rent Expense	3,900
Net Fixed Assets	10,500	Owner's Equity	$24,000	Wage Expense	9,700
Total Assets	$24,000	Tot. Liabs. & Owner's Eq.	$24,000	Depreciation Exp.	1,500
				Misc. Expenses	2,900
				Total Op. Exp.	$18,000
				Net Profit (Loss)	$(1,000)

COMPARING GADGETS ETC. BALANCE SHEETS AND INCOME STATEMENTS

As we complete the Gadgets Etc. accounting refresher, we show the accrual-basis and cash-basis balance sheets and income statements side by side to facilitate comparison of the results. Figure 5.22 shows both balance sheets and income statements.

FIGURE 5.22 GADGETS ETC. COMPARATIVE BALANCE SHEETS AND INCOME STATEMENTS FOR YEAR ENDED OCTOBER 31, 20xy

Accrual Method		Cash Method	
Assets		**Assets**	
Cash	$1,500	Cash	$1,500
Accounts Rec.	15,600	Inventory	12,000
Inventory	12,000	Current Assets	$13,500
Prepaid Assets	300	Net Fixed Assets	10,500
Current Assets	29,400	Total Assets	$24,000
Net Fixed Assets	10,500		
Total Assets	$39,900		
Liabilities		**Liabilities**	
Accounts Payable	$10,000	Total Liabilities	$0
Accrued Expenses	600	Capital Stock	$25,000
Current Liabilities	$10,600	Retained Earnings	(1,000)
Total Liabilities	$10,600	Owner's Equity	$24,000
Capital Stock	$25,000	Tot. Liabs. & Owner's Equity	$24,000
Retained Earnings	4,300		
Owner's Equity	$29,300		
Tot. Liabs. & Owner's Equity	$39,900		
Income Statement		**Income Statement**	
Sales	$53,000	Sales	$37,000
Cost of Sales	30,000	Cost of Sales	20,000
Gross Profit	$23,000	Gross Profit	$17,000
Rent Expense	3,600	Rent Expense	3,900
Wage Expense	10,300	Wage Expense	9,700
Bad Debt Expense	400	Depreciation Exp.	1,500
Depreciation Exp.	1,500	Misc. Expenses	2,900
Misc. Expenses	2,900	Total Op. Exp.	$18,000
Total Op. Exp.	$18,700	Net Profit (Loss)	($1,000)
Net Profit	$4,300		

The following observations can be made:

- The same set of business transactions yielded very different balance sheets and income statements at year-end, depending on the accounting method used.
- Total assets are significantly lower under the cash method, since accounts receivable and accounts payable are not recorded, and inventory increases only as vendors are paid for the merchandise.
- Sales or revenue is also lower under the cash method, since sales are not booked until the cash is collected.
- Cost of sales is also lower under the cash method, and resulting gross profit is lower.
- Expense levels are mixed, since more cash was disbursed (expensed under cash method) for rent than was expensed under the accrual method, and less cash was disbursed (expensed under the cash method) for wages than was expensed under the accrual method. The cash-basis method did not recognize bad debt expense.
- Beginning and ending cash did not change, regardless of accounting method used. As you will see in, Chapter 9, because beginning and ending cash did not change, neither did the cash flow of the business. In the later section, we will build the statement of cash flows for Gadgets Etc. on both an accrual and a cash basis.

BUILD FINANCIAL STATEMENTS

One of the keys to successfully analyzing business financial statements is to know the accountant's approach to financial reporting. This enables a business banker to interpret the information presented, especially when a particular reporting situation is encountered for the first time. In practice, accountants record events and transactions that affect the business during a specific accounting period in accounts representing individual asset, liability, and equity items. These accounts are summarized at the end of the period, with the results shown in financial statements.

As a business banker learns about the cash flow cycle and industry characteristics of a business in the early stages of the Commercial Lending Decision Tree, he or she also learns that it is equally important to understand the accounting methods and procedures being used. This section walked you through a typical accounting process, providing you with an opportunity to practice using the accrual method of accounting.

In this section, you used a typical accounting process to practice constructing a balance sheet and income statement using the accrual method of accounting. By knowing an accountant's approach to financial reporting and how to interpret the information, you should now feel more confident about how business financial statements are constructed.

SUMMARY

The accounting method a business uses will greatly affect the nature of its financial statements. Just as the types of businesses (agricultural, wholesale, retail, etc.) have unique operating characteristics that a business banker should understand, different accounting methods have special characteristics that affect the balance sheet and income statement.

In this chapter, you learned that accounting methods refer to the basic rules and guidelines used to record transactions and prepare financial statements. You are now able to compare and contrast the two primary methods used by businesses—the cash method and accrual method. You also learned how to construct a balance sheet and income statement using the accrual basis, and now have a better understanding of how to explain your entries.

EXERCISE 1

Instructions

Complete the following two steps:
1. Take the Widgets, Inc. First Year Transactions information below and add it to the Accounting Transactions Worksheet (on the following page) to make the entries for Widgets Inc. first year in business using the accrual basis of accounting
2. Explain your entries and how they affected the balance sheet and income statement

Widgets, Inc. First Year Transactions

A. Mr. Jones starts Widgets, Inc. by issuing shares of capital stock for $7,500 on January 1, 20xx. The business elects to use the accrual basis of accounting.

B. Widgets, Inc. purchases equipment costing $6,000. A cash down payment of $2,000 is made upon delivery of the equipment, and a note for $4,000 was signed for the remaining balance of the purchase price. No interest accrues and payments do not start until January 1, 20xy.

C. Widgets, Inc. purchases merchandise for resale, all on account, for $30,000 during the year.

D. Widgets Etc. sells merchandise costing $26,000 for $42,000. All sales are on account.

E. Widgets, Inc. collects $33,000 of cash on accounts (from customers) during the year.

F. Widgets, Inc. disburses cash of $25,000 to creditors (on account) during the year.

G. Widgets, Inc. disburses cash of $9,400 for miscellaneous operating expenses during the year.

H. Widgets, Inc. recognizes depreciation expense for the year of $2,600.

I. Widgets, Inc. declares and pays $1,200 of dividends during the year.

Widgets, Inc. Accounting Transactions Worksheet

WIDGETS, INC. T-ACCOUNTS WORKSHEET — ACCRUAL BASIS

BALANCE SHEET

ASSETS | LIABILITIES

Beginning Bal.
Ending Balance

Beginning Bal.
Transactions:
Ending Balance

Beginning Bal.
Transactions:
Ending Balance

Beginning Bal.
Transactions:
Ending Balance

Beginning Bal.
Transactions:
Ending Balance

Beginning Bal.
Transactions:
Ending Balance

Total Liabilities

OWNER'S EQUITY

Beginning Bal.
Transactions:
Ending Balance

Beginning Bal.
Transactions:
Ending Balance **

Owner's Equity

Total Assets

Total Liabs. & Owner's Eq.

INCOME STATEMENT

Transactions:
Cumulative Total

Transactions:
Cumulative Total

Transactions:
Cumulative Total

Transactions:
Cumulative Total

Transactions:
Cumulative Total

Net Income **

Section 2
Analyzing Business Financial Statements and Tax Returns

Income Statement Analysis

OBJECTIVES

After studying *Income Statement Analysis*, you will be able to—

- Explain the components of revenue and cost of goods sold
- Describe operating expenses and net profit analysis

INTRODUCTION

Financial analysis begins with obtaining and processing statements. The business banker applies technical and analytical skills to spread the statements in various ways to obtain a more precise understanding of the company's financial position and operations. In many cases, tax returns serve as the financial statements, but with the data arranged in a different format.

Regardless of the format, a key ingredient of financial analysis is the income statement (see Figure 6.1). Dissecting the income statement reveals the underlying structure and helps the business banker become familiar with the entries and what they reveal about a firm's financial performance. This chapter divides the income statement analysis into two parts. In Part 1, you will learn about analyzing sales and cost of goods sold. In Part 2, you will learn how to analyze operating expenses and net profit.

FIGURE 6.1 INCOME STATEMENT STRUCTURE

Account lines		Amount	Percentage of sales
Part 1	Gross sales		
	− discounts, allowances, and returns		
	= net sales		
	− cost of goods sold		
	= gross profit		
Part 2	− operating expenses		
	= operating profit		
	+ other income		
	− other expenses		
	− interest expense		
	= net profit before taxes		
	− taxes		
	= net profit after taxes		

Relationship to the Commercial Lending Decision Tree

In the textbook Introduction, we explored the Commercial Lending Decision Tree as a way to think about the stages and steps involved in the commercial lending process. Although these steps do not necessarily occur in a particular order, the Decision Tree places them in a likely sequence. As shown in the illustration in this textbook's Introduction, this process emphasizes early screening and qualifying steps, which were covered in Section 1 – Understanding Business Borrowers (Chapters 1–5).

In the early stage of the process, the lender also begins assessing the business's financial and nonfinancial qualifications to borrow from the bank. In Section 2, you will move into the analytical process that occurs after detailed financial statements and other data about the business and its owners (as likely guarantors) have been received. Specifically, you are entering Stage Two, as shown in the Commercial Lending Decision Tree illustration in this book's Introduction.

INCOME STATEMENT ANALYSIS—PART 1: SALES AND COST OF GOODS SOLD ANALYSIS

The income statement is a treasure chest of information for a business banker. As an integral part of a financial statement, the income statement reflects a firm's revenues from sales and its operating costs. In preparing income statements, businesses can use either accrual or cash accounting methods. With accrual accounting, revenues are matched with expenses over a stated period of time (usually 12 months). With cash-basis accounting, revenue is recognized when received, and expenses are recorded when paid in cash. An income statement is also sometimes called a profit and loss (P&L) statement or earnings statement.

Income statements consist of revenues and expenses. When revenues exceed expenses, a business is profitable. If expenses exceed revenues, then business will have a net loss. Because income statements are a gauge of a firm's ability to convert its resources into profits, business bankers regard income statements as an important tool for evaluating a company's long-range profitability and cash flow. For most businesses, profits are the primary component of the cash flow available to repay creditors (principal and interest). Therefore, the analysis of a company's income statement is a major factor in a business banker's decision to extend credit.

Income statement analysis starts with examining the income, or revenue, which is at the top of the income statement. The figure below shows a typical income statement structure. Each income section has two main parts: revenues and expenses. The income statement normally begins with net sales, a figure that is derived by subtracting discounts, returns, and allowances from gross sales. Cost of goods sold appears directly under net sales and is deducted from revenue to calculate a company's gross profit. Cost of goods sold is the cost of producing or purchasing a product. In this section, you will learn about Part 1 of the income statement analysis—the sales and cost of goods sold (Figure 6.2).

FIGURE 6.2 INCOME STATEMENT STRUCTURE

Account lines		Amount	Percentage of sales
Part 1	Gross sales		
	− discounts, allowances, and returns		
	= net sales		
	− cost of goods sold		
	= gross profit		
Part 2	− operating expenses		
	= operating profit		
	+ other income		
	− other expenses		
	− interest expense		
	= net profit before taxes		
	− taxes		
	= net profit after taxes		

The Income Statement Structure and Preliminary Considerations

Before we examine sales and cost of goods sold, we need to review the importance of the entire income statement and how your work in Stage One of the Commercial Lending Decision Tree will help you in analyzing financial statements. In the first section of the textbook, you explored the basic types of businesses, such as wholesalers and retailers, and how their operating cycles were different. You also looked at cash cycles and other characteristics. You will apply this knowledge to income statement analysis throughout this chapter.

The income statement reveals the results of the company's operation and management. This usually is the first section of the financial statement to be analyzed, because, among other things, it directly or indirectly affects most of the components of the balance sheet. For example, businesses selling products on credit have accounts receivable on the balance sheet. If credit sales change, either in volume or in repayment terms offered to purchasers, so should accounts receivable.

The chart below (Figure 6.3) shows the typical income statement structure. The left side shows the account lines and the various additions and subtractions made in order to calculate the net profit or income. The right side shows the same items, but in the order usually found in a tax return.

FIGURE 6.3 INCOME STATEMENT STRUCTURE

Account Lines on Financial Statement	Account Lines on Tax Return
Gross sales	Gross sales
− discounts, allowances, and returns	− discounts, allowances, and returns
= net sales	= net sales
− cost of goods sold	− cost of goods sold
= gross profit	= gross profit
− operating expenses	+ other income
= operating profit	= total income
+ other income	− operating expenses
− other expenses	− other expenses
− interest expense	− interest expense
= net profit before taxes	= ordinary income* or taxable income**
− taxes	− taxes**
= net profit after taxes	= net profit after taxes

* Partnerships, LLCs, and S corporations
** C corporations

In both financial statement and tax returns, the income statement begins with net sales, which is derived by subtracting discounts, returns, and allowances from gross sales. Cost of goods sold is the cost of producing or purchasing a product, and varies somewhat by type of business. Subtracting cost of goods sold from net sales determines gross profit. Gross margin is gross profit expressed as a percentage of net sales.

Some costs are fixed or semivariable, and also controlled by the owner, such as lease costs. Other costs are variable, such as cost of goods sold. Operating expenses are more in the control of the business owner. These expenses include advertising, selling, salaries, and other expenses for the ongoing operation of the business. The relationship of fixed costs, total costs, and net sales is called operating leverage.

Operating income is calculated by subtracting total operating expenses from gross profit. If a company has an operating loss, then it may not be able to repay its loans. Other income and other expenses also must be considered. Some of these expenses may be extraordinary or nonrecurring. Notice that in the tax return format, other income is added to gross profit to determine total income. Other expenses and interest expense are included in the operating expenses category.

Finally, when applicable, taxes are calculated, and net profit after tax is determined. Reconciling net worth shows whether net profit was retained as a future source of funding for the business, or was distributed among its owners. Earnings retained in a business increase net worth, while money taken out as dividends decreases net worth.

An income statement may be called a *P&L statement*, an *earnings statement*, or an *operating statement*. Whatever the designation, it provides a summary of a firm's total revenues and expenses recognized in the generation of profit for a specific period. For comparative purposes, income statements reflect the normal operating cycle of a business. A financial statement covering an operating cycle of 12 months is a fiscal year statement. Tax returns also usually cover a 12-month period. A financial statement prepared for a period of less than 12 months (that is, semiannual, quarterly, or monthly) is called an *interim statement*.

How the Type of Business Affects the Structure

Income statement analysis is affected by the type of business. Service and agricultural businesses generally have little or no cost of goods sold. Components of the cost of goods sold are different for manufacturers, wholesalers, retailers, and construction businesses. The accounting method used for reporting revenue (accrual or cash basis) and for reporting inventory (LIFO, FIFO, or weighted average) ultimately affects various profit subtotals. The lender must understand and know the following major accounts of an income statement:

- Net sales
- Cost of goods sold
- Operating expenses
- Other income and other expense
- Interest expense
- Net profit/income

Preliminary Considerations

A feature of most income statement spreads (Figure 6.4) is to express each account as a percentage of net sales. As part of a comprehensive analysis, each account is further evaluated. The first step is to understand the company's business and some basics about its income statements by asking the following questions:

- How are the statements prepared?
- What operating strategy and objectives are employed?
- Under what conditions does the company operate?
- What methods are used to recognize revenue and expenses?

FIGURE 6.4 INCOME STATEMENT SPREAD: DRY SUPPLY

Income Statement ($ in 000s)	Review 20xx Amount	%	Review 20xy Amount	%	Review 20xz Amount	%
Net sales	$895	100.0	$937	100.0	$918	100.0
Cost of goods sold	645	72.1	667	71.2	631	68.7
Gross profit	250	27.9	270	28.8	287	31.3
Selling, gen. and admin. expense	157	17.5	173	18.5	180	19.6
Officer's compensation	36	4.0	31	3.3	28	3.1
Rent expenses	15	1.7	18	1.9	20	2.2
Bad debt expense	2	0.2	1	0.1	0	0.0
Profit-sharing expense	7	0.8	7	0.7	0	0.0
Depreciation expense	12	1.3	12	1.3	13	1.4
Total operating expenses	229	25.6	242	25.8	241	26.3
Operating income	21	2.3	28	3.0	46	5.0
Other income	0	0.0	0	0.0	0	0.0
Interest income	2	0.2	2	0.2	2	0.2
Rental income	3	0.3	3	0.3	3	0.3
Interest expense	6	0.7	7	0.7	11	1.2
Net profit before tax	20	2.2	26	2.8	40	4.4
Taxes	11	1.2	12	1.3	17	1.9
Net profit after tax	$ 9	1.0	$ 14	1.5	$ 23	2.5

Types of Businesses

Income statements reflect the different operating characteristics of agricultural, wholesaling, retailing, manufacturing, service, and construction businesses. For example, relative to other types of businesses, manufacturing and retailing companies realize a higher gross profit as a percentage of net sales. Because of substantial operating expenses, a greater gross profit margin typically is more necessary for a manufacturer or a retailer than for a wholesaler. Because the product cost is generally not marked up substantially, a wholesaler has a low gross profit. Furthermore, because it sells products faster, a wholesaler is in less danger of absorbing significant losses when a product becomes obsolete or loses consumer acceptance. Service and agricultural businesses often have no cost of goods sold, so gross profit margin and net sales are the same.

Many other differences between businesses appear on the income statement. Selling expenses are a large item on a retailer's income statement, whereas salaries and general and administrative expenses make up a significant part of a professional service company's operating budget. A business banker should be aware of the typical differences among businesses and industries, and consider the financial statements of a borrower within the proper context.

Management Objectives

Business operating strategies and objectives also shape income statements. If Dry Supply wanted to penetrate or capture a large share of a market, then it might reduce the selling price of its products without lowering costs. Over one or more years, this action likely would result in a decrease in net profits. Similarly, introducing a new product (such as a new cleaning powder) may increase selling expenses and temporarily depress the company's earnings. By understanding these considerations before analyzing an income statement, a business banker will be able to more accurately interpret trends.

Revenue Analysis

Many income statements start with net sales and do not show gross sales and deductions to get to net sales. An exception to this tendency is manufacturers. In any event, a lender should inquire about discounts, returns and allowances, if they are not shown on the income statement.

For agricultural, wholesaling, and retailing businesses, the first entry on the income statement is often net sales. For service businesses, the first entry is net sales or net revenues. For construction businesses, the first entry is contract revenues. Net sales, net revenues, and contract revenues all mean the same thing. Net sales are revenue that a business realizes from the products it sells or the services it renders. Every invoice or cash receipt issued represents a sale. When compiled and tabulated for a given period—a year for a fiscal statement or a shorter interval for an interim statement—gross sales are reported for that period. With the accrual method of accounting, sales do not necessarily reflect cash collected. Sales for manufacturers, wholesalers, service, and construction businesses generally are on credit. Agribusiness and retail sales are typically cash. A business banker should take into consideration the following factors when analyzing sales:

- Net sales
- Method of accounting for revenue and expenses
- Sales volume and price trends
- Sales mix
- Order-backlogs
- Large, nonrecurring sales
- Sales on extended terms or to marginal customers

Net Sales

Gross sales are a firm's total sales before subtracting deductions (discounts, allowances, and returns) to get to net sales because not all of the sales result in full payment.
- Discounts are price reductions offered in return for early payment of a sales invoice, to move out-of-date stock, to reward valuable customers, to encourage very large purchases, or even to promote a product.

- Allowances are amounts deducted from the total sale price when a shipment is made incorrectly.
- Returns are price reductions due to the return of the product for quality concerns or other reasons.

Example

Dry Supply offers customers a discount for paying invoices within 10 days of the billing date. When shipments are made incorrectly, customers receive credit on future bills (allowances) or have orders returned and bills canceled (returns). Some mistakes and returns are normal and acceptable. Too many adjustments, however, reflect on the quality of operations and could signal a management problem.

Figure 6.5 (below) shows Dry Supply's net sales calculation.

FIGURE 6.5 NET SALES CALCULATION: DRY SUPPLY ($ IN 000s)			
	20xx	20xy	20xz
Gross sales	$912	$954	$944
Less discounts	8	12	11
Less allowances	5	2	8
Less returns	4	3	7
Net sales	$895	$937	$918

With Dry Supply's customers receiving allowances and returns, it appears that shipments are not always prepared to order or the quality of the product may be a problem. However, in this case, allowances and returns are each less than 1 percent of sales and combined total about 1.6 percent. Based on net profit after tax margins of 1 percent to 2.5 percent, profits would almost double had there been no returns and allowances.

Method of Accounting for Revenues and Expenses

When the accrual method of accounting is used, revenues usually are recognized when products are delivered for payment or sold directly to the end user, or the service is provided, or in the case of construction, partially completed. The method of accruing revenues, however, may vary from statement to statement or industry to industry. It is important to differentiate between the accrual basis of accounting and the cash basis of accounting.

The accrual method (see Chapter 4) accounts for revenues when a sale is made and for expenses when an expense is incurred. This is called the *matching principle*. The cash method recognizes income and expense when cash is received or paid. For many businesses, the accrual method is a better measure of profitability over time and reveals more about management strategies and practices in the timing of purchases, sales, and expenses.

Sales Volume and Price Trends

A good indicator of a company's performance is the change in net sales level over several statements. By scanning an income statement spreadsheet from left to right, the dollar value in net sales may be readily noted and compared. Yet, as previously mentioned, numbers can be misleading. A consistent 3 percent to 6 percent increase in net sales may not be noteworthy when a competitor's net sales increased by 10 percent over the same period. Also, a 3 percent to 6 percent increase may be due primarily to inflation, rather than to an increase in the quantity of products sold or services rendered.

For example, Dry Supply's net sales over the past three years were the following:

Year	Sales
20xx	$895
20xy	$937
20xz	$918

The annual increase in net sales on both a numerical and percentage basis was the following:

Period	Growth	Percentage Growth
20xx–20xy	$42	4.7%
20xy–20xz	($19)	(2.0%)

Another way of looking at net sales is on a unit basis, because net sales are determined by volume and price. For instance, in the Dry Supply example, suppose that the $937,000 of revenues in 20xy was based on the sale of 18,019 pounds of liquid cleaner at about $52 per pound. In 20xz, revenues were $918,000. If the price of liquid cleaner had dropped to about $50 per pound, then the $19,000 decrease in revenues occurred despite selling more units. However, if the price of the cleaner increased to $54 per pound during 20xz, then net sales on a unit basis did not increase. The following table summarizes these possible changes. Breaking down net sales by units sold and price adds insight into the causes of an increase (or decrease) in net sales.

Year	Units and Price	Net Sales
20xy	18,019 × $52	$937,000
20xz	18,360 × $50	$918,000
20xz	17,000 × $54	$918,000

Businesses that sell numerous products, such as hardware stores, are often analyzed by looking at average dollar net sales and number of customers in each department. For example, if customers in a hardware store purchase more paint and paint supplies than household products, the retailer should have more inventories in the paint product department. When comparing net sales from one year to the next, another item to consider is whether the company added or closed any stores or offices, or whether they added or removed any products.

Sales Mix

Businesses often differentiate net sales by new accounts, product lines, sales territories, old accounts, and/or operating divisions. These breakdowns help a business banker focus on precise factors that influence net sales. If Dry Supply generates 70 percent of its revenues from selling dry-cleaning products and only 10 percent from selling laundry products, yet devotes equal time and other resources to selling both, a business banker might question the owner's managerial decision-making abilities (Figure 6.6). The net sales mix also may affect gross margin.

FIGURE 6.6 DRY SUPPLY SALES MIX ($ IN 000s)

		20xy		20xz
Net Sales				
Dry-Cleaning	15,000 units $43.33 per unit	$ 650	8,077 units $43.33 per unit	$ 350
Laundry Products	3,019 units $95.00 per unit	$ 287	5,979 units $95.00 per unit	$ 568
Total Net Sales		$ 937		$ 918
Cost of Goods Sold				
Dry-Cleaning	15,053 units $19.93 per unit	$ 300	8,077 units $19.93 per unit	$ 161
Laundry Products	3,030 units $47.52 per unit	$ 144	5,979 units $47.52 per unit	$ 284
Total Cost of Goods Sold		$ 444		$ 445
Percentage of Sales		47.4%		48.5%

Order Backlogs

Most customers can provide indicators of future net sales. Trends in order backlogs provide some insight into revenue growth and the capacity of a business to supply its product. If order backlogs are not special orders, the business banker might question why the customer does not routinely carry more of the products. With $150,000 in order backlogs, Dry Supply's revenue growth should remain strong for the next year.

Large, Nonrecurring Sales

A substantial jump in the level of net sales from one year to the next may indicate a one-time sale of an unusually costly product, an event unlikely to be repeated in the future. A business banker should make sure that all large, nonrecurring sales are identified and taken into account when reviewing sales trends. For example, if Dry Supply had a one-time nonrecurring order in 20xy for $200,000, then net sales would have decreased without this order.

Sales on Extended Terms or to Marginal Customers

To increase net sales, a business may relax normal credit criteria for some customers. For example, a business normally sells products on credit with payment due in 30 days, but in an effort to improve net sales it extends the payment period to 60 days. This practice ends up absorbing some of the company's working capital. In addition, the same business could increase net sales by selling products or providing services to customers that have a higher risk of nonpayment, such as new businesses. This increased credit risk would likely cause slowing collections of accounts receivable, also absorbing working capital. By examining the aged listing of accounts receivable and its trends, a business banker can determine if these practices exist.

Cost of Goods Sold

Cost of goods sold is the amount expensed to the income statement for the purchase and production of goods sold. Calculating cost of goods sold is different for manufacturers, wholesalers, retailers, and construction businesses (Figure 6.7).

- A manufacturer has three types of inventory: raw material, work-in-process, and finished goods. The first step is to determine all direct manufacturing costs over the course of the year: material costs, labor expense, factory overhead, and taxes. Work-in-process is then added to this number to arrive at the total cost of goods manufactured. Because some goods are unfinished at the end of the year and unsold inventory remains, these costs must be deducted to arrive at total cost of goods sold. Therefore, the cost of goods sold is the total of the costs directly related to the manufacturing and purchase of goods, plus any work-in-process inventory, less finished goods inventory.
- A wholesaler, retailer, or construction business buys products from one party and sells to another, or uses the products to construct something. Agricultural and service companies may not have significant costs of goods sold to calculate.

FIGURE 6.7 CALCULATIONS OF COST OF GOODS FOR BUSINESSES

Manufacturer	Wholesale/Retail/Construction	Service/Agriculture
Sales − Cost of goods sold = Gross profit − Operating expenses − Total operating expenses = Operating profit + Other income − Other expense − Interest expense = Net profit before tax	Sales − Cost of goods sold = Gross profit − Operating expenses − Total operating expenses = Operating profit + Other income − Other expense − Interest expense = Net profit before tax	Sales = Gross profit − Operating expenses − Total operating expenses = Operating profit + Other income − Other expense − Interest expense = Net profit before tax
Cost of goods sold calculations		
Beginning raw material + purchases − ending raw material = raw material used Beginning work-in-process + raw material used + labor + manufacturing overhead − ending work-in-process = cost of goods manufacturing Beginning finished goods + cost of goods manufacturing − ending inventory = cost of goods sold Beginning inventory + raw materials + labor costs + manufacturing overhead = cost of goods available for sale − work in process − closing inventory = cost of goods sold	Beginning raw material + purchases − ending raw material = cost of goods sold	Same as net sales unless the company has inventory, then same as wholesale, retail, or construction

When the cost of goods sold is deducted from net sales, the resulting amount is the gross profit, which is the amount of profit available to cover all other operating expenses. For analysis, the cost of goods sold and the gross profit as percentages of net sales are calculated. The percentage of gross profit to net sales is referred to as gross margin. For a business with net sales of $120,000, a cost of goods sold of $90,000 and a gross profit of $30,000, the cost of goods sold percentage is 75 percent and the gross margin is 25 percent. For every dollar generated by a sale of goods or services, 75 cents is the cost of producing, purchasing, or providing the goods or services, while 25 cents is the profit with which to pay all other operating expenses. With these considerations in mind, some areas of inquiry within the analysis of cost of goods sold are inventory valuation, product costs, pricing philosophy, and supplier relationships.

Inventory Valuation

Inventory is a key component in the cost of goods sold for all companies. Balance sheets show the dollar value of the inventory. A business banker must realize that this dollar value is an estimate based on the cost of a number of inventory items being purchased by the company over a period of time and having different prices because of various factors, including inflation. Therefore, it is important to remember that most companies use an estimate to identify the value of inventory on interim balance sheets.

Inventory is generally valued by one of two accounting methods—LIFO or FIFO—although another method, weighted-average cost, is increasing in use.

- LIFO (last-in, first-out) uses the most recent purchases first in when determining cost of goods sold. As such, ending inventory is valued assuming the earliest purchases remain in ending inventory. In times of inflation, the LIFO method results in a lower gross profit. LIFO, because it more closely matches current costs with current selling prices, is a more accurate gauge of profits during inflationary periods.
- FIFO (first-in, first-out) accounts for a firm's operations as if it will use first those items purchased earliest. Therefore, on the firm's financial statements, the cost of the items purchased most recently is assigned to ending inventory. During a period of rising prices, FIFO accounting overstates gross profit.

LIFO and FIFO inventory methods are simply accounting conventions and do not have to match the actual flow or usage of inventory in a business.

One way to visualize LIFO accounting is a *pile of sand* or *gravel*. Inventory is added to the top of the pile as it is purchased. As inventory is used, it is taken from the top of the pile. Over time, a layer of sand or gravel at the bottom of the pile may be untouched and rather old. These lower layers of ending inventory are at older costs. Still, the actual flow of inventory in a business may not match this theoretical pile, but the LIFO accounting method matches it.

One way to visualize FIFO accounting is a *pipeline*. Inventory is added at the back end of the pipeline and then emerges from the front end as it is used. Depending on the length of the pipeline, the inventory items used may have been purchased some time ago. However, the ending inventory sitting in the pipeline was purchased more recently. The actual flow of inventory in a business may not match this theoretical pipeline, but the FIFO accounting method matches it.

Changing the Inventory Method Used

If a business changes the way it values inventory, many income statement accounts may be significantly different before and after the change. Generally accepted accounting principles (GAAP) require the customer's accountant to disclose any change in inventory valuation in the footnotes to the financial statements. The inventory valuation method used has no relationship to the physical movement of inventory; however, it does affect reported profits and post-tax cash flow. Depending on the inventory valuation method used, inflation or rising product costs can have a differing impact on reported earnings. The time needed to complete the operating cycle also can influence the selection of the appropriate inventory valuation method.

A company may switch from FIFO to LIFO inventory valuation without Internal Revenue Service (IRS) approval or notification. A switch from LIFO to FIFO, however, requires IRS notification. Any gain realized from the switch must be amortized over twice the number of years the company used LIFO.

Reconciling LIFO to FIFO

If a firm uses LIFO, GAAP requires a footnote to the financial statements that attempts to reconcile inventory valued at LIFO for financial reporting purposes to the inventory's value if FIFO (replacement cost) had been used. This approach creates a LIFO reserve. The annual adjustment to the LIFO reserve is made at the end of the fiscal year. Interim financial statements are therefore distorted.

The LIFO reserve represents earnings that have been sheltered from taxes. Assuming that the inventory can be sold for replacement cost and income taxes are paid, the residual can be considered "hidden inventory profits." In a period of rising inventory prices, some companies suspend purchase or production and sell out of inventory. This "dipping into the LIFO reserve" effectively increases earnings on a temporary basis.

Inventory as a Deferred or Capitalized Cost

The cost of inventory, whether purchased or manufactured, is aggregated or capitalized on the balance sheet in inventory until sold. Inventory is therefore a deferred cost that will remain on the balance sheet until sold or expensed. This further reinforces the importance of having a clear understanding of the borrower's inventory management systems and of periodically inspecting the borrower's inventory.

To illustrate the impact inventory valuation has on ending inventory, cost of goods sold, gross profit, gross margin, and net profit, consider a simple example (Figure 6.8) in which inflation is at an extraordinarily high rate.

FIGURE 6.8 INVENTORY PURCHASES ILLUSTRATION			
Day	No. of Units	Unit Cost	Total Purchases
1	10,000	$1.00	$10,000
2	5,000	$1.50	$ 7,500
3	10,000	$2.00	$20,000
Total	25,000		$37,500

In this example, 10,000 units were sold at $4.00 per unit by the end of Day 3. Ending inventory is 15,000 units. Based on this data, the accounts on two income statements—one prepared using the LIFO method, the other using FIFO—are shown in the example. Figure 6.9 below shows how the choice of inventory valuation method will have a significant effect on the income statement.

FIGURE 6.9 LIFO AND FIFO INVENTORY VALUATION COMPARISON			
LIFO			**FIFO**
Sales (10,000 @ $4.00)	$40,000	Sales (10,000 @ $4.00)	$40,000
Opening inventory	$ 0	Opening inventory	$ 0
Purchases	$37,500	Purchases	$37,500
Cost of goods available for sale	$37,500	Cost of goods available for sale	$37,500
Less ending inventory (15,000 units)		Less ending inventory (15,000 units)	
10,000 units @ $1.00	($10,000)	5,000 units @ $1.50	($7,500)
5,000 units @ $1.50	(7,500)	10,000 units @ $2.00	(20,000)
Total ending inventory	($17,500)	Total ending inventory	(27,500)
Cost of goods sold	$20,000	Cost of goods sold	$10,000
Gross profit	$20,000	Gross profit	$30,000
Gross margin	50%	Gross margin	75%
Income taxes at 30%	$ 6,000	Income taxes at 30%	$ 9,000
Net profit after tax	$14,000	Net profit after tax	$21,000
Summary Comparison LIFO versus FIFO in Period of Rising Inventory Costs			
	LIFO		**FIFO**
Cost of goods sold	$20,000	Cost of goods sold	$10,000
Gross profit	$20,000	Gross profit	$30,000
Gross margin	50%	Gross margin	75%
Net profit after tax	$14,000	Net profit after tax	$21,000

Inventory Valuation—Weighted-average Cost Method

With bar codes, scanners, and other computerized inventory tracking, the weighted-average cost method is becoming more popular. Businesses with fluctuating inventory levels use weighted-average inventory accounting because it effectively combines the other two methods, thereby reducing the inventory holding gains of FIFO and limiting the gains in a LIFO windfall. The weighted-average unit cost (Figure 6.10) is calculated as cost of goods for sale (beginning inventory and net purchases) divided by units available for sale.

FIGURE 6.10 WEIGHTED-AVERAGE COST INVENTORY VALUATION EXAMPLE (COST OF GOODS FOR SALE ÷ UNITS AVAILABLE FOR SALE)		
Sales (10,000 units @ $4.00)		$40,000
Purchases	$37,500	
Less ending inventory—15,000 units @ $1.50 [($37,500÷25,000 = $1.50]	(22,500)	
Cost of goods sold		$15,000
Gross profit		$25,000
Gross margin		62.5%

The weighted-average cost method shows results about halfway between the LIFO and FIFO methods.

Figure 6.11 below compares the weighted-average cost inventory valuation methodwith LIFO and FIFO.

FIGURE 6.11 INVENTORY VALUATION COMPARISON: WEIGHTED-AVE. COST, LIFO, FIFO			
	Weighted-ave. Cost	LIFO	FIFO
Sales (10,000 x 4.00)	$40.000	$40.000	$40.000
Purchases	$37,500	$37,500	$37,500
Less ending inventory	*22,500	**17,500	***27,500
Cost of goods sold	$15,000	$20,000	$10,000
Gross profit	$25,000	$20,000	$30,000
Gross margin	62.5%	50.0%	75.0%
* 15,000 units @ $1.50 [(37,500÷25,000) = $1.50] ** 10,000 units @ $1.00 + 5,000 @ $1.50 *** 5,000 units @ $1.50 + 10,000 @ $2.00			

Inventory Valuation—Retail Method

Another way to value inventory is the retail method, which retailers use to estimate the ending inventory cost. The retailer can take a physical inventory at retail prices (or estimate ending inventory), then convert the ending inventory from retail price to cost using the cost-to-retail ratio. This method eliminates the need to review original invoices or other documents to determine the original cost of each inventory item. The retail method can be used with any of the cost-flow assumptions discussed earlier—FIFO, LIFO, or weighted-average cost. The business banker should understand which method is being used because the valuation method affects net profit and the inventory balance sheet (and collateral) value.

Gross Profit

Once net sales and cost of goods sold have been calculated, it is easy to determine the gross profit, which is the difference between the two. Gross profit usually reflects the type of industry in which the company operates. Dry Supply's gross profit for the following three years was as follows (Figure 6.12):

- 20xx = $250,000
- 20xy = $270,000
- 20xz = $287,000

FIGURE 6.12 DRY SUPPLY GROSS PROFIT ($ IN 000s)						
	20xx		20xy		20xz	
Net sales	$895	100.0%	$937	100.0%	$918	100.0%
Less: cost of goods sold	645	72.1%	667	72.1%	631	68.7%
Gross profit	$250	27.9%	$270	28.8%	$287	31.3%

Dry Supply's cost of goods sold were 72.1 percent, 71.2 percent, and 68.7 percent of net sales in 20xx, 20xy, and 20xz, respectively. Although it appears somewhat consistent, the 3.4 percent decrease over the two-year period translated into additional profits of $31,212 in 20xz compared with 20xx ($918,000 x 0.034).

The following are questions a business banker might ask:
- Were prices increased?
- Did the product mix change?
- What changes are expected to occur in subsequent year(s)?

The answers to these questions would reveal additional information about the company's operations. For example, if Dry Supply had increased sales prices by 5 percent in 20xz, then its gross margin would have actually declined by about 1.6 percent. This could have been caused by a change in the product mix, or product costs that increased by more than 5 percent.

Gross Margin Trends

A final step in analyzing sales and cost of goods sold is investigating changes in gross margin levels. Sharp changes should be explained. For example, deteriorating margins indicate purchasing difficulties, manufacturing or service inefficiencies, pricing issues, or inventory accumulation. Also, acceptable gross margin levels vary among industries. So, in order to assess the sufficiency of margins, a business banker should compare them with other businesses in the particular market or industry. Gross margin trends usually are compared best as percentage trends and not as dollar trends.

In fact, when analyzing cost of goods sold, gross profits, and operating expenses, it is helpful to think of them as percentages of net sales and not actual dollars. For example, the gross margin for Dry Supply for 20xy was 28.8 percent of net sales. A change of 1 percent would result in $9,370 of extra or lost income (1 percent of $937,000). Because the gross margin increased 2.5 percent from 20xy to 20xz, this resulted in increased gross profit over 20xy of $22,950 (0.025 x $918,000).

To summarize, the income statement is a key component of financial analysis. You learned the basic structure of the income statement along with some preliminary considerations you need to understand before spreading a company's income statement. You also learned about the factors that need to be considered when analyzing sales and how to determine the cost of goods sold for various business types. You can now define the three common types of inventory valuation, which is important because the valuation method affects net profit and the inventory balance sheet (and collateral) value. You have gained a better understanding of the gross profit calculation and how to investigate changes in the gross margin levels by looking at market or industry trends.

INCOME STATEMENT ANALYSIS—PART 2: OPERATING EXPENSE AND NET PROFIT ANALYSIS

After you have analyzed the revenues shown on the income statement, the next step is to analyze the corresponding expenses incurred. You should always examine the expenses with the two following objectives in mind:

- To determine whether any expenses are excessive

- To identify trends over time by comparing changes in sales to changes in expenses

Once you identify changes, you can seek explanations for them.

In this section, you will learn about Part 2 of the income statement analysis—the operating expense and net profit analysis (Figure 6.13).

FIGURE 6.13 INCOME STATEMENT STRUCTURE

Account lines		Amount	Percentage of sales
Part 1	Gross sales		
	− discounts, allowances, and returns		
	= net sales		
	− cost of goods sold		
	= gross profit		
Part 2	− operating expenses		
	= operating profit		
	+ other income		
	− other expenses		
	− interest expense		
	= net profit before taxes		
	− taxes		
	= net profit after taxes		

Other than the costs incurred in purchasing inventory and direct manufacturing expenses previously discussed, operating expenses are those incurred by a business in the normal course of conducting its operations. These expenses are often categorized as selling, general, and administrative expenses (S, G & A). This category includes everything from salaries of office staff to postage stamps. For some industries, this can be the largest category of expenses on the income statement.

Operating Expense Analysis

Operating expenses (selling, general, and administrative expenses) represent costs not directly related to the production of goods and services. Wages paid to laborers to ship products, for example, are usually an expense allocated to cost of goods sold, while salaries paid to the office manager of Dry Supply are an operating expense. Usually, the customer can supply a detailed breakdown of operating expenses, including salaries by type of personnel, insurance premiums, repairs and maintenance, utilities, and automobile, entertainment, profit-sharing, legal, accounting, advertising, and postage costs.

The owner often has more control over operating expenses than cost of goods sold. For example, the owner can decide how much to pay administrative employees, whether to lease or own the location, how much to pay himself or herself, and if the company should have an employee retirement plan. These expenses reflect management decisions that provide some insight into management's style and ability to adjust to change (Figure 6.14).

FIGURE 6.14 DRY SUPPLY OPERATING EXPENSE TRENDS ($ IN 000s)						
	20xx		20xy		20xz	
Net sales	$895	100.0%	$937	100.0%	$918	100.0%
Gross profit	$250	27.9%	$270	28.8%	$287	31.3%
Operating expenses (selling, general, and administrative costs)	$157	17.5%	$173	18.5%	$180	19.6%
Officers compensation	36	4.0%	31	3.3%	28	3.1%
Rent expense	15	1.7%	18	1.9%	20	2.2%
Bad debt expense	2	0.2%	1	0.1%	0	0.0%
Profit-sharing	7	0.8%	7	0.7%	0	0.0%
Depreciation	12	1.3%	112	1.3%	13	1.4%
Total operating expenses	$229	25.6%	$242	25.8%	$241	26.3%
Operating income	$ 21	2.3%	$ 28	3.0%	$ 46	5.0%

Depreciation can be a significant, non-cash expense for many businesses, especially manufacturers and retailers that have significant investments in fixed assets. Except for land, fixed assets are assumed to lose their economic value over their estimated useful or productive lives. For purposes of valuing assets on financial statements and tax returns, both GAAP and the IRS require businesses to recognize depreciation expense within the income statement. The accumulated depreciation expense, over time, is collected into an asset account as a reduction to the fixed asset values.

The following are accounting issues for depreciating fixed assets:
- Costs at which the assets are recorded on the balance sheet
- Amortization period at which the cost should be allocated to future periods
- Salvage value of the asset

As with inventory, businesses can use several methods to depreciate fixed assets in financial statements. These include straight-line and double-declining balance. Additional methods that are considered **accelerated** (depreciate the asset faster) are available for use in tax returns.

Small Businesses Benefit from Accelerated Depreciation and Section 179 Deduction

Typically, if property for business has a useful life of more than one year, the cost must be depreciated across several tax years with a portion of the cost deducted each year. But there are ways to accelerate the depreciation and even receive these income tax benefits in the year of purchase.

For acceleration of depreciation, the tax code allows the Modified Accelerated Cost Recovery System (MACRS) approach, where equipment purchases made near the end of a quarter or year can be depreciated as if in place for the entire period.

Electing Section 179 allows immediate write-off, in the year of purchase, of qualifying equipment purchases. (See IRS Publication Section 946 for details of both MACRS and Section 179.)

Starting with tax year 2002, the previous and long-standing Investment Tax Credit of $25,000 for small business equipment purchases was expanded by Congress to $100,000 and indexed to inflation. By tax year 2008, the write-off had increased to $125,000 and was doubled by Congress to $250,000. Again in tax year 2010 Congress doubled it again to $500,000. As a company's purchases of qualifying equipment begin to exceed $2,000,000 there is a dollar-for-dollar reduction in the deduction is allowed.

Business bankers also should examine Schedule M-1 of a business tax return to locate operating expenses recorded on the books of the business, but not deducted on the tax return and not included in the amounts shown in the tax return's income statement that is usually the first page. Examples include depreciation, charitable contributions, and travel and entertainment. If material, these amounts shown on Schedule M-1 should be added to the amounts shown on the first page of the tax return.

Operating Income

To calculate operating income (loss), subtract total operating expenses from gross profit. A loss occurs if the total operating expenses exceed the gross profit. As shown in the example, in 20xz, Dry Supply's gross profit was $287,000 (31.3 percent of net sales), total operating expense was $241,000 (26.3 percent of net sales), and operating income was $46,000 (5 percent of net sales). This calculation excludes other income, other expenses, and interest expenses, which usually are shown after operating income or operating profit on a financial statement. However, in business tax returns, other income is included with gross profit to derive "total income." Similarly, other expenses and interest expenses are included in tax returns with operating expenses.

Operating Leverage

The control a business has over its costs is in part determined by the nature of those costs. Changes in volume affect each type of cost in a different way.

- Fixed costs are generally defined as selling, general, and administrative expenses, as well as other operating expenses. Business owners may collectively call these expenses "overhead." These costs are considered fixed or semivariable because once they are established, the business needs to pay them. For example, a business owner can decide whether to buy or lease a building, thus affecting rent expense. Once the lease is signed or the mortgage taken out, the monthly payment becomes fixed for the term of the lease or mortgage. Advertising and other expenses also are fixed or semivariable costs controlled by the owner. Another way to think of fixed costs is that they do not automatically adjust as sales increase or decrease. Therefore, some expenses within cost of goods sold can have fixed or semivariable characteristics.
- Variable costs are generally the cost of goods sold, since the owner does not need to purchase additional products if sales do not materialize. Because the cost of goods varies by the cost of each product sold, cost of goods also varies due to sales mix. Another way to think of variable costs is that they tend to automatically adjust as sales increase or decrease. Therefore, some costs within operating expenses can have variable characteristics.

Operating leverage describes the relationship among fixed costs, total costs, and net sales. The higher the percentage of fixed costs to total costs, then the higher the operating leverage. Insufficient net sales volume coupled with high operating leverage can affect gross profit and net profit margins by increasing sensitivity to economic changes, resulting in greater volatility of earnings, uncertainty, and risk. In such situations, profits or losses fluctuate disproportionately to changes in volume. As the net sales volume increases, fixed costs are spread across more units, thereby lowering per-unit costs and improving gross margin. Figure 6.15 below demonstrates the effect of operating leverage on profitability. Once fixed costs are covered, the incremental per-unit contribution to fixed costs is added to net profit, even if variable costs increase and remain the same percentage of net sales.

FIGURE 6.15 OPERATING LEVERAGE EXAMPLES ($ IN 000s)

Net sales	$1,000	100%	$2,000	100%	$4,000	100%
Fixed costs	$1,000	100%	$1,000	50%	$1,000	25%
Gross profit	$ 0	0%	$1,000	50%	$3,000	75%
Variable costs	$ 250	25%	$ 500	25%	$1,000	25%
Net profit	($ 250)	(25%)	$ 500	25%	$2,000	50%

Industries with high operating leverage, such as agricultural businesses, are more susceptible to changes in the economy and have more volatile earnings than those with low operating leverage. High operating leverage, therefore, introduces increased uncertainty and risk into a loan. The operating expenses increase because of the increased depreciation expense for the machinery. Fixed asset additions tend to occur in stair-steps. Initially, gross and net margins are reduced, reflecting increased operating leverage. Figure 6.16 shows how margins improve as sales expand over time.

FIGURE 6.16 OPERATING LEVERAGE AND FIXED ASSETS EXAMPLE*

	Year 0		Year 1		Year 2	
Net sales	$300,000	100%	$330,000	100%	$360,000	100%
Cost of goods sold	225,000	75%	247,500	75%	270,000	75%
Gross profit margin	$ 75,000	25%	$ 82,500	25%	$ 90,000	25%
Operating expense	45,000	15%	49,500	15%	54,000	15%
Depreciation	15,000	5%	33,000	10%	33,000	9%
Operating profit	$ 15,000	5%	$ 0	5%	$ 3,000	1%

*Assumptions: Company has completed Year 0. Machines purchased in Year 1 for $90,000 to be depreciated over 5 years with no salvage value using straight-line depreciation.

Another way of measuring whether costs are reasonable is to calculate cost of goods sold and operating expenses as a percentage of net sales and compare the results to a similar company or to the industry average. For example, if officer salaries, as a percentage of net sales, generally average 10 percent to 15 percent for a closely held business, then a 30-percent figure may indicate owners are generously compensating themselves and perhaps others at the expense of the firm's long-term profitability.

As shown page 160, Dry Supply's income statement analysis reveals that operating expenses were 25.6 percent, 25.8 percent, and 26.3 percent of net sales for 20xx, 20xy and 20xz, respectively. The 0.7 percent increase in operating expenses from 20xx to 20xz, as a percentage of net sales, decreased profits by $6,426 ($918,000 x 0.007). The increase in operating expenses as a percentage of net sales is partially caused by decreased sales—when net sales decrease and operating expenses remain the same (in dollar terms), the percentage of operating expenses to net sales increases.

Other Income and Expense Analysis

Income and expenses that occur outside normal business operations are listed in the other income and other expense accounts on the income statement. Other income and other expenses also may be referred to as *extraordinary recurring* and *nonrecurring income* or *expense*. Possible sources of other income are gains on the sale of fixed assets, plus interest income, dividend income, and rental income from leasing excess facilities and equipment to other parties. Other expenses include losses on the sale of fixed assets, losses on the sale of investments or discontinued operations, and interest expense.

Some companies have income sources in addition to sales and expenses other than those included in cost of goods sold or operating expenses. After evaluating the operating profit or loss of a business, a lender should look at these income and expense items that lie outside of the business' normal operations. This enables the business banker to determine if these items significantly affect the overall net profit or loss of the business, and whether or not they are consistently recurring items.

Other Income

Other income is income generated outside the normal operating activities of the business. This income does not result from sales of the firm's products or services, but from other, unrelated activities. Some businesses have a dependable source of other income that should be analyzed as recurring income. Other income that is nonrecurring is often labeled *extraordinary income*. Typical sources of other income include the following:

- **Rental income**—It is often generated from excess building facilities or equipment. Renting or leasing excess capacity without interrupting operational efficiency is a prudent action. However, the lender needs to consider whether the income will continue or if the company will soon need to use the space or equipment and, thereby, halt this income source.
- **Interest income**—It can be generated from excess cash placed in bank accounts or other investments, or perhaps from a loan to another business. If such investments recur, the level of market interest rates will affect the level of income generated over time.
- **Gain on sale of fixed assets**—A business can generate income by selling its excess fixed assets at a profit. For instance, after upgrading its fixed assets with more efficient equipment, a company may want to sell its used equipment. A gain results when the sale price exceeds the net book value (asset's cost less accumulated depreciation) of the asset sold.
- **Dividend income**—Businesses may own stock in related operating companies or in publicly traded companies. Any dividends received constitute a source of non-operating income. Because dividends are based on the profitability of another company, without first analyzing the other company, a business banker should not assume that the dividends constitute a dependable source of future income. A lender also might investigate the reason for the investment. Was it a temporary use of excess funds, some form of speculation, or to gain a business advantage?
- **Extraordinary recurring and nonrecurring income**—If other income constitutes a significant portion of the total income of a company, then the business

banker determines the sources of the other income and whether they can be relied on in the future. For example, Dry Supply rents extra office space to another business for $3,000 per year. Alternatively, income from interest is usually recurring, although the amount may fluctuate depending on market interest rates. Dry Supply earns $2,000 in interest income each year. Besides helping a business banker anticipate future profitability, information about other income can present a portrait of a company's operations. An increase in income from renting excess facilities or equipment or by selling fixed assets, for example, may indicate that a business has excess capacity.

Business bankers also should examine Schedule M-1 of a business tax return to locate other income that is recorded on the books of the business but not included in the amounts shown in the tax return's income statement that is usually the first page. An example of tax-exempt income is interest income on certain state and municipal bonds. If material, these amounts shown on Schedule M-1 should be added to the amount shown for *other income* on the first page of the tax return.

Note also that in business tax returns *other income* is included with gross profit to derive "total income."

Other Expenses

A business may have other expenses (also called non-operating expenses) as well as non-operating income. Similarly, these expenses arise outside the normal business operations and may be recurring or nonrecurring in nature. Typical sources of other expenses include the following:

- **Loss on sale of fixed assets**—If a business sells any of its fixed assets below book value, then the loss associated with the sale is recognized as a non-operating expense. When such losses show up on the income statement, a business banker needs to determine if additional losses are expected. Additional losses are more likely if the company has consistently underestimated depreciation on the used equipment by overestimating its useful life. If a sudden jump in technology has rendered just a few assets obsolete, then continued losses on the sale of fixed assets are unlikely.
- **Loss on discontinued operations**—It occurs when certain undertakings have not been as profitable as management would like, and the assets could be more efficiently used in some other area of the business. When it decides to discontinue an operation, a business usually establishes a reserve on the balance sheet to cover estimated losses related to liquidating the assets and contracts. The analytical challenge is to determine whether the business will face additional losses in the future on other undertakings—some that might not be within management's control.
- **Interest expense**—It is shown as a non-operating expense because not all companies borrow money or at least not the same amount at the same time. Because it is related to a discretionary source of funding, interest expense is listed separately from other expenses. The cost of borrowing money depends both on the company's overall level of borrowings and on whether debt is at fixed or floating rates. In the latter case, the market interest rate at any particular

time can have serious consequences. Therefore, depending on the company's borrowing requirements and interest rates, interest expense can fluctuate dramatically.

- **Extraordinary recurring and nonrecurring expenses**—Just as with other income, any significant other expenses should be identified as recurring or nonrecurring. Losses from selling fixed assets, from stock, or from discontinued operations do not occur regularly. Even so, the business banker should ask whether any future sale of assets is contemplated or whether any additional losses from discontinued operations will be forthcoming. Interest expense, which is a recurring expense, fluctuates along with market interest rates and the amount of company debt. In 20xy, Dry Supply's interest expense increased to $11,000. The company either used its credit line more or underlying interest rates increased.

Business bankers also should examine Schedule M-1 of a business tax return to locate *other expenses* that are recorded on the books of the business but not included in the amounts shown in the tax return's income statement that is usually the first page. Some of the expenses listed on Schedule M-1 should be included in the appropriate operating expense categories and will have been handled already. If material items remain that match the *other expenses* discussed in this reading, then these amounts should be added to the amount shown for *other expenses* on the first page of the tax return.

Analysis of Net Profit Before Tax and After Tax

Net Profit Before Tax

By adding other income and subtracting other expense from operating profit (or loss), the result is net profit before tax, net income before tax, or pretax profit. Accountants, customers, bankers, and investors often use the terms "net profit" and "net income" interchangeably. Because S corporations, LLCs, partnerships, and sole proprietorships are not taxed on the income statement, net profit is the same as net profit before tax and is labeled ordinary income.

Income Taxes

For C corporations, income taxes are the final entry on the income statement before reaching the bottom line. To anticipate the future tax rate of a business and its effect on profitability requires an understanding of business and personal tax issues. Many factors affect the amount of taxes reported on the income statement, and this amount does not necessarily match that cited on personal or corporate tax returns. Job credits, loss carryovers, different federal and state tax brackets, and varying state tax requirements all make it difficult to draw useful comparisons among businesses and to assess the ability of a company to manage its tax burden.

Net Profit After Tax

The quality and consistency of a company's earnings essentially determine its ability to repay debt. Tracing the trend in net profits for several years also provides some insight into the future profitability of a business. It is important to compare a firm's net profit record with those of similar businesses and with the industry as a whole. This comparison helps the business banker determine if a change reflects only that business, or if other factors, such as a booming economy, also played a role. A business that realized a 10 percent annual increase in net profits after tax, when the industry average over the same period was a 25 percent annual increase, made a comparatively poor showing.

Reconciliation of Net Worth

Many income statements continue beyond net profit to show how the business accumulated and used those profits. Profits are dispensed in one of the following two ways:
- Profits can remain in the business as retained earnings
- Profits can be paid out as distributions or dividends to its owners

The net worth reconciliation statement provides insight into management's objectives about retaining earnings and building equity. An increase in net worth may be a sign that a business is committed to future expansion through retained earnings. For a C corporation, the dividend payout and earnings retention policies should be compared to those of similar corporations.

As a formatting preference, the reconciliation of net worth can appear separately from the income statement. The reconciliation of net worth is required in a reviewed or audited financial statement by an outside accountant either as an extension of the income statement or as a separate item. As you learned in Chapter 5, a reconciliation of net worth can be excluded in a compiled (by an outside accountant) financial statement if its cover letter states that certain disclosures have been omitted. Interim and fiscal-year financial statements provided directly from the business usually exclude a reconciliation of net worth as well. Business tax returns provide a Schedule M-2 that reconciles net worth, and this schedule appears below the balance sheet, which is Schedule L in the tax returns.

In cases where the financial statement or tax return does not provide a reconciliation of net worth, lenders generally create their own as part of the statement spreading process. A key reason for doing this is to discover any distributions or dividends paid from the net profits of the period. Distributions and dividends are not otherwise disclosed in either the balance sheet or income statement.

> **Did You Know?**
>
> Net worth also may be referred to as *equity* or *capital*. Net worth is the difference between total assets and total liabilities.

Reconciling Net Worth

The first entry to reconcile net worth is beginning net worth. In a corporation or company, net worth primarily represents common stock, paid in capital and retained earnings. With a partnership or a sole proprietorship, net worth represents the equity investment of its owners.

In the accounts that follow beginning net worth, earnings retained in a business increase net worth; losses reduce it. Owner withdrawals (in partnerships, sole proprietorships, LLCs, and S corporations) decrease net worth as well as dividends (C corporations). In publicly traded corporations, dividends can help attract additional equity from investors seeking a high stock dividend return. These corporations must strike a balance between paying dividends (reducing net worth) and attracting investors (increasing net worth).

In determining the net profit after tax at year end, privately held companies strike a balance by varying what is paid into pension and profit-sharing plans and what is allocated to officer bonuses, salary increases, or other compensation. By increasing or lowering these expenses, net profit after tax and, therefore, additions to net worth can be held fairly constant each year. For example, in a year where sales and preliminary profits of a privately held business are much higher than previous years, if the owners decide to pay themselves a large, one-time bonus, then the result of this action would decrease net profit to earlier levels and, thus, hold net worth steady.

Retained Earnings

Retained earnings are not distributed to stockholders. Retained earnings are a part of the company's net worth. At the beginning of 20xx, Dry Supply's retained earnings were $57,000. All the income the company made for that year [$14,000] was kept in the company, resulting in retained earnings of $71,000 at year end. This number is then the company's retained earnings at the start of 20xy. Again, the income earned by Dry Supply during 20xy was kept in the company—leaving a balance of $94,000 in the company's retained earnings account at the end of 20xy (previous year's retained earnings balance of $71,000 plus current year's net profit of $23,000).

As the income statements are analyzed, Schippel addresses these and other questions. The right questions will help her "get behind" the numbers and better predict the company's future ability to repay debt.

Based on her analysis of Dry Supply's income statements, Schippel has drawn some preliminary conclusions about the company's strengths, weaknesses and uncertainties. Bearing in mind the formula for an acceptable credit risk, she has listed her observations in the following table:

Strengths	Weaknesses	Uncertainties
• Length of time in business • Established customer base • Cost of goods sold • Increasing profits • Retained earnings • Management	• Reaching maximum shipping capacity • Continued future customer growth • Lack of sales growth	• New customers' ability to pay • Fixed asset needs

In Income Statement Analysis – Part 2, you learned about the operating expenses that represent costs not directly related to the production of goods and services, and how to analyze this section of the income statement. You also learned how to identify other income and expenses that occur outside the normal business operations that may be referred to as extraordinary recurring and nonrecurring income or expense. You now know that analyzing the company's net profit before and after tax will help to determine its ability to repay debt and that the net worth reconciliation statement provides insight into management's objectives about retaining earnings and building equity.

SUMMARY

In the chapter, you learned that income statements are considered a gauge of a company's ability to convert its resources to cash flow. For this reason, these statements are important tools for evaluating a company's long-range profitability. You learned that the key component of financial analysis is the income statement. You are now able to explain and analyze the sales revenue section and cost of goods sold elements that make up the first part of the income statement. In addition, you learned how to analyze the second part of the income statement—the operating expenses and the net profit before and after tax—which provides insight into the company's style and ability to adjust to change, and management's objectives about retaining earnings and building equity. You also learned that there are formatting differences with how some accounts are shown in the income statement and in the first page of a business tax return.

QUESTIONS FOR DISCUSSION

1. Which two business types generally have little or no cost of goods sold?
2. What factors can influence the gross profit of a business?
3. What may be the causes of a deteriorating trend in the gross margin level of a business?
4. What information does the net worth reconciliation statement provide?

EXERCISE 1

Background

Dry Supply Case Study

Having covered key issues to address on the income statement, now look at an example of the analytical process, featuring Anne Schippel, the business banker. From previous interviews with the owners of Dry Supply, Schippel has learned that the wholesale company was founded in 1949 by the father, who sold it 20 years later to his daughters; they are the current owners and managers of the company. Four grandchildren also are employed by the company. In short, this is a family-run business and likely to remain so in the foreseeable future.

Dry Supply began as a wholesaler of powdered laundry products. Twenty years later, the operation changed its focus to dry-cleaning supplies, such as liquid cleaners, plastic bags, and metal hangers. The company continues in that capacity today. Historically, the company has had a very good operating and credit record, and a check on its dealings with suppliers and customers reveals no notable problems.

Having obtained this and other background information, Schippel prepares to analyze Dry Supply's income statements. Adhering to a consistent process, Schippel begins by first reviewing the statements presented by the customer, noting the overall quality and completeness of the data. Applicable information, taken from the statements, then is entered into a computer, which generates a standard spreadsheet. At Schippel's bank, all financial statements, regardless of the preparer, are analyzed by using a standard format. The bank has discovered that a key to effective analysis is consistency in both the presentation and evaluation of information.

With spreadsheet in hand, Schippel begins a comprehensive financial analysis of Dry Supply's income statements.

INCOME STATEMENT SPREAD: DRY SUPPLY

Income Statement ($ in 000s)	Review 20xx		Review 20xy		Review 20xz	
	Amount	%	Amount	%	Amount	%
Net sales	$895	100.0	$937	100.0	$918	100.0
Cost of goods sold	645	72.1	667	71.2	631	68.7
Gross profit	250	27.9	270	28.8	287	31.3
Selling, gen. and admin. expense	157	17.5	173	18.5	180	19.6
Officer's compensation	36	4.0	31	3.3	28	3.1
Rent expenses	15	1.7	18	1.9	20	2.2
Bad debt expense	2	0.2	1	0.1	0	0.0
Profit-sharing expense	7	0.8	7	0.7	0	0.0
Depreciation expense	12	1.3	12	1.3	13	1.4
Total operating expenses	229	25.6	242	25.8	241	26.3
Operating income	21	2.3	28	3.0	46	5.0
Other income	0	0.0	0	0.0	0	0.0
Interest income	2	0.2	2	0.2	2	0.2
Rental income	3	0.3	3	0.3	3	0.3
Interest expense	6	0.7	7	0.7	11	1.2
Net profit before tax	20	2.2	26	2.8	40	4.4
Taxes	11	1.2	12	1.3	17	1.9
Net profit after tax	$ 9	1.0	$ 14	1.5	$ 23	2.5

QUESTIONS FOR DISCUSSION

1. For the last three years, sales have shown a moderate increase from approximately $895,000 to $918,000. Sales have declined, however, during the most recent year. Schippel sees this decrease as more of a concern than the three-year increase: What are some questions Schippel should ask Dry Supply to help explain this sales decrease?

2. Dry Supply's cost of goods sold has decreased over the three-year period. What questions should Schippel develop to ask Dry Supply regarding the cost of goods sold?

3. Operating expenses increased from $157,000 to $180,000 in two years. What questions should Schippel ask about the operating expenses?

4. Overall, Dry Supply has been consistently profitable, with after-tax profits rising each year. What questions should Schippel ask Dry Supply about the growing profitability?

7

BALANCE SHEET ANALYSIS

OBJECTIVES

After studying *Balance Sheet Analysis,* you will be able to—

- Identify balance sheet considerations
- Describe the different types of assets—current, other, and noncurrent
- Explain the components involved in liability and equity analysis

INTRODUCTION

A balance sheet, also known as a *statement of financial condition*, is like a digital photograph of a point in time and shows a summary of a company's or individual's assets, liabilities, and equity on a given day. Just as the real world changes day by day, so does the financial picture presented in balance sheet accounts. Because the amount and mix of assets, liabilities, and equity change, a business banker should not assume the balance sheet picture is frozen in time.

Generally, a firm's balance sheet is prepared as of the close of business on the last day of a month, quarter, or year. Balance sheets reported in tax returns usually will be for the last day of the fiscal year of the business. During the balance sheet analysis process, the business banker notes unusual amounts, spots trends, draws comparisons with other balance sheets, and responds to the numbers with questions in an effort to fully understand the picture being presented.

Relationship to the Commercial Lending Decision Tree

In the Introduction to this textbook, you explored the Commercial Lending Decision Tree as a way to think about the stages and steps involved in the commercial lending process. Although these steps do not necessarily occur in a particular order, the Decision Tree places them in a likely sequence. As shown in the illustration in the Introduction, this process emphasizes early screening and qualifying steps, which was covered in Section 1. As you move into Section 2, you will begin making a detailed analysis of various financial information as shown in the Commercial Lending Decision Tree for Stage Two.

In Chapter 6, you explored business income statements. Chapter 7 begins with an overview of the business balance sheet and then details the balance sheet equation. The components of the balance sheet are defined and explained. Later in this section, you will learn various financial ratios and measures that help to assess the financial condition and trends of the business. In Chapter 9, you will develop and analyze a cash flow statement, and Chapters 10 and 11 will cover the UCA model along with cash budgets and pro forma statements.

BUSINESS BALANCE SHEET CONSIDERATIONS

Balance sheet analysis examines specific characteristics of a firm's financial performance. Before analyzing the balance sheets, considerations that should be made include knowing who prepared the sheets, when they were prepared, and the type of business and its industry. This information will help the lender understand the entries and formulate appropriate questions and investigations.

Key Considerations

To analyze business balance sheets effectively, a business banker must know the answers to the following questions:

- Who prepared the balance sheets?

    Business balance sheets may be prepared internally by a company controller or the business owner, or externally by an accountant. Although business bankers prefer external statements, the size of the firm may not warrant the time and expense for this level of detail and oversight. In many cases, the business banker will work from the balance sheet shown on Schedule L in the business tax return.

- When were they prepared?

    A retailer, for example, may carry an unusually large amount of inventory. To finance that inventory, the retailer may have a correspondingly large amount of short-term debt in the months preceding certain seasons. A balance sheet prepared just prior to a major selling season may be entirely different from one prepared after the season, when inventory and short-term debt are lower and cash is higher. To get a more complete picture of the firm's finances, a business banker usually examines several interim balance sheets.

- What type of business and industry is being reported?

    As you learned in Chapter 1, agricultural, manufacturing, wholesaling, retailing, service, and construction businesses differ significantly in their asset and liability structures. Most agricultural businesses and manufacturers carry a relatively large amount of fixed assets and a correspondingly large long-term debt to finance those assets. Most wholesalers carry high levels of accounts receivable and inventory. Because retailers sell a finished product for cash, they work with low levels of accounts receivable and high levels of inventory. Whereas service businesses, such as physicians, carry little inventory: their primary current assets are cash and accounts receivable. Other service entities, such as churches, have few accounts receivable and high fixed assets. Construction businesses carry inventory in the form of land held for development and fixed assets used to construct projects. Figure 7.1 illustrates key balance sheet accounts by industry type.

FIGURE 7.1 KEY BALANCE SHEET ACCOUNTS BY INDUSTRY TYPE					
AGRICULTURE BUSINESS	MANUFACTURER	WHOLESALER	RETAILER	SERVICE BUSINESS	CONSTRUCTION BUSINESS
Inventory	Accounts receivable	Accounts receivable	Inventory	Accounts receivable	Inventory
Fixed assets	Inventory	Inventory	Fixed assets	Fixed assets	Fixed assets
Short-term bank debt	Fixed assets	Fixed assets	Accounts payable	Short-term bank debt	Short-term bank debt
Long-term debt	Accounts payable	Accounts payable	Seasonal bank debt	Long-term debt	Long-term debt
	Long-term debt	Long-term debt			

- What business strategies and objectives are being reflected?

    Managerial policies and objectives also shape a company's balance sheet. A business with a conservative operating policy that emphasizes profits rather than growth generally has relatively strict accounts receivable and inventory controls, and limited debts. In its drive to grow and capture market share, a more aggressive company emphasizes sales growth, incurs more debt, and favors higher levels of accounts receivable and inventory.

Strategies and objectives can be a function of where the business is within a particular life cycle (see Chapter 3). For instance, the conservative operating policy discussed is likely to be displayed by a business in the mature phase of its life cycle. Conversely, the aggressive strategy is more likely to be displayed by a firm in its growth stage.

Balance Sheet Equation

Another consideration is the balance sheet equation. Because a balance sheet is a statement of a firm's financial position, it lists assets owned, liabilities owed, and equity invested as of a specific date. The following is the balance sheet equation:

$$\text{Assets (owned)} = \text{Liabilities (owed)} + \text{Equity (invested)}$$

This equation, a basic principle of accounting, applies to all balance sheets regardless of business type, complexity, or structure. Consider a business whose sole asset is one account receivable with a balance of $500,000, of which $400,000 is financed by a short-term bank loan. The remaining $100,000 represents the owner's equity. The following is a resulting balance sheet equation of this business:

$$\textit{Assets} = \textit{Liabilities} + \textit{Equity}$$
$$\text{or} \quad \textit{Accounts Receivable} = \textit{Short-Term Debt} + \textit{Owner's Equity}$$
$$\text{or} \quad \$500,000 = \$400,000 + \$100,000$$

In this section, you learned about the key considerations you need to know in order to analyze business balance sheets effectively. You also learned about the balance sheet equation—a basic principle of accounting that applies to all balance sheets regardless of business type, complexity, or structure.

In summary, the balance sheet equation is a constant; however, the components and amounts of assets, liabilities, and equity may change daily.

ASSET ANALYSIS

A balance sheet lists assets first, in order of liquidity, followed by liabilities listed in order of payment priority, and then equity (net worth). Assets are anything a business owns that has commercial, exchange, or monetary value. Businesses usually carry the assets at cost unless fair market value is lower. Assets may be property or claims against others (accounts receivable). They may be tangible (physical in character), such as land, buildings and equipment, or intangible, such as goodwill, copyrights, and patents.

Dry Supply is a wholesaler of dry-cleaning and laundry products, and its balance sheet will be used to demonstrate the concepts in this textbook. For Dry Supply, total assets equal total liabilities (debt) plus net worth. Figure 7.2 shows a summary of Dry Supply's balance sheet.

FIGURE 7.2 BALANCE SHEET SPREAD: DRY SUPPLY

Common-sized report ($ in $000s)	Review 12/31/20xx		Review 12/31/20xy		Review 12/31/20xz	
Assets	Amount	%	Amount	%	Amount	%
Cash	$ 3	1.2	$ 12	4.6	$ 22	8.1
Accounts receivable	114	46.9	118	45.4	117	43.3
Less: allowance for doubtful accounts	5	2.1	5	1.9	5	1.9
Net accounts receivable	109	44.9	113	43.5	112	41.5
Inventory	73	30.0	72	27.7	67	24.8
Total current assets	185	76.1	197	75.8	201	74.4
Furniture and fixtures	76	31.3	75	28.8	78	28.9
Leasehold improvements	1	0.4	1	0.4	0	0.0
Transportation equipment	53	21.8	70	26.9	85	31.5
Gross fixed assets	130	53.5	146	56.2	163	60.4
Less: Accum. depreciation	85	35.0	97	37.3	110	40.7
Net fixed assets	45	18.5	49	18.8	53	19.6
Cash-value life insurance	13	5.3	14	5.4	16	5.9
Total assets	$243	100.0	$260	100.0	$270	100.0
	Review 12/31/20xx		Review 12/31/20xy		Review 12/31/20xz	
Liabilities	Amount	%	Amount	%	Amount	%
Notes payable bank short-term	$81	33.3	$68	26.2	$59	21.8
Accounts payable—trade	42	17.3	46	17.7	31	11.5
Income taxes payable	5	2.1	6	2.3	7	2.6
Accrued bonuses	10	4.1	11	4.2	12	4.4
Total current liabilities	138	56.8	131	50.4	109	40.4
Subordinated debt officers	48	19.8	58	22.3	67	24.8
Total liabilities	186	76.5	189	72.7	176	65.2
Net worth						
Common stock	2	0.8	2	0.8	2	0.7
Retained earnings	55	22.6	69	26.5	92	34.1
Total net worth	57	23.5	71	27.3	94	34.8
Total liabilities and net worth	$243	100.0	$260	100.0	$270	100.0

Current Assets

Current assets are expected to convert to cash within 12 months or within the normal operating cycle of the business. A temporary investment in current assets, to be converted to cash within one year, usually is financed by short-term bank debt and accounts payable (suppliers). A permanent investment in current assets, which may be converted to cash but requires reinvestment to maintain the viable core business, is financed either with long-term debt or with the firm's net worth. Current assets are listed on the balance sheet in relation to their liquidity or convertibility to cash. Cash, which is the most liquid asset, is followed by marketable securities, accounts receivable (which must be collected to be converted to cash), and inventory (which, when sold, usually becomes cash or an account receivable that, when collected, is converted to cash).

Cash

The cash account includes petty cash a business keeps on hand to process transactions that cannot be paid by check or credit card. Most businesses hold operating cash in checking accounts, either non-interest-bearing or interest-bearing accounts.

Although generally cash holdings are small in comparison to other current assets, it is worthwhile to determine their availability as a source of funds for a business. Also, the level of cash provides some insight into the philosophy of the firm's management. For example, a conservatively managed company may keep a larger balance of cash on hand as a hedge against unforeseen developments. A lender should be careful and avoid making decisions based solely on high cash volumes because the cash may be used to fund operations when problems begin.

Because the level of available cash can vary from day to day, looking at the average cash balance in the company's bank accounts usually provides a more realistic figure. When assessing the cash available to a business, a lender discounts cash held at banks to satisfy a minimum requirement to avoid service charges or as a pledge against existing debt (sometimes called **compensating balances**).

> **Compensating balance**
> The balance that a customer must keep on deposit with a bank to ensure a credit line, to gain unlimited checking privileges, and to offset the bank's expenses in providing various operating services.

Most businesses need a minimum amount of cash to operate. This minimum varies by the type of business. With $22,000 on hand, Dry Supply's cash seems adequate for this type of business.

Marketable Securities

For most businesses, marketable securities represent temporary investments of excess funds in U.S. government or high-grade corporate stocks and bonds. For balance sheet purposes, investments in a closely held business, an affiliated business, and low-grade public companies are considered noncurrent assets and listed as *other securities*. Because an investment in a closely held business is not readily marketable, converting it to cash usually takes longer than one year. Similarly, most affiliated businesses are also closely held, with ownership that is not readily marketable and the tendency to maintain the affiliation for periods of time longer than one year. Low-grade stocks are generally those that are valued at less than $1 per share, trade at low volumes, or are listed on a regional or informal stock exchange.

To be listed as a current asset, the intent must be to sell or to cash in the marketable security as it matures in the coming year and then to use the proceeds in operations.

If the securities continue to be held, the business banker asks the following questions:

- Does the company truly have excess funds for investment?
- Are the securities subject to decline in value due to trading or interest rate risk?
- Is the company borrowing money from the bank to carry the securities?

Business tax returns list marketable securities in two categories—U.S. government obligations and tax-exempt securities. They are positioned below accounts receivable and inventory in the listing of assets on Schedule L in the tax return or balance sheet.

Accounts Receivable

Accounts receivable include amounts owed—as of the balance sheet date—from customers of the business resulting from extensions of credit for the products or services. The account debtor is the party responsible for paying the accounts receivable. Because they take time to collect (usually 30 to 90 days) and because they may never be collected, accounts receivable are considered less liquid than cash and marketable securities. For accounting purposes, *trade accounts receivable* are created by a business when credit is granted for selling a product or rendering a service only. Credit extended to officers, employees, affiliates, or for the sale of other assets is considered *other receivables* and should be listed as a noncurrent asset on the balance sheet.

In addition to being a less liquid form of current assets than cash and marketable securities, accounts receivable are also riskier since they must be collected before cash is available to repay debts. Further, the size of this balance sheet account, as well as the corresponding credit quality, is of great interest to a business banker because accounts receivable often are used as collateral for bank loans.

The size of accounts receivable is a function of sales growth and credit terms the business offers. If accounts receivable have increased rapidly, a business banker looks first at the income statement to determine whether there has been a corresponding increase in sales. If not, then the increase may be attributable to a liberalization of credit terms or the lack of good collection efforts. If the borrower is relying on the collection of these receivables to repay bank debt, then an increase in the outstanding receivables without a corresponding increase in sales poses a greater risk of delayed repayment or even non-repayment of bank debt.

Business tax returns include trade notes receivable along with accounts receivable as listed in the balance sheet. If the business maintains an *allowance for bad debts* (discussed later), then this amount is subtracted from accounts receivable on the tax return balance sheet.

For Dry Supply, the company's accounts receivable and sales have remained level. Apparently, new and existing customers are offered similar terms.

Figure 7.3 shows the income statement for spread Dry Supply. Sales have been fairly consistent at about $900,000 for the three years shown. Accounts receivable show a similar pattern over the three years shown.

FIGURE 7.3 INCOME STATEMENT SPREAD: DRY SUPPLY

Income Statement ($ in 000s)	Review 20xx Amount	%	Review 20xy Amount	%	Review 20xz Amount	%
Net sales	$895	100.0	$937	100.0	$918	100.0
Cost of goods sold	645	72.1	667	71.2	631	68.7
Gross profit	250	27.9	270	28.8	287	31.3
Selling, gen. and admin. expense	157	17.5	173	18.5	180	19.6
Officer's compensation	36	4.0	31	3.3	28	3.1
Rent expenses	15	1.7	18	1.9	20	2.2
Bad debt expense	2	0.2	1	0.1	0	0.0
Profit-sharing expense	7	0.8	7	0.7	0	0.0
Depreciation expense	12	1.3	12	1.3	13	1.4
Total operating expenses	229	25.6	242	25.8	241	26.3
Operating income	21	2.3	28	3.0	46	5.0
Other income	0	0.0	0	0.0	0	0.0
Interest income	2	0.2	2	0.2	2	0.2
Rental income	3	0.3	3	0.3	3	0.3
Interest expense	6	0.7	7	0.7	11	1.2
Net profit before tax	20	2.2	26	2.8	40	4.4
Taxes	11	1.2	12	1.3	17	1.9
Net profit after tax	$ 9	1.0	$ 14	1.5	$ 23	2.5

Accounts Receivable: Aged Listings and Concentrations

An aged listing of accounts receivable (often called an *aging* or *ageing*) is simply a list of the customers to whom the company sells, the amount owed by each, and the length of time the amount has been outstanding. This listing helps identify older and past-due receivables, plus any concentrations.

When reviewing an aged listing of accounts receivable, lenders must know whether the list was prepared from the invoice issuance date or from the due date. The preferred format is from the invoice date, so if 30-day terms are offered to customers, then accounts are not past due until shown in the "31–60 day" column, which follows a "1–30 day" column. If aged from due date, those same accounts are past due if shown in the "1–30 day" column, which follows a "current" column. The aged listing also should include the customer address, phone number, and contact person—information needed to facilitate collection in a liquidation situation.

A primary consideration is the overall trend in amounts in the different aged columns. If the proportions of accounts in the older columns are increasing, then the overall age of the receivables is getting older. The older the receivables, the less likely they will be paid. Further, accounts that are severely past due (usually 90 days past due) may never be collected. For such delinquent accounts, many lenders discount the value of any receivables generated from more recent sales. This exclusion is called a *cross-aging*.

A business banker also must be sensitive to concentrations, generally defined as individual customer receivables exceeding 20 to 25 percent of the total receivables. Both concentrations and relative age of receivables influence credit risk. In most situations, the more diversified the customer base of a business, the less likely a few defaults will severely affect the ability of the business to generate cash.

A high concentration in accounts receivable makes the business economically dependent on those concentrations. If the business loses a large customer, then the effect is felt more deeply in the income statement and the sales volume may be more difficult to replace with multiple customers. With some businesses, such concentrations may be hard to avoid—or they may even be a strategic decision by management. The business banker should assess the scope of concentrations and the relative risk involved.

Another risk is dealing with a large account where invoices remain unpaid or are paid late. A few larger accounts generally pose more risk, compared to a larger base of small accounts. Smaller accounts are not always preferable if any resulting unpaid accounts are so small that they do not justify the costs to collect them. Also, smaller firms with smaller accounts may have more credit risk than larger firms with larger accounts.

In analyzing a company's accounts receivable, a business banker looks beyond the mere numbers involved and considers the following key characteristics of the customers:

- Credit quality
- Length of relationship
- Size of relationship
- Adherence to payment terms

Beyond the risk of concentrations and relative age of accounts receivable, a lender should inquire about any written or unwritten agreements about those accounts. For example, if the owners of a retail furniture store agree to supply their external accountant with office desks and chairs in exchange for services, then the payment of the receivables is not collected as cash but rather as the value of work done (a form of bartering). Where such agreements exist, accounts receivable may be offset by entries to trade payables. This example demonstrates that the amount of receivables does not always represent cash to be collected.

Figure 7.4 shows an *abbreviated listing* of the accounts receivable for Dry Supply at the end of 20xz. About 90 percent of Dry Supply's receivables are 30 days old or less, and the accounts shown appear to be paying in a timely manner, since they have few invoices older than 60 days. Only 2 percent of all accounts were seriously delinquent. Assuming that its credit terms are 30 days, Dry Supply's accounts receivable appear to be of a good quality. Furthermore, with access to the entire list, you can determine if there are any concentrations of receivables. Even without the entire list, problem or delinquent accounts are small and pose little risk. For the one account shown that is over

FIGURE 7.4 ABBREVIATED ACCOUNTS RECEIVABLE AGED LISTING FOR DRY SUPPLY AS OF DECEMBER 31, 20xz (FROM INVOICE DATE)

Customer	0–30 days	31–60 days	61–90 days	Over 90 days
ABC Cleaners	$ 4	$ 6		
Anytown Quick Clean				$ 1
Better Cleaners		$ 1	$ 1	
Cleaners R Us	$ 8	$ 1		
. . . .	. . . .	. . . .	. . . .	. . . .
. . . .	. . . .	. . . .	. . . .	. . . .
. . . .	. . . .	. . . .	. . . .	. . . .
Yours Next	$ 3			
Total	$105	$ 8	$ 2	$ 2

90 days past invoice issue date, Dry Supply appears to have not been making current sales until the delinquency is resolved. Or, it could be that current sales to Anytown Quick Clean have been paid and an older sale is under dispute.

Allowance for Doubtful Accounts

Businesses have two options for handling accounts that are determined to be uncollectible:
- Direct write-off—Uncollected receivables are recognized as a bad debt expense on the income statement. Sales that occurred in a prior period may not be written off until a subsequent year, causing a potential overstatement of profits in the earlier year and understatement in the later year. Also, earnings can be more volatile if large amounts of write-offs occur at the same time, followed by periods of fewer write-offs.
- Establish an allowance for doubtful accounts—To reduce earnings volatility (potential overstatements and understatements of profits), many businesses using the accrual method of accounting will establish an allowance for doubtful accounts, where the amount of the bad debt expense to the income statement usually is determined by considering the historical losses and the quality of existing accounts receivable. The bad debt expense is actually a provision for bad debts that is added to the allowance account. Then, as accounts are deemed uncollectible, they are charged off and the reserve is decreased.

The amount of write-offs (net of recoveries) is calculated in the following way:
Previous year-end balance, allowance for doubtful accounts
+ *current year bad debt expense [provision]*
− *current year-end balance, allowance for doubtful accounts*
= *net charge-offs of uncollectible accounts receivable*

Whether the business uses direct write-offs or an allowance, the percentage of charge-offs each year help to assess not only the quality of the customer base of a business but also the effectiveness of credit and collection procedures. For 20xz, Dry Supply has no current year bad debt expense ($0), and its current year allowance for bad debt is the same as the previous year-end ($5,000). This results in no charge-offs of uncollectible accounts receivable during 20xz.

Inventory

Inventory consists of merchandise purchased for resale, or finished goods manufactured and held for sale, together with related raw materials and work-in-process. In general, inventory is intended for internal consumption or sale. Raw materials, work-in-process, and finished goods are the three basic components of inventory. If the financial statement or tax return does not provide a breakout of these components, then the business banker should get this information from the customer. In addition, the business banker needs to know the **inventory valuation method used**. Depending on the method used, inflation or rising product costs can have a differing impact on reported earnings.

Because businesses need liquidity, they often avoid tying up cash by holding excess inventory. In particular, if bank financing is required, then holding onto inventory during periods of high interest rates can be expensive. However, if management is concerned about the ongoing availability of raw materials or products, then they may decide to purchase large quantities of inventory.

> **Inventory Valuation Methods**
>
> The choice of an inventory accounting method is important in determining the collateral value; however, the actual physical flow of inventory is not a key consideration. LIFO charges to expenses the most recent (last-in) cost of inventory because the company has to replace the used inventory at current values or costs. This leaves ending inventory, a balance sheet asset, at an older, lower value, assuming rising prices. FIFO expenses the old inventory costs first and leaves the current value of ending inventory on the balance sheet. Assuming rising prices, FIFO inventory would be valued higher than LIFO inventory on a balance sheet. A third inventory valuation method, the weighted-average method, values ending inventory on the balance sheet approximately halfway between the LIFO and FIFO methods.
>
> Some businesses adjust inventory values up or down to control net profit levels. Although this may be valid, only CPA-prepared audits and reviews provide adequate footnotes to fully explain such adjustments. Sometimes an interim statement uses an estimated number or an unchanged year-end number for inventory. If so, the business banker should question the income statement and balance sheet. The cost of goods sold listed will be inaccurate, and it will be impossible to determine the correct net profit or loss. Any subsequent adjustment to net profit or loss will change the retained earnings on the balance sheet.

Since the majority of accounts payable are created by purchases of inventory, the level of accounts payable tends to move in the same direction as inventory levels. A business that stockpiles inventory may need to stretch the accounts payable repayment time frame as a source of financing. This is sometimes called "riding the trade."

Whenever management competes more aggressively by keeping inventory levels high, the risks are that demand for the product will drop suddenly or prices may drop significantly. Because obtaining goods from overseas is often difficult or entails lengthy delivery times, companies may keep large inventories of items ordered from abroad.

Raw Materials Inventory

Manufacturers purchase raw materials inventory to use in the manufacturing process. Agricultural, wholesaling, retailing, service, and construction businesses generally do not have significant holdings of raw materials.

Lenders evaluate raw material inventory on the same basis as finished goods—that is, in terms of marketability. The end use of raw materials determines the marketability. Raw materials sold to various industries have better marketability than do raw materials used in a single manufacturing process. A manufacturer of custom draperies, for example, carries bolts of fabric and specialized materials for opening and closing drapes. The fabric is readily salable to fabric retailers, but the specialized materials can be sold only to another manufacturer of draperies.

A large raw materials inventory account can result from speculation in inventory due to expected price increases or concern over the potential loss of a supplier or some other type of disruption in supply. A business may try to hedge on prices by buying inventory in bulk at a low price with hopes of selling it later at a higher price, or to avoid having to purchase it at a higher price in the future. If the price of the raw materials, however, decreases unexpectedly, then the company may suffer a large loss. For this reason, it is important for the business banker to understand management's approach to raw materials purchases, especially how they manage price risk.

Work-in-process

Generally, as with raw materials, manufacturers are the only type of businesses that have significant levels of work-in-process inventory. From a lender's standpoint, work-in-process inventory is the most problematic. If liquidating inventory, it may be hard to sell since the product is not finished, nor are the materials in a raw state that can be used by other businesses.

Beyond being more difficult to sell, partially completed products have a market value that is less than the accumulated costs to produce them. Additional costs are needed for completion and achieving the value of finished goods, and not all purchasers may have the internal capabilities to convert the work-in-process to finished goods. Lenders, therefore, typically do not assign a value to work-in-process inventory as loan collateral.

The amount of work-in-process inventory depends primarily on the length of the production process. With a short production cycle, the value of the company's work-in-process should be small in relation to its raw materials and finished goods inventories. But if the production process is longer and more complex, a more significant portion of a company's assets may be tied up in work-in-process.

A manufacturer of customized products usually has a large work-in-process inventory but a much smaller finished goods inventory—its products are delivered almost immediately to the buyer upon completion. Because the general marketability of custom-made products is low, the manufacturer may require substantial up-front deposits or progress payments while producing the items in order to reduce the risk of custom orders not being accepted. For most lenders, custom-made inventory has almost no collateral value due its limited marketability.

Finished Goods Inventory

Finished goods are salable merchandise. Wholesale and retail finished goods are purchases of a product for resale and are the primary type of inventory. For manufacturers, finished goods inventory includes finished products not yet shipped or sold.

In a service or construction business, consumable supplies used to provide a service or for construction are considered finished goods inventory, but usually they are relatively small in relation to other assets. Occasionally, finished goods for a construction/development (that is, a firm that does not build for its own account but for others under contract) business include land held for sale or completed buildings for sale. For an agricultural business, finished goods are the harvested crop or livestock.

For many businesses, the risk that finished goods inventory will not sell is related primarily to the style sensitivity or utility of the merchandise. A lender, therefore, assesses a company's inventory account in terms of the present and future marketability of the inventory. Some items have more predictable and longer-term marketability.

For example, an office retailer sells paper and pens that are staple items and hold their value because they are a basic need subject to continuous demand. But if the company's inventory included specialized software that has a limited need and is subject to obsolescence, then a sudden drop in market demand could render the inventory worthless. Perishable inventory adds an unusual degree of risk, and a business banker has to move quickly to liquidate product inventory that is subject to spoilage or that requires refrigeration or freezing.

In evaluating a company's inventory account, a business banker should determine whether it includes obsolete inventory that fails to meet market specifics and/or demand. If so, then the value of the company's inventory and profits in recent years may have been overstated. Inventory is not expensed until sold or is considered obsolete and written off. Obsolete inventory does not represent liquidity for the company or good collateral value for a lender to support or secure debt repayment. Most companies write off obsolete inventory annually as a part of taking the physical count of the inventory.

In the Dry Supply example, inventory is growing at about the same rate as sales. This means that management is doing a consistently good job of converting products into sales.

Other Current Assets

Other current assets, including income tax refunds due, are generally insignificant. Categorizing these assets may vary from bank to bank, depending on the bank's method of spreading statements. Dry Supply lists no other current assets, so the line is omitted in the computer-generated spreadsheet.

According to the balance sheet, Dry Supply had the following current assets at the end of 20xx, 20xy, and 20xz:

Financial statements usually provide a subtotal for current assets, but the business tax return format does not.

Current Assets: Dry Supply ($ in 000s) As of December 31st	20xx	20xy	20xz
Cash	$ 3	$ 12	$ 22
Accounts receivable, net	109	113	112
Inventory	73	72	67
Other current assets	0	0	0
Total current assets	$185	$197	$201

Noncurrent Assets

Noncurrent assets either will not be converted to cash within 12 months (or the normal operating cycle of the business) or may have little or no liquidation value. A prepaid annual, term life insurance premium, for example, is considered by most lenders to be a noncurrent asset because it has little liquidation value. Fixed assets, other securities, notes receivable, amounts due from officers and employees, amounts due from affiliates, prepaid expenses, cash-value life insurance, and intangibles are noncurrent assets.

Fixed Assets

Fixed assets—items of a long-term nature required to operate a business—are not expected to convert to cash within 12 months or the normal operating cycle of a business. Fixed assets consist primarily of land, buildings and improvements, equipment, vehicles, furniture, and leasehold improvements used in operating a business. Depending on the type of business, the size of the fixed assets can vary significantly.

In financial statements, land usually is listed along with machinery, equipment, and other fixed assets. However, because land is not depreciated, it is listed separately on business tax returns. Similarly, depletable assets (usually natural resources) are listed separately because they are amortized rather than depreciated. Depreciation will be explained later in this chapter.

Most manufacturing companies and agricultural businesses must invest heavily in fixed assets before producing that first widget or bale of hay. At the other end of the spectrum, many service businesses begin operations with a comparatively small fixed-asset base. A small law firm, for instance, may have minimal fixed assets—perhaps books, computer equipment, and nominal leasehold improvements. Some businesses own their land and buildings; others rent.

Fixed-asset Valuation

In analyzing fixed assets, it is important to consider how they are accounted for on the balance sheet. Issues include the following:
- Cost at which the assets are recorded—All costs needed to bring the fixed asset into operating condition are recorded as part of the cost of the asset. Examples include freight costs, installation costs, and set-up costs that may or may not add value to the asset.
- Rate at which the cost is allocated to future periods—A fixed asset's recorded cost is depreciated each year after it is acquired. Depreciation is the process of allocating the cost of the fixed asset (less salvage value, if any) over its estimated useful or depreciable life, whichever is less. A depreciation charge on the income statement is treated as a non-cash expense because no cash has been paid out for the expense.

A $25,000 company car depreciated over five years, for example, could be partially expensed at $5,000 per year, depending on the depreciation method. Each year, the depreciation is expensed on the income statement, and the company car listed on the balance sheet as a fixed asset is reduced by a like amount. The value on the balance sheet is called book value. Finally, when the asset is fully depreciated, the asset is considered to be without value or to have reached a salvage value below which it cannot fall.
- Record of asset's eventual disposal—When a fixed asset is sold, there can be a gain or loss, depending on whether the proceeds exceed the book value of the asset at the time of sale. Some assets may be fully depreciated but remain in use in the operations of the business, and may have value in the open market.

Depreciation

Companies often calculate depreciation differently for financial reporting purposes than for tax purposes. The following are the two primary methods of calculating depreciation:
- Straight line—To calculate straight-line depreciation, divide the cost of a fixed asset, less salvage value, by its initially estimated useful economic life. This amount is recorded on the income statement as depreciation each year.
- Double-declining balance—To calculate double-declining balance depreciation, multiply two times the straight-line rate by the declining asset balance.

Using straight-line and double-declining balance methods, Figure 7.5 compares calculations for depreciation of a fixed asset that costs $100,000 and has a useful life of five years. The annual depreciation expense, which appears on the company's income statement as an operating expense, and the asset's value are reduced to zero during a five-year period.

FIGURE 7.5 DEPRECIATION CALCULATION EXAMPLES

Depreciation Method	Straight-Line		Double-Declining Balance	
Cost of asset	$100,000		$100,000	
Useful life	5 years		5 years	
Salvage value	$10,000		$10,000	
Depreciation/year	20%		40%	
End of Year	Depreciation	Book Value	Depreciation	Book Value
1	$18,000	$82,000	$40,000	$60,000
2	18,000	64,000	24,000	36,000
3	18,000	46,000	14,400	21,600
4	18,000	28,000	8,640	12,960
5	18,000	10,000	5,148	7,776
Formula	Each year: 20% x ($100,000 - $10,000)		Each year: 40% x (Book Value at Beginning of Year)	

The following are accounting entries to record depreciation:

- Debit depreciation expense (as is the case with any expense)
- Credit accumulated depreciation (reduces the value of fixed assets)

Debit	Credit
+ Depreciation expense	+ Accumulated depreciation

Notice that in the above accounting entries, cash is not involved. The business pays out cash only when the fixed asset is purchased. Because depreciation is a non-cash, tax-deductible expense, it is a tax advantage to depreciate the asset as quickly as possible. Businesses can do this if they have taxable income or can deduct current year losses from a previous year's taxable income (known as a tax loss carry-back) and receive a tax refund. To assist businesses, the Internal Revenue Service (IRS) has published guidelines for how quickly companies can depreciate fixed assets for tax purposes.

A company may use the straight-line method for internal reporting and a more accelerated method (such as double-declining balance) for tax purposes. This results in having two different income amounts in a current year. In most cases, the accelerated method initially produces lower taxes due but ends up giving a business a higher taxable income in the future—if it did not continue to purchase any more equipment and it runs out of depreciation expense. To prevent this situation, Generally Accepted Accounting Principles (GAAP) requires a business using the accrual method of accounting to establish a liability for deferred taxes to offset the actual tax savings. The deferred taxes are essentially a reserve that goes on the balance sheet as a noncurrent liability.

For specific asset categories, the **IRS code on depreciation** specifies the length of the depreciation period (depreciable life) and the depreciation method. Despite this basis for standardization, variations in the way companies depreciate fixed assets make it difficult to analyze the account. Although land is not depreciated, all other fixed assets are depreciated over time. Some may be worth less than reported. Others—primarily land and buildings—usually appreciate and can represent hidden asset value. A business banker, by obtaining current valuations or appraisals to support fixed asset values, can sometimes justify lending to a business where leverage appears higher because the value of land and buildings is understated on the balance sheet.

IRS guidelines define depreciation with the following questions:

What can be depreciated?

A business can depreciate many different kinds of property. The property can be depreciated if it meets all of the following requirements:
- It must be owned by the business.
- It must be used in the business or held to produce income.
- It must have a useful life that extends substantially beyond the year it is placed in service.
- It must be something that wears out, decays, gets used up, becomes obsolete, or loses its value from natural causes.

What cannot be depreciated?
- Land
- Property placed in service and disposed of in the same year
- Equipment used to build capital improvements
- Inventory
- Repairs and replacements that do not increase the value of property, make it more useful, appreciably lengthen its useful life, or adapt it to a different use

The amount of the deduction depends on the following:
- How much the property cost
- When the owner began using the property
- How long it will take to recover the cost
- Which of the several depreciation methods is used

For more information, see Publication 946, *How to Depreciate Property*.

Fixed-asset Capacity, Efficiency, and Specialization

Business bankers also assess the efficiency, capacity, and specialization of fixed assets. Inefficient or technically obsolete equipment limits a firm's ability to compete, unless substantial capital outlays will be made in the near future. Furthermore, outdated or specialized equipment offers little marketability as collateral. A specialized bread-cutting machine, for example, has a lower resale value than a lathe, which can be used by many types of businesses. Idle equipment, however, may indicate that a business can increase future sales-generating capacity without additional fixed-asset purchases.

Certain expenses recorded as fixed assets are called capitalized expenses. Costs incurred in overhauling a major piece of equipment usually are capitalized, whereas minor repairs and routine maintenance typically are treated as current year expenses. This treatment depends on the timing of when the benefits will be received. Benefits from a complete overhaul will be received for several years, so they are to the cost basis of the machine and allocated by means of depreciation expense. For a minor repair, benefits are derived in the current period, and the expense is charged against current income.

> ### Small Business Equipment Purchases
> ### Section 179 Provisions
>
> Starting with tax year 2002, the long-standing Investment Tax Credit of $25,000 for small business equipment purchases was renamed and expanded by Congress to $100,000 and indexed to inflation. By tax year 2008, the write-off had increased (due to inflation) to $125,000 and was doubled by Congress to $250,000. Again in tax year 2010, Congress doubled it to $500,000. As a company's purchases of qualifying equipment begin to exceed $2,000,000, there is a dollar-for-dollar reduction in the deduction allowed.
>
> The following is property that may be written off in the tax year of purchase rather than depreciated over the asset's useful life:
>
> - Machinery and equipment
> - Furniture and fixtures
> - Most storage facilities
> - Single-purpose agricultural or horticultural structures

Leasehold Improvements

Leasehold improvements—costs to improve a leased building, such as carpeting, special lighting, general renovations, and decorating—are not directly expensed on the income statement. They are capitalized on the balance sheet and amortized. Amortization, like depreciation, is a non-cash expense, and allocated on the fixed asset costs on the income statement over their useful or depreciable life, whichever is less.

An important risk with leasehold improvements is that they usually stay with the building and become the property of the building's owner should the tenant company move to a new location. For this reason, banks generally give very little value to leasehold improvements as collateral. It is not unusual for some retail and service businesses to have leasehold improvements as the largest category of fixed assets. When calculating tangible net worth, some lenders include the discount to the value of leasehold improvements as a reduction to net worth.

Valuing Fixed Assets

One of the best ways to value fixed assets is to look to credible independent appraisers who have experience in identifying the proper value range of an asset. If a borrower has recently arranged for an appraisal of its physical assets, then the appraiser's value can be a starting point.

The following are other resources that lenders use to conduct their own independent valuation:
- Calling companies in the same industry to randomly verify the values presented
- Employing specialized appraisers with experience valuing similar fixed assets
- Contacting the company's insurance agent for current values

A lender explains to the appraiser precisely the type of valuation sought. Valuations are prepared on several bases: liquidation, auction, market value, or replacement value.

Dry Supply's Fixed Assets

Dry Supply's fixed assets are summarized below. The company does not own its land or building. Fixed assets are composed primarily of company vehicles and equipment used to test products. With fixed assets heavily depreciated, the lender better understands the request for new equipment.

Also, with the fixed assets depreciated approximately two-thirds, a business banker will want to determine the future fixed asset needs and if the pending loan request includes all needs over the next year or so. In 20xz, Dry Supply added a used delivery truck at a cost of $15,000. This purchase raises the question of whether the company might need other vehicle replacements in the future.

Dry Supply Fixed Assets as of December 31 ($ in 000s)	20xx		20xy		20xz	
Furniture and fixtures	$ 76	31.3%	$ 75	28.8%	$ 78	28.9%
Leasehold improvements	1	0.4%	1	0.4%	0	0.0%
Transportation equipment	53	21.8%	70	26.9%	85	31.5%
Gross fixed assets	$130	53.5%	$146	56.2%	$163	60.4%
Less: Accum. depreciation	85	35.0%	97	37.3%	110	40.7%
Net total fixed assets	$ 45	18.5%	$ 49	18.8%	$ 53	19.6%
Percent depreciated	65.0%		66.0%		67.0%	

Other Securities

Other securities include stock in closely held companies, investments in affiliates, and stocks with marginal value. If a publicly held stock falls below $1 per share, it is usually considered an *other security* because the market has become limited. Also, most investors purchasing low-grade stock generally hold the stock for a long time. Other securities can be listed within *other investments* on business tax returns.

Notes Receivable

A note receivable is written with terms for repaying credit extended by a business. It may be used for selling costly merchandise or for resolving slow-paying accounts receivable. Generally, the amount carried for notes receivable is insignificant on a balance sheet. Because the terms are generally more than one year, notes receivable are classified as noncurrent assets.

Due from Officers and Employees, or Loans to Shareholders

Due from officers and employees represents loans or advances made by a business to its owners, officers, or employees. These loans are classified as noncurrent assets because often there is less pressure on an owner, officer, or employee to repay the debt on time. It is, therefore, less liquid than debts from other parties and is not considered as having collateral value.

Whenever there is a large change in this account, a business banker should determine the cause. Sometimes small business owners borrow from the company to inflate earnings (via additional interest income paid to the company) and decrease personal taxes (via additional interest expense incurred by the owner), and also to maintain their lifestyle rather than take a salary. This action, however, would reduce net income and might result in a loss. To avoid payroll withholding taxes, owners also will make a loan to themselves rather than take a salary distribution. Since the amounts are not likely to be collected promptly, they usually are deducted from net worth to determine tangible net worth.

Due from Affiliates

Affiliated businesses are related to each other by common ownership. Due from affiliates represents an obligation of a related business. As with loans to officers, the close relationship between the creditor and the debtor relegates this loan to the status of a noncurrent asset. Without pressure to pay, due from affiliates may not be available for timely conversion to cash. A business banker should obtain and analyze the financial statements of the appropriate affiliated companies in order to assess the quality of this asset, particularly if the amount due from affiliates is large.

Prepaid Expenses

Prepaid expenses (sometimes called prepaid assets) are items paid but not yet expensed on the income statement. Classified as noncurrent assets, they have little liquidation value for a lender. Many accountants classify prepaid expenses as a current asset, so a lender will need to reclassify the account when spreading financial statements. Examples include insurance premiums paid at the start of the year and rent paid at the first of the month or one or more months in advance.

Cash-value Life Insurance

Cash-value life insurance is the amount a whole life insurance policy is worth if the policy is surrendered. It also is added to the amount payable (face value) upon the death of the insured person. Many businesses carry life insurance on the owners or key officers. The company receives the benefit of the cash value and face value. If needed, the company can even borrow against the cash value. It is usually considered a noncurrent asset because it is unknown when the cash value will be realized. Insurance policies, unlike accounts receivable and inventory, generally are not converted to cash during the course of an operating cycle.

Intangibles

Assets with no physical existence are reported as intangibles. Intangibles include many items referred to as intellectual property, which has become a specialty area within many law firms. In general, intangibles include the following items:

- Goodwill arises when the purchase price of an acquired company exceeds its book value or the value of its tangible assets. This occurs during a merger or acquisition because a company's good reputation, favorable location, or customer base may be of great value even though they do not appear as an asset account on a balance sheet. The value of intangibles, excluding goodwill (which is governed by regulatory, governmental, and Securities and Exchange Commission rules), generally is amortized over an estimated life of the patent or copyright.
- Patents give a company the exclusive right to manufacture a product. The intangibles account reflects only the purchase price of the patent or the legal cost of recording internally developed patents, although the value of a patent for a highly successful product may be greater than these costs.
- Trademarks are the registered names of products or services. Trademarks can be bought and sold or licensed in exchange for royalty payments. Although the

current value of a trademark may be greater, the balance sheet account reflects the purchase price or legal cost of recording the trademark only.
- Copyrights are exclusive rights to make copies, license, distribute, or sell a literary, musical, or artistic work, whether printed, audio, video, etc. Similar to patents and trademarks, the value shown on the balance sheet usually reflects the purchase price or legal cost of obtaining the copyright.
- Operating rights include special rights granted by government regulatory agencies. Telephone companies, airlines, and television stations are examples of businesses that must obtain operating rights for their geographic areas. Because companies sell or lease these rights, they often represent a value greater than shown on the balance sheet.
- Customer lists have considerable operational value, but due to uncertain dollar value, they are classified as intangibles without value.

Other than fixed assets, the only noncurrent asset for Dry Supply is cash-value life insurance. Having proceeded through all of the current and noncurrent asset accounts on the balance sheet, the total assets of Dry Supply can now be determined for the following December 31, 20xx, 20xy, and 20xz:

Current Assets + Noncurrent Assets = Total Assets   ($ in 000s)
    December 31, 20xx $185 + $58   = $243
    December 31, 20xy $197 + $63   = $260
    December 31, 20xz $201 + $69   = $270

You have learned the definition of current assets as assets that are expected to convert to cash within 12 months or within the normal operating cycle of the business. This includes such assets as cash, marketable securities, accounts receivable, and inventory. You have also learned about other current assets, which are generally insignificant. Categorizing these assets may vary from bank to bank, but typically they include items like income tax refunds due. In addition, you learned how to define noncurrent assets as assets that either will not be converted to cash within 12 months (or the normal operating cycle of the business) or may have little or no liquidation value, such as prepaid insurance premiums, notes receivables, and intangible assets.

LIABILITIES AND EQUITY ANALYSIS

Now that you have dealt with assets in the balance sheet equation (assets = liabilities + equity), the next areas to examine are liabilities and equity accounts. Liabilities are listed in order of payment priority, usually grouped as current and noncurrent. As a basic definition, liabilities are amounts owed. Equity (net worth) accounts are listed next.

Current Liabilities

Current liabilities are amounts due for repayment within 12 months. They are usually repaid with cash generated from converting current assets during the normal operating cycle of the business. Current liabilities indicate a company's short-term ability to finance operations. In analyzing any liability, a business banker determines

the following:
- To whom the money is owed
- Reason for borrowing or obligation
- Repayment terms
- Any assets pledged as collateral
- Any debt agreements in place that may restrict the business

Current liabilities include overdrafts, notes payable to banks, accounts payable, notes payable to others, due to affiliates and officers, current maturities of long-term debt, accrued expenses, and other current liabilities. Any liability with no stated maturity date, such as a demand loan, is also classified as a current liability.

Overdrafts

Overdrafts—checks written in excess of the bank deposit balance—effectively are short-term unsecured loans. If the checks, however, have not been mailed or cleared, a business will show a balance sheet overdraft on its books, while the bank does not show an overdraft on the checking account.

Accountants generally will show an overdraft as a negative cash balance. When spreading financial statements, most bankers will net any negative cash balances against any positive balances. If the net balance remains negative, then the amount is reclassified as a liability and one of four following options is used:

- Show as an overdraft—This approach recognizes that the checks may be for multiple purposes.

- Add to any line of credit amount—If an actual overdraft occurs at the bank, and if a line of credit is available from that bank to the business, then the checks would likely be paid via a draw on the line of credit. Some businesses utilize cash management systems where this would occur automatically.

- Add to accounts payable—Businesses such as wholesalers or manufacturers with larger amounts of accounts payable are more likely to have paid on those accounts with the checks that created the overdraft. This approach effectively reverses the payments for analytical purposes, since the accounts payable balance was reduced by funds that were not really available to the business.

- Add to accrued expenses—Service businesses or contractors with larger amounts of payroll or accrued expenses are more likely to have paid on those accounts with the checks that created the overdraft. This approach effectively reverses the payments for analytical purposes, since the accrued expenses (including payroll) balance was reduced by funds that were not really available to the business.

Selecting from these approaches depends on the lender's knowledge of the type of business and the nature of its operating cycle and banking relationship.

Notes Payable to Banks

This category includes short-term bank loans for periods of less than one year, lines of credit, and installment loans that mature within 12 months with a balance remaining. Short-term bank loans are often for 90, 120, or 180 days, and are secured by accounts receivable and/or inventory. These notes usually fund temporary or seasonal increases in accounts receivable and inventory purchases. In some cases, a short-term bank loan is used to finance multiple pieces of equipment or temporarily finance fixed assets until renewed and rewritten as a long-term loan.

For example, an owner of a lawn and garden store borrows heavily from a bank just before and during the summer season to purchase lawn mowers for resale. As the inventory of lawn mowers is sold, cash is generated to repay the loan. The store owner's notes payable to the bank would be high during the spring and summer, then low (or zero) the rest of the year.

If the note represents a line of credit, a business banker needs to determine the purpose, expiration date, interest rate, security (collateral), and other terms of the debt. Evaluating lines of credit can help a business banker understand a company's plans for bank borrowings and determine whether the loan being considered will meet anticipated financing needs. This evaluation relies heavily on the average or seasonal line usage, remaining funds available under the line, and any related loan covenants or restrictions placed on the business.

One area of confusion with notes payable involves how accountants handle installment loans that mature within 12 months with a balance remaining. In such cases, for credit or interest rate risk reasons, the bank has structured a long-term loan with maturity that precedes the full repayment. This is a common structure for loans that finance real estate, such as a manufacturing plant or distribution warehouse.

For example, the lawn and garden store that was discussed earlier acquired its land and building three years ago. The bank structured the loan to amortize (periodic payments) over 15 years or 180 months. However, at that time the store had exclusive distribution rights for a national mower brand that would be up for renewal in 36 months. Further, the bank (similar to most banks) could not offer a fixed interest rate for the full 180 months. To deal with credit risk of the customer losing a major product line and to keep the interest rate commitment short-term (to match the bank's funding sources), the bank set a three-year **balloon maturity** on the loan. Two and a half years have passed, and the store is rendering its fiscal year-end financial statement. Since the loan is maturing within 12 months from the date of the financial statement, the accountant should show the loan as a short-term note payable. If a lender anticipates that the loan will be renewed, or if a lender is dealing with an earlier financial statement and the loan has, in fact, been renewed, then it should be reclassified for spreading purposes into respective long-term debt and current maturities portions at each financial statement date. Long-term debt and current maturities are discussed later in this chapter.

Returning to the Dry Supply example, its notes payable to banks decreased. Dry Supply's very good earnings for the year, together with a stable level of accounts receivable and inventory, allowed the company to reduce its short-term borrowing needs. In fact, for more than 180 days in 20xz, the company actually had a zero balance on its line of credit.

> ### Balloon vs. Bullet Maturity
>
> While lenders tend to use the terms interchangeably, there is a subtle difference.
>
> - Balloon maturity refers to a loan that requires the remaining principal balance to be paid at a specific point in time, after some amortization of the principal balance has occurred. For example, a loan may be amortized over a 15-year period but requires that at the end of the fifth year, the entire remaining principal balance must be paid. Most lenders use this structure if they intend to review the loan for renewal on similar terms and conditions.
>
> - Bullet maturity refers to a one-time lump-sum repayment of an outstanding loan, typically made by the borrower after very little, if any, amortization of the loan. This also refers to a loan that requires a disproportionately large portion (or even all) of the loan to be repaid at maturity. Such loans generally require periodic payment of interest prior to maturity, even if no principal amortization is being required. Most lenders use this structure if they anticipate reviewing the loan for renewal on different terms and conditions, usually tied to some other financial event happening with the borrower on or about the same time.
>
> Because each maturity structure involves a large, lump-sum amount due, they give a lender an important means of reducing interest rate risk in a loan. Most banks do not have access to longer-term sources of funding and should not take the risk of offering a long-term fixed interest rate on a real estate loan. By using a three- or five-year maturity along with a longer amortization of 15 years, a bank can offer a fixed interest rate and payment that better matches the useful life of the asset and the borrower's cash flow while reducing the bank's interest rate risk. Even if offering a variable interest rate, the bank may need to adjust the index or spread to better match current market conditions.
>
> A repricing option built into the loan structure can achieve the same pricing goals, but most lenders prefer a balloon or bullet maturity structure because it can also potentially reduce credit risk and help meet portfolio management targets. The maturity gives the lender the option to refinance the remaining balance on adjusted terms, beyond the interest rate, such as additional collateral or guarantees if the credit risk profile of the borrower has deteriorated. The interest rate, in addition to being reset to market levels, can further be adjusted to reflect the changed risk profile of the borrower.
>
> If the borrower's risk profile is not within the lender's parameters, then the borrower can be asked to refinance that debt with another creditor, bank, or non-bank. Of course, other creditors may not offer to refinance, leaving the original bank with a difficult situation.
>
> Similarly, even if the credit risk remains acceptable, the original lender may choose not to refinance if the loan no longer fits its portfolio management targets and goals.

Accounts Payable

Also referred to as trade credit, trade payables, or simply payables, accounts payable are amounts owed to vendors and suppliers for delivered products or services used in normal operations, and other bills that must be paid within one year. For many businesses, accounts payable, which represent an ongoing debt obligation, are a crucial, non-interest-bearing source of financing.

Analyzing accounts payable involves the relationship between payables and inventory, the diversity and stability of suppliers, and payment terms. Payables normally have shorter payment terms than the time the related inventory will be held by business. Therefore, the percentage change in these two accounts should be similar. As inventory levels fall or rise, so should payables. Any significant deviations should be investigated and will likely create cash flow changes.

By obtaining a list of the company's main suppliers, a lender periodically can examine the vendor relationships. An aged listing of accounts payable will identify the name of the vendor, amount due, and length of time it has been outstanding. This list can show the numbers of vendors and any reliance (concentrations of purchases) on a narrow group of suppliers. Other considerations include credit terms and the ability of the borrower to take advantage of discounts, if any, or least staying current. In most cases where payables become delinquent, the supplier will suspend shipments, with resulting disruptions to the operations of a business.

For Dry Supply, accounts payable decreased by $15,000 and inventory decreased by $5,000 in 20xz. The most recent aged listing of accounts payable did not show any delinquent accounts, and there were no concentrations of purchases with a single vendor.

Notes Payable to Others

Notes payable to others represent amounts owed to a creditor that is neither a bank nor an investor in commercial paper. Examples include a short-term loan obtained from a commercial finance company to purchase a small piece of equipment or a note payable to a supplier to finance a seasonal increase in inventory. Commercial paper is an option for larger, publicly held companies with established credit ratings. It is an unsecured, short-term borrowing issued by companies for up to 270 days in amounts of $100,000 or more. Although unsecured, commercial paper usually is supported by a line of credit at a bank.

Due to Affiliates or Officers, or Loans from Shareholders

These liabilities represent amounts owed by a business to its affiliated businesses or its officers. The business banker should obtain a copy of the note to determine the repayment details. Most lenders consider this account a current liability, even if repayment terms extend beyond one year, because a company's officers can get repaid first when faced with a difficult situation.

A lender can consider amounts due from related parties as **subordinated debt** (a long-term liability) when the debt is subordinated to the lender or other creditors. The underlying agreement may subordinate payment priority, lien priority, or both. If the debt is subordinated to a particular lender, and if the terms are fairly restrictive for repayment, then that lender may further consider the subordinated debt to be equity, for analysis purposes. Subordinated debt will be discussed in more detail later in this reading.

> **Subordinated debt**
> Long-term debt that is paid off only after depositors and other creditors have been paid.

In any event, a business banker should investigate the purpose for the loan and terms. An increase in this account often is traced to the company expensing a large salary to its owner, who, in turn, has loaned it back to the company. This usually is done for tax considerations.

Current Maturities of Long-term Debt

Also known as the current portion of long-term debt, current maturities of long-term debt (CMLTD) is the principal portion of long-term or installment debt that will be paid within one year. For example, at the fiscal year-end of a business, a $400,000 loan for manufacturing equipment is outstanding. The loan is to be paid in 48 equal monthly installments of principal, plus interest due. Of the $400,000 total loan amount, $100,000 is due within one year and is listed at fiscal year-end as CMLTD. In situations where there is a level payment of combined principal and interest, the CMLTD amount at any financial statement date will be based on an amortization schedule of the loan.

Installment debt analysis includes identification of its repayment terms, maturity schedules, conditions, security (collateral), and creditors. Debt financed with balloon or bullet maturities faces the possibility that in future years current maturities might increase substantially. The lender must determine whether future earnings can repay balloon notes and, if not, what refinancing provisions have been made. Covenants written into the balloon note's agreement might be triggered by certain events that cause the debt to be accelerated and become due and payable. For example, the debt might become due immediately if the company fails to meet certain profit levels.

Business tax returns combine notes payable and CMLTD as a single line item within the balance sheet or Schedule L in the tax returns.

Accrued Expenses

Accrued expenses (sometimes called accruals) are operating expenses and other expenses recognized on the income statement but not yet paid, or paid in arrears. They include various operating expenses that have not been allocated to cost of goods sold (and inventory). For many companies the largest accrued expense is for payroll and related benefits. Operating expenses paid for in advance, such as rent and insurance, become **prepaid expenses**, an asset account. Generally, accrued expenses excludes income taxes payable and deferred taxes, which have separate accounts. Business tax returns do not have a separate line item for accrued expenses, so they are generally included with other current liabilities on Schedule L.

> **Prepaid expenses**
>
> A classification of expenditure made to benefit future periods. Such items are classified as current assets and constitute a part of a firm's working capital. Prepaid expenses include prepaid rent, certain taxes, royalties, and unexpired insurance premiums.

Other Current Liabilities

The amounts reported in other current liabilities usually are not material. Some of these incidental items include deposits received before products are manufactured or shipped.

Current Liabilities: Dry Supply ($ in 000s)

As of December 31st,	20xx	20xy	20xz
Notes payable-bank	$ 81	$ 12	$ 22
Accounts payable-trade	42	113	112
Accrued taxes	5	72	67
Accrued bonuses	10	0	0
Total current liabilities	$185	$197	$201

The balance sheet spread for Dry Supply below shows the current liability accounts for December 31, 20xx, 20xy, and 20xz.

Although the company's short-term bank debt and accounts payable have declined, a business banker should examine the inventory account to see if it also declined and how the company repaid the debt. In addition, the company has $19,000 of accrued liabilities in 20xz. A lender should determine when these liabilities need to be paid and the source of funding for the repayment. As with current assets, business tax return formats do not provide a subtotal for current liabilities.

Noncurrent Liabilities

Noncurrent or long-term liabilities are amounts due beyond one year. They include long-term debt, bonds and debentures, subordinated debt, and reserves. With any long-term obligation, the portion of debt due within one year is classified separately as a current liability.

Unlike current liabilities, which generally are repaid by the conversion of current assets to cash, long-term liabilities are usually repaid from excess cash generated over a series of operating cycles. Therefore, an assessment of future profitability accompanies any evaluation of a business's ability to sustain repeated operating cycles to support its long-term obligations. Further, long-term liabilities are evaluated for terms, purposes, interest rates, security (collateral) pledged, and whether current levels supply adequate financing support for fixed assets or permanent working capital levels.

Long-term Debt

Land, buildings, equipment, and permanent increases in levels of inventory and receivables are among the items financed with long-term debt. Loans secured by land and buildings are also called mortgage loans or deed of trust loans, and generally they are repaid over 15 to 20 years. Equipment usually is financed over the shorter of depreciable life or the useful life, which is generally 3 to 10 years. Permanent increases in inventory and accounts receivable normally are financed over three to five years.

When incurring long-term debt, most businesses are required to enter into a loan agreement that essentially supplements the basic terms and conditions in the note. The addition provisions can include financial covenants and other expectations of the business over the loan term. Most long-term loans are secured by collateral because the longer the term of the loan, the higher the risk. Also, because these loans often finance or refinance the purchase of assets, the assets are available as collateral. Only companies with exceptionally strong balance sheets and consistent profits merit a long-term, unsecured note.

Bonds and Debentures

Bonds are interest-bearing or discounted certificates of indebtedness, paying a fixed rate of interest to the creditors or holders over the life of the obligation. Maturities generally are longer than five years. Debentures are unsecured promises to pay, backed by the general credit of the issuer. Some debentures can be exchanged for common stock at a specific price. In terms of the financing they provide for a company, bonds and debentures function the same as long-term debt; however, bonds and debentures are securities that can be traded by investors and have a market value. Section 1, Chapter 2, covers industrial revenue bonds, a form of tax advantaged financing often available to customers of community banks.

Subordinated Debt

Subordinated debt is a liability that has a lien against the borrower's assets that is secondary (or junior) to other obligations or a claim for payment, only after holders of the primary (or senior) debt obligations are paid. When debt is subordinated, an agreement is created that stipulates whether nothing, or a limited amount of principal and interest, will be paid on the subordinated debt until the terms of certain other debts are satisfied.

Most lenders use the subordinated debt category, for spreading purposes, only for debts subordinated to the lender and under acceptable conditions. If the debt is from the officers or owners of the business, and adequately subordinated, then some banks add the amount to total equity when calculating tangible net worth. For example, a bank may, as a condition of extending credit to a business, specify that any loans from the owners be subordinated to the bank's loans. Payments on the owner loans are prohibited as specified in the subordination agreement. Also, in a liquidation, the bank will be repaid in full before any payment is made on the subordinated debt. The subordinating of collateral results when one lien holder takes a junior position to another lien holder, and it is often a key feature of a subordination agreement.

In lending to a privately held company, it is often required that any owner debts be subordinated because the company's owners have the ability to pre-pay these loans, regardless of the written commitment in place between the owners and the business. To effectively freeze these loan amounts, the original note(s) signed by the business are held by the bank, along with a subordination agreement establishing when and how these loans can be repaid.

Long-term debt, bonds/debentures, and subordinated debt can be shown together on a business tax return as mortgages, notes, bonds payable in 1 year, or more. If subordinated debt is from a shareholder, then it should be listed as "loans from shareholders" account on Schedule L.

Reserves

Although reserves are not a formal debt owed to any one or several creditors, they are recognized as a long-term liability because they represent an obligation that theoretically must be met some time in the future. Two more common uses of reserves are to pay deferred income taxes and provide product warranties.

Deferred income taxes arise when a business uses one depreciation method for tax reporting that accelerates depreciation expense faster than another method used for preparing financial statements. It is accepted by GAAP to prepare financial statements and tax returns using different depreciation methods. Product warranties arise when a business guarantees its product for a period of time. The estimated costs to repair a product under warranty are classified as a long-term liability usually labeled "warranty reserves."

Referring to Dry Supply's balance sheet for 20xx, 20xy, and 20xz, its total for long-term liabilities consists of a single line item—subordinated debt-officers—of $48,000,

$58,000, and $67,000, respectively. With the liability portion of the balance sheet equation now complete, the composition of current and noncurrent liabilities is as follows:

Current Liabilities + Noncurrent Liabilities = Total Liabilities ($ in 000s)
    December 31, 20xx: $138 + $48   = $186
    December 31, 20xy: $131 + $58   = $189
    December 31, 20xz: $109 + $67   = $176

Equity (Net Worth)

You have learned about all the assets and liabilities, and what remains is the equity held by the ownership of the business, whether it is a sole proprietor or thousands of corporate shareholders. Assets less liabilities equals equity is a variation on the standard balance sheet equation. Equity also is referred to as **net worth** or net assets.

> **Net worth**
> Assets minus liabilities of a business. This is the owners' equity. *Also called* shareholders' equity.

Think of equity as the claims of the owners, rather than creditors, against the assets of a business. Unlike creditors, business owners must absorb all losses in assets, and their claims are recognized only after all creditor obligations are fulfilled. This is why, in bankruptcy, all creditors are paid before owners receive any assets upon liquidation.

An analysis of equity accounts begins by determining the amount of equity available and how it has changed over time. The amount of equity represents a cushion available to creditors before assets are liquidated. If there is little or no equity, full repayment of all liabilities is questionable.

Dry Supply's equity on December 31, 20xx, 20xy, and 20xz consists of the following:

Equity: Dry Supply ($ in 000s) As of December 31st,	20xx	20xy	20xz
Common stock	$ 2	$ 2	$ 2
Retained earnings	55	69	92
Total equity	$ 57	$ 71	$ 94

If the balance sheet is prepared correctly, then the equation will balance as shown in the following example:

Assets = Liabilities + Equity ($ in 000s)
    December 31, 20xx: $243 = $186 + $57
    December 31, 20xy: $260 = $189 + $71
    December 31, 20xz: $270 = $176 + $94

Equity can vary by the type of business. For example, a sole proprietorship in a service business, such as a dentist, might take most of the equity (net worth) out of the business as salaries or distributions. A wholesaler, on the other hand, would likely leave some equity in the business to finance inventory purchases or other needs.

Equity (Net Worth) for Different Business Entities

Equity accounts found on a balance sheet vary by the type of business entity that is represented. This reading will first discuss C corporations, which have some of the most commonly-known equity categories, then examine categories specific to the other major legal entities that businesses utilize.

C Corporations

For C corporations, equity consists of forms of stock (common, preferred, treasury, and paid-in capital) and retained earnings. When considering stock accounts, a business banker identifies the principal shareholders, their percentages of ownership, and the terms of issuance (such as any individual buy–sell agreements). If an agreement exists by which the company may repurchase the stock of a shareholder, a business banker needs to understand the terms and conditions of the agreement and how it will be funded.

- Common and preferred stock—This balance sheet account represents the nominal value of all common and preferred stock issued by a company. Common stock represents ownership in a corporation and carries voting rights, whereas preferred stock usually does not have voting rights. Although holders of common stock have the right to elect directors and collect dividends, common stock claims are subordinate to preferred stock in liquidation. Further, preferred stockholders receive dividend payments before common stockholders. Privately held companies generally start with a limited amount of common stock.

- Paid-in capital (or surplus)—When stock is sold in excess of its nominal or par value, the extra equity generated is paid-in capital. To illustrate, suppose a company has been authorized to issue 10,000 shares of stock at a par or face value of $10 per share. It issues 5,000 shares, generating $50,000 of equity, which is reported in the common stock account on the balance sheet. A few profitable years later, the company decides to issue the remaining shares, but because it has done so well and investors are willing to pay for future earnings, the company is able to sell its remaining 5,000 shares for $20 per share. Of the $100,000 in proceeds from the stock issuance, $50,000 (par value) is added to the common stock account, while the other $50,000 is recorded as paid-in capital. Stock issuance, whether at par value or higher, always increases owner equity.

- Treasury stock—Sometimes a company may repurchase or buy back some of its outstanding shares of stock. To fund stock options, stock grants, and mergers, publicly held companies often repurchase shares "into the treasury" (treasury stock). Public companies also use this technique if they believe their stocks are undervalued or priced too low by investors. As time passes, if a company continues to be profitable, then it can sell the shares on the open market to raise capital. The projected return on the repurchased shares may exceed other options a company has for deploying excess cash.

If the company is closely held, the firm may use this account to buy out individual owners, whether as part of succession planning or formal ownership transition, or as a way to buy out an owner who wants to exit voluntarily from the company. Common stock documents may mandate that sellers first offer the stock back to the company.

Stock repurchased but not retired (in other words, locked up in a vault and held for the treasury) is treasury stock. Because it has been repurchased from shareholders, treasury stock represents a reduction in equity, just as an issuance of stock increases it. If treasury stock is retired later and thus is no longer outstanding, then the decline in equity is transferred to the common stock and paid-in capital accounts, as shown in the following illustration:

Debit	Credit
+ Treasury stock account	+ Common stock and/or + Paid-in capital account

- Retained earnings—A firm's net profit after tax is either allocated to its owners, such as in dividends paid to stockholders, or kept in the business to build equity value and to act as a future source of financing. Profits left in a business are called retained earnings.

Equity Accounts for Other Entities

- Sole proprietorships—They have the following two unique equity accounts:
  - The **owner capital account** shows the combination of cash contributions, non-cash contributions, and retained earnings. Cash contributions are any funds used to start the business or provided by the owner over the years. Non-cash contributions include inventory or fixed assets converted to business use, recorded at fair market value.
  - The **owner draw account** shows money and other assets the owner takes from the business to use personally. This is how the owner gets compensated, since a sole proprietor does not receive a paycheck with payroll and income taxes withheld. The owner writes a check, adding to the draw account and reducing the equity of the business.

- Partnerships—The **partners' capital account**, similar to a sole proprietorship, shows the combination of cash contributions and non-cash contributions of the partners, plus retained earnings. This account is also a combination of a running balance maintained for each partner, based on each partner's cash and non-cash contribution. Net income (or losses) of the partnership are allocated proportionately based on what is in the partnership agreement. The **partners' draw account** shows the combined money and other assets the partners have taken from the business to use personally. The amount of draws a partner is allowed to take can be different than his or her partnership interest (ownership percentage). So, even though a business may have two equal partners, it does not mean they have to take the same draw amount. As with the partners' capital account, a running balance is maintained for each partner.

- Limited Liability Companies (LLCs)—The LLCs have a **members' capital account** that functions in a similar fashion to partnerships. The account is effectively a combination of the individual capital accounts of each owner or member. LLC members can also make draws or distributions, but they can be on a basis that is different from their ownership interests.
- S corporations—The equity section of the balance sheet for an S corporation is almost the same as the equity section for a regular or C corporation, because the S corporation designation is a tax, rather than accounting, issue. The one major difference is that an S corporation is limited to one class of stock, so there is a single **capital stock account** instead of potentially separate common stock and preferred stock accounts. For accounting purposes, most S corporations maintain running capital account balances for each owner, but owner draws are required to be in proportion with their ownership interests.

Concept of Tangible Net Worth

> **Tangible net worth**
> Ordinarily, the total capital accounts (equity) less intangibles.

When evaluating the equity of a business, intangibles and other assets of limited value should be deducted from the reported total equity (net worth) to obtain **tangible net worth.** This gives a truer picture of the value of the owner's investment in the business. The following intangibles and other items are typically deducted from total equity to obtain tangible net worth:

- Leasehold improvements
- Due from officers and employees
- Intangibles
  - Goodwill
  - Patents
  - Customer lists
  - Copyrights
  - Operating rights

In most cases, intangibles have limited value, but it is important to note that some intangibles (e.g., patents, customer lists, copyrights, operating rights) **may** have significant value in a loan workout situation, especially when the business is still operating. Lenders should always consider including these assets in the bank's collateral package, which will be covered later.

On December 31, 20xz, Dry Supply had no leasehold improvements, due from officers or intangible assets, so the total equity and tangible net worth were the same. If the lending bank considers subordinated debt as part of equity, then this liability account would be added to equity when calculating the tangible net worth of Dry Supply. Figure 7.6 summarizes the balance sheet categories.

FIGURE 7.6 SUMMARY OF BALANCE SHEET CATEGORIES

Classification	Account	Comments
Current asset	Cash	Checking accounts, interest-bearing accounts, and petty cash
	Marketable securities	U.S. government securities and high-grade corporate stocks
	Accounts receivable	Trade accounts only, net of allowance for doubtful accounts
	Inventory	Includes raw materials, work-in-process, and finished goods
	Other current assets	Conversion to cash expected within one year, such as an income tax refund
Fixed asset (noncurrent)	Land	Shown at cost (separate line item on tax returns, since land is not depreciated; included with other fixed assets on conventional financial statements)
	Buildings	Shown at cost less accumulated depreciation
	Equipment	
	Vehicles	
	Furniture	
	Leasehold improvements	
Noncurrent asset	Other securities	Stocks in privately held companies, affiliates, and low-grade stocks
	Notes receivable	Notes from sale of large assets or to resolve slow accounts receivable
	Due from officers and employees	Loans made to business owners, officers, and employees
	Due from affiliates	Amounts due from related businesses
	Prepaid expenses	Shown as actual amount paid for future service
	Cash-value life insurance	Shown as verified amount from issuer
	Intangibles	Includes goodwill, patents, trademarks, copyrights, operating rights, and customer lists
Current liability	Overdrafts	Checks written in excess of bank balances
	Notes payable to banks, or short-term debt	Amounts due on short-term notes to fund temporary or seasonal increases in accounts receivable and inventory, and temporary financing of fixed assets
	Accounts payable	Amounts owed to suppliers
	Accrued expenses	Actual expenses recognized and not paid
	Notes payable to others	Short-term financing for other purposes
	Due to affiliates or officers	Nonsubordinated financing due in less than one year
	Current maturities of long-term debt	Shown as the principal portion due in the coming year
	Other current liabilities	Unusual or smaller items not previously listed
Noncurrent liability	Bonds and debentures	Shown as amount owed by maturity net of any payments
	Long-term debt	Shown net of current maturities
	Subordinated debt	Amounts owed that are junior to bank debt
	Reserves	Long-term obligations, such as deferred taxes
Equity (net worth)	Common stock	Shown at cost
	Preferred stock	Shown at cost
	Paid-in capital	Stock sold at higher than par value, shown at sales price
	Treasury stock	Shown in amount paid to redeem stock
	Retained earnings	Profits left in the business

You have learned that current liabilities are amounts due for repayment within 12 months and include items such as overdrafts, notes payable to banks, and accounts payable. You have also learned about noncurrent or long-term liabilities, which are amounts due beyond one year. They include long-term debt, bonds and debentures, subordinated debt, and reserves. In addition to liabilities, you increased your knowledge about equity (net worth) and retained earnings. You learned that equity can vary by the type of business, and certain types of business entities have owner capital accounts and owner draw accounts that are the main components of equity.

SUMMARY

By completing this chapter, you have learned the balance sheet considerations necessary to analyze business balance sheets effectively. You now know that a company's assets are divided into current assets and noncurrent assets (total assets = current assets + noncurrent assets), and liabilities are divided into current liabilities and noncurrent liabilities (total liabilities = current liabilities + noncurrent liabilities). You also learned the components involved in a liability and equity analysis—specifically, that total equity (or net worth) is reported as shareholders' equity. These major sections are then further subdivided into specific accounts as line entries on the balance sheet.

Balance sheet analysis begins with the equation *assets = liabilities + equity (net worth)*. For any increase or decrease in an asset account, there must be a corresponding change in another asset account or in one or more liability or equity accounts. Evaluating each balance sheet account provides insight into asset quality, solvency, liquidity, collateral availability, and debt repayment requirements.

EXERCISE 1

Background

For several years, Anne Schippel has been the business banker for the company, Dry Supply. After reviewing the company balance sheet, she makes the following observations. Three major asset accounts are on the books of Dry Supply: accounts receivable, inventory, and fixed assets. The amount of accounts receivable and inventory are characteristic of a wholesaler.

Please review the Dry Supply Income Statement Spread and Balance Sheet Spread on the next two pages and follow the instructions below:

Instructions

For each of Anne Schippel's observations listed below, develop questions you would ask Dry Supply in order to complete your balance sheet analysis.
- Observation 1: Accounts receivable have remained in the $114,000 to $118,000 range.
- Observation 2: Inventory decreased during the period, while sales and accounts receivable increased.
- Observation 3: Fixed assets increased from $130,000 on December 31, 20xx, to $163,000 on December 31, 20xy.

- Observation 4: Accounts payable showed a larger decrease than inventory. Some of the decrease is to be expected because inventory usually is financed by trade creditors.
- Observation 5: Loans to shareholders has grown from $48,000 on December 31, 20xx, to $67,000 in December 31, 20xy.
- Observation 6: With regard to equity, what two questions immediately come to mind?

INCOME STATEMENT SPREAD: DRY SUPPLY

Income Statement ($ in 000s)	Review 20xx Amount	%	Review 20xy Amount	%	Review 20xz Amount	%
Net sales	$895	100.0	$937	100.0	$918	100.0
Cost of goods sold	645	72.1	667	71.2	631	68.7
Gross profit	250	27.9	270	28.8	287	31.3
Selling, gen. and admin. expense	157	17.5	173	18.5	180	19.6
Officer's compensation	36	4.0	31	3.3	28	3.1
Rent expenses	15	1.7	18	1.9	20	2.2
Bad debt expense	2	0.2	1	0.1	0	0.0
Profit-sharing expense	7	0.8	7	0.7	0	0.0
Depreciation expense	12	1.3	12	1.3	13	1.4
Total operating expenses	229	25.6	242	25.8	241	26.3
Operating income	21	2.3	28	3.0	46	5.0
Other income	0	0.0	0	0.0	0	0.0
Interest income	2	0.2	2	0.2	2	0.2
Rental income	3	0.3	3	0.3	3	0.3
Interest expense	6	0.7	7	0.7	11	1.2
Net profit before tax	20	2.2	26	2.8	40	4.4
Taxes	11	1.2	12	1.3	17	1.9
Net profit after tax	$ 9	1.0	$ 14	1.5	$ 23	2.5

BALANCE SHEET SPREAD: DRY SUPPLY						
Common-sized report ($ in $000s)	Review 12/31/20xx		Review 12/31/20xy		Review 12/31/20xz	
Assets	Amount	%	Amount	%	Amount	%
Cash	$ 3	1.2	$ 12	4.6	$ 22	8.1
Accounts receivable	114	46.9	118	45.4	117	43.3
Less: allowance for doubtful accounts	5	2.1	5	1.9	5	1.9
Net accounts receivable	109	44.9	113	43.5	112	41.5
Inventory	73	30.0	72	27.7	67	24.8
Total current assets	185	76.1	197	75.8	201	74.4
Furniture and fixtures	76	31.3	75	28.8	78	28.9
Leasehold improvements	1	0.4	1	0.4	0	0.0
Transportation equipment	53	21.8	70	26.9	85	31.5
Gross fixed assets	130	53.5	146	56.2	163	60.4
Less: Accum. depreciation	85	35.0	97	37.3	110	40.7
Net fixed assets	45	18.5	49	18.8	53	19.6
Cash-value life insurance	13	5.3	14	5.4	16	5.9
Total assets	$243	100.0	$260	100.0	$270	100.0
	Review 12/31/20xx		Review 12/31/20xy		Review 12/31/20xz	
Liabilities	Amount	%	Amount	%	Amount	%
Notes payable bank short-term	$81	33.3	$68	26.2	$59	21.8
Accounts payable—trade	42	17.3	46	17.7	31	11.5
Income taxes payable	5	2.1	6	2.3	7	2.6
Accrued bonuses	10	4.1	11	4.2	12	4.4
Total current liabilities	138	56.8	131	50.4	109	40.4
Subordinated debt officers	48	19.8	58	22.3	67	24.8
Total liabilities	186	76.5	189	72.7	176	65.2
Net worth						
Common stock	2	0.8	2	0.8	2	0.7
Retained earnings	55	22.6	69	26.5	92	34.1
Total net worth	57	23.5	71	27.3	94	34.8
Total liabilities and net worth	$243	100.0	$260	100.0	$270	100.0

8

Ratio Analysis

OBJECTIVES

After studying *Ratio Analysis*, you will be able to—

- Describe the considerations a lender needs to take into account when using ratios to evaluate financial performance
- Identify, calculate, and interpret liquidity, financial leverage, profitability, efficiency, and debt coverage ratios
- Explain how to use industry data when performing a ratio analysis

INTRODUCTION

Income statements (Chapter 6) and balance sheets (Chapter 7) provided the raw material for analysis—the details needed to create a financial picture of a business. Ratios, however, let the business banker move beyond the raw material by helping to tell the story about the business, adding another dimension to the analytical process.

Ratios allow a business banker to examine the relationship between two or more accounts on the financial statement. The general performance of a business can be analyzed one way by looking at how liquidity has changed over several years. To gain an in-depth perspective of the firm's liquidity, a lender reviews and analyzes how the components of various liquidity ratios evolved.

Ratios also permit a business banker to compare the financial performance of different companies of various sizes in the same industry. Where a large company is expected to generate more liquidity (as measured in dollars) than is a small company, liquidity ratios place both companies on equal footing and enable meaningful comparison.

Finally, ratios help a business banker to begin learning about the management of the business. Management's actions or inaction (whether responding to the competition, industry conditions, or the economy) drives the financial statements, which, in turn, determines the ratios.

This chapter covers the various ratios used within the financial analysis process, including how they are calculated and how they can be interpreted. You will learn about liquidity ratios as well as ratios that measure liquidity, financial leverage, profitability, efficiency, and debt coverage.

Relationship to the Commercial Lending Decision Tree

In the textbook Introduction, we explored the Commercial Lending Decision Tree (as shown in the illustration in the Introduction) as a way to think about the stages and steps involved in the commercial lending process. As you have already learned, the first stage in this process emphasizes early screening and qualifying steps, such as general fit with the portfolio and goals of your bank, and the initial assessment of financial and nonfinancial qualifications of the business. These preliminary steps allow a business banker to anticipate various issues and conduct a more efficient and accurate financial analysis.

The second stage moves into the detailed analysis of financial data gathered from the business and any owners that may serve as guarantors. An important part of the business financial assessment is ratio analysis, and in this textbook you will learn the process. Ratio analysis typically follows income statement (Chapter 6) and balance sheet (Chapter 7) analysis within the overall financial statement analysis process and steps.

RATIO ANALYSIS CONSIDERATIONS

Lenders cannot fully compare the performance of a business against itself or industry standards simply by reviewing actual account line items and results on income statements and balance sheets. The financial statement picture is too complex and too varied. Ratio analysis, however, allows business bankers to compare the financial performance of businesses of different sizes as well as the various components of the financial statements.

Ratios are used to examine other facets of a business in addition to profitability.

How quickly inventory is sold, how rapidly accounts receivable are collected, how efficiently assets are used, and other related questions are explored and analyzed using ratio calculations and interpretation.

Although ratios are valuable tools for financial analysis, they have limitations. A single ratio provides but a small amount of information about a business. To improve the financial analysis, multiple ratios are used in conjunction with one another. They are analyzed over time, preferably fixed periods, to determine trends and consistency. Several years of ratios provide a better tool for analysis than do ratios for one year.

Ratios and Accounting Methods

Complete and accurate financial statements are crucial for performing a valid ratio analysis. Understanding the underlying accounting techniques is also critical because rarely do all businesses in a given industry use the same accounting principles. While comparisons can be drawn against an industry, due to the variances within the data of the various firms, findings should be viewed as general indicators of performance rather than absolute rankings.

Dry Supply's financial statement spreads will be used to demonstrate raio analysis.

Income Statement

FIGURE 8.1 INCOME STATEMENT SPREAD: DRY SUPPLY						
Income Statement ($ in 000s)	Review 20xx		Review 20xy		Review 20xz	
	Amount	%	Amount	%	Amount	%
Net sales	$895	100.0	$937	100.0	$918	100.0
Cost of goods sold	645	72.1	667	71.2	631	68.7
Gross profit	250	27.9	270	28.8	287	31.3
Selling, gen. and admin. expense	157	17.5	173	18.5	180	19.6
Officer's compensation	36	4.0	31	3.3	28	3.1
Rent expenses	15	1.7	18	1.9	20	2.2
Bad debt expense	2	0.2	1	0.1	0	0.0
Profit-sharing expense	7	0.8	7	0.7	0	0.0
Depreciation expense	12	1.3	12	1.3	13	1.4
Total operating expenses	229	25.6	242	25.8	241	26.3
Operating income	21	2.3	28	3.0	46	5.0
Other income	0	0.0	0	0.0	0	0.0
Interest income	2	0.2	2	0.2	2	0.2
Rental income	3	0.3	3	0.3	3	0.3
Interest expense	6	0.7	7	0.7	11	1.2
Net profit before tax	20	2.2	26	2.8	40	4.4
Taxes	11	1.2	12	1.3	17	1.9
Net profit after tax	$ 9	1.0	$ 14	1.5	$ 23	2.5

As you can see on Dry Supply's income statement (Figure 8.1), for 20xz, Dry Supply's net profit before taxes was $40,000. This figure is not measured against a much larger dry-cleaning supply wholesale company because a larger company would be expected to earn more net profits.

A better comparison is the net profit each company realized as a percent of total sales. Dry Supply, with sales of about $918,000, earned a net profit before taxes of about 4.4 percent ($40,000 ÷ $918,000) on each sales dollar. By comparing this figure to another company or an industry average, a business banker can determine if Dry Supply's profitability performance is below average, about average, or above average.

When examining a balance sheet (Figure 8.2), you will discover different businesses within the same industry may use last-in, first-out (LIFO); first-in, first-out (FIFO); or the weighted-average cost method for valuing inventory. For fixed assets, the business may use straight line, double-declining balance, or other depreciation methods. To prepare financial statements, the business may use the cash or accrual accounting method.

FIGURE 8.2 BALANCE SHEET SPREAD: DRY SUPPLY

Common-sized report ($ in $000s)	Review 12/31/20xx		Review 12/31/20xy		Review 12/31/20xz	
Assets	Amount	%	Amount	%	Amount	%
Cash	$ 3	1.2	$ 12	4.6	$ 22	8.1
Accounts receivable	114	46.9	118	45.4	117	43.3
Less: allowance for doubtful accounts	5	2.1	5	1.9	5	1.9
Net accounts receivable	109	44.9	113	43.5	112	41.5
Inventory	73	30.0	72	27.7	67	24.8
Total current assets	185	76.1	197	75.8	201	74.4
Furniture and fixtures	76	31.3	75	28.8	78	28.9
Leasehold improvements	1	0.4	1	0.4	0	0.0
Transportation equipment	53	21.8	70	26.9	85	31.5
Gross fixed assets	130	53.5	146	56.2	163	60.4
Less: Accum. depreciation	85	35.0	97	37.3	110	40.7
Net fixed assets	45	18.5	49	18.8	53	19.6
Cash-value life insurance	13	5.3	14	5.4	16	5.9
Total assets	$243	100.0	$260	100.0	$270	100.0

	Review 12/31/20xx		Review 12/31/20xy		Review 12/31/20xz	
Liabilities	Amount	%	Amount	%	Amount	%
Notes payable bank short-term	$81	33.3	$68	26.2	$59	21.8
Accounts payable—trade	42	17.3	46	17.7	31	11.5
Income taxes payable	5	2.1	6	2.3	7	2.6
Accrued bonuses	10	4.1	11	4.2	12	4.4
Total current liabilities	138	56.8	131	50.4	109	40.4
Subordinated debt officers	48	19.8	58	22.3	67	24.8
Total liabilities	186	76.5	189	72.7	176	65.2
Net worth						
Common stock	2	0.8	2	0.8	2	0.7
Retained earnings	55	22.6	69	26.5	92	34.1
Total net worth	57	23.5	71	27.3	94	34.8
Total liabilities and net worth	$243	100.0	$260	100.0	$270	100.0

Each method is an acceptable accounting practice but can generate variations in financial results. Further, the combination of differences in methods within a single business adds to the potential for results that vary from other similar businesses. Chapter 5 covered information about accounting methods and how financial results can vary using different methods.

In addition to the variances caused by different accounting methods, ratios may portray an incomplete picture of nonfinancial performance. For example, one of the profitability ratios is return on sales. If the return on sales is 3 percent, then it does not tell the business banker if the 3 percent was earned on one sale or a little on each sale, or if some sales were unprofitable.

Ratio Characteristics

Ratios are a means to an end and not an end in itself. They are analytical tools and have the following characteristics:

- Ratios express *relationships between two related accounts*. Calculating accounts receivable to rent, for example, gives a ratio that lacks significant meaning because the two accounts are unrelated. However, accounts receivable to sales does express a relationship between two related items and is a meaningful ratio.

- Ratios are expressed in *whole numbers, percentages, or multiples,* such as $2, 2 percent, or 2-to-1 (2:1 or 2.0x). Whole numbers generally are used to express working capital and cash flow measures. Percentages are used with profitability ratios, such as a gross margin of 30 percent. Multiples are used when comparing balance sheet items to each other as well as when performing calculations that combine income statement items with balance sheet items, such as sales being "five times" [5.0x] fixed assets.

- Ratios *have their own syntax*—"to" means "divided by." For example, current assets to current liabilities is the same as *current assets ÷ current liabilities.*

Ratios are important to the financial analysis process, but a business banker should not rely too heavily on ratios to the exclusion of considering nonfinancial or qualitative items. All steps of the commercial lending decision process are necessary to make a good credit decision.

In this section, you learned that a business banker must take into consideration certain factors when performing a ratio analysis. One of those considerations is that it is crucial for you to understand the different accounting methods when analyzing ratios because not all businesses in a given industry use the same accounting principles. In addition, you now know to consider ratios as analytical tools, and you have increased your awareness of their characteristics.

TYPES OF RATIOS

Ratios usually are grouped into categories that represent major financial analysis concepts. The most common ratio categories are liquidity, leverage, profitability, efficiency, and coverage.

Liquidity Ratios

Liquidity indicates a company's ability to meet current obligations and sustain its operations by using cash or converting current assets to cash. There are no clear standards for an acceptable level of liquidity for a business. A small manufacturer with an uncertain or highly variable cash flow, for example, may need more cash on hand (liquidity) than a large utility company with a highly predictable level of cash inflow.

The following liquidity ratios are most commonly used in commercial lending:

- Current ratio
- Quick ratio
- Dollar amount of working capital

Current Ratio

Current ratio(x) = *Current assets ÷ current liabilities*

The current ratio is used to analyze the financial stability of a business. It offers an approximate measure of a firm's ability to pay its current obligations (represented by current liabilities) on time or within its operating cycle. Generally, the higher the current ratio, the greater the liquidity cushion a business has to meet its current obligations.

At one time, a current ratio of 2.0x was considered a sign that a business was doing well. Today, however, other factors such as industry standards and the composition and quality of current assets are considered. If much of the current assets of a business are comprised of slow-moving or obsolete inventory, then a current ratio of 3.5x may be needed. Alternatively, a current ratio of less than 2.0x, or even closer to 1.0x, may be satisfactory for a business holding a high percentage of its current assets in cash, marketable securities, and non-delinquent accounts receivable.

Referring to Dry Supply's balance sheet for year-end 20xz, its current ratio is calculated as (in thousands of dollars) the following:

$$\text{Current ratio} = \frac{\text{Current assets}}{\text{Current liabilities}} = \frac{\$201}{\$109} = 1.8x$$

Dry Supply's current ratio of 1.8x means that it has $1.80 worth of current assets for every $1.00 of current liabilities. Dry Supply's current assets could shrink approximately 46 percent in value before they no longer could be converted to sufficient cash to pay its short-term creditors. This figure is calculated by subtracting current liabilities from current assets ($201 − $109 = $92) and dividing the result by current assets ($92 ÷ $201 = 45.8%).

The current ratio, however, does not tell the business banker about the quality of the current assets or the timing of the liabilities. For example, it does not show if the $1.80 of current assets is cash (favorable), uncollectible accounts receivable (unfavorable), or obsolete inventory (also unfavorable). Neither does the ratio indicate whether the liabilities are due in one day or 10 months. For Dry Supply, the current assets are cash of $22,000, net accounts receivable of $112,000, and inventory of $67,000. Because cash and accounts receivable are more liquid than inventory, it appears Dry Supply has a good current ratio.

At 12/31/20xx, Dry Supply's current ratio was 1.3x, and at 12/31/20xz it was 1.8x. The company has improved its liquidity, as measured by the current ratio, over the past three years. A business banker will want to determine if this trend will continue or at least hold steady.

Quick Ratio

Quick ratio (x) = *(Cash + marketable securities + net accounts receivable) ÷ current liabilities*

Also known as the *acid test ratio*, the quick ratio is a narrower measure of liquidity because it counts only the current assets that can quickly be converted to cash. Unlike the current ratio, inventory and other less liquid current assets are excluded from the quick ratio. By eliminating inventory from consideration, lenders no longer need to determine how it was valued or how fast it could be liquidated.

Historically, a quick ratio of 1.0x has been accepted as a sign that a business has a good liquid condition. As with all ratios, however, there are exceptions. If a substantial portion of the accounts receivable are past due, then a quick ratio greater than 1.0x may be necessary. A ratio of less than 1.0x may be acceptable in a business selling inventory entirely for cash, such as a grocery store or retail store, because there will not be a material amount of accounts receivable.

The following is Dry Supply's quick ratio calculation at the end of 20xz (in thousands of dollars):

$$\text{Quick ratio} = \frac{\text{Cash+mkt. securities+accounts rec.}}{\text{Current liabilities}} = \frac{\$22+\$0+\$112}{\$109} = \frac{\$134}{\$109} = 1.2x$$

Dry Supply's quick ratio of 1.2x means that it has $1.20 of liquid current assets for each dollar of current liabilities. This quick ratio, which is above the 1.0x guideline, should be compared with others in the industry. For Dry Supply, this ratio was 0.81x at 12/31/20xx and 0.95x at 12/31/20xy. Because the value of this ratio has been increasing, Dry Supply has reduced its dependency on inventory to cover current liabilities for three consecutive years.

Dollar Amount of Working Capital

Working capital ($) = *Current assets – current liabilities*

Although working capital is a dollar amount and not stated as a ratio, it is a measure of liquidity. Working capital, calculated as current assets minus current liabilities, reflects a company's net investment in current assets—cash, marketable securities, accounts receivable, and inventory. A company's ability to meet current obligations or to take advantage of business opportunities depends on having an adequate supply of working capital. For a business banker, working capital represents the cushion a business has to work with in repaying short-term debt.

At the end of 20xz, Dry Supply's working capital (in thousands of dollars) was the following:

Working capital = Current assets – current liabilities = $201–$109 = $92

Dry Supply's current assets exceeded its current liabilities by $92,000 at year-end 20xz—an amount almost equal to the total level of current liabilities. This represents a fairly large cushion to work with as the business meets its current obligations. At year-end 20xx and 20xy, this cushion was $47,000 and $66,000, respectively, showing growth over the three years while the level of current liabilities decreased.

Financial Leverage Ratios

Financial leverage measures the degree of risk shouldered by the owners of a business versus that of its creditors. Assets are financed by either owners' equity (net worth) or debt provided by creditors (liabilities). Risk to creditors increases the higher the financial leverage. Highly leveraged businesses, for example, are generally less equipped to deal with business cycle fluctuations and, therefore, are more prone to failure. In the absence of net worth as a source of funding, a business may be unable to sustain its operations during an economic downturn unless it can procure additional debt financing. Such a prospect certainly poses more risk for a commercial lender. And, if liquidation does occur, creditors potentially have more to lose than do owners.

> **Financial Leverage vs. Operating Leverage**
>
> Financial leverage measures the degree of risk creditors take versus that taken by owners. Operating leverage is the relationship of fixed costs to total costs and net sales on the income statement. Firms that have higher financial leverage have a higher proportion of debt on the balance sheet, compared to equity. Firms with higher operating leverage have a higher proportion of fixed costs to variable costs on the income statement. In general, higher levels of either leverage measure indicate higher risk for lenders. When bankers use the word "leverage" they are usually referring to financial leverage.

For many firms, financial leverage increases and decreases are often related to fixed asset purchases and repayment of the long-term debt used to purchase the fixed assets. If a business recently purchased significant fixed assets, then the financial leverage may be temporarily higher than that of the industry. The analytical issue for a business banker is whether the business has sufficient cash flow to repay the debt, which will cause financial leverage to decrease again to acceptable levels. Businesses whose financial leverage is consistently higher than normal industry levels are in need of additional equity and are a high lending risk.

In assessing financial leverage, three key ratios are debt-to-worth and two variations called tangible leverage and tangible effective leverage.

Debt-to-worth or Leverage Ratio

Debt-to-worth or Leverage Ratio (x) = *Total liabilities ÷ net worth*

This ratio is the primary measurement of leverage by most lenders; it is often called the *leverage ratio*. It is the simple ratio of total liabilities to net worth (or owners' equity). When this ratio exceeds 1.0x, the risk of the creditors is greater than that of the owners. Leverage levels of up to 2.0x are acceptable in many lending situations; however, the typical debt-to-equity ratio varies by industry. Some businesses, such as banks, have total liabilities far in excess of their equity.

For Dry Supply at 12/31/20xz, the debt-to-worth ratio (calculated in thousands of dollars) is the following:

$$\text{Debt-to-worth} = \frac{\text{Total liabilities}}{\text{Net worth}} = \frac{\$176}{\$94} = 1.9x$$

With a ratio of 1.9x, it appears that over the short term, Dry Supply's creditors are incurring a larger share of the financing risk than its owners. At 12/31/20xx, this ratio was 3.3x; at 12/31/20xy, it was 2.7x, showing a decreasing trend over the three year-ends as total liabilities remained fairly stable and earnings increased net worth. A key issue for a business banker is whether this positive trend is expected to continue.

Tangible Leverage Ratio

Tangible Leverage Ratio (x) = *Total liabilities ÷ (net worth – intangible assets)*

The concept of tangible net worth involves reducing the stated net worth or owners' equity by assets with no physical existence, such as goodwill, patents, trademarks, copyrights, operating rights, and customer lists. Because intangible assets may be of little value in liquidation, lenders often subtract them in order to determine the true net worth of the business. In some cases, lenders further subtract from net worth other assets of limited value, such as due from officers and employees, receivables from affiliated businesses, and leasehold improvements.

The following illustration is the tangible leverage ratio (calculated in thousands of dollars) for Dry Supply at 12/31/20xz:

$$\text{Tangible leverage ratio} = \frac{\text{Total liabilities}}{\text{Net worth – intangible assets}} = \frac{\$176}{\$94 - \$0} = \frac{\$176}{\$94} = 1.9x$$

Because Dry Supply did not have any intangible assets at 12/31/20xx, 12/31/20xy, and 12/31/20xz, the values of the tangible leverage ratio were the same as the leverage ratio.

Tangible Effective Leverage Ratio

Tangible Effective Leverage Ratio (x) =
(Total liabilities – subordinated debt) ÷ (net worth + subordinated debt – intangible assets)

The concepts of unsubordinated liabilities and capital funds are used for this ratio. Subordinated debt is a liability having a lien against the borrower's assets that is secondary (or *junior*) to other obligations or a claim for payment only after holders of the primary (or *senior*) debt obligations are paid. When debt is subordinated, an agreement is created that stipulates whether nothing, or a limited amount of principal and interest, will be paid on the subordinated debt until the terms of certain other debts are satisfied.

Most lenders use the subordinated debt category, for spreading purposes, only for debts subordinated to the lender and under acceptable conditions. The amount of subordinated debt is subtracted from total liabilities to obtain *unsubordinated liabilities*, and then subordinated debt is added to tangible net worth to obtain *tangible capital funds*.

For Dry Supply at 12/31/20xz, the following illustration is the tangible effective leverage ratio (calculated in thousands of dollars):

$$\frac{\text{Tangible effective}}{\text{leverage ratio}} = \frac{\text{Total liabilities} - \text{subordinated debt}}{\text{Net worth} + \text{sub. debt} - \text{intangible assets}} = \frac{\$176 - \$67}{\$94 + \$67 - \$0} = \frac{\$109}{\$161} = 0.7x$$

Because Dry Supply had subordinated debt at 12/31/20xx, 12/31/20xy, and 12/31/20xz, the values of the tangible effective leverage ratio were lower at each year-end. At 12/31/20xx, the value was 1.3x; at 12/31/20xy, it was 1.0x. This decreasing trend shows less risk to creditors, especially the creditors that benefit directly from the subordinated debt. A business banker will want to know the terms of the subordination and whether the bank's debt is superior to the subordinated debt or can be added as one of the senior creditors to the subordinated debt.

As we mentioned in Chapter 7, in lending to a privately held company, it is often required that any owner debts be subordinated because the company's owners have the ability to pre-pay these loans, regardless of the written commitment in place between the owners and the business. To effectively freeze these loan amounts, the original note(s) signed by the business are held by the bank, along with a subordination agreement establishing when and how these loans can be repaid. It is important to note that business bankers should always monitor the financial statements of borrowers with debt subordinated to the bank's debt to insure that the firm's subordinated debt is not paid in advance of the firm's obligations to the bank. Keeping the subordinated notes at the bank may not stop a borrower from repaying the subordinated notes instead of his obligations to the bank first. Reclaiming improperly paid-out funds to subordinated debt holders, especially in workout situations, may prove to be a challenge.

Profitability Ratios

Profitability ratios, also called *operating ratios*, evaluate a company's ability to realize its objectives. Whether the objective is to maintain a certain percent share of the market or to expand as rapidly as possible, the yardstick by which all businesses ultimately are measured is their bottom line or their record in making a profit. The most commonly used profitability ratios look at the relationship between various income statement profit categories (gross profit, operating profit, pretax profit, and net profit) and sales, then comparisons of pretax profit to total assets and to equity. Taken together, they give the business banker a good indication of the ability of a business to grow, remain solvent, and repay debt. Many bankers use pretax profit in calculating the ratios that compare profit to total assets and to equity in order to provide a more meaningful comparison with other businesses that may use different accounting methods or have a legal structure where profits are passed through to the owners (legal structures such as partnerships, S corporations, and limited liability companies). Profit ratios are usually expressed as percentages.

- Gross profit margin (%) = *Gross profit ÷ net sales*
- Operating profit margin (%) = *Operating profit ÷ net sales*

- Pretax profit margin (%) = *Pretax profit ÷ net sales*
- Net profit margin (%) = *Net profit ÷ net sales*

These ratios allow a business banker to compare the profitability of a business from year to year, as well as see where net profits are generated. As you read in Chapter 1, certain firms in certain industries tend to have different levels of profit margins. Because service businesses and retailers tend to have more costs and expenses in the operating expenses category on the income statement, these types of firms tend to have higher gross profit margins than do agricultural businesses, manufacturers, and wholesalers. Agricultural businesses, manufacturers, and wholesalers tend to have more expenses within the cost of goods sold category. At the operating profit level, wholesalers tend to lag agricultural businesses, manufacturers, and retailers. Service businesses, among all of the other business types, tend to have the highest levels of operating profits.

For Dry Supply, the following first group of profitability ratios for 20xz (calculated in thousands of dollars) was:

$$\text{Gross profit margin} = \frac{\text{Gross profit}}{\text{Net sales}} = \frac{\$287}{\$918} = 31.3\%$$

$$\text{Operating profit margin} = \frac{\text{Operating profit}}{\text{Net sales}} = \frac{\$46}{\$918} = 5.0\%$$

$$\text{Pretax profit margin} = \frac{\text{Pretax profit}}{\text{Net sales}} = \frac{\$40}{\$918} = 4.4\%$$

$$\text{Net profit margin} = \frac{\text{Net profit}}{\text{Net sales}} = \frac{\$23}{\$918} = 2.5\%$$

As a wholesaler, Dry Supply shows somewhat typical levels of cost of goods sold (resulting in gross profit) and operating expenses (resulting in operating profit). The chart below shows the following same ratios over the past three years:

Year	20xx	20xy	20xz
Gross profit margin	27.9%	28.8%	31.3%
Operating profit margin	2.3%	3.0%	5.0%
Pretax profit margin	2.2%	2.8%	4.4%
Net profit margin	1.0%	1.5%	2.5%

Over the three years shown, Dry Supply improved its gross profit margin, and along with relatively steady operating expense levels, the improvement in gross profit margin resulted in better operating profits margins and net profit margins. Although these trends are very positive, a business banker should find out the key cost and expense categories that are responsible for the improvements. Most customers can provide detailed line-item reports for areas not broken out in the formal income statement.

The net profit margin shows the profit earned on each dollar of sales and is, therefore, the most quoted measure of a business's overall efficiency. It reflects management's decisions on product pricing, plant efficiency, ability to control overhead expenses, and attitude toward earnings retention. This ratio, using either pretax profit or net profit as the basis, is sometimes referred to as *return on sales*.

Just as with the other ratios, there is no general benchmark figure to be achieved. A business in a relatively volatile industry where profits can rise or fall rapidly should exhibit a higher ratio than a business that has a record of modest but steady profitability over the years. To determine the acceptability of these ratios, the business banker should look at the overall trend of ratios for the business being analyzed and compare those ratios with other businesses in the same industry.

Return-on-assets Ratio

Return-on-assets ratio (%) = *Pretax profit ÷ total assets*

The return-on-assets ratio measures the profitability of a business in relation to its efficiency in using its assets. It reflects management's decisions on credit policies, inventory controls, fixed asset utilization, and profit.

Although the return-on-assets ratio can be calculated in several ways, the formula shown above is the simplest—but it can distort the true picture. Replacing ending or total assets with average total assets is a more precise measure of this variable. Other considerations include asset valuation (for example, land as a fixed asset usually is valued at historical or acquisition cost, which is often below current market value) and imbalances. These factors may occur from timing differences between a point-in-time value (assets) and a period of time value (net profit).

Dry Supply's return-on-assets ratio for 20xz (calculated using thousands of dollars) was the following:

$$Return\text{-}on\text{-}assets = \frac{Pretax\ profit}{Total\ assets} = \frac{\$40}{\$270} = 14.8\%$$

Dry Supply's return-on-assets is, therefore, about 15 cents for every dollar of assets. This figure is meaningful only in comparison to previous years (8.2 percent in 20xx and 10 percent in 20xy) or to others in its industry. The three-year improvement is certainly a positive sign; however, with Dry Supply requesting to increase its equipment, this ratio may decline temporarily next year.

Return-on-equity Ratio

Return-on-equity ratio (%) = *Pretax profit ÷ net worth*

The return-on-equity ratio shows the efficiency with which owners' equity or net worth is being used to generate profit. For example, if owners' equity is small relative to total liabilities (resulting in a higher leverage ratio), then a business banker should expect to see a higher return-on-equity ratio.

What constitutes an adequate return to the owners (investors) depends on the perceived risk of their investment, as compared with something fairly risk-free, such as an FDIC-insured deposit at a bank or U.S. Treasury securities. When the average return on federally insured bank deposits is, for example, 4 percent, the return demanded on a non-insured, private company investment should be much higher.

Another way to gauge the return is through the relative level of owners' funds in the business. Returning to our earlier example, if owners' equity is small relative to total liabilities, then a high return-on-equity ratio does not necessarily indicate good performance if pretax profit is below industry averages. At a higher net worth position, the same pretax profit results in a lower return-on-equity. So, sometimes a high return-on-equity indicates an undercapitalized rather than an efficient business, especially if the leverage ratio is fairly high. In this respect, the return-on-equity ratio, however, does provide some insight into management's strategy regarding pretax profit targets and financial leverage goals.

Referring to Dry Supply's 20xz income statement, the following is its return-on-equity (in thousands of dollars):

$$\text{Return-on-equity} = \frac{\text{Pretax profit}}{\text{Net worth}} = \frac{\$40}{\$94} = 42.6\%$$

In 20xy, Dry Supply returned about 43 cents for every dollar invested by its owners, compared with about 35 cents in 20xx and 37 cents in 20xy. This is certainly a good performance by almost any standard, but particularly noteworthy in this case because Dry Supply's debt-to-equity is low. On the other hand, if subordinated debt is counted as equity, then the return drops to 24.8 percent for 20xz [$40 ÷ ($94 + $67)].

Efficiency Ratios

Of course, calculating the current ratio, quick ratio, and working capital does not address the issue of the timing of debt payment versus the timing of inventory sales and the collection of accounts receivable. To determine these timing issues, three ratios—expressed as days—measure management's ability to use company assets efficiently. They compare sales or cost of goods sold to three balance sheet accounts: accounts receivable, inventory, and accounts payable—or, in other words, how many days (on average) it takes to do the following:

- Manufacture, hold, and then sell inventory
- Collect accounts receivable
- Pay accounts payable (vendors)

Some bankers use the same relationships to determine how many times in a year the balance sheet accounts "turnover" by taking a year (365 days) and dividing by the days calculated above.

One additional ratio measures efficiency by comparing sales to total assets. This ratio is not expressed in days but shows the overall efficiency of the entire asset base of a firm.

Accounts Receivable Turnover

Accounts receivable turnover (days) = *(Net accounts receivable x 365 days)* ÷ *net sales*

Sometimes called the *accounts receivable collection period* or *day's accounts receivable ratio*, this measurement gives the average number of days it takes for a business to collect credit sales made to its customers. To make any worthwhile observations, the accounts receivable performance is compared with its own historical record as well as to others in the industry. For example, most retailers have few receivables, whereas a manufacturer's receivables often are expected to amount to one or two months of average sales, depending on the typical credit terms extended to its customers. If credit terms normally are payment in 30 days, then it is difficult to expect the average holding period to be a shorter timeframe.

A ratio that increases over time, or is high relative to an industry-wide average, may indicate that some accounts receivable are delinquent or uncollectible. As part of the analysis of this ratio, a business banker may request an aged listing of accounts receivable, itemized by individual accounts. (An example aged listing of accounts receivable is provided in Chapter 7.) In addition to analyzing this on an account-by-account basis, a high ratio also prompts a business banker to examine the credit terms and collection practices of the business.

Although it is ideal to use credit sales when calculating this ratio, in most instances a business banker simply uses net sales (after returns and allowances) along with net accounts receivable (after deducting any allowance for doubtful accounts). In 20xz, the following accounts receivable holding period calculation for Dry Supply (in thousands of dollars) was:

$$\text{Acc. rec. turnover} = \frac{\text{Accounts receivable} \times 365 \text{ days}}{\text{Net sales}} = \frac{\$112 \times 365d}{\$918} = \frac{40,880d}{918} = 44.5d$$

On average, Dry Supply's accounts receivable were collected in 45 days (rounded to a whole day). For this time frame to be relevant, compare Dry Supply's performance for 20xz with earlier years (44 days in 20xx and 44 days in 20xy) and with other wholesaling companies of similar asset size. With payments received within 44 to 45 days, Dry Supply's customer base has been consistent in payment and generally pays its bills on time, if we can assume that most customers receive payment terms of 30 days.

Nevertheless, the accounts receivable turnover ratio does not tell the business banker whether the company, for example, is owed a total of $112,000 by only two customers—one customer is one day past due (31 days from invoice date, based on 30-day payment terms) and the other 29 days (almost a month) past due (59 days from invoice date) for an average of 45 days from invoice date. This is where an aged listing of accounts receivable allows an analysis of the overall size and quality of each account receivable.

Inventory Turnover Ratio

Inventory turnover ratio (days) = *(Inventory x 365 days) ÷ cost of goods sold*

Sometimes called the *inventory holding period ratio* or *day's inventory ratio*, the inventory turnover ratio measures the average length of time inventory is held, including storage time for raw materials or components, time to manufacture or convert the materials, then the shipment and/or storage of finished goods until sold.

To provide an accurate picture of the actual physical turnover of inventory, cost of goods sold is used in the formula rather than net sales, thus excluding profit and overhead expense. As we have seen in earlier chapters, the inventory valuation method used (LIFO, FIFO, or weighted-average cost) may differ among businesses and can affect industry comparisons.

The following is Dry Supply's inventory holding period at year end 20xz (calculated in thousands of dollars):

$$\text{Inventory turnover} = \frac{\text{Inventory} \times 365 \text{ days}}{\text{Cost of goods sold}} = \frac{\$67 \times 365d}{\$631} = \frac{24{,}455d}{631} = 38.8d$$

According to this ratio, Dry Supply's inventory is held and sold/utilized within about 39 days. The significance of this timeframe rests on a comparison to its own performance in previous years (41 days in 20xx and 39 days in 20xy) as well as to the performance of similar wholesalers. A comparatively low inventory holding period indicates an efficient use of resources and excellent liquidity. Inherent in an extremely low inventory holding period is the danger of the business becoming understocked and a potential loss of sales if customer demand goes unfulfilled. Conversely, a comparatively high holding period indicates possible inventory buildup, which can be costly and unproductive. Dry Supply's ratio shows the company to be managing its inventory consistently (39 days for the past two years and a small decrease from 41 days in 20xx) and is likely carrying the correct amount of inventory.

The inventory turnover ratio does not tell a business banker the makeup of the inventory. For example, if Dry Supply's supply inventory is comprised of 25 percent as plastic bags, 25 percent as hangers, 40 percent as laundry products, and 10 percent as dry-cleaning supplies, then it may be difficult to determine whether the company has a good mix of inventory. The inventory turnover ratio tells a business banker the average holding time only, not the components of the inventory mix. If the company has only a few lines of inventory, then separate ratios by inventory component may be helpful. In the auto industry, for example, a business banker should calculate separate holding periods for a car dealer's new and used vehicle inventory.

Accounts Payable Turnover Ratio

Accounts payable turnover ratio (days) = *(Accounts payable x 365 days) ÷ cost of goods sold*

Sometimes called *accounts payable payment period ratio* or *day's payables ratio*, this formula measures how quickly a company pays its trade creditors. Ideally, inventory purchases, as calculated in the statement of cash flows, is used for this ratio. If the inventory purchases figure is not available, then cost of goods sold can be used in the denominator of the ratio.

Because credit terms vary considerably from industry to industry, the accounts payable turnover ratio is used primarily in relation to past performance and industry-wide performance. Over time, a significant increase in this ratio may indicate a cash flow problem, or it may mean an easing of credit terms offered by vendors. A decrease in the payment period may indicate that trade credit is being paid early and discounts are being taken, or it may be an indication that suppliers are withdrawing credit or shortening payment terms.

Using cost of goods sold for 20xz, at the end of 20xz the following is Dry Supply's ratio calculated (in thousands of dollars) as:

$$\text{Acc. pay. turnover} = \frac{\text{Accounts payable} \times 365 \text{ days}}{\text{Cost of goods sold}} = \frac{\$31 \times 365d}{\$631} = \frac{11,315d}{631} = 17.9d$$

On average, Dry Supply pays trade creditors in 18 days. Again, this figure should be compared with previous years (24 days in 20xx and 25 days 20xy). Dry Supply shortened its payment time between 20xx and 20xz. A business banker will want to determine if this action will continue into the future, since it has an effect on the firm's cash flow.

At 18 to 25 days, Dry Supply probably is within expected trade terms of 30 days. However, the accounts payable turnover ratio does not tell a business banker if Dry Supply owes money to twenty trade creditors or just two. Nor does it clarify whether the business is within terms with all trade creditors.

Sales to Total Assets

Sales to total assets = *Net sales ÷ total assets*

The ratio of sales to total assets measures how efficiently a business uses its entire base of assets. In this calculation, net sales is divided by total assets. The resulting ratio measures the dollars of net sales that each dollar of assets produces. For example, a ratio of 5.0x for sales-to-total assets indicates a business is producing $5 of net sales for each dollar of assets—the higher the ratio, the more efficient the business. However, if the ratio is very high compared with the industry, then the business may have a large percentage of assets comprised of equipment that is getting too old, obsolete, or fully depreciated, and may not be serviceable in the near future. On the other hand, if the ratio is too low compared with the industry, then the business may have just acquired new fixed assets and may be poised for growth and expansion.

At year-end 20xz, the following sales-to-total-assets ratio for Dry Supply (calculated in thousands of dollars) was:

$$\text{Sales to total assets} = \frac{\text{Net sales}}{\text{Total assets}} = \frac{\$918}{\$270} = 3.4x$$

For Dry Supply, the sales-to-total-assets ratio is relatively high because the fixed assets are almost 70 percent depreciated. This might explain the need for equipment financing. At the previous two year-ends, the ratio was 3.7x (20xx) and 3.6x (20xy). This trend shows that slightly fewer sales dollars are being generated for each dollar of assets over the last three years. In other words, the utilization of the entire base of assets—from accounts receivable to inventory to net fixed assets—has not been as efficient, although the relative level of efficiency appears to be good.

Coverage Ratios

Coverage ratios measure the extent a firm's fixed charges from debt obligations are met or exceeded by the cash flow from its operations. The ability to cover principal and interest payments is of crucial concern to business bankers and other creditors. In contrast to financial leverage ratios, which assess the bank's margin of comfort in the event of liquidation, coverage ratios indicate the cash flow margin of comfort while the business is a going concern. Traditional cash flow coverage, interest coverage, fixed charge coverage, and dividend payout are the most common coverage ratios used by business bankers.

Traditional Cash Flow Coverage

Traditional cash flow coverage = *(Net profit + depreciation + non cash expenses) ÷ CMLTD**

*CMLTD = Current maturities of long-term debt

Sometimes called the *gross cash flow coverage ratio*, the traditional cash flow coverage ratio compares cash-based net income with principal payments due on debt obligations in the coming year. Cash-based net income is determined by adding depreciation and any other non-cash expenses to net income. Some bankers, as well as some statement spreading programs, use the previous year-end's CMLTD as the denominator.

For Dry Supply at 12/31/20xz and using current year-end CMLTD, the following traditional cash flow coverage (calculated in thousands of dollars) was:

$$\text{Traditional cash flow coverage} = \frac{\text{Net profit} + \text{depreciation} + \text{non-cash expenses}}{\text{CMLTD}} = \frac{\$23 + \$13 + \$0}{\$0} = \frac{\$36}{\$0} = n/a$$

The traditional cash flow coverage ratio cannot be computed for Dry Supply because it does not have any long-term debt over the three-year period (as shown in the balance sheet spread).

Interest Coverage

Interest coverage = *(Pretax income + interest expense) ÷ interest expense*

The interest coverage ratio, sometimes called *times interest earned*, shows the proportion of a firm's earnings needed to pay interest on its debt. This is used when a business, like Dry Supply, has debt that consists of a revolving line of credit or short-term bank notes that do not have monthly principal payments or other types of formal amortization. Many larger companies and governmental entities also fit this profile, and the ratio is important to the evaluation process used by debt-rating agencies and large banks involved in public bond issues and large, revolving lines of credit that do not require amortization. For bonds issued by highly rated companies, the repayment usually comes from new bonds issued with the express purpose of paying off the old bond a couple of years prior to its maturity. For a revolving line of credit, if the borrower maintains adequate financial performance, then the line of credit commonly is used for another year. As a result, the only debt service issue is assurance that interest expense will be paid on time.

Although this ratio has limited application to businesses that have substantial amounts of amortizing debt, it provides a valuable picture of the potential effect of an increase in interest rates on the cash flow of a business, and the extent to which earnings are penalized to pay the financing costs of the business. A ratio greater than 1.0x is almost mandatory because a lower ratio indicates the earnings of the business are insufficient to cover its interest expense. Because interest expense is tax-deductible, most formulas start with pretax profit. Some bankers refer to the pretax profit plus interest expense as earnings before interest and taxes (EBIT).

The following interest coverage ratio for Dry Supply for 20xz (calculated in thousands of dollars) was:

$$\text{Interest coverage} = \frac{\text{Pretax profit + interest expense}}{\text{Interest expense}} = \frac{\$40 + \$11}{\$11} = \frac{\$51}{\$11} = 4.6x$$

With an interest coverage ratio of 4.6x, Dry Supply's interest expense could increase significantly before the company—at its current level of earnings—would be unable to pay its interest expense from profits. In 20xx, this ratio was 4.3; in 20xy, it was 4.7, for a favorable trend over three consecutive years.

TIP
Debt Service Coverage Ratio

None of the coverage ratios listed in this section has been labeled "debt service coverage." In a sense, all of the ratios contribute to a business banker's understanding of a business's ability to pay its various obligations. The fixed charge coverage ratio shown in this section is perhaps the most common definition of debt service coverage (DSC) by bankers, but even then there is not uniform agreement on how to handle dividends within the numerator, and some bankers add rent payment (for debt equivalents) into both the numerator and denominator.

We encourage you to learn the DSC formula preferred by your bank—or even what may be customary in your geographical region.

Fixed Charge Coverage

Fixed charge coverage = (Net profit + interest expense + depreciation) ÷ (CMLTD + interest exp.)

The fixed charge coverage ratio shows the proportion of a firm's cash flow available to cover various fixed charges. The lower the ratio, the smaller the margin of safety to repay debt and other fixed charges. If a firm's fixed charge coverage ratio falls below 1.0x, then it is not generating enough cash to repay its fixed obligations and will need additional funding (perhaps borrowed funds) in the coming year to service these obligations.

The numerator of this ratio serves as the lender's definition of cash flow available for debt service and other fixed obligations. Most business bankers start with net profit and interest expense so as not to double count the interest expense, since it is part of the debt service in the denominator of the formula. As with the traditional cash flow coverage ratio, non-cash expenses are also added to net profit. Some lenders refer to this cash flow figure as *earnings before interest, depreciation, and amortization* (EBIDA). Some lenders prefer to start with pretax profit and call the cash flow figure *earnings before interest, taxes, depreciation, and amortization* (EBITDA).

Because business bankers often are concerned with recurring distributions or dividend payouts to owners of small businesses, some formulas subtract distributions and dividends from the numerator. Pass-through entities (such as partnerships, S corporations, and LLCs) usually make distributions to their owners for tax purposes and need to be handled effectively as tax expenses and deducted from cash flow available to meet obligations. Similarly, most business-entity formats can pay dividends to owners as a return on their investment (not for taxation purposes), especially for C corporations. These dividends also can be subtracted from cash flow. Because dividends normally are a discretionary outflow, business bankers often restrict dividend payouts when structuring a commercial loan.

The fixed obligations usually include the components of debt service, which are principal payments (CMLTD) and interest expense. Because many firms can rent key assets that would otherwise be financed by a loan, business bankers can add rent payments that serve essentially as loan payments to both the numerator and denominator of the fixed charge coverage ratio's formula. The numerator becomes *earnings before interest, taxes, depreciation, amortization, and rent* (EBITDAR).

As one final variation, some bankers take loans that have no stated amortization and impute some level of principal payments for purposes of calculating this ratio.

The following is Dry Supply's 20xz fixed charge coverage ratio (calculated in thousands of dollars):

$$\text{Fixed charge coverage} = \frac{\text{Net profit + interest exp. + deprec.}}{\text{CMLTD + interest expense}} = \frac{\$23 + \$11 + \$13}{\$0 + \$11} = \frac{\$47}{\$11} = 4.3x$$

Because Dry Supply does not have any long-term debt, no current maturities are factored into the calculation above. However, if a business banker where to impute an amortization for the $59,000 of short-term notes payable, then the ratio would change. For instance, if the short-term debt had an imputed amortization of roughly five years, then CMLTD would be approximately $12,000 and the ratio would decrease to 2.0x [$47 ÷ ($12 + $11)].

Using the imputed loan amortization and if the ratio is further adjusted for rent expense, assuming it serves as a debt payment alternative, then the result is 1.6x [($47 + $20) ÷ ($23 + $20)]. Even with these adjustments, Dry Supply has a fairly strong cushion before coverage of fixed obligations becomes a problem.

> **Coverage Ratios versus Cash Flow Analysis**
>
> These coverage ratios work well for firms with a fairly steady balance sheet, as we see in Dry Supply. That is, the key asset and liability accounts for Dry Supply are not growing or shrinking rapidly. However, these coverage ratios could cause a business banker to come to some incorrect conclusions if the business is experiencing rapid growth or is shrinking dramatically in size. As we study cash flow statements later in this textbook, you will see how changes in balance sheet accounts can create additional sources and uses of cash flow, beyond the debt service and fixed charges used in these coverage ratios. Cash flow analysis will be an important extension of the ratio analysis process.

Dividend Payout Ratio

Dividend payout ratio = *Cash dividend paid ÷ net profit*

The dividend payout ratio does not show a coverage; it shows the percentage of net profit a business pays to owners as dividends. These funds are not available for paying fixed obligations, so this ratio usually is calculated along with the coverage ratios, as well as dividends or distributions sometimes serving as an adjustment to the fixed charge coverage ratio. One reason to separately calculate this ratio is to understand that the funds paid as dividends or distributions also are not available to support growth in accounts receivable, inventory, or fixed assets on the balance sheet.

With audited or reviewed financial statements, the amount of dividends or distributions will be found in the reconciliation of retained earnings or in the footnotes to the financial statement. In other situations, dividends paid or distributions made will need to be calculated. For example, if a business had a net profit $50 (in thousands of dollars), then the calculation would be the following:

Previous year-end retained earnings	$10
+ current year net profit	+ 50
− current year-end retained earnings	− 44
= dividends paid	$16

$$\text{Dividend payout ratio} = \frac{\textit{Dividends paid}}{\textit{Net profit}} = \frac{\$16}{\$50} = 32.0\%$$

Dry Supply has not paid dividends for the three years that we have been analyzing, so the dividend payout ratio is 0 percent. All of the earnings of the business have been retained and are available to cover debt service and fixed obligations, as well as to support growth in current assets and fixed assets.

Listed below in Figure 8.3 is a summary of definitions of the most common ratio categories.

FIGURE 8.3 DEFINITIONS OF RATIOS

Liquidity

Liquidity ratios show the ability of a business to meet current obligations and sustain its operations by using cash or converting current assets to cash. No rule determines an acceptable level of liquidity for a business, but depends on other risks such as the degree of financial leverage.

Current ratio (x): *Current assets ÷ Current liabilities*
The current ratio is used to analyze the financial stability of a business. This ratio does not tell the business banker the quality of the current assets or the timing of the current liabilities.

Quick ratio (x): *(Cash + Marketable securities + Accounts receivable) ÷ Current liabilities*
Also known as the acid-test ratio, the quick ratio is a more precise measure of liquidity because it counts only those current assets that can be converted to cash quickly. A quick ratio of 1.0x has been accepted as a sign that a business has a good liquid condition.

Working capital ($): *Current assets − Current liabilities*
Although working capital is not stated as a ratio, it is a measure of liquidity. The ability to meet current obligations or to take advantage of business opportunities depends on having an adequate supply of working capital. From a business banker's viewpoint, working capital represents a cushion a business has to work with in repaying debt.

Leverage

Leverage ratios, also known as financial leverage ratios, measure the degree of risk borne by the owners of the business versus its creditors. Assets are financed by either owner's equity (net worth) or debt (liabilities). The risk to the creditors increases as the proportion of debt to equity (financial leverage) increases.

Debt to net worth ["leverage"] ratio (x): *Total liabilities ÷ Net worth*
The basic leverage or debt to net worth ratio is a measure of the share of business funding from creditors compared to the share provided by the owners of the business. When this ratio exceeds 1.0x, then the claims of the creditors are greater than that of the owners. This ratio varies greatly by industry.

Tangible leverage ratio (x): *Total liabilities ÷ (Net worth − Intangible assets)*
The tangible leverage ratio adjusts net worth for various assets that may have little value, such as intangible assets (goodwill, patents, trademarks, copyrights, operating rights and customer lists), due from officers and employees, receivables from affiliated businesses, and leasehold improvements. As with the basic leverage ratio, tangible leverage measures the proportion of tangible assets funded by creditors versus the share funded by the owners of the business.

Tangible effective leverage ratio (x):
(Total liabilities − Subordinated debt) ÷ (Net worth − Intangible assets + Subordinated debt)
The tangible effective leverage ratio takes the tangible leverage ratio and further adjusts both total liabilities and tangible net worth by subordinated debt in cases where the debt is subordinated to the bank making the analysis. The amount of subordinated debt is subtracted from total liabilities to obtain unsubordinated liabilities, and then subordinated debt is added to tangible net worth to obtain tangible capital funds.

FIGURE 8.3 DEFINITIONS OF RATIOS (CONTINUED)

Profitability

Profitability ratios, also called operating ratios, evaluate a company's ability to realize its operational objectives. Whether the objective is to maintain a certain percent share of the market or to expand as rapidly as possible, the yardstick by which all businesses ultimately are measured is the "bottom line" or net profit. The most commonly used profitability ratios look at the relationship between net profit and sales, net profit and assets, or net profit and equity. Taken together, these ratios give the business banker a good indication of the ability of a business to grow, remain solvent, and repay debt.

Gross profit margin (%): *Gross profit ÷ Net sales*
The gross profit margin shows the gross profit earned on each dollar of sales. It primarily reflects management's decisions on product pricing, plant efficiency and costs related to inventory and production.

Operating profit margin (%): *Operating profit ÷ Net sales*
The operating profit margin shows the operating profit earned on each dollar of sales, and reflects management's decisions on product pricing, plant efficiency and cost related to inventory and production, plus overhead or fixed expenses not directly related to inventory and production.

Pretax profit margin (%): *Pretax profit ÷ Net sales*
The pretax profit margin shows the pretax profit earned on each dollar of sales and it encompasses all the costs and expenses of the business, except for income taxes. It reflects management's decisions on product pricing, plant efficiency, ability to control expenses, and attitude toward earnings retention.

Net profit margin (%): *Net Profit ÷ Net Sales*
The net profit margin shows the net profit earned on each dollar of sales and is the most quoted measure of a business's overall efficiency. It reflects management's decisions on product pricing, plant efficiency, ability to control expenses, and attitude toward income taxes (if applicable) and earnings retention.

Return-on-assets ratio (%): *Pretax profit ÷ Total assets*
The return-on-assets ratio measures the profitability of a business in relation to its efficiency in using its assets. It reflects management's decisions on credit policies, inventory controls, fixed asset efficiency, and profit.

Return-on-equity ratio (%): *Pretax profit ÷ Net worth*
The return-on-equity ratio shows the efficiency with which owners' equity is being used to generate profit. The higher the leverage, the higher the return-on-equity ratio for a given level of profits. What constitutes an adequate return to investors depends on the risk of the capital structure of the business. The return-on-equity ratio provides some insight into management's strategy regarding profit retention and financial leverage.

Efficiency

Efficiency ratios, also called turnover ratios, show how quickly receivables are collected, how quickly inventory is sold as well as how many dollars of sales are generated by fixed assets and total assets. These ratios measure management of the utilization of the assets of the business and can vary among different business types.

Accounts receivable turnover (d): *(Accounts receivable x 365) ÷ Net sales*
Accounts receivable turnover gives the average number of days it takes for a business to collect credit sales made to its customers. It does not tell the business banker the mix of the accounts and overall quality and relative sizes, which can come from an aged listing of accounts receivable.

Inventory turnover (d): *(Inventory x 365) ÷ Cost of goods sold*
The inventory turnover ratio measures the average length of time required to sell inventory. To provide an accurate picture of the actual physical turnover of inventory, cost of goods sold is used in the formula rather than sales, thus excluding profit and overhead expense. This ratio does not tell the business banker what comprises the inventory or the mix or salability of the inventory. It tells the average selling time only. If the business has a few categories of inventory only, separate ratios by type are helpful in order to make a complete analysis.

Accounts payable turnover (d): *(Accounts payable x 365) ÷ Cost of goods sold*
Accounts payable turnover measures how quickly a business pays its trade creditors. A significant increase in this ratio over time may indicate a cash flow problem, or it may mean an easing of credit terms. A decrease in this ratio may indicate that trade credit is being paid early and discounts are being taken, or it may be a reflection that suppliers are withdrawing credit. The ratio does not tell the business banker if a business owes money to twenty or only two trade creditors, nor does it clarify whether a business is within terms with all trade creditors.

Sales to total assets (x): *Net sales ÷ Total assets*
The ratio of sales to total assets measures how efficiently a business uses its entire base of assets. In this calculation, net sales is divided by total assets. The resulting ratio measures the dollars of net sales that each dollar of assets produces.

> ### FIGURE 8.3 DEFINITIONS OF RATIOS *(CONTINUED)*
>
> #### Coverage
>
> **Debt coverage ratios** measure the extent to which the fixed charges from debt obligations of a business are met or exceeded by the cash flow from operations. The ability of a business to "cover" principal and interest payments is a key indicator of financial health and important to the business banker considering a new loan request or monitoring an existing lending arrangement.
>
> Traditional cash flow coverage (x):
> *(Net profit + Depreciation + Noncash expenses) ÷ Current maturities of long-term debt*
> The traditional cash flow coverage ratio shows the proportion of a firm's net profit and noncash expenses needed to pay the principle due on long-term debt in the coming year (current maturities of long-term debt, or CMLTD). The lower the ratio, the smaller the margin of safety to repay debt. This ratio may be a fairly reliable indicator of the future performance of a business in a "steady state" (that is not growing or shrinking rapidly), provided profitability and non-cash expenses are expected to remain the same or increase.
>
> Interest coverage ratio (x): *(Pretax profit + Interest expense) ÷ Interest expense*
> The interest coverage ratio shows the proportion of the earnings of a business needed to pay interest on its debt. Public bond rating agencies and regional banks that make revolving lines of credit to large companies use this ratio. Although this ratio has its drawbacks, it provides a valuable picture of the potential impact of an increase in interest rates on the company's cash flow and the extent to which earnings are penalized to pay the financing costs of the company. A ratio greater than 1 is almost mandatory, because a lower ratio indicates a company's earnings are insufficient to cover the interest on its debt.
>
> Fixed charge coverage ratio (x):
> *(Net profit + interest expense + depreciation) ÷ (CMLTD + interest expense)*
> The fixed charge coverage ratio shows the proportion of a firm's cash flow available to cover various fixed charges. The numerator of this ratio serves as the lender's definition of cash flow available for debt service and other fixed obligations. It is sometimes referred to as earnings before interest, depreciation and amortization (EBIDA). Some lenders prefer to start with pretax profit and call the cash flow figure and call it earnings before interest, taxes, depreciation and amortization (EBITDA). Some formulas further subtract distributions and dividends from the numerator. Even other variations treat rent expense as a fixed obligation added to both the numerator and denominator, and the numerator becomes earnings before interest, taxes, depreciation, amortization and rent (EBITDAR). As one final variation, some bankers take loans that have no stated amortization and impute some level of principal payments for purposes of calculating this ratio. Despite all of these possible variations in the basic formula, fixed charge coverage is perhaps the most frequently used ratio for debt service coverage.
>
> Dividend payout ratio (x): *Cash dividend paid × 100 Net profit after tax*
> The dividend payout ratio does not show a coverage, but shows the percentage of net profit a business pays to owners as dividends. These funds are not available for paying fixed obligations, so this ratio usually is calculated along with the coverage ratios, as well as dividends or distributions sometimes serving as an adjustment to the fixed charge coverage ratio. One reason to separately calculate this ratio is to understand that the funds paid as dividends or distributions also are not available to support growth in accounts receivable, inventory or fixed assets.

Financial ratios measure many aspects of a business and are a fundamental part of the financial statement analysis. In this section, you learned the definitions of the most common ratio categories—liquidity, financial leverage, profitability, efficiency, and debt coverage. You also learned how to calculate and interpret these ratios. By understanding that financial ratios are categorized according to which financial aspect of the business the ratio measures, you are now prepared to successfully analyze ratios.

INDUSTRY DATA

By comparing an individual business with industry data, it is possible to determine which balance sheet or income statement items are out of line. In many industries, smaller businesses are less profitable because their owners are less interested in net profit and more interested in total payout from the business, including salaries and perks.

Smaller companies often have older, more fully depreciated equipment. A lender can verify this by looking at the common-size percentages. Larger businesses often achieve real productivity gains with newer equipment. Consequently, the common-size analysis for these companies shows a higher percentage of total assets invested in fixed assets.

For comparing the trends of a business with industry norms, lenders refer to industry data and compare the customer's performance level against the high-, mid-, and low-performance-level averages for the industry. Other important industry data, that is different from basic financial ratios, can be obtained from industry and trade associations, as well as from colleges and universities. Used along with basic financial ratios, a business banker can explore the performance of a business in terms of its ability to handle existing or proposed debt obligations and its ability to weather inevitable business disruptions or downturns.

Primary Sources of Industry Data

Bankers rely on the following two primary sources of industry data:
- The Annual Statement Studies published by the Risk Management Association (RMA)
- Industry and trade associations

RMA's Annual Statement Studies

RMA's Annual Statement Studies is a compilation of business financial ratios (similar to those you have studied in this textbook), based on spreads submitted by member banks. The data is organized into North American Industry Classification System (NAICS) codes, as sample sizes allow. That is, some industries can be broken into fairly narrow branches within the NAICS code structure if sufficient data has been submitted.

- Data for the ratios is grouped three ways. The first grouping is the most recent year by relevant asset size ranges, depending on the asset sizes within the data. The second grouping is the most recent year by relevant revenue sizes. The third grouping format is the entire industry for the most recent three years.

- Three values or quartiles are presented for each ratio. The middle number is the median (middle) score for the appropriate grouping of businesses (asset size, revenue size, or entire sample). The top number is the median score for the top half of all companies. The lower number is the median for the bottom half. These three medians give rise to four quartiles. The quartiles are used for calculating the three ratios in each category. The first quartile of businesses has values for the given ratio that are entirely above the top number; businesses in the second quartile have values for the given ratio that appear between the top and middle number; the ratio value of businesses in the third quartile appear between the middle and lower number; ratio values for fourth-quartile businesses are below the lowest number. This means that only 50 percent of the businesses have ratios between the top and bottom numbers. Many business bankers refer to the quartile position of the business they are analyzing in their credit analysis reports because there is no "average" figure to cite.

Industry and Trade Associations

Industry and trade associations—plus governmental entities, colleges and universities—can provide similar data based on basic financial ratios but more often cover statistics or ratios that are somewhat unique to their own industry. The following are examples:

A. The website for the National Association of Motorcoach Operators (www.namocoaches.org) provides unique data and statistics, such as the industry having about 4,000 companies, with 90 percent operating fewer than 25 buses. About 50 percent of the active job positions in the industry are with firms with fewer than 50 total employees. The association also tracks such items as annual revenue per bus. This is information that goes far beyond current ratios and leverage ratios, and is equally important to understanding a commercial borrower that is in this industry.

B. Governmental entities, such as the U.S. Department of Agriculture, provide extensive information on crop yields and pricing. Most major commodities also have a dedicated industry group. For example, the National Cotton Council of America (www.cotton.org) provides data on production, production history and yield from the county and state level in the United States, and worldwide data. It also provides technical resources that would be ideal for a business banker attempting to learn the industry, such as:

- Bale packaging (standards, specifications, and updates);
- Biotechnology (reports and studies on biotechnology, plus links to other resources);
- Cottonseed (information on cottonseed and cottonseed products);
- Flow-shipment (warehouse reporting information, shipping standards, rack sample study, and related reports); and
- Pest management (information on boll weevils, cotton nematodes, and cotton seedling diseases).

C. Colleges and universities also can be a source of data, sometimes in cooperation with an industry group. Since 1980, the Recreational Vehicle Industry Association (RVIA) has commissioned the University of Michigan Survey Research Center to update various industry statistics every four years. The most recent study cited a 15 percent increase over the four years in numbers of RV owners, now reaching 1 in 12 households in the United States.

Trend and Comparative Analysis

Trend analysis is measuring the performance of a business against itself over time. Comparative analysis is evaluating the performance of a business against other companies in the industry.

Figure 8.4 summarizes Dry Supply's trend analysis for the past three years and provides a comparative analysis for the current year for a number of important ratios. It also compares Dry Supply's most recent results with the wholesale dry-cleaning equipment industry.

FIGURE 8.4 TREND AND COMPARATIVE ANALYSIS: DRY SUPPLY						
	Dry Supply, Inc. Trend Analysis			Wholesale Dry-Cleaning Equipment Industry Quartiles 20xz		
Ratio	20xx	20xy	20xz	Higher	Median	Lower
Current	1.3x	1.5x	1.8x	2.4x	1.5x	1.2x
Quick	0.8x	1.0x	1.2x	1.2x	0.8x	0.4x
Tangible leverage	3.3x	2.7x	1.9x	0.9x	2.5x	5.1x
Interest coverage	4.3x	4.7x	4.6x	5.5x	2.1x	1.0x
Pretax profit margin	2.2%	2.8%	4.3%	n/a	2.1%	n/a
Return-on-assets	8.2%	10.0%	14.8%	10.7%	3.2%	(0.3%)

Trend Analysis

From fiscal year-end 20xx to 20xz, Dry Supply's current ratio increased from 1.3x to 1.8x. An examination of Dry Supply's balance sheets shows that although current liabilities decreased, current assets remained somewhat level. This situation reduced the company's need for short-term borrowings to support its current asset base, thus increasing its current ratio at 12/31/20xz. During the same period, Dry Supply's quick ratio improved from 0.8x to 1.2x. This was due to increases in cash and accounts receivable without a corresponding increase in current liabilities.

The decreasing tangible leverage (debt to tangible net worth) ratio suggests that Dry Supply's net worth (consisting primarily of retained earnings) has been sufficient to fund its balance sheet growth in the same or in better proportions over the three-year period. This could have resulted from a conscious management decision to use the company's leverage less aggressively. Dry Supply's increasing net profits for fiscal years 20xx to 20xz, together with its dividend policy (a dividend payout ratio of zero), appears to support this conclusion.

For the past three years, Dry Supply's coverage ratios have been consistent. The company's 20xz interest coverage ratio of 4.6x remains at an acceptable level. During this period, pretax profit margin improved from 2.2 percent to 4.3 percent, and return-on-assets improved from 8.2 percent to 14.8 percent. The net profit margin improvement may indicate a lack of competition, improved sales mix, good expense control, or some combination of the three. The return-on-assets improvement is due to limited growth of assets compared with improved net profits.

Comparative Analysis

Dry Supply's 20xz current ratio is in the third quartile and above the median for the industry. The ratio of 1.8x suggests that in liquidation, Dry Supply's current assets, even after discounts of almost 50 percent, would be sufficient to current liabilities. Moreover, its 20xz quick ratio is in the top quartile for its industry. An experienced business banker would recognize that Dry Supply's liquidity compares favorably to the industry; however, because the primary purpose of a ratio is to reflect trends, it is difficult to be conclusive about any single ratio in isolation. This is why a business banker needs to understand the business and its industry.

Dry Supply's tangible leverage ratio of 1.9x at 12/31/20xz indicates that creditors continue to have more risk than do owners. Although this ratio has improved over the three years, it is still fairly high and may limit the company's ability to borrow additional funds. At 12/31/20xz, this ratio is in the second quartile for its industry, which means that, in general, Dry Supply has a lower (more favorable) tangible leverage ratio than do most of its competitors.

The coverage ratio available for the industry is interest coverage, which shows Dry Supply to be higher than the median for the industry. This is the result of having a lower leverage position than its peers, which likely includes having fewer borrowed funds to generate interest expense, together with favorable levels of profits compared with the industry.

Dry Supply's pretax profit margin for 20xz is well above the median for the industry, with full quartiles not available from the industry data. A business banker should look further at the common-size income statement data for the industry to see which components cause the favorable position relative to the industry. Dry Supply could have a higher gross profit margin, lower operating expense levels, or a combination of both.

The relatively high levels of profits contribute to Dry Supply being in the top quartile for the return-on-assets ratio for 20xz. It is possible that Dry Supply uses its assets more efficiently than others in the industry to produce profits, but perhaps Dry Supply does not have as much new equipment as its competitors do. If industry data for the sales-to-assets ratio is available, as well as the other efficiency ratios, then a business banker can make better conclusions about this ratio.

In summary, Dry Supply compares favorably to its industry in this sample of ratios, in addition to exhibiting positive trends over the past three years.

Ratios are generally meaningless unless they are compared against something else, like a firm's past performance or those of another company in the same industry. In this section, you learned that bankers rely on the following two primary sources of industry data—the Annual Statement Studies published by the Risk Management Association (RMA), and industry and trade associations—for ratio comparisons. You now have a greater understanding of how trend and comparative analysis is used in measuring and evaluating a business' ratios.

SUMMARY

The financial analysis process would not be complete without a thorough understanding of ratio analysis. Ratios allow a business banker to examine the relationship between two or more items on the income statement and balance sheet. Through trend and comparative analysis of ratios, a business banker can evaluate the performance of a business in terms of liquidity, financial leverage, profitability, efficiency, and coverage.

By completing this chapter, you have learned that when using ratios to evaluate financial performance, a business banker needs to take into consideration the accounting methods used and the characteristics of ratios. You also learned the definitions of the various ratios used within the financial analysis process, including how they are calculated and how they can be interpreted. You have now gained a better perspective of how industry data are paired with trend and comparative analysis to analyze ratios of a business.

QUESTION FOR DISCUSSION

1. When comparing a firm's ratios to its industry, why is it important to understand the underlying accounting methods used by the business?

EXERCISE 1

Match the following terms with the definitions.

___ 1. Liquidity ratios A. Evaluate a company's ability to realize its operational objectives

___ 2. Leverage ratios B. Measure the extent to which the fixed charges from debt obligations of a business are met or exceeded by the cash flow from operations

___ 3. Profitability ratios C. Show the ability of a business to meet current obligations and sustain its operations by using cash or converting current assets to cash

___ 4. Efficiency ratios D. Show how quickly receivables are collected, how quickly inventory is sold, and how many sales dollars are generated by fixed assets and total assets

___ 5. Coverage ratios E. Measure the degree of risk borne by the owners of the business versus its creditors

EXERCISE 2

It is now time for you to apply what you have learned by performing a ratio analysis.

Background

Dry Supply Case Study

Anne Schippel, business banker, is analyzing Dry Supply's financial statements. When calculating ratios, many commercial lenders use a ratio summary. Figure 8.5 summarizes the key ratios as they might appear on her spreadsheet.

In reviewing the Ratio Summary and Comparative Data for Dry Supply for 12/31/20xx through 12/31/20xz, Anne Schippel has developed some questions and observations regarding the ratios. It is now your turn to do the same.

FIGURE 8.5 RATIO SUMMARY: DRY SUPPLY	12/31/20xx	12/31/20xy	12/31/20xz
Liquidity			
Current ratio	1.3x	1.5x	1.5x
Quick ratio	0.8x	1.0x	1.0x
Working capital	$47,000	$66,000	$92,000
Leverage			
Debt to net worth	3.3x	2.7x	1.9x
Tangible leverage	3.3x	2.7x	1.9x
Tangible effective leverage	1.3x	1.0x	0.7x
Profitability			
Gross profit margin	27.9%	28.8%	31.3%
Operating profit margin	2.3%	3.0%	5.0%
Pretax profit margin	2.2%	2.8%	4.4%
Net profit margin	1.0%	1.5%	2.5%
Return-on-assets	8.2%	10.0%	14.8%
Return-on-equity	35.1%	36.6%	42.6%
Efficiency			
Accounts receivable turnover	44.5d	44.0d	44.5d
Inventory turnover	41.3d	39.4d	38.8d
Accounts payable turnover	17.9d	17.9d	17.9d
Sales to total assets	3.4x	3.4x	3.4x
Coverage			
Traditional cash flow coverage	n/a	n/a	n/a
Interest coverage	4.3x	4.7x	4.6x
Fixed charge coverage	4.5x	4.7x	4.3x
Dividend payout ratio	0.0%	0.0%	0.0%

Figure 8.6 shows available comparative data for Dry Supply's industry for the most recent year.

FIGURE 8.6 COMPARATIVE ANALYSIS: DRY SUPPLY			
Wholesale Dry-Cleaning Equipment Industry Quartiles 20xz			
Ratio	Higher	Median	Lower
Current	2.4x	1.5x	1.2x
Quick	1.2x	0.8x	0.5x
Tangible leverage	0.9x	2.5x	5.1x
Pretax profit margin	n/a	2.1x	n/a
Return-on-assets	10.7x	3.2x	(0.3x)
Interest coverage	5.5x	2.1x	1.0x

Part 1

For each of the ratios listed below, perform your own ratio analysis by stating your observation and develop any necessary questions you would ask Dry Supply to complete your analysis.

    A. Liquidity ratios
    B. Financial leverage ratios
    C. Profitability ratios
    D. Efficiency ratios
    E. Coverage ratios

Part 2

Using Stage One of the Commercial Lending Decision Tree in the textbook Introduction, Schippel determined that Dry Supply, as a wholesaler, would likely show certain financial characteristics when she began to analyze the financial statements. What are some examples of these characteristics within the ratios for 20xx through 20xz?

9

Cash Flow Analysis

OBJECTIVES

After studying *Cash Flow Analysis*, you will be able to—

- Identify cash flow statements and reports
- Describe the two dominant types of cash flow statement or model formats—indirect and direct method
- Explain and calculate operating cash flows using the direct method
- Describe how to complete and use an abbreviated cash flow report and other tools

INTRODUCTION

Income statements (Chapter 6) and balance sheets (Chapter 7) provide the raw material for financial analysis—the details needed to build a financial picture of a business. Ratios (Chapter 8) tell a story about the commercial business—adding another dimension to the analytical process. However, income statements, balance sheets, and ratios do not necessarily repay loans. Cash repays loans, so it is critical to develop an understanding of the cash flow of a business in order to complete the analysis.

Relationship to the Commercial Lending Decision Tree

In the textbook Introduction, we explored the Commercial Lending Decision Tree (as shown in the illustration in the Introduction) as a way to think about the stages and steps involved in the commercial lending process. As you have already learned, the first stage in this process emphasizes early screening and qualifying steps, such as general fit with the portfolio and goals of your bank, and initial assessment of financial and non-financial qualifications of the business. These preliminary steps allow a business banker to anticipate various issues and conduct a more efficient and accurate financial analysis.

The second stage moves into the detailed analysis of financial data gathered from the business and any owners that may serve as guarantors. An important part of the business financial assessment is cash flow analysis, and this chapter will help you learn this process. Cash flow analysis typically follows the income statement, balance sheet analysis, and ratio analysis within the overall financial statement analysis process and steps.

Cash flow statements are part of a complete set of financial statements. For businesses that have externally prepared financials, accountants prepare cash flow statements according to **GAAP**, with the exception of compiled statements that usually omit a statement of cash flows (Chapter 4). In situations where a business submits internally prepared financial statements, tax returns, or an accountant's compilation, a business banker should prepare a cash flow statement or model. The lender has the option of replicating the GAAP format for a statement of cash flows (SCF) or making use of the UCA cash flow model developed by bankers and embedded in financial spreading software. Although the formats vary somewhat, they focus on organizing the sources and uses of cash, allowing a business banker to determine how a business uses cash to cover operating expenses, fund growth, and debt repayment.

> **Generally Accepted Accounting Principles (GAAP)**
>
> The rules, conventions, practices, and procedures that form the foundation for financial accounting.

Cash flow analysis also helps a business banker understand the history of the business, where things stood in the past and where they stand today. By studying pro forma statements and cash budgets, which will be covered in more detail later, a business banker may be able to anticipate future trends for the business. This chapter continues the financial analysis process by exploring cash flow statements and analyzing cash flow.

OVERVIEW OF CASH FLOW STATEMENTS AND REPORTS

The cash flow statement shows all of the cash resources available to a business. It also shows the flow of cash that results from the company's use of its cash resources during a given period, typically one year. Because it spans an entire year, the cash flow statement does not reveal the peak or low point of debt during a year. Nevertheless, it allows the lender to evaluate managerial decisions regarding cash. Management's actions and inactions are responsible for the results found in the income statement and balance sheet; the same holds true for the cash flow statement.

Similar to the way the income statement identifies the flow of revenues and expenses, the cash flow statement shows the total cash resources employed from the balance sheet and the income statement, how these resources became available, and how efficiently they were used. Cash flow statements can help a lender predict whether and why a business would seek a loan, and whether it has the capacity to repay debt.

To create a cash flow statement, information is drawn from one income statement, two balance sheets, and other financial records of the business. The cash flow statement is reconciled to changes in cash and cash equivalents, such as marketable securities and other assets that can quickly convert to cash. When all of the transactions over the course of a year are totaled, the result will equal the change in cash and cash equivalents from the beginning to the end of the year.

Why Bankers Focus on Cash Flow

Borrowers, investors, and lenders often differ in how they look at loan repayment. Borrowers often believe that loans are evaluated based on collateral. Investors tend to look at the long-term profitability of the business when evaluating loan repayment. Lenders, who know that cash (and only cash) repays loans, focus more on a company's ability to produce cash that is used to repay debt, invest in fixed assets, and support sales growth.

Business bankers focus on cash flow statements for the following reasons:
- To assess management decisions made over time;
- To evaluate the sources and uses of cash—where from and how used;
- To explain the disposition or use of profits;
- To evaluate the size, composition, and stability of operating cash flows; and
- To determine how wisely and prudently the business manages its cash.

Profit

One of the primary goals of a business is to maximize profits by increasing sales and reducing costs. Profits are generally the primary source of cash flow used to repay long-term debt. Profit, working capital, and cash have different functions in analyzing a company's operating cycle and cash flow.

Profit is recognized on the income statement when inventory is converted to an account receivable or cash. The income statement, which reports the effects of net profit on total assets, does not report the effect of cash on total assets. Nor does it consider the timing of cash flows. As such, profit relates to past and present management decisions.

Working Capital

Working capital does not change in the operating cycle, except for the net profit margin added as sales are made. There is only a change in its character. Working capital requirements grow as sales grow or as the operating cycle lengthens.

Cash Flows

Cash flows occur when inventory is purchased for cash and when receivables are converted to cash. These events reflect current management decisions. Bankers are primarily interested in the flow of cash, not profits or working capital, because cash flow shows financing requirements and the ability to repay loans.

The following are some additional concepts to remember when analyzing the cash flow statement:

- Accrual accounting recognizes a sale when products or services are provided in exchange for cash or for increases in accounts receivable, rather than as cash received only.
- Accrual accounting recognizes cash outlays for services with benefits anticipated in future periods as assets (prepaid expenses) on the balance sheet, rather than as expenses on the income statement.
- Cash-basis accounting recognizes cash outlays for inventory and labor in the inventory account and cash outlays for plant and equipment in the fixed asset account.
- The income statement contains charges for expenses that do not incur any outlay of cash; these include depreciation, amortization, and provision for taxes.

Sources and Uses of Cash—Liabilities and Equity Accounts

In developing a cash flow statement, it is important to understand the difference between transactions that use cash and transactions that supply cash to the operations of a business. Assume, for example, Dry Supply purchases plastic bags from its suppliers and receives the goods under the condition that the supplier will be paid within 30 days. Under this trade credit arrangement, Dry Supply has the use of its suppliers' funds for 30 days. Because inventory is increasing without expenditures in cash, accounts payable effectively becomes a source of cash for Dry Supply. Similarly, if Dry Supply borrows funds from a bank with a promise to repay the debt with interest over time, then the loan proceeds represent a source of cash. Therefore, an increase in bank debt is another source of cash for Dry Supply. Both accounts payable and long-term debt are liabilities. An increase in either one, or any other liability account, represents a source of cash to a business.

The examples show how an increase in a liability is a source of cash. The same relationship holds true for equity—that is, when equity in a business increases, cash available to a company increases. For example, selling stock or an increase in retaining earnings (usually from net profits) increases a company's cash.

Returning to the Dry Supply example, suppose it is the 30th of the month and payroll is issued. Electronically, cash is transferred from the company's account to those of its employees. Dry Supply also draws on cash when it makes a payment on its bank debt or repays a trade creditor. Similarly, stock repurchased from shareholders requires cash payments—a transaction that also decreases equity.

On the balance sheet, using cash to pay employees appears as a decrease in the accrued expenses or wages payable account. Using cash corresponds to a decline in accruals or any other liability.

So far, we have considered the relationship between sources and uses of cash for liabilities and equity only. An increase in any liability or equity account represents a source of cash, and a decrease in any liability or equity account represents a use of cash.

Asset Accounts

Referring now to the asset side of the financial statement, for the equation to balance, assets must have an opposite effect on cash flow. Whenever Dry Supply increases its accounts receivable, it uses cash. In essence, the company is granting its customers the use of its funds until the account or invoice is paid. An increase in assets, therefore, corresponds to a use of cash. Furniture and fixtures represent another asset of Dry Supply. Their asset value appears in the fixed-asset account on the balance sheet. When the business sells an unused desk, the amount in the fixed asset account declines, but the money received from the transaction represents an inflow of cash. A decrease in assets, therefore, corresponds to a source of funds.

Summary of Balance Sheet Sources and Use of Cash		
Accounts	Sources of Cash	Uses of Cash
Assets	Decrease	Increase
Liabilities	Increase	Decrease
Equity	Increase	Decrease

In summary, changes in asset, liability, and equity accounts have the following effects on cash:

In this section, you learned why a banker focuses on the cash flow of a business. It is cash (and only cash) that repays loans, so it is critical to focus on a company's ability to produce cash that is used to repay debt, invest in fixed assets, and support sales growth. You also learned about the relationship between sources and uses of cash for liabilities and equity. An increase in accounts payable, or any other liability account, represents a source of cash to a business, and the same relationship is true for equity—when equity in a business increases, cash available to that company increases. In addition, you learned about the relationship between sources and uses of cash for assets—an increase in accounts receivables is a use of cash, and selling an asset, for example, is a source of cash. You should now feel more confident about the overview of cash flow statements and reports.

STATEMENT OF CASH FLOWS—INDIRECT METHOD

Prior to November 1987, businesses provided a *statement of changes in financial position* along with the balance sheet and income statement. This report had many preparation options, including a cash basis and a working capital basis. The lack of a standard format led bankers to begin developing their own cash-based reports, with the UCA cash flow model emerging as a standard tool within most statement spreading software. The label "UCA" comes from the Risk Management Association's training course called *Uniform Credit Analysis*, where the model was introduced.

At about the same time, the Financial Accounting Standards Board (FASB) issued SFAS 95, *Statement of Cash Flows*, effective in 1988. The SFAS 95

> **Indirect method**
>
> A method used to prepare a statement of cash flows (SCF) that starts with net profit and adjusts for any non-cash items (depreciation and amortization) expensed on the income statement. This amount is further adjusted for changes in assets (other than cash), liabilities, and equity (other than net profits). These changes are grouped into operating, investing, and financing cash flow. The result from all three sections equals the change in cash during the year.

report is cash-based only and greatly reduced the formatting options to just two—**indirect** and **direct method**—with the indirect method being the dominant choice by businesses and their accountants. Interestingly, the UCA model uses the direct method, as you will learn later.

CASH FLOW FORMATS: INDIRECT VS. DIRECT METHOD

The banking industry has evolved to use the following two primary formats for cash flow statements and models:

(1) In situations where a business provides accountant-prepared financial statements (reviews and audits, in particular, as covered in Section 1, Chapter 4), a business banker can utilize a statement of cash flows (SCF) prepared in accordance with SFAS 95, *Statement of Cash Flows*, effective in 1988. As explained in this reading, an SCF usually is prepared using the indirect method.

(2) In most situations—including accountant-prepared reviews and audits, plus customer-prepared financial statements and tax returns—bankers use statement spreading software to create the UCA cash flow model (UCA model). This report is generated using the direct method.

Statement of Cash Flows (SCF)—Indirect Method

In SFAS 95, the Financial Accounting Standards Board (FASB) expressed a preference for, but did not require, the use of the direct method. Both the direct and indirect methods require cash flows to be classified according to operating, investing, and financing activities. The different presentation affects the operating section only. The investing and financing sections do not differ between the two presentations.

> **Direct method**
>
> A method used to prepare a statement of cash flows (SCF) that identifies cash receipts and payments, organized into operating, investing, and financing cash flows. It starts with *cash collected from sales*, which is one of several operating activities that involve receipts and payments from normal business operations. Essentially, the various income statement items that generate net profit are matched with changes to their counterparts in the balance sheet. So, sales is matched to the change in accounts receivable to derive *cash collected from sales*. Cost of goods sold is matched to changes in both inventory and accounts payable to derive *cash paid to suppliers*. Beyond the operating cash flows section, the format of a direct method SCF is the same as in indirect SCF. Both formats generate a result that equals the change in cash during the year.

> **DID YOU KNOW?**
>
> Cash inflows and outflows for most cash flow reports and models, including the statement of cash flows, are classified into the following categories:
>
> • Operating activities
>
> • Investing activities
>
> • Financing activities

Although both the direct and indirect approaches produce the same subtotal for cash provided from operating activities, the internal composition of the statements differ substantially. A major advantage of the direct method is that the primary sources and uses of cash are listed. A major advantage of the indirect method is that the reasons for the difference between net income and cash generated by operations are detailed.

On the practical side, the indirect approach is used more frequently, partly because of historical convention, and the indirect approach is similar to the statement that was required prior to SFAS 95. Additionally, a firm using the direct approach must provide a schedule that reconciles net income with cash provided by operating activities. This reconciliation essentially consists of the information contained in the indirect approach. Thus, a firm that opts for the direct approach must really provide both methods. Some firms are reluctant to do this, either because additional costs are involved or because they feel that the statement will become too cluttered and, therefore, less informative.

The indirect cash flow method under SFAS 95 will be demonstrated later, using the financial data from Dry Supply, a wholesaler of powdered laundry products. The operating activities section of the SCF will be demonstrated from the same financial data but will employ the direct method. Because the investing and financing activities sections of the SCF are the same using both methods, they will not be repeated using the direct method.

Survey of User Preferences

A survey published several years ago by *The CPA Journal* reported that 82 percent of CEOs, CFOs, and managers preferred the indirect method, compared with 70.3 percent of investors and analysts. Overall, 78.9 percent of users prefer the indirect method. The following four possible reasons for the preferred format were (in order of importance):

1. Familiarity with the format, since it more closely resembles the statement of changes in financial position previously required.
2. Consistency.
3. Seeing changes in accounts receivable and accounts payable, for example, was important. (Seeing actual cash received [from customers, for instance] and cash paid [to suppliers, for instance] was not important.)
4. Ability to see the difference between net income and cash from operations.

The following trends were found by business type:

- Manufacturing favored the indirect method (85.9%).
- Merchandising (retailers) preferred the indirect method but by a much lesser percentage than did other business types (63.6%).
- Service businesses preferred the indirect method (76.7%).

The survey did not provide data for agricultural businesses, wholesalers, and construction businesses.

UCA Cash Flow Model—Direct Method

Most of the cash flow models developed by bankers have used the direct method as well as the operating, investing, and financing cash flows categories. The Uniform Credit Analysis (UCA) model, introduced in The Risk Management Association's training course, *Uniform Credit Analysis*, is perhaps the most popular version and is provided by most of the financial spreading software programs.

Banker-developed models focus on seeing where cash was acquired and expended rather than on simple changes in balance sheet accounts. Most attempt to isolate or exclude interest payments from operating activities in order to create a cash flow available for debt service number. They also pair the interest paid with scheduled payments on bank debt (current maturities of long-term debt) as a measure of required debt service. Later, when the model presents the overall change in bank debt, the current maturities are excluded from the underlying calculation, since they have already been paid.

Cash Flows from Operating Activities—Indirect Method

In this section, the statement of cash flows will be demonstrated for Dry Supply, a wholesaler of powdered laundry products. The spreadsheets for the most recent three

FIGURE 9.1 INCOME STATEMENT SPREAD: DRY SUPPLY

Income Statement ($ in 000s)	Review 20xx Amount	%	Review 20xy Amount	%	Review 20xz Amount	%
Net sales	$895	100.0	$937	100.0	$918	100.0
Cost of goods sold	**645**	**72.1**	**667**	**71.2**	**631**	**68.7**
Gross profit	250	27.9	270	28.8	287	31.3
Selling, gen. and admin. expense	157	17.5	173	18.5	180	19.6
Officer's compensation	36	4.0	31	3.3	28	3.1
Rent expenses	15	1.7	18	1.9	20	2.2
Bad debt expense	2	0.2	1	0.1	0	0.0
Profit-sharing expense	7	0.8	7	0.7	0	0.0
Depreciation expense	**12**	**1.3**	**12**	**1.3**	**13**	**1.4**
Total operating expenses	229	25.6	242	25.8	241	26.3
Operating income	21	2.3	28	3.0	46	5.0
Other income	0	0.0	0	0.0	0	0.0
Interest income	2	0.2	2	0.2	2	0.2
Rental income	3	0.3	3	0.3	3	0.3
Interest expense	**6**	**0.7**	**7**	**0.7**	**11**	**1.2**
Net profit before tax	20	2.2	26	2.8	40	4.4
Taxes	**11**	**1.2**	**12**	**1.3**	**17**	**1.9**
Net profit after tax	$ 9	1.0	$ 14	1.5	$ 23	2.5

years for Dry Supply are shown in Figure 9.1 and Figure 9.2.

Cash flows from operating activities is the first category on the indirect method SFAS 95 *statement of cash flows* (SCF) (Figure 9.3). It shows the cash coming into the business through the incomes statement by starting with the firm's net income, then adding depreciation, since it is a non-cash charge. Next, changes in various current asset and current liability accounts are presented, including accounts receivable, inventory, accounts payable, and accrued expenses. Changes in cash are not included in operating activities because cash is the final balancing account. Also,

> **Cash flows from operating activities**
>
> The amount of cash generated from a business enterprise's normal, ongoing operations during an accounting period. Cash flow from operations excludes extraordinary income and expense.

changes in short-term debt are not included because they will are related to financing cash flow later in the format.

FIGURE 9.2 BALANCE SHEET SPREAD: DRY SUPPLY

Common-sized report ($ in $000s)	Review 12/31/20xx		Review 12/31/20xy		Review 12/31/20xz	
Assets	Amount	%	Amount	%	Amount	%
Cash	$ 3	1.2	$ 12	4.6	$ 22	8.1
Accounts receivable	114	46.9	118	45.4	117	43.3
Less: allowance for doubtful accounts	5	2.1	5	1.9	5	1.9
Net accounts receivable	109	44.9	113	43.5	112	41.5
Inventory	73	30.0	72	27.7	67	24.8
Total current assets	185	76.1	197	75.8	201	74.4
Furniture and fixtures	76	31.3	75	28.8	78	28.9
Leasehold improvements	1	0.4	1	0.4	0	0.0
Transportation equipment	53	21.8	70	26.9	85	31.5
Gross fixed assets	130	53.5	146	56.2	163	60.4
Less: Accum. depreciation	85	35.0	97	37.3	110	40.7
Net fixed assets	45	18.5	49	18.8	53	19.6
Cash-value life insurance	13	5.3	14	5.4	16	5.9
Total assets	$243	100.0	$260	100.0	$270	100.0
	Review 12/31/20xx		Review 12/31/20xy		Review 12/31/20xz	
Liabilities	Amount	%	Amount	%	Amount	%
Notes payable bank short-term	$81	33.3	$68	26.2	$59	21.8
Accounts payable—trade	42	17.3	46	17.7	31	11.5
Accrued taxes	5	2.1	6	2.3	7	2.6
Accrued bonuses	10	4.1	11	4.2	12	4.4
Total current liabilities	138	56.8	131	50.4	109	40.4
Subordinated debt officers	48	19.8	58	22.3	67	24.8
Total liabilities	186	76.5	189	72.7	176	65.2
Net Worth						
Common stock	2	0.8	2	0.8	2	0.7
Retained earnings	55	22.6	69	26.5	92	34.1
Total net worth	57	23.5	71	27.3	94	34.8
Total liabilities and net worth	$243	100.0	$260	100.0	$270	100.0

The amounts for net income and depreciation are taken directly from the income statement for 20xz. The balance sheet account changes are computed from the ending balances for December 31, 20xy, and December 31, 20xz. As discussed earlier, increases in assets are a use of cash (shown as a negative number). Decreases in liabilities also are a use of cash (shown as a negative number). Positive numbers are decreases in assets and increases in liabilities.

Many financial statement users find the operating activities section to be quite informative. Business bankers and other creditors, for example, recognize that loans and accounts payable can only be repaid with cash and that a firm's operations are a likely

FIGURE 9.3 DRY SUPPLY STATEMENT OF CASH FLOWS FOR THE YEAR ENDING 12/31/20xz ($ IN 000s)

CASH FLOW FROM OPERATING ACTIVITIES

Cash Flow from Operating Activities	
Net income	$ 23
Adjustments to reconcile net income to net cash	
Depreciation	13
Changes in current assets and current liabilities	
Accounts receivable (increase) decrease	1
Inventory (increase) decrease	5
Accounts payable – trade increase (decrease)	(15)
Accrued taxes increase (decrease)	1
Accrued bonuses increase (decrease)	1
Net cash provided by operating activities	$ 29

source of cash for these repayments. Because the ability to generate cash determines dividends and share price, shareholders and investors are also interested in cash provided by **operating activities.**

Cash Flows from Investing Activities—Indirect Method

The second section of the SCF summarizes the purchase and sale of fixed assets (Figure 9.4). Because they can be delayed and are controlled more closely by management, **investing activitie**s are more discretionary than operating activities.

Most of the **cash flows from investing activities** are related to the following capital expenditures:

- Proceeds from sale of equipment—The amount of cash received from selling equipment the business no longer needs (for example, vehicles and other equipment used in the operation of the business)

- Payment received on note for sale of plant—The amount of cash received from selling land and buildings

- Capital expenditures—The amount of cash used to purchase equipment, vehicles, fixtures, land, buildings, and leasehold improvements

> **Operating activities**
>
> Operating activities measure, through net income and receivables, cash generated by the current operating cycle and short-term changes in current accounts requiring cash for purchases, accounts payable, and payments to employees.

> **Investing activities**
>
> Investing activities measure payments received from selling fixed assets and capital expenditures for new fixed assets.

FIGURE 9.4 DRY SUPPLY STATEMENT OF CASH FLOWS FOR THE YEAR ENDING 12/31/20xz ($ IN 000s)

CASH FLOW FROM INVESTING ACTIVITIES

Cash Flow from Investing Activities	
Proceeds from sale of equipment	$ 0
Payment received on note for sale of plant	0
Cash value life insurance decrease (increase)	(2)
Capital expenditures	(17)
Net cash provided by investing activities	($ 19)

> **Cash flows from investing activities**
>
> Discretionary cash flows that can be delayed are controlled more closely by management and summarize the purchase and sale of fixed goods.

Proceeds from sale of equipment are shown on the income statement as gains or losses on sale of fixed assets. Dry Supply had no sales of equipment in 20xz. Payment received on note for sale of plant would be indicated as reductions on notes receivable. A lender will need to verify these notes were from sale of plant and not from some other purpose. Dry Supply had no payments on note from sale of plant during 20xz. The investing section of the SCF also captures changes in other non-current assets, such as cash-value life insurance, which increased by $2,000 in 20xz. The capital expenditure purchases are calculated using the change in net fixed assets plus depreciation expense. Depreciation expense is a non-cash charge, and a lender is always concerned with cash flow.

Figure 9.5 illustrates the 20xz capital expenditures calculation for Dry Supply.

FIGURE 9.5 DRY SUPPLY CAPITAL EXPENDITURES FOR THE YEAR ENDING 12/31/20xz ($ IN 000s)

20xy net fixed assets	$ 49
Less: 20xz net fixed assets	53
Net fixed assets (increase) decrease	($ 4)
Depreciation expense	(13)
Capital expenditures	($17)

The $17,000 increase in gross fixed assets is considered a use of cash. Because fixed assets were a use of cash, the increase is shown as a negative number.

Cash Flows from Financing Activities—Indirect Method

Cash flows from financing activities on the SCF include debt or equity activities directly related to the external **financing activities** of the business. For example, an increase in a company's common stock and paid-in capital accounts is a positive sign because it generally lowers the company's financial leverage, which may reduce the risk to the lender. Retaining profits is the primary source of equity growth and cash flow to repay debt.

The company's dividend policy is important to examine because dividends diminish the amount of cash available to repay loans. The cash also could be used to fund growth and reduce the amount of cash available for equity or debt repayment.

A lender compares the amount of the **dividend** to the operating cash flows and debt requirements. Partnerships, S corporations, and LLCs often make distributions to fund the personal tax liability of the owners. A lender compares the amount of the distribution to the actual tax liability.

> **Cash flows from financing activities**
>
> The amount of cash that directly relates to the business's external financing, involving debt or equity.

> **Financing activities**
>
> Financing activities measure cash flows from debt, debt payments, and proceeds from and payments to shareholders, the external financing of a business.

> **Dividends vs. Distributions**
>
> In common discussion, bankers tend to interchange the words *dividend* and *distribution.*
>
> - *Dividends* are company profits paid pro rata to stockholders, either in cash or in more shares. Dividends generally are limited to C corporations and are taxable income to the stockholders who receive them. Dividends are not a tax-deductible expense to the corporation.
>
> - *Distributions* are cash or other assets taken out of the business by its owners (partners, members, or shareholders of pass-through entities such as partnerships, LLCs, and S corporations) and are not necessarily a distribution of profits. In general, as long as cumulative distributions are less than the cumulative net taxable income passed through to the owners from the business, distributions are not taxable income to the recipients. This is because the net taxable income passed through to the owners has already been taxed as personal income to them.

Cash flows from financing activities relate to the following instances of bank debt, leases, and equity:

- Proceeds from sale of stock—Proceeds received from the sale of common or preferred stock

- Proceeds from notes payable short-term debt—The amount of new or repaid short-term bank debt

- Proceeds from long-term debt—The net amount of new long-term debt

- Repayment of debt—The current maturities of long-term debt from the previous year plus any other payments on long-term debt

- Payments under capital lease obligations—Payments on capitalized leases and usually disclosed in the footnotes in reviewed and audited financial statements

- Dividends paid—The amount of distributions to owners and dividends paid

Figure 9.6 shows the third section of an SCF, with the cash flow from financing activities for Dry Supply.

FIGURE 9.6 DRY SUPPLY STATEMENT OF CASH FLOWS FOR THE YEAR ENDING 12/31/20xz ($ IN 000s)

CASH FLOW FROM FINANCING ACTIVITIES

Cash Flow from Financing Activities	
Proceeds from sale of stock	$ 0
Proceeds from short-term debt	(9)
Proceeds from subordinated debt	9
Repayment of debt	0
Payment under capital lease obligations	0
Dividends paid	0
Net cash provided by financing activities	$ 0

Because the debt was reduced in 20xz, the amount of change in short-term bank debt is a negative number. Dry Supply, which has no long-term debt, does have subordinated long-term debt. Because the owners loaned the company more money, the net change of $9,000 is a positive number.

Figure 9.7 shows the calculations for the debt changes.

FIGURE 9.7 DRY SUPPLY DEBT CHANGE CALCULATIONS FOR THE YEAR ENDING 12/31/20xz ($ IN 000s)

20xz short-term debt	$ 59
−20xy short-term debt	68
Short-term debt increase (decrease)	($ 9)
20xz subordinated debt	$ 67
− 20xy subordinated debt	58
Subordinated debt increase (decrease)	$ 9

Dry Supply has no capitalized leases and has not paid out dividends to the owners for three years. Even though the company does not pay dividends, it still provides salary and other benefits to the owners that reduce net profit. Either way—higher profits than pay dividends, or higher salaries and benefits to owners and no dividends—the effect on the resulting increase to retained earnings can be very similar.

Figure 9.8 shows the calculation for the dividends paid by Dry Supply.

FIGURE 9.8 DRY SUPPLY DIVIDENDS PAID CALCULATION FOR THE YEAR ENDING 12/31/20xz ($ IN 000s)

20xy retained earnings	$ 69
+ 20xz net profit (loss)	23
− 20xz retained earnings	92
= Dividends paid	$ 0

Completed Statement of Cash Flows—Indirect Method

When used in conjunction with the income statement and balance sheet, the SCF is a key tool in financial analysis. It helps the business banker evaluate a company's ability to generate positive cash flows from operations, which is essential to meeting financial obligations and paying dividends. In addition, a SCF helps answer a business banker's questions about a company's need for financing and the effect a company's investing and financing transactions have had on its cash position.

Using the results from the calculations, the income statement, and balance sheet, Figure 9.9 shows the completed SCF for 20xz for Dry Supply. The increase (or decrease) in cash and cash equivalents is the total of the net cash provided (or used) by operating, investing, and financing activities. Thus, $29,000 + ($19,000) + $0 = $10,000.

In this section, you learned about the two formatting options for cash flow reports—indirect and direct methods—that have evolved. From the indirect method, you can now explain that cash flow from operating activities is cash generated from a business enterprise's normal, ongoing operations during a specific accounting period. You also learned that cash flow from investing activities summarizes the purchase and sale of fixed assets and that cash flow from financing activities includes debt or equity activities directly related to the external financing activities of the business.

In addition to knowing the types of reports and the three categories on the SCF,

FIGURE 9.9 DRY SUPPLY STATEMENT OF CASH FLOWS FOR THE YEAR ENDING 12/31/20xz ($ IN 000s)

Cash Flow from Operating Activities	
Net income	$ 23
Adjustments to reconcile net income to net cash	
Depreciation	13
Changes in current assets and current liabilities	
Accounts receivable (increase) decrease	1
Inventory (increase) decrease	5
Accounts payable – trade increase (decrease)	(15)
Income taxes payable increase (decrease)	1
Accrued bonuses increase (decrease)	1
Net cash provided by operating activities	$ 29
Cash Flow from Investing Activities	
Proceeds from sale of equipment	$ 0
Payment received on note for sale of plant	0
Cash value life insurance decrease (increase)	(2)
Capital expenditures	(17)
Net cash provided by investing activities	($ 19)
Cash Flow from Financing Activities	
Proceeds from sale of stock	$ 0
Proceeds from short-term debt	(9)
Proceeds from subordinated debt	9
Repayment of debt	0
Payment under capital lease obligations	0
Dividends paid	0
Net cash provided by financing activities	$ 0
Net increase (decrease) in cash	$ 10
Cash at beginning of year	12
Cash at end of year	$ 22

you are now able to explain why a completed statement of cash flows is a critical tool in financial analysis: it helps the business banker evaluate a company's ability to generate positive cash flows from operations, which as you know, is essential to meeting financial obligations and paying dividends.

STATEMENT OF CASH FLOWS (OPERATING ACTIVITIES)—DIRECT METHOD

Now you will explore the direct method SCF section for operating activities, since the investing and financing activities calculations do not differ from the indirect method. It is important for a business banker to understand the direct method for operating activities because it is very similar to the UCA cash flow model that bankers have developed.

The underlying approach of the direct method is to take net profit—which is at the start of the indirect method—and break it apart into its components, such as sales and operating expenses. These income statement items are then grouped with the related balance sheet accounts. For instance, sales is considered along with the decrease (increase) in accounts receivable to calculate cash received from customers. This way, cash flow from operating activities includes the following types of activities normally involved in producing and delivering goods and services:

- Cash received from customers—The collection of accounts receivable and short- and long-term notes receivable from customers
- Cash paid to suppliers—Cash expenditures for acquiring materials and making payments to vendors, including net payments to accounts payable
- Cash paid for operating expenses—Cash expenditures for selling, general, and administrative expenses, including net payments to prepaid assets and accrued expenses
- Interest received—Interest income earned on excess funds or other sources of investment
- Interest paid—Interest expense, shown on the income statement presentation
- Income taxes paid—Amounts expensed on the income statement as paid taxes and changes on the balance sheet in accrued and deferred taxes
- Extraordinary items—Items such as lawsuit settlements and insurance claims, which usually are one-time events and are not related to the operation of the business

Some cash flow reports and models used by business bankers show the operating cash flows prepared with the direct method. The UCA model that has evolved as the primary cash flow report used by bankers is prepared on the direct method. This report is provided by most statement spreading programs. The UCA model also is prepared on the direct method.

Calculations Using the Direct Method

The following are the calculations of cash flows from Dry Supply operating activities using the direct method:

- Cash received from customers—This line is calculated as net sales, plus or minus the change in accounts receivable.

A decrease in accounts receivable is a source of cash. The change from 20xy to 20xz, therefore, is a positive number. If the accounts receivable had grown in 20xz, then the change would have been a use of cash and, therefore, a negative number. Total cash received from customers is calculated as net sales, plus or minus the change in accounts receivable ($918 + $1= $919).

Figure 9.10 shows the 20xz cash received from customers calculation for Dry Supply.

FIGURE 9.10 DRY SUPPLY CASH RECEIVED FROM CUSTOMERS CALCULATION FOR THE YEAR ENDING 12/31/20xz ($ IN 000s)

20xz net sales	$ 918
+ 20xy accounts receivable	$ 113
− 20xz accounts receivable	112
+ Accounts receivable (increase) decrease	$ 1
= Cash received from customers	$ 919

- Cash paid to suppliers—This line is calculated as cost of goods sold (net of depreciation), plus or minus changes in inventory and accounts payable.

Because they are expenses from the income statement, cost of goods sold is always a negative number (net of depreciation). The $5,000 decrease in inventory is a source of cash and, therefore, a positive number. The $15,000 decrease in accounts payable is a use of cash and a negative number.

Figure 9.11 shows the 20xz cash paid to suppliers calculation for Dry Supply.

FIGURE 9.11 DRY SUPPLY CASH PAID TO SUPPLIERS CALCULATION FOR THE YEAR ENDING 12/31/20xz ($ IN 000s)

220xz cost of goods sold (net of depreciation)	($ 631)
+ 20xy inventory	$ 72
− 20xz inventory	67
+ Inventory (increase) decrease	$ 5
+ 20xz accounts payable	$ 31
− 20xy accounts payable	46
+ Accounts payable increase (decrease)	($ 15)
= Cash paid to suppliers	($ 641)

- Cash paid for operating expenses—This line is calculated as selling, general, and administrative expenses (both net of depreciation), plus or minus changes in prepaid expenses (asset account for items paid in advance, such as rent and insurance) and accrued expenses (liability account for items paid in arrears).

Because they are expenses from the income statement, selling, general, and administrative expenses are always a negative number (net of depreciation). The $5,000 decrease in inventory is a source of cash and, therefore, a positive number. The $15,000 decrease in accounts payable is a use of cash and a negative number. The $1,000 increase in accrued expenses is a source of cash and a positive number. The accrued taxes account will be used later in the operating activities format.

Figure 9.12 shows the 20xz cash paid for operating expenses calculation for Dry Supply.

FIGURE 9.12 DRY SUPPLY CASH PAID FOR OPERATING EXPENSES CALCULATION FOR THE YEAR ENDING 12/31/20xz ($ IN 000s)

20xz selling, general, and administrative expenses (net of depreciation)		($ 228)
+ 20xy prepaid expenses	$ 0	
– 20xz prepaid expenses	0	
+ Prepaid expenses (increase) decrease		$ 0
+ 20xz accrued expenses	$ 12	
– 20xy accrued expenses	11	
+ Accrued expenses increase (decrease)		$ 1
= Cash paid for operating expenses		($ 227)

- Cash paid for interest, income taxes, and extraordinary items—This line is calculated using various income and expenses that have not already been used in our previous calculations.

Interest received is always a positive number, and it is the interest income amount from the income statement. Interest paid is always a negative number. It is the interest expense figure from the income statement, adjusted for the changes in interest payable. Income taxes paid may be a positive or negative number, depending on the income tax expense on the income statement, adjusted for the changes in deferred taxes and income taxes payable liability accounts.

Extraordinary items may be a positive or negative number, and will be the figure from the income statement. In a direct method SCF, an accountant will likely include extraordinary items in the operating section; however, some cash flow models within statement spreading software do not show extraordinary items in the operating section.

Figure 9.13 shows the calculation for this section of the SCF (direct method) for Dry Supply.

FIGURE 9.13 DRY SUPPLY CASH PAID FOR INTEREST, INCOME TAXES, AND EXTRAORDINARY ITEMS CALCULATION FOR THE YEAR ENDING 12/31/20xz ($ IN 000s)

20xz interest received			$ 2
20xz interest paid			(11)
– 20xz income tax expense		(17)	
+ 20xz income taxes payable	$ 7		
– 20xy income taxes payable	6		
+ Income taxes payable increase (decrease)		$ 1	
+ Cash paid for income taxes			(16)
Extraordinary/Miscellaneous items			
+ 20xz rental income			3
= Cash paid for interest, income taxes and extraordinary items			($ 22)

The $2,000 in interest received, a positive number, represents interest income on excess or temporary cash during the year. The $11,000 in interest expense, a negative number, is the interest paid during the year for loans. The $16,000 cash paid for income taxes starts with the current year income tax expense of $17,000 on the income statement (a use of cash), plus the change in the income taxes payable liability account of $1,000 from 20xy to 20xz. Because the account increased, the change is a source of cash, for taxes paid of $16,000 as a use of cash. The rental income of $3,000, a positive number, is from the income statement and is the only extraordinary or miscellaneous item.

Using the direct method, we can now show the entire operating activities SCF section for Dry Supply. As mentioned earlier, the cash flow from operating activities is the same as when using the indirect method but with a format that better matches the actual activities of the underlying business—that is, most managers do not consciously set out to increase or decrease receivables. However, they do attempt to collect cash from sales. Figure 9.14 below shows the direct-method operating activities SCF section for Dry Supply.

FIGURE 9.14 DRY SUPPLY STATEMENT OF CASH FLOWS OPERATING ACTIVITIES (DIRECT METHOD) FOR THE YEAR ENDING 12/31/20xz ($ IN 000s)

Cash Flow from Operating Activities	
Cash received from customers	$ 919
Cash paid to suppliers	(641)
Cash paid for operating expenses	(227)
Cash paid for interest, income taxes and extraordinary items	(22)
Net cash provided by operating activities	$ 29

You can now look at the two SCF versions side by side. Notice that the investing and financing sections are the same. Figure 9.15 shows the completed SCFs for Dry Supply, using both the indirect and direct methods.

You explored the direct method SCF section for operating activities. You learned how to calculate operating cash flows using the direct method and how to identify similarities and differences between the SCF methods. You now know why it is important for a business banker to understand the direct method for operating activities: it is very similar to the UCA cash flow model that bankers have developed.

CASH FLOW REPORTS AND OTHER TOOLS

Some cash flow reports and models used by business bankers recast the entire indirect method SCF into a simpler format. In some cases, the operating activities section of the indirect method SCF can help to explore the effect of sales growth and other significant financial changes on cash flow.

Abbreviated Cash Flow Report

The indirect method SCF, which starts with net profit (loss) and then uses the calculated changes between two balance sheets, is the basis for a more streamlined way to look at cash flow. For smaller loan requests, some lenders use an abbreviated cash flow report that summarizes the sources and uses of cash flow, and covers two consecutive fiscal years of balance sheets and the current year income statement. By completing this format, a lender can determine how the business used the profits, how it structured its debt, and potential questions to ask the business.

FIGURE 9.15 DRY SUPPLY FOR THE YEAR ENDING 12/31/20xz ($ IN 000s) STATEMENT OF CASH FLOWS

INDIRECT METHOD		DIRECT METHOD	
Cash Flow from Operating Activities		*Cash Flow from Operating Activities*	
Net income	$ 23		
Adjustments to reconcile net income to net cash Depreciation	13	Cash received from customers	$ 919
Changes in current assets and current liabilities		Cash paid to suppliers	(641)
Accounts receivable (increase) decrease	1	Cash paid for operating expenses	(227)
Inventory (increase) decrease	5		
Accounts payable – trade increase (decrease)	(15)	Cash paid for interest, income taxes and extraordinary items	(22)
Income taxes payable increase (decrease)	1		
Accrued bonuses increase (decrease)	1	Net cash provided by operating activities	$ 29
Net cash provided by operating activities	$ 29		

Cash Flow from Investing Activities	
Proceeds from sale of equipment	$ 0
Payment received on note for sale of plant	0
Cash value life insurance decrease (increase)	(2)
Capital expenditures	(17)
Net cash provided by investing activities	$ 19
Cash Flow from Financing Activities	
Proceeds from sale of stock	$ 0
Proceeds from short-term debt	(9)
Proceeds from subordinated debt	9
Repayment of debt	0
Payment under capital lease obligations	0
Dividends paid	0
Net cash provided by financing activities	$ 0
Net increase (decrease) in cash	$ 10
Cash at beginning of year	12
Cash at end of year	$ 22

Figure 9.16 shows a completed abbreviated cash flow report for Dry Supply for 20xz.

Using the report, we can see that Dry Supply had $53,000 of cash inflows and $43,000 of cash outflows, for a resulting $10,000 increase in its cash balances. The primary cash inflow was from cash profit. Additionally, Dry Supply decreased inventory by $5,000, which was used to partially reduce accounts payable $5,000. The remaining $10,000 reduction to accounts payable came from cash profits. Dry Supply purchased $17,000 of fixed assets, also paid from cash profits. It appears that the subordinated debt increase of $9,000 was used to pay down notes payable by $9,000.

By using an abbreviated cash flow report, a lender can quickly answer the following questions about cash flow as related to the Commercial Lending Decision Tree concept:

- What is causing more cash to go out than to come in? (The cause of borrowing)

FIGURE 9.16 ABBREVIATED CASH FLOW REPORT FORMAT: DRY SUPPLY FOR THE YEAR ENDING 12/31/20xz ($ IN 000s)

Cash Sources—Inflows			Cash Uses—Outflows	
Cash profit (net income plus depreciation expense)	$ 36	-or-	Cash loss (net loss, offset by depreciation expense)	$ 0
Decrease in accounts receivable	1	-or-	Increase in accounts receivable	0
Decrease in inventory	5	-or-	Increase in inventory	0
Increase in accounts payable	0	-or-	Decrease in accounts payable	15
Increase in notes payable	0	-or-	Decrease in notes payable	9
			Dividends	0
Disposals of fixed assets	0	-or-	Fixed asset additions	17
Increase in subordinated debt	9	-or-	Decrease in subordinated debt	0
New capital stock issued	0	-or-	Increase in treasury stock	0
Decrease in all other assets	0	-or-	Increase in all other assets	2
Increase in all other liabilities	2	-or-	Decrease in all other liabilities	0
Total cash sources – inflows	$ 53	-or-	Total cash uses – outflows	$ 43
Result: Decrease in cash balance	$ 0	-or-	Increase in cash balance	$ 10

- What has changed in the company's business operations? (The repayment sources)
- What is the possibility that these changes will continue in the future? (The risk of nonpayment)
- What is the proper loan structure? (The term of the loan)

Impact of Sales Growth and Other Significant Changes on Cash Flow

So far, as we have applied cash flow statements and models to Dry Supply, there have not been significant changes in cash flow beyond the cash profits generated by the income statement. In fact, the company has not shown significant changes in sales levels, while the balance sheet has been fairly steady in relation to sales. Profits have been consistent and growing modestly. The result is an overall cash flow situation where cash profits are the main driver, since there have not been significant cash flow demands from balance sheet changes.

In many lending situations, a business banker will encounter a much more dynamic set of financial statements, including high levels of sales growth, or changes in efficiency that amplify changes in accounts receivable, inventory, and accounts payable. Such factors have led to a common saying in banking that "cash profits or EBITDA are not cash flow." We studied earnings before interest, taxes, depreciation, and amortization (EBITDA) as part of the debt coverage ratios in Chapter 8. The danger in using cash profits or EBITDA in debt coverage ratios is the assumption that this portion of cash flow can be directed or funneled exclusively to the debt service needs of the business.

As an example, let's explore Dry Supply if it had experienced a sharp, 15-percent increase in sales for 20xz over 20xy. The new level of net sales would be $1,078,000, with profits of about $27,000 if we assume the same net profit margin of 2.5 percent. To support the sales growth, assume that Dry Supply had to increase inventory levels by 20 percent, and the higher level of accounts receivable generated by the sales slowed down its collection efforts such that accounts receivable grew 20 percent. Support from vendors kept pace with sales, with accounts payable growing 15 percent. As a result, these accounts will become $90,000, $136,000, and $55,000, respectively. Finally, we will assume the same changes to other assets and liabilities as originally shown for 20xz.

Figure 9.17 shows the operating activities section of an indirect SCF for Dry Supply for 20xz that factors in the discussed changes in profits, accounts receivable, inventory, and accounts payable.

FIGURE 9.17 DRY SUPPLY STATEMENT OF CASH FLOWS FOR THE YEAR ENDING 12/31/20xz ($ IN 000s)

Cash Flow from Operating Activities	Original Data	With 15% Sales Growth
Net income	$ 23	$ 27
Adjustments to reconcile net income to net cash		
Depreciation	13	13
Changes in current assets and current liabilities		
Accounts receivable (increase) decrease	1	(23)
Inventory (increase) decrease	5	(15)
Accounts payable – trade increase (decrease)	(15)	7
Accrued taxes increase (decrease)	1	1
Accrued bonuses increase (decrease)	1	1
Net cash provided by operating activities	$ 29	$ 11

At first glance, the resulting $11,000 of operating cash flow does not appear to cause concern; however, it is important to note how growth in receivables and inventory created cash outflows not fully offset by the inflows from cash profits and accounts payable. This reduced operating cash flow by almost two-thirds, and operating cash flow now cannot support the expansion of fixed assets unless Dry Supply can borrow funds, find another source of cash inflows (no reduction to short-term notes payable), or reduce cash on hand.

Further, we see that cash profits, once adjusted in either the UCA model or SCF, may not be fully available to cover debt service or investments in a business with a dynamic financial situation. Even in the original data shown above, Dry Supply's $36,000 of cash profits are reduced slightly to $29,000 of operating cash flow, given a steady balance sheet and nominal sales growth. Some of the cash profits are siphoned away to other, competing cash needs. More dramatically, with stronger sales growth, cash profits of $40,000 are reduced to $11,000 of operating cash flow.

As related to the Commercial Lending Decision Tree, the concept of expanding and improving the definition of cash flow from cash profits or EBITDA to cash from operating activities (SCF) or net cash from operations (UCA) allows a business banker to move beyond simple coverage ratios and develop the following questions:

- What is causing more cash to go out than to come in? (The cause of borrowing)
- What has changed in the company's business operations? (The repayment sources)
- What is the possibility that these changes will continue in the future? (The risk of nonpayment)

- What is the proper loan structure? (The term of the loan)

You learned how to complete and use an abbreviated cash flow report—which is used for smaller loan requests—that summarizes the sources and uses of cash flow, and covers two consecutive fiscal years of balance sheets and the current year income statement. You now know that when reviewing the cash flow reports, you may witness the impact of sales growth or changes in efficiency that can cause changes in accounts receivable, inventory, and accounts payable. This information provides you, as a business banker, with an opportunity to move beyond simple coverage ratios and develop clarifying questions for the customer.

SUMMARY

Cash flow analysis examines how cash is generated and used in a business, thus giving another perspective of the financial management of a business. Cash flow statements help a lender predict whether and why a business would seek a loan, and whether it has the capacity to repay debt.

By completing this chapter, you learned how to identify cash flow statements and now know how they can help a lender predict whether and why a company would seek a loan, and whether it has the capacity to repay debt. You are now able to describe the two formats used for a statement of cash flows (SCF): indirect method and direct method.

You also learned how the operating cash flows section of an SCF is derived using the direct method, which is an option seldom used by accountants, but more similar to the UCA cash flow model available to bankers in computerized statement spreading programs. Regardless of the format used, cash flow analysis reconciles the changes in cash and cash equivalents, and addresses cash flows from operating, investing, and financing activities of a business. It deepens your understanding of the impact of management's actions and inactions while running the business.

Many companies experience sales growth and other changes that can have a significant effect on cash flow, beyond profits shown on the income statement. All too frequently, customers do not know how much money they really need or how to structure the loan. A thorough financial analysis (historic and projected) encompassing income statement analysis, balance sheet analysis, ratio analysis, and cash flow analysis gives a business banker critical information to determine how much credit a business may need, the timing of those needs, and whether the business can repay the loan according to proposed terms. The next chapter will cover the UCA cash flow model (Chapter 10). Cash budgets and pro forma statements will be discussed in more detail in Chapter 11.

QUESTION FOR DISCUSSION

1. What are some key items a business banker should look for in a full statement of cash flows?

EXERCISE 1

It is now time for you to apply what you have learned by analyzing operating cash flow.

Background

Anne Schippel, business banker, is analyzing Dry Supply's financial statements and has compiled a statement of cash flows for 20xz. The operating activities section is shown below.

DRY SUPPLY STATEMENT OF CASH FLOWS FOR THE YEAR ENDING 12/31/20xz ($ IN 000s)	
CASH FLOW FROM OPERATING ACTIVITIES	
Cash Flow from Operating Activities	
Net income	$ 23
Adjustments to reconcile ne income to net cash Depreciation	13
Changes in current assets and current liabilities	
Accounts receivable (increase) decrease	1
Inventory (increase) decrease	5
Accounts payable – trade increase (decrease)	(15)
Income taxes payable increase (decrease)	1
Accrued bonuses increase (decrease)	1
Net cash provided by operating activities	$ 29

What are some questions Anne Schippel might ask Dry Supply to better understand the operating cash flows of the business?

EXERCISE 2

It is now time for you to apply what you have learned by analyzing investing cash flow.

Background

Anne Schippel, business banker, is analyzing Dry Supply's financial statements and has compiled a statement of cash flows for 20xz. The investing activities section is shown below.

DRY SUPPLY STATEMENT OF CASH FLOWS FOR THE YEAR ENDING 12/31/20xz ($ IN 000s)	
CASH FLOW FROM INVESTING ACTIVITIES	
Cash Flow from Investing Activities	
Proceeds from sale of equipment	$ 0
Payment received on note for sale of plant	0
Cash value life insurance decrease (increase)	(2)
Capital expenditures	(17)
Net cash provided by investing activities	($ 19)

What are some questions Anne Schippel should ask Dry Supply to better understand the investing cash flows of the business?

EXERCISE 3

It is now time for you to apply what you have learned by analyzing financing cash flow.

Background

Anne Schippel, business banker, is analyzing Dry Supply's financial statements and has compiled a statement of cash flows for 20xz. The financing activities section is shown below.

What are some questions Anne Schippel should ask Dry Supply or be thinking about to better understand the financing cash flows of the business?

DRY SUPPLY STATEMENT OF CASH FLOWS FOR THE YEAR ENDING 12/31/20xz ($ IN 000s)

CASH FLOW FROM FINANCING ACTIVITIES

Cash Flow from Financing Activities	
Proceeds from sale of stock	$ 0
Proceeds from short-term debt	(9)
Proceeds from subordinated debt	9
Repayment of debt	0
Payment under capital lease obligations	0
Dividends paid	0
Net cash provided by financing activities	$ 0

EXERCISE 4

Instructions

For this exercise, you will complete a worksheet for the statement of cash flows for 20xy, an abbreviated cash flow report for 20xy, and explain how Dry Supply generated and used cash during 20xy.

PART 1

Dry Supply Statement of Cash Flows for 20xy

1. Fill out the *Dry Supply Statement of Cash Flows* worksheet for 20xy.

2. Fill out the *Dry Supply Abbreviated Cash Flow Report* for 20xy.

PART 2

3. Based on your cash flow analysis, explain how Dry Supply generated and used cash during 20xy.

4. Referring to the Commercial Lending Decision Tree, how does cash flow analysis improve the process?

WORKSHEET: DRY SUPPLY ABBREVIATED CASH FLOW REPORT FOR THE YEAR ENDING 12/31/20xy ($ IN 000s)

Cash Sources—Inflows			Cash Uses—Outflows	
Cash profit (net income plus depreciation expense)	$	-or-	Cash loss (net loss, offset by depreciation expense)	$
Decrease in accounts receivable		-or-	Increase in accounts receivable	
Decrease in inventory		-or-	Increase in inventory	
Increase in accounts payable		-or-	Decrease in accounts payable	
Increase in notes payable		-or-	Decrease in notes payable	
			Dividends	
Disposals of fixed assets		-or-	Fixed asset additions	
Increase in subordinated debt		-or-	Decrease in subordinated debt	
New capital stock issued		-or-	Increase in treasury stock	
Decrease in all other assets		-or-	Increase in all other assets	
Increase in all other liabilities	___	-or-	Decrease in all other liabilities	___
Total cash sources – inflows	$	-or-	Total cash uses – outflows	$
Result: Decrease in cash balance	$	-or-	Increase in cash balance	$

WORKSHEET: DRY SUPPLY STATEMENT OF CASH FLOWS FOR THE YEAR ENDING DECEMBER 31 ($ IN 000s)

Cash Flow from Operating Activities		
Net income	$ __	$ 23
Adjustments to reconcile net income to net cash		
Depreciation	__	13
Changes in current assets and current liabilities		
Accounts receivable (increase) decrease	__	1
Inventory (increase) decrease	1	5
Accounts payable – trade increase (decrease)	__	(15)
Income taxes payable increase (decrease)	__	1
Accrued bonuses increase (decrease)	1	1
Net cash provided by operating activities	$	$ 29
Cash Flow from Investing Activities		
Proceeds from sale of equipment	$ 0	$ 0
Payment received on note for sale of plant	0	0
Cash value life insurance decrease (increase)	__	(2)
Capital expenditures	__	(17)
Net cash provided by operating activities	($ 17)	($ 19)
Cash Flow from Financing Activities		
Proceeds from sale of stock	$ 0	$ 0
Proceeds from short-term debt	__	(9)
Proceeds from subordinated debt	__	9
Repayment of debt	0	0
Payment under capital lease obligations	0	0
Dividends paid	0	0
Net cash provided by financing activities	($ 3)	$ 0
Net increase (decrease) in cash	$ __	$ 10
Cash at beginning of year	__	12
Cash at end of year	$ 12	$ 22

10

THE UCA MODEL

OBJECTIVES

After studying *The UCA Model*, you will be able to—

- Compare the formats of the banker-prepared *Uniform Credit Analysis* (UCA) cash flow model and the accountant-prepared statement of cash flows (SCF)
- Construct a UCA model and interpret the results
- Explain the advantages of the UCA model.

INTRODUCTION

Because cash repays loans, cash flow analysis is an important step after understanding income statements (Chapter 6), balance sheets (Chapter 7), and ratios (Chapter 8). Cash flow analysis helps to explain not only various trends in income statement items and balance sheet accounts, but also why ratios have changed. Understanding the sources and uses of a business also helps a business banker improve loan structuring by more clearly showing why funds were borrowed and how funds can be generated for repayment. In this chapter, you will expand your knowledge of cash flow analysis (Chapter 9) to the UCA model used by bankers.

Relationship to the Commercial Lending Decision Tree

In the textbook Introduction, we discussed the Commercial Lending Decision Tree as a way to think about the stages and steps involved in the commercial lending process. As you have already learned, the first stage in this process emphasizes early screening and qualifying steps—such as a general fit with the portfolio and goals of your bank and initial assessment of financial and nonfinancial qualifications of the business. These preliminary steps allow a business banker to anticipate various issues and conduct a more efficient and accurate financial analysis.

The second stage moves into the detailed analysis of financial data gathered from the business and any owners who may serve as guarantors. An important part of the business financial assessment is cash flow analysis, particularly the UCA model as demonstrated in this chapter.

As you studied earlier, cash flow statements are part of a complete set of financial statements. For businesses that have externally prepared financials, accountants prepare cash flow statements according to GAAP—except for compiled statements that usually omit a statement of cash flows. In situations where a business submits internally prepared financial statements, tax returns, or an accountant's compilation, business bankers typically prepare a cash flow statement or model. The preferred model is the UCA cash flow model developed by bankers and available in most financial spreading software programs. By exploring the UCA model, this chapter takes the next step in the process of business financial statement analysis.

UCA CASH FLOW MODEL—DIRECT METHOD

Some cash flow reports and models used by business bankers show the operating cash flows prepared with the direct method. We will examine the most commonly used model: the UCA model. As mentioned earlier in the textbook, the label "UCA" comes from the Risk Management Association's course, *Uniform Credit Analysis*, where the model was introduced.

In this chapter, the UCA cash flow model will be demonstrated for Dry Supply, a wholesaler of powdered laundry products. The spreadsheets for the most recent three years of financial data for Dry Supply are shown below. We will refer back to Figure 10.1 and Figure 10.2 throughout the chapter readings and various exercises.

FIGURE 10.1 INCOME STATEMENT SPREAD: DRY SUPPLY						
Income Statement ($ in 000s)	Review 20xx		Review 20xy		Review 20xz	
	Amount	%	Amount	%	Amount	%
Net sales	$895	100.0	$937	100.0	$918	100.0
Cost of goods sold	645	72.1	667	71.2	631	68.7
Gross profit	250	27.9	270	28.8	287	31.3
Selling, gen. and admin. expense	157	17.5	173	18.5	180	19.6
Officer's compensation	36	4.0	31	3.3	28	3.1
Rent expenses	15	1.7	18	1.9	20	2.2
Bad debt expense	2	0.2	1	0.1	0	0.0
Profit-sharing expense	7	0.8	7	0.7	0	0.0
Depreciation expense	12	1.3	12	1.3	13	1.4
Total operating expenses	229	25.6	242	25.8	241	26.3
Operating income	21	2.3	28	3.0	46	5.0
Other income	0	0.0	0	0.0	0	0.0
Interest income	2	0.2	2	0.2	2	0.2
Rental income	3	0.3	3	0.3	3	0.3
Interest expense	6	0.7	7	0.7	11	1.2
Net profit before tax	20	2.2	26	2.8	40	4.4
Taxes	11	1.2	12	1.3	17	1.9
Net profit after tax	$ 9	1.0	$ 14	1.5	$ 23	2.5

UCA Format Compared to SCF

The UCA cash flow model uses the same major categories for cash flow as SCF—operating, investing, and financing. However, components involved in business debt service (interest expense and current maturities of long-term debt, or CMLTD) are isolated after operating activities, and dividends are treated as a financing cost (along with interest expense) rather than as a component within the equity account changes. The following items are also handled differently or placed in a different location in the UCA format:

- Interest expense is not included in the computation of operating cash flow or net cash after operations (NCAO) in the UCA model. Therefore, the model's net cash from operations represents operating cash flow available to cover debt service.

- Dividends are not included within the equity change components of the financing cash flow of the UCA model. Instead, they are considered a financing cost, along with interest expense.

- CMLTD from the previous year-end is not included in the computation of financing cash flow in the UCA model. This particular number, moved to a position immediately below interest expense, represents the scheduled reductions of loan principal that should have been made during the year.

FIGURE 10.2 BALANCE SHEET SPREAD: DRY SUPPLY

Common-sized report ($ in $000s)	Review 12/31/20xx		Review 12/31/20xy		Review 12/31/20xz	
Assets	Amount	%	Amount	%	Amount	%
Cash	$ 3	1.2	$ 12	4.6	$ 22	8.1
Accounts receivable	114	46.9	118	45.4	117	43.3
Less: allowance for doubtful accounts	5	2.1	5	1.9	5	1.9
Net accounts receivable	109	44.9	113	43.5	112	41.5
Inventory	73	30.0	72	27.7	67	24.8
Total current assets	185	76.1	197	75.8	201	74.4
Furniture and fixtures	76	31.3	75	28.8	78	28.9
Leasehold improvements	1	0.4	1	0.4	0	0.0
Transportation equipment	53	21.8	70	26.9	85	31.5
Gross fixed assets	130	53.5	146	56.2	163	60.4
Less: Accum. depreciation	85	35.0	97	37.3	110	40.7
Net fixed assets	45	18.5	49	18.8	53	19.6
Cash-value life insurance	13	5.3	14	5.4	16	5.9
Total assets	$243	100.0	$260	100.0	$270	100.0

	Review 12/31/20xx		Review 12/31/20xy		Review 12/31/20xz	
Liabilities	Amount	%	Amount	%	Amount	%
Notes payable bank short-term	$81	33.3	$68	26.2	$59	21.8
Accounts payable—trade	42	17.3	46	17.7	31	11.5
Income taxes payable	5	2.1	6	2.3	7	2.6
Accrued bonuses	10	4.1	11	4.2	12	4.4
Total current liabilities	138	56.8	131	50.4	109	40.4
Subordinated debt officers	48	19.8	58	22.3	67	24.8
Total liabilities	186	76.5	189	72.7	176	65.2
Net worth						
Common stock	2	0.8	2	0.8	2	0.7
Retained earnings	55	22.6	69	26.5	92	34.1
Total net worth	57	23.5	71	27.3	94	34.8
Total liabilities and net worth	$243	100.0	$260	100.0	$270	100.0

The report uses different descriptions for many of the same calculations made in a direct method SCF. Although the number of statement spreading programs has grown, there are slight variations in the wording of the following UCA terms:

- **Cash from sales** is the portion of the present year's sales collected in the present year, plus any amounts from previous years' sales collected during the present year.

- **Cash production costs** are cash expended during the present year to produce goods for sale (manufacturer) or to acquire merchandise (wholesaler or retailer).

- **Gross cash profit** is the difference between cash from sales and cash production costs.

- **Cash operating expenses** is actual cash spent during the year for selling and general and administrative expenses. This figure is adjusted for depreciation as well as for changes in prepaid and accrued expenses.

- **Cash operating profit** is the result of subtracting cash operating expenses from gross cash profit.

- **Net cash after operations (NCAO)** is cash remaining after adjusting cash operating profit to reflect net cash inflow (or outlay) arising from changes in income taxes and in miscellaneous assets and liabilities. It is the amount available for servicing interest on bank debt.

- **Net cash income** is the result of subtracting financing costs (interest as the cost of debt and dividends/withdrawals as the cost of equity) from NCAO. On a cash basis, this number is comparable to the amount of net income (on an accrual basis) that is retained after dividends. To this end, consider spreading as "income taxes" the portion of partnership/LLC/S corporation dividends that equate to the owners' personal income tax on the entity's net income.

- **Cash after debt amortization (CADA)** is computed by subtracting the CMLTD at the end of the previous year from net cash income. If, after this step, there is still a positive figure, then it means the company has been able to generate sufficient cash from its operations to meet all its obligations to bank lenders, including interest and principal. If, on the other hand, this figure is negative, the firm must resort to additional sources of financing to meet these obligations as well as to make any capital expenditures

- **Financing surplus (requirement)** is the result of subtracting fixed asset expenditures and other long-term investments from CADA. This measures either the magnitude of excess cash generated beyond all needs of the business, or the amount of external financing needed.

- **Cash after external financing**—"External financing" refers to the provision of additional cash to the company from new loans (short-term and/or long-term) or equity capital (from shareholders). The cash after external financing is the excess or shortfall of cash after adjusting for the amount of external financing or lump-sum repayments (excluding scheduled CMLTD from the previous year-end).

- **Actual change in cash** is the year-to-year change as shown on the company's balance sheet. If the cash flow statement has been calculated correctly, this will be the same as cash after external financing.

The chart below compares the UCA and SCF formats (Figure 10.3)

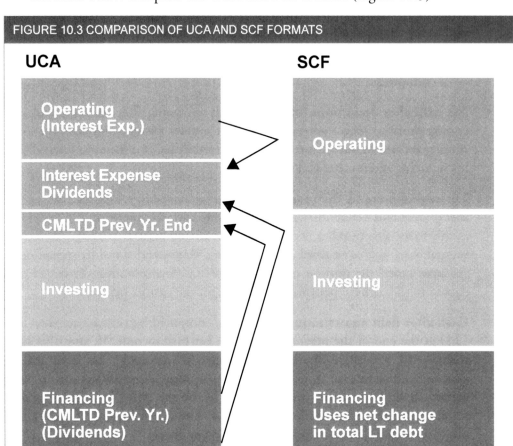

FIGURE 10.3 COMPARISON OF UCA AND SCF FORMATS

By utilizing the UCA model as part of the financial analysis process, you will be able to answer the following questions:

- For the year shown, can internally generated funds, represented by net cash from operations, cover debt service?
- After investments in equipment, what is the surplus cash flow (or deficit to be financed)?
- How was the surplus utilized (or deficit financed)?

UCA Calculations Using the Direct Method—Net Cash from Operations (NCAO)

The following are the calculations for net cash after operations (NCAO) for Dry Supply using the UCA format:

- **Cash from sales**—This line in the UCA model is calculated as net sales, plus or minus the change in accounts receivable, and is the same as the SCF cash received from customers. Note that net sales is the first item in the UCA model, compared to net income as the first item in a statement of cash flows.

A decrease in accounts receivable is a source of cash. The change from 20xy to 20xz, therefore, is a positive number. If the accounts receivable had grown in 20xz, then the change would have been a use of cash and, therefore, a negative number. Total cash received from customers is calculated as net sales, plus or minus the change in accounts receivable ($918 + $1= $919).

Figure 10.4 shows the 20xz cash from sales UCA calculation for Dry Supply.

FIGURE 10.4 DRY SUPPLY CASH FROM SALES UCA CALCULATION FOR 20xz ($ IN 000s)

20xz net sales	$ 918
+ 20xy accounts receivable	$ 113
− 20xz accounts receivable	112
+ Accounts receivable (increase) decrease	$ 1
= Cash received from customers	$ 919

- **Cash production costs**—This line is calculated as cost of goods sold (net of depreciation), plus or minus changes in inventory and accounts payable. It is similar to the SCF cash paid to suppliers.

Because they are expenses from the income statement, cost of goods sold is always a negative number (net of depreciation). The $5,000 decrease in inventory is a source of cash and, therefore, a positive number. The $15,000 decrease in accounts payable is a use of cash and a negative number.

Figure 10.5 shows the 20xz cash production costs UCA calculation for Dry Supply.

FIGURE 10.5 DRY SUPPLY CASH PRODUCTION COSTS UCA CALCULATION FOR 20xz ($ IN 000s)

220xz cost of goods sold (net of depreciation)		($ 631)
+ 20xy inventory	$ 72	
− 20xz inventory	67	
+ Inventory (increase) decrease		$ 5
+ 20xz accounts payable	$ 31	
− 20xy accounts payable	46	
+ Accounts payable increase (decrease)		($ 15)
= Cash paid to suppliers		($ 641)

- **Cash operating expenses**—This line is calculated as selling, general, and administrative expenses (both net of depreciation), plus or minus changes in prepaid expenses (asset account for items paid in advance, such as rent and insurance), and accrued expenses (liability account for items paid in arrears).

Because they are expenses from the income statement, selling, general, and administrative expenses are always a negative number (net of depreciation). Prepaid expenses did not change; it is not a source or use of cash. The $1,000 increase in accrued expenses is a source of cash and positive number. The accrued taxes account will be used later in the operating activities format.

Figure 10.6 shows the 20xz cash operating expenses calculation for Dry Supply.

FIGURE 10.6 DRY SUPPLY CASH OPERATING EXPENSES UCA CALCULATION FOR 20xz ($ IN 000s)

20xz selling, general, and administrative expenses (net of depreciation)	($ 228)	
+ 20xy prepaid expenses	$ 0	
− 20xz prepaid expenses	0	
+ Prepaid expenses (increase) decrease		$ 0
+ 20xz accrued expenses	$ 12	
− 20xy accrued expenses	11	
+ Accrued expenses increase (decrease)		$ 1
= Cash paid for operating expenses		($ 227)

- **Total miscellaneous**—This line is calculated using various income and expenses that have not already been used in our previous calculations (excluding income tax expense and interest expense), plus changes in other current assets, other noncurrent assets, other current liabilities, and other noncurrent liabilities.

Other income is always a positive number, and it can include the interest income and rental income amounts from the income statement. Other expenses will include miscellaneous expense items from the income statement and will be a negative number.

Extraordinary items may be a positive or negative number, and will be the figure from the income statement. In a direct method SCF, an accountant will likely include extraordinary items in the operating section; however, some cash flow models within statement spreading software do not show extraordinary items in the operating section.

Figure 10.7 shows the UCA calculation for this section for Dry Supply.

FIGURE 10.7 DRY SUPPLY TOTAL MISCELLANEOUS UCA CALCULATION FOR 20xz ($ IN 000s)

20xz other income		$ 5
20xz other expenses		(0)
+ 20xy other current assets	$ 0	
− 20xz other current assets	0	
+ Other current assets (increase) decrease		$ 0
+ 20xz other current liabilities	$ 0	
− 20xy other current liabilities	0	
+ Other current liabilities increase (decrease)		$ 0
+ 20xy other current assets	$ 0	
− 20xz other current assets	0	
+ Other current assets (increase) decrease		$ 0
+ 20xz other current liabilities	$ 0	
− 20xy other current liabilities	0	
+ Other current liabilities increase (decrease)		$ 0
= Total miscellaneous		$ 5

- **Cash paid for taxes**—This line is calculated using income tax expense, plus or minus the change in income taxes payable (a liability) and deferred taxes (also a liability). Income taxes paid may be a positive or negative number, depending on the income tax expense on the income statement, adjusted for the changes in deferred taxes and income taxes payable liability accounts.

Figure 10.8 shows the calculation for this section of the SCF (direct method) for Dry Supply.

FIGURE 10.8 DRY SUPPLY CASH PAID FOR TAXES UCA CALCULATION FOR 20xz ($ IN 000s)

20xz income tax expense		(17)
+ 20xz income taxes payable	$ 7	
− 20xy income taxes payable	6	
+ Income taxes payable increase (decrease)		$ 1
= Cash paid for taxes		(16)

The $16,000 cash paid for income taxes starts with the current year income-tax expense of ($17,000) on the income statement (a use of cash), plus the change in the income taxes payable liability account of $1,000 from 20xy to 20xz. Because the account increased, the change is a source of cash for taxes paid of ($16,000) as a use of cash.

We can now show the entire NCAO UCA section for Dry Supply. As mentioned earlier, the direct method better matches the actual activities of the underlying business—that is, most managers do not consciously set out to increase or decrease receivables. However, they do attempt to collect cash from sales. From a calculation standpoint, NCAO differs from the SCF operating cash flow because NCAO does not include interest expense and extraordinary expenses. For Dry Supply in 20xz, there were no extraordinary expenses, so the difference between NCAO of $40,000 and SCF operating cash flow of $29,000 is the interest expense of $11,000.

Figure 10.9 shows the NCAO UCA section for Dry Supply.

FIGURE 10.9 DRY SUPPLY UCA CASH FLOW MODEL NET CASH AFTER OPERATIONS FOR 20xz ($ IN 000s)

Cash from sales	$ 919
Cash production costs	(641)
Cash operating expenses	(227)
Total miscellaneous	5
Cash paid for taxes	(16)
Net cash after operations	$ 40

UCA Calculations Using the Direct Method—Cash After Debt Amortization

The next step in the UCA model is to show the cash outflow for debt service. Along the way, two subtotals are created. The first is net cash income (after financing costs, including cash paid for interest expense and dividends), then cash after debt amortization, or CADA (after CMLTD from the previous year end).

- **Financing costs**—This line in the UCA model is calculated as interest expense, plus or minus the change in interest payable, along with dividends and distributions, plus or minus dividends payable. For large companies, dividends are a return to investors, similar to interest expense being a return to lenders. For many smaller firms that are pass-through entities, the dividend amount is more closely related to the tax obligations that owners incur when the businesses earn a profit.

  Dry Supply does not have an interest payable or dividend payable liability account at either 12/31/20xy or 12/31/20xz, and no dividends were paid during the year. This leaves interest expense as the sole component of financing costs. Interest paid is always a negative number and is the interest expense figure from the income statement.

- **CMLTD-previous year**—This line represents the scheduled reductions of loan principal that should have been made during the current year. This figure generally includes any current amounts due on capitalized lease obligations. Dry Supply does not have any long-term debt or related current maturities.

Figure 10.10 shows the 20xz cash after debt amortization (CADA) UCA calculation for Dry Supply.

FIGURE 10.10 DRY SUPPLY CASH AFTER DEBT AMORTIZATION UCA CALCULATION FOR 20xz ($ IN 000s)

Net cash after operations	$ 40
– 20xz interest expense	($ 11)
– 20xz dividends or distributions	0
= Financing costs	($ 11)
= Net cash income	$ 29
– 20xy CMLTD	($ 0)
= Cash after debt amortization	$ 29

Because CADA is positive for Dry Supply, the company has been able to generate sufficient cash from its operations to meet all its obligations to bank lenders, including interest and principal, plus any dividends paid to investors.

As mentioned earlier, the UCA model shows several important things, including whether internally generated funds, represented as *net cash after operations*, can cover debt service. This can be represented by a ratio that is often provided along with other conventional ratios in statement spreading programs.

- **Cash Coverage Ratio (x)** is calculated by dividing NCAO by the sum of interest expense and the previous year-end CMLTD. Just like a positive figure for CADA, a cash coverage ratio ≥ 1.0x means that the company has been able to generate sufficient cash from its operations to meet all of its obligations to bank lenders, including interest and principal.

Another way to think about debt service from the UCA model is that NCAO must be positive in order to cover any of the possible components of debt service, plus any dividends paid. If the business can successfully cover all of its debt service and dividend payments, then CADA must be positive, or at least $0.

UCA Calculations Using the Direct Method—Financing Surplus (Requirement)

The next step in the UCA model is to show the cash outflow for capital expenditures and other long-term investments. This calculation is very similar to the process used for the indirect method SCF section for investing activities.

Proceeds from sale of equipment are shown on the income statement as gains or losses on sale of fixed assets. This extraordinary item is included in many UCA model formats within the investing activities section. Dry Supply had no sales of equipment in 20xz. Payment received on a note for sale of plant or equipment would be indicated as reductions on notes receivable. Dry Supply had no payments on notes receivable during 20xz. The investing section of the UCA model also captures changes in other noncurrent assets, such as cash surrender value life insurance (CSVLI), which increased by $2,000 in 20xz. The capital expenditures are calculated using the change in net fixed assets, plus depreciation expense. Depreciation expense is a noncash charge and, therefore, a source of cash for Dry Supply.

Figure 10.11 shows the 20xz capital expenditures and financing surplus (requirement) UCA calculation for Dry Supply.

FIGURE 10.11 DRY SUPPLY FINANCING SURPLUS (REQUIREMENT) UCA CALCULATION FOR 20xz ($ IN 000s)

Cash after debt amortization	$ 29
20xz depreciation expense	($ 13)
+ 20xy net fixed assets	$ 49
− 20xz net fixed assets	(53)
+ Other current assets (increase) decrease	($ 4)
= Capital expenditures	($ 17)
+ 20xy investments (CSVLI)	14
− 20xz investments (CSVLI)	(16)
= Total long-term investments	($ 19)
= Financing surplus (requirement)	$ 10

For Dry Supply, the $19,000 use of cash for long-term investments in the UCA model matches the cash from investing activities section of the SCF on both the indirect and direct methods. This may not always be the case, depending on how extraordinary expenses and miscellaneous assets (such as CSVLI) are classified in a statement spreading program. Changes in some miscellaneous assets and liabilities can be included in the NCAO calculation. Therefore, it is important to know how a particular model directs these cash flows.

With a $10,000 financing surplus, Dry Supply has generated excess cash beyond all operating and investing needs of the business.

UCA Calculations Using the Direct Method—Cash After External Financing

The next step in the UCA model is to show the cash inflows and outflows related to financing and owner's equity. This will not include CMLTD from the previous year, which was used to determine CADA. In the equivalent SCF section, dividends are included. The UCA model does not include dividends because dividends were already subtracted to obtain CADA. In most situations, long-term debt will include the long-term portion of capitalized leases. Subordinated debt can also be included in long-term debt unless spread as an equity equivalent, as discussed earlier in this curriculum.

Figure 10.12 shows the 20xz calculation capital expenditures and financing surplus (requirement) UCA calculation for Dry Supply.

FIGURE 10.12 DRY SUPPLY CASH AFTER EXTERNAL FINANCING UCA CALCULATION FOR 20xz ($ IN 000s)

Financing surplus (requirement)			$ 10
− 20xy notes payable bank short-term	($ 68)		
+ 20xz notes payable bank short-term	59		
+ Short-term debt increase (decrease)		($ 9)	
+ 20xz CMLTD	$ 0		
+ 20xz long-term debt	67		
− 20xy long-term debt	(58)		
+ Incremental long-term debt		$ 9	
− 20xy stockholders equity (excl. retained earnings)	($ 2)		
+ 20xz stockholders equity (excl. retained earnings)	2		
+ stockholders equity increase (decrease)		$ 0	
= Total external financing			$ 0
= Cash after external financing			$ 10

For Dry Supply, the $9,000 in proceeds from stockholder loans (spread as subordinated debt officers) was offset by $9,000 in pay downs on short-term bank debt. The result is no cash inflow or outflow from external financing. The cash after external financing is $10,000, which matches the year-to-year change in Dry Supply's cash balance.

Advantages of UCA

Now that you have learned the various cash flow formats, Figure 10.13 shows a side by side comparison of the indirect and direct SCF, plus the direct UCA model for Dry Supply for 20xz.

All three formats can enhance the cash flow analysis process, but the UCA format has the following advantages:

- It provides a business banker with more information to track where cash was generated and absorbed by the operations of a business. It highlights management's actions and inactions regarding the following various cash flow drivers of—

FIGURE 10.13 DRY SUPPLY FOR THE YEAR ENDING 12/31/20xz ($ IN 000s)

STATEMENT OF CASH FLOWS

INDIRECT METHOD		DIRECT METHOD	
Cash Flow from Operating Activities		*Cash Flow from Operating Activities*	
Net income	$ 23	Cash received from customers	$ 919
Adjustments to reconcile income to net cash Depreciation	13	Cash paid to suppliers	(641)
Changes in current assets and current liabilities		Cash paid for operating expenses	(227)
Accounts receivable (increase) decrease	1	Cash paid for interest, income taxes and extraordinary items	(22)
Inventory (increase) decrease	5	Net cash provided by operating activities	$ 29
Accounts payable – trade increase (decrease)	(15)		
Income taxes payable increase (decrease)	1		
Accrued bonuses increase (decrease)	1		
Net cash provided by operating activities	$ 29		

Cash Flow from Investing Activities
- Proceeds from sale of equipment $ 0
- Payment received on note for sale of plant 0
- Cash value life insurance decrease (increase) (2)
- Capital expenditures (17)
- Net cash provided by investing activities $ 19

Cash Flow from Financing Activities
- Proceeds from sale of stock $ 0
- Proceeds from short-term debt (9)
- Proceeds from subordinated debt 9
- Repayment of debt 0
- Payment under capital lease obligations 0
- Dividends paid 0
- Net cash provided by financing activities $ 0
- Net increase (decrease) in cash $ 10
- Cash at beginning of year 12
- *Cash at end of year* $ 22

UCA CASH FLOW MODEL

DIRECT METHOD		
Cash from sales		$ 919
Cash production costs		(641)
Cash operating expenses		(227)
Total miscellaneous		5
Cash paid for taxes		(16)
Net cash after operations		$ 40
Interest costs paid	($ 11)	
Dividends or distributions paid	0	
Financing costs		($ 11)
Net cash income		$ 29
Current maturities of LTD		($ 0)
Cash after debt amortization		$ 29
Capital expenditures		($ 17)
Change in long-term investments		($ 19)
Financing surplus (requirement)		$ 10
Change in short-term debt		($ 9)
Incremental long-term debt		$ 9
Change in stockholders equity		$ 0
Total external financing		$ 0
Cash after external financing		$ 10
Cash at beginning of year		12
Cash at end of year		$ 22

American Bankers Association   The UCA Model   275

- Sales
- Gross profit margin
- Operating expenses
- Accounts receivable levels and turnover
- Inventory levels and turnover
- Accounts payable levels and turnover

- It shows whether the business was able to cover its debt service (principal and interest) and dividends with internally generated funds.

- It treats dividends and distributions (withdrawals) as a cost of financing the firm, whereas the two SCF cash flow formats treat these two items as an adjustment to the firm's equity section. This is an important distinction between the three cash flow formats; many borrowers are pass-through entities (partnerships, LLCs, S corporations, and others) where dividends and distributions, depending on their size, can have a significant effect on net cash income.

- It highlights the firm's financing surplus (or requirement) after considering its debt repayment, dividends/distributions, and capital expenditures.

- It shows the operating and financing activities that were funded by new debt.

In this section, you learned the similarities and differences between the UCA cash flow model and the statement of cash flows (SCF). You also learned about operating activities in the UCA model and how some of them differ from SCF. You are now able to describe the cash flow outcomes from debt service activities and how capital expenditures and other long-term investments are calculated in the UCA model. You are now able to show the cash inflows and outflows related to financing and owner's equity, and explain the advantages for business bankers to use the UCA format for cash flow analysis rather than the SCF.

SUMMARY

By completing this chapter, you are now able to explain the comparison between the banker-prepared UCA cash flow model and the statement of cash flow format. You learned that the UCA cash flow model uses the same major categories for cash flow as SCF—operating, investing, and financing. However, some components are handled differently; there are different descriptions for many of the same calculations; and some items are in a different location in the UCA format. You also learned how to construct, perform calculations, and interpret results for the UCA model. In this chapter, you gained a better understanding of the advantages of the UCA model.

QUESTION FOR DISCUSSION

1. What three items are included in the SCF format but reclassified or handled differently in the UCA model?

EXERCISE 1

It is now time for you to apply what you have learned by analyzing operating cash flow using the UCA cash flow model.

You will need to refer to Dry Supply's balance sheet and income statements spreads to complete the exercise.

BALANCE SHEET SPREAD: DRY SUPPLY

Common-sized report ($ in $000s)	Review 12/31/20xx		Review 12/31/20xy		Review 12/31/20xz	
Assets	Amount	%	Amount	%	Amount	%
Cash	$ 3	1.2	$ 12	4.6	$ 22	8.1
Accounts receivable	114	46.9	118	45.4	117	43.3
Less: allowance for doubtful accounts	5	2.1	5	1.9	5	1.9
Net accounts receivable	109	44.9	113	43.5	112	41.5
Inventory	73	30.0	72	27.7	67	24.8
Total current assets	185	76.1	197	75.8	201	74.4
Furniture and fixtures	76	31.3	75	28.8	78	28.9
Leasehold improvements	1	0.4	1	0.4	0	0.0
Transportation equipment	53	21.8	70	26.9	85	31.5
Gross fixed assets	130	53.5	146	56.2	163	60.4
Less: Accum. depreciation	85	35.0	97	37.3	110	40.7
Net fixed assets	45	18.5	49	18.8	53	19.6
Cash-value life insurance	13	5.3	14	5.4	16	5.9
Total assets	$243	100.0	$260	100.0	$270	100.0
	Review 12/31/20xx		Review 12/31/20xy		Review 12/31/20xz	
Liabilities	Amount	%	Amount	%	Amount	%
Notes payable bank short-term	$81	33.3	$68	26.2	$59	21.8
Accounts payable—trade	42	17.3	46	17.7	31	11.5
Income taxes payable	5	2.1	6	2.3	7	2.6
Accrued bonuses	10	4.1	11	4.2	12	4.4
Total current liabilities	138	56.8	131	50.4	109	40.4
Subordinated debt officers	48	19.8	58	22.3	67	24.8
Total liabilities	186	76.5	189	72.7	176	65.2
Net worth						
Common stock	2	0.8	2	0.8	2	0.7
Retained earnings	55	22.6	69	26.5	92	34.1
Total net worth	57	23.5	71	27.3	94	34.8
Total liabilities and net worth	$243	100.0	$260	100.0	$270	100.0

INCOME STATEMENT SPREAD: DRY SUPPLY						
Income Statement ($ in 000s)	Review 20xx		Review 20xy		Review 20xz	
	Amount	%	Amount	%	Amount	%
Net sales	$895	100.0	$937	100.0	$918	100.0
Cost of goods sold	645	72.1	667	71.2	631	68.7
Gross profit	250	27.9	270	28.8	287	31.3
Selling, gen. and admin. expense	157	17.5	173	18.5	180	19.6
Officer's compensation	36	4.0	31	3.3	28	3.1
Rent expenses	15	1.7	18	1.9	20	2.2
Bad debt expense	2	0.2	1	0.1	0	0.0
Profit-sharing expense	7	0.8	7	0.7	0	0.0
Depreciation expense	12	1.3	12	1.3	13	1.4
Total operating expenses	229	25.6	242	25.8	241	26.3
Operating income	21	2.3	28	3.0	46	5.0
Other income	0	0.0	0	0.0	0	0.0
Interest income	2	0.2	2	0.2	2	0.2
Rental income	3	0.3	3	0.3	3	0.3
Interest expense	6	0.7	7	0.7	11	1.2
Net profit before tax	20	2.2	26	2.8	40	4.4
Taxes	11	1.2	12	1.3	17	1.9
Net profit after tax	$ 9	1.0	$ 14	1.5	$ 23	2.5

Background

Anne Schippel, business banker, is analyzing Dry Supply's financial statements and has compiled a UCA cash flow model for 20xz. The net cash after operations (NCAO) section is shown in the chart below.

DRY SUPPLY UCA CASH FLOW MODEL NET CASH AFTER OPERATIONS FOR 20xz ($ IN $000s)	
Cash from sales	$ 919
Cash production costs	(641)
Cash operating expenses	(227)
Total miscellaneous	5
Cash paid for taxes	(16)
Net cash after operations	$ 40

What are some questions that Anne Schippel should ask Dry Supply to better understand the net cash after operations of the business?

EXERCISE 2

It is now time for you to apply what you have learned about cash after debt amortization (CADA) using the UCA cash flow model.

Background

Anne Schippel, business banker, is analyzing Dry Supply's financial statements and has compiled a UCA cash flow model for 20xz. The calculation of cash after debt amortization is shown in the image below.

DRY SUPPLY CASH AFTER DEBT AMORTIZATION FOR 20xz ($ IN $000s)	
Net cash after operations	$ 40
Interest costs paid	($ 11)
Dividends or distributions paid	0
Financing costs	($ 11)
Net cash income	$ 29
Current maturities of LTD	($ 0)
Cash after debt amortization	$ 29

What is Dry Supply's cash coverage ratio for 20xz?

EXERCISE 3

It is now time for you to apply what you have learned by analyzing the financing surplus (or requirement).

You will need to refer to Dry Supply's balance sheet and income statements spreads to complete the exercise.

Background

Anne Schippel, business banker, is analyzing Dry Supply's financial statements and has compiled a statement of cash flows for 20xz. The investing activities section and resulting financing surplus (or requirement) is shown in the chart below.

DRY SUPPLY FINANCING SURPLUS (REQUIREMENT) UCA CALCULATION FOR 20xz ($ IN $000s)	
Cash after debt amortization	$ 29
Change in long-term investments	($ 19)
Financing surplus (requirement)	$ 10

What are some questions that Anne Schippel should ask Dry Supply to better understand the financing surplus (requirement)?

EXERCISE 4

It is now time for you to apply what you have learned by analyzing financing cash flow.

You will need to refer to Dry Supply's balance sheet and income statements spreads to complete the exercise.

Background

Anne Schippel, business banker, is analyzing Dry Supply's financial statements and has compiled a statement of cash flows for 20xz. The financing activities section and resulting cash after external financing is shown in the chart below.

DRY SUPPLY CASH AFTER EXTERNAL FINANCING FOR 20xz ($ IN $000s)	
Financing surplus (requirement)	$ 10
Change in short-term debt	($ 9)
Incremental long-term debt	$ 9
Change in stockholders' equity	$ 0
Total external financing	$ 0
Cash after external financing	$ 10

What are some questions that Anne Schippel should ask Dry Supply to better understand the financing cash flows of the business?

EXERCISE 5

Instructions

You will need to refer to Dry Supply's balance sheet and income statements spreads to complete the exercise.

For this exercise, you will complete a worksheet for the UCA cash flow model for 20xy and explain how Dry Supply generated and used cash during 20xy.

Part 1

Dry Supply UCA Cash Flow Model for 20xy

1. Using the 20xy balance sheet and income statement information for Dry Supply, complete the worksheet for the UCA cash flow model for 20xy.

Part 2

2. Based on your cash flow analysis, explain how Dry Supply generated and used cash during 20xy.

3. With regard to the Commercial Lending Decision Tree in the textbook Introduction, how does UCA cash flow analysis improve the process?

DRY SUPPLY UCA CASH FLOW WORKSHEET FOR 20xy ($ IN $000s)		20xz
20xy net sales	_____	$ 918
+ 20xx accounts receivable	_____	$ 113
− 20xy accounts receivable	_____	112
+ Accounts receivable (increase) decrease	_____	$ 1
= **Cash from sales**	_____	$ 919
20xy cost of goods sold (net of depreciation)	_____	($631)
+ 20xx inventory	_____	$ 72
− 20xy inventory	_____	67
+ Inventory (increase) decrease	_____	$ 5
+ 20xy accounts payable	_____	$ 31
− 20xx accounts payable	_____	46
+ Accounts payable increase (decrease)	_____	($ 15)
= **Cash productions costs**	_____	($641)
20xy selling, gen. & admin. exp. (net of deprec.)	_____	($ 228)
+ 20xy accrued expenses	_____	$ 12
− 20xx accrued expenses	_____	11
+ Accrued expenses increase (decrease)	_____	$ 1
= **Cash operating expenses**	_____	($227)
20xy other income	_____	$ 5
20xy other expenses	_____	($ 0)
= **Total miscellaneous**	_____	$ 5
20xz income tax expense	_____	($ 17)
+ 20xy income taxes payable	_____	$ 7
− 20xx income taxes payable	_____	6
+ Income taxes payable increase (decrease)	_____	$ 1
= **Cash paid for taxes**	_____	($ 16)
NET CASH AFTER OPERATIONS	_____	$ 40
20xy interest expense	_____	($ 11)
20xy dividends or distributions	_____	0
= Financing costs	_____	($ 11)
= **Net cash income**	_____	$ 29
− 20xx CMLTD	_____	($ 0)
CASH AFTER DEBT AMORTIZATION	_____	$ 29
20xy depreciation expense	_____	($ 13)
+ 20xx net fixed assets	_____	$ 49
− 20xy net fixed assets	_____	(53)
+ Other current assets (increase) decrease	_____	($ 4)
= Capital expenditures	_____	($ 17)
+ 20xx investments (CSVLI)	_____	14
− 20xy investments (CSVLI)	_____	(16)
= **Total long-term investments**	_____	($ 19)
FINANCING SURPLUS (REQUIREMENT)	_____	$ 10
− 20xx notes payable bank short-term	_____	($ 68)
+ 20xy notes payable bank short-term	_____	59
+ Short-term debt increase (decrease)	_____	($ 9)
+ 20xy CMLTD	_____	$ 0
+ 20xy long-term debt	_____	67
− 20xx long-term debt	_____	(58)
+ Incremental long-term debt	_____	$ 9
− 20xx stockholders equity (excl. ret. earnings)	_____	($ 2)
+ 20xy stockholders equity (excl. ret. earnings)	_____	2
+ stockholders equity increase (decrease)	_____	$ 0
TOTAL EXTERNAL FINANCING	_____	$ 0
CASH AFTER EXTERNAL FINANCING	_____	$ 10

11

Cash Budgets and Pro Forma Statements

OBJECTIVES

After studying *Cash Budgets and Pro Forma Statements*, you will be able to—

- Describe the role and use of cash budgets in financial statement analysis
- Explain the importance of pro forma statements for projecting cash flow and loan repayment

INTRODUCTION

So far, your analysis of business financial statements and tax returns has focused on history, using four important components: income statements, balance sheets, ratios, and cash flow statements, which include the UCA model. Although cash repays loans and historical analysis helps a business banker understand the current financial health of a business, you also need to predict what will happen in the future. More specifically, future cash flow is what repays loans, and you need to learn about forward-looking tools, such as cash budgets and pro forma or projected statements.

Relationship to the Commercial Lending Decision Tree

In the textbook Introduction, we explored the Commercial Lending Decision Tree as a way to think about the stages and steps involved in the commercial lending process. As you have already learned, the first stage in this process emphasizes early screening and qualifying steps, such as a general fit with the portfolio and goals of your bank, and initial assessment of financial and nonfinancial qualifications of the business. These preliminary steps allow a business banker to anticipate various issues and conduct a more efficient and accurate financial analysis.

The second stage moves into the detailed analysis of financial data gathered from the business and any owners who may serve as guarantors. In moving beyond the historical analysis of income statements, balance sheets, ratios, and cash flow (including the UCA model), you complete the financial statement analysis process by utilizing cash budgets and pro forma statements. Based on earlier steps in the lending process, we set the stage for cash budgets and pro forma statements. For instance, a cash budget is a better fit for businesses in the start-up or growth stages of the business life cycle, and it focuses heavily on the operating cycle of the business.

Although much of financial analysis helps a business banker understand the history of the business, studying cash budgets and pro forma statements prepares him or her to anticipate future trends. For businesses that are seasonal or have short-term funding needs, a cash budget helps predict maximum and minimum financing needs on a month-to-month basis. Pro forma statements provide a multi-year look at cash needs and the effect of sales growth and other long-term trends.

Year Sequence for Dates in Textbook Cases

This chapter uses the following order or sequence of years for the dates in the financial statements:
- 20xx, 20xy, and 20xz

For projected years, the following sequence is used:
- 20yx, 20yy, 20yz, and so on

ANALYZING CASH BUDGETS

A cash budget provides an estimate of the short-term cash position and funding requirements of a business. For a business that reports income using the accrual method of accounting, the income statement makes it difficult to determine the amounts of cash generated and used from month to month. Consequently, a business banker trying to structure a short-term loan request may have difficulty determining the borrower's ability to generate cash and repay debt. It is particularly useful in determining the credit needs of businesses in the start-up or growth stages of the business life cycle as well as businesses with seasonal variations in operations. A cash budget clarifies the monthly cash flow and sources of repayment. It is used to estimate the flow of cash through the accounts of a business during a designated time period.

Cash budgets are useful to both bankers and businesses. Bankers use cash budgets to review the periods between the origination and repayment of short-term loans. Businesses develop cash budgets to forecast and better control monthly, weekly, or daily cash requirements. By projecting the schedule of receipts and disbursements on a monthly, weekly, or daily basis, a business banker can identify the cause, timing, and magnitude of a company's peak borrowing needs and its repayment capabilities for short-term debt.

Cash Budget Overview

Ideally, most businesses should use cash budgets as a part of their own internal financial planning process. When a borrower prepares a cash budget, a business banker should examine the underlying realism of the assumptions. A business banker should ask the following questions:

- Has the past performance of the business supported the projections?

- Are the projections conservative and dependable, with proper consideration given to external factors (such as the economy, the industry, or government regulations)?

- Are the assumptions within management's control?

- Is the past data reliable?

Many small businesses are not able to provide a cash budget for analysis because they do not employ a chief financial officer (CFO) or controller who can prepare such a report. The cost of having an outside accountant prepare this analysis may be too great in relation to the amount of the loan requested. Larger companies may not need to prepare a cash budget because they employ a CFO or controller to forecast and manage the day-to-day cash needs. So, in many cases, business bankers prepare a cash budget based on interviews, past financial statements, accounts receivable turnover, inventory management, and accounts payable terms. If the business creates accrual-basis financial statements, then a business banker will need to convert this information to cash-basis information. However it is prepared, a cash budget is only a rough estimate of cash needs. This is because the budget is based on estimates and numerous other variables that could easily change.

Inflows and Outflows of Cash, Plus Other Building Blocks of a Cash Budget

A cash budget is used to examine a company's inflows and outflows on a cash basis rather than on an accrual basis. The timing of these cash flows and the actual cash requirements of the business are taken into account. This means that although a business income statement recognizes sales at delivery, a cash budget recognizes only cash sales or collections of accounts receivable. If a business makes credit sales on 30-day terms, a cash budget recognizes the collection of cash 30 days after the sale (assuming the customer pays in 30 days) rather than on the day of sale.

An accrual income statement recognizes expenditures as an expense when a purchase is delivered or, in the case of cost of goods sold, when a sale is made. This does not necessarily mean that the cash has been paid. The amount due can be charged to accounts payable and eventually paid when the cash is available. The time at which the expenditure is paid is the focus in a cash budget; the issue of recognizing it as an expense is not important. For example, an insurance premium paid annually, rather than expensed evenly throughout the year, is entered as a cash expenditure during the month it is paid.

To construct a cash budget for an existing company, business bankers use the ratios (in days) of receivables turnover, inventory turnover, and payables turnover because one of the primary assumptions in a cash budget is that these ratios will remain steady. Business bankers should be able to rely on the relationships between a company's various current assets and current liability accounts to its sales. If alterations were to be made in these relationships—as would occur in a change in collection terms—then the business banker needs to know of them to properly complete the budget.

A cash budget should also include detailed cash flow information about the timing of any equipment purchases, the repayment of long-term debt, and when interest and principal payments on loans are due.

Simply put, companies use cash budgets to keep their checking accounts from running out of cash. Business bankers use cash budgets to determine when customers will likely need to borrow—and to assure themselves that borrowers will be able to repay short-term loans. Sometimes the business banker will want to rework the cash budget to determine how unexpected changes in cash flow assumptions affect it. This procedure, commonly referred to as scenario analysis, could enable the business banker to uncover financing needs not foreseen by the business.

Further, a cash budget allows management to control the company's performance on an interim basis and lets a business banker analyze that performance by identifying the various components of cash flow. Management can react quickly if the actual cash flow varies significantly from the expected cash budget. Management's effectiveness in dealing with such deviations depends on the time increment (monthly or weekly) that is used to prepare the cash budget and how often the company's performance is reviewed.

To summarize, cash budgets forecast a company's cash receipts and disbursements between statement dates, usually monthly. The most common sources of cash are cash sales, the collection of accounts receivable, and proceeds from new loans or lines of credit. The most common uses of cash include operating expenses, payments of accounts payable (for inventories), interest, taxes, labor (payroll), and capital expenditures.

Use of Cash Budgets

When considering a loan request from a company with seasonal sales, business bankers find the cash budget to be a critical tool for financial statement analysis. Seasonal financing requirements are spurred by increases in inventory and accounts receivable, which are associated with periodic peaks in sales, production, or purchasing. This interim need might not be apparent in a company's year-end financial statements, because a true short-term need will be self-liquidating. The assets being financed will convert to cash to repay debt.

For example, a company purchases lawn mowers during the winter. The repayment source is the sale of the asset purchased (lawn mowers) during the spring. The company should be able to pay the interim loan during the course of an operating cycle. The operating cycle defines the time period during which cash converts into inventory, then into accounts receivable (or cash), and, finally—through the collection of accounts receivable—back into cash. If the company cannot pay its interim loan by converting its assets into cash during the operating cycle, then its borrowing need is not short-term. Because seasonal borrowing is self-liquidating, the company does not have to be profitable to repay the debt, provided its cash flow is not negative and the accounts receivable are collected.

For start-up companies, a cash budget is essential in the early months. New companies typically have one-time expenses, such as rental deposits. Start-up companies that provide a product or service on credit also are not able to collect cash from accounts receivable in the early weeks. Therefore, the company will have expenses that are due during a time when little cash is collected.

When approving a short-term loan request, the business banker must have confidence in the company's cash budgets. For established companies, this confidence is a direct result of how well management has performed against its previous plans and how dependable the company's cash flows have been in the past. For start-up companies, the quality of the supporting information, the assessment of management, and the amount of initial capital assist in providing the confidence needed. A cash budget shows absolute cash needs; however, because the budget is only a forecast and a single short-term event could delay a receipt of cash, the business banker should be ready to finance more than the budget estimates.

Cash Budget Format

When a cash budget is completed, the business banker's job is to check the timing and magnitude of the projected cash flows of the business based on other available financial information. Prior to the preparation or interpretation of a cash budget, the business banker reviews all of the financial information, including ratios. The assumptions behind the cash budget projections are a critical part of the cash budget and should be realistic.

Whether constructing a cash budget or reviewing an existing one, a business banker should identify the following areas:

- Timing and amount of cash sales revenues, credit sales, and collection of accounts receivable
- Accounts receivable turnover compared with established credit terms of the business
- Suppliers' credit terms and the payment practices of the business, with respect to purchased materials

- Magnitude and timing of direct labor and overhead costs, and of various operating expenditures of the business, including its general, administrative, and selling expenses
- Nonoperating expenditures (dividend payment policies, loan repayment schedules, and interest payments).

The specific format that companies use for their monthly cash budgets varies. The following is a typical format:

- Line 1: beginning cash (including marketable securities) at the start of each period
- Line 2: receipts, including cash sales, collections of accounts receivable, new loan proceeds, injection of owner's equity, and other cash proceeds
- Line 3: total cash available, the sum of lines 1 and 2
- Lines 4–8: operating cash paid out, including inventory (raw material) purchases; labor and overhead expenses; selling, general, and administrative expenses; owner's salary; and interest expense
- Line 9: total disbursements—the sum of lines 4 through 8
- Lines 10–12: other cash outflows, including loan principal payments, capital expenditures (net of any long-term financing), and dividends
- Line 13: total cash paid out, the sum of lines 9 through 12
- Line 14: net cash position (total cash available [line 3], minus projected total cash paid out [line 13])
- Line 15: minimum cash position (the amount required for ongoing operations)
- Line 16: Loan required—the amount needed to bring the company's cash position up to its minimum cash requirement; negative funding requirements indicate amounts available for repayment of previous funding needs
- Line 17: cumulative borrowing/reduction—the amount of current short-term debt, plus or minus any additional funds needed

Example: Cash Budget for a Growing Company (Designs by Dezine, Inc.)

As an example, this section uses Designs by Dezine, Inc., to show a cash budget for a growing company with some seasonality. Figure 11.1 shows Designs by Dezine's historical and projected sales on a monthly basis for the years 20xz and 20yx.

On January 2, 20yx, the company requested bank financing for a new computer system that costs $10,000. Designs by Dezine plans to pay $2,000 down and finance the balance over five years (the depreciable life of the equipment). The company requested a loan with payments on a five-year amortization.

The bank's examination of the company's financial statements made the business banker wonder if the company also might need permanent funding or a line of credit to support the growth in sales projected for 20yx. The business banker decided to construct a new cash budget.

trying to structure a short-term loan request may have difficulty determining the borrower's ability to generate cash and repay debt. It is particularly useful in determining the credit needs of businesses in the start-up or growth stages of the business life cycle as well as businesses with seasonal variations in operations. A cash budget clarifies the monthly cash flow and sources of repayment. It is used to estimate the flow of cash through the accounts of a business during a designated time period.

Cash budgets are useful to both bankers and businesses. Bankers use cash budgets to review the periods between the origination and repayment of short-term loans. Businesses develop cash budgets to forecast and better control monthly, weekly, or daily cash requirements. By projecting the schedule of receipts and disbursements on a monthly, weekly, or daily basis, a business banker can identify the cause, timing, and magnitude of a company's peak borrowing needs and its repayment capabilities for short-term debt.

Cash Budget Overview

Ideally, most businesses should use cash budgets as a part of their own internal financial planning process. When a borrower prepares a cash budget, a business banker should examine the underlying realism of the assumptions. A business banker should ask the following questions:

- Has the past performance of the business supported the projections?

- Are the projections conservative and dependable, with proper consideration given to external factors (such as the economy, the industry, or government regulations)?

- Are the assumptions within management's control?

- Is the past data reliable?

Many small businesses are not able to provide a cash budget for analysis because they do not employ a chief financial officer (CFO) or controller who can prepare such a report. The cost of having an outside accountant prepare this analysis may be too great in relation to the amount of the loan requested. Larger companies may not need to prepare a cash budget because they employ a CFO or controller to forecast and manage the day-to-day cash needs. So, in many cases, business bankers prepare a cash budget based on interviews, past financial statements, accounts receivable turnover, inventory management, and accounts payable terms. If the business creates accrual-basis financial statements, then a business banker will need to convert this information to cash-basis information. However it is prepared, a cash budget is only a rough estimate of cash needs. This is because the budget is based on estimates and numerous other variables that could easily change.

Inflows and Outflows of Cash, Plus Other Building Blocks of a Cash Budget

A cash budget is used to examine a company's inflows and outflows on a cash basis rather than on an accrual basis. The timing of these cash flows and the actual cash requirements of the business are taken into account. This means that although a business income statement recognizes sales at delivery, a cash budget recognizes only cash sales or collections of accounts receivable. If a business makes credit sales on 30-day terms, a cash budget recognizes the collection of cash 30 days after the sale (assuming the customer pays in 30 days) rather than on the day of sale.

An accrual income statement recognizes expenditures as an expense when a purchase is delivered or, in the case of cost of goods sold, when a sale is made. This does not necessarily mean that the cash has been paid. The amount due can be charged to accounts payable and eventually paid when the cash is available. The time at which the expenditure is paid is the focus in a cash budget; the issue of recognizing it as an expense is not important. For example, an insurance premium paid annually, rather than expensed evenly throughout the year, is entered as a cash expenditure during the month it is paid.

To construct a cash budget for an existing company, business bankers use the ratios (in days) of receivables turnover, inventory turnover, and payables turnover because one of the primary assumptions in a cash budget is that these ratios will remain steady. Business bankers should be able to rely on the relationships between a company's various current assets and current liability accounts to its sales. If alterations were to be made in these relationships—as would occur in a change in collection terms—then the business banker needs to know of them to properly complete the budget.

A cash budget should also include detailed cash flow information about the timing of any equipment purchases, the repayment of long-term debt, and when interest and principal payments on loans are due.

Simply put, companies use cash budgets to keep their checking accounts from running out of cash. Business bankers use cash budgets to determine when customers will likely need to borrow—and to assure themselves that borrowers will be able to repay short-term loans. Sometimes the business banker will want to rework the cash budget to determine how unexpected changes in cash flow assumptions affect it. This procedure, commonly referred to as scenario analysis, could enable the business banker to uncover financing needs not foreseen by the business.

Further, a cash budget allows management to control the company's performance on an interim basis and lets a business banker analyze that performance by identifying the various components of cash flow. Management can react quickly if the actual cash flow varies significantly from the expected cash budget. Management's effectiveness in dealing with such deviations depends on the time increment (monthly or weekly) that is used to prepare the cash budget and how often the company's performance is reviewed.

To summarize, cash budgets forecast a company's cash receipts and disbursements between statement dates, usually monthly. The most common sources of cash are cash sales, the collection of accounts receivable, and proceeds from new loans or lines of credit. The most common uses of cash include operating expenses, payments of accounts payable (for inventories), interest, taxes, labor (payroll), and capital expenditures.

Use of Cash Budgets

When considering a loan request from a company with seasonal sales, business bankers find the cash budget to be a critical tool for financial statement analysis. Seasonal

FIGURE 11.1 DESIGNS BY DEZINE—MONTHLY SALES ($ IN 000s)		
Month	Historical 20xz	Projected 20yx
January	$ 0	$ 20
February	$ 0	$ 30
March	$ 0	$ 40
April	$ 0	$ 50
May	$ 15	$ 60
June	$ 30	$ 60
July	$ 40	$ 60
August	$ 55	$ 70
September	$ 60	$ 80
October	$ 74	$ 90
November	$ 90	$110
December	$ 20	$ 30
Total	$384	$700

Figure 11.2 summarizes the major accounts from Designs by Dezine's 20xz tax return.

FIGURE 11.2 DESIGNS BY DEZINE SUMMARY FINANCIAL INFORMATION		
	20xz (in 000s)	Common-sized %
Income Statement		
Sales	$ 384	100.0%
Raw materials purchases	$ 330	85.9%
Depreciation	$ 12	3.1%
Owner's salary	$ 43	11.2%
S, G, & A expenses	$ 22	5.7%
Interest expense	$ 3	0.8%
Net profit before tax	($ 26)	(6.7%)
Balance Sheet—Assets		
Cash	$ 6	9.4%
Accounts receivable	$ 8	12.5%
Inventory	$ 1	1.6%
Total current assets	$ 15	23.4%
Net fixed assets	$ 49	76.5%
Total assets	$ 64	100.0%
Liabilities and Equity		
Accounts payable	$ 3	4.7%
Notes payable shareholder	$ 46	71.9%
Long-term debt	$ 40	62.5%
Net worth	($ 25)	(39.1%)
Total liabilities and equity	$ 64	100.0%

The financial information above provides the basis for the development of the company's 20yx cash budget as shown in Figure 11.3. An explanation of each line of the budget follows.

- **Beginning cash**—On Designs by Dezine's 20xz income tax return, cash at year-end was $6,053. The business banker enters this amount on Line 1 as beginning cash. Line 15 on the cash budget shows the minimum cash balance required for ongoing operations as $5,000. If cash is higher than $5,000 at the end of any month, it is because all short-term debt (shown as *loan required* on Line 16, with a cumulative balance on Line 17) has been repaid.

FIGURE 11.3 DESIGNS BY DEZINE 20yx CASH BUDGET ($ IN 000s)													
		Jan	Feb	Mar	April	May	June	Jul	Aug	Sep	Oct	Nov	Dec
1	Beginning Cash	6	5	5	5	5	5	5	5	5	5	14	27
2	Receipts	18	25	35	45	55	60	60	65	75	85	100	70
3	Total Cash Avail.	24	30	40	50	60	65	65	70	80	90	114	97
4	Materials purchases	8	8	12	16	20	24	24	24	28	32	36	44
5	Labor (non-S, G, & A)	7	11	14	18	21	21	21	25	28	32	39	11
6	S, G, & A expenses	4	4	4	4	4	4	4	4	4	4	4	4
7	Owner's salary	5	5	5	5	5	5	5	5	5	5	5	5
8	Interest expense	1	1	1	1	1	1	1	1	1	1	1	1
9	Total disbursements	25	29	36	44	51	55	55	59	66	74	85	65
10	Loan principal paid	1	2	2	2	2	2	2	2	2	2	2	2
11	Net capital expend.	2	0	0	0	0	0	0	0	0	0	0	0
12	Distributions or div.	0	0	0	0	0	0	0	0	0	0	0	15
13	Total cash paid out	28	31	38	46	53	57	57	61	68	76	87	82
14	Net cash position	(4)	(1)	2	4	7	8	8	9	12	14	27	15
15	Minimum cash	5	5	5	5	5	5	5	5	5	14	27	15
16	S-T loan required	9	6	3	1	(2)	(3)	(3)	(4)	(7)	0	0	0
17	Cumulative loan req.	9	15	18	19	17	14	11	7	0	0	0	0

- **Receipts**—As summarized in monthly sales chart above, Designs by Dezine projects a sales increase for 20yx. The growth is from one full year of operations and projected larger contracts. The company is somewhat seasonal, with large sales levels in the summer and fall. As a construction company, Designs by Dezine obtains a 50 percent down payment with each contract. Most contracts are completed in 30 to 45 days. The remaining 50 percent is collected on completion. The company ended 20xz with $8,000 of accounts receivable. The first month's receipts would include $10,000 of down payments for the projected January sales. Therefore, the receipts are $18,000 ($8,000 accounts receivable collections and $10,000 down payments). Thus, Line 2 reflects the accounts receivable collections and sales down payments, totaling $18,000.

- **Total cash available**—Total cash receipts on Line 3 equal the following items:

- $24,000 for January ($6,000 cash, $8,000 accounts receivable collections, and $10,000 down payment of projected January sales)

- $27,000 for February ($10,000 collected on the balance of January sales, 50 percent down on projected February sales $12,000, plus beginning cash $5,000)

- $38,000 for March ($13,000 collected on the balance of February sales, 50 percent down on projected March sales $20,000, plus beginning cash of $5,000)

- Additional months thereafter, as shown in the chart above (receipts from down payments and the balance of sales from the previous month, plus beginning cash or excess net cash position)

- **Total cash paid out**—The cash-paid-out figures typically are estimated expenditures, using expenses as a percentage of sales, which is calculated from the company's previous income statement. The business banker might wish to discuss with the borrower what effect the new equipment and projected sales growth will have on the company's financial performance. Moreover, the business banker should analyze the expense categories to determine which of them are fixed and might remain stable in the face of growing sales. Cash budget expenditures might also be based on company-provided estimates of proposed expenditures.

- **Materials purchases and labor**—Because the analysis shows growing sales for Designs by Dezine, it is logical for the business banker to assume that many of the company's costs will grow at a similar rate. The next step is to calculate materials purchases and labor expenses. Designs by Dezine's material expenses were 85.9 percent of sales last year. This amount also includes labor for each job. The company is projecting 75 percent of sales for materials and labor expenses. After a discussion with the owners, the business banker calculates the amount of materials costs at 40 percent and labor costs at 35 percent.

  When creating a cash budget, a business banker must take into account the actual timing of a company's accounts payable for raw materials or inventory payments. Designs by Dezine's accounts payable for materials are paid 30 days after the start of a job. Generally, raw materials are delivered early in the job, with payment due 30 days after receipt of the raw materials. Therefore, January material purchases are $8,000 (December sales of $20,000 x 0.40 = $8,000), and labor expenses are $7,000 (projected sales of $20,000 x 0.35 = $7,000). February materials purchases are $8,000 (January projected sales of $20,000 x 0.40 = $8,000), and labor expenses are $11,000 (February projected sales of $30,000 x 0.35 = $10,500 rounded to $11,000). For each month following, materials purchases will continue to be 40 percent of the previous month's sales and labor will be 35 percent of the current month's sales.

- **Selling, general, and administrative (S, G, & A) expenditures**—An income statement often lists the individual expense categories that make up its S, G, &

A expenses, including office employees' salaries, office supplies, advertising, transportation, accounting, and so on. These expenditures support sales and generally are incurred in the same month as the sales and are paid for in that same month. It is not necessary to expect these expenditures to take place in advance of the sales date. S, G, & A expenses are calculated as a percentage of sales if no major changes are anticipated. For 20xz, Designs by Dezine's S, G & A expenses were 5.7 percent of sales; however, this number is distorted because 20xz was a partial year, and sales are projected to increase substantially. The company is projecting S, G & A expenses of $46,000 for 20yx. After discussing this with the owner, the business banker determines that this amount is reasonable. Therefore, the cash budget uses $4,000 per month on Line 6.

- **Owner's salary**—Last year, Linda Dezine drew an officer's compensation of $42,700 for eight months. She is expecting to draw up to $80,000 this year if the company's performance allows. However, she has agreed to limit her salary to $5,000 each month until the company can afford to pay her more. The $5,000 draw is listed on Line 7 of the projected cash budget. Because the cash budget shows excess cash in November and December, she may choose to increase her salary during those months.

- **Interest expense**—The new loan for $8,000 and a shareholder loan taken out late last year will increase interest expense and the cash flow required for principal repayment compared with 20xz. Assuming that the interest rate will be 8 percent, the new interest expense would be about $546 for the first year of the computer loan, with payments starting in February (based on an amortization schedule). The amount of the shareholder loan is obtained from the company tax return ($46,172 at 12/31/20xz). If $1,000 principal reductions are made, beginning in February, total interest expense for the 20yx will be about $3,743. The remaining debt is a loan for vehicles (trucks), shown as a $40,064 balance at 12/31/20xz. The loans started at $43,000 at 8 percent, with payments of $872 over 60 months. Based on an amortization schedule, interest paid in 20yx should be about $2,880.

  For cash budget purposes, the interest on the existing loans (vehicles and shareholder) is added together and divided by 12. This results in $552 of monthly interest for all 12 months. The interest on the computer loan is about $50 per month, beginning in February. Because the cash budget is presented in even thousands, the business banker will round the monthly amount up to $1,000 for the cash budget.

- **Total disbursements**—The sum of Lines 4 through 8 equals total disbursements on Line 9. This sum should total the cash expenditures for cost of goods sold; selling, general, and administrative expenses; and interest expense.

- **Loan principal**—As mentioned in the interest expense calculations, Designs by Dezine's balance sheet shows long-term debt of $40,064 for vehicles and a $46,172 shareholder loan at 12/31/20xz. Using an amortization schedule, the 20xz principal reduction for the vehicles loan will be about $7,582.

(The loan started at $43,000 at 8 percent for payments of $872 over 60 months. Six payments had been made during 20xz.) For cash budgeting, this amount will be divided by 12, resulting in $632 per month. This will be rounded up to $1,000 for January.

Starting in February, the company is hoping to begin repaying shareholders $1,000 per month on the principal portion of the debt. Also in February, payments will begin on the $8,000 computer loan. Using an 8 percent interest rate and payments of $162 over 60 months, the principal reduction during 20yx (11 months) would be about $1,238, or $112 per month. So, principal reductions in February and the following months will include an additional $1,112. Together with the $632 per month for the vehicles loan, total monthly principal reduction is about $1,744, which will be rounded to $2,000.

- **Net capital expenditures**—Computer equipment is the company's only projected capital equipment purchase for 20yx. The amount on Line 11 is shown net of any long-term financing, which is expected to be $8,000. This leaves $2,000 as the net capital expenditure for cash budget purposes. The business banker will need to adjust this amount if the loan is not approved or is obtained for a different dollar amount.

- **Income taxes and dividends**—Income taxes sometimes can be a problem for businesses preparing cash budgets. Designs by Dezine is an S corporation, with Linda Dezine as the sole owner and personally liable for any taxable income. Therefore, the company will show no taxes paid. However, most S corporations make a distribution to the owner to fund any income taxes on the business income that is passed through to the owner's personal tax return. Because the company showed an operating loss last year (20xz), the amount of the distribution for this year (20yx) needs to be based on projected earnings. Linda Dezine is projecting a $45,000 profit for 20yx, so a distribution of $15,000 is projected for December.

- **Total cash paid out**—The business banker has now accounted for all of the anticipated cash expenditures for each month for Designs by Dezine. The company's projected total cash outlays are listed for each month on Line 13.

- **Net cash position**—This line of the cash budget is calculated by subtracting total cash paid out (Line 13) from total cash available (Line 3). It shows that Designs by Dezine's net cash position does not exceed its minimum cash required (Line 15) until May.

- **Short-term loan required**—This is the amount of cash the company needs to maintain its stated minimum cash position of $5,000. The amount of a loan required is calculated by subtracting the company's net cash position (Line 14) from its minimum cash requirement (Line 15). From January through April, the company needs additional short-term borrowings to maintain its cash position. In January the net cash position is ($4000), so $9,000 must be borrowed to end up with a positive minimum cash position of $5,000. In February the net cash position is ($1,000), so $6,000 must be borrowed to reach the minimum cash position of $5,000. Starting in May, the net cash position exceeds the minimum cash level, so new borrowings are required. The negative numbers show the amount of cash (above the minimum level) that can be used to pay down short-term loans.

- **Cumulative loan required**—This is the running balance of the short-term borrowing needed to maintain the company's minimum cash position. In January $9,000 must be borrowed to end up with a positive minimum cash position of $5,000, leaving a cumulative loan balance of $9,000. In February another $6,000 must be borrowed to reach the minimum cash position of $5,000, leaving a cumulative loan balance of $15,000. Monthly borrowings occur through April, with the cumulative balance reaching a peak of $19,000 in that same month.

In May, the net cash position is $7,000, so $2,000 of the loan can be repaid. In June the net cash position is $8,000, so $3,000 of the loan can be repaid. Through September, loan repayments of $19,000 will have been made, totally repaying any short-term borrowings. Cash balances begin to build from October to December.

Cash Budget Analysis

Overall, Designs by Dezine's cash budget shows that the business will have short-term borrowing needs as its sales grow early in 20yx and before the resulting receivables are collected. Borrowings reach a peak of $19,000 in April, with reductions projected to start in May and the loan balance dropping to $0 by September. The business banker will want to see if the company has planned for these short-term borrowings and perhaps consider offering a line of credit for this purpose. Once this short-term borrowing need is realized, Linda Dezine may want to delay making principal payments on the shareholder loan or even reconsider the timing of the computer purchases. Also, she may rethink the level of salary she intends to pay from the business. She may even be able to obtain higher down payments on contracts. All of these items will serve to reduce the firm's borrowing needs. These insights into the firm's overall borrowing needs are generated by an analysis of the Designs by Dezine's cash budget.

The Role of a Cash Budget

The business banker analyzes the cash budget to determine the effect on operating cycle, working capital, and capital expenditures. Each of these items affects the cash flow, profit margins, and amount of debt needed.

Interrelationship Between the Operating Cycle and Cash Needs

As mentioned before, the cash conversion (or operating) cycle will help determine whether a business needs to prepare a cash budget. For example, a restaurant probably will not need a cash budget because its operating cycle is short, possibly only a few days. The distinction between its accrual-basis income and its cash-basis income will be slight. Further, a review of its monthly statements is practically mandatory for a business banker because the capability of generating income can change quickly.

The longer operating cycles of manufacturing and certain wholesaling businesses can be a problem because they require sizable amounts of working capital. A considerable amount of cash is needed to acquire raw materials inventories, pay employee wages, and maintain an inventory of finished goods. For these businesses, cash budgets are essential.

Interrelationship Between Working Capital and Capital Expenditures

Sales growth or replacement of capital equipment requires careful planning. When sales grow, accounts receivable and inventory tend to grow as well. Working capital is defined as current assets, minus current liabilities. With accounts receivable and inventory being the primary current assets, the cash budget will help determine the effect on the working capital requirements of a business.

Replacing and adding fixed assets often accompanies sales growth. If a business can schedule repayment of any related loans in accordance with the useful life of the equipment, then the working capital cash needs can be addressed by drawing a cash budget that includes these new loan payments.

The cash budget also addresses the issue of separating financing for permanent expansion of fixed assets from financing for working capital needs. The focus on cash flow makes a cash budget an exceptionally good demonstration of the difference between accounting for income and determining debt repayment capacity. Convincing borrowers to use this approach for their own understanding is invaluable. If a business has a substantial profit margin, then it frequently can finance most, if not all, of its working capital needs and fixed assets.

In this section, you learned that the monthly cash budget is an important tool of financial statement analysis because it helps identify the cause, timing, and magnitude of a company's peak borrowing needs during interim periods—needs that may not show up on year-end financial statements. You also learned that a cash budget is used to examine a company's inflows and outflows on a cash basis, and why it is a critical tool of financial statement analysis for businesses that use accrual-basis accounting. You are now familiar with the typical cash-budget format along with financial information you should identify when constructing or reviewing a cash budget. A cash budget can help business bankers avoid the pitfall of inadvertently lending for long-term periods when the borrower actually has a short-term need. You should now feel more confident when analyzing a cash budget and determining its effect on the operating cycle, working capital, and capital expenditures.

CALCULATING AND INTERPRETING PRO FORMA FINANCIAL STATEMENTS

Some companies prepare forecasted financial statements as part of routine financial planning. Pro forma or forecasted income statements and balance sheets represent management's best estimates about how a business will perform in the future. It also considers the expected economic, competitive, and regulatory environments in which the business will operate.

Business bankers typically require commercial term-loan applicants to submit forecasted financial statements that show the projected financial results and repayment capacity of the business for one to three years or the term of the loan, whichever is shorter. The number of years covered in a pro forma forecast is entirely up to the business banker. Some business bankers work from just a one-year forecast because a particular business environment might be too uncertain to put any reliability in a longer forecast. This chapter uses a one-year forecast for convenience, but the principles expressed can be extended easily for up to five years.

Business bankers also request copies of past forecasted statements so that they can compare management's past predictions with the actual results. Business bankers sometimes prepare their own pro forma balance sheets and income statements based on the company's past performance and expectations for the future.

Regardless of the source, even at their best, pro forma statements have shortcomings. No one can predict the future with certainty, and many unforeseen factors can dramatically affect a company's projected financial plans.

Considerations for Constructing and Reviewing Projections

Pro forma financial statements are similar to historical financial statements in appearance and use, except that they focus on the future instead of the past and are based upon assumptions rather than hard facts.

Projection Assumptions

One of the business banker's first tasks in reviewing the forecasts of a business is to determine how optimistic the company's plan is. Hastily reviewing an optimistic plan from a business could draw the business banker into a problem loan. First and foremost, business bankers need to consider whether pro forma statements appear to be realistic.

Business bankers use conceptual and mechanical tools to decide whether a company's pro forma is reasonable. They also use these tools to create their own projections of business performance and loan repayment capacity. The conceptual part of the analysis is based on the past performance of the business as evidenced by its prior financial statements, various ratios, and the banker's cash flow analysis. The pro forma forecast—taking into consideration both internal and external forces that affect the business—must assess the financial consequences of management's plans and strategies, actions and inactions, and how they are likely to affect the borrowing needs, repayment capacity, and general credit worthiness of the business.

One way business bankers enhance their analysis of projections is to think of the following three scenarios:
- Best case
- Most likely case
- Worst case

Another tool business bankers use to improve the likelihood of creating realistic assessments is constructing multiple one-year forecasts, either manually or with a software program or spreadsheet. A good electronic format allows a business banker to change assumptions and easily fit various scenarios into a spreadsheet. It also allows the business banker to run simulations of changes in important variables to see the results.

Ideally, this electronic tool uses the same output format, ratios and cash flow model as found in the spread of historical financial statements. This facilitates an orderly comparison of the results.

Pro Forma Framework

The pro forma framework is the basic framework for forecasting financial statements, and it involves paying attention to the following elements:

- The past performance of the business, its continued reliability, and the consistency of past projections
- The external factors that affect the operations of the business, such as the economy, industry trends, the market, competition, and government regulations
- The internal factors that affect the operations of the business, such as management, physical plant, financial controls, marketing strategy, and managerial reports

A business banker who considers these elements will be able to determine not only whether a company's financial projections are technically correct but also whether the projections are based on realistic and reasonable assumptions.

Realistic Assumptions

A business banker reviewing a business-prepared forecast should not rely totally on the assumptions made by the business; he or she should introduce other assumptions that might be more realistic or that fit within the three scenarios of best case, most likely case, or worst case. The company's and business banker's forecasted results are compared in a process that is similar to analyzing financial statements. The basis of both sets of projections and the resulting analysis is the company's past financial results and its plans for sales, expense controls, capital equipment, and plant expenditures for the coming years.

In addition to reviewing the financial documents submitted by the business, a business banker usually will have already visited the business in person to meet key personnel and see the operations. The business banker also should get references and information from outside sources, such as suppliers, customers, and trade associations.

Financial Statement Background

To ensure that a forecast analysis is comprehensive and credible, a business banker should have the following items on hand:

- A complete set of income statements, balance sheets, and statements of cash flows for the past three to five years;
- The debt schedule (loan balances, payments, and other details) of the business; and
- Any previous projections made by the business (if available).

Dependability of Performance

A thorough understanding of the business, its industry, and its market helps the business banker determine the reliability of the financial projections and assumptions made by the business. Long-term forecasts are most dependable for businesses that have consistent performance trends and have closely tracked the industry. Much of this information will have been derived from analyzing the company's balance sheets and income statements, industry trends, and ratios. At this point in the review, the business banker should have a solid grasp of the operations of the business and its past and current performance.

Creating a meaningful forecast is exceedingly difficult for new businesses and those with brief histories or a record of inconsistent performance. For new companies, business bankers can obtain information on the products or services to determine what level of sales may be expected. For a business that provides products or services for a highly competitive market, there can be a rapid loss of the market share. Therefore, extending credit to such firms also is difficult. As you have studied, such businesses require special care and attention early in the lending process.

Time Intervals

The time interval represented by the forecasted statements should match the purpose and the repayment period for the proposed loan. For example, in projecting seasonal borrowing needs, the business usually should construct a cash budget (on a monthly, weekly, or daily basis) and not a pro forma financial statement for annual periods.

Projections that support long-term financing requests should indicate the ability of the business to repay the debt and also extend far enough into the future to reassure the business banker that current trends will continue. These projections should be consistent with trends established over the same period of time in the past. The business banker compares past projections with the past performance of the business. If the projections are not consistent with trends established over the same period of time in the past, then the owner or senior management should provide substantive explanations for these discrepancies.

External Factors

External factors affect both the operations of a business and the analysis of its forecast statements. A business banker should consider how these various factors might change over time and possibly influence the future performance of the business in unexpected ways.

Although management cannot control most of the external factors that make up the operating environment, it must anticipate and plan for such factors in order to achieve financial objectives. In making or analyzing projections, the company or business banker takes into consideration the following major external factors:

- The economy—predictions for general business conditions, interest rates, and economic fluctuations

- The industry—its growth or stagnancy, the ease of entry into it, its degree of competitiveness and number of competitors, and the position of the business in the industry (whether it is a leader or a marginal producer)

- The market—its degree of diversification (number of buyers), the cost of entry into it, the basis of competition (price, quality, technology), the competition from complementary products, and sociological trends (consumer preferences, environmental concerns, and so on)

- Government regulations—prospects for regulatory changes (deregulation), particular environmental issues, and future vulnerability to imports or protection by import restrictions
- Labor—the future availability and cost of labor; if non-unionized, prospects for unionization; if unionized, likelihood of strikes and anticipated costs of new contract negotiations

Businesses using price-sensitive materials and commodities, such as the airline and travel industries, can have their entire inventory source or service process disrupted by an unforeseen event. Even well-established companies can be affected by unanticipated events. For example, the U.S. airlines and the entire travel industry were hurt financially after the terrorist attacks on September 11, 2001, and the resulting severe downturn over the next six months in both leisure and business travel was due to security concerns.

Internal Factors

Internal factors include the human, financial, and physical resources available to the business. Management can control most of these factors and use them to enhance operational performance. The following are major internal factors to consider:

- Management—experience, past performance, ability to project performance and to perform according to projections, ability to achieve objectives, and ability to grow with the business
- Physical plant and equipment—capacity, condition, and efficiency compared with that of competitors; technological sophistication
- Financial controls—accounts receivable systems (approval and collection), inventory and purchasing systems, accounts payable systems, expense controls, and budgetary provisions
- Marketing strategy—the company's niche or broad marketing plan and market territory, adequacy of financial and human resources to support the plan distribution system
- Managerial reports—quality and adequacy of financial and other managerial reports, which are the basis for decision making

The essence of good management is the ability to plan for an uncertain future, to react to adverse or favorable events, and to employ the resources of the business to achieve its objectives. This requires a thorough knowledge of both the external and internal factors that affect a business—and the requirements and limitations these factors impose.

Example: Designs by Dezine, Inc.

Designs by Dezine, Inc.'s forecasted financial statements for 20yx, summarized in Figure 11.4, will be used to demonstrate pro forma analysis. On January 2, 20yx, the company requested bank financing for a computer system that cost $10,000. Designs by Dezine plans to pay $2,000 down and finance the balance over five years. The company has requested a loan with a five-year amortization of principal and interest. A one-year forecast will be used to demonstrate pro forma analysis.

FIGURE 11.4 COMPANY-PREPARED PRO FORMA STATEMENT ($ IN 000s)

Designs by Dezine, Inc., for 20yx	Amount ($)	
Income Statement		
Net Sales	$700	100.0%
Cost of Goods Sold	525	75.0%
Gross Profit	$175	25.0%
S, G, & A Expenses	46	6.6%
Owner's Salary	60	8.6%
Depreciation	14	2.0%
Total Operating Expenses	$120	17.1%
Operating Profit	$ 55	7.8%
Interest Expense	10	1.4%
Pretax Profit	$ 45	6.4%
Income Taxes	0	
Net Profit	$ 45	6.4%
Dividend/Distribution for Taxes	$ 15	2.1%
Balance Sheet—Assets	$ 22	25.3%
Cash	18	30.7%
Accounts Receivable	2	2.3%
Inventory	$ 42	48.3%
Total Current Assets	45	51.7%
Net Fixed Assets	$ 87	100.0%
Total Assets		
Liabilities and Owner's Equity		
Short-Term Bank Debt	$ 0	0.0%
Accounts Payable	7	16.1%
Long-Term Debt	40	37.9%
Shareholder Debt	35	40.2%
Total Liabilities	$ 82	94.2%
Capital Stock	$ 1	1.1%
Retained Earnings	4	4.6%
Total Owner's Equity	$ 5	5.7%
Total Liabilities and Owners Equity	$ 87	100.0%

The bank has provided various services to Designs by Dezine for several years. As part of the commercial relationship, the company provides the bank with copies of its monthly and annual financial statements. Because of these past dealings, the business banker has a good feel for the company's strengths and weaknesses, and knows a number of its officers. The company's borrowings traditionally have been term loans for vehicles. To supplement the company's financial statements, the business banker also has obtained industry information from the company's trade association.

Summary of External Factors

The economy is currently weak. All economic indicators are flat or down, and are projected to remain so for the next year. Monetary growth and inflation appear stable for the immediate future. Industry predictions show that the value of residential real estate will increase by 5 percent in the current year.

The remodeling industry is expected to do well, as individuals will likely remodel their existing homes rather than move during an economic downturn. The remodeling industry expects to grow by 15 percent next year. Federal government regulations have little direct effect on the remodeling industry. State regulations vary by state, with most states raising air-quality levels in homes and requiring better insulating materials and better-built homes.

Summary of Internal Factors

Management's goal is for the company to become a leader in the industry. For its first year, Designs by Dezine performed satisfactorily. Now management wants to create a growth-oriented company with quality projects that are larger in size. Management's primary weakness lies in its lack of a sales manager. The president currently functions in that position. The company also will need to consider renting its own facility in the coming year.

Although the company's management intends to take an aggressive position in the market, it is unwilling to lower price in order to achieve an increased market share. This approach requires the company to hire very skilled laborers and to compensate them well.

Analyzing Pro Forma Statements

Forecasting analysis enables the company's management and the business banker to anticipate the financial consequences of the company's plans and strategies. It has been said that the "the past may provide significant clues to the future." By analyzing the firm's past performance, the business banker can get a better feel for what might happen to the firm in the future.

Past Performance

The company's past history offers a basis on which to judge the reasonableness of the assumptions used to construct the projected statements. Figure 11.5 summarizes Designs by Dezine's common-sized balance sheet and income statement for 20xz.

FIGURE 11.5 DESIGNS BY DEZINE SUMMARY FINANCIAL INFORMATION		
	20xz (in 000s)	**Common-sized %**
Income Statement	$ 384	100.0%
Sales	$ 330	85.9%
Raw materials purchases	$ 12	3.1%
Depreciation	$ 43	11.2%
Owner's salary	$ 22	5.7%
S, G, & A expenses	$ 3	0.8%
Interest expense	($ 26)	(6.7%)
Net profit before tax		
Balance Sheet—Assets	$ 6	9.4%
Cash	$ 8	12.5%
Accounts receivable	$ 1	1.6%
Inventory	$ 15	23.4%
Total current assets	$ 49	76.5%
Net fixed assets	$ 64	100.0%
Total assets		
Liabilities and Equity	$ 3	4.7%
Accounts payable	$ 46	71.9%
Notes payable shareholder	$ 40	62.5%
Long-term debt	($ 25)	(39.1%)
Net worth	$ 64	100.0%
Total liabilities and equity		

- *Past income statements*—Designs by Dezine had only eight months of sales last year, during which it generated sales of $384,000. The income statement also shows that the company's gross margin was 14.1 percent. The gross profit varies, depending on the mix of products sold. For example, the company makes more money on decks and custom cabinets than it does on large additions. S, G, & A expenses were 5.7 percent of sales. The company had an operating loss its first year, which is not unusual.

- *Past balance sheets*—An examination of past years' balance sheets should help to shape expectations for the company's future financing needs. Designs by Dezine's balance sheet shows that the company's financial position is funded primarily by the owner.

The company's sales terms are 50 percent down at signing of the contract and the balance upon completion of the project. Most work is done in 30 to 45 days. During 20xz, receivables were collected upon completion of all work. The company's inventory is nominal, consisting of nuts, bolts, nails, and lumber. The fixed assets consist of two company trucks.

Forecasting an Income Statement

The income statement is the first statement forecasted because the income statement largely drives the balance sheet. The following examples show how the balance sheet is based on the income statement:

- Net profit and dividends are used to calculate retained earnings.
- Accounts receivable are calculated from projected credit sales.
- Inventory is calculated using cost of goods sold.
- Fixed assets are lowered by the amount of depreciation expense.

Sales

The sales projection is the cornerstone of the entire forecasted financial statement. An unrealistic sales figure causes the rest of the projection to be of questionable value because the forecasted income statement accounts are usually calculated as a percentage of sales. The sales projection also affects many balance sheet accounts, such as accounts receivable and inventory. The basis for the estimation of sales can vary—from a very precise, detailed sales budget to a more simplistic percentage increase over the previous year's figures.

Designs by Dezine has projected a large sales increase for the next year. This is based on a full year of operations and completion of some larger projects. Based on eight months' sales in 20xz of $384,000 and now forecasting a full year of operations, management predicts sales to be $700,000 for 20yx. We saw a breakout of the historical and projected sales by month in Reading 1.

From comments in the credit file, the business banker notes that first-year sales were originally projected at $500,000. Because the company did not achieve its first-year sales, the business banker feels that sales in the $650,000 range are more appropriate than the $700,000 listed in the company's forecast. For the first year, sales averaged about $50,000 per month. With the company operating for a full year, this allows an approximated increase of 8 percent, which the business banker feels is more realistic based on industry data.

Figure 11.6 shows a side-by-side comparison of the company's projected income statement to the bank's adjusted income statement.

FIGURE 11.6 DESIGNS BY DEZINE, INC.				
	Company		Bank	
FOR 20yx	Amount ($000s)		Amount ($000s)	
Income Statement				
Net Sales	$700	100.0%	$650	100.0%
Cost of Goods Sold	525	75.0%	510	78.5%
Gross Profit	$175	25.0%	$140	21.5%
S, G, & A Expenses	46	6.6%	58	8.9%
Owner's Salary	60	8.6%	60	9.2%
Depreciation	14	2.0%	14	2.1%
Total Operating Expenses	$120	17.1%	$132	20.3%
Operating Profit	$ 55	7.8%	$ 8	1.2%
Interest Expense	10	1.4%	10	1.5%
Pretax Profit	$ 45	6.4%	($ 2)	(0.3%)
Income Taxes	0		0	
Net Profit	$ 45	6.4%	($ 2)	(0.3%)
Dividend/Distribution for Taxes	$ 15	2.1%	0	

Cost of Goods Sold

Cost of goods sold usually ranks second in importance (behind sales) on the forecast income statement. It is usually calculated as a percentage of projected sales, taking into consideration both past and anticipated performance. When a business must trim its selling prices to remain competitive, the cost of goods sold as a percentage of sales increases. Therefore, if the number of units sold remains the same, then the cost of goods sold, as a percent of sales, will increase.

Management's projected cost of goods sold should be consistent with the previous year's figures. The company is projecting a 10 percent improvement. Designs by Dezine's cost of goods sold ranged from 82 to 90 percent per project last year. The percentage varies, depending on the product sold. Management projects cost of goods sold at 75 percent of projected sales for the following year. Management hopes to achieve this by keeping its labor busy on a more consistent basis.

The business banker believes that the company's projected cost of goods sold as a percentage of its sales is not realistic and reasonable because it is not consistent with past performance. Also, the company has stated that it does not make as much on larger projects yet is targeting larger projects to achieve the sales growth. Therefore, the business banker applies 78.5 percent to the cost of goods sold projected by the bank. At this point, the forecast income statements already differ, as illustrated in the comparison chart above.

The bank's conservative forecast of lower sales and higher cost of goods sold produces a gross profit of $35,000 less than the customer's projection. Each 1 percent change on the banker's forecast in the cost of goods sold lowers the gross profit by $6,500.

Operating Expenses

Designs by Dezine's operating expenses include S, G, & A expenses, depreciation, and officers' salaries. These expenses differ from those included in the cost of goods sold because they are not directly related to the purchase or production of goods or services. However, the operating expenses are usually more difficult to control when sales change rapidly. A company normally projects its operating expenses as a percentage of projected sales or as a percentage change from the previous year's operating expenses.

Selling expenses include the cost of advertising, market research, sales training, promotion, and commissions. Management can vary these expenses at its discretion, as warranted by changing conditions in the marketplace. For instance, when a company introduces a new product or encounters increased competition in the industry, management might increase its sales commissions or promotional outlays.

General and administrative (G and A of S, G, & A) expenses include rent, utilities, real estate, taxes (other than income taxes), depreciation of assets not used in production (such as administrative offices and equipment), telephones, staff and officers' salaries and benefits, and subscriptions. If the company anticipates no dramatic changes, then these items can be calculated as a percentage of sales based on past history. The business banker should evaluate the assumptions behind each figure in this category.

In the past, management consistently held S, G, & A expenses to 5.7 percent of sales. The company is forecasting these expenses at 6.6 percent of sales for next year. A modest increase in expenses is due to increased advertising cost. The bank projects these expenses at 8.9 percent of sales because of its lower sales forecast and a possible need to rent space next year.

The owner has forecasted a personal salary of $60,000 per year. This is close to the annualized amount taken last year. The bank agrees with this amount. The depreciation expense was $12,000 (rounded up) last year. Depreciation expense is expected to be $12,000 on the existing trucks and $2,000 for the new computer, for a total of $14,000.

Operating Profit

After the operating expenses have been subtracted from the gross revenues, the company's operating profit remains. The company projection of sales and expense figures results in an operating profit of $55,000, or 7.9 percent of sales. The bank's projections result in an operating profit of 1.2 percent of sales, or $8,000. The increased cost of goods sold percentage and increased S, G, & A expenses have caused a difference of $47,000 between the two forecasts.

Other Income and Expense

Income statements often include other income and other expense items that do not result from normal business operations. Although these accounts typically are quite small, the business banker must determine what specific items are included and whether they are recurring or nonrecurring. These accounts are not usually predictable as a percentage of a company's sales. Designs by Dezine has not had other income in the past and does not anticipate any in the coming year. Its only non-operating expense is interest.

Interest expense is often listed separately on the income statement. This is a relatively predictable expense because a range of interest rates can be assumed for term debt and short-term (seasonal) borrowings. It is estimated by the projected average amount of term and seasonal debt outstanding during the year.

The increased interest expense for the new loan is added to the historical interest expense. The historical interest expense is low. The shareholder advanced about $46,000 late in the year. This loan was to fund the company during the first year of operation. The forecast includes interest expense on the existing vehicles debt of about $3,000, shareholder debt of $4,000, and the new computer loan of $500. Although it appears that the company might need more money to fund its growth, the amount is unknown until the balance sheet is constructed. Therefore, both the company and the business banker have added another $2,500 of interest expense for a total of $10,000 for interest expense forecasted.

Income Taxes

Income taxes often are projected using current business income tax tables. But because Designs by Dezine is an S corporation, income taxes are not forecasted for its income statement. Instead, the company has forecasted a $15,000 distribution to the owner to be used to pay the tax liability generated at the personal level on the company's projected $45,000 of taxable income. Because the business banker is forecasting a net loss, there will not be a tax liability for Linda Dezine from S corporation earnings, so the bank's projection does not include a distribution.

Forecasting the Balance Sheet

After analyzing and reworking Designs by Dezine's forecasted income statement, the business banker constructs the pro forma balance sheet, as shown in the chart below. Like the income statement forecast, the chart compares the customer's sheet with the one made by the business banker. The assumptions made and conclusions reached in projecting the various income statement accounts affect several entries on the forecasted balance sheet. Therefore, the assumptions used in composing and analyzing the forecasted balance sheet must be consistent with those used for the income statement.

Figure 11.7 shows a side-by-side comparison of the company's projected balance sheet to the bank's adjusted balance sheet forecast.

The cash account in the assets section of the balance sheet or the notes payable short term to bank account in the liabilities section will be the plug figure used to balance the forecasted balance sheet. In other words, one of these accounts is used to balance the statement after all of the other accounts have been calculated. After the forecast balance sheet has been calculated—if assets exceed total liabilities and net worth (stockholders' equity)—any differences are "plugged" by increasing the notes payable to bank account. However, if total liabilities and net worth exceed assets, then the difference is added to the cash account to balance the statement or subtracted from the notes payable if any short-term loans are outstanding.

The changes on the balance sheet will include planned changes in the levels of capital expenditures, long-term debt, and other long-term assets and liabilities. In addition, the business banker will be able to identify certain liquidity, leverage, efficiency, and profit ratios, and test the relationship of those ratios to past figures and to those within the industry.

FIGURE 11.7 DESIGNS BY DEZINE, INC., FOR 12/31/20yx

	Company		Bank	
	Amount ($000s)		Amount ($000s)	
Balance Sheet—Assets				
Cash	$ 22	25.3%	$ 5	25.3%
Accounts Receivable	18	30.7%	18	30.7%
Inventory	2	2.3%	2	2.3%
Total Current Assets	$ 42	48.3%	$ 25	48.3%
Net Fixed Assets	45	51.7%	45	51.7%
Total Assets	$ 87	100.0%	$ 70	100.0%
Liabilities and Owner's Equity				
Short-Term Bank Debt	$ 0	0.0%	$ 10	0.0%
Accounts Payable	7	16.1%	12	16.1%
Long-Term Debt	40	37.9%	40	37.9%
Shareholder Debt	35	40.2%	35	40.2%
Total Liabilities	$ 82	94.2%	$ 97	94.2%
Capital Stock	$ 1	1.1%	$ 1	1.1%
Retained Earnings	4	4.6%	(28)	4.6%
Total Owner's Equity	$ 5	5.7%	($ 27)	5.7%
Total Liabilities and Owner's Equity	$ 87	100.0%	$ 70	100.0%

Assets

Asset forecasts are based on past trends and estimated changes. For example, a company might install a new collection system, which would reduce the level of accounts receivable. The fixed-asset account normally grows in relationship to the plant and equipment capacity. The fixed assets also can grow to replace outdated equipment. Each asset account should be compared with past trends.

- **Cash and marketable securities**—Every business needs a minimum cash balance. For forecasting purposes, cash and marketable securities accounts are combined. The forecast is based on past cash balances, since certain cash balances are derived from the level of the firm's operations (e.g., check float).

  In the borrower's loan agreement, it is possible that additional balances will be required as compensating balances. In that case, they should be added to the calculated amount above. The company forecasts its minimum cash needs at $5,000. Management attributes its ability to live within the projected cash rate to its improved management of inventory and receivables. The business banker agrees with this assessment of its minimum cash needs. Because the company is projecting greater profits, the company forecast has plugged cash at $22,000. The bank is forecasting an operating loss so the minimum cash of $5,000 is used.

- **Accounts receivable** reflects the amount owed to the company by its customers at the end of the period covered by the forecasted income statement. The company's past performance with respect to receivables turnover (in days) is used to assess a company's projected accounts receivable.

The business banker should thoroughly understand management's sales, credit, and collection policies. Credit terms should be compared with actual collection periods to determine the effectiveness of a company's collection policies. The sales goals of a business can have an effect on accounts receivable. For example, management could try to increase sales by offering longer credit terms, by offering credit terms for products formerly sold for cash only, or by lowering prices. The accounts receivable calculation considers trends from previous statements. For most companies, the calculation for accounts receivable uses the following formula:

$$\frac{(Proj.\ accounts\ rec.\ turnover\ (d) \times Proj.\ sales)}{365\ day} = Projected\ accounts\ receivable$$

For example, if Designs by Dezine decided not to obtain down payments and allow credit terms of 45 days after completion, then the following calculation would be for accounts receivable:

$$(45d \times \$700{,}000) \div 365d = \$86{,}301$$

Sometimes, receivables turnover analysis alone can be misleading and can fail to reveal problems with uncollectible receivables or disputed invoices. By comparing several months of accounts receivable aged listings, the business banker can determine new accounts and predict collection times of existing accounts. This is particularly helpful if a business has a concentration of sales to one company. An aged listing of accounts receivable should be used to evaluate management's assumptions for future receivables because the aging reflects management's actual practices and successes with respect to collecting receivables.

Designs by Dezine, Inc., requires payment when the project is completed. Accounts receivable represent the 50 percent of the sales not collected at the time of the signing of the contract. For example, December sales are projected to be $35,000. The company will collect $17,500 at the signing of the contract. The balance of the December sales will be listed as accounts receivable of $17,500 ($18,000 rounded) on the forecasted statement. This is the estimated amount of work that will be done on December sales but not paid. This is an estimate only and is likely to be on the high side because the company probably will not complete all the December sales prior to the end of the month.

- **Inventory** on a forecasted basis usually is calculated using past inventory turnover in days. The following is the formula:

$$\frac{(Projected\ inventory\ turnover\ (d) \times Projected\ cost\ of\ goods\ sold)}{365\ days} = Projected\ inventory$$

For example, if a retail lumber yard carried 90 days of inventory and had projected cost of goods sold of $1,200,000, then the following would be the projected inventory calculation:

$$(90d \times \$1,200,000) \div 365d = \$295,890$$

In addition to considering past performance, a business banker preparing an inventory projection should take into account anticipated changes in the sales and purchasing policies of the business. For example, if a supplier changes the minimum purchase requirement from one case to ten cases per order, then the amount of inventory forecasted on the balance sheet should likely be increased. Designs by Dezine carries a nominal inventory consisting of nails, screws, and other small items. Both the company and bank forecast inventory of $2,000.

- **Fixed assets**—Many companies routinely prepare a capital expense or acquisitions budget, which lists planned projects, their costs, and anticipated sources of funding. If no such budget exists, then business management usually can provide a schedule of fixed assets and depreciation (used for income tax return purposes) to the bank. This information also can be included in the footnotes of a business financial statement reviewed or audited by an external accountant. The fixed asset schedule includes the purchase date, useful life, cost, method of depreciation, and depreciation taken to date for each major asset. Any projected increases in fixed assets (that is, anticipated purchases) are shown in the acquisitions budget.

Businesses usually need to replace their fully depreciated assets (which are carried at $0) at a cost higher than the origin cost. Business bankers should know the age and useful life of the fixed assets to determine the replacement needs. A manufacturing facility with considerable excess capacity distorts the need, since the business can increase sales without a corresponding increase in the size of its base of fixed assets. Thus, the capacity of the company's existing plant and equipment, relative to projected production and space needs, must be taken into consideration. Some companies show no fixed assets on their balance sheet (or a very small amount relative to sales) because they lease their equipment or the company's principals own the fixed assets and rent them back to the business.

Figure 11.8 shows Designs by Dezine's assumptions for its fixed assets account in 20yx.

FIGURE 11.8 DESIGNS BY DEZINE FIXED ASSET PROJECTION FOR 20yx ($ IN 000s)	
Beginning gross fixed assets	$ 61
+ New purchases	10
= Total gross fixed assets	$ 71
− Accumulated depreciation	(12)
− Depreciation per year for existing fixed assets	(12)
− Depreciation per year on new purchases	(2)
= Ending net fixed assets	$ 45

The new depreciation is calculated using the purchase price of the new computer equipment and is based on the depreciable life of the equipment, which is five years ($10,000 ÷ 5 years = $2,000 per year).

Depreciable fixed assets are evaluated by using one or both of the following methods:

- Asset usage—measures loss of useful life

$$\frac{Accumulated\ depreciation}{Fixed\ assets\ at\ gross\ or\ historical\ cost} = Percent\ Used\ (\%)$$

- Remaining useful life—measures number of years of depreciable life remaining

$$\frac{Net\ fixed\ assets}{Annual\ depreciation\ expense} = Remaining\ Useful\ Life\ (y)$$

For Designs by Dezine for 20xz, the asset usage is 20 percent ($12,000 ÷ $61,000 = 20%), which means that 20 percent of the fixed assets have been depreciated. The company should not have to provide funds to replace the company vehicles (primary component of fixed assets) to maintain productivity. The remaining useful life is 4.1 years ($49,000 ÷ $12,000 per year = 4.1 years). This tells the business banker that the remaining useful life of the company vehicles is still very close to the original expectation of about five to six years.

- **Total assets**—The business banker forecasts total assets of $70,000, compared with the company's forecast of $87,000. The key driver is the difference in the amount of current assets, which also affects the total assets.

Liabilities and Net Worth

Having completed the review of the asset side of the company's forecasted balance sheet, the first item on the liability side of the balance sheet—short-term notes payable—will be considered.

- **Short-term notes payable**—As mentioned earlier, short-term notes payable serves as a plug figure in balancing forecasted balance sheets. Therefore, other projected liability accounts are completed before calculating this figure. The business banker is forecasting a net operating loss; therefore, notes payable short term are plugged at $10,000. The company is forecasting excess cash and thus indicates that no short-term debt is needed, and even applies $5,000 of excess cash to paying down accounts payable.

- **Accounts payable and accruals**—The amount of accounts payable is a function of the dollar limits and other terms of trade credit that is extended by suppliers as well as the actual payment practices of the business. The forecasted payables turnover (in days) is compared with the past turnover ratios. Accrual estimates are based on past trends.

It is often difficult for a business banker to obtain a listing of purchased raw materials, which is needed to calculate a payables turnover ratio and to enter it onto a balance sheet forecast. As an alternative, a business banker can relate accounts payable to cost of goods sold as follows:

$$\frac{\text{Proj. acc. payable turnover (d)} \times \text{Proj. cost of goods sold}}{365 \text{ days}} = \text{Projected accounts payable}$$

Designs by Dezine is expecting to pay its suppliers upon completion of each job. Materials costs are estimated to be 40 percent of each sale. The projected accounts payable of $7,000 at year-end is less than the $12,000 expected, based on 40 percent of the forecasted December sales of $30,000. The company expects to be able to use some of its excess cash balance (over the minimum desired level of cash) to reduce amounts owed to suppliers. Since the business banker is not projecting any excess cash balances at year-end, the accounts payable level will remain at $12,000, which is higher than the company forecast.

- **Current maturities of long-term debt (CMLTD)** represents the principal amounts of long-term debt due in the next 12 months. This figure can be calculated with the schedule of debt in the footnotes of a company's financial statement or with the previous year's current maturities. Any current maturities resulting from the proposed loan also should be included. The current maturities for the new loans might be principal payments, a custom-designed schedule, or payments (including interest and principal, like installment loans) in which amortization tables would be used.

    The 20xz tax return for Designs by Dezine did not break out CMLTD. Therefore, the company forecast does not use this account. This is misleading for cash flow purposes because some portion of the existing term debt and the new computer loan will be due in the coming year. The company has projected long-term debt principal payments of $18,000 on the company vehicles and shareholder loan, plus another $1,000 on the new computer loan. The existing vehicle debt has two years remaining on the amortization. The new computer loan will be financed for five years. For projection purposes, both the company and the bank will use $19,000 for CMLTD for 20xz. For 20yx, CMLTD has not been estimated, but this will not have an effect on determining UCA cash flow for 20xz.

- **Long-term debt** is the portion of the debt scheduled to be repaid at time periods more than a year away from the financial statement date. Designs by Dezine and the bank use the same amounts for forecasted long-term debt at 12/31/20yx, without an adjustment for estimated CMLTD.

- **Net worth or total owner's equity**—Generally, the equity section of the balance sheet is easily projected. Common stock figures (for preferred and common stock) can be picked up from previous balance sheets unless additions or deletions to the stock were made in the current year. The retained earnings account is increased by the amount of projected after-tax profits from the forecast income statement, less projected dividends. If a loss is projected, then the retained earnings account is decreased by the amount of the loss.

The Plug Accounts

As discussed previously, the short-term notes payable account is one of two possible plug (balancing) figures on the balance sheet; the cash account is the other one. If assets exceed liabilities and net worth on the forecasted balance sheet, then the difference is added to the short-term notes payable in order to balance the statement. But if liabilities and net worth exceed assets, then the difference is added to cash to balance the statement. The company plugs the cash account and the bank plugs the notes payable short-term due to differences in the projections.

The mere balancing of amounts into short-term notes payable may not be a realistic alternative in this procedure unless the financing need is truly short-term rather than long-term. The company may have permanent working capital needs and, therefore, may require long-term financing. The business banker should consider the appropriate type of financing after preparing a cash flow statement or model, and then reviewing the overall financial condition of the company.

In addition, the additional interest expense usually has not been calculated if the plug is short-term notes payable. When this additional interest expense is included in a revised income statement, net income is decreased and the plug figure of short-term notes payable increases a little more.

Analyzing Each Scenario

When multiple-year, forecasted statements are prepared at the low point in the operating cycle of a business (which is the typical point for a fiscal year-end), any need for seasonal debt to finance a seasonal buildup in accounts receivable and inventory will not be shown. Businesses that have seasonal sales or production peaks should prepare monthly cash budgets. Further, the business banker or company should prepare a cash budget before preparing the long-term forecast.

By preparing a cash budget first, the amount of peak debt needed and the potential loan structure can be determined—regardless of whether the company needs short-term or long-term debt, and how much.

Designs by Dezine and the business banker have constructed two different sets of forecast financial statements, as shown earlier. The bank's projections show that the company needs more debt than it has requested. The following are some of the more significant changes made by the business banker to the company's forecasted statements:

- The bank projects less in sales revenues than the company does
- The bank projects more cost of goods sold expense than the company does
- The bank projects more in S, G, & A expenses than the company does
- The bank projects significantly less cash flow compared with the company's projection because the bank projects lower net profits

Because cash and only cash repays loans, a projected cash flow statement or model should also be prepared. Figure 11.9 shows the UCA cash model for 20yx for Designs by Dezine based on the company's projection.

FIGURE 11.9 DESIGNS BY DEZINE UCA CASH FLOW WORKSHEET FOR YEAR ENDED 12/31/20yx COMPANY-PREPARED PROJECTION ($ IN $000s)

20yx net sales		$ 700
+ 20xz accounts receivable	$ 8	
− 20yx accounts receivable	18	
+ Accounts receivable (increase) decrease		($ 10)
= **Cash from sales**		**$ 690**
20yx cost of goods sold (net of depreciation)		($ 525)
+ 20xz inventory	$ 1	
− 20yx inventory	2	
+ Inventory (increase) decrease		($ 1)
+ 20yx accounts payable	$ 7	
− 20xz accounts payable	3	
+ Accounts payable increase (increase)		$ 4
= **Cash productions costs**		**($ 522)**
20yx selling, gen. & admin. exp. (net of deprec.)		($ 106)
= **Cash operating expenses**		**($ 106)**
= **Total miscellaneous**		$ 0
20yx income tax expense		$ 0
= Cash paid for taxes		$ 0
NET CASH AFTER OPERATIONS		**$ 62**
20yx interest expense		($ 10)
20yx dividends or distributions		($ 15)
= Financing costs		($ 25)
= **Net cash income**		**$ 37**
− 20xz CMLTD		($ 19)
CASH AFTER DEBT AMORTIZATION		**$ 18**
20xy depreciation expense		($ 14)
+ 20xz net fixed assets	$ 49	
− 20yx net fixed assets	(45)	
+ Other current assets (increase) decrease		$ 4
= Capital expenditures		($ 10)
= Total long-term investments		($ 10)
FINANCING SURPLUS (REQUIREMENT)		**$ 8**
+ Short-term debt increase (decrease)		$ 0
+ 20yx CMLTD	$ 0	
+ 20yx long-term debt	75	
− 20xz long-term debt (less CMLTD of $19)	(67)	
+ Incremental long-term debt		$ 8
+ Stockholders equity increase (decrease)		$ 0
TOTAL EXTERNAL FINANCING		**$ 8**
CASH AFTER EXTERNAL FINANCING		**$ 16**
Beginning cash balance		6
Ending cash balance		$ 22

According to the company's projection, the cash flow is sufficient to fund operations, debt service, and capital expenditures in the next year (20yx). The company-prepared cash flow indicates that short-term debt will not be needed at fiscal year-end, even though the cash budget from earlier in this chapter showed short-term borrowings during the fiscal year peaking at $19,000 but being fully repaid by September.

The business banker's projection indicates that cash flow is not sufficient, even though we have not examined the banker's projection using the UCA cash flow model. However, the bank-prepared balance sheet was plugged with $10,000 of short-term debt at the end of 20yx. The bank currently does not have a line of credit approved for the company. A primary concern is to determine how the company will fund its growth if the profits do not materialize as projected.

Uncertainties in Forecasts

Forecasted statements attempt to estimate the financial future of a business in an uncertain environment. These uncertainties include the economy, competition, government regulations, technological change, and management's ability to perform effectively. Although uncertainty increases the longer the projection extends into the future, the offsetting factor is that feedback received by management in the interim allows the plan to be changed.

Another shortcoming of analyzing forecasts is that a business banker can overlook the interim financing needs of the business. Because a multiple-year, forecasted balance sheet reflects the financial state of a business at a given point in time (usually the fiscal year-end, and also the low point of the operating cycle), it does not reveal any funding needs that might arise between fiscal year-end balance sheet dates. These hidden funding needs typically involve seasonal asset buildups in preparation for heavy sales periods and are better analyzed with monthly cash budgets.

In this section, you learned about the considerations that a business banker must make when he or she reviews pro forma statements. Pro forma financial statements should be based on accurate knowledge of the past performance of a business, coupled with knowledge of the external and internal factors that affect the future operations of the business. You also learned how to construct and analyze pro forma forecasts of income statements and balance sheets. In addition, you now know how to analyze different pro forma scenarios with short-term and long-term forecasts, which will enable you to reach conclusions about the probable financing needs and repayment ability of a business.

Although pro forma analysis has a number of limitations, such as its failure to reveal seasonal financing needs, it remains very important to the lending decision process because future cash flows—not historical cash flows—repay loans. In this section, you learned about uncertainties that can affect forecasted statements. Because the future is unpredictable, all projections should be tempered with appropriate conservatism.

SUMMARY

By completing this chapter, you learned about the role and use of cash budgets in financial statement analysis and the importance of pro forma statements for projecting cash flow and loan repayment. For businesses in the start-up and growth phases of the business life cycle, or with seasonal variations in the operating cycle, cash budgets play an important part in determining short-term credit needs. A business banker's job is to check the timing and magnitude of the projected cash flows based on other available financial information. Historical analysis, including ratios, helps determine whether the assumptions behind the cash budget are realistic.

Pro forma statements are formatted like historical statements, but they also are based on assumptions and long-term projections of business trends that must be realistic. Because of increased uncertainty with long-term forecasts, many bankers and customers prefer to develop best case, worst case, and most likely sets of assumptions, which generate different sets of projected financial statements. Past performance is tempered with external factors (such as government regulations) and internal factors (experience of management, for instance) that are expected to influence the business. You learned the specific steps that go into creating pro forma statements, plus issues surrounding the inherent uncertainties as you analyze the results.

Many companies experience sales growth and other changes that can have a significant effect on cash flow, beyond profits shown on the income statement. All too frequently, customers do not know how much money they really need or how to structure the loan. A thorough financial analysis (historical and projected) encompassing income statement analysis, balance sheet analysis, ratio analysis, and cash flow analysis gives a business banker critical information to determine how much credit a business may need, the timing of those needs, and whether the business can repay the loan according to proposed terms.

EXERCISE 1

Instructions

In this exercise you will practice analyzing a cash budget for Designs by Dezine, Inc.

Part 1

If raw material purchases need to be paid at the time of purchase, how would Designs by Dezine's cash budget be affected? Use the Cash Budget worksheet to recalculate the cash budget for 20xy.

Part 2

- Explain how was Designs by Dezine's cash budget was affected by the raw material purchases paid at the time of purchase.
- How does the short-term borrowing amount change?

Year Sequence for Dates in Textbook Cases
This chapter uses the following order or sequence of years for the dates in the financial statements:
- 20xx, 20xy, and 20xz

For projected years, the following sequence is used:
- 20yx, 20yy, 20yz, and so on

WORKSHEET: DESIGNS BY DEZINE 20yx CASH BUDGET (IN $000s)		Jan	Feb	Mar	April	May	June	Jul	Aug	Sep	Oct	Nov	Dec
1	Beginning Cash	6											
2	Receipts	18											
3	Total Cash Avail.	24											
4	Materials purchases	8											
5	Labor (non-S, G, & A)	7											
6	S, G, & A expenses	4											
7	Owner's salary	5											
8	Interest expense	1											
9	Total disbursements	25											
10	Loan principal paid	1											
11	Net capital expend.	2											
12	Distributions or div.	0											
13	Total cash paid out	28											
14	Net cash position	(4)											
15	Minimum cash	5											
16	S-T loan required	9											
17	Cumulative loan req.	9											

EXERCISE 2

This exercise allows you to test your understanding of considerations for reviewing projections.

Instructions

Based on the information in the chapter on *Cash Budgets and Pro Forma Statements*, answer the following questions:

1. A company requests financing for its seasonal inventory. What type of forecast should be prepared?
2. What is the most important part of a long-term forecast?
3. What should be considered when forecasting accounts receivable and inventory?
4. What are the two possible balance sheet accounts to plug in a forecast?
5. Who should prepare pro forma financial statements?

EXERCISE 3

In this exercise you will test your understanding of analyzing pro forma statements.

Instructions

- Complete the blank UCA Cash Flow Worksheet on the following page for 20yx using the financial information from the income statement and balance sheet comparison chart for Designs by Dezine, Inc.

- Explain your results and compare them with the cash flow using the company-prepared forecast

DRY SUPPLY UCA CASH FLOW WORKSHEET FOR 20xy ($ IN $000s)		20xy
20xy net sales	___	$ 918
+ 20xx accounts receivable	___	$ 113
− 20xy accounts receivable	___	112
+ Accounts receivable (increase) decrease	___	$ 1
= Cash from sales	___	**$ 919**
20xy cost of goods sold (net of depreciation)	___	($631)
+ 20xx inventory	___	$ 72
− 20xy inventory	___	67
+ Inventory (increase) decrease	___	$ 5
+ 20xy accounts payable	___	$ 31
− 20xx accounts payable	___	46
+ Accounts payable increase (decrease)	___	($ 15)
= Cash productions costs	___	**($641)**
20xy selling, gen. & admin. exp. (net of deprec.)	___	($ 228)
+ 20xy accrued expenses	___	$ 12
− 20xx accrued expenses	___	11
+ Accrued expenses increase (decrease)	___	$ 1
= Cash operating expenses	___	**($227)**
20xy other income	___	$ 5
20xy other expenses	___	($ 0)
= Total miscellaneous	___	**$ 5**
20xz income tax expense	___	($ 17)
+ 20xy income taxes payable	___	$ 7
− 20xx income taxes payable	___	6
+ Income taxes payable increase (decrease)	___	$ 1
= Cash paid for taxes	___	**($ 16)**
NET CASH AFTER OPERATIONS	___	**$ 40**
20xy interest expense	___	($ 11)
20xy dividends or distributions	___	0
= Financing costs	___	($ 11)
= Net cash income	___	**$ 29**
− 20xx CMLTD	___	($ 0)
CASH AFTER DEBT AMORTIZATION	___	**$ 29**
20xy depreciation expense	___	($ 13)
+ 20xx net fixed assets	___	$ 49
− 20xy net fixed assets	___	(53)
+ Other current assets (increase) decrease	___	($ 4)
= Capital expenditures	___	($ 17)
+ 20xx investments (CSVLI)	___	14
− 20xy investments (CSVLI)	___	(16)
= Total long-term investments	___	**($ 19)**
FINANCING SURPLUS (REQUIREMENT)	___	**$ 10**
− 20xx notes payable bank short-term	___	($ 68)
+ 20xy notes payable bank short-term	___	59
+ Short-term debt increase (decrease)	___	($ 9)
+ 20xy CMLTD	___	$ 0
+ 20xy long-term debt	___	67
− 20xx long-term debt	___	(58)
+ Incremental long-term debt	___	$ 9
− 20xx stockholders equity (excl. ret. earnings)	___	($ 2)
+ 20xy stockholders equity (excl. ret. earnings)	___	2
+ stockholders equity increase (decrease)	___	$ 0
TOTAL EXTERNAL FINANCING	___	**$ 0**
CASH AFTER EXTERNAL FINANCING	___	**$ 10**

Section 3
Analyzing Personal Financial Statements and Tax Returns

12

Types of Personal Financial Statements

OBJECTIVES

After studying *Types of Personal Financial Statements*, you will be able to—

- Explain the basic formats and the preliminary analysis of a personal financial statement (PFS)
- Describe the components of a PFS

INTRODUCTION

Where it is difficult to separate business and personal assets, or when the loan request is contingent on the business owners guaranteeing the debt, business bankers should obtain personal financial statements (PFSs) from the proposed guarantors. PFSs, similar to business financial statements, report the assets, liabilities, net worth, income and expenses, and other personal information relevant to the owners or principals. In the case of a small-business owner or self-employed borrower, the assets and income of the person and the business are often combined and analyzed together in what is called a global cash flow.

This chapter covers both the formats and the basic components of the various types of PFSs. In subsequent chapters, you will learn about ratios used within the personal financial analysis process, including how they are calculated and how they can be interpreted.

Relationship to the Commercial Lending Decision Tree

In the textbook Introduction, we explored the Commercial Lending Decision Tree as a way to think about the stages and steps involved in the commercial lending process. As you have already learned, the first stage in this process emphasizes early screening and qualifying steps, such as general fit with the portfolio and goals of your bank and initial assessment of financial and nonfinancial qualifications of the business. These preliminary steps allow a business banker to anticipate various issues and conduct a more efficient and accurate financial analysis.

The second stage moves into the detailed analysis of financial data gathered from the business and any owners who may serve as guarantors. In Section 2, you learned about business financial statements, tax returns, and the related analytical process. You will now turn your attention to PFSs and tax returns.

PERSONAL FINANCIAL STATEMENT OVERVIEW

A PFS is a summary of personal assets, liabilities, and net worth. It also provides information on income, expenditures, contingent liabilities, asset ownership and values, and liabilities owed, plus a set of representations and warranties.

Basic Formats

When an independent accountant prepares a PFS, the criteria are defined by the American Institute of Certified Public Accountants (AICPA) in Statement of Position (SOP) Number 82-1, *Accounting and Financial Reporting for Personal Financial Statements*. However, in most situations the borrower prepares his or her own PFS. Generally, the borrower completes a form provided by the bank, or even a form from another bank. Some borrowers may use a printout from personal finance software. Using a standard form helps to ensure consistency in presentation.

When a borrower prepares a PFS in any format other than your bank's own format, the borrower should also partially complete the following sections on your bank's form:

- Address the statement to the bank

- Answer questions on income, expenditures, and contingent liabilities

- Provide **representations** and **warranties** required by your bank

- Sign and date the form

- Indicate "see attached" on the asset and liability section and attach the other format that was completed

> **Representation**
> A statement of fact included in a document to influence opinion. For example, the applicant represents that the information is true and correct.

> **Warranty**
> An assurance, promise, or guaranty by one party that a particular statement of fact is true and may be relied upon by the other party. For example, the applicant warrants that the supporting schedules are complete and correct, and will notify the lender of any material changes.

In addition to having different formats, the basic components may not be very clear to many borrowers, and they may need assistance in filling out a PFS, or an explanation of the key components in order to complete it properly.

To analyze the information properly, a business banker will need to understand how the form was prepared and the format used. With two completed PFSs and a current-year personal tax return, a business banker can further calculate personal cash flow. Also, a business banker can calculate a debt-to-income (DTI) ratio to determine if personal debt levels are excessive. These calculations and other tools will be covered in upcoming chapters.

Sample Format and Preliminary Analysis

The PFS format used by banks varies. This chapter uses a two-page PFS format to demonstrate the typical PFS content and analytical process.

Figure 12.1 shows a PFS for Kaitlyn Nieson, one of the owners of Dry Supply, Inc., as part of a recent loan request. Recall that we have been analyzing the business financial statements of Dry Supply, a wholesaler of dry-cleaning supplies and equipment.

The first page of this sample PFS form requires the following information:
- The name of the bank that will be receiving the information
- The personal information on the applicant and co-applicant, such as name, address, telephone number, and names of employers
- The income and expense data
- The summary of the balance sheet and contingent liabilities

The second page has schedules for details on certain assets and liabilities, states the representations and warranties, and provides space for signatures and submission dates.

FIGURE 12.1 PERSONAL FINANCIAL STATEMENT FORMAT FOR KAITLYN NIESON

PERSONAL FINANCIAL STATEMENT AS OF   October 10, 20xz
Date

SUBMITTED TO: Your Bank

PERSONAL INFORMATION

APPLICANT (NAME) **Kaitlyn Nieson**	CO-APPLICANT (NAME)
Employer and Address **Dry Supply, Inc. Salina, KS**	Employer and Address

Business Phone No. **785-447-0300**	No. of Years with Employer **20**	Title/Position **President**	Business Phone No.	No. of Years with Employer	Title/Position

Home Address **4566 North Lynn Court, Salina, KS**	Home Address

Home Phone No. **785-445-0236**	Social Security No. **111-33-4444**	Date of Birth **09/14/19xz**	Home Phone No.	Social Security No.	Date of Birth
Marital Status: **X** Single __ Married __ Divorced __ Widowed			Marital Status: __ Single __ Married __ Divorced __ Widowed		

CASH INCOME & EXPENDITURE STATEMENT FOR THE YEAR ENDED   20xy   (OMIT CENTS)

ANNUAL INCOME	Applicant	Co-Applicant	ANNUAL EXPENDITURES	Applicant	Co-Applicant
Salary	14,000		Mortgage/Rent - Residence	3,600	
Bonuses & Commissions			All Other Debt Service	6,600	
Interest & Dividends	5,000		Federal Income & Other Taxes	8,800	
Rental Income (Net of Expenses)	6,000		State Income & Other Taxes	2,200	
Partner or Owner Draws/Distributions			Insurance (Home, Health, Vehicles)		
Other Income (List) **gifts, trusts (family trust income)**	19,000		Other Expenses (List) **prop. taxes – residence and investment RE**	1,800	
			Other Living Expenses	5,000	
TOTAL INCOME ($)	**44,000**		**TOTAL EXPENDITURES ($)**	**28,000**	

BALANCE SHEET AS OF   Sept. 30, 20xz

ASSETS	AMOUNT ($)	LIABILITIES	AMOUNT ($)
Cash* in This Bank	30,000	Notes Payable to Banks – Secured (Schedule E)	
Cash* in Other Financial Institutions	20,000	Notes Payable to Banks – Unsecured (Schedule E)	
Readily Marketable Securities (Schedule A)	150,000	Notes Payable to Others – Secured (Schedule E)	
Non-Readily Marketable Securities (Schedule A)	100,000	Notes Payable to Others – Unsecured (Schedule E)	
Accounts and Notes Receivable		Accounts Payable (including credit cards)	1,000
Cash Surrender Value of Life Ins. (Schedule B)		Margin Accounts	
Residential Real Estate (Schedule C)	150,000	Notes Due: Partnerships/Other Entities (Schedule D)	
Real Estate Investments (Schedule C)	75,000	Mortgage Debt (Schedule C)	74,000
Partnerships/LLCs/S Corporations (Schedule D)		Loans on Life Insurance Policies (Schedule B)	
Personal Property (Including Automobiles)	30,000	Taxes Payable	
IRAs, Keoghs and Other Qualified Plans		Other Liabilities (List)	
Sole Proprietorship Assets:		**TOTAL LIABILITIES ($)**	**75,000**
Accounts Receivable		Estimated Tax Liability If All Major Assets Sold	25,000
Inventory		**SUBTOTAL ($)**	**100,000**
Fixed Assets		**NET WORTH ($)**	**455,000**
Other Assets (List)			
TOTAL ASSETS ($)	**555,000**	**TOTAL LIABS. & NET WORTH ($)**	**555,000**

* Including money market accounts and CDs.

CONTINGENT LIABILITIES (Must be Completed; If None, Then Write "None" Below	YES	NO	AMOUNT ($)
Are you a guarantor, co-maker, or endorser for any debt of an individual, corporation or partnership?	X		250,000
Do you have any outstanding letters of credit or surety bonds?		X	
Are there or any lawsuits or legal actions pending against you?		X	
Are you contingently liable on any lease or contract?		X	
Are any of your tax obligations past due?		X	
Are you obligated to pay alimony and/or child support?		X	
Other contingent liabilities (describe):		X	

OTHER QUESTIONS	YES	NO	
Have you, or any firm in which you were a major owner, ever filed a petition in bankruptcy or has one been filed individually against you? If yes, please provide details below:		X	
Are you an executive officer, director or principal shareholder of a bank?		X	Bank:

FIGURE 12.1 PERSONAL FINANCIAL STATEMENT FORMAT FOR KAITLYN NIESON (CONTINUED)

SCHEDULE A—ALL SECURITIES (Including Non-Money Market Mutual Funds)*

# of Shares (Stock) or Face Value (Bonds)	Description	Owner(s)	Where Held	Cost	Current Market Value	PLEDGED YES	PLEDGED NO
READILY MARKETABLE SECURITIES (Including U.S. Government And Municipals)*							
1,500 shares	Giant Public C0.	Kaitlyn Nieson	brokerage	$30,000	$150,000		X
NON-READILY MARKETABLE SECURITIES (Closely Held Businesses, Thinly Traded or Restricted Stocks)*							
1,000 shares	Dry Supply, Inc.	Kaitlyn Nieson	safe dep. box	$500	$100,000		

If not enough space, attach a separate schedule or brokerage statement and enter totals only.

SCHEDULE B – LIFE INSURANCE (Use Additional Sheets If Necessary)

Insurance Company	Face Amount	Type of Policy	Beneficiary	Cash Surrender Value	Amount Borrowed	Ownership
Big Life Company	250,000	term	Dry Supply	n/a	n/a	Kaitlyn Nieson

Disability Insurance	Applicant	Co-Applicant
Monthly Distribution if Disabled		
Number of Years Covered		

SCHEDULE C—PERSONAL RESIDENCE & REAL ESTATE INVESTMENTS, MORTGAGE DEBT

Personal Residence Address	Legal Owner	Purchase Year	Purchase Price	Market Value	Present Loan Bal.	Interest Rate	Maturity Date	Monthly Payment	Lender
4566 N. Lynn Ct.	KN	19x3	40,000	150,000	24,000	6%	20yz	300	Your Bank

Investment Property Address	Legal Owner	Purchase Year	Purchase Price	Market Value	Present Loan Bal.	Interest Rate	Maturity Date	Monthly Payment	Lender
Florida Condo	KN	19x9	60,000	75,000	50,000	8%	20yx	550	Other Bank

SCHEDULE D—PARTNERSHIPS/LLCS/S CORPORATIONS (less than majority ownership for real estate partnerships)*

Type of Investment	Date of Initial Investment	Cost or Initial Investment	% Owned	Current Market Value	Bal. Due on Partnerships: Notes or Cash Calls	Current Year Investments
Business/Professional (indicate name)						
Investments (including tax shelters)						

Note: For investments listed above that represent a material portion of your total assets, please include financial statements or tax returns of the entities, plus any Schedule K-1s provided to you.

SCHEDULE E—NOTES PAYABLE

Due To	Type of Facility	Maximum Amount of Facility	Secured Yes	Secured No	Collateral	Interest Rate	Maturity	Unpaid Balance

** Immediately above the signature blocks, most banks place a paragraph of text called *representations and warranties*. This information differs from bank to bank and from state to state, depending on state laws and other issues. You are encouraged to read and to understand your bank's particular wording that is used. **

Kaitlyn Nieson   _Oct 10, 20xz_

Applicant Signature   Date   Co-Applicant Signature   Date

Regardless of the form used, the following information is reviewed and verified before analyzing the PFS:

- The financial statement is submitted to the lending bank. If this is not the case, it is the policy of many banks to have the statement readdressed to them. This ensures that the representations and warranties are intended to cover the lending (named) bank.

- The form and all applicable supporting schedules are completed. Before a credit decision is made, the borrower must fill in all appropriate lines on the form, including income and expense items.

- The form contains no math errors. The statement is checked for accurate addition and subtraction of assets and liabilities. Totals in supporting schedules must match the assets and liabilities listed.

- All contingent liabilities are itemized. If no contingent liabilities exist, the words "none" should appear, rather than leaving the section blank.

- The appropriate representations and warranties are in place, including that the information is true and correct, the applicant and co-applicant are obligated to provide updates, and the lending bank may make inquiries about the information being provided.

- The statement is signed and dated by the applicant and co-applicant (often a spouse) as applicable, or if major assets are owned jointly. The statement should be dated prior to the loan date, unless it is provided during ongoing monitoring of an existing loan.

The business banker verifies the methodology used to value assets, and may need to obtain supporting documents. For example, the business banker may request a copy of a brokerage firm's statement to verify the value of marketable securities. As part of the review, the business banker requires the applicant to supply any incomplete information. In our example situation, Anne Schippel, the business banker analyzing the Dry Supply loan request, has made sure that any sections left blank on Nieson's PFS are not needed or are not applicable.

You have learned about the basic formats for personal financial statements. You now know that when an independent accountant prepares a PFS, certain criteria must be met as defined by the AICPA, and when the borrower prepares his or her own PFS, the borrower may use a bank form or a printout from personal financial software.

In addition, you learned what information is reviewed and verified prior to analyzing the PFS. You should now understand that you will need to verify the methodology used to value assets, obtain any supporting documents, ask the applicants to supply any incomplete information, and make sure that any sections left blank on the PFS are not needed or are not applicable.

PERSONAL FINANCIAL STATEMENT COMPONENTS

The preliminary analysis establishes the method and format, and to some degree, helps develop the expectations that a business banker will have for the components that should be present. We now move into the detailed analysis of the various PFS components, including personal information, a listing of annual income and expenditures, a balance sheet and supporting schedules, a listing of contingent liabilities, then some questions, and representations/warranties. In some cases, the lender may need to assist the borrower in understanding these components—both what they mean and how they should be reported.

Personal Information

The first section of this example PFS format requests the applicant's and co-applicant's names, addresses, employer names, occupations, telephone numbers, Social Security numbers, and other personal information. If a borrower is new to the bank, the business banker should ask for identification to verify that the individual presenting the statement and the name on the financial statement are the same. Further, the correct addresses and Social Security numbers facilitate obtaining credit bureau reports (CBRs) on the individuals.

Income & Expenditure Statement

The second section of the example PFS shows the annual income and expenditures of the applicants.

Income Analysis

Information about income is requested in most PFS formats. If it is not requested, or if a business banker wishes to verify the income listed on the PFS, a copy of the applicant's personal tax return (U.S. Individual Tax Return, Form 1040 and supporting schedules) both provide and verify income. Other sources of salary and wage verification include W-2s and pay stubs.

Typical income categories include salary, bonuses and commissions, interest and dividend income, rental income, partnership or owner draws/distributions, and then other types of income that may not fit the listed categories. These types of income can be derived from employment with businesses not owned by the applicants, as well as investments in readily marketable securities and real estate. They can also be derived from privately held businesses.

When analyzing the income that the owner is taking out of a business, a business banker considers the following types of items, other than salary, that may be paid for by the business and will not need to be paid from the owner's personal income. These categories, except for rent, do not appear in most PFS formats, so it may help to ask a business owner the following questions if any of these types of income are applicable:

- **Travel expenses**—Are they excessive and material to the business? What amount is paid for by the business when personal time is added to the expense? For example, a company convention may include additional personal vacation time, yet the company only pays the travel expenses during the business portion of the trip.

- **Auto expenses**—Is the auto available for personal use? What type of auto or truck, how old, and how much is it used personally?

- **Office expenses**—Are personal expenses for telephones, cell phones, and correspondence included?

- **Insurance**—What type of insurance is carried (health, property, and life)? Who is insured and who are the beneficiaries?

- **Pension**—How is it determined? What is the age of the borrower? When can payments begin?

- **Profit-sharing**—What is the formula for payout? Is the owner vested in the plan? When is it available as income?

- **Rent**—Is rent paid to the owner for equipment or buildings? Is it excessive compared to market amounts? If so, what amount is available for personal use over and above any debt service related to the assets leased?

- **Loans to officers**—When do these loans need to be paid? What are the terms? Are they subordinated to any other obligations?

When analyzing personal income, the business banker addresses the following questions:

- **Will it continue?** Is the reported income reliable, and are sufficient assets listed on the financial statement to support or to create the income? In terms of reliability, bonuses and commissions may be tied to certain performance objectives and may or may not recur. In terms of support, the income received must be validated by the assets owned, such as dividend income being adequately supported by common stocks that pay dividends. Further, if a borrower lists substantial income and nominal cash on hand, that may mean that the borrower's spending or investing habits exceed the income and may not be sustainable.

- **Is it verifiable?** As mentioned earlier, sources of verification include W-2s and personal tax returns, plus other documents such as business financial statements and brokerage account statements.

- **Is it material?** Does a particular type of income represent a significant portion of the borrower's total income? If the income is not reliable and yet material, it may adversely affect the borrower's ability to repay debt (or support business loans as a personal guarantor) if the income does not continue.

- **What type of income is it?** Is it salary, bonuses and commissions, rental income, interest income, dividend income, capital gains, business income, or other investment income that is fairly reliable and expected to recur? Or is it other, nonrecurring income?

- **Does the income provide cash to the borrower?** We will study cash flow more closely in Section 3, but for now, understand that some types of income reported by the applicant may not be the same as cash received. For instance, an applicant may sell an asset and report a capital gain as taxable income, but the transaction may not have yielded any actual cash proceeds to the applicant. We tend to use the words income and cash flow interchangeably at the personal level, but it is important for the business banker to distinguish between the two.

In the example, Nieson reports income of $44,000 per year, consisting of her salary of $14,000 from Dry Supply and other income of $30,000. The $19,000 listed as gifts and trusts should be explained to determine whether it will continue.

Expenditures Analysis

Annual expenditures are listed on most PFS formats. If they are not listed, a business banker needs to obtain the following personal expense information and ask questions in order to assess personal cash flow:

- **Mortgage/rent (residence)**—What are the terms of the mortgage? Is a long-term maturity or balloon payment coming due? Does the payment include taxes, insurance, and association fees, if any? How does the principal balance compare to the current value of the residence and its original cost? If the residence or apartment is leased, what are the terms of the lease? Are any special assessments pending?

- **All other debt service (interest and principal payments)**—When are payments due and to whom? If this is an existing bank customer, do the bank's records agree with the amount reported? If a mortgage is involved, how does the principal balance compare to the current value of the real estate and its original cost? For other secured loans, how does the principal balance compare to the current value of the asset and its original cost?

- **Taxes (federal and state)**—What amounts are due? Are estimated payments needed? Are tax payments current?

- **Insurance**—What is the annual expense, and what type of insurance is being purchased?

- **Other expenses** can include the following:

    - *Real estate taxes*—When are taxes payable? What has been the trend in the tax amount due?

    - *Investments*—What is the frequency of this activity and the reason?

    - *Alimony and child support*—What are the terms of the divorce decree? The lender may need to obtain a copy of the divorce decree to verify the information.

    - *Tuition*—How much longer will it need to be paid? When are payments due?

- *Medical expenses*—What is the cause? What type of health insurance is carried? Will the expenses be recurring?

- *Other expenses*—What are these expenses? Will the expenses be recurring?

In addition to analyzing individual line items, the business banker compares total expenses with total income. A very high total expense in relation to income affects the borrower's ability to repay debt and provide further support as a personal guarantor on a commercial loan. The owner may have a lifestyle that results in taking out excessive salaries and dividends, or there may be a temporary need for excessive salaries, such as to pay a child's college tuition.

Most banks have a maximum DTI percentage used for underwriting consumer loans. Assuming a 40 percent DTI limit, a borrower with $1,500 of monthly income should have monthly loan payments of no more than $600 [$1,500 × 0.40 = $600]. This leaves the other 60 percent of income to cover expenditures that are not loan payments (or leases, such as for automobiles, that are a loan equivalent). For a borrower with $1,500 of monthly income, living expenses (expenditures that are not loan payments) should not exceed $600 per month.

In the example PFS, Nieson reported $28,000 in annual expenditures. A lender will verify the tax and mortgage expense. The personal living expenses seem low, and the lender should discuss this item with Nieson.

Balance Sheet

The third section of the example PFS shows the balance sheet of the applicants. This particular format shows all of the assets, whether jointly or individually owned. Some formats break out the jointly and individually owned assets into separate columns, or use a letter code (such as J for joint, A for applicant, or C for co-applicant) to indicate ownership of assets and responsibility for liabilities. The balance sheet is dated, to determine when the balance sheet was constructed. It can have a date that is different from the signature date, usually a recent month-end.

Asset Analysis

The analysis of a borrower's assets is based on liquidity, solvency, and marketability. Just as with a business financial statement, assets on the balance sheet are listed in order of liquidity, but are valued at current market or estimated amounts, compared with the historical cost that overrides the valuation of business assets.

- Liquidity answers the question *Can the borrower generate enough cash to pay personal living expenses and other obligations as they come due?*

- Solvency, on the other hand, answers the question *Can the borrower sell the assets for sufficient cash to repay all debt?*

- Marketability answers the question *Does a market exist in which to sell the assets, and at what price?* Not all assets have a ready market. Investments in partnerships, for example, may be marketable only to the other partners, who determine the price due to the limited market.

Just as with a business balance sheet, assets may be current or noncurrent. Current assets are expected to convert to cash in 12 months or less. Noncurrent assets are not expected to convert to cash after one year. Current liabilities are debts due in one year or less; long-term liabilities are due in more than one year.

- **Cash** is listed first on the balance sheet because it is the most liquid. A business banker needs to know where the cash is on deposit, in what type of account, and the amount. Because it is a balance sheet, the amount reported is the cash on hand that day, not necessarily the amount of cash always on deposit.

  The total cash listed is weighed against the amount of total income earned. The lower the income, generally the less cash the borrower has available. The greater the income, the greater the amount of liquid cash a borrower should have on hand. Depending on the lifestyle of the borrower, the amount of cash will vary.

  As a test of reasonableness, you can also compare the cash on the balance sheet to the interest income reported on Form 1040. For illustration purposes, if market interest rates for deposit accounts are 5 percent, then reported cash balances of $10,000 should generate about $500 of interest income on the borrower's tax return. If a higher amount of interest income is shown on the tax return, then the borrower's average cash levels may be higher than the reported amount.

  For the PFS example, Nieson reports $50,000 cash in banks, an amount that seems high in comparison to her income. Schippel notes that $20,000 of this is on deposit with another financial institution and plans to cross-sell this opportunity at their next meeting.

- **Readily marketable securities** are listed next. Schedule A on the second page details the number of shares, description of the securities, owner, where the securities are held, cost, current market value, and if the securities are pledged as collateral. The sum of Schedule A current market values should equal the amount of readily marketable securities listed on the balance sheet.

  Readily marketable securities are those listed on a major stock exchange. They are traded daily. A business banker wants to know the high and low value per share in the past year and the number of shares traded daily. This information indicates how much the value may vary in the future. If the borrower owns a large number of shares, the stock may not be liquid. For example, if the borrower lists 50,000 shares of stock in ABC Inc., and the number of shares traded daily is 1,000, the borrower cannot readily liquidate the shares. Moreover, selling excessive shares in a short period could drive down the value of the stock.

  Unlike a business entity that invests in marketable securities to employ excess funds on a temporary basis until needed in the business, individuals usually invest in order to gain wealth or to generate additional income. These investments are treated as current assets.

In margin accounts, securities held by brokers are readily marketable. However, usually they are pledged against margin loans made by the broker. Amounts owed on securities are listed as liabilities or margin loans due to brokers.

Another variation of marketable securities is restricted securities. As the name implies, these securities owned by the borrower are restricted in terms of ability to sell, both in timing and amounts. For example, the borrower might list stock options that cannot be exercised until some future date.

In the PFS example, Nieson reports $150,000 in readily marketable securities owned, which seems high in relation to income. Nieson may have purchased these securities some time ago and may owe taxes on the gain in value if sold. With $150,000 of securities and $50,000 in cash, she could obtain a very favorable interest rate if she were willing to pledge these assets as collateral to secure the loans to Dry Supply.

- **Non-readily marketable securities** are common stock in privately held companies, partnerships, and limited liability companies (LLCs). They are also listed on Schedule A. Most business owners list the value of their business here. Some banks may deduct this value from the individual's net worth in order to isolate financial strength outside the business for purposes of gauging support available from a personal guarantee of the owner. A key question for non-readily marketable securities is the method of valuation. It can be based on sales volume, a multiple of net profits, or even a multiple of net worth. In the PFS example, Nieson values her 50 percent ownership in Dry Supply at $100,000. Dry Supply showed total equity of $94,000 on December 31, 20xz. A 50 percent interest therefore is $47,000. By indicating a value of $100,000, Nieson is valuing her interest at slightly more than twice the book value.

- **Accounts and notes receivable** are amounts owed to the borrower by other individuals or businesses. A business banker needs to know when the loan originated, terms of repayment, collateral, and ability of the individual or business to repay the debt. The amounts listed often are notes receivable from a privately held company owned by the borrower. In the PFS example, Nieson does not list notes receivable.

- **Life insurance** is summarized in Schedule B. The cash surrender value of life insurance (CSVLI) is listed on the balance sheet as an asset. Schedule B summarizes the insurance company, face amount of the policy, type of policy, beneficiary, cash surrender value, amount borrowed, and the owner.

With a privately held business, estate planning often is complex. One issue is whether the insurance proceeds will be sufficient to pay estate taxes upon the death of the business owner. The customer's personal attorney usually can verify the estimate of estate taxes (the lender should ask the customer for permission to contact the attorney). If the life insurance is insufficient, the company or other assets have to be liquidated or sold to pay the estate taxes. In the PFS example,

Nieson indicates $100,000 face value of life insurance owned with no cash value.

The amount of disability insurance is analyzed to determine whether monthly benefits are sufficient to pay current expenditures in the event the owner becomes disabled. Nieson does not list a disability insurance policy, and the lender will want to discuss this omission with her.

- **Real estate** is listed on Schedule C. Residential real estate includes the personal residence and secondary residences. Investment real estate property includes real estate owned for business purposes, such as apartment buildings and commercial buildings. The schedule is completed with the property address, legal owner, purchase year and price, market value, present loan balance, interest rate, loan maturity date, monthly payment, and the name of the lender. The legal owner is compared with the person(s) providing the PFS. If the financial statement is from one individual, and the property is owned by two individuals, then the asset and the equity in the property usually cannot be considered unless the co-owner also is a joint borrower. The equity in the real estate is deducted from the net worth because the individual cannot convert the asset to cash without the permission of the other owner.

    Because real estate values vary over time, the year purchased, purchase price, and condition of the property are important considerations. Although real estate usually increases in value over time, there can be sharp decreases in the short term. If the owner purchased real estate in a high market, the property could be worth less than the purchase price. Nevertheless, in most cases, real estate is a possible source of equity available to the borrower, although it is not very liquid collateral for the bank because of the time it usually takes to foreclose and liquidate it. When analyzing investment property, a lender considers the amount of rental income, expenses to maintain the property, and debt service requirements.

    In the PFS example, Nieson reports $225,000 in real estate owned. She values her personal residence at $150,000 and a Florida condominium at $75,000. The values reported are higher than the original cost. A business banker should determine the method and source of the valuation, and whether the market value of the real estate has declined. It appears that new appraisals have not been completed to support her stated value.

- **Partnerships, LLCs, and S corporation ownerships** are listed in Schedule D. This is the amount of equity held in private businesses, tax shelters, and other investments. A business banker determines the type of investment, cost, percentage owned, current market value, balance due on partnership notes, and future contributions due. A copy of the financial statements or tax returns of each entity should be obtained, as well as any Schedule K-1s provided by the entity to the borrower. The K-1s can verify partner or owner draws/distributions shown as income.

    There are two types of partnerships: general and limited. General partners of both types of partnerships carry contingent liability, and the total amount of that liability is the total debt of the partnership. The liability for a limited partner in a limited partnership is the amount of equity invested in the partnership.

Because there usually is not a market for partnership investments, they are not liquid or readily marketable. The amount listed as an asset commonly is deducted from stated net worth to determine adjusted net worth, which we will study later in this curriculum. In the PFS example, Nieson does not list any investments from partnerships.

- **Personal property** is the value of household furnishings, automobiles, and other personal items, such as boats, recreational vehicles, art, and collectibles. Because it is difficult to determine the real value, this amount usually is a deduction when determining adjusted net worth, which we will study later in this curriculum. Used household furnishings are more valuable to the owner than at an auction. If the borrower is married, most personal property is considered jointly owned. In the PFS example, Nieson reports $30,000 of personal property.

- **Retirement accounts** are usually listed as a noncurrent asset. The figure is based on the current value of individual retirement accounts, Keogh, 401(k), profit-sharing, pensions, and other retirement accounts. A business banker will want to determine the likely amount of future contributions, when distributions can begin, in what type of account the funds are held, and if vesting is required. If the owner is not near retirement age, retirement accounts are not liquid and remain listed as a noncurrent asset. The penalties for early withdrawal from most retirement accounts are severe, and the income tax consequences are significant. In the PFS example, Nieson does not list any retirement accounts at this time. Schippel makes a note to discuss Nieson's retirement planning at their next meeting.

- **Sole proprietorship assets** include accounts receivable, inventory, and equipment. Because the assets and liabilities of a sole proprietorship are simply an extension of the owner, they should be listed on the owner's PFS. The example PFS format has a dedicated section for listing sole proprietorship assets, but many PFS formats do not provide a reminder or dedicated section. And, because the owners often mix personal and business assets and liabilities, a business banker should determine which assets and liabilities are associated with the business and which are personal. In formal financial reporting, accounting convention requires that business and personal assets and liabilities be separated in order to present the business entity. However, because most PFSs are prepared informally by individuals, the separation of business assets and liabilities may not be clear.

- **Other assets** may include antiques and collectibles not listed as personal property. A commercial lender should verify the ownership and value of these assets. Asset values can be verified by obtaining copies of recent appraisals or by the lender's review of (and concurrence with) the valuation method used to establish the asset's value. If asset appraisals are not available, the assets can be treated as personal assets and the value deducted to obtain an adjusted net worth. Another asset that may be listed is deferred income, or the amount of income the borrower has deferred from his or her employer. Borrowers in high tax brackets may defer income until they are in a lower tax bracket, or even to simply move the income into the next tax year.

Liability Analysis

Liabilities are amounts owed by the borrower and are listed roughly in the order of maturity or payment due date. Loans owed to the bank to which the statement is addressed usually are listed first.

- **Notes payable**—Loans are either secured or unsecured. Secured notes have collateral pledged to the note. Personal collateral includes cash, marketable securities, residence, CSVLI, autos, boats, and motorcycles. Unsecured notes are usually for less than one year.

    Notes payable are detailed in Schedule E, showing the lender, the type of facility, the amount of the debt, if secured or unsecured, collateral (if secured), interest rate, maturity, and the unpaid balance. It also is important to know the terms and conditions under which the maturity of any of the loans can be accelerated.

    A business banker should compare the monthly amount due with the available income to service the debt. Further, loans to other lenders are a potential sales opportunity to refinance debt. For classification purposes, lines of credit are usually listed as current liabilities. Many other personal loans are noncurrent because the maturities are usually longer than one year. In the example PFS, Nieson reports no notes payable to banks or others.

- **Accounts payable**—Personal accounts payable are amounts owed on revolving credit, primarily personal credit card balances. A business banker will want to know the amount of credit available and amount not used. Interest rates may be high compared to bank financing, so significant amounts owed on credit cards adversely affect the borrower. Many small businesses now use credit cards as a source of financing. Credit cards in the company name are not listed here. It is possible that the credit card debt in the individual name was used to lend money to the business. Nieson owes $1,000 on credit cards. By using credit bureau reports, a lender can confirm debts owed and monthly obligations.

- **Margin accounts** are amounts owed to brokerage firms, secured by marketable securities. A borrower who appears to have high liquidity may actually owe large amounts on readily marketable securities. If the value of the securities drops, the borrower may have to raise cash quickly to pay down the amount owed on the margin loan or pledge additional securities, or the securities already pledged may be sold to maintain the margin (the percentage loaned against the total value of the pledged securities). In the PFS example, Nieson reports no amounts owing on margin accounts.

- **Notes due to partnerships** (as well as any other similar entities) are summarized in Schedule D. A business banker should determine the amount and timing of future payments. Also, a business banker should review the partnership or entity's cash flow to determine if any additional, nonrequired payments need to be made. In our PFS example, Nieson does not list any entries for this line.

- **Mortgage debt**—Mortgages payable are listed on Schedule C, along with the various real estate properties owned. The mortgage principal balance is evaluated against the original cost of the property and its current value. Amounts owed beyond the original cost may indicate that the property has been refinanced since it was purchased, and loans against the increased value were obtained. A business banker should understand the reasons for any refinancing that has taken place. Also, the bank should verify that real estate taxes are current and insurance is being maintained for at least the amount of the debt. In the PFS example, Nieson owes a total of $74,000 on her two properties.

- **Loans on life insurance** are amounts borrowed on life insurance policies that have a cash value. These loans, usually at a low interest rate, have no scheduled principal payment due, and if not repaid at the time of death of the insured, the loan amount is subtracted from the total death benefit. Bankers prefer that the customer list the full cash value of the life insurance policy as an asset, then show the loan separately as a liability. Some borrowers simply report the net cash value. That is, they show as an asset the difference between the cash value and any related loan. In the PFS example, Nieson does not list any amounts borrowed against the life insurance policy.

- **Taxes payable** are the amounts owed for federal, state, and local income taxes on current or most recent period income. Any amounts owed for prior years may be a warning sign of illiquidity or disagreements with the taxing authority. In any case, a business banker should understand the reasons and proceed with caution. In the PFS example, Nieson does not list any amounts for taxes payable.

In addition to this line-by-line analysis, a business banker should compare the mix of liabilities with the mix of assets. Also, the terms or maturities of a liability are compared with the useful life of any related or pledged asset. For example, residential real estate has a long useful life, and therefore the term of the related mortgage is expected to be longer than the term of a credit card account.

Net Worth

An applicant's net worth is the difference between total assets and total liabilities. In some cases, as shown in the PFS example, the applicant is asked to estimate any capital gains taxes that would be paid should any of the assets be sold. This is reported as estimated tax liability if all major assets sold. Accountants make this estimate when engaged to prepare a PFS under SOP No. 82-1, discussed earlier in this chapter. It involves determining the gain by subtracting the cost of an asset from its current estimated value. A tax rate is then applied to any gain, and all gains totaled.

Contingent Liabilities

One of the most important disclosures on a PFS is contingent liabilities, or amounts for which the borrower is not directly liable but may need to pay some time in the future based on events that may or may not be within the borrower's control. Contingent liabilities include guarantees of loans and leases, outstanding letters of credit, legal actions pending, and past-due tax obligations. Listing contingent liabilities in the PFS format helps remind the borrower of these items, as is the case with the example format.

Any amounts listed are compared to annual income to determine the borrower's ability to repay the debt, if needed. Any particularly large amounts should be investigated further, to understand the terms or conditions that could trigger direct liability. In the PFS example, Nieson lists her personal guarantee of a $250,000 obligation of Dry Supply as her only contingent liability. This indirect liability should be understood more fully, since the amount is large relative to her reported annual income.

Other Information Requested

Most PFS forms include borrower questions and a paragraph above the signature line stating that the information reported is true and correct. The following are two common borrower questions:

- Have you (or any entity that you have owned in a major capacity) ever declared bankruptcy?

- Are you an executive officer, director, or principal shareholder of a bank?

The second question is necessary to help determine if Regulation O may apply to a relationship between the borrower and your bank. Other questions (noted below) are used in some formats, and they may assist with underwriting and provide cross-selling opportunities:
- Have you filed income tax returns?
- Do you have a will?
- Have you prepared a financial or estate plan?
- Do you anticipate any upcoming material changes in your financial condition?

Representations and Warranties

When signing the statement, the borrower represents and warrants the items listed on the statement. This includes verifying that the information is true and correct, providing information for the purpose of obtaining or continuing a credit request, authorizing the bank to make credit inquiries, and agreeing to supply annual updates of financial statements. This section usually includes the signature, date, and room for the applicant and co-applicant to sign the PFS.

These disclosures are important for a couple of legal reasons. First, a borrower can be criminally prosecuted for knowingly submitting a fraudulent financial statement to a federally insured financial institution for purposes of obtaining credit. This is another reason to address the PFS to the lending bank. Second, debts incurred fraudulently are not dischargeable in bankruptcy.

In this section, you learned about the various components of the PFS. You now know the personal information needed on the PFS and that you should verify the applicants' identification if they are not known to you. You also learned about the income and expenditure statement and what questions to ask the applicant. You have a better understanding of the areas on the balance sheet that need to be reviewed and analyzed along with calculating the net worth—the balance sheet must balance, with assets equaling liabilities plus net worth. In addition, you learned why contingent liabilities are important, the purpose of the other information requested, and the importance of representations and warranties.

SUMMARY

Personal financial statements summarize all assets, liabilities, net worth, income, expenditures, and contingent liabilities of the individuals providing the statement. The borrower usually prepares the statement on a bank-approved form or a computer-generated form, which is attached to the bank form after all key questions on the bank form are answered. All PFSs are addressed to the lending bank, signed, dated, and checked for mathematical errors.

By completing this chapter, you learned the basic formats for a PFS and the information to review and verify prior to analyzing the statement. You also learned about the various components of a PFS—the personal information, the income and expenditure statement, the balance sheet, net worth, contingent liabilities, other information that is requested, and representations and warranties.

QUESTIONS FOR DISCUSSION

Complete the following three statements:
a. _____ is listed first on the PFS because it is the most _____.
b. Equity in a privately held company is listed as a _____ on a PFS.
c. _____ liabilities are amounts for which the applicant is not directly liable.

EXERCISE 1

In this exercise you will construct a personal financial statement

Instructions

Construct a PFS for Michael Richards as of September 30, 20xx, using the following information and the blank PFS:

Residence mortgage	$ 155,000
Value of privately held company	$ 200,000
Credit cards	$ 5,000
Boat	$ 20,000
Autos owned	$ 25,000
Mutual fund	$ 20,000
Due from parents	$ 10,000
Auto debt	$ 15,000
Personal property	$ 35,000
401(k)	$ 135,000
Cash	$ 15,000
Boat loan	$ 12,000
Home/residence	$ 225,000
Receivable due from friends	$ 10,000

PERSONAL FINANCIAL STATEMENT OF MICHAEL RICHARDS AS OF SEPTEMBER 30, 20xx			
Assets:		Liabilities:	
	$		$
		Total Liabilities:	
		Net Worth:	
Total Assets:	$	Total Liabilities and Net Worth	$

13

Key Ratios and Adjusted Net Worth

OBJECTIVES

After studying *Key Ratios and Adjusted Net Worth*, you will be able to—

- Calculate and interpret the liquidity ratio, unsecured debt ratio, and debt-to-income (DTI) ratio
- Perform an analysis using ratios to determine a personal financial condition
- Use adjusted net worth to perform an analysis of key personal asset and liability accounts
- Describe the components, adjustments and steps associated with adjusted net worth

INTRODUCTION

Understanding the various formats of personal financial statements (PFSs) and their components is the first step in analyzing the financial condition of the owners who will likely guarantee the debt of a business borrower. The second step is to develop a few ratios and determine the adjusted net worth of the owners. Similar to business financial statement analysis, ratios allow a business banker to examine the relationship between two or more accounts on the PFS. The general financial condition of an individual can be analyzed by comparing income to debt service. To gain an in-depth perspective of the individual's balance sheet, a lender reviews and analyzes assets and liabilities to develop an adjusted net worth.

Ratios and other measures also permit a business banker to compare the financial performance of different individuals, as well as develop trends of individuals compared to their own past performance.

This chapter covers the key ratios used within the personal financial analysis process, including how they are calculated and how they can be interpreted. You will also learn to develop adjusted net worth.

Relationship to the Commercial Lending Decision Tree

In the textbook Introduction, we explored the Commercial Lending Decision Tree as a way to think about the stages and steps involved in the commercial lending process. As you have already learned, the first stage in this process emphasizes early screening and qualifying steps, such as general fit with the portfolio and goals of your bank, and the initial assessment of financial and nonfinancial qualifications of the business. These preliminary steps allow a business banker to anticipate various issues and conduct a more efficient and accurate financial analysis.

The second stage moves into the detailed analysis of financial data gathered from the business and any owners who may serve as guarantors. This chapter will build on your knowledge of the format and component of PFSs and tax returns by adding key ratios and other ways to measure personal financial performance.

KEY RATIOS FROM PERSONAL FINANCIAL STATEMENTS

A PFS is a summary of personal assets, liabilities, and net worth. It also provides information on income, expenditures, contingent liabilities, asset ownership and values, and liabilities owed, plus a set of representations and warranties.

Perhaps the primary ratio used in the PFS analysis is the DTI ratio, which compares monthly personal income to monthly debt service for an individual. Two other ratios are used to examine other aspects, in addition to the ability to make loan payment. One is the amount of liquid assets as part of total assets, and the other is the level of unsecured debt outstanding to annual income.

Although they are valuable tools for financial analysis, ratios have limitations. A single ratio provides but a small amount of information about a person. To improve the financial analysis, ratios are used in conjunction with one another, as well as another calculation called **adjusted net worth**. The ratios are analyzed over time, preferably fixed periods, to determine trends and consistency. Several years of ratios provide a better tool for analysis than ratios for one year. Complete and accurate financial statements are also crucial for performing a valid ratio analysis.

As you learned in Section 2, ratios are a means to an end and not an end to themselves. They are analytical tools and have their own characteristics.

> **Adjusted net worth**
>
> The amount of an individual's net worth after making adjustments for the overstated value of assets and understated amount of liabilities.

- Ratios express *relationships between two related accounts*. The ratio of accounts receivable to rent, for example, lacks significance because the two amounts are not related. However, accounts receivable to sales does express a relationship between two related items and is a meaningful ratio.

- Ratios are expressed in whole *numbers, percentages, or multiples*, such as $2, 2 percent, or 2-to-1 (2:1 or 2.0x). Whole numbers generally are used to express working capital and cash flow measures. Percentages are used with profitability ratios, such as a gross margin of 30 percent. Multiples are used when comparing balance sheet items to each other, as well as calculations that combine income statement items with balance sheet items, such as sales being "five times" [5.0x] fixed assets.

- Ratios *have their own syntax*—"to" means "divided by." For example, current assets to current liabilities is the same as current assets ÷ current liabilities.

Although ratios are important to the financial analysis process, a business banker should not rely too heavily on ratios to the exclusion of considering nonfinancial or qualitative items. All steps of the commercial lending decision process are necessary to make a good credit decision.

Sample PFS Format

The PFS formats used by banks vary. In this chapter, a two-page PFS format is used to demonstrate the typical PFS content and analytical process. The PFS shown in Figure 13.1 is for Ed and Linda Dezine and is dated December 31, 20xz. Later in this chapter, you will work with the PFS for Kaitlyn Nieson, one of the owners of Dry Supply, Inc., introduced in the previous chapter.

Liquidity Ratio

Liquidity indicates a person's ability to generate enough cash to pay personal living expenses and other obligations as they come due. Beyond recurring monthly income, liquidity focuses on availability of current assets that can be converted to cash. Liquid assets on a personal balance sheet are considered to be cash, readily marketable securities, and the cash surrender value of life insurance (CSVLI). For a retired borrower, many lenders consider retirement accounts (the current value of individual retirement account (IRA), Keogh, 401(k), profit-sharing, pension, and other retirement accounts) as liquid assets.

There are no clear standards for an acceptable level of liquidity. A young couple saving for their first home or for their first child may have relatively low levels of liquid assets compared with a retired couple. Nevertheless, many lenders like to see a mini-

FIGURE 13.1 PFS FOR ED AND LINDA DEZINE

PERSONAL FINANCIAL STATEMENT AS OF January 17, 20yx
Date

SUBMITTED TO: **Your Bank**

PERSONAL INFORMATION					
APPLICANT (NAME) **Linda C. Dezine**			CO-APPLICANT (NAME) **Edward G. Dezine**		
Employer and Address **Designs by Dezine, Hometown, MN**			Employer and Address **Structural Engineering, Inc., Hometown, MN**		
Business Phone No. **612-123-4567**	No. of Years with Employer **5**	Title/Position **President**	Business Phone No. **612-234-5566**	No. of Years with Employer **12**	Title/Position **VP Engineering**
Home Address **9425 Norwood Ave., Hometown, MN**			Home Address **9425 Norwood Ave., Hometown, MN**		
Home Phone No. **612-617-9526**	Social Security No. **123-45-6789**	Date of Birth **03/07/19xx**	Home Phone No. **612-617-9526**	Social Security No. **234-55-6677**	Date of Birth **09/16/19xy**
Marital Status: __Single **X** Married __Divorced __Widowed			Marital Status: __Single **X** Married __Divorced __Widowed		

CASH INCOME & EXPENDITURE STATEMENT FOR THE YEAR ENDED 20xz (OMIT CENTS)

ANNUAL INCOME	Applicant	Co-Applicant	ANNUAL EXPENDITURES	Applicant	Co-Applicant
Salary	42,700	80,000	Mortgage/Rent - Residence	45,600	
Bonuses & Commissions			All Other Debt Service car loan	4,800	
Interest & Dividends	2,400		Federal Income & Other Taxes	24,000	
Rental Income (Net of Expenses)			State Income & Other Taxes	9,000	
Partner or Owner Draws/Distributions			Insurance (Home, Health, Vehicles)	2,400	
Other Income (List) **consulting**	40,000		Other Expenses (List) meals/food, contributions, medical and other	69,000	
			Other Living Expenses	5,000	
TOTAL INCOME ($)	**85,100**	**80,000**	**TOTAL EXPENDITURES ($)**	**159,800**	

BALANCE SHEET AS OF December 31, 20xz

ASSETS	AMOUNT ($)	LIABILITIES	AMOUNT ($)
Cash* in This Bank	45,000	Notes Payable to Banks – Secured (Schedule E)	11,000
Cash* in Other Financial Institutions		Notes Payable to Banks – Unsecured (Schedule E)	
Readily Marketable Securities (Schedule A)	32,000	Notes Payable to Others – Secured (Schedule E)	
Non-Readily Marketable Securities (Schedule A)	100,000	Notes Payable to Others – Unsecured (Schedule E)	
Accounts/Notes Receivable from Designs by Dezine	46,000	Accounts Payable (including credit cards)	3,000
Cash Surrender Value of Life Ins. (Schedule B)	20,000	Margin Accounts	
Residential Real Estate (Schedule C)	700,000	Notes Due: Partnerships/Other Entities (Schedule D)	
Real Estate Investments (Schedule C)		Mortgage Debt (Schedule C)	410,000
Partnerships/LLCs/S Corporations (Schedule D)		Loans on Life Insurance Policies (Schedule B)	
Personal Property (Including Automobiles)	85,000	Taxes Payable	
IRAs, Keoghs and Other Qualified Plans	440,000	Other Liabilities (List)	
Sole Proprietorship Assets:		**TOTAL LIABILITIES ($)**	**424,000**
Accounts Receivable		Estimated Tax Liability If All Major Assets Sold	
Inventory		**SUBTOTAL ($)**	**424,000**
Fixed Assets		**NET WORTH ($)**	**1,079,000**
Other Assets (List)	35,000		
TOTAL ASSETS ($)	**1,503,000**	**TOTAL LIABS. & NET WORTH ($)**	**1,503,000**

* Including money market accounts and CDs.

CONTINGENT LIABILTIES (Must be Completed; If None, Then Write "None" Below	YES	NO	AMOUNT ($)
Are you a guarantor, co-maker, or endorser for any debt of an individual, corporation or partnership?	X		40,000
Do you have any outstanding letters of credit or surety bonds?		X	
Are there or any lawsuits or legal actions pending against you?		X	
Are you contingently liable on any lease or contract?		X	
Are any of your tax obligations past due?		X	
Are you obligated to pay alimony and/or child support?		X	
Other contingent liabilities (describe):		X	

OTHER QUESTIONS	YES	NO	
Have you, or any firm in which you were a major owner, ever filed a petition in bankruptcy or has one been filed individually against you? If yes, please provide details below:		X	
Are you an executive officer, director or principal shareholder of a bank?		X	Bank:

FIGURE 13.1 PFS FOR ED AND LINDA DEZINE *(CONTINUED)*

SCHEDULE A—ALL SECURITIES (Including Non-Money Market Mutual Funds)*

# of Shares (Stock) or Face Value (Bonds)	Description	Owner(s)	Where Held	Cost	Current Market Value	PLEDGED YES	PLEDGED NO
READILY MARKETABLE SECURITIES (Including U.S. Government And Municipals)*							
100 shares	National Fund	Linda & Ed	brokerage	$45,000	$32,000		X
NON-READILY MARKETABLE SECURITIES (Closely Held Businesses, Thinly Traded or Restricted Stocks)*							
1,000 shares	Designs by Dezine	Linda		$1,000	$100,000		

If not enough space, attach a separate schedule or brokerage statement and enter totals only.

SCHEDULE B – LIFE INSURANCE (Use Additional Sheets If Necessary)

Insurance Company	Face Amount	Type of Policy	Beneficiary	Cash Surrender Value	Amount Borrowed	Ownership
Mutual Ins. Co.	200,000	whole life	Ed	10,000	0	Linda
Mutual Ins. Co.	200,000	whole life	Linda	10,000	0	Ed

Disability Insurance	Applicant	Co-Applicant
Monthly Distribution if Disabled	none	none
Number of Years Covered		

SCHEDULE C—PERSONAL RESIDENCE & REAL ESTATE INVESTMENTS, MORTGAGE DEBT

Personal Residence Address	Legal Owner	Purchase Year	Purchase Price	Market Value	Present Loan Bal.	Interest Rate	Maturity Date	Monthly Payment	Lender
9425 Norwood Ave.	L&E	19x3	600,000	700,000	410,000	7%	20zz	3,800	Mortgage, Inc.

Investment Property Address	Legal Owner	Purchase Year	Purchase Price	Market Value	Present Loan Bal.	Interest Rate	Maturity Date	Monthly Payment	Lender

SCHEDULE D—PARTNERSHIPS/LLCS/S CORPORATIONS (less than majority ownership for real estate partnerships)*

Type of Investment	Date of Initial Investment	Cost or Initial Investment	% Owned	Current Market Value	Bal. Due on Partnerships: Notes or Cash Calls	Current Year Investments
Business/Professional (indicate name)						
Investments (including tax shelters)						

Note: For investments listed above that represent a material portion of your total assets, please include financial statements or tax returns of the entities, plus any Schedule K-1s provided to you.

SCHEDULE E—NOTES PAYABLE

Due To	Type of Facility	Maximum Amount of Facility	Secured Yes	Secured No	Collateral	Interest Rate	Maturity	Unpaid Balance
Car Lender	car loan		X		auto	8%	20yz	11,000

** Immediately above the signature blocks, most banks place a paragraph of text called *representations and warranties*. This information differs from bank to bank and from state to state, depending on state laws and other issues. You are encouraged to read and to understand your bank's particular wording that is used. **

Linda C. Dezine	*Jan. 17, 20yx*	*Edward G. Dezine*	*Jan. 17, 20yx*
Applicant Signature	Date	Co-Applicant Signature	Date

mum of 10 percent for the ratio of liquid assets to total assets on a PFS.

Liquidity Ratio(x) = Liquid assets ÷ total assets

Referring to the Dezines' balance sheet for December 31, 20xz, the liquidity ratio is calculated as follows (in thousands of dollars):

$$\text{Liquidity ratio (\%)} = \frac{\text{Liquid assets}}{\text{Total assets}} = \frac{\text{Cash} + \text{mkt. sec.} + \text{CSVLI}}{\$1,503} = \frac{\$97}{\$1,503} = 6.5\%$$

The Dezines' liquidity ratio of 6.5 percent means that they have $6.50 worth of liquid assets for every $100.00 of total assets. As a cash flow source to supplement recurring income, if needed, this amount is relatively small compared to total assets. This means that should the Dezines experience a disruption in income, fewer liquid assets may need to be used to help meet personal expenses and debt payments.

A positive aspect of the Dezines' liquidity is that about half of the liquid assets are in cash. As you saw in the previous chapter, the total cash listed on a PFS can be weighed against the amount of total income earned. The lower the income, generally the less cash the borrower has available. The higher the income, the more liquid cash a borrower should have on hand. Depending on the borrower's lifestyle, the amount of cash will vary.

Unsecured Debt Ratio

Another relationship that many bankers focus on is the level of personal unsecured debt to annual income. Because the majority of consumer debt is secured (such as residences and automobiles), lenders tend to focus less on the total levels of liabilities to net worth (the business financial analysis concept of leverage). Unsecured debt, which sometimes includes credit card balances that are carried for more than one month and is usually at the highest interest rates, presents the most risk to individuals. As with the liquidity ratio, there are no clear standards for an acceptable level, but many bankers prefer the unsecured debt ratio to be 20 percent or less.

Unsecured Debt Ratio (%) = Unsecured notes payable ÷ annual income

Referring to the Dezines' PFS for December 31, 20xz, their unsecured debt ratio is calculated as (in thousands of dollars) follows:

$$\text{Unsecured debt ratio (\%)} = \frac{\text{Unsecured Notes Payable}}{\text{Annual Income}} = \frac{\$0}{\$165} = 0\%$$

The Dezines' unsecured debt ratio is 0 percent because they do not have any unsecured notes payable. Even if it is determined that their accounts payable of $3,000 consists of balances on credit cards (balances that are not paid off each month), the unsecured ratio is still a little less than 2 percent, which is very low. This means that they have loans that are primarily secured, which should be at better interest rates, and with collateral to support the loans in addition to recurring income.

Debt-to-Income Ratio

This ratio compares monthly gross income to monthly debt service, and is perhaps the most common ratio used in consumer lending and personal financial analysis. Not only does it allow a lender to compare current income levels to existing debt service, it shows whether added debt will require too much of an individual's income. Unlike the liquidity and unsecured debt ratios, there is a clear standard of 40 percent or less for an acceptable DTI level.

Debt-to-Income Ratio (%) = Monthly debt service ÷ monthly income

Referring to the Dezines' PFS for December 31, 20xz, the following is a calculation of their DTI ratio (in actual dollars):

$$DTI\ ratio\ (\%) = \frac{Monthly\ debt\ service}{Monthly\ gross\ income} = \frac{\$3,800 + \$400}{(\$165,100 \div 12)} = \frac{\$4,200}{\$13,758} = 30.5\%$$

The Dezines' DTI ratio is 30.5 percent, which is well below the consumer lending standard. However, a business banker will want to consider the loan applicant's lifestyle to determine if the DTI is low. For example, if the Dezines typically take three vacations per year, each costing $15,000, it is possible that their 30 percent DTI is not low.

If you assume that the Dezines' accounts payable is $3,000 of credit card balances that are carried month to month, then many bankers would add a payment of 5 percent each month on the carried balances. This adds $150 per month to debt service ($3,000 x 5% = $150), and increases the DTI ratio to about 32 percent ($4,350 ÷ $13,758 = 31.6%).

Another use of the DTI ratio is to determine how much additional debt service the Dezines can be allowed to have personally.

Maximum additional debt service ($) = (Monthly gross income x 40%) − existing debt service

For the Dezines, the following is the maximum additional debt service at a 40 percent DTI limit and considering the accounts payable to be credit card balances carried month to month (in actual dollars):

Monthly additional debt service ($) = (Monthly gross income x 40%) − existing debt service
= ($13,758 x 40%) − $4,350 = $5,503 − $4,350 = $1,153

At a 6 percent interest rate, a monthly payment of $1,153 can support a loan amount of about $49,000 on a 48-month amortization, and about $192,000 on a 30-year mortgage amortization. In short, the Dezines have substantial additional borrowing capacity against their monthly income.

In this section, you learned about ratios used to analyze a PFS—a summary of personal assets, liabilities, and net worth. You now know how to calculate and interpret the liquidity ratio, the unsecured debt ratio, and the primary ratio used in the PFS analysis, the DTI ratio. These ratios help a business banker determine the amount of liquid assets as part of the total assets, the ratio of unsecured debt outstanding to annual income, and an individual's monthly personal income to monthly debt service. You have gained a better understanding of how to perform an analysis using ratios to interpret a PFS.

ADJUSTED NET WORTH

A borrower's reported net worth is the difference between total assets and total liabilities. However, some of the asset values may not be realistic, while a number of personal assets have little or no value in a lending situation. Similarly, some liabilities may be omitted or not correctly reported. For these reasons, most bankers develop an *adjusted net worth* to take into account any inaccuracies or omissions among assets and liabilities.

Components of Adjusted Net Worth

The borrower's PFS must be adjusted for any overstated valuations of assets and any understated liabilities. Most financial statement adjustments focus on assets, because their values in many cases are the opinion of the borrower. While liabilities are easily verifiable, assets can be overstated for the following reasons:

- **A lack of liquidity**—Liquidity deals with how quickly an asset can be converted to cash to help pay personal living expenses and other obligations as they come due. Some assets are very illiquid, and their values heavily discounted or entirely eliminated.

- **A lack of marketability**—Marketability deals with the existence of a formal or informal market in which to sell the assets, and even the related price for comparable assets in that market. Not all assets have a ready market. Investments in closely held businesses, for example, may be marketable only to the other owners, who determine the price due to the limited market.

The business banker should verify the methodology used to value assets, and may need to obtain supporting documents. For example, a copy of a brokerage firm's statement can verify the value of marketable securities. As part of the review, the business banker requires the applicant to supply any incomplete information.

Specifically, a business banker should take the following steps:

- Verify that all assets are owned and all liabilities are owed by the individual(s) presenting the statement.

- Compare reported values of marketable securities to the most recently quoted prices.

- Be sure that all marketable securities are properly identified as to where they were traded, what type of security was traded, and how they were valued.

- Compare liabilities to a recent personal credit report.

- Compare the cost of real estate and the date it was acquired against current market value and test the value for reasonableness.

- Verify cash balances and where they are held.

- Verify that the borrower has properly distinguished between the face value and the cash value of any insurance policies owned.

- Verify that all loans are listed and have not been netted (in netted amounts, the applicant lists only the net value of the asset after subtracting the liability).

The process of adjusting asset and liability values actually results in two numbers in situations where the borrower is guaranteeing the debt of a business—*outside net worth and adjusted net worth*. You will learn more about these two items below.

Outside Net Worth

In situations where individuals are guaranteeing the debt of a business that they own, lenders attempt to determine the individuals' net worth outside or beyond the borrowing business. This is done because the value of the borrowing business generally will be exhausted or depleted by the time a lender relies on the owner's personal guarantee, and any value the owner assigned to the business now will be negligible or zero.

Outside Net Worth ($) = Stated net worth – value of closely held business being guaranteed

Referring to the Dezines' balance sheet for December 31, 20xz (Figure 13.1), and assuming that your bank is making a loan to their business called Designs by Dezine, their outside net worth is calculated as (in thousands of dollars):

Stated net worth	*$1,079*
Less: value of closely held business (being guaranteed)	*$ 100*
Outside net worth	*$ 979*

Calculating Adjusted Net Worth

Any remaining issues a business banker encounters when verifying and analyzing personal assets and liabilities (using the steps in Chapter 12) can be used to construct an adjusted personal net worth statement. In this process, the following deductions are taken from the net worth indicated by the applicant:

- Properties held in names other than the applicant's

- Personal property not supported by appraisals or independent valuations

- Excessive values of real estate, both residence and investment real estate

- Excessive values of privately held businesses not already adjusted in computing outside net worth

- Amounts due from relatives, friends, and privately held companies

- Any income taxes incurred to access values of IRAs, Keoghs, 401(k)s, and other retirement accounts, and any penalties if applicant's age is less than 59½

- CSVLI that is pledged as collateral
- Fractional ownership interests in investments
- Unlisted securities not supported with financial statements and independent valuations

The following are other deductions or additions to net worth:

- Changes in values of marketable securities, based on updated listings
- Liabilities shown on credit bureau reports or other resources, but not shown on the PFS
- Estimated tax liability if all major assets are sold (if not provided in PFS format used)

Referring to the Dezines' balance sheet for December 31, 20xz, and assuming that your bank is making a loan to their business called Designs by Dezine, the following is their outside net worth and adjusted net worth (calculated in thousands of dollars):

Stated net worth		$1,079
Less: value of closely held business (being guaranteed)		$ 100
Outside net worth		$ 979
Adjustments		
Note receivable from Designs by Dezine	($ 46)	
Value of personal property	($ 85)	
Taxes and penalties on retirement withdrawals*	($ 154)	
Total adjustments		($ 285)
Adjusted net worth		$ 694

* 10% penalty + 25% income taxes paid, $440,000 x 35% = $154,000

The Dezines' adjusted net worth is $694,000, compared with their stated net worth $1,079,000. Extending beyond the outside net worth already computed, the note receivable from their business was deducted, plus the value of personal property. An adjustment was also made for penalties and income taxes that would result from liquidating their retirement accounts prior to age 59½. Although there is no uniform way to handle this, most banks deduct at least the 10 percent penalty for early withdrawal and a 25 percent income tax burden. For the Dezines, this is at least a $154,000 reduction in the value of the retirement assets. (Generally, retirement accounts may be withdrawn at age 59½ without penalty.)

Despite this adjustment process, the "true" value of the assets cannot be determined until the Dezines sell the assets or the bank liquidates the assets. Nevertheless, from a business banker's assessment, the Dezines' net worth is not liquid, since the equity in their residence ($290,000) and adjusted value of retirement accounts ($286,000) comprise most of their adjusted or remaining net worth ($694,000). Another observation is that their profile is not atypical for the owners of a privately held business or individuals with large amounts of retirement assets.

In this section, you learned about the components, adjustments, and steps associated with adjusted net worth. As part of the review process, the business banker should take steps to verify and compare the asset and liability information on the PFS and adjust for any overstated valuations of assets and any understated liabilities. You also learned about outside net worth, whereby lenders attempt to determine an individual's net worth outside or beyond the borrowing business. You can now identify personal asset and liability issues that can be used to calculate an adjusted personal net worth, which is typically lower than the stated net worth on the PFS.

SUMMARY

Like a business balance sheet, a personal financial statement is a summary of an individual's personal assets, liabilities, and net worth. Along with the individual's income and expenditures, a business banker should explore the relationships between various accounts and line items, similar to ratio analysis of a business. In addition to liquidity and debt levels, bankers focus on adjusted net worth because individuals generally do not adhere to strict accounting standards, and many assets may have incorrect or negligible values that contribute to reported net worth. This process is very similar to the analysis of intangible assets reported by a business.

By completing this chapter, you learned how to calculate and interpret the three key ratios associated with analyzing a personal financial statement—liquidity ratio, unsecured debt ratio, and DTI ratio. You can now use these ratios to analyze a borrower's personal financial condition. You also learned about the components of adjusted net worth and how to determine if there are any overstated valuations of assets or any understated liabilities. In addition, you learned how to use adjusted net worth to perform an analysis of key personal asset and liability accounts.

QUESTIONS FOR DISCUSSION

1. Why does unsecured debt present the most risk?
2. Why are asset values adjusted when developing an adjusted net worth?
3. Why is an owner's valuation of a borrowing business excluded from stated net worth to arrive at outside net worth?

EXERCISE 1

In this exercise you will perform an analysis of a personal financial statement using ratios.

Background

In the last chapter, you analyzed the business financial statements of Dry Supply, a wholesaler of dry-cleaning supplies and equipment. Using the personal financial statement of Kaitlyn Nieson (on the following pages), one of the owners of Dry Supply, Inc. you will now calculate the key ratios and explain what they reveal.

Instructions

Using the PFS of Kaitlyn Nieson, calculate the following ratios and explain what they reveal:

1. Liquidity ratio
2. Unsecured debt ratio
3. DTI ratio

PERSONAL FINANCIAL STATEMENT AS OF   October 10, 20xz
Date

SUBMITTED TO: **Your Bank**

PERSONAL INFORMATION

APPLICANT (NAME) **Kaitlyn Nieson**			CO-APPLICANT (NAME)		
Employer and Address **Dry Supply, Inc. Salina, KS**			Employer and Address		
Business Phone No. **785-447-0300**	No. of Years with Employer **20**	Title/Position **President**	Business Phone No.	No. of Years with Employer	Title/Position
Home Address **4566 North Lynn Court, Salina, KS**			Home Address		
Home Phone No. **785-445-0236**	Social Security No. **111-33-4444**	Date of Birth **09/14/19xz**	Home Phone No.	Social Security No.	Date of Birth
Marital Status: **X** Single __ Married __ Divorced __ Widowed			Marital Status: __ Single __ Married __ Divorced __ Widowed		

CASH INCOME & EXPENDITURE STATEMENT FOR THE YEAR ENDED   20xy   (OMIT CENTS)

ANNUAL INCOME	Applicant	Co-Applicant	ANNUAL EXPENDITURES	Applicant	Co-Applicant
Salary	14,000		Mortgage/Rent - Residence	3,600	
Bonuses & Commissions			All Other Debt Service	6,600	
Interest & Dividends	5,000		Federal Income & Other Taxes	8,800	
Rental Income (Net of Expenses)	6,000		State Income & Other Taxes	2,200	
Partner or Owner Draws/Distributions			Insurance (Home, Health, Vehicles)		
Other Income (List) **gifts, trusts** (family trust income)	19,000		Other Expenses (List) prop. taxes – residence and investment RE	1,800	
			Other Living Expenses	5,000	
TOTAL INCOME ($)	**44,000**		**TOTAL EXPENDITURES ($)**	**28,000**	

BALANCE SHEET AS OF   Sept. 30, 20xz

ASSETS	AMOUNT ($)	LIABILITIES	AMOUNT ($)
Cash* in This Bank	30,000	Notes Payable to Banks – Secured (Schedule E)	
Cash* in Other Financial Institutions	20,000	Notes Payable to Banks – Unsecured (Schedule E)	
Readily Marketable Securities (Schedule A)	150,000	Notes Payable to Others – Secured (Schedule E)	
Non-Readily Marketable Securities (Schedule A)	100,000	Notes Payable to Others – Unsecured (Schedule E)	
Accounts and Notes Receivable		Accounts Payable (including credit cards)	1,000
Cash Surrender Value of Life Ins. (Schedule B)		Margin Accounts	
Residential Real Estate (Schedule C)	150,000	Notes Due: Partnerships/Other Entities (Schedule D)	
Real Estate Investments (Schedule C)	75,000	Mortgage Debt (Schedule C)	74,000
Partnerships/LLCs/S Corporations (Schedule D)		Loans on Life Insurance Policies (Schedule B)	
Personal Property (Including Automobiles)	30,000	Taxes Payable	
IRAs, Keoghs and Other Qualified Plans		Other Liabilities (List)	
Sole Proprietorship Assets:		**TOTAL LIABILITIES ($)**	**75,000**
Accounts Receivable		Estimated Tax Liability If All Major Assets Sold	25,000
Inventory		**SUBTOTAL ($)**	**100,000**
Fixed Assets		**NET WORTH ($)**	**455,000**
Other Assets (List)			
TOTAL ASSETS ($)	**555,000**	**TOTAL LIABS. & NET WORTH ($)**	**555,000**

* Including money market accounts and CDs.

CONTINGENT LIABILTIES (Must be Completed; If None, Then Write "None" Below	YES	NO	AMOUNT ($)
Are you a guarantor, co-maker, or endorser for any debt of an individual, corporation or partnership?	X		250,000
Do you have any outstanding letters of credit or surety bonds?		X	
Are there or any lawsuits or legal actions pending against you?		X	
Are you contingently liable on any lease or contract?		X	
Are any of your tax obligations past due?		X	
Are you obligated to pay alimony and/or child support?		X	
Other contingent liabilities (describe):		X	

OTHER QUESTIONS	YES	NO	
Have you, or any firm in which you were a major owner, ever filed a petition in bankruptcy or has one been filed individually against you? If yes, please provide details below:		X	
Are you an executive officer, director or principal shareholder of a bank?		X	Bank:

SCHEDULE A—ALL SECURITIES (Including Non-Money Market Mutual Funds)*

# of Shares (Stock) or Face Value (Bonds)	Description	Owner(s)	Where Held	Cost	Current Market Value	PLEDGED YES	NO
READILY MARKETABLE SECURITIES (Including U.S. Government And Municipals)*							
1,500 shares	Giant Public C0.	Kaitlyn Nieson	brokerage	$30,000	$150,000		X
NON-READILY MARKETABLE SECURITIES (Closely Held Businesses, Thinly Traded or Restricted Stocks)*							
1,000 shares	Dry Supply, Inc.	Kaitlyn Nieson	safe dep. box	$500	$100,000		

If not enough space, attach a separate schedule or brokerage statement and enter totals only.

SCHEDULE B – LIFE INSURANCE (Use Additional Sheets If Necessary)

Insurance Company	Face Amount	Type of Policy	Beneficiary	Cash Surrender Value	Amount Borrowed	Ownership
Big Life Company	250,000	term	Dry Supply	n/a	n/a	Kaitlyn Nieson

Disability Insurance	Applicant	Co-Applicant
Monthly Distribution if Disabled		
Number of Years Covered		

SCHEDULE C—PERSONAL RESIDENCE & REAL ESTATE INVESTMENTS, MORTGAGE DEBT

Personal Residence Address	Legal Owner	Purchase Year	Purchase Price	Market Value	Present Loan Bal.	Interest Rate	Maturity Date	Monthly Payment	Lender
4566 N. Lynn Ct.	KN	19x3	40,000	150,000	24,000	6%	20yz	300	Your Bank

Investment Property Address	Legal Owner	Purchase Year	Purchase Price	Market Value	Present Loan Bal.	Interest Rate	Maturity Date	Monthly Payment	Lender
Florida Condo	KN	19x9	60,000	75,000	50,000	8%	20yx	550	Other Bank

SCHEDULE D—PARTNERSHIPS/LLCS/S CORPORATIONS (less than majority ownership for real estate partnerships)*

Type of Investment	Date of Initial Investment	Cost or Initial Investment	% Owned	Current Market Value	Bal. Due on Partnerships: Notes or Cash Calls	Current Year Investments
Business/Professional (indicate name)						
Investments (including tax shelters)						

Note: For investments listed above that represent a material portion of your total assets, please include financial statements or tax returns of the entities, plus any Schedule K-1s provided to you.

SCHEDULE E—NOTES PAYABLE

Due To	Type of Facility	Maximum Amount of Facility	Secured Yes	No	Collateral	Interest Rate	Maturity	Unpaid Balance

** Immediately above the signature blocks, most banks place a paragraph of text called *representations and warranties*. This information differs from bank to bank and from state to state, depending on state laws and other issues. You are encouraged to read and to understand your bank's particular wording that is used. **

Kaitlyn Nieson   *Oct 10, 20xz*
Applicant Signature   Date   Co-Applicant Signature   Date

EXERCISE 2

In this exercise you will practice computing outside and adjusted net worth.

Instructions

Complete the following using the personal financial statement of Kaitlyn Nieson, a 50 percent owner of Dry Supply, Inc.

1. Compute an outside and adjusted net worth for October 10, 20xz.
2. Comment on the liquidity of the adjusted net worth.
3. If your bank does not compute outside net worth, is there an excess value of Dry Supply that should be deducted to reach Nieson's adjusted net worth? Assume that the latest net worth reported for Dry Supply was $94,000.
4. In terms of the Commercial Lending Decision Tree, what conclusions can Ann Schipel, the business banker handling the Dry Supply account, make regarding Nieson's personal financial situation and support as a likely guarantor?

EXERCISE 3

In this exercise you will practice computing the liquidity ratio, and the outside and adjusted net worth.

Instructions

Using the PFS that was constructed earlier for Michael Richards as of September 30, 20xx (Chapter 12):

PERSONAL FINANCIAL STATEMENT OF MICHAEL RICHARDS AS OF SEPTEMBER 30, 20xx			
Assets:		Liabilities:	
Cash	$ 15,000	Credit cards	$ 5,000
Mutual fund	$ 20,000	Auto debt	$ 15,000
401(k)	$ 135,000	Boat loan	$ 12,000
Receivable due from friends	$ 10,000	Residence mortgage	$ 155,000
Due from parents	$ 10,000	Total Liabilities:	$ 187,000
Home/residence	$ 225,000		
Value of privately held company	$ 200,000		
Personal property	$ 35,000	Total Liabilities:	
Auto	$ 25,000		
Boat	$ 20,000	Net Worth:	
Total Assets:	$ 695,000	Total Liabilities and Net Worth	$ 695,000

1. Compute the liquidity ratio.
2. Compute outside net worth and adjusted net worth, assuming that your bank is making a loan to a privately held business that is valued at $200,000 on his statement, and Richards will be fully guaranteeing the loan.

14

Personal Tax Returns and Cash Flow

OBJECTIVES

After studying *Personal Tax Returns and Cash Flow*, you will be able to—

- Describe the key components of a personal tax return
- Use tax return information to develop a personal cash flow

INTRODUCTION

Personal tax returns provide a final piece to the puzzle of understanding the financial strength of a business owner as a guarantor in a commercial lending situation. So far in Section 3, we have focused on the various formats of personal financial statements and their components, then developed some ratios and an adjusted net worth. We now turn to personal tax returns and personal cash flow.

Similar to the process of developing business cash flow, you will need a current-year tax return (basically an income statement at the personal level) and two personal balance sheets (with dates near the beginning and end of the tax year) to calculate personal cash flow. This figure can be used to develop a more comprehensive debt-to-income (DTI) ratio in order to determine if personal debt levels are excessive. It also assists in assessing the financial strength of the owner/guarantor relative to the business debt being considered.

This chapter covers the key portions of a personal tax return that are used to develop personal cash flow. You will also learn to develop a personal cash flow. In the next chapter, you will use personal cash flow, combined with business cash flow, to develop a global cash flow. Most business bankers compare this global cash flow to the combined personal and business debt to determine a global debt service coverage ratio.

Relationship to the Commercial Lending Decision Tree

In the textbook Introduction, we explored the Commercial Lending Decision Tree as a way to think about the stages and steps involved in the commercial lending process. As you have already learned, the first stage in this process emphasizes early screening and qualifying steps, such as general fit with the portfolio and goals of your bank and initial assessment of financial and nonfinancial qualifications of the business. These preliminary steps allow a business banker to anticipate various issues and conduct a more efficient and accurate financial analysis.

The second stage moves into the detailed analysis of financial data gathered from the business and any owners who may serve as guarantors. This chapter will build on your knowledge of personal financial statements and key ratios by adding a comprehensive personal cash flow developed from personal tax returns.

INTRODUCTION TO PERSONAL TAX RETURNS

A personal tax return (PTR) can be used to verify income and ownership of assets, and also provide information needed to construct a personal cash flow for a business owner who will likely serve as a guarantor of business debt. Reported income also is used to test the reasonableness of values assigned to assets, while reported expenses can validate some liabilities.

Key Uses of Personal Tax Returns and Common Forms

The PTR is a hybrid form of cash accounting. Many line items are prepared on a cash basis, except for depreciation and various items of taxable income that did not involve cash. The PTR also details the major sources of income, net of expenses, which are detailed in supporting schedules. It is important that the borrower supply the complete tax return and all supporting schedules.

The following are key components of a typical business-owner PTR:

- Form 1040—U.S. Individual Income Tax Return
- Schedule A—Itemized Deductions
- Schedule B—Interest and Ordinary Dividends
- Schedule C—Profit or Loss from Business (Sole Proprietorship)
- Schedule D—Capital Gains and Losses
- Schedule E—Supplemental Income and Loss
- Schedule F—Profit or Loss from Farming
- Form 4562—Depreciation and Amortization
- Form 4794—Sales of Business Property
- Form 6252—Installment Sale Income

The following components are not included with the PTR submitted to the Internal Revenue Service (IRS), but they are important to obtain for cash flow purposes:

- Schedule K-1 (Form 1065)—Partner's Share of Income, Deductions, Credits, etc.
- Schedule K-1 (Form 1120S)—Shareholder's Share of Income, Deductions, Credits, etc.

You will be examining these various schedules and forms as they interact with or feed lines within the main Form 1040.

Income vs. Cash

When analyzing the cash flow of business owners, it is important to understand that many items listed on their personal tax returns do not involve the actual inflow or outflow of personal cash. This contrasts with most consumer lending situations, where reported income is very close to cash flow, especially when the applicant does not own a business or rental properties. For business owners, adjusted gross income (AGI), a key number for tax purposes, is not a good number for cash flow purposes for the following reasons:

- Some forms of income are exempt from taxes.
- Other types of income may be deferred.
- Some deductions do not involve cash expenditures.
- Income reported from the sale of assets is net of expenses incurred from the sale and other expenses and accumulated depreciation during the holding period.
- Various income tax consequences [income (loss), credits, and deductions] come into the owner's return from pass-through entities, such as partnerships, limited liability companies (LLCs), and S corporations.

To analyze a business owner, Schedule C (sole proprietorships) and Schedule E (income or loss from rental properties and closely held, pass-through entities) are areas of focus for a business banker. However, a more accurate picture of cash flow for pass-through entities (contributions, distributions, and repayments of debt to partners or shareholders) is available only from Schedule K-1, and these items are not reported anywhere in the actual PTR.

In this chapter, you will be using the 20xz PTR for Edward G. and Linda C. Dezine (See Appendix A in this chapter). In addition to this chapter, IRS Publication 583, *Starting a Business and Keeping Records*, and Publication 334, *Tax Guide for Small Businesses*, are excellent resources for examining personal tax returns for business income and cash flow.

> Year Sequence for Dates in Chapter Cases
> This chapter uses the following order or sequence of years for the dates in the financial statements:
>
> • 20xx, 20xy, and 20xz
>
> For projected years, it uses the following sequence:
>
> • 20yx, 20yy, 20yz, and so on.

Personal Tax Return Components

Initial Review

The business banker should first confirm that the names on the PTR are correct and whether the return is joint or individual. The name(s), address, and Social Security number(s) should match the personal financial statement (PFS) and bank records. In the initial review, a business banker verifies that all supporting schedules are included. Pages 1 and 2 of the Form 1040 can serve as a table of contents for this review. As large numbers are located in the right-hand column, the business banker can scan to the left of the row to see the schedule that should be attached. Further, the business banker should ask for any Schedule K-1s if business income (or loss) from pass-through entities is listed on the second page of Schedule E.

Analysis of Income and Form 1040

Income received is listed on lines 7 through 21 of the 20xz PTR Form 1040. The following key questions are on income:

- Was it really cash received?
- What was the source?
- Will it be recurring?
- What amount is noncash income or expense (such as depreciation)?
- What amount is available to the individual?

> Note about line numbers on tax forms
>
> The various line numbers can change from year to year, although there have been very few changes in recent years. As you work with tax returns in the future, understand that lines can shift or even be combined with other lines.

Line 7: Wages and salaries—This line includes wages paid by employers, including firms that may be owned by the taxpayer, but excludes sole proprietorships or partnerships. The amount reported on line 7 is net of pretax deductions, such as 401(k) contributions. Reported income can include noncash benefits, such as personal use of a company vehicle. A business banker should verify the mix and amount of income for this line, using the W-2 for verification.

In our example for 20xz, the Dezines reported total wages of $159,588 from a combination of Designs by Dezine, Inc. (an S corporation owned by Linda) and Structured Engineering, Inc. (Ed's employer). The business tax return for Designs by Dezine showed compensation paid to Linda of $42,700, which matches the amount reported on their PFS. Also on the PFS, Ed reported $80,000 of income, so approximately $37,000 came from another source. A business banker should ask for W-2s to clarify the income and sources. Some state tax return formats have separate lines for each employer, and it is not necessary to obtain W-2s.

Line 8: Taxable interest income—The amount on lines 8a and 8b is itemized on Schedule B. Total interest income includes taxable (line 8a) and tax-exempt (line 8b) interest earned on deposits, bonds, notes, mortgages, and accounts receivable. Compare the amounts reported on line 8 to the PFS to ensure that the income will continue. The reported interest amount, based on current interest rates, gives a business banker an idea of the average level of deposits during the year, and should be close to the amounts reported on the PFS (or shown on your bank's deposit system, if the account is with your bank). Historical levels of cash shown on earlier PFSs and interest income shown on earlier Schedule Bs can help determine whether the deposits are expected to remain the same in the future. Anticipated changes in interest rates can also be a factor in the stability of this income. If rates are expected to fall, the interest income may decrease even if the deposits remain the same.

In our example for 20xz, the Dezines received $2,428 in interest income from a bank account, which is listed on Schedule B and appears reasonable, if interest rates for deposits in 20xz were about 5 percent, because they listed $45,000 of cash on their PFS.

Line 9: Dividend income—The amount of dividend income also is itemized on Schedule B. A distinction should be made between dividends, distributions, and capital gains. Dividends generally are amounts paid out of the profits or earnings of a corporation to its investors. Dividends paid to owners of C corporations usually are taxable income to the recipient. However, dividends or distributions paid to owners of partnerships, LLCs, and S corporations usually are not taxable income to the recipient. Capital gains, but not dividends and distributions, arise from the sale of assets, and are reported on Schedule D.

Ordinary dividends (line 9a) are the most common type of distribution from a corporation. They are paid out of the earnings and profits of the corporation. Ordinary dividends are taxable as ordinary income unless they are qualified dividends. Qualified dividends (line 9b) are a portion of ordinary dividends that meet certain requirements to be taxed at lower rates. So, total dividend income is shown on line 9a, and need not include any amounts shown on line 9b.

Note that some dividends, particularly from banks and large companies, can be involved in a dividend reinvestment program where the proceeds are used to purchase additional shares of common stock of the bank or large company, and the taxpayer does not actually receive cash for the dividends. The dividend income, however, is still reported on Schedule B, even if the taxpayer did not receive the cash.

In our example for 20xz, the Dezines own a mutual fund account that paid them $8 in ordinary dividends.

Line 10: State income tax refunds—Verify the amount reported on line 10 with the previous year's state income tax return. Generally, amounts reported on line 10 are not recurring and are not considered as cash available to service future debt. In many cases, they are small and not material to a cash flow analysis. In our 20xz example, the Dezines did not list state income tax refunds.

Line 11: Alimony—Verify the terms of the alimony payments with the divorce decree. If the payment is to be discontinued in the near future, the business banker needs to take that into account when assessing the ability to repay long-term loans. Review the divorce decree to determine if there are any escalation clauses in the payments.

Line 12: Business income—Schedule C details all income and expenses from sole proprietorships. In most cases, business bankers take net profit (or loss) from line 31 and add back depletion from line 12, depreciation expense from line 13 (both noncash items), and interest expense from line 16 (to avoid double-counting with debt service). Depreciation also can be included in cost of goods sold, which is detailed on page 2 of Schedule C. Specifically, look for line 39, "other costs," and supporting information attached to the PTR or provided by the customer.

In some cases, where a business banker is providing debt to purchase an asset to replace one that has been leased, it may be necessary to adjust or add back some of the rental expense from line 20. One more adjustment involves meal and entertainment expenses. Because only 50 percent of these expenses is deductible, it is necessary for cash flow purposes to reduce reported net income (or loss) by the other 50 percent that was expended and not deducted.

In our example for 20xz, Linda Dezine shows ownership of a teaching and consulting business that provides seminars to contractor associations and consults with other contractors on remodeling projects. The business has gross receipts of $39,587 and net profits of $39,518. No depletion, depreciation, interest, rental, or meals/entertainment expense is shown.

Line 13: Capital gain or (loss)—Gains and losses occur when assets are sold for more or less than their book or depreciated value. Determine from Schedule D if cash was received and whether the transactions will be a continuing source of cash flow. If they are not going to continue, the cash flow usually will not be counted when determining the ability to repay future loans. Further, if the cash proceeds, net of any debt repaid, are reinvested in another asset, the cash flow may not be counted. Access to a PFS and questions to the individual can clarify the true nature of any proceeds.

Starting in 2011, Form 8949 was implemented to list transaction details (previously listed directly on Schedule D) of the various short-term and long-term asset sales as an attachment to Schedule D. As many as three copies of this form can be used, depending on whether the taxpayer (a) received a Form 1099-B for the transaction reporting the cost basis of the asset sold, (b) received a Form 1099-B that did not include the cost basis, or (c) did not receive a Form 1099-B for the transaction.

Sales of business assets and depreciable assets, such as rental real estate held personally, are reported on Form 4797, with the gain or loss shown on line 11 of Schedule D. Some gains and losses reported with form 4797 are reported directly on line 14 of Form 1040 (see below). As with Schedule D, a business banker will need to determine the cash generated from the transaction, as well as whether such a transaction will be recurring.

In some cases, there are tax advantages for breaking a large capital gain into smaller amounts of taxable income. This is called an *installment sale*, reported on Form 6252 and also summarized on line 11 of Schedule D. Form 6252 shows the principal payments received during the year, and any interest received will be shown on Schedule B. Depending on the structure of the installments, what is usually considered a nonrecurring transaction can actually generate a series of cash flows over several years that can be included in a cash flow analysis.

In our 20xz example, on Form 8949 the Dezines reported a loss on the sale of shares of a mutual fund (National Fund) of ($1,324), but with proceeds of $9,728. The proceeds represent the cash flow for 20xz, while an outflow of $11,052 occurred in 20xy. We do not know if the Dezines reinvested the proceeds into another mutual fund, although they have shown dividend income from the fund and listed the fund as a holding on their PFS.

Tax returns can be a puzzle

In addition to the complexity of tax laws, the tax return forms and schedules often do not provide bankers all of the information needed to determine the cash flow impact of various reported income and expense items. Therefore, tax return analysis is difficult to complete from tax returns alone. It requires access to previous tax returns, current and previous personal financial statements, brokerage statements, and credit bureau reports—as well as access to the customer for questions. Especially for capital gains and losses, a banker needs information about the actual cash involved in the asset sale, whether any debt was repaid from proceeds, and what was done with the net proceeds. To count the transaction as recurring, levels of similar asset holdings (such that transactions can happen again in the future) and the customer's plans are important.

Line 14: Other gains and losses—Amounts listed on line 14 are from the sale of business assets and depreciable assets reported on Form 4797, but not included on Schedule D. As with capital gains and losses discussed earlier, a business banker will need to determine the cash generated from the transaction, plus whether such a transaction will be recurring.

Lines 15a and 16a: Individual retirement account (IRA) distributions and pensions and annuities—This is the total amount distributed to the taxpayer, with the taxable portion shown on lines 15b and 16b. If the individual is retired, distributions should be received in the future and significant portions may not be subject to taxes. The amount to be received depends on the value of retirement accounts. Verify distributions with the amount listed on the PFS for retirement assets. If the individual is not eligible for retirement, then amounts taken out early are subject to substantial penalties and taxes. Also, the amount shown on line 15a can be a rollover distribution from an IRA or other qualified retirement plan, and should not be counted as cash flow.

Line 17: Rental real estate, royalties, partnerships, estates, and trusts—This line includes several items commonly used by business bankers, including rental real estate and taxable income or loss from pass-through entities shown on Schedule E. Reported income from all of these activities is not necessarily cash. For rental real estate, amounts reported are net of depreciation and amortization (noncash expenses) that need to be added back. Any interest expense is added back to prevent double-counting with debt service.

> **Annualizing certain income or loss items for debt coverage ratios**
>
> Income or loss reported on several tax forms may need to be annualized or rendered on a monthly basis for only the months of operation when computing cash flow to use in a debt coverage ratio. Schedule C (sole proprietorships), Schedule E (rental real estate), and Schedule F (farms) are examples of business schedules that do not clearly indicate whether the business operated for the entire tax period. In such cases, a business banker will need to consult the customer or other resources to determine the appropriate number of months or weeks of operations in order to properly adjust the income or loss prior to developing a monthly DTI ratio or annual debt service coverage (DSC) ratio.

For partnerships, LLCs, and S corporations, use the appropriate Schedule K-1 (using tax identification numbers shown on the second page of Schedule E) to determine the actual amount of cash inflow or outflow involved:

- **Schedule K-1 (Form 1065)** is used by both partnerships and LLCs, because LLCs are taxed as partnerships in most situations. Box 1 will show the ordinary income or loss that appears on Schedule E. Actual cash inflow to the taxpayer will be shown in box 4 (compensation or salary labeled as guaranteed payments) and box 19 (distributions, usually with the letter code A). Any contributions from the taxpayer into the partnership or LLC will be shown in section L in the bottom left-hand corner, along with the distributions repeated. Business bankers use the net distribution (contribution) for personal cash flow.

- **Schedule K-1 (Form 1120S)** is used by S corporations. Box 1 will show the ordinary income or loss passed through to Schedule E. Distributions do not have a dedicated box, but are a part of box 16 labeled *items affecting shareholder basis*, with amounts designated with letter code D being distributions, usually as cash. However, this K-1 does not have a section L to show any offsetting contributions by the owner into the S corporation, so a business banker should ask the borrower if any contributions have been made, as well as if any distributions were made in cash, instead of other assets or property.

In our 20xz example, the Dezines do not have rental real estate, so page 1 of Schedule E is blank. They reported a net loss of $26,031 on Schedule E Part II on the second page. This is the net amount of taxable loss from Designs by Dezine, Inc., after allowable deductions. Since the related K-1 did not show any distributions, based on the information in the tax returns and forms, we do not have any cash inflow or outflow to use in our analysis.

Line 18: Farm income (or loss)—Schedule F for farms is very similar in format and analysis to Schedule C for sole proprietorships. In most cases, business bankers take net profit (or loss) from line 34 and add back depreciation expense from line 14 (a noncash items) and interest expense from line 21 (to avoid double-counting with debt service). In some cases, where a business banker is providing debt to purchase an asset to replace one that has been leased, it may be necessary to adjust or add back some of the rental expense from line 24. In considering the cash flow from farming, a business banker should assess future crop prices, crops on hand, future livestock prices, and other variables.

Lines 19–21: Unemployment, Social Security benefits, and other income— Verify any amounts listed on these lines to determine if they will continue. Unemployment benefits, which carry a maximum payment time frame, usually are not considered a recurring source of income. Other income may not be recurring, and the source should be verified. In most cases, business bankers use line 20a for the total cash flow from Social Security benefits. In our 20xz example, the Dezines reported $8,900 of other income. Details are not available in the schedules that have been provided, and since the amount is only 5 percent of AGI, it does not appear to be material. If it is larger, a business banker should obtain more information.

Line 22: Total income—Line 22 is the total of lines 7 through 21. For the Dezines, the total income listed is $183,087. A business banker should determine how much of that income was cash received and how much income was reduced by noncash deductions for depreciation and amortization. We have been discussing some of these adjustments for cash flow purposes, and will formalize them later in this chapter.

Lines 23–35: Adjustments to income—Usually, adjustments to income are not recurring, except for IRA and retirement plan contributions. The $2,791 the Dezines listed on line 27 represents a credit for half of the self-employment tax due for the consulting/teaching business and does not affect cash flow. Line 29 is a credit for apportion of self-employed health insurance expenses and does not affect cash flow.

Lines 37–38 Adjusted gross income—This is an important number that affects the thresholds for a number of deductions and credits throughout a PTR. However, as we have already pointed out, for business owners this may not be an accurate indication of actual personal cash flow.

Line 40: Itemized deductions—Itemized deductions listed on Schedule A primarily are cash expenditures, with a few noncash deductions. Medical and dental expenses on line 1 rarely exceed the amount to be deducted, yet are a cash outlay. Compare the state income taxes listed on line 5 with the W-2s or the general sales tax tables. Use local county records to verify real estate taxes shown on line 6. Line 7 has the amount of state personal property taxes, often charged in conjunction with vehicle and boat registrations. Check the home interest on line 10 with the information given on the PFS for the related mortgage. Discuss the contributions on lines 16 and 17 with the borrower to determine whether these commitments will continue in the future. Amounts on line 17 usually do not involve cash expenditures. Finally, line 24 lists job expenses and other deductions that usually are cash outlays.

Line 61: Total tax—The amount of taxes due is taken from one of the tax rate schedules and adjusted for credits (lines 47–53) and other taxes (lines 56–60), including self-employment tax based on earnings from a sole proprietorship and guaranteed payments (an equivalent to salary) from a partnership. A business banker should compare this amount with the total tax payments on line 72. Tax payments may be withheld from salary, as indicated and verified on a W-2, or estimated taxes may have been paid during the tax year. To avoid a penalty, estimated tax payments must be fairly close to the total tax due.

Related Analysis of Income and Form 1120S (S Corporation)

Our 20xz case example includes the tax return of the business owned by Linda Dezine, called Designs by Dezine, Inc. Page 1 of Form 1120S serves as the income statement, with a balance sheet provided in Schedule L on page 4.

For the first eight months of operations, Designs by Dezine had sales of $384,332 and showed a net loss of ($26,031). Many new companies show an operating loss the first year of operations. The business banker will want to understand which expenses were one-time, start-up expenses and which were fixed and likely to be ongoing. The major expenses for Designs by Dezine were cost of goods sold, which included employee wages and materials for remodeling projects. Line 14 lists a noncash expense of $11,866 for depreciation.

As the Dezines are the 100 percent owners of the business, the loss was shown in box 1 of the Schedule K-1 (Form 1120S) and passed through to the Dezines' PTR. However, this amount did not involve any cash outflow or inflow to the Dezines, because no distribution was indicated in box 16 of the Schedule K-1. When the company becomes profitable, a dividend or distribution may be paid to the Dezines to reimburse them for personal income taxes due on the company profits that pass through to their personal Schedule E. As you learned in Section 1 of this textbook, an S corporation does not pay income taxes at the entity level, and all tax liability occurs at the personal level of the owners.

The balance sheet (Schedule L) on page 4 of Form 1120S indicates that the company owns $60,822 in buildings and other depreciable assets, which are two company vehicles provided to employees. Line 20 of page 4 has the related debt for the company vehicles. The company also owes Linda Dezine $46,172, which is listed on her personal financial statement as a note receivable in the amount of $46,000. Many customers round PFS amounts to the nearest thousand, so this difference is not material. Nevertheless, this transaction appears to have happened in 20xz, so this is a personal cash outflow for that year. It more than offsets the personal cash inflow from Linda's salary, which is listed as officer's compensation on line 7 of Form 1120S and included as wages on the PTR line 7.

In this section, you learned the key uses and common forms associated with personal tax returns. You also learned that when analyzing the cash flow of business owners, it is important to understand that many items listed on their PTRs do not involve inflows or outflows of personal cash, which can affect debt repayment. You can identify the components and line items needed when analyzing the Form 1040 and its supporting documentation. You should now feel more confident in explaining to a potential borrower why you need more than the first two pages of a PTR.

PERSONAL CASH FLOW ANALYSIS

The business banker should perform a personal cash flow analysis using the applicant's individual tax return and other documents, such as PFSs. In this example you will use two years of PFS information from the Dezines, assuming that the 12/31/20xy and 12/31/20xz statements are before and after, respectively, the 6/7/20xz example from Chapter 13.

Figure 14.1 summarizes the Dezines' personal financial information:

FIGURE 14.1 SUMMARY OF PERSONAL BALANCE SHEETS OF LINDA C. AND EDWARD G. DEZINE

($ in 000s)	12/31/20xy	12/31/20xz	Change
Assets			
Cash	$ 40	$ 45	$ 5
Marketable securities	42	32	(10)
Non-readily marketable securities	0	100	100
Accounts and notes receivable	0	46	46
CSVLI	20	20	0
Real estate	700	700	0
Personal property and automobiles	70	85	15
Retirement accounts	430	440	10
Other assets	35	35	0
Total Assets	$1,337	$1,503	$ 166
Liabilities			
Notes payable—banks	$ 0	$ 11	$ 11
Others and accounts payable	2	3	1
Real estate mortgages	420	410	(10)
Total Liabilities	$ 422	$424	$ 2
Net Worth	$ 915	$1,079	$ 164
Total Liabilities and Net Worth	$1,337	$1,503	$ 166

Calculating Personal Cash Flow

Business bankers have different formats for compiling a personal cash flow (see Figure 14.2).

For this chapter, the Dezines' personal cash flow statement will be used as one type of format. This format computes cash flow available for debt service in two ways, which can be used for a DTI or DSC ratio. Since a consumer DTI ratio is based on gross income or cash flow before taxes and living expenses, the example format provides a gross cash flow number. Then taxes and living expenses are deducted to arrive at a net cash flow number to be used for a DSC ratio.

FIGURE 14.2 DEZINES' PERSONAL CASH FLOW STATEMENT

Personal Cash Flow Available for Debt Service Worksheet

Name: __Edward G. and Linda C. Dezine__   For: __20xz__

Line Item	Source	Amount	
Gross Wages Received			
Wages, salaries	Form 1040, line 7	$159,888	
Guaranteed payments	Sched. K-1 (Form 1065), box 4	-	
Other	Form 1040, PFS, other	-	
Gross Cash Flow from Wages			$159,888
Other Personal Cash Flow			
Interest and dividend income	Form 1040, lines 8a, 8b, and 9a	$2,436	
State/local income tax refund	Form 1040, line 10	-	
Alimony received and other income	Form 1040, lines 11 and 21	8,900	
Net proceeds from asset sales	Sched. D, Forms 8949, 4797, etc.	9,728	
Asset purchases (net of related loans)	Form 1040, PFS, other	(2,000)	
Miscellaneous income	Form 1040, PFS, other	-	
IRA/pension/Social Sec. distributions	Form 1040, lines 15a, 16a, and 20a	-	
Total Other Personal Cash Flow			$19,064
Cash Flow from Businesses Interests			
Sole proprietorship income	Sched. C, line 31	$39,518	
Add: Depreciation and depletion	Sched. C, lines 12 and 13	-	
Add: Interest expense	Sched. C, lines 16a and 16b	-	
Other (meals/ent., rent, etc.)	Sched. C, line 24b, 20a, 20b, etc.	-	
Rental real estate income	Sched. E, line 26	-	
Add: Interest expense	Sched. E, lines 12 and 13	-	
Add: Depreciation	Sched. E, line 18	-	
Farm income	Sched. F, line 34	-	
Add: Depreciation	Sched. F, line 14	-	
Add: Interest expense	Sched. F, lines 21a and 21b	-	
Other (rent, livestock/crop sales, etc.)	Sched. F, Form 4797, other	-	
Partnership/LLC net distributions	Sched. K-1 (Form 1065), section L	-	
S corporation net distributions	Sched. K-1 (Form 1120S), box 16	-	
Other: Cap stock and loan to S corp.	Form 1040, PFS, other	(46,472)	
Total Cash Flow from Business Interests			($6,954)
Gross Personal Cash Flow Available for Debt Service, DTI (40%) Basis			**$171,998**
Taxes, Living Expenses, and Other Expenses			
Federal income tax withheld	Form 1040, line 62	($22,359)	
Estimated Fed. tax payments	Form 1040, line 63	-	
FICA tax withheld or paid	W-2 or 7.65% of wages	(12,231)	
State/local income taxes	Sched. A, line 5	(8,866)	
State/local real estate taxes	Sched. A, line 6	(3,221)	
Personal property and other taxes	Sched. A, lines 7 and 8	(188)	
Medical expenses	Sched. A, line 1	(1,318)	
Gifts to charity and other expenses	Sched. A, line 16 and 24	(30,885)	
Other living expenses	PFS or best estimate	(41,797)	
Other: Insurance expense	Form 1040, PFS or other	(2,400)	
Total Taxes, Living Expenses and Other			($123,265)
Net Personal Cash Flow Available for Debt Service, DSC (1.25x) Basis			**$48,733**
	Various Living Expenses/Gross Personal Cash Flow	($76,400)	44%

Key Sections and Calculations

Key sections of the example format with sample calculations are explained below.

- **Gross wages received**—To calculate the amount of gross wages received, add all sources of personal wages and salaries, including guaranteed payments (a salary equivalent) from partnerships. In our example, the Dezines reported $159,888 in wages and salaries on line 7 of the 20xz Form 1040.

Gross wages received—Dezine 20xz			
Wages, salaries	Form 1040, line 7	$ 159,888	
Guaranteed payments	Sched. K-1 (Form 1065), box 4	0	
Other	Form 1040, PFS, other	0	
Gross cash flow from wages			$ 159,888

- **Other personal cash flow** includes all other income except wages and salaries. The business banker should determine whether the income will continue, what are the sources of income, and whether the income is available for future debt service. This section includes items presented earlier, such as interest and dividend income, plus IRA, pension, and Social Security distributions. For the Dezines, other personal income includes interest income of $2,428, dividend income of $8, and other income (from Form 1040, line 21) of $8,900. From their capital loss of ($1,324) reported on Form 1040, line 13, we find net proceeds of $9,728 from the mutual fund sale. For this exercise, we are assuming that this will be a recurring item for the Dezines, and that no related debt had to be repaid upon sale of the shares as reported on Form 8949.

From the summary balance sheets, it appears that the Dezines purchased an automobile for approximately $15,000 financed with a loan of approximately $13,000 (balance of $11,000 at year-end). This asset purchase had a cash outflow effect of ($2,000).

Other personal cash flow—Dezine 20xz			
Interest and dividend income	Form 1040, line 7	$ 24,036	
State/local income tax refund	Form 1040, line 10	0	
Alimony received and other income	Form 1040, lines 11 and 21	8,900	
Net proceeds from asset sales	Sched. D, Forms 8949, 4797, etc.	9,728	
Asset purchases (net of related loans)	Form 1040, PFS, other	(2,000)	
Miscellaneous income	Form 1040, PFS, other	0	
IRA/pension/Soc. Sec. distributions	Form 1040, lines 15a, 16a, and 20a	0	
Total other personal cash flow			$19,064

The Dezines have about $179,000 in gross personal cash flow to support their personal debt, business interests, and personal expenses.

- **Cash flow from business interests**—This section covers various types of business ownerships and the related cash flow to the owners, starting with sole proprietorships. For a customer with numerous business ownerships, this section can be expanded. Most business bankers use net income or loss, adjusted for depreciation and interest expense, for determining the cash flow to the owners of sole proprietorships, real estate shown on Schedule E, and farms. For pass-through entities (partnerships, LLCs, and S corporations), most business bankers use the net distribution (contribution) as shown on the Schedule K-1 provided to the owner.

Cash flow from business interests—Dezine 20xz			
Sole proprietorship income	Sched. C, line 31	$ 39,518	
Add: Depreciation and depletion	Sched. C, lines 12 and 13	0	
Add: Interest expense	Sched. C, lines 16a and 16b	0	
Other (meals/ent., rent, etc.)	Sched. C, lines 24b, 20a, 20b, etc.	0	
Rental real estate income	Sched. E, line 26	0	
Add: Interest expense	Sched. E, lines 12 and 13	0	
Add: Depreciation	Sched. E, line 18	0	
Farm income	Sched. F, line 34	0	
Add: Depreciation	Sched. F, line 14	0	
Add: Interest expense	Sched. E, lines 21a and 21b	0	
Other (rent, livestock/crop sales, etc.)	Sched. F, Form 4797, other	0	
Partnership/LLC net dist. (contr.)	Sched. K-1 (Form 1065), section L	0	
S Corporation net dist. (contribution)	Sched. K-1 (Form 1120S), box 16	0	
Other: Cap. stock and loan to S corp.	Form 1040, PFS, other	($46,472)	
Total cash flow from business interests			($ 6,954)

The calculation of cash flow from business interests can be complicated, depending on the number of tax schedules involved. For the Dezines, two business ownerships are involved. First, there is the consulting business shown as a sole proprietorship on Schedule C. The net income is $39,518 with no adjustments for depreciation or interest expense. The worksheet format allows for adjusting rent, as discussed earlier, and also for the nondeductible portion of meals and entertainment expense (Schedule C, line 24b).

Second, there is the S corporation Designs by Dezine. Although it had a loss of ($26,031) that passed through to Schedule E, there was no cash flow effect to the Dezines since the Schedule K-1 (Form 1120S) did not show any distributions. Nevertheless, Linda Dezine invested $300 in capital stock and loaned $46,172 to the business during the year. The total of these two items is shown in the chart above.

Overall, the Dezines had a net outflow of about ($7,000) for their businesses, leaving about $172,000 to support personal debt and personal expenses.

- **Gross personal cash flow available for debt service** includes gross cash flow from wages and the total cash flow from businesses interests. For the Dezines, the total gross cash flow is $171,998. Since it does not include taxes and living expenses, this is the appropriate cash flow figure to use when calculating a DTI ratio. Using monthly debt service of $4,200 for the Dezines (Chapter 13), then their DTI ratio is about 29 percent [$4,200 ÷ ($171,998 ÷ 12) = 29.3%]. Another way to think about this gross cash flow figure is that the Dezines have about $172,000 in cash flow to support personal debt and personal expenses.

- **Taxes, living expenses, and other expenses**—This section includes all taxes (income, real estate, and personal property), personal living expenses, and other expenses, excluding interest payments and debt payments. At this point in the worksheet, you will also make sure you have considered all of the asset and liability changes between the two PFSs.

Taxes, living expenses, and other expenses—Dezine 20xz			
Federal income tax withheld	Form 1040, line 62	($ 22,359)	
Est. Fed. tax payments	Form 1040, line 63	0	
FICA tax withheld or paid	W-2 or 7.65% of wages	(12,231)	
State/local income taxes	Sched. A, line 5	(8,866)	
State/local real estate taxes	Sched. A, line 6	(3,221)	
Personal property and other taxes	Sched. A, lines 7 and 8	(188)	
Medical expenses	Sched. A, line 1	(1,318)	
Gifts to charity and other expenses	Sched. A, lines 16 and 24	(30,885)	
Other living expenses	PFS or best estimate	(41,797)	
Other: Insurance	Form 1040, PFS, other	(2,400)	
Total Taxes, living expenses, and other expenses			($123,265)

For the Dezines, the various tax expenses are taken from the tax return. W-2 forms from the Dezines' employers would have shown Federal Insurance Collection Act (FICA) withholdings for Social Security and Medicare. Without the W-2, these were estimated at 7.65 percent of wages shown ($159,888 x 7.65% = $12,231). The Social Security portion of FICA (6.2 percent) is limited to roughly the first $110,000 of wages for each taxpayer. The actual limit is increased for inflation each year and published by the IRS. Neither of the Dezines appears to have combined wages above the Social Security limit.

For self-employed taxpayers, the FICA equivalent is called self-employment tax and is 15.3 percent of earnings for sole proprietorships and rental real estate, plus a 15.3 percent assessment on guaranteed payments from a partnership. As with FICA, the 12.4 percent Social Security portion is limited to roughly the first $110,000 of self-employment income. Linda Dezine has $4,853 of self-employment taxes due, shown on Schedule SE and Form 1040, line 56. Along with federal income tax due of $16,019, the Dezines show total tax due of $20,872. For cash flow purposes, most business bankers focus on the taxes actually withheld and/or paid, instead of the amount due. Therefore, lines 55, 56, and 61 will not be used in the personal cash flow worksheet. Linda Dezine will use the projected self-employment tax for the next year, along with projected income taxes due on the same business earnings, to make quarterly estimated tax payments.

Personal living expenses can vary depending on lifestyle and general price levels in the community where the borrower lives. Some business bankers use a set percentage of gross income to avoid subjectivity. Either the applicant provides this information or the business banker estimates it using PFS trends. For example, if the PFS shows no personal liquidity but good income, the applicant probably spends all income or invests it in nonliquid assets. If the earlier analysis reveals any investment income, assume that it is spent on personal living expenses.

The example worksheet has four shaded rows that comprise most of the common living expenses that can be listed, in either a PTR or PFS. These items are totaled and compared with gross personal cash flow in order to give an idea of the appropriateness of the total amount being considered.

For the Dezines, medical expenses, gifts to charity, and other expenses were shown on Schedule A of Form 1040. Their PFS lists the same items within "other expenses" of $69,000. This leaves $36,797 of additional personal expenses that we will show on the worksheet as "other living expenses," along with $5,000 categorized as "other living expenses" on the PFS. The PFS lists insurance expense of $2,400, which will be shown on the final row of this section.

- **Year-to-year balance sheet changes** are now considered, if such changes affected cash flow and have not already been used. As with business cash flow, increases in assets other than cash will be considered uses of cash. However, individuals are allowed to value assets at market, which may create an increase in the asset that did not involve cash.

  The following quick review lists the asset and liability changes for the Dezines from 12/31/20xy to 12/31/20xz:

  o Marketable securities decreased from $42,000 to $32,000. This appears to have already been used via the proceeds from asset sales of $9,728 from Schedule D and Form 8949.

  o Nonmarketable securities increased from $0 to $100,000. This represents the value of Linda Dezine's ownership in Designs by Dezine and did not involve a cash outlay, except for $300 of capital stock shown on the business tax return.

  o Accounts & notes receivable increased by $46,000 and it includes the $46,172 loan by Linda Dezine to Designs by Dezine. This is a use of cash and was recognized in the worksheet in the business interests section, along with the $300 of capital stock she invested as shown on the business tax return.

  o Personal property and automobiles increased by $15,000 and was included, net of $13,000 loan in the asset purchases row, within *other personal cash flow* in the worksheet. The loan's ending balance at 12/31/20xz was $10,000.

  o Retirement accounts increased from $430,000 to $440,000 and appears to be a valuation increase, not a cash outlay, since no contributions were reported on Form 1040. It is possible that nondeductible contributions were made, but not likely, given the Dezines' income level.

  o Notes payable banks increased by $11,000 and appears to be the 12/31/20xz amortized balance of the car loan mentioned above. The inflow of $13,000 of loan proceeds was netted against the $15,000 car purchase in the *other personal cash flow* section of the worksheet.

  o Real estate mortgages decreased by $10,000 and appears to have occurred from scheduled monthly payments. Because this is part of personal debt service, it was not included to calculate cash flow available for debt service (to avoid double-counting).

Overall, the Dezines have about $123,000 in personal expenses.

- **Net personal cash flow available for debt service** includes the gross cash flow of about $172,000 calculated earlier, less the taxes and living expenses of about $123,000. The result is net cash flow of about $49,000. Since it includes taxes and living expenses, this is the appropriate cash flow figure to use when calculating a DSC ratio. Using annual debt service of $50,400 for the Dezines (Chapter 13), then their DSC ratio is less than 1.0x.

Another way to think about this net cash flow figure is that the Dezines do not have recurring cash flow available (beyond personal debt service) to support their business interests. However, an argument can be made that the loan to Designs by Dezine is not a recurring transaction, and net personal cash flow should be higher at about $95,000. This changes the DSC ratio to 1.9x. From this perspective it appears the Dezines have more than sufficient income to service their debt, plus room to further support external businesses.

In this section, you learned about the key sections on a personal cash flow statement. You can now identify these areas and perform calculations to determine a borrower's cash flow. It is important for you to know how to do a personal cash flow analysis with these calculations so you can verify that borrowers have enough income to service their debt and additional cash for possible emergencies or further business expansion.

SUMMARY

By completing this chapter, you learned the key components of a personal tax return and how to use that information to develop a personal cash flow. Personal tax returns are a key element in the analysis of owners and guarantors of commercial loans. PTRs summarize most of the income and expenses, while providing information about cash inflows and outflow, plus noncash items that affect the income and expenses. Personal cash flow is calculated primarily from PTRs and the supporting schedules. Cash flow is analyzed based on its type, source, and frequency (recurring). Most business bankers focus on cash flow available for debt service, which can be rendered on a gross basis (for use with DTI ratios) and a net basis (for use with DSC ratios).

QUESTION FOR DISCUSSION

1. Why is it important for the borrower to submit a complete tax return and all the supporting schedules when serving as a guarantor on a business debt?

APPENDIX A: DEZINE PERSONAL TAX RETURN

Form 1040 Department of the Treasury—Internal Revenue Service (99)
U.S. Individual Income Tax Return 20XZ OMB No. 1545-0074 IRS Use Only—Do not write or staple in this space.

For the year Jan. 1–Dec. 31, 20XZ or other tax year beginning , 20XZ ending , 20 See separate instructions.

Your first name and initial: Edward G.	Last name: Dezine
Your social security number: 2 3 4 5 5 6 6 7 7	
If a joint return, spouse's first name and initial: Linda C.	Last name: Dezine
Spouse's social security number: 1 2 3 4 5 6 7 8 9	
Home address (number and street): 9425 Norwood Ave.	Apt. no.
City, town or post office, state, and ZIP code: Hometown, MN	

Make sure the SSN(s) above and on line 6c are correct.

Presidential Election Campaign Check here if you, or your spouse filing jointly, want $3 to go to this fund. Checking a box below will not change your tax or refund. ☐ You ☐ Spouse

Filing Status
Check only one box.
1. ☐ Single
2. ✓ Married filing jointly (even if only one had income)
3. ☐ Married filing separately. Enter spouse's SSN above and full name here. ▶
4. ☐ Head of household (with qualifying person). (See instructions.) If the qualifying person is a child but not your dependent, enter this child's name here. ▶
5. ☐ Qualifying widow(er) with dependent child

Exemptions
6a ✓ **Yourself.** If someone can claim you as a dependent, do not check box 6a
6b ✓ **Spouse**

6c Dependents: (1) First name Last name	(2) Dependent's social security number	(3) Dependent's relationship to you	(4) ✓ if child under age 17 qualifying for child tax credit (see instructions)
Kathy Dezine	3 4 5 6 6 7 7 8 8	parent	☐
			☐
			☐
			☐

If more than four dependents, see instructions and check here ▶ ☐

Boxes checked on 6a and 6b: **2**
No. of children on 6c who:
• lived with you: ___
• did not live with you due to divorce or separation (see instructions): ___
Dependents on 6c not entered above: **1**
Add numbers on lines above ▶ **3**

6d Total number of exemptions claimed

Income

Attach Form(s) W-2 here. Also attach Forms W-2G and 1099-R if tax was withheld.

If you did not get a W-2, see instructions.

Enclose, but do not attach, any payment. Also, please use Form 1040-V.

Line	Description	Amount		Total
7	Wages, salaries, tips, etc. Attach Form(s) W-2		7	159,588
8a	Taxable interest. Attach Schedule B if required		8a	2,428
8b	Tax-exempt interest. Do not include on line 8a	8b		
9a	Ordinary dividends. Attach Schedule B if required		9a	8
9b	Qualified dividends	9b		
10	Taxable refunds, credits, or offsets of state and local income taxes		10	
11	Alimony received		11	
12	Business income or (loss). Attach Schedule C or C-EZ		12	39,518
13	Capital gain or (loss). Attach Schedule D if required. If not required, check here ▶ ☐		13	(1,324)
14	Other gains or (losses). Attach Form 4797		14	
15a	IRA distributions 15a	b Taxable amount	15b	
16a	Pensions and annuities 16a	b Taxable amount	16b	
17	Rental real estate, royalties, partnerships, S corporations, trusts, etc. Attach Schedule E		17	(26,031)
18	Farm income or (loss). Attach Schedule F		18	
19	Unemployment compensation		19	
20a	Social security benefits 20a	b Taxable amount	20b	
21	Other income. List type and amount		21	8,900
22	Combine the amounts in the far right column for lines 7 through 21. This is your **total income** ▶		22	183,087

Adjusted Gross Income

Line	Description	Amount		Total
23	Educator expenses	23		
24	Certain business expenses of reservists, performing artists, and fee-basis government officials. Attach Form 2106 or 2106-EZ	24		
25	Health savings account deduction. Attach Form 8889	25		
26	Moving expenses. Attach Form 3903	26		
27	Deductible part of self-employment tax. Attach Schedule SE	27	2,791	
28	Self-employed SEP, SIMPLE, and qualified plans	28		
29	Self-employed health insurance deduction	29	1,978	
30	Penalty on early withdrawal of savings	30		
31a	Alimony paid b Recipient's SSN ▶	31a		
32	IRA deduction	32		
33	Student loan interest deduction	33		
34	Tuition and fees. Attach Form 8917	34		
35	Domestic production activities deduction. Attach Form 8903	35		
36	Add lines 23 through 35		36	4,769
37	Subtract line 36 from line 22. This is your **adjusted gross income** ▶		37	178,318

For Disclosure, Privacy Act, and Paperwork Reduction Act Notice, see separate instructions. Cat. No. 11320B Form **1040** (2011)

Form 1040 (20xz) Page 2

Tax and Credits	38	Amount from line 37 (adjusted gross income)		38	178,318
	39a	Check if: ☐ You were born before January 2, 19rz, ☐ Blind. ☐ Spouse was born before January 2, 19rz, ☐ Blind. Total boxes checked ▶ 39a			
Standard Deduction for—	b	If your spouse itemizes on a separate return or you were a dual-status alien, check here ▶ 39b☐			
• People who check any box on line 39a or 39b or who can be claimed as a dependent, see instructions.	40	Itemized deductions (from Schedule A) or your **standard deduction** (see left margin)		40	72,119
	41	Subtract line 40 from line 38		41	106,199
	42	**Exemptions.** Multiply $3,700 by the number on line 6d		42	11,100
	43	**Taxable income.** Subtract line 42 from line 41. If line 42 is more than line 41, enter -0-		43	95,099
	44	**Tax** (see instructions). Check if any from: a ☐ Form(s) 8814 b ☐ Form 4972 c ☐ 962 election		44	16,019
• All others: Single or Married filing separately, $5,800	45	**Alternative minimum tax** (see instructions). Attach Form 6251		45	
	46	Add lines 44 and 45 ▶		46	16,019
	47	Foreign tax credit. Attach Form 1116 if required	47		
	48	Credit for child and dependent care expenses. Attach Form 2441	48		
Married filing jointly or Qualifying widow(er), $11,600	49	Education credits from Form 8863, line 23	49		
	50	Retirement savings contributions credit. Attach Form 8880	50		
	51	Child tax credit (see instructions)	51		
	52	Residential energy credits. Attach Form 5695	52		
Head of household, $8,500	53	Other credits from Form: a ☐ 3800 b ☐ 8801 c ☐	53		
	54	Add lines 47 through 53. These are your **total credits**		54	
	55	Subtract line 54 from line 46. If line 54 is more than line 46, enter -0- ▶		55	16,019
Other Taxes	56	Self-employment tax. Attach Schedule SE		56	4,853
	57	Unreported social security and Medicare tax from Form: a ☐ 4137 b ☐ 8919		57	
	58	Additional tax on IRAs, other qualified retirement plans, etc. Attach Form 5329 if required		58	
	59a	Household employment taxes from Schedule H		59a	
	b	First-time homebuyer credit repayment. Attach Form 5405 if required		59b	
	60	Other taxes. Enter code(s) from instructions		60	
	61	Add lines 55 through 60. This is your **total tax** ▶		61	20,872
Payments	62	Federal income tax withheld from Forms W-2 and 1099	62	22,359	
	63	20xz estimated tax payments and amount applied from 20xy return	63		
If you have a qualifying child, attach Schedule EIC.	64a	**Earned income credit (EIC)**	64a		
	b	Nontaxable combat pay election	64b		
	65	Additional child tax credit. Attach Form 8812	65		
	66	American opportunity credit from Form 8863, line 14	66		
	67	First-time homebuyer credit from Form 5405, line 10	67		
	68	Amount paid with request for extension to file	68		
	69	Excess social security and tier 1 RRTA tax withheld	69		
	70	Credit for federal tax on fuels. Attach Form 4136	70		
	71	Credits from Form: a ☐ 2439 b ☐ 8839 c ☐ 8801 d ☐ 8885	71		
	72	Add lines 62, 63, 64a, and 65 through 71. These are your **total payments** ▶		72	22,359
Refund	73	If line 72 is more than line 61, subtract line 61 from line 72. This is the amount you **overpaid**		73	1,487
	74a	Amount of line 73 you want **refunded to you.** If Form 8888 is attached, check here ▶ ☐		74a	1,487
Direct deposit? See instructions.	b	Routing number		▶ c Type: ☐ Checking ☐ Savings	
	d	Account number			
	75	Amount of line 73 you want **applied to your 20yx estimated tax** ▶	75		
Amount You Owe	76	**Amount you owe.** Subtract line 72 from line 61. For details on how to pay, see instructions ▶		76	
	77	Estimated tax penalty (see instructions)	77		
Third Party Designee	Do you want to allow another person to discuss this return with the IRS (see instructions)? ☐ **Yes.** Complete below. ☐ **No**				
	Designee's name ▶	Phone no. ▶	Personal identification number (PIN) ▶		

Sign Here

Under penalties of perjury, I declare that I have examined this return and accompanying schedules and statements, and to the best of my knowledge and belief, they are true, correct, and complete. Declaration of preparer (other than taxpayer) is based on all information of which preparer has any knowledge.

Joint return? See instructions.
Keep a copy for your records.

Your signature	Date	Your occupation	Daytime phone number
		engineer	612-617-9526
Spouse's signature. If a joint return, **both** must sign.	Date	Spouse's occupation	If the IRS sent you an Identity Protection PIN, enter it here (see inst.)
		consulting	

Paid Preparer Use Only

Print/Type preparer's name	Preparer's signature	Date	Check ☐ if self-employed	PTIN
Firm's name ▶			Firm's EIN ▶	
Firm's address ▶			Phone no.	

Form **1040** (2011)

SCHEDULE A (Form 1040)		**Itemized Deductions**		OMB No. 1545-0074	
Department of the Treasury Internal Revenue Service (99)		▶ Attach to Form 1040. ▶ See Instructions for Schedule A (Form 1040).		**20XZ** Attachment Sequence No. 07	
Name(s) shown on Form 1040 Edward G. and Linda C. Dezine				Your social security number 234-55-6677	

Section	#	Description		Amount	Total
Medical and Dental Expenses		Caution. Do not include expenses reimbursed or paid by others.			
	1	Medical and dental expenses (see instructions)	1	1,318	
	2	Enter amount from Form 1040, line 38	2	178,318	
	3	Multiply line 2 by 7.5% (.075)	3	13,374	
	4	Subtract line 3 from line 1. If line 3 is more than line 1, enter -0-			4 0
Taxes You Paid	5	State and local (check only one box):			
		a ☑ Income taxes, or			
		b ☐ General sales taxes	5	8,866	
	6	Real estate taxes (see instructions)	6	3,221	
	7	Personal property taxes	7	188	
	8	Other taxes. List type and amount ▶	8		
	9	Add lines 5 through 8			9 12,275
Interest You Paid	10	Home mortgage interest and points reported to you on Form 1098	10	29,410	
	11	Home mortgage interest not reported to you on Form 1098. If paid to the person from whom you bought the home, see instructions and show that person's name, identifying no., and address ▶	11		
Note. Your mortgage interest deduction may be limited (see instructions).	12	Points not reported to you on Form 1098. See instructions for special rules	12		
	13	Mortgage insurance premiums (see instructions)	13		
	14	Investment interest. Attach Form 4952 if required. (See instructions.)	14		
	15	Add lines 10 through 14			15 29,410
Gifts to Charity	16	Gifts by cash or check. If you made any gift of $250 or more, see instructions	16	30,530	
If you made a gift and got a benefit for it, see instructions.	17	Other than by cash or check. If any gift of $250 or more, see instructions. You must attach Form 8283 if over $500	17	500	
	18	Carryover from prior year	18		
	19	Add lines 16 through 18			19 31,030
Casualty and Theft Losses	20	Casualty or theft loss(es). Attach Form 4684. (See instructions.)			20
Job Expenses and Certain Miscellaneous Deductions	21	Unreimbursed employee expenses—job travel, union dues, job education, etc. Attach Form 2106 or 2106-EZ if required. (See instructions.) ▶	21		
	22	Tax preparation fees	22	250	
	23	Other expenses—investment, safe deposit box, etc. List type and amount ▶	23	105	
	24	Add lines 21 through 23	24	355	
	25	Enter amount from Form 1040, line 38	25	178,318	
	26	Multiply line 25 by 2% (.02)	26	3,566	
	27	Subtract line 26 from line 24. If line 26 is more than line 24, enter -0-			27 0
Other Miscellaneous Deductions	28	Other—from list in instructions. List type and amount ▶			28
Total Itemized Deductions	29	Add the amounts in the far right column for lines 4 through 28. Also, enter this amount on Form 1040, line 40			29 72,119
	30	If you elect to itemize deductions even though they are less than your standard deduction, check here ▶ ☐			

For Paperwork Reduction Act Notice, see Form 1040 instructions.   Cat. No. 17145C   Schedule A (Form 1040) 2011

SCHEDULE B
(Form 1040A or 1040)

Department of the Treasury
Internal Revenue Service (99)

Interest and Ordinary Dividends

▶ Attach to Form 1040A or 1040.   ▶ See instructions on back.

OMB No. 1545-0074

20XZ

Attachment Sequence No. **08**

Name(s) shown on return: Edward G. and Linda C. Dezine

Your social security number: 234-55-6677

Part I — Interest

(See instructions on back and the instructions for Form 1040A, or Form 1040, line 8a.)

Note. If you received a Form 1099-INT, Form 1099-OID, or substitute statement from a brokerage firm, list the firm's name as the payer and enter the total interest shown on that form.

		Amount
1	List name of payer. If any interest is from a seller-financed mortgage and the buyer used the property as a personal residence, see instructions on back and list this interest first. Also, show that buyer's social security number and address ▶	
	Your Bank	2,428
2	Add the amounts on line 1	2,428
3	Excludable interest on series EE and I U.S. savings bonds issued after 1989. Attach Form 8815	
4	Subtract line 3 from line 2. Enter the result here and on Form 1040A, or Form 1040, line 8a ▶	2,428

Note. If line 4 is over $1,500, you must complete Part III.

Part II — Ordinary Dividends

(See instructions on back and the instructions for Form 1040A, or Form 1040, line 9a.)

Note. If you received a Form 1099-DIV or substitute statement from a brokerage firm, list the firm's name as the payer and enter the ordinary dividends shown on that form.

		Amount
5	List name of payer ▶	
	National Fund	8
6	Add the amounts on line 5. Enter the total here and on Form 1040A, or Form 1040, line 9a ▶	8

Note. If line 6 is over $1,500, you must complete Part III.

Part III — Foreign Accounts and Trusts

(See instructions on back.)

You must complete this part if you **(a)** had over $1,500 of taxable interest or ordinary dividends; **(b)** had a foreign account; or **(c)** received a distribution from, or were a grantor of, or a transferor to, a foreign trust.

		Yes	No
7a	At any time during 2011, did you have a financial interest in or signature authority over a financial account (such as a bank account, securities account, or brokerage account) located in a foreign country? See instructions		✓
	If "Yes," are you required to file Form TD F 90-22.1 to report that financial interest or signature authority? See Form TD F 90-22.1 and its instructions for filing requirements and exceptions to those requirements		
b	If you are required to file Form TD F 90-22.1, enter the name of the foreign country where the financial account is located ▶		
8	During 2011, did you receive a distribution from, or were you the grantor of, or transferor to, a foreign trust? If "Yes," you may have to file Form 3520. See instructions on back		✓

For Paperwork Reduction Act Notice, see your tax return instructions.   Cat. No. 17146N   Schedule B (Form 1040A or 1040) 2011

SCHEDULE C (Form 1040)

Department of the Treasury
Internal Revenue Service (99)

Profit or Loss From Business
(Sole Proprietorship)

▶ For information on Schedule C and its instructions, go to *www.irs.gov/schedulec*
▶ Attach to Form 1040, 1040NR, or 1041; partnerships generally must file Form 1065.

OMB No. 1545-0074

20XZ

Attachment Sequence No. 09

Name of proprietor: Linda C. Dezine

Social security number (SSN): 123-45-6789

A Principal business or profession, including product or service (see instructions)
consulting and teaching

B Enter code from instructions ▶ 6 1 1 0 0 0

C Business name. If no separate business name, leave blank.

D Employer ID number (EIN), (see instr.)

E Business address (including suite or room no.) ▶ 9425 Norwood Ave.
City, town or post office, state, and ZIP code   Hometown, MN

F Accounting method: (1) ☑ Cash (2) ☐ Accrual (3) ☐ Other (specify) ▶

G Did you "materially participate" in the operation of this business during 2011? If "No," see instructions for limit on losses ☑ Yes ☐ No

H If you started or acquired this business during 2011, check here ▶ ☐

I Did you make any payments in 2011 that would require you to file Form(s) 1099? (see instructions) ☐ Yes ☑ No

J If "Yes," did you or will you file all required Forms 1099? ☐ Yes ☐ No

Part I Income

1a	Merchant card and third party payments. For 2011, enter -0-	1a	
b	Gross receipts or sales not entered on line 1a (see instructions)	1b	39,587
c	Income reported to you on Form W-2 if the "Statutory Employee" box on that form was checked. **Caution.** See instr. before completing this line	1c	
d	**Total gross receipts.** Add lines 1a through 1c	1d	39,587
2	Returns and allowances plus any other adjustments (see instructions)	2	
3	Subtract line 2 from line 1d	3	
4	Cost of goods sold (from line 42)	4	
5	**Gross profit.** Subtract line 4 from line 3	5	
6	Other income, including federal and state gasoline or fuel tax credit or refund (see instructions)	6	
7	**Gross income.** Add lines 5 and 6 ▶	7	

Part II Expenses   Enter expenses for business use of your home only on line 30.

8	Advertising	8		18	Office expense (see instructions)	18	69
9	Car and truck expenses (see instructions)	9		19	Pension and profit-sharing plans	19	
10	Commissions and fees	10		20	Rent or lease (see instructions):		
11	Contract labor (see instructions)	11		a	Vehicles, machinery, and equipment	20a	
12	Depletion	12		b	Other business property	20b	
13	Depreciation and section 179 expense deduction (not included in Part III) (see instructions)	13		21	Repairs and maintenance	21	
				22	Supplies (not included in Part III)	22	
				23	Taxes and licenses	23	
				24	Travel, meals, and entertainment:		
14	Employee benefit programs (other than on line 19)	14		a	Travel	24a	
15	Insurance (other than health)	15		b	Deductible meals and entertainment (see instructions)	24b	
16	Interest:			25	Utilities	25	
a	Mortgage (paid to banks, etc.)	16a		26	Wages (less employment credits)	26	
b	Other	16b		27a	Other expenses (from line 48)	27a	
17	Legal and professional services	17		b	Reserved for future use	27b	
28	**Total expenses** before expenses for business use of home. Add lines 8 through 27a ▶					28	69
29	Tentative profit or (loss). Subtract line 28 from line 7					29	39,518
30	Expenses for business use of your home. Attach **Form 8829.** Do **not** report such expenses elsewhere					30	
31	Net profit or (loss). Subtract line 30 from line 29.						
	• If a profit, enter on both **Form 1040, line 12** (or **Form 1040NR, line 13**) and on **Schedule SE, line 2.** If you entered an amount on line 1c, see instr. Estates and trusts, enter on **Form 1041, line 3.**					31	39,518
	• If a loss, you **must** go to line 32.						
32	If you have a loss, check the box that describes your investment in this activity (see instructions).						
	• If you checked 32a, enter the loss on both **Form 1040, line 12,** (or **Form 1040NR, line 13**) and on **Schedule SE, line 2.** If you entered an amount on line 1c, see the instructions for line 31. Estates and trusts, enter on **Form 1041, line 3.**					32a ☐ All investment is at risk. 32b ☐ Some investment is not at risk.	
	• If you checked 32b, you **must** attach **Form 6198.** Your loss may be limited.						

For Paperwork Reduction Act Notice, see your tax return instructions.   Cat. No. 11334P   Schedule C (Form 1040) 2011

Schedule C (Form 1040) 20xz   Page **2**

Part III Cost of Goods Sold (see instructions)

33   Method(s) used to
     value closing inventory: **a** ☐ Cost   **b** ☐ Lower of cost or market   **c** ☐ Other (attach explanation)

34   Was there any change in determining quantities, costs, or valuations between opening and closing inventory?
     If "Yes," attach explanation . . . .   ☐ Yes   ☐ No

35	Inventory at beginning of year. If different from last year's closing inventory, attach explanation	35
36	Purchases less cost of items withdrawn for personal use	36
37	Cost of labor. Do not include any amounts paid to yourself	37
38	Materials and supplies	38
39	Other costs	39
40	Add lines 35 through 39	40
41	Inventory at end of year	41
42	**Cost of goods sold.** Subtract line 41 from line 40. Enter the result here and on line 4	42

Part IV Information on Your Vehicle. Complete this part **only** if you are claiming car or truck expenses on line 9 and are not required to file Form 4562 for this business. See the instructions for line 13 to find out if you must file Form 4562.

43   When did you place your vehicle in service for business purposes? (month, day, year) ▶ ____/____/____

44   Of the total number of miles you drove your vehicle during 20xz, enter the number of miles you used your vehicle for:

     a Business _____   **b** Commuting (see instructions) _____   **c** Other _____

45   Was your vehicle available for personal use during off-duty hours? . . . . ☐ Yes   ☐ No

46   Do you (or your spouse) have another vehicle available for personal use? . . . . ☐ Yes   ☐ No

47a Do you have evidence to support your deduction? . . . . ☐ Yes   ☐ No

  b If "Yes," is the evidence written? . . . . ☐ Yes   ☐ No

Part V Other Expenses. List below business expenses not included on lines 8–26 or line 30.

----------------------------------		
48 **Total other expenses.** Enter here and on line 27a	48	

Schedule C (Form 1040) 2011

SCHEDULE D (Form 1040)	Capital Gains and Losses	OMB No. 1545-0074
Department of the Treasury Internal Revenue Service (99)	▶ Attach to Form 1040 or Form 1040NR. ▶ See Instructions for Schedule D (Form 1040). ▶ Use Form 8949 to list your transactions for lines 1, 2, 3, 8, 9, and 10.	20XZ Attachment Sequence No. 12
Name(s) shown on return: Edward G. and Linda C. Dezine		Your social security number: 234-55-6677

Part I — Short-Term Capital Gains and Losses—Assets Held One Year or Less

Complete Form 8949 before completing line 1, 2, or 3. This form may be easier to complete if you round off cents to whole dollars.	(e) Sales price from Form(s) 8949, line 2, column (e)	(f) Cost or other basis from Form(s) 8949, line 2, column (f)	(g) Adjustments to gain or loss from Form(s) 8949, line 2, column (g)	(h) Gain or (loss) Combine columns (e), (f), and (g)
1 Short-term totals from all Forms 8949 with **box A** checked in **Part I**	9,728	(11,052)		(1,324)
2 Short-term totals from all Forms 8949 with **box B** checked in **Part I**		( )		
3 Short-term totals from all Forms 8949 with **box C** checked in **Part I**		( )		

4 Short-term gain from Form 6252 and short-term gain or (loss) from Forms 4684, 6781, and 8824	4	
5 Net short-term gain or (loss) from partnerships, S corporations, estates, and trusts from Schedule(s) K-1	5	
6 Short-term capital loss carryover. Enter the amount, if any, from line 8 of your **Capital Loss Carryover Worksheet** in the instructions	6	( )
7 **Net short-term capital gain or (loss).** Combine lines 1 through 6 in column (h). If you have any long-term capital gains or losses, go to Part II below. Otherwise, go to Part III on the back	7	(1,324)

Part II — Long-Term Capital Gains and Losses—Assets Held More Than One Year

Complete Form 8949 before completing line 8, 9, or 10. This form may be easier to complete if you round off cents to whole dollars.	(e) Sales price from Form(s) 8949, line 4, column (e)	(f) Cost or other basis from Form(s) 8949, line 4, column (f)	(g) Adjustments to gain or loss from Form(s) 8949, line 4, column (g)	(h) Gain or (loss) Combine columns (e), (f), and (g)
8 Long-term totals from all Forms 8949 with **box A** checked in **Part II**		( )		
9 Long-term totals from all Forms 8949 with **box B** checked in **Part II**		( )		
10 Long-term totals from all Forms 8949 with **box C** checked in **Part II**		( )		

11 Gain from Form 4797, Part I; long-term gain from Forms 2439 and 6252; and long-term gain or (loss) from Forms 4684, 6781, and 8824	11	
12 Net long-term gain or (loss) from partnerships, S corporations, estates, and trusts from Schedule(s) K-1	12	
13 Capital gain distributions. See the instructions	13	
14 Long-term capital loss carryover. Enter the amount, if any, from line 13 of your **Capital Loss Carryover Worksheet** in the instructions	14	( )
15 **Net long-term capital gain or (loss).** Combine lines 8 through 14 in column (h). Then go to Part III on the back	15	

For Paperwork Reduction Act Notice, see your tax return instructions.   Cat. No. 11338H   Schedule D (Form 1040) 2011

Schedule D (Form 1040) 20xz Page 2

Part III Summary

16 Combine lines 7 and 15 and enter the result **16** (1,324)

- If line 16 is a **gain**, enter the amount from line 16 on Form 1040, line 13, or Form 1040NR, line 14. Then go to line 17 below.
- If line 16 is a **loss**, skip lines 17 through 20 below. Then go to line 21. Also be sure to complete line 22.
- If line 16 is **zero**, skip lines 17 through 21 below and enter -0- on Form 1040, line 13, or Form 1040NR, line 14. Then go to line 22.

17 Are lines 15 and 16 **both** gains?
☐ **Yes.** Go to line 18.
☐ **No.** Skip lines 18 through 21, and go to line 22.

18 Enter the amount, if any, from line 7 of the **28% Rate Gain Worksheet** in the instructions ▶ **18**

19 Enter the amount, if any, from line 18 of the **Unrecaptured Section 1250 Gain Worksheet** in the instructions . . . . ▶ **19**

20 Are lines 18 and 19 **both** zero or blank?
☐ **Yes.** Complete Form 1040 through line 43, or Form 1040NR through line 41. Then complete the **Qualified Dividends and Capital Gain Tax Worksheet** in the instructions for Form 1040, line 44 (or in the instructions for Form 1040NR, line 42). **Do not** complete lines 21 and 22 below.

☐ **No.** Complete Form 1040 through line 43, or Form 1040NR through line 41. Then complete the **Schedule D Tax Worksheet** in the instructions. **Do not** complete lines 21 and 22 below.

21 If line 16 is a loss, enter here and on Form 1040, line 13, or Form 1040NR, line 14, the **smaller** of:
- The loss on line 16 or
- ($3,000), or if married filing separately, ($1,500) **21** (1,324)

Note. When figuring which amount is smaller, treat both amounts as positive numbers.

22 Do you have qualified dividends on Form 1040, line 9b, or Form 1040NR, line 10b?

☐ **Yes.** Complete Form 1040 through line 43, or Form 1040NR through line 41. Then complete the **Qualified Dividends and Capital Gain Tax Worksheet** in the instructions for Form 1040, line 44 (or in the instructions for Form 1040NR, line 42).
☑ **No.** Complete the rest of Form 1040 or Form 1040NR.

Schedule D (Form 1040) 2011

Form 8949 — Sales and Other Dispositions of Capital Assets

Form 8949
Department of the Treasury
Internal Revenue Service (99)

▶ See Instructions for Schedule D (Form 1040).
▶ For more information about Form 8949, see www.irs.gov/form8949
▶ Attach to Schedule D to list your transactions for lines 1, 2, 3, 8, 9, and 10.

OMB No. 1545-0074
20XZ
Attachment Sequence No. **12A**

Name(s) shown on return: Edward G. and Linda C. Dezine
Your social security number: 234-55-6677

Part I — Short-Term Capital Gains and Losses—Assets Held One Year or Less

Note: You **must** check **one** of the boxes below. Complete a *separate* Form 8949, page 1, for **each** box that is checked.

*****Caution.** Do not complete column (b) or (g) until you have read the instructions for those columns (see the Instructions for Schedule D (Form 1040)). Columns (b) and (g) do not apply for most transactions and should generally be left blank.

- ☑ **(A)** Short-term transactions reported on Form 1099-B with basis reported to the IRS
- ☐ **(B)** Short-term transactions reported on Form 1099-B but basis not reported to the IRS
- ☐ **(C)** Short-term transactions for which you cannot check box A or B

1	(a) Description of property (Example: 100 sh. XYZ Co.)	(b) Code, if any, for column (g)*	(c) Date acquired (Mo., day, yr.)	(d) Date sold (Mo., day, yr.)	(e) Sales price (see instructions)	(f) Cost or other basis (see instructions)	(g) Adjustments to gain or loss, if any*
	330 shares National Fund		06/01/xy	02/01/xz	9,728	11,052	

| 2 | **Totals.** Add the amounts in columns (e) and (f). Also, combine the amounts in column (g). Enter here and include on Schedule D, **line 1** (if **box A** above is checked), **line 2** (if **box B** above is checked), or **line 3** (if **box C** above is checked). ▶ | | | | 9,728 | 11,052 | (1,324) |

For Paperwork Reduction Act Notice, see your tax return instructions. Cat. No. 37768Z Form **8949** (2011)

Form 8949 (20xz)   Attachment Sequence No. **12A**   Page **2**

Name(s) shown on return. Do not enter name and social security number if shown on other side. | Your social security number

Part II   Long-Term Capital Gains and Losses—Assets Held More Than One Year

Note: You **must** check **one** of the boxes below. Complete a *separate* Form 8949, page 2, for **each** box that is checked.

*Caution. Do not complete column (b) or (g) until you have read the instructions for those columns (see the Instructions for Schedule D (Form 1040)). Columns (b) and (g) do not apply for most transactions and should generally be left blank.

☐ **(A)** Long-term transactions reported on Form 1099-B with basis reported to the IRS
☐ **(B)** Long-term transactions reported on Form 1099-B but basis not reported to the IRS
☐ **(C)** Long-term transactions for which you cannot check box A or B

3	(a) Description of property (Example: 100 sh. XYZ Co.)	(b) Code, if any, for column (g)*	(c) Date acquired (Mo., day, yr.)	(d) Date sold (Mo., day, yr.)	(e) Sales price (see instructions)	(f) Cost or other basis (see instructions)	(g) Adjustments to gain or loss, if any*

| 4 | **Totals.** Add the amounts in columns (e) and (f). Also, combine the amounts in column (g). Enter here and include on Schedule D, **line 8** (if **box A** above is checked), **line 9** (if **box B** above is checked), or **line 10** (if **box C** above is checked) ▶ | 4 | | | |

Form **8949** (2011)

SCHEDULE E (Form 1040)	**Supplemental Income and Loss**	OMB No. 1545-0074
Department of the Treasury Internal Revenue Service (99)	(From rental real estate, royalties, partnerships, S corporations, estates, trusts, REMICs, etc.) ▶ Attach to Form 1040, 1040NR, or Form 1041. ▶ See separate instructions.	20XZ Attachment Sequence No. **13**
Name(s) shown on return Edward G. and Linda C. Dezine		Your social security number 234-55-6677

A Did you make any payments in 20xz that would require you to file Form(s) 1099? (see instructions) ☐ Yes ☑ No
B If "Yes," did you or will you file all required Forms 1099? ☐ Yes ☐ No

Part I   Income or Loss From Rental Real Estate and Royalties Note. If you are in the business of renting personal property, use Schedule **C** or **C-EZ** (see instructions). If you are an individual, report farm rental income or loss from **Form 4835** on page 2, line 40.

Caution. For each rental property listed on line 1, check the box in the last column only if you owned that property as a member of a qualified joint venture (QJV) reporting income not subject to self-employment tax.

1	Physical address of each property–street, city, state, zip	Type-from list below	2	For each rental real estate property listed, report the number of days rented at fair rental value and days with personal use. See instructions.		Fair Rental Days	Personal Use Days	QJV
A					A			
B					B			
C					C			

Type of Property:
1 Single Family Residence   3 Vacation/Short-Term Rental   5 Land   7 Self-Rental
2 Multi-Family Residence   4 Commercial   6 Royalties   8 Other (describe)

			Properties		
			A	B	C
Income:					
3a	Merchant card and third party payments. For 20xz, enter -0-	3a			
b	Payments not reported to you on line 3a	3b			
4	Total not including amounts on line 3a that are not income (see instructions)	4			
Expenses:					
5	Advertising	5			
6	Auto and travel (see instructions)	6			
7	Cleaning and maintenance	7			
8	Commissions	8			
9	Insurance	9			
10	Legal and other professional fees	10			
11	Management fees	11			
12	Mortgage interest paid to banks, etc. (see instructions)	12			
13	Other interest	13			
14	Repairs	14			
15	Supplies	15			
16	Taxes	16			
17	Utilities	17			
18	Depreciation expense or depletion	18			
19	Other (list) ▶	19			
20	Total expenses. Add lines 5 through 19	20			
21	Subtract line 20 from line 4. If result is a (loss), see instructions to find out if you must file **Form 6198**	21			
22	Deductible rental real estate loss after limitation, if any, on **Form 8582** (see instructions)	22	( )	( )	( )
23a	Total of all amounts reported on line 3a for all rental properties		23a		
b	Total of all amounts reported on line 3a for all royalty properties		23b		
c	Total of all amounts reported on line 4 for all rental properties		23c		
d	Total of all amounts reported on line 4 for all royalty properties		23d		
e	Total of all amounts reported on line 12 for all properties		23e		
f	Total of all amounts reported on line 18 for all properties		23f		
g	Total of all amounts reported on line 20 for all properties		23g		
24	**Income.** Add positive amounts shown on line 21. **Do not** include any losses			24	
25	**Losses.** Add royalty losses from line 21 and rental real estate losses from line 22. Enter total losses here			25	( )
26	**Total rental real estate and royalty income or (loss).** Combine lines 24 and 25. Enter the result here. If Parts II, III, IV, and line 40 on page 2 do not apply to you, also enter this amount on Form 1040, line 17, or Form 1040NR, line 18. Otherwise, include this amount in the total on line 41 on page 2			26	

For Paperwork Reduction Act Notice, see your tax return instructions.   Cat. No. 11344L   Schedule E (Form 1040) 2011

Schedule E (Form 1040) 20xz Attachment Sequence No. 13 Page 2
Name(s) shown on return. Do not enter name and social security number if shown on other side. Your social security number

Caution. The IRS compares amounts reported on your tax return with amounts shown on Schedule(s) K-1.

Part II — Income or Loss From Partnerships and S Corporations
Note. If you report a loss from an at-risk activity for which any amount is **not** at risk, you **must** check the box in column (e) on line 28 and attach **Form 6198**. See instructions.

27 Are you reporting any loss not allowed in a prior year due to the at-risk or basis limitations, a prior year unallowed loss from a passive activity (if that loss was not reported on Form 8582), or unreimbursed partnership expenses? If you answered "Yes," see instructions before completing this section. ☐ Yes ☐ No

28

(a) Name	(b) Enter P for partnership; S for S corporation	(c) Check if foreign partnership	(d) Employer identification number	(e) Check if any amount is not at risk
A Designs by Dezine, Inc.	S	☐	41-1234567	☐
B		☐		☐
C		☐		☐
D		☐		☐

	Passive Income and Loss		Nonpassive Income and Loss		
	(f) Passive loss allowed (attach Form 8582 if required)	(g) Passive income from Schedule K-1	(h) Nonpassive loss from Schedule K-1	(i) Section 179 expense deduction from Form 4562	(j) Nonpassive income from Schedule K-1
A			26,031		
B					
C					
D					
29a Totals					
b Totals			26,031		

30 Add columns (g) and (j) of line 29a **30**
31 Add columns (f), (h), and (i) of line 29b **31** (26,031)
32 **Total partnership and S corporation income or (loss).** Combine lines 30 and 31. Enter the result here and include in the total on line 41 below **32** (26,031)

Part III — Income or Loss From Estates and Trusts

33

(a) Name	(b) Employer identification number
A	
B	

	Passive Income and Loss		Nonpassive Income and Loss	
	(c) Passive deduction or loss allowed (attach Form 8582 if required)	(d) Passive income from Schedule K-1	(e) Deduction or loss from Schedule K-1	(f) Other income from Schedule K-1
A				
B				
34a Totals				
b Totals				

35 Add columns (d) and (f) of line 34a **35**
36 Add columns (c) and (e) of line 34b . . . . **36** ( )
37 **Total estate and trust income or (loss).** Combine lines 35 and 36. Enter the result here and include in the total on line 41 below **37**

Part IV — Income or Loss From Real Estate Mortgage Investment Conduits (REMICs) — Residual Holder

38

(a) Name	(b) Employer identification number	(c) Excess inclusion from Schedules Q, line 2c (see instructions)	(d) Taxable income (net loss) from Schedules Q, line 1b	(e) Income from Schedules Q, line 3b

39 Combine columns (d) and (e) only. Enter the result here and include in the total on line 41 below . . **39**

Part V — Summary

40 Net farm rental income or (loss) from **Form 4835**. Also, complete line 42 below **40**
41 **Total income or (loss).** Combine lines 26, 32, 37, 39, and 40. Enter the result here and on Form 1040, line 17, or Form 1040NR, line 18 ▶ **41** (26,031)
42 **Reconciliation of farming and fishing income.** Enter your **gross** farming and fishing income reported on Form 4835, line 7; Schedule K-1 (Form 1065), box 14, code B; Schedule K-1 (Form 1120S), box 17, code U; and Schedule K-1 (Form 1041), line 14, code F (see instructions) . . **42**
43 **Reconciliation for real estate professionals.** If you were a real estate professional (see instructions), enter the net income or (loss) you reported anywhere on Form 1040 or Form 1040NR from all rental real estate activities in which you materially participated under the passive activity loss rules . . **43**

Schedule E (Form 1040) 2011

American Bankers Association — *Personal Tax Returns and Cash Flow* 385

SCHEDULE SE
(Form 1040)

Department of the Treasury
Internal Revenue Service (99)

▶ Attach to Form 1040 or Form 1040NR.   ▶ See separate instructions.

Self-Employment Tax

OMB No. 1545-0074

20**XZ**

Attachment Sequence No. **17**

Name of person with **self-employment** income (as shown on Form 1040)
Linda C. Dezine

Social security number of person with **self-employment** income ▶ 123-45-6789

Before you begin: To determine if you must file Schedule SE, see the instructions.

May I Use Short Schedule SE or Must I Use Long Schedule SE?

Note. Use this flowchart **only if** you must file Schedule SE. If unsure, see *Who Must File Schedule SE* in the instructions.

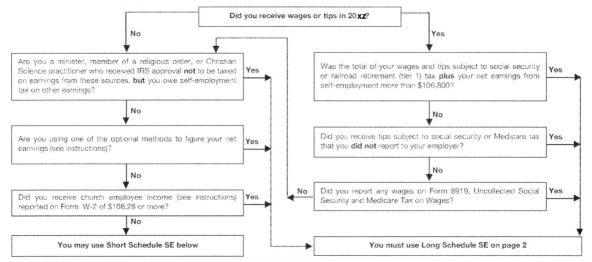

Section A—Short Schedule SE. Caution. Read above to see if you can use Short Schedule SE.

1a	Net farm profit or (loss) from Schedule F, line 34, and farm partnerships, Schedule K-1 (Form 1065), box 14, code A	**1a**	
b	If you received social security retirement or disability benefits, enter the amount of Conservation Reserve Program payments included on Schedule F, line 4b, or listed on Schedule K-1 (Form 1065), box 20, code Y	**1b**	( )
2	Net profit or (loss) from Schedule C, line 31; Schedule C-EZ, line 3; Schedule K-1 (Form 1065), box 14, code A (other than farming); and Schedule K-1 (Form 1065-B), box 9, code J1. Ministers and members of religious orders, see instructions for types of income to report on this line. See instructions for other income to report	**2**	39,518
3	Combine lines 1a, 1b, and 2	**3**	39,518
4	Multiply line 3 by 92.35% (.9235). If less than $400, you do not owe self-employment tax; **do not** file this schedule unless you have an amount on line 1b ▶	**4**	36,495
	Note. If line 4 is less than $400 due to Conservation Reserve Program payments on line 1b, see instructions.		
5	**Self-employment tax.** If the amount on line 4 is: • $106,800 or less, multiply line 4 by 13.3% (.133). Enter the result here and on **Form 1040, line 56,** or **Form 1040NR, line 54** • More than $106,800, multiply line 4 by 2.9% (.029). Then, add $11,107.20 to the result. Enter the total here and on **Form 1040, line 56,** or **Form 1040NR, line 54**	**5**	4,853
6	**Deduction for employer-equivalent portion of self-employment tax.** If the amount on line 5 is: • $14,204.40 or less, multiply line 5 by 57.51% (.5751) • More than $14,204.40, multiply line 5 by 50% (.50) and add $1,067 to the result. Enter the result here and on **Form 1040, line 27,** or **Form 1040NR, line 27**	**6**	2,791

For Paperwork Reduction Act Notice, see your tax return instructions.   Cat. No. 11358Z   Schedule SE (Form 1040) 2011

Schedule K-1
(Form 1120S)
Department of the Treasury
Internal Revenue Service

For calendar year 20**xz**, or tax year beginning _____, 20**xz** ending _____, 20 _____

20 **XZ**

☐ Final K-1 ☐ Amended K-1   OMB No. 1545-0130

671111

Shareholder's Share of Income, Deductions, Credits, etc.
▶ See back of form and separate instructions.

Part I — Information About the Corporation

A Corporation's employer identification number
41-1234567

B Corporation's name, address, city, state, and ZIP code

Designs by Dezine, Inc.
9425 Norwood Avenue
Hometown, MN

C IRS Center where corporation filed return
Ogden, UT

Part II — Information About the Shareholder

D Shareholder's identifying number
234-55-6677

E Shareholder's name, address, city, state, and ZIP code

Linda C. Dezine
9425 Norwood Avenue
Hometown, MN

F Shareholder's percentage of stock ownership for tax year . . . . _____100_____ %

Part III — Shareholder's Share of Current Year Income, Deductions, Credits, and Other Items

#	Item	Amount	#	Item
1	Ordinary business income (loss)	(26,031)	13	Credits
2	Net rental real estate income (loss)			
3	Other net rental income (loss)			
4	Interest income			
5a	Ordinary dividends			
5b	Qualified dividends		14	Foreign transactions
6	Royalties			
7	Net short-term capital gain (loss)			
8a	Net long-term capital gain (loss)			
8b	Collectibles (28%) gain (loss)			
8c	Unrecaptured section 1250 gain			
9	Net section 1231 gain (loss)			
10	Other income (loss)		15	Alternative minimum tax (AMT) items
11	Section 179 deduction		16	Items affecting shareholder basis
12	Other deductions			
			17	Other information

* See attached statement for additional information.

For Paperwork Reduction Act Notice, see Instructions for Form 1120S.   Cat. No. 11520D   Schedule K-1 (Form 1120S) 2011

Schedule K-1 (Form 1120S) 20 xz

This list identifies the codes used on Schedule K-1 for all shareholders and provides summarized reporting information for shareholders who file Form 1040. For detailed reporting and filing information, see the separate Shareholder's Instructions for Schedule K-1 and the instructions for your income tax return.

1. **Ordinary business income (loss).** Determine whether the income (loss) is passive or nonpassive and enter on your return as follows:

	Report on
Passive loss	See the Shareholder's Instructions
Passive income	Schedule E, line 28, column (g)
Nonpassive loss	Schedule E, line 28, column (h)
Nonpassive income	Schedule E, line 28, column (j)

2. **Net rental real estate income (loss)** — See the Shareholder's Instructions
3. **Other net rental income (loss)**
    - Net income — Schedule E, line 28, column (g)
    - Net loss — See the Shareholder's Instructions
4. **Interest income** — Form 1040, line 8a
5a. **Ordinary dividends** — Form 1040, line 9a
5b. **Qualified dividends** — Form 1040, line 9b
6. **Royalties** — Schedule E, line 3b
7. **Net short-term capital gain (loss)** — Schedule D, line 5
8a. **Net long-term capital gain (loss)** — Schedule D, line 12
8b. **Collectibles (28%) gain (loss)** — 28% Rate Gain Worksheet, line 4 (Schedule D instructions)
8c. **Unrecaptured section 1250 gain** — See the Shareholder's Instructions
9. **Net section 1231 gain (loss)** — See the Shareholder's Instructions
10. **Other income (loss)**

Code		
A	Other portfolio income (loss)	See the Shareholder's Instructions
B	Involuntary conversions	See the Shareholder's Instructions
C	Sec. 1256 contracts & straddles	Form 6781, line 1
D	Mining exploration costs recapture	See Pub. 535
E	Other income (loss)	See the Shareholder's Instructions

11. **Section 179 deduction** — See the Shareholder's Instructions
12. **Other deductions**

Code		
A	Cash contributions (50%)	
B	Cash contributions (30%)	
C	Noncash contributions (50%)	
D	Noncash contributions (30%)	See the Shareholder's Instructions
E	Capital gain property to a 50% organization (30%)	
F	Capital gain property (20%)	
G	Contributions (100%)	
H	Investment interest expense	Form 4952, line 1
I	Deductions—royalty income	Schedule E, line 19
J	Section 59(e)(2) expenditures	See the Shareholder's Instructions
K	Deductions—portfolio (2% floor)	Schedule A, line 23
L	Deductions—portfolio (other)	Schedule A, line 28
M	Preproductive period expenses	See the Shareholder's Instructions
N	Commercial revitalization deduction from rental real estate activities	See Form 8582 instructions
O	Reforestation expense deduction	See the Shareholder's Instructions
P	Domestic production activities information	See Form 8903 instructions
Q	Qualified production activities income	Form 8903, line 7b
R	Employer's Form W-2 wages	Form 8903, line 17
S	Other deductions	See the Shareholder's Instructions

13. **Credits**

Code		
A	Low-income housing credit (section 42(j)(5)) from pre-2008 buildings	
B	Low-income housing credit (other) from pre-2008 buildings	
C	Low-income housing credit (section 42(j)(5)) from post-2007 buildings	
D	Low-income housing credit (other) from post-2007 buildings	See the Shareholder's Instructions
E	Qualified rehabilitation expenditures (rental real estate)	
F	Other rental real estate credits	
G	Other rental credits	
H	Undistributed capital gains credit	Form 1040, line 71, box a
I	Alcohol and cellulosic biofuel fuels credit	
J	Work opportunity credit	See the Shareholder's Instructions
K	Disabled access credit	
L	Empowerment zone and renewal community employment credit	

Code		Report on
M	Credit for increasing research activities	See the Shareholder's Instructions
N	Credit for employer social security and Medicare taxes	See the Shareholder's Instructions
O	Backup withholding	Form 1040, line 62
P	Other credits	See the Shareholder's Instructions

14. **Foreign transactions**

A	Name of country or U.S. possession	
B	Gross income from all sources	Form 1116, Part I
C	Gross income sourced at shareholder level	

    Foreign gross income sourced at corporate level

D	Passive category	
E	General category	Form 1116, Part I
F	Other	

    Deductions allocated and apportioned at shareholder level

G	Interest expense	Form 1116, Part I
H	Other	Form 1116, Part I

    Deductions allocated and apportioned at corporate level to foreign source income

I	Passive category	
J	General category	Form 1116, Part I
K	Other	

    Other information

L	Total foreign taxes paid	Form 1116, Part II
M	Total foreign taxes accrued	Form 1116, Part II
N	Reduction in taxes available for credit	Form 1116, line 12
O	Foreign trading gross receipts	Form 8873
P	Extraterritorial income exclusion	Form 8873
Q	Other foreign transactions	See the Shareholder's Instructions

15. **Alternative minimum tax (AMT) items**

A	Post-1986 depreciation adjustment	
B	Adjusted gain or loss	See the Shareholder's Instructions and the Instructions for Form 6251
C	Depletion (other than oil & gas)	
D	Oil, gas, & geothermal—gross income	
E	Oil, gas, & geothermal—deductions	
F	Other AMT items	

16. **Items affecting shareholder basis**

A	Tax-exempt interest income	Form 1040, line 8b
B	Other tax-exempt income	
C	Nondeductible expenses	See the Shareholder's Instructions
D	Distributions	
E	Repayment of loans from shareholders	

17. **Other information**

A	Investment income	Form 4952, line 4a
B	Investment expenses	Form 4952, line 5
C	Qualified rehabilitation expenditures (other than rental real estate)	See the Shareholder's Instructions
D	Basis of energy property	See the Shareholder's Instructions
E	Recapture of low-income housing credit (section 42(j)(5))	Form 8611, line 8
F	Recapture of low-income housing credit (other)	Form 8611, line 8
G	Recapture of investment credit	See Form 4255
H	Recapture of other credits	See the Shareholder's Instructions
I	Look-back interest—completed long-term contracts	See Form 8697
J	Look-back interest—income forecast method	See Form 8866
K	Dispositions of property with section 179 deductions	
L	Recapture of section 179 deduction	
M	Section 453(l)(3) information	
N	Section 453A(c) information	
O	Section 1260(b) information	
P	Interest allocable to production expenditures	See the Shareholder's Instructions
Q	CCF nonqualified withdrawals	
R	Depletion information—oil and gas	
S	Amortization of reforestation costs	
T	Section 108(i) information	
U	Other information	

Form 1120S — U.S. Income Tax Return for an S Corporation

OMB No. 1545-0130

Department of the Treasury — Internal Revenue Service

20**XZ**

▶ Do not file this form unless the corporation has filed or is attaching Form 2553 to elect to be an S corporation.
▶ See separate instructions.

For calendar year 20xz or tax year beginning , 20xz, ending , 20

A S election effective date: 04/29/20xz
B Business activity code number (see instructions): 236110
C Check if Sch. M-3 attached ☐

Name: Designs by Dezine, Inc.
Number, street, and room or suite no. 9425 Norwood Avenue
City or town, state, and ZIP code: Hometown, MN

D Employer identification number: 41-1234567
E Date incorporated: 04/29/20xz
F Total assets (see instructions): $ 63,017

G Is the corporation electing to be an S corporation beginning with this tax year? ☐ Yes ☑ No If "Yes," attach Form 2553 if not already filed
H Check if: (1) ☐ Final return (2) ☐ Name change (3) ☐ Address change (4) ☐ Amended return (5) ☐ S election termination or revocation
I Enter the number of shareholders who were shareholders during any part of the tax year ▶ 1

Caution. Include **only** trade or business income and expenses on lines 1a through 21. See the instructions for more information.

Income

1a	Merchant card and third-party payments. For 20xz, enter -0-.	1a	
b	Gross receipts or sales not reported on line 1a (see instructions)	1b	384,332
c	Total. Add lines 1a and 1b	1c	384,332
d	Returns and allowances plus any other adjustments (see instructions)	1d	
e	Subtract line 1d from line 1c	1e	384,332
2	Cost of goods sold (attach Form 1125-A)	2	329,976
3	Gross profit. Subtract line 2 from line 1e	3	54,356
4	Net gain (loss) from Form 4797, Part II, line 17 (attach Form 4797)	4	
5	Other income (loss) (see instructions—attach statement)	5	
6	**Total income (loss).** Add lines 3 through 5 ▶	6	54,356

Deductions (see instructions for limitations)

7	Compensation of officers	7	42,700
8	Salaries and wages (less employment credits)	8	
9	Repairs and maintenance	9	
10	Bad debts	10	
11	Rents	11	786
12	Taxes and licenses	12	6,428
13	Interest	13	3,414
14	Depreciation not claimed on Form 1125-A or elsewhere on return (attach Form 4562)	14	11,866
15	Depletion (**Do not deduct oil and gas depletion.**)	15	
16	Advertising	16	592
17	Pension, profit-sharing, etc., plans	17	
18	Employee benefit programs	18	2,353
19	Other deductions (attach statement)	19	12,248
20	**Total deductions.** Add lines 7 through 19 ▶	20	80,387
21	**Ordinary business income (loss).** Subtract line 20 from line 6	21	(26,031)

Tax and Payments

22a	Excess net passive income or LIFO recapture tax (see instructions)	22a		
b	Tax from Schedule D (Form 1120S)	22b		
c	Add lines 22a and 22b (see instructions for additional taxes)		22c	
23a	2011 estimated tax payments and 2010 overpayment credited to 2011	23a		
b	Tax deposited with Form 7004	23b		
c	Credit for federal tax paid on fuels (attach Form 4136)	23c		
d	Add lines 23a through 23c		23d	
24	Estimated tax penalty (see instructions). Check if Form 2220 is attached ▶ ☐		24	
25	**Amount owed.** If line 23d is smaller than the total of lines 22c and 24, enter amount owed		25	
26	**Overpayment.** If line 23d is larger than the total of lines 22c and 24, enter amount overpaid		26	
27	Enter amount from line 26 **Credited to 2012 estimated tax** ▶ **Refunded** ▶		27	

Sign Here

Under penalties of perjury, I declare that I have examined this return, including accompanying schedules and statements, and to the best of my knowledge and belief, it is true, correct, and complete. Declaration of preparer (other than taxpayer) is based on all information of which preparer has any knowledge.

▶ Signature of officer   Date   ▶ Title

May the IRS discuss this return with the preparer shown below (see instructions)? ☐ Yes ☐ No

Paid Preparer Use Only

Print/Type preparer's name	Preparer's signature	Date	Check ☐ if self-employed	PTIN
Firm's name ▶			Firm's EIN ▶	
Firm's address ▶			Phone no.	

For Paperwork Reduction Act Notice, see separate instructions.   Cat. No. 11510H   Form **1120S** (2011)

Form 1120S (20xz) Page **2**

Schedule B — Other Information (see instructions)

		Yes	No
1	Check accounting method: **a** ☐ Cash **b** ☑ Accrual **c** ☐ Other (specify) ▶ _____		
2	See the instructions and enter the: **a** Business activity ▶ 236110 **b** Product or service ▶ residential remodeling		
3	At the end of the tax year, did the corporation own, directly or indirectly, 50% or more of the voting stock of a domestic corporation? (For rules of attribution, see section 267(c).) If "Yes," attach a statement showing: **(a)** name and employer identification number (EIN), **(b)** percentage owned, and **(c)** if 100% owned, was a qualified subchapter S subsidiary election made?		✓
4	Has this corporation filed, or is it required to file, **Form 8918**, Material Advisor Disclosure Statement, to provide information on any reportable transaction?		✓
5	Check this box if the corporation issued publicly offered debt instruments with original issue discount ▶ ☐ If checked, the corporation may have to file **Form 8281**, Information Return for Publicly Offered Original Issue Discount Instruments.		
6	If the corporation: **(a)** was a C corporation before it elected to be an S corporation **or** the corporation acquired an asset with a basis determined by reference to the basis of the asset (or the basis of any other property) in the hands of a C corporation **and (b)** has net unrealized built-in gain in excess of the net recognized built-in gain from prior years, enter the net unrealized built-in gain reduced by net recognized built-in gain from prior years (see instructions) ▶ $ _____		
7	Enter the accumulated earnings and profits of the corporation at the end of the tax year. $ (26,031)		
8	Are the corporation's total receipts (see instructions) for the tax year **and** its total assets at the end of the tax year less than $250,000? If "Yes," the corporation is not required to complete Schedules L and M-1		✓
9	During the tax year, was a qualified subchapter S subsidiary election terminated or revoked? If "Yes," see instructions		✓
10a	Did the corporation make any payments in 20xz that would require it to file Form(s) 1099 (see instructions)?		✓
b	If "Yes," did the corporation file or will it file all required Forms 1099?		

Schedule K — Shareholders' Pro Rata Share Items

			Total amount
	1	Ordinary business income (loss) (page 1, line 21)	**1** (26,031)
	2	Net rental real estate income (loss) (attach Form 8825)	**2**
	3a	Other gross rental income (loss) **3a**	
	b	Expenses from other rental activities (attach statement) . . **3b**	
	c	Other net rental income (loss). Subtract line 3b from line 3a	**3c**
Income (Loss)	4	Interest income	**4**
	5	Dividends: **a** Ordinary dividends	**5a**
		b Qualified dividends **5b**	
	6	Royalties	**6**
	7	Net short-term capital gain (loss) (attach Schedule D (Form 1120S))	**7**
	8a	Net long-term capital gain (loss) (attach Schedule D (Form 1120S))	**8a**
	b	Collectibles (28%) gain (loss) **8b**	
	c	Unrecaptured section 1250 gain (attach statement) . . **8c**	
	9	Net section 1231 gain (loss) (attach Form 4797)	**9**
	10	Other income (loss) (see instructions) Type ▶	**10**

Form **1120S** (2011)

Form 1120S (20xz) Page **3**

		Shareholders' Pro Rata Share Items (continued)		Total amount	
Deductions	11	Section 179 deduction (attach Form 4562)	11		
	12a	Contributions	12a		
	b	Investment interest expense	12b		
	c	Section 59(e)(2) expenditures (1) Type ▶ _____ (2) Amount ▶	12c(2)		
	d	Other deductions (see instructions) . . . Type ▶	12d		
Credits	13a	Low-income housing credit (section 42(j)(5))	13a		
	b	Low-income housing credit (other)	13b		
	c	Qualified rehabilitation expenditures (rental real estate) (attach Form 3468)	13c		
	d	Other rental real estate credits (see instructions) Type ▶	13d		
	e	Other rental credits (see instructions) . . . Type ▶	13e		
	f	Alcohol and cellulosic biofuel fuels credit (attach Form 6478)	13f		
	g	Other credits (see instructions) . . . . Type ▶	13g		
Foreign Transactions	14a	Name of country or U.S. possession ▶			
	b	Gross income from all sources	14b		
	c	Gross income sourced at shareholder level	14c		
		Foreign gross income sourced at corporate level			
	d	Passive category	14d		
	e	General category	14e		
	f	Other (attach statement)	14f		
		Deductions allocated and apportioned at shareholder level			
	g	Interest expense	14g		
	h	Other	14h		
		Deductions allocated and apportioned at corporate level to foreign source income			
	i	Passive category	14i		
	j	General category	14j		
	k	Other (attach statement)	14k		
		Other information			
	l	Total foreign taxes (check one): ▶ ☐ Paid ☐ Accrued	14l		
	m	Reduction in taxes available for credit (attach statement)	14m		
	n	Other foreign tax information (attach statement)			
Alternative Minimum Tax (AMT) Items	15a	Post-1986 depreciation adjustment	15a	2,966	
	b	Adjusted gain or loss	15b		
	c	Depletion (other than oil and gas)	15c		
	d	Oil, gas, and geothermal properties—gross income	15d		
	e	Oil, gas, and geothermal properties—deductions	15e		
	f	Other AMT items (attach statement)	15f		
Items Affecting Shareholder Basis	16a	Tax-exempt interest income	16a		
	b	Other tax-exempt income	16b		
	c	Nondeductible expenses	16c		
	d	Distributions (attach statement if required) (see instructions)	16d		
	e	Repayment of loans from shareholders	16e		
Other Information	17a	Investment income	17a		
	b	Investment expenses	17b		
	c	Dividend distributions paid from accumulated earnings and profits	17c		
	d	Other items and amounts (attach statement)			
Reconciliation	18	**Income/loss reconciliation.** Combine the amounts on lines 1 through 10 in the far right column. From the result, subtract the sum of the amounts on lines 11 through 12d and 14l	18	(26,038	)

Form **1120S** (2011)

Form 1120S (20xz) Page **4**

Schedule L — Balance Sheets per Books

	Assets	Beginning of tax year (a)	(b)	End of tax year (c)	(d)
1	Cash				6,053
2a	Trade notes and accounts receivable			8,000	
b	Less allowance for bad debts	(	)	( )	8,000
3	Inventories				16
4	U.S. government obligations				
5	Tax-exempt securities (see instructions)				
6	Other current assets (attach statement)				
7	Loans to shareholders				
8	Mortgage and real estate loans				
9	Other investments (attach statement)				
10a	Buildings and other depreciable assets			60,822	
b	Less accumulated depreciation	(	)	(11,866)	48,956
11a	Depletable assets				
b	Less accumulated depletion	(	)	( )	
12	Land (net of any amortization)				
13a	Intangible assets (amortizable only)				
b	Less accumulated amortization	(	)	( )	
14	Other assets (attach statement)				
15	Total assets				63,025
	Liabilities and Shareholders' Equity				
16	Accounts payable				
17	Mortgages, notes, bonds payable in less than 1 year				
18	Other current liabilities (attach statement)				2,520
19	Loans from shareholders				46,172
20	Mortgages, notes, bonds payable in 1 year or more				40,064
21	Other liabilities (attach statement)				
22	Capital stock				300
23	Additional paid-in capital				
24	Retained earnings				(26,031)
25	Adjustments to shareholders' equity (attach statement)				
26	Less cost of treasury stock		( )		( )
27	Total liabilities and shareholders' equity				63,025

Schedule M-1 — Reconciliation of Income (Loss) per Books With Income (Loss) per Return

Note. Schedule M-3 required instead of Schedule M-1 if total assets are $10 million or more — see instructions

1	Net income (loss) per books	(26,037)	5	Income recorded on books this year not included on Schedule K, lines 1 through 10 (itemize): a Tax-exempt interest $	
2	Income included on Schedule K, lines 1, 2, 3c, 4, 5a, 6, 7, 8a, 9, and 10, not recorded on books this year (itemize):				
3	Expenses recorded on books this year not included on Schedule K, lines 1 through 12 and 14l (itemize):		6	Deductions included on Schedule K, lines 1 through 12 and 14l, not charged against book income this year (itemize):	
a	Depreciation $		a	Depreciation $	
b	Travel and entertainment $				
			7	Add lines 5 and 6	9
4	Add lines 1 through 3	(26,028)	8	Income (loss) (Schedule K, line 18). Line 4 less line 7	(26,028)

Schedule M-2 — Analysis of Accumulated Adjustments Account, Other Adjustments Account, and Shareholders' Undistributed Taxable Income Previously Taxed (see instructions)

		(a) Accumulated adjustments account	(b) Other adjustments account	(c) Shareholders' undistributed taxable income previously taxed
1	Balance at beginning of tax year			
2	Ordinary income from page 1, line 21			
3	Other additions		3	
4	Loss from page 1, line 21	(26,031)		
5	Other reductions	( )	(9)	
6	Combine lines 1 through 5	(26,037)		
7	Distributions other than dividend distributions			
8	Balance at end of tax year. Subtract line 7 from line 6	(26,037)		

Form **1120S** (2011)

SCHEDULE F
(Form 1040)
Department of the Treasury
Internal Revenue Service (99)

Profit or Loss From Farming

▶ Attach to Form 1040, Form 1040NR, Form 1041, Form 1065, or Form 1065-B.
▶ See Instructions for Schedule F (Form 1040).

OMB No. 1545-0074

20 **XZ**

Attachment Sequence No. **14**

Name of proprietor | Social security number (SSN)

A Principal crop or activity | **B** Enter code from Part IV ▶ | **C** Accounting method: ☐ Cash ☐ Accrual | **D** Employer ID number (EIN), (see instr)

E Did you "materially participate" in the operation of this business during 20xz? If "No," see instructions for limit on passive losses. ☐ Yes ☐ No
F Did you make any payments in 20xz that would require you to file Form(s) 1099 (see instructions) ☐ Yes ☐ No
G If "Yes," did you or will you file all required Forms 1099? ☐ Yes ☐ No

Part I — Farm Income—Cash Method. Complete Parts I and II (Accrual method. Complete Parts II and III, and Part I, line 9.)

1a	Specified sales of livestock and other resale items (see instructions)	1a	
b	Sales of livestock and other resale items not reported on line 1a	1b	
c	Total of lines 1a and 1b (see instructions)	1c	
d	Cost or other basis of livestock or other items reported on line 1c	1d	
e	Subtract line 1d from line 1c		1e
2a	Specified sales of products you raised (see instructions)		2a
b	Sales of products you raised not reported on line 2a		2b
3a	Cooperative distributions (Form(s) 1099-PATR)	3a	3b Taxable amount	3b
4a	Agricultural program payments (see instructions)	4a	4b Taxable amount	4b
5a	Commodity Credit Corporation (CCC) loans reported under election		5a
b	CCC loans forfeited	5b	5c Taxable amount	5c
6	Crop insurance proceeds and federal crop disaster payments (see instructions)		
a	Amount received in 20xz	6a	6b Taxable amount	6b
c	If election to defer to 20yx is attached, check here ▶ ☐	6d Amount deferred from 2010	6d
7a	Specified custom hire (machine work) income (see instructions)		7a
b	Custom hire income not reported on line 7a		7b
8a	Specified other income (see instructions)		8a
b	Other income not reported on line 8a (see instructions)		8b
9	**Gross income.** Add amounts in the right column (lines 1e, 2a, 2b, 3b, 4b, 5a, 5c, 6b, 6d, 7a, 7b, 8a, and 8b). If you use the accrual method, enter the amount from Part III, line 50 (see instructions) ▶		9

Part II — Farm Expenses—Cash and Accrual Method. Do not include personal or living expenses (see instructions).

10	Car and truck expenses (see instructions). Also attach Form 4562	10		23	Pension and profit-sharing plans	23
11	Chemicals	11		24	Rent or lease (see instructions):	
12	Conservation expenses (see instructions)	12		a	Vehicles, machinery, equipment	24a
13	Custom hire (machine work)	13		b	Other (land, animals, etc.)	24b
14	Depreciation and section 179 expense (see instructions)	14		25	Repairs and maintenance	25
				26	Seeds and plants	26
				27	Storage and warehousing	27
15	Employee benefit programs other than on line 23	15		28	Supplies	28
16	Feed	16		29	Taxes	29
17	Fertilizers and lime	17		30	Utilities	30
18	Freight and trucking	18		31	Veterinary, breeding, and medicine	31
19	Gasoline, fuel, and oil	19		32	Other expenses (specify):	
20	Insurance (other than health)	20		a		32a
21	Interest:			b		32b
a	Mortgage (paid to banks, etc.)	21a		c		32c
b	Other	21b		d		32d
				e		32e
22	Labor hired (less employment credits)	22		f		32f
33	**Total expenses.** Add lines 10 through 32f. If line 32f is negative, see instructions ▶					33
34	**Net farm profit or (loss).** Subtract line 33 from line 9					34

If a profit, stop here and see instructions for where to report. If a loss, complete lines 35 and 36.

35 Did you receive an applicable subsidy in 20xz? (see instructions) ☐ Yes ☐ No
36 Check the box that describes your investment in this activity and see instructions for where to report your loss.
a ☐ All investment is at risk. **b** ☐ Some investment is not at risk.

For Paperwork Reduction Act Notice, see your tax return instructions. Cat. No. 11346H Schedule F (Form 1040) 2011

Schedule F (Form 1040) 20xz   Page 2

Part III Farm Income—Accrual Method (see instructions).

37a	Specified sales of livestock, produce, grains, and other products (see instructions)		37a	
b	Sales of livestock, produce, grains, and other products not reported on line 37a		37b	
38a	Cooperative distributions (Form(s) 1099-PATR)	38a	38b Taxable amount	38b
39a	Agricultural program payments	39a	39b Taxable amount	39b
40	Commodity Credit Corporation (CCC) loans:			
a	CCC loans reported under election		40a	
b	CCC loans forfeited	40b	40c Taxable amount	40c
41	Crop insurance proceeds		41	
42a	Specified custom hire (machine work) income from merchant card or third party payments (see instructions)		42a	
b	Other custom hire income not reported on line 42a		42b	
43a	Specified other income (see instructions)		43a	
b	Other income not reported on line 43a		43b	
44	Add amounts in the right column for lines 37a through 43b (lines 37a, 37b, 38b, 39b, 40a, 40c, 41, 42a, 42b, 43a, and 43b)		44	
45	Inventory of livestock, produce, grains, and other products at beginning of the year. Do not include sales reported on Form 4797	45		
46	Cost of livestock, produce, grains, and other products purchased during the year	46		
47	Add lines 45 and 46	47		
48	Inventory of livestock, produce, grains, and other products at end of year	48		
49	Cost of livestock, produce, grains, and other products sold. Subtract line 48 from line 47*		49	
50	**Gross income.** Subtract line 49 from line 44. Enter the result here and on Part I, line 9 ▶		50	

*If you use the unit-livestock-price method or the farm-price method of valuing inventory and the amount on line 48 is larger than the amount on line 47, subtract line 47 from line 48. Enter the result on line 49. Add lines 44 and 49. Enter the total on line 50 and on Part I, line 9.

Part IV Principal Agricultural Activity Codes

Do not file Schedule F (Form 1040) to report the following.
- *Income from providing agricultural services such as soil preparation, veterinary, farm labor, horticultural, or management for a fee or on a contract basis. Instead file Schedule C (Form 1040) or Schedule C-EZ (Form 1040).*
- *Income from breeding, raising, or caring for dogs, cats, or other pet animals. Instead file Schedule C (Form 1040) or Schedule C-EZ (Form 1040).*
- *Sales of livestock held for draft, breeding, sport, or dairy purposes. Instead file Form 4797.*

These codes for the Principal Agricultural Activity classify farms by their primary activity to facilitate the administration of the Internal Revenue Code. These six-digit codes are based on the North American Industry Classification System (NAICS).

Select the code that best identifies your primary farming activity and enter the six digit number on line B.

Crop Production
111100 Oilseed and grain farming
111210 Vegetable and melon farming
111300 Fruit and tree nut farming
111400 Greenhouse, nursery, and floriculture production
111900 Other crop farming

Animal Production
112111 Beef cattle ranching and farming
112112 Cattle feedlots
112120 Dairy cattle and milk production
112210 Hog and pig farming
112300 Poultry and egg production
112400 Sheep and goat farming
112510 Aquaculture
112900 Other animal production

Forestry and Logging
113000 Forestry and logging (including forest nurseries and timber tracts)

Schedule F (Form 1040) 2011

☐ Final K-1 ☐ Amended K-1   OMB No. 1545-0099

651111

Schedule K-1
(Form 1065)

Department of the Treasury
Internal Revenue Service

For calendar year 20**XZ** or tax
year beginning _____, 20**XZ**
ending _____, 20

20 **XZ**

Partner's Share of Income, Deductions, Credits, etc.

► See back of form and separate instructions.

Part I Information About the Partnership

A Partnership's employer identification number

B Partnership's name, address, city, state, and ZIP code

C IRS Center where partnership filed return

D ☐ Check if this is a publicly traded partnership (PTP)

Part II Information About the Partner

E Partner's identifying number

F Partner's name, address, city, state, and ZIP code

G ☐ General partner or LLC member-manager   ☐ Limited partner or other LLC member

H ☐ Domestic partner   ☐ Foreign partner

I What type of entity is this partner? _____

J Partner's share of profit, loss, and capital (see instructions):

	Beginning	Ending
Profit	%	%
Loss	%	%
Capital	%	%

K Partner's share of liabilities at year end:
- Nonrecourse . . . . $ _____
- Qualified nonrecourse financing . $ _____
- Recourse . . . . $ _____

L Partner's capital account analysis:
- Beginning capital account . . . $ _____
- Capital contributed during the year $ _____
- Current year increase (decrease) . $ _____
- Withdrawals & distributions . . $ (_____)
- Ending capital account . . . . $ _____

☐ Tax basis ☐ GAAP ☐ Section 704(b) book
☐ Other (explain)

M Did the partner contribute property with a built-in gain or loss?
☐ Yes ☐ No
If "Yes," attach statement (see instructions)

Part III Partner's Share of Current Year Income, Deductions, Credits, and Other Items

1	Ordinary business income (loss)		15	Credits
2	Net rental real estate income (loss)			
3	Other net rental income (loss)		16	Foreign transactions
4	Guaranteed payments			
5	Interest income			
6a	Ordinary dividends			
6b	Qualified dividends			
7	Royalties			
8	Net short-term capital gain (loss)			
9a	Net long-term capital gain (loss)		17	Alternative minimum tax (AMT) items
9b	Collectibles (28%) gain (loss)			
9c	Unrecaptured section 1250 gain			
10	Net section 1231 gain (loss)		18	Tax-exempt income and nondeductible expenses
11	Other income (loss)			
			19	Distributions
12	Section 179 deduction			
13	Other deductions			
			20	Other information
14	Self-employment earnings (loss)			

*See attached statement for additional information.

For IRS Use Only

For Paperwork Reduction Act Notice, see Instructions for Form 1065.   Cat. No. 11394R   Schedule K-1 (Form 1065) 2011

Schedule K-1 (Form 1065) 20xz

This list identifies the codes used on Schedule K-1 for all partners and provides summarized reporting information for partners who file Form 1040. For detailed reporting and filing information, see the separate Partner's Instructions for Schedule K-1 and the instructions for your income tax return.

1. **Ordinary business income (loss).** Determine whether the income (loss) is passive or nonpassive and enter on your return as follows.

	Report on
Passive loss	See the Partner's Instructions
Passive income	Schedule E, line 28, column (g)
Nonpassive loss	Schedule E, line 28, column (h)
Nonpassive income	Schedule E, line 28, column (j)

2. **Net rental real estate income (loss)** — See the Partner's Instructions
3. **Other net rental income (loss)**
    - Net income — Schedule E, line 28, column (g)
    - Net loss — See the Partner's Instructions
4. **Guaranteed payments** — Schedule E, line 28, column (j)
5. **Interest income** — Form 1040, line 8a
6a. **Ordinary dividends** — Form 1040, line 9a
6b. **Qualified dividends** — Form 1040, line 9b
7. **Royalties** — Schedule E, line 3b
8. **Net short-term capital gain (loss)** — Schedule D, line 5
9a. **Net long-term capital gain (loss)** — Schedule D, line 12
9b. **Collectibles (28%) gain (loss)** — 28% Rate Gain Worksheet, line 4 (Schedule D instructions)
9c. **Unrecaptured section 1250 gain** — See the Partner's Instructions
10. **Net section 1231 gain (loss)** — See the Partner's Instructions
11. **Other income (loss)**

Code		
A	Other portfolio income (loss)	See the Partner's Instructions
B	Involuntary conversions	See the Partner's Instructions
C	Sec. 1256 contracts & straddles	Form 6781, line 1
D	Mining exploration costs recapture	See Pub. 535
E	Cancellation of debt	Form 1040, line 21 or Form 982
F	Other income (loss)	See the Partner's Instructions

12. **Section 179 deduction** — See the Partner's Instructions
13. **Other deductions**

Code		
A	Cash contributions (50%)	
B	Cash contributions (30%)	
C	Noncash contributions (50%)	
D	Noncash contributions (30%)	See the Partner's Instructions
E	Capital gain property to a 50% organization (30%)	
F	Capital gain property (20%)	
G	Contributions (100%)	
H	Investment interest expense	Form 4952, line 1
I	Deductions—royalty income	Schedule E, line 19
J	Section 59(e)(2) expenditures	See the Partner's Instructions
K	Deductions—portfolio (2% floor)	Schedule A, line 23
L	Deductions—portfolio (other)	Schedule A, line 28
M	Amounts paid for medical insurance	Schedule A, line 1 or Form 1040, line 29
N	Educational assistance benefits	See the Partner's Instructions
O	Dependent care benefits	Form 2441, line 12
P	Preproductive period expenses	See the Partner's Instructions
Q	Commercial revitalization deduction from rental real estate activities	See Form 8582 instructions
R	Pensions and IRAs	See the Partner's Instructions
S	Reforestation expense deduction	See the Partner's Instructions
T	Domestic production activities information	See Form 8903 instructions
U	Qualified production activities income	Form 8903, line 7b
V	Employer's Form W-2 wages	Form 8903, line 17
W	Other deductions	See the Partner's Instructions

14. **Self-employment earnings (loss)**

    Note. If you have a section 179 deduction or any partner-level deductions, see the Partner's Instructions before completing Schedule SE.

A	Net earnings (loss) from self-employment	Schedule SE, Section A or B
B	Gross farming or fishing income	See the Partner's Instructions
C	Gross non-farm income	See the Partner's Instructions

15. **Credits**

A	Low-income housing credit (section 42(j)(5)) from pre-2008 buildings	
B	Low-income housing credit (other) from pre-2008 buildings	
C	Low-income housing credit (section 42(j)(5)) from post-2007 buildings	See the Partner's Instructions
D	Low-income housing credit (other) from post-2007 buildings	
E	Qualified rehabilitation expenditures (rental real estate)	
F	Other rental real estate credits	
G	Other rental credits	
H	Undistributed capital gains credit	Form 1040, line 71; check box a
I	Alcohol and cellulosic biofuel fuels credit	See the Partner's Instructions
J	Work opportunity credit	
K	Disabled access credit	
L	Empowerment zone and renewal community employment credit	See the Partner's Instructions
M	Credit for increasing research activities	
N	Credit for employer social security and Medicare taxes	
O	Backup withholding	Form 1040, line 62
P	Other credits	See the Partner's Instructions

16. **Foreign transactions**

A	Name of country or U.S. possession	
B	Gross income from all sources	Form 1116, Part I
C	Gross income sourced at partner level	

    Foreign gross income sourced at partnership level

D	Passive category	
E	General category	Form 1116, Part I
F	Other	

    Deductions allocated and apportioned at partner level

G	Interest expense	Form 1116, Part I
H	Other	Form 1116, Part I

    Deductions allocated and apportioned at partnership level to foreign source income

I	Passive category	
J	General category	Form 1116, Part I
K	Other	

    Other information

L	Total foreign taxes paid	Form 1116, Part II
M	Total foreign taxes accrued	Form 1116, Part II
N	Reduction in taxes available for credit	Form 1116, line 12
O	Foreign trading gross receipts	Form 8873
P	Extraterritorial income exclusion	Form 8873
Q	Other foreign transactions	See the Partner's Instructions

17. **Alternative minimum tax (AMT) items**

A	Post-1986 depreciation adjustment	
B	Adjusted gain or loss	See the Partner's Instructions and the Instructions for Form 6251
C	Depletion (other than oil & gas)	
D	Oil, gas, & geothermal—gross income	
E	Oil, gas, & geothermal—deductions	
F	Other AMT items	

18. **Tax-exempt income and nondeductible expenses**

A	Tax-exempt interest income	Form 1040, line 8b
B	Other tax-exempt income	See the Partner's Instructions
C	Nondeductible expenses	See the Partner's Instructions

19. **Distributions**

A	Cash and marketable securities	
B	Distribution subject to section 737	See the Partner's Instructions
C	Other property	

20. **Other information**

A	Investment income	Form 4952, line 4a
B	Investment expenses	Form 4952, line 5
C	Fuel tax credit information	Form 4136
D	Qualified rehabilitation expenditures (other than rental real estate)	See the Partner's Instructions
E	Basis of energy property	See the Partner's Instructions
F	Recapture of low-income housing credit (section 42(j)(5))	Form 8611, line 8
G	Recapture of low-income housing credit (other)	Form 8611, line 8
H	Recapture of investment credit	See Form 4255
I	Recapture of other credits	See the Partner's Instructions
J	Look-back interest—completed long-term contracts	See Form 8697
K	Look-back interest—income forecast method	See Form 8866
L	Dispositions of property with section 179 deductions	
M	Recapture of section 179 deduction	
N	Interest expense for corporate partners	
O	Section 453(l)(3) information	
P	Section 453A(c) information	
Q	Section 1260(b) information	See the Partner's Instructions
R	Interest allocable to production expenditures	
S	CCF nonqualified withdrawals	
T	Depletion information—oil and gas	
U	Amortization of reforestation costs	
V	Unrelated business taxable income	
W	Precontribution gain (loss)	
X	Section 108(i) information	
Y	Other information	

15

COMBINING BUSINESS AND PERSONAL CASH FLOW INTO GLOBAL CASH FLOW

OBJECTIVES

After studying *Combining Business and Personal Cash Flow into Global Cash Flow,* you will be able to—

- Explain why global cash flow is critical when making credit decisions
- Develop a global cash flow and global debt service coverage for a borrower

INTRODUCTION

So far in Section 3, we have focused on the various formats of personal financial statements and their components, developed ratios, and adjusted net worth, then analyzed personal tax returns and personal cash flow. You have seen how the value a business owner assigns to a closely held business on his or her personal financial statement (PFS) can affect the personal balance sheet, as well as how income and cash received from business interests can affect personal cash flow.

Because it is often difficult to separate business and personal assets and income, or when the personal financial strength of the owner—as a guarantor—is important to the credit situation, many business bankers compute what is called a **global cash flow (GCF)** for comparison to combined personal and business debt service obligations. This chapter covers the concepts and key steps to developing GCF from personal and business financial information.

> **Global cash flow (GCF)**
> GCF analysis blends personal cash flow, business income, and business cash flow into a single model that attempts to demonstrate a business owner's ability to generate cash flow sufficient to cover expenses such as business debt, capital expenditures, income taxes, personal debt service, and living expenses.

Relationship to the Commercial Lending Decision Tree

In the textbook Introduction, we explored the Commercial Lending Decision Tree as a way to think about the stages and steps involved in the commercial lending process. As you have already learned, the first stage in this process emphasizes early screening and qualifying steps, such as general fit with the portfolio and goals of your bank and initial assessment of financial and nonfinancial qualifications of the business. These preliminary steps allow a business banker to anticipate various issues and conduct a more efficient and accurate financial analysis.

The second stage moves into the detailed analysis of financial data gathered from the business and any owners who may serve as guarantors. This chapter will build on your knowledge of personal financial statements and business financial statements by adding a comprehensive GCF developed primarily from personal and business tax returns.

GLOBAL CASH FLOW OVERVIEW

Some of the first "global" underwriting models were developed in the 1990s as large banks automated the small business lending process. These models were based primarily on business and personal tax returns, and combined business and personal cash flow into total cash flow. This was compared with all business and personal debt.

The models were applied to small business situations where it was common for the business owner to be a co-borrower or full guarantor of the business debts, in many cases pledging personal collateral to the loans. In a sense, the business and personal cash flow, as well as the business and personal collateral, were tied together.

Because some of the same interconnections exist with larger business loans and many private banking situations, the GCF concept has been extended to almost all business lending situations where a personal co-borrower or guarantor (full or partial) is needed to support the credit. The owners and the businesses may not have as many interconnections, but this comprehensive analysis is consistent with the regulatory concepts discussed later in this chapter.

In fact, regardless of interconnections, the need to comprehensively analyze all business holdings and their effect on a borrower or guarantor was made clear in the economic and commercial real estate downturn of 2008–2010. Knowledge of both contingent liabilities and potential claims on owner/guarantor resources from all businesses and real estate projects is critical to making informed credit decisions.

Why Is Global Cash Flow Needed?

In many business lending situations, it is difficult to separate the business and its owners on a financial basis. Assets may be used both personally and for the business. The owner may be a co-borrower with the business on many of its loans. From year to year, as tax rules and incentives change, an owner may elect to recognize income or take out cash out of the business in a variety of ways.

To remedy the intermingled nature of the owner and the business, most business bankers attempt to go beyond simply analyzing the business and the owners separately. Instead, the business banker takes the analysis to the next level and combines business and personal cash flow into a GCF for comparison to both business and personal tax debt service capacity. When analyzing the "big picture" in this fashion, how much or how little salary the business owner pays him- or herself is not material. Whether the business owner is a full guarantor or co-borrower is not critical. What matters is that total business and personal cash flow, combined without double-counting, is sufficient to cover combined business and personal debt service.

Beyond this underwriting approach used by most business bankers, bank regulators have developed an expectation of a full, global analysis in business and commercial lending situations. This was spelled out in the interagency *Policy Statement on Prudent Commercial Real Estate Loan Workouts* issued in October 2009. Within the context of loan workouts, this document cites the need for "An analysis of the borrower's global debt service," where "global debt represents the aggregate of a borrower's or guarantor's financial obligations, including contingent obligations." This is one of the few interagency statements that discuss the concept of global analysis. The following appears later in the document, when it extends the discussion to guarantors:

> *The institution should have sufficient information on the guarantor's global financial condition, income liquidity, cash flow, contingent liabilities, and other relevant factors (including credit ratings, when available) to demonstrate the guarantor's financial capacity to fulfill the obligation. This assessment includes consideration of the total number and amount of guarantees currently extended by a guarantor in order to assess whether the guarantor has the financial capacity to fulfill the contingent claims that exist.*

Again, even though the context is loan workouts, the regulatory definitions and discussion of GCF are important to understand and should be applied to all lending situations for two reasons. First, developing the GCF is part of a broader, global analysis of financial condition. Second, it is important to understand the following differences between contingent claims and contingent liabilities:

- Contingent liability (Chapter 12)—Contingent liabilities are amounts for which the borrower is not directly liable but may need to pay some time in the future based on events that may or may not be within the borrower's control. Contingent liabilities include guarantees of loans and leases, outstanding letters of credit, legal actions pending, and past-due tax obligations.

- Contingent claims, while not specifically defined by the policy statement, go beyond the face amount of a loan or lease guarantee, letter of credit, and so forth, and attempt to identify a contingency that is likely to become a direct liability in the short term.

For example, a person may have a 50 percent limited guarantee on a $1 million loan secured by a business or real estate project. If a global analysis determines that the business or project has very strong debt service coverage (DSC) ratios and a very strong financial condition overall, this contingent liability is not likely to be a contingent claim in the short term. For purposes of a GCF, there is no immediate contingent claim to include in the business and personal debt service calculation.

If, however, the business or project has weak or insufficient DSC ratios, or has a very weak financial condition overall, a contingent claim should be developed, based on the guarantee percentage, the loan amount, any collateral or reserves pledged, and any knowledge of the relative financial strength of any other guarantors. This estimated contingent claim should be included in the business and personal debt service calculation within the global analysis.

Two Analytical Issues

At its most basic level, a global analysis will involve a combination of business and personal cash flow, plus business and personal debt service, which brings up at least two of the following analytical issues:

1. Mixing business DSC and personal DTI–Business and personal debt service ratios are computed in ways that make it difficult to combine the equations without some sort of adjustment. A business DSC ratio usually is based on annual net income after all operating expenses and taxes as the numerator, with annual debt service the denominator. Target levels for this ratio generally are 1.25x or higher, as you learned earlier.

A personal debt-to-income (DTI) ratio usually is based on monthly gross income before living expenses (the personal equivalent of business operating expenses) and taxes as the denominator, with monthly debt service as the numerator. Target levels for this ratio generally are 40 percent or lower, as you learned earlier.

Figure 15.1 shows several differences between DSC and DTI:

FIGURE 15.1 DIFFERENCES BETWEEN DSC AND DTI		
Factor	Business DSC	Personal DTI
Time Period for Data	Annual	Monthly
Numerator	**Net** cash flow	Debt service
Denominator	Debt service	Gross cash flow
Target levels	≥ 1.25x	≤ 40%

Because of the cash flow difference—a net basis for business DSC and gross basis for personal DTI—you cannot simply reverse the numerator or denominator, and then annualize. Most banks resolve the issue by further deducting from gross personal cash flow the appropriate living expenses and taxes, as demonstrated in the Personal Cash Flow Available for Debt Service Worksheet in Chapter 14. The result is a combined GCF available for debt service with all items expressed on an annual basis.

2. Crediting personal cash flow for business cash flow received only or for all cash flow generated—This is another area where the calculations can vary from situation to situation. In general, when an individual (or couple filing a joint personal tax return) has a controlling interest in a business, personal cash flow should include the full cash flow of the business, and personal debt service should include the debt service of the controlled business. The *Personal Cash Flow Available for Debt Service Worksheet* uses this approach for sole proprietorships, rental real estate, and farms as reported on a personal tax return, because these businesses are owned totally by the taxpayer, and the owner can withdraw any cash at any time. Further, the debt is a direct obligation of the taxpayer. Many bankers use the same approach for other controlled businesses (C corporations, S corporations, partnerships, and limited liability corporations (LLCs)) when the owner(s) fully guarantee the business debt.

In situations where there is a minority ownership in a business, most bankers include in personal cash flow only distributions (net of any contributions) from the business, and then include only a portion of debt service if a contingent claim exists.

Beyond the business cash flow or distributions from controlling and minority business interests, it usually is accurate to include personal cash flow resulting from any salaries (and guaranteed payments from partnerships), interest income (on funds loaned to the business), dividends, rent, or other income received from the business. When compiling a GCF, these items of personal income usually can stay in place, and should not result in double-counting because these same items will be offsetting expenses to a controlled business, while distributions from a minority interest generally come from net income after the same offsetting expenses.

No Single "Correct" Method for GCF

Because business ownerships and the exact nature of cash flow between the owners and the business can vary greatly, it is difficult to create a single format to use with every GCF analysis a business banker can encounter. What has been described so far can work well with a limited number of business interests, including some commercial real estate (CRE).

However, for borrowers or guarantors with extensive CRE holdings, many bankers use a format similar to the first page of the *Personal Cash Flow Available for Debt Service Worksheet*, add a detailed chart with rows or columns for each CRE project, and develop cash flows and valuations for each property in order to determine if a contingent claim exists. The results of the various properties are totaled to give a portfolio-level view of cash flows and performance. Further, the contingent claims can be compared to the individual's cash flow as calculated separately.

Global Cash Flow Example

This section will provide a detailed example of a GCF calculation, along with the development of global debt service coverage (global DSC). As mentioned earlier, there is no single, standard format for GCF and global DSC. This example format works well for many commercial borrowers whose businesses are privately held. For this example, you will be using the Personal Cash Flow Available for Debt Service Worksheet (Appendix A) and the 20xz personal tax return for Edward G. and Linda C. Dezine (Appendix A) at the end of chapter 14.

The personal cash flow derived for the Dezines also was based on the following chart (Figure 15.2) that summarizes two years of PFS information from the Dezines for 12/31/20xy and 12/31/20xz, which matches the beginning and end of the year covered by the personal tax return.

Year Sequence for Dates in Chapter Cases
This chapter uses the following order or sequence of years for the dates in the financial statements:

- 20xx, 20xy, and 20xz

For projected years, the following sequence is used:

- 20yx, 20yy, 20yz, and so on

FIGURE 15.2 SUMMARY OF PERSONAL BALANCE SHEETS OF LINDA C. AND EDWARD G. DEZINE

($ in 000s)	12/31/20xy	12/31/20xz	Change
Assets			
Cash	$ 40	$ 45	$ 5
Marketable securities	42	32	(10)
Non-readily marketable securities	0	100	100
Accounts and notes receivable	0	46	46
CSVLI	20	20	0
Real estate	700	700	0
Personal property and automobiles	70	85	15
Retirement accounts	430	440	10
Other assets	35	35	0
Total Assets	$1,337	$1,503	$ 166
Liabilities			
Notes payable—banks	$ 0	$ 11	$ 11
Others and accounts payable	2	3	1
Real estate mortgages	420	410	(10)
Total Liabilities	$ 422	$424	$ 2
Net Worth	$ 915	$1,079	$ 164
Total Liabilities and Net Worth	$1,337	$1,503	$ 166

Calculating Global Cash Flow

As mentioned earlier, business bankers have different formats for compiling personal and global cash flows. As an example, we will use the format shown on the second page of Appendix A, the Personal Cash Flow Available for Debt Service Worksheet.

The first page of this format computes cash flow available for debt service in two ways, which can be used for a DTI or DSC ratio. Because a consumer DTI ratio is based on gross income or cash flow before taxes and living expenses, the example format provides a gross cash flow number. Then taxes and living expenses are deducted to arrive at a net cash flow number to be used for a DSC ratio.

The second page of this format computes the respective DTI and DSC ratios from the cash flows developed on the first page. The remaining portions of the second page compute GCF and global DSC.

The following explains the key sections of the example format, plus sample calculations:

- **Net personal cash flow available for debt service**—This figure comes from the same line item on the first page of the worksheet. For the Dezines, the net personal cash flow is $48,733.

- **Adjust for net distributions**—This section allows for an adjustment to net personal cash flow for controlled entities where the full business cash flow and business debt service will be used later in the GCF calculation. If the personal cash flow includes any distributions (net of contributions) from such entities, these amounts need to be taken out of personal cash flow, using this section. This avoids double-counting of net distributions with the cash flow of the business. For the Dezines, there are no adjustments, because there was no cash flow impact to them from ownerships in pass-through entities.

- **Other adjustments**—The complex nature of personal cash flow and personal tax returns can create many one-time or unique situations. This section allows for adjustments and explanations.

For the Dezines, their 20xz personal cash flow included outflows for the $300 capital stock investment into Designs by Dezine, plus the $46,172 loan to the business. There can be several reasons to adjust for these transactions. First, they may be considered one-time or nonrecurring. In such a case, the transactions can be excluded from personal cash flow and there is no need for adjustment.

Second, if business cash flow for the entity will be represented by a simple formula such as net income + depreciation expense + interest expense (as we will use in this example), then the inflow of $46,472 into the business is not present to offset the personal outflow, and the personal cash outflow (if recorded) needs to be eliminated. This is achieved by adjusting the personal cash flow by a positive $46,472.

Net Personal Cash Flow Available for Debt Service			$48,733

Adjust for Net Distributions IF Using All Cash Flow and Debt Service of the Entity Below			
Partnership/LLC net dist. (contrib.)	Sched. K-1 (Form 1065), sect. L	$ 0	
S Corporation net dist. (contrib.)	Sched. K-1 (Form 1120S), box 16		

Other Adjustments	*Explanation*		
Capital stock and loan to S Corp.	Not included in bus. cash flow	46,472	
Total Adjustments			$ 46,472

- **Business cash flow available for debt service**—This section lists the businesses and related cash flow being used in the global analysis. As we have seen, there are several ways to express business cash flow, from earnings before interest, taxes, depreciation and amortization (EBITDA), to operating cash flow in a statement of cash flows and net cash after operations from the UCA model (Chapter 10). We will use EBITDA in this example.

Using the 20xz tax return for Designs by Dezine, you start with net income. It generally is preferable to use net income (or loss) per books, as shown on Schedule M-1 of the tax return. For 20xz, this is a net loss of ($26,037), compared to a loss of ($26,031) shown as ordinary income on the first page of the tax return. We then take depreciation of $11,866 from line 14 together with interest expense of $3,414 from line 13.

When loans from the owner to the business are involved, as with Linda Dezine and her business, it may be necessary to adjust the interest expense shown at the business level, also depending on whether the debt is included as business debt service. In this example, you will not be including amortization of the shareholder loan within business debt service, so any interest expense shown on the business tax return and added back for EBITDA needs to be adjusted or reduced by the amount applicable to the shareholder loan.

For Designs by Dezine, all of the $3,414 of interest expense appears to be related to bank loans, not the shareholder loan, on the basis of the following clues:

- First, the Dezines did not report interest income from the business on their personal tax return Schedule B, so it appears that the business did not pay any interest expense to the Dezines. Also, we noted in Chapter 11 that the loan was made very late in the year.

- Second, the interest amount is about 8.5 percent of the ending loan balances of the bank loans as reported on the business tax return ($3,414 ÷ $40,064 = 8.5%). This appears to be reasonable and is close to the interest levels discussed as we developed the Dezines' personal cash flow.

Global cash flow available for debt service includes the adjusted personal cash flow and the business cash flow. For the Dezines, this amount is $84,448.

Business Cash Flow Available for Debt Service			
Business Name	Basis or Source	Amount	
Designs by Dezine	20xz net income per books	($26,037)	
Designs by Dezine	20xz depreciation expense	11,866	
Designs by Dezine	20xz interest expense (bank debt)	$3,414	
Total business cash flow available for debt service			($ 10,757)
Global Cash Flow Available for Debt Service			$84,448

- **Business debt service**—This section can be used for debt service of businesses controlled by the individual(s), as well as any partial amounts or contingent claims arising for guarantees of businesses where there is a minority ownership position. Most business bankers would exclude any debt such as the shareholder loan from Linda Dezine to her business.

For the Dezines, it shows the loans listed on line 20 of Schedule L (the balance sheet) on page 4 of the business tax return for Designs by Dezine. In Chapter 11, you learned that these were vehicle loans with about $21,000 per year in total debt service, principal, and interest. However, because the business was in operation for only about eight months during 20xz, we estimate the actual debt service for 20xz at about $14,000 [$21,000 x (8 months ÷ 12 months) = $14,000] against the partial year of cash flow. The debt service could be even lower if the vehicle were placed into service for less than the eight months estimated.

- **Global annual debt service** includes both business and personal debt service. For the Dezines, total business and personal debt service is $66,200 ($52,200 + $14,000 = $66,200).

- **Global DSC** is computed by dividing GCF by global debt service. For the Dezines, global DSC is 1.28x ($84,448 ÷ $66,200 = 1.28x).

- **Excess (deficit) global cash flow after debt service** shows the actual dollar amount by which GCF exceeds debt obligations. For the Dezines, this amount is $18,248 ($84,448 − $66,200 = $18,248).

Most business bankers prefer to have global at or above 1.25x, similar to business debt coverage ratios discussed in Chapter 8. The extent to which the ratio exceeds 1.25x, as well as the excess (deficit) GCF after debt service, both give a business banker an indication of two things.

Business Debt Service			
Lender	Purpose/Type	Annual Pmts	
Anytown Bank	Vehicle (8 months of $21,000)	$14,000	
Total Annual Business Debt Service			$14,000
Total Annual Personal Debt Service			$84,448
Global Annual Debt Service			$66,200
	Global DSC		1.28x
	Excess (Deficit) GCF After Debt Service		$18,248

First, without significant changes being expected in cash flow and debt service, how much room exists to handle unexpected cash flow problems or operating cycle disruptions? Second, if the business is expanding, how much additional debt can the owners/guarantors support as a second or third level of possible repayment?

In this section, you learned the importance of global analysis in business and commercial lending. You now understand the significance of performing a global analysis by combining business and personal cash flow into a GCF for comparison to both business and personal tax debt service capacity. You can describe the two analytical issues associated with GCF—mixing business DSC and personal DTI and crediting personal cash flow for business cash flow received only or for all cash flow generated. You learned how to calculate a GCF and also learned the difference between contingent liabilities and potential claims on owner/guarantor resources. All of these aspects of a global analysis are critical to making informed credit decisions.

SUMMARY

Many commercial lending situations involve businesses in which the personal financial condition of the owners is important to the lending decision, with the owners serving as co-borrowers or guarantors. Because of the complex and interconnected nature of these businesses and their owners, most business bankers attempt to take a comprehensive look at the combined business and personal cash flow compared to combined business and personal debt service. This comprehensive look is called a global cash flow or global analysis.

By completing this chapter, you have learned how global analysis has evolved, why it is critical when making credit decisions, some regulatory guidance concerning global analysis, plus two of the analytical issues encountered when mixing business and personal financial data. You have worked through the key sections and steps in compiling a GCF and had an opportunity to develop, calculate, and interpret a GCF and a global DSC ratio.

QUESTION FOR DISCUSSION

1. A GCF analysis involves a combination of business and personal cash flow, plus business and personal debt service. What are the two analytical issues associated with GCF?

EXERCISE 1

In this exercise you will develop a global cash flow and global DSC for Edward and Linda Dezine for 20xz.

Instructions

Use the Dezines' Personal Cash Flow Available for Debt Service Worksheet (Appendix A) to develop a global cash flow and DSC for Edward and Linda Dezine for 20xz. To complete this exercise you should use cash flow from the UCA Cash Flow Model (Chapter 10) as the source for the business cash flow of Designs by Dezine, instead of EBITDA used in the examples earlier. As you saw in Calculating Global Cash Flow and in Section 2 of this textbook, EBITDA is one of several ways to express business cash flow.

PART 1

Complete the second page of the Personal Cash Flow Available for Debt Service Worksheet to develop global cash flow and global DSC.

PART 2

Explain how these results differ from the example using EBITDA for business cash flow, plus any other adjustments that were made.

APPENDIX A: PERSONAL CASH FLOW

Personal Cash Flow Available for Debt Service Worksheet

Name: __Edward G. and Linda C. Dezine__   For: __20xz__

Line Item	Source	Amount	
Gross Wages Received			
Wages, salaries	Form 1040, line 7	$159,888	
Guaranteed payments	Sched. K-1 (Form 1065), box 4	-	
Other	Form 1040, PFS, other	-	
Gross Cash Flow from Wages			$159,888
Other Personal Cash Flow			
Interest and dividend income	Form 1040, lines 8a, 8b, and 9a	$2,436	
State/local income tax refund	Form 1040, line 10	-	
Alimony received and other income	Form 1040, lines 11 and 21	8,900	
Net proceeds from asset sales	Sched. D, Forms 8949, 4797, etc.	9,728	
Asset purchases (net of related loans)	Form 1040, PFS, other	(2,000)	
Miscellaneous income	Form 1040, PFS, other	-	
IRA/pension/Social Sec.distributions	Form 1040, lines 15a, 16a, and 20a	-	
Total Other Personal Cash Flow			$19,064
Cash Flow from Businesses Interests			
Sole proprietorship income	Sched. C, line 31	$39,518	
Add: Depreciation and depletion	Sched. C, lines 12 and 13	-	
Add: Interest expense	Sched. C, lines 16a and 16b	-	
Other (meals/ent., rent, etc.)	Sched. C, line 24b, 20a, 20b, etc.	-	
Rental real estate income	Sched. E, line 26	-	
Add: Interest expense	Sched. E, lines 12 and 13	-	
Add: Depreciation	Sched. E, line 18	-	
Farm income	Sched. F, line 34	-	
Add: Depreciation	Sched. F, line 14	-	
Add: Interest expense	Sched. F, lines 21a and 21b	-	
Other (rent, livestock/crop sales, etc.)	Sched. F, Form 4797, other	-	
Partnership/LLC net distributions	Sched. K-1 (Form 1065), section L	-	
S corporation net distributions	Sched. K-1 (Form 1120S), box 16	-	
Other: Cap stock and loan to S corp.	Form 1040, PFS, other	(46,472)	
Total Cash Flow from Business Interests			($6,954)
Gross Personal Cash Flow Available for Debt Service, DTI (40%) Basis			**$171,998**
Taxes, Living Expenses, and Other Expenses			
Federal income tax withheld	Form 1040, line 62	($22,359)	
Estimated Fed. tax payments	Form 1040, line 63	-	
FICA tax withheld or paid	W-2 or 7.65% of wages	(12,231)	
State/local income taxes	Sched. A, line 5	(8,866)	
State/local real estate taxes	Sched. A, line 6	(3,221)	
Personal property and other taxes	Sched. A, lines 7 and 8	(188)	
Medical expenses	Sched. A, line 1	(1,318)	
Gifts to charity and other expenses	Sched. A, line 16 and 24	(30,885)	
Other living expenses	PFS or best estimate	(41,797)	
Other: Insurance expense	Form 1040, PFS or other	(2,400)	
Total Taxes, Living Expenses and Other			($123,265)
Net Personal Cash Flow Available for Debt Service, DSC (1.25x) Basis			**$48,733**
	Various Living Expenses/Gross Personal Cash Flow	($76,400)	44%

Personal Debt Service Coverage (DTI and DSC)

Personal Debt Service, Including Sole Proprietorships, Rental RE and Farms

Lender	Purpose/Type	Payment	
First National Bank	residential mortgage	$3,800	
Anytown Bank	car loan	400	
various credit cards	imputed at 5%	150	
		-	
Total Monthly Personal Debt Service			$4,350
Total Annual Personal Debt Service			$52,200

Gross Personal Cash Flow Available for Debt Service, DTI (40%) Basis		$171,998
	Monthly Gross CFADS	$14,333
	DTI (Debt-to-Income)	30.3%
Net Personal Cash Flow Available for Debt Service, DSC (1.25x) Basis		$48,733
	DSC	0.93 x

Global Cash Flow and Global DSC

Net Personal Cash Flow Available for Debt Service, DSC (1.25x) Basis	$48,733

Adjust for Net Distributions IF Using All Cash Flow and Debt Service of Entity Below

Partnership/LLC net distributions	Sched. K-1 (Form 1065), section L	
S corporation net distributions	Sched. K-1 (Form 1120S), box 16	

Other Adjustments   Explanation

Total Adjustments		

Business Cash Flow Available for Debt Service

Business Name	Basis or Source	Amount
Total Business Cash Flow Available for Debt Service		

Global Cash Flow Available for Debt Service	

Business Debt Service

Lender	Purpose/Type	Annual Pmts	
Anytown Bank	vehicles (8 mos. of $21,000)	$14,000	
		-	
		-	
		-	
Total Annual Business Debt Service			$14,000
Total Annual Personal Debt Service			$52,200
Global Annual Debt Service			$66,200
	Global DSC		
	Excess (Deficit) GCF after Debt Service		

Glossary Terms

Accounts payable
Amounts owed to vendors and suppliers for delivered products or services used in normal operations and bills that must be paid in one year or less. *Also called* payables.

Accounts receivable
Assets on a balance sheet that arise from the extension of trade credit to a company's customers where the customers have not paid by the reporting date. These are generally short-term assets. *Also called* receivables.

Accrual basis
A method of accounting in which revenue is recognized when earned, expenses are recognized when incurred, and other changes in financial condition are recognized as they occur, without regard to the timing of the actual cash receipts and expenditures.

Accrued expenses
Expenses incurred but not yet paid during an accounting period.

Adverse audit opinion
An adverse audit opinion is issued when the auditor determines that the financial statements of a business are materially misstated and, considered as a whole, do not conform with GAAP.

Adjusted net worth
The amount of an individual's net worth after making adjustments for the overstated value of assets and understated amount of liabilities.

Audited statement
A financial statement that has been audited in conformity with generally accepted auditing standards by a certified public accountant and is accompanied by the auditor's opinion.

Business life cycle
The business life cycle is a macro look at how most businesses typically change and develop over time. Every business starts as a concept or idea. After that stage, businesses "age" through four main life cycle stages (start-up, growth, mature, and decline), which affect the need for particular bank products and services.

Capital
The funds invested in a firm by the owners for use in conducting business.

Capital stock
(1) All the outstanding shares of a company's stock representing ownership, including preferred and common stock. (2) The total amount of stock, common and preferred, that a corporation is authorized to issue under its certificate of incorporation or charter. It is typical to have more shares authorized than are issued.

Cash basis
Income and expenses recorded when cash is received or paid out, regardless of when income was earned or expenses were incurred.

Cash flows from financing activities
The amount of cash that directly relates to the business's external financing, involving debt or equity.

Cash flows from investing activities
Discretionary cash flows that can be delayed are controlled more closely by management and summarize the purchase and sale of fixed goods.

Cash flows from operating activities
The amount of cash generated from a business enterprise's normal, ongoing operations during an accounting period. Cash flow from operations excludes extraordinary income and expense.

Common-sizing
A form of financial ratio analysis that allows the comparison of companies with different levels of sales or total assets by introducing a common denominator. A common-sized balance sheet expresses each item on the balance sheet as a percentage of total assets and each item on the income statement as a percentage of net sales.

Compensating balance
The balance that a customer must keep on deposit with a bank to ensure a credit line, to gain unlimited checking privileges, and to offset the bank's expenses in providing various operating services.

Compiled statement
The least informative externally CPA-prepared financial statement, in which the numbers are restated from company records with little or no verification. These statements are available to nonpublic entities only.

dba
An abbreviation for "doing business as." Some entities may have one name but conduct business under another name.

Depreciation
In accounting, a process of allocating the cost of a fixed asset less salvage value, if any, over its estimated useful life. A depreciation charge is treated as a noncash expense. For income tax purposes, depreciation is determined by a formula, not by any actual loss of value. This aspect of depreciation applies to many types of assets, not just real property.

Direct method
A method used to prepare a statement of cash flows (SCF) that identifies cash receipts and payments, organized into operating, investing, and financing cash flows. It starts with *cash collected from sales*, which is one of several operating activities that involve receipts and payments from normal business operations. Essentially, the various income statement items that generate net profit are matched with changes to their counterparts in the balance sheet. So, sales is matched to the change in accounts receivable to derive *cash collected from sales*. Cost of goods sold is matched to changes in both inventory and accounts payable to derive *cash paid to suppliers*. Beyond the operating cash flows section, the format of a direct method SCF is the same as in indirect SCF. Both formats generate a result that equals the change in cash during the year.

Financial Accounting Standards Board (FASB)
The public accounting profession's private self-regulatory organization that is authorized to establish financial accounting and reporting standards, commonly referred to as generally accepted accounting principles (GAAP). FASB publishes the widely used Statements of Financial Accounting Standards (SFAS).

Financial statement analysis
The examination and interpretation of financial data to evaluate a business's past performance, present condition, and future prospects.

Financing activities
Financing activities measure cash flows from debt, debt payments, and proceeds from and payments to shareholders, the external financing of a business.

Fixed assets
Those items of a long-term nature required for the normal conduct of a business and not converted into cash during a normal operating period. Fixed assets include furniture, buildings, and machinery, and are subject to depreciation.

Footnotes
A detailed explanation attached to and considered an integral part of audited or reviewed financial statements prepared by a certified public accountant that allow the auditor to comment on the statements relative to GAAP.

Generally Accepted Accounting Principles (GAAP)
The rules, conventions, practices, and procedures that form the foundation for financial accounting.

Global cash flow (GCF)
GCF analysis blends personal cash flow, business income, and business cash flow into a single model that attempts to demonstrate a business owner's ability to generate cash flow sufficient to cover expenses such as business debt, capital expenditures, income taxes, personal debt service, and living expenses.

Going concern disclosure
A going concern disclosure opinion is issued when the auditor considers that the business is not a going concern, or will not be a going concern in the near future. The auditor is then required to include an explanatory paragraph before the opinion paragraph or following the opinion paragraph in the audit report explaining the situation. Such an opinion is called an "unqualified modified opinion."

Indirect method
A method used to prepare a statement of cash flows (SCF) that starts with net profit and adjusts for any non-cash items (depreciation and amortization) expensed on the income statement. This amount is further adjusted for changes in assets (other than cash), liabilities, and equity (other than net profits). These changes are grouped into operating, investing, and financing cash flow. The result from all three sections equals the change in cash during the year.

International Financial Reporting Standards (IFRS)
International Financial Reporting Standards (IFRS) are principles-based standards, interpretations, and the framework (1989)[1] adopted by the International Accounting Standards Board (IASB).

Inventory
The materials owned and held by a business, such as raw materials, intermediate products and parts, work-in-progress, and finished goods. These materials may be intended for sale or internal consumption.

Investing activities
Investing activities measure payments received from selling fixed assets and capital expenditures for new fixed assets.

Management letter
Letter sent to the board of directors or management of the company expressing concerns or deficiencies not referred to in the audit. The auditing CPA includes information describing the reportable condition, as well as information about any material weaknesses that do not reduce risk of error or irregularities.

Net worth
Assets minus liabilities of a business. This is the owners' equity. *Also called* shareholders' equity.

Operating activities
Operating activities measure, through net income and receivables, cash generated by the current operating cycle and short-term changes in current accounts requiring cash for purchases, accounts payable, and payments to employees.

Operating agreement
The document that sets forth how the business of a limited liability company will be conducted. It is similar to a corporation's bylaws.

Operating cycle
The time required to purchase or manufacture inventory or provide service, sell the product or provide the service, and collect the cash.

Paid assets
Assets that you have paid for in advance, but whose benefits you do not realize the benefits until later. The easiest examples to understand are insurance or rent.

Participation
An interest in a loan acquired by a third party, such as another lender or a group of lenders, from the lender that originates and services the loan.

Prepaid expenses
A classification of expenditure made to benefit future periods. Such items are classified as current assets and constitute a part of a firm's working capital. Prepaid expenses include prepaid rent, certain taxes, royalties, and unexpired insurance premiums.

Qualified audit opinion
A qualified audit opinion is issued when the auditor encountered one of two types of situations that do not comply with generally accepted accounting principles; however, the rest of the financial statements are fairly presented.

Representation
A statement of fact included in a document to influence opinion. For example, the applicant represents that the information is true and correct.

Retainage
The amount of a contractor's bill that is withheld until the job has been completed.

Reviewed statement
The degree of work performed by a public accounting firm in conjunction with the issuance of financial statements of a nonpublic entity that is greater in scope than a compilation but less in scope than an audit and does not provide a basis for the expression of an opinion on the financial statements. The accountant's report would generally state, however, that, based on his or her review, the accountant is not aware of any material modifications that should be made to the financial statements for them to conform to generally accepted accounting principles.

Securities and Exchange Commission (SEC)
The federal agency that regulates the public sale of securities and related disclosures. The SEC monitors issuers, underwriters, exchanges, and over-the-counter dealers and publishes regulations pertaining to financial information submitted by businesses reporting the results of their financial condition and their operations.

Subcontractor
One who takes a portion of a contract from the principal contractor or from another subcontractor.

Subordinated debt
Long-term debt that is paid off only after depositors and other creditors have been paid.

Syndication
A loan made by a group of banks to one borrower. In most cases, the dollar amount requested exceeds the amount the individual banks are either willing or able to lend. Each bank receives a pro-rated share of the income based on its level of participation of credit.

Tangible net worth
Ordinarily, the total capital accounts (equity) less intangibles.

Trade credit
Credit extended to a company by its suppliers, usually to cover inventory purchases or other normal operating expenses.

Unqualified audit opinion
An unqualified audit opinion is issued when the auditor concludes that the financial statements give a true and fair view in accordance with the financial reporting framework used for the preparation and presentation of the financial statements. The auditor does not have any significant reservation in respect of matters contained in the financial statements.

Warranty
An assurance, promise, or guaranty by one party that a particular statement of fact is true and may be relied upon by the other party. For example, the applicant warrants that the supporting schedules are complete and correct, and will notify the lender of any material changes.

Working capital
A firm's investment in current assets, namely cash, marketable securities, accounts receivable, and inventory. Working capital is liquid and therefore is available to meet current business needs. The difference between a firm's current assets and current liabilities is called working capital.

INDEX

A

Abbreviated accounts receivable listing, 179–180
Abbreviated cash flow report, 254–258
Accelerated depreciation, 160
Accounting
    accrual method, 110–111, 112–127, 136–137
    cash method, 110–115, 128–137
    Financial Accounting Standards Board, 87–88
    generally accepted accounting principles, 87–88, 93–97, 100, 112
    income tax basis, 112–113
    methods, 82, 110–111
    overview, 115
    ratio analysis, 209–211
    standards, 86–88
Accounting and Financial Reporting for Personal Financial Statements, 322
Accounts payable, 115, 193–194, 309–310
    definition of, 115
Accounts payable turnover ratio, 221–222
Accounts receivable
    abbreviated listing, 179–180
    aged listings and concentrations, 178–179
    definition of, 115
    forecasting, 306–307
    trade accounts receivable, 177
Accounts receivable turnover, 220
Accrual accounting method, 110–111, 112–127
Accrual basis, 110–111
    definition of, 110
Accruals, 29
Accrued expenses, 195
    definition of, 23
Adjusted gross income, 359
Adjusted net worth, 342–343, 348–351
    definition of, 343
Adverse audit opinions, 96–97, 98
    definition of, 96
Aged accounts receivable listings, 178–179
Aggregate accounts, 83–84
AGI. *See* Adjusted gross income
Agricultural businesses
    borrowing needs, 33
    lending summary, 5
    operating cycle, 4–5
AICPA. *See* American Institute of Certified Public Accountants
Alimony payments, 362
American Institute of Certified Public Accountants, 87, 91, 322
Angel investing, 42
Annual Statement Studies, 75, 230
Annualizing income, 364

Articles of incorporation, 55–56
    definition of, 56
Asset accounts
    cash flow analysis, 241
Assets
    balance sheet analysis, 174–190
    current assets, 175–183
    fixed, 117
    noncurrent assets, 183–190
    prepaid, 123
Assumed names, 51–52
Audited financial statements, 93–101
Audited statements
    definition of, 93

B

Balance sheet equation, 174
Balance sheets
    accounts by industry type, 173
    accrual basis, 127, 136–137
    analysis of, 103
    asset analysis, 174–190
    balance sheet equation, 174
    cash basis, 136–137
    categories, 202
    considerations, 172–174
    description of, 78
    equity analysis, 198–203
    forecasting, 305–313
    liabilities, 190–198
    personal financial statements, 330–335
    relationships to Commercial Lending Decision Tree, 172
Balloon maturity, 192–193
Bonds, 196–197
Borrowers. *See* Business borrowers
Brokerage firms, 40
Budgets. *See* Cash budgets
Bullet maturity, 193
Business borrowers
    borrowing arrangement types, 36–38, 39
    borrowing needs by business type or industry, 32–34
    business sectors, 4–18
    operating cycles, 3–4
    reasons businesses borrow, 32–36
    relationship to the Commercial Lending Decision Tree, 22
    strengths, weaknesses and uncertainties, 85–86
Business cash flow. *See* Cash flow analysis; Global cash flow
Business income, 362, 378–379, 414–415
Business legal structures. *See* Legal structures
Business life cycles
    characteristics of, 58–59, 65
    decline stage, 59, 63, 64–65
    definition of, 58
    growth stage, 59, 61, 64, 65
    matching products, 58
    mature stage, 59, 62, 64, 65
    relationship to the Commercial Lending Decision Tree, 48
    risk factors, 64–65

start-up stage, 59, 60, 64, 65
Business loans
    borrowing arrangement types, 36–38, 39
    borrowing needs by business type or industry, 32–34
    brokerage firms, 40
    captive finance companies, 41
    cash flow cycles, 22–25
    commercial finance companies, 40
    competitors to banks, 39–42
    complementary financing, 39, 42–44
    credit card issuers, 41
    credit unions, 40
    factoring, 40–41
    government loan programs, guarantees and grants, 42–43
    industrial revenue bonds, 43
    investors, 42
    lease financing, 38
    leasing companies, 41
    lending sources, 39–44
    life insurance companies, 41
    long-term sources of cash, 32
    long-term uses of cash, 30–32
    matching purpose to repayment sources, 39
    operating line of credit, 36–37
    participation, 43–44
    reasons businesses borrow, 32–36
    sources of cash, 26–30
    special commitment loans, 36
    standby letter of credit, 37–38, 43
    syndication, 43–44
    term loans, 38
    trade credit, 42
    uses of cash, 23–25
Business sectors
    agricultural businesses, 4–5, 33
    Commercial Lending Decision Tree considerations, 2–3
    construction businesses, 12, 14–15, 34
    manufacturers, 5–7, 33
    retailers, 9–11, 34
    risk evaluation, 17–18
    service businesses, 11–12, 34
    wholesalers, 7–9, 33

C

C corporations
    articles of incorporation, 55–56
    difference from other entities, 55
    equity analysis, 199–200
    income taxes for owners, 54–55
    liability, 55
    overview, 50
CADA. *See* Cash after debt amortization
Capital. *See also* Net worth
    definition of, 26
    paid-in capital, 199
Capital accounts, 200–201
Capital gains and losses, 362–363, 380–384, 416–419
Capital stock

definition of, 116
Captive finance companies, 41
Cash
    accruals, 29
    capital, 26–27
    fixed asset cycle, 31
    flow cycles, 22–25
    forecasting, 306
    long-term sources of, 32
    long-term uses of, 30–32
    reduction of credit sale terms, 29–30
    sources of, 26–30
    trade credit, 23, 28
    uses of, 23–25
Cash accounting method, 110–115, 128–136
Cash accounts, 176
Cash after debt amortization, 267, 271–273
Cash basis, 110–111
    definition of, 110
Cash budget statements, 104
Cash budgets
    analysis of, 294
    analyzing, 284–295
    format, 287–294
    inflows and outflows of cash, 285–286
    overview, 285
    relationship to Commercial Lending Decision Tree, 284
    role of, 294–295
    uses of, 286–287
Cash flow. *See* Global cash flow; Personal cash flow
Cash flow analysis. *See also* Global cash flow
    abbreviated report, 254–258
    asset accounts, 241
    cash flows from financing activities, 247–249
    cash flows from investing activities, 246–247
    cash flows from operating activities, 244–246
    completed statement, 249–250
    coverage ratios and, 226
    direct method, 242–254
    equity accounts, 240
    impact of sales growth, 256–258
    indirect method, 241–250
    liabilities, 240
    overview, 238–241
    relationship to Commercial Lending Decision Tree, 238
    statement of cash flows, 241–254
Cash flow cycles, 22–25
Cash flows from financing activities, 247–249
    definition of, 247
Cash flows from investing activities, 246–247
    definition of, 246
Cash flows from operating activities, 244–246
    definition of, 244
Cash surrender value of life insurance, 332–333
Cash-value life insurance, 189
Certificate of limited partnership
    definition of, 54
Certified public accountants, 86–101
"Clean" audit opinions, 94–95

CMLTD. *See* Current maturities of long-term debt
Commercial finance companies, 40
Commercial Lending Decision Tree
    balance sheets, 172
    business borrowing, 22
    business life cycles, 48
    business sector considerations, 2–3
    cash budgets, 284
    cash flow analysis, 238
    financial statements, 70–71, 110
    global cash flow, 398
    income statements, 144
    key ratios, 342
    legal structures, 48
    personal cash flow, 358
    personal financial statements, 322
    personal tax returns, 358
    pro forma statements, 284
    ratio analysis, 208
    stages of, xx
    UCA Model, 264
Commercial real estate
    global cash flow, 401–402
    project financing, 41
Common-sizing, 75, 76–77
    definition of, 76
Common stock, 199
Community banks
Compensating balances
    definition of, 176
Compiled financial statements, 89–92
Compiled statements
    definition of, 89
Construction businesses
    borrowing needs, 34
    financial risks, 14–15
    financial statements, 15
    lending summary, 15
    operating cycle, 14
    subcontractors, 12, 14
Contingent liabilities, 337
Corporations. *See* C corporations; S corporations
Cost of goods sold, 153–154
Coverage ratios, 223–226, 230
CPA. *See* Certified public accountants
CRE. *See* Commercial real estate
Credit card issuers, 41
Credit files, 74
Credit sales
    reduction of terms, 29–30
Credit scoring, 86
Credit unions, 40
CSVLI. *See* Cash surrender value of life insurance
Current assets
    accounts receivable, 177–180
    allowance for doubtful accounts, 180
    cash, 176
    conversion to cash, 175
    inventory, 180–183

    marketable securities, 176–177
Current liabilities
    accounts payable, 193–194
    accrued expenses, 195
    balloon maturity, 192–193
    bullet maturity, 193
    current maturities of long-term debt, 194–195
    definition of, 190
    due to affiliates or officers, 194
    loans from shareholders, 194
    notes payable to banks, 192–193
    notes payable to others, 194
    overdrafts, 191
    prepaid expenses, 195
    subordinated debt, 194
Current maturities of long-term debt, 194–195, 225, 265, 310
Current ratio, 212–213

D

Day's accounts receivable ratio, 220
DBA. *See* Doing business as
Debentures, 196–197
Debt coverage ratios, 229, 364
Debt service coverage ratio, 224, 364, 367, 400–401
Debt service coverage worksheet, 408–409
Debt-to-income ratio, 342, 347–348, 364, 367, 400–401
Debt-to-worth leverage ratio, 214–215
Decision Tree. *See* Commercial Lending Decision Tree
Depreciation
    balance sheets, 184–187
    definition of, 125
    income statements, 160
    IRS code, 185–187
Direct cash flow analysis, 242–254
    definition of, 242
Disclaimer of opinion, 99–101
Discontinued operations loss, 164
Distributions
    definition of, 248
Dividend income, 163, 361, 377, 413
Dividend payout ratio, 226, 230
Dividends
    definition of, 248
DLOC. *See* Documentary letter of credit
Documentary letter of credit, 38
Doing business as, 51–52
    definition of, 51
Doubtful accounts, 180
Draw accounts, 200–201
DSC. *See* Debt service coverage ratio
DTI. *See* Debt-to-income ratio

E

Earnings before interest, depreciation, and amortization, 225, 256–257, 404
Earnings before interest, taxes, depreciation, amortization and rent, 225
Earnings before interest, taxes, depreciation, and amortization, 225
Earnings statements, 145, 147

EBIDA. *See* Earnings before interest, depreciation, and amortization
EBITDA. *See* Earnings before interest, taxes, depreciation, and amortization
EBITDAR. *See* Earnings before interest, taxes, depreciation, amortization and rent
Efficiency ratios, 219–223, 228
Equity. *See also* Net worth
    analysis of, 198–203
Equity accounts
    cash flow analysis, 240
Estates, 363, 420–421
Externally prepared financial statements, 89
Extraordinary recurring/nonrecurring expenses, 165
Extraordinary recurring/nonrecurring income, 163–164

F

Factoring, 40–41
Farm income, 364, 393–394, 429–430
FASB. *See* Financial Accounting Standards Board
Federal Insurance Collection Act, 371
FICA. *See* Federal Insurance Collection Act
FIFO. *See* First-in, first-out
Financial Accounting Standards Board, 87–88, 241–242
    definition of, 87
Financial leverage ratios, 214–216, 227, 228
Financial statement analysis
    definition of, 70, 71–72
Financial statements. *See also* Personal financial statements; Pro forma statements
    accounting methods, 82
    accounting standards, 86–88
    aggregate accounts, 83–84
    analysis process, 71–78
    analytical techniques, 84
    analyzing financial statements, 103–104, 137
    audited statements, 93–101
    balance sheets, 78, 103
    basics of, 78–79
    borrower strengths, weaknesses and uncertainties, 85–86
    cash flow analysis, 104
    common-sizing, 75, 76–77
    comparative analysis, 75
    compiled statements, 89–92
    continuity analysis, 76
    data analysis, 70, 71–72
    distortion in numbers, 83
    external environment, 82
    externally prepared statements, 89
    factors to consider, 80–81
    financial analysis components, 102
    footnotes, 79
    forecasts, 104–105
    income statements, 79, 103
    internally prepared statements, 88–89
    interpretive analysis, 72, 76–78, 81
    limitations of, 82–84
    limitations of analysis, 105–106
    management letters, 92, 101–102
    management plans and reports, 102
    obtaining, 73–74
    processing, 74

    purpose of analysis, 71
    quality and reliability of, 86
    quality of information, 82
    ratio analysis, 104
    relationship to the Commercial Lending Decision Tree, 70–71, 110
    reviewed statements, 92–93
    spreadsheet guidelines, 74, 79–80
    statement of cash flows, 79
    technical analysis, 72, 75, 81
    trend analysis, 75
    types of preparation, 88–102
    unlisted information, 83
    written analysis, 76
Financing activities
    definition of, 247
Finished goods inventory, 182–183
First-in, first-out, 82, 154–157
Fixed asset cycle, 31
Fixed assets
    capacity, efficiency and specialization, 186–187
    cash conversion, 183–184
    definition of, 117
    depreciation, 184–186
    forecasting, 308–309
    leasehold improvements, 187
    valuation, 184
    valuing, 187
Fixed charge coverage, 224–226
Footnotes
    definition of, 79
Forecasting
    balance sheets, 305–313
    cash budgets, 104
    income statements, 302–305
    pro forma statements, 105
    uncertainties, 313
Form 1040, 360–365, 374–386, 410–422
Form 1120S, 366, 387–392, 423–428

G

GAAP. *See* Generally accepted accounting principles
Gain on sale of fixed assets, 163
GCF. *See* Global cash flow
General contractors, 12, 14
General partnership
    activities, 53
    business responsibility, 53
    liability, 53
    overview, 50
    partnership agreement, 52–53
    taxation, 53
Generally accepted accounting principles, 87–88, 93–97, 100, 112, 238
    definition of, 87, 112, 238
Global cash flow
    analytical issues, 400–402
    calculating, 402–406
    crediting personal cash flow, 401–402
    definition of, 398

importance of, 399–400
mixing business DSC and personal DTI, 400–401
overview, 398–399
relationships to Commercial Lending Decision Tree, 398
worksheet, 409
Glossary terms, 433–435
Going concern disclosures, 97, 99
    definition of, 97
Government loan and grant programs, 42–43
Gross profit, 157–158

I

IFRS. *See* International financial reporting standards
Income adjustments, 365
Income statements
    accounting method, 150
    accrual basis, 127, 136–137
    analysis of, 103
    analysis overview, 145
    cash basis, 136–137
    cost of goods sold, 153–154
    description of, 79
    forecasting, 302–305
    gross profit, 157–158
    inventory valuation, 154–157
    large, nonrecurring sales, 152
    management objectives, 149
    net profit analysis, 165–166
    net sales, 149–150
    operating expenses, 158–165
    order backlogs, 152
    price trends, 150–151
    reconciliation of net worth, 166–168
    relationship to Commercial Lending Decision Tree, 144
    retained earnings, 167–168
    revenue analysis, 149–152
    sales mix, 151–152
    sales on extended terms, 152
    sales volume, 150–151
    structure, 146–147
    type of business considerations, 147–149
Income tax basis, 112–113
Indirect cash flow analysis, 241–250
    definition of, 241
Individual retirement accounts, 363
Industrial revenue bonds, 43
Intangibles, 189–190
Interest coverage, 223–224
Interest expense, 164–165
Interest income, 163, 361, 377, 413
Internal Revenue Service. *See also* Personal tax returns
    depreciation code, 185–187
    depreciation methods, 160
Internally prepared financial statements, 88–89
International financial reporting standards, 87–88
    definition of, 87
Interpretive financial statement analysis, 72, 76–78, 81
Inventory

definition of, 113
finished goods inventory, 182–183
forecasting, 307–308
raw materials inventory, 181
valuation methods, 82, 154–157, 180–183
work-in-process, 182
Inventory turnover ratio, 221
Investing activities
definition of, 246
Investment Tax Credit, 187
Investors, 42
IRA. *See* Individual retirement accounts
IRB. *See* Industrial revenue bonds
IRS. *See* Internal Revenue Service
Itemized deductions, 365, 376, 412

K

Key ratios
personal financial statements, 342–348
relationships to Commercial Lending Decision Tree, 342

L

Last-in, first-out, 82, 154–157
Lease financing, 38
Leasehold improvements, 187
Leasing companies, 41
Legal structures
C corporation, 50, 54–56
general partnership, 50, 52–53
limited liability company, 50, 57–58
limited partnership, 50, 53–54
overview, 48–49
relationship to the Commercial Lending Decision Tree, 48
S corporation, 50, 56–57
sole proprietorship, 50, 51–52
types of, 49–50
Lending decision tree. *See* Commercial Lending Decision Tree
Lending sources, 39–44
Leverage ratios, 214–216, 227, 228
Liabilities
accounts payable, 193–194
accrued expenses, 195
balloon maturity, 192–193
bonds, 196–197
bullet maturity, 193
cash flow analysis, 240
current, 190–196
current maturities of long-term debt, 194–195
debentures, 196–197
due to affiliates or officers, 194
loans from shareholders, 194
long-term debt, 196
noncurrent, 196–198
notes payable to banks, 192–193
notes payable to others, 194
overdrafts, 191
personal financial statements, 335–337

prepaid expenses, 195
reserves, 197–198
subordinated debt, 194, 197
Life cycles. *See* Business life cycles
Life insurance
cash surrender value, 332–333
cash-value, 189
companies, 41
LIFO. *See* Last-in, first-out
Limited liability companies
equity analysis, 201
lending to, 57–58
limited liability partnership, 57
operating agreement, 57–58
overview, 50
ownership, 57
personal financial statements, 333–334
Limited liability partnerships, 57
Limited partnership
certificate of limited partnership, 54
liability, 54
overview, 50, 53
taxation, 54
Line of credit, 36–37
Liquidity ratios, 212–214, 227, 343, 346
LLC. *See* Limited liability companies
LLP. *See* Limited liability partnerships
Loans. *See* Business loans
Long-term debt, 196, 310
Loss on sale of fixed assets, 164

M

MACRS. *See* Modified Accelerated Cost Recovery System
Management letters, 92, 101–102
definition of, 92
Manufacturers
borrowing needs, 33
characteristics, 6
lending summary, 7
operating cycle, 5–6
Marketable securities, 176–177, 306
Members' capital accounts, 201
Modified Accelerated Cost Recovery System, 160

N

NAICS. *See* North American Industry Classification System
NCAO. *See* Net cash after operations
Net cash after operations, 265, 267–271
Net profit analysis, 165–166
Net worth. *See also* Equity
adjusted net worth, 342–343, 348–351
definition of, 198
forecasting, 310
outside net worth, 349
personal financial statements, 336
Non-readily marketable securities, 332
Noncurrent assets

cash-value life insurance, 189
depreciation, 184–186
fixed assets, 183–188
intangibles, 189–190
leasehold improvements, 187
notes receivable, 188–189
prepaid expenses, 189
securities, 188
valuing fixed assets, 187
Noncurrent liabilities
bonds, 196–197
debentures, 196–197
long-term debt, 196
reserves, 197–198
subordinated debt, 197
North American Industry Classification System, 13, 75, 230
Notes payable to banks, 192–193
Notes payable to others, 194
Notes receivable, 188–189

O

Operating activities
definition of, 246
Operating agreements, 57–58
definition of, 57
Operating cycles
agricultural businesses, 4–5
analyzing financial data, 16–17
application, 17
construction businesses, 14
definition of, 3, 22
evaluating risks, 17–18
financial data from, 16–17
manufacturers, 5–6
purpose of, 3–4
retailers, 9–10
service businesses, 11–12
wholesalers, 7–8
working capital and, 3–4
Operating expenses, 158–165
Operating income, 161
Operating leverage, 161–162, 214
Operating line of credit, 36–37
Operating ratios, 216–219
Operating statements, 147
Outside net worth, 349
Overbillings, 15
Overdrafts, 191
Owner capital account, 200
Owner draw account, 200
Owner's equity, 198, 310

P

Paid-in capital, 199
Participations, 43–44
definition of, 43
Partners' capital account, 200

Partners' draw account, 200–201
Partnership agreement
    definition of, 52
Partnerships
    agreement, 52–53
    equity analysis, 200–201
    income, 363, 384–385, 420–421
    personal financial statements, 333–334
Permanent working capital line of credit, 37
Personal cash flow. *See also* Global cash flow
    analysis of, 367
    calculating, 367–373
    debt service worksheet, 408–409
    income, 359–360
    relationship to the Commercial Lending Decision Tree, 358
Personal financial statements
    balance sheet, 330–335
    basic formats, 322–323
    components, 327–338
    contingent liabilities, 337
    expenditures analysis, 329–330
    format, 322–326
    income analysis, 327–329
    key ratios, 342–348
    liability analysis, 335–336
    net worth, 336
    overview, 322–326
    personal information, 327
    preliminary analysis, 323–326
    relationship to Commercial Lending Decision Tree, 322
    representations, 337–338
    warranties, 337–338
Personal property, 334
Personal tax returns
    cash flow, 359–360
    components of, 360–365
    Form 1040, 360–365, 374–386, 410–422
    Form 1120S, 366
    forms, 359
    income, 359–360
    income analysis, 360–365
    initial review, 360
    related analysis of income, 366
    relationship to the Commercial Lending Decision Tree, 358
    uses of, 358–359
PFS. *See* Personal financial statements
P&L statement. *See* Profit and loss statements
Policy Statement on Prudent Commercial Real Estate Loan Workouts, 399
Preferred stock, 199
Prepaid assets
    definition of, 123
Prepaid expenses, 189, 195
    definition of, 195
Pro forma statements
    analyzing, 301
    calculating and interpreting, 295–313
    external factors, 298–301
    forecasting a balance sheet, 305–313
    forecasting an income statement, 302–305

framework, 297
internal factors, 299–301
past performance and, 301–302
performance dependability, 297–298
preparing forecasts, 105
projection assumptions, 296–297
realistic assumptions, 297
relationship to Commercial Lending Decision Tree, 284
time intervals, 298
Profit
gross, 157–158
net profit analysis, 165—166
Profit and loss statements, 145, 147
Profitability ratios, 216–219, 228
PTR. *See* Personal tax returns

Q

Qualified audit opinions, 95–96
definition of, 95
Quick ratio, 213

R

Ratio analysis. *See also* specific ratios
accounting methods, 209–211
Annual Statement Studies, 230
comparative analysis, 231–233
considerations, 208–211
coverage ratios, 223–226, 230
debt service coverage ratios, 224, 229
definitions of ratios, 227—229
efficiency ratios, 219–223, 228
financial leverage ratios, 214–216, 228
industry and trade associations, 230–231
industry data, 229–233
liquidity ratios, 212–214, 227
profitability ratios, 216–219, 228
ratio characteristics, 211
relationship to Commercial Lending Decision Tree, 208
trend analysis, 231–233
types of ratios, 211–229
Raw materials inventory, 181
Readily marketable securities, 331–332
Real estate, 333
Rental real estate income, 163, 363, 384–385, 420–421
Representations, 323, 337–338
definition of, 323
Reserves, 197–198
Retailers
borrowing needs, 34
financial statements, 10–11
lending summary, 10
operating cycle, 9–10
Retainage
definition of, 14
Retained earnings, 167–168
Retirement accounts, 334
Return-on-assets ratio, 218

Return-on-equity ratio, 218–219
Revenue analysis, 149–152
Reviewed financial statements, 92–93
Reviewed statements
    definition of, 92
Risk Management Association, 75, 230, 241–244
RMA. *See* Risk Management Association
Rounding
    definition of, 75
Royalties, 363, 384–385, 420–421

S

S corporations
    distribution of income and cash, 56–57
    equity analysis, 201
    Form 1120S, 366, 389–392, 425–428
    overview, 50
    ownership, 56
    personal financial statements, 333–334, 420–421
    taxation, 56
Salaries, 361
Sales to total assets ratio, 222–223
SAS. *See Statements on Auditing Standards*
SBA. *See* Small Business Administration
SCF. *See* Statement of cash flows
Schedule K-1, 56, 364, 387–388, 395–396, 423–424, 431–432
Seasonal line of credit, 37
SEC. *See* Securities and Exchange Commission
Section 179 deduction, 160, 187
Securities and Exchange Commission, 87–88
    definition of, 87
Self-employment tax, 386, 422
Service businesses
    borrowing needs, 34
    financial statements, 11–12
    lending summary, 12
    operating cycle, 11–12
    other service-related businesses, 12, 13
SFAS 95, *Statement of Cash Flows*, 241–243
Shareholders' equity, 198
Short-term notes payable, 309
SLOC. *See* Standby letter of credit
Small Business Administration, 42
Small businesses
    SBA business loans, 42
    Section 179 deduction, 160, 187
Social Security benefits, 365
Sole proprietorships
    assumed name, 51–52
    business income, 362, 378–379
    business responsibility, 51
    equity analysis, 200
    liability, 51
    overview, 50
    personal financial statements, 334
    taxation, 51

SOP. *See* Statement of Position
Special commitment loans, 36
Spreadsheets, 74, 79–80
SSARS 19. *See Statement on Standards for Accounting and Review Services, Compilation and Review Engagements*
Standby letter of credit, 37–38, 43
State income tax refunds, 362
Statement of cash flows, 79, 241–254, 265–268
Statement of Position, 322
Statement on Standards for Accounting and Review Services, Compilation and Review Engagements, 91–92
Statements on Auditing Standards, 99
Stock
    preferred, 199
    treasury, 199–200
Stock accounts, 201
Subcontractors
    definition of, 12, 14
Subordinated debt, 194, 197
    definition of, 194
Supplemental income, 384–385, 420–421
Surplus capital, 199
Syndications, 43–44
    definition of, 43

T

Tangible effective leverage ratio, 215–216
Tangible leverage ratio, 215
Tangible net worth
    definition of, 201
Tax returns. *See* Personal tax returns
Technical financial statement analysis, 72, 75, 81
Term loans, 38
Terms, 433–435
Trade accounts receivable, 177
Trade credit, 28, 42
    definition of, 23
Traditional cash flow coverage, 223
Treasury stock, 199–200
Trusts, 363

U

UCA Model
    advantages of, 274, 276
    cash after debt amortization, 271–273
    cash after external financing, 273–274
    compared to statement of cash flows, 265–268
    direct cash flow analysis, 243–244
    direct method, 264–276
    financing surplus, 273
    indirect cash flow analysis, 241–243
    net cash after operations, 267–271
    relationship to Commercial Lending Decision Tree, 264
Underbillings, 15
Unemployment benefits, 365
Uniform Credit Analysis, 241–244. *See also* UCA Model
Unqualified audit opinions, 94–95
    definition of, 94
Unsecured debt ratio, 346

W

Wages, 361
Warranties, 323, 337–338
    definition of, 323
Weighted average costs, 82
Wholesalers
    assessing borrower risk, 8
    borrowing needs, 33
    lending summary, 9
    operating cycle, 7–8
Work-in-process inventory, 182
Working capital
    definition of, 3
    dollar amount of, 213–214
    operating cycles and, 3–4
    permanent working capital line of credit, 37
Write-offs, 180